The Political Economy of Regionalism, Trade, and Infrastructure

Southeast Asia and the Belt and Road Initiative in a New Era

Series on China's Belt and Road Initiative

Print ISSN: 2591-7730
Online ISSN: 2591-7749

This book series showcases the most up-to-date and significant research on China's Belt and Road Initiative (BRI) by leading scholars from inside and outside China. It presents a panoramic view on the BRI, from the perspectives of China's domestic policy, China's foreign investment, international relations, cultural cooperation and historical inheritance. As the first English book series on the BRI, this series offers a valuable English-language resource for researchers, policymakers, professionals and students to better understand the challenges and opportunities brought by the BRI.

Published:

Vol. 13 *The Political Economy of Regionalism, Trade, and Infrastructure: Southeast Asia and the Belt and Road Initiative in a New Era*
edited by LIU Hong, TAN Kong Yam and Guanie LIM

Vol. 12 *Belt and Road Initiative: Interregional Cooperation Between Asia and Europe*
by RONG Xinchun

Vol. 11 *21st-Century Maritime Silk Road Initiative: Aims and Objectives, Implementation Strategies and Policy Recommendations*
by ZHAO Jianglin

Vol. 10 *China's Belt and Road Initiative, the Eurasian Landbridge, and the New Mega-Regionalism*
by Richard POMFRET

Vol. 9 *China's Belt and Road Initiative and RMB Internationalization*
by MENG Gang

For the complete list of volumes in this series, please visit
www.worldscientific.com/series/scbri

Series on China's Belt and Road Initiative – Vol. 13

The Political Economy of Regionalism, Trade, and Infrastructure

Southeast Asia and the Belt and Road Initiative in a New Era

Edited by

Hong LIU
Nanyang Technological University, Singapore

Kong Yam TAN
Nanyang Technological University, Singapore

Guanie LIM
National Graduate Institute for Policy Studies, Japan

World Scientific

NEW JERSEY • LONDON • SINGAPORE • BEIJING • SHANGHAI • HONG KONG • TAIPEI • CHENNAI • TOKYO

Published by

World Scientific Publishing Co. Pte. Ltd.
5 Toh Tuck Link, Singapore 596224
USA office: 27 Warren Street, Suite 401-402, Hackensack, NJ 07601
UK office: 57 Shelton Street, Covent Garden, London WC2H 9HE

Library of Congress Cataloging-in-Publication Data
Names: Liu, Hong, 1962– editor. | Tan, Kong Yam, editor. | Lim, Guanie, editor.
Title: The political economy of regionalism, trade, and infrastructure : Southeast Asia and the Belt and Road Initiative in a new era / Edited by Hong Liu, Kong Yam Tan, Guanie Lim.
Description: Hackensack : World Scientific, 2022. | Series: Series on China's Belt and Road Initiative, 2591-7730 ; vol. 13 | Includes bibliographical references.
Identifiers: LCCN 2021028961 | ISBN 9789811233142 (hardcover) | ISBN 9789811233159 (ebook) | ISBN 9789811233166 (ebook other)
Subjects: LCSH: Yi dai yi lu (Initiative : China) | Regional economics--Southeast Asia. | Southeast Asia--Foreign economic relations--China. | China--Foreign economic relations--Southeast Asia.
Classification: LCC HC441 .P644 2022 | DDC 338.959--dc23
LC record available at https://lccn.loc.gov/2021028961

British Library Cataloguing-in-Publication Data
A catalogue record for this book is available from the British Library.

For any available supplementary material, please visit
https://www.worldscientific.com/worldscibooks/10.1142/12183#t=suppl

Desk Editor: Jiang Yulin

Typeset by Stallion Press
Email: enquiries@stallionpress.com

About the Book

Since its launch in late 2013, the Belt and Road Initiative (BRI) has become a significant factor in shaping China's economic and diplomatic relations with the world. China's increasing clout presents opportunities as well as challenges, especially for the developing economies of the Association of Southeast Asian Nations (ASEAN) which constitute major sites for investment and trade alongside the BRI routes.

This edited volume examines whether and to what extent China's economic ascendancy has impacted the proposed ASEAN Economic Community and the respective nations in the region. It deals with this question by grounding the analysis along three themes — institutions at a regional level, industry/sector, and particular ASEAN countries' economic relationship with China. Sixteen articles are presented to illuminate the state of affairs at the regional level and in specific ASEAN economies. They point to the importance of managing trade and investment flows stemming from China's increasingly sophisticated national firms. This in turn hinges on forging 'rules of the game' at both the multilateral and bilateral levels, which potentially leads to mutually beneficial industrialization and long-term wealth creation.

The Political Economy of Regionalism, Trade, and Infrastructure will be of great interest to scholars of political economy and industrial policy in East Asia, as well as to scholars and policy professionals analyzing approaches to development strategy more broadly.

About the Editors

Professor Hong Liu is the Tan Lark Sye Chair Professor of Public Policy and Global Affairs at Nanyang Technological University (NTU) in Singapore, where he also serves as the Director of the Nanyang Centre for Public Administration. He had previously taught at the University of Manchester as Chair of Chinese Studies and the Founding Director of the Centre for Chinese Studies (2006–2010) and at the Faculty of Arts and Social Sciences at the National University of Singapore (1995–2006).

Professor Liu's research areas include Asian governance, Sino-Southeast Asian relations, international migration, global talent management, and the Belt and Road Initiative. He has authored/edited more than 20 books and about 100 academic articles, including in leading international journals such as the *World Politics*, *Journal of Asian Studies*, *Critical Asian Studies*, *Journal of Southeast Asian Studies*, *The China Quarterly*, *Journal of Contemporary China*, *Nature and Culture*, *International Journal of Comparative Sociology*, and *Ethnic and Racial Studies*. His publications also appear in the Chinese, French, Dutch, Japanese, Indonesian and Korean languages.

Professor Kong Yam Tan is presently a Professor of Economics at NTU, Singapore. He is also the board member of Changi Airport Group, Surbana-Jurong and CapitaMall REIT.

From 1985 to 1988, he was an assistant director in the Monetary Authority of Singapore in charge of exchange rate policy. He was the chief assistant to Dr Goh Keng Swee, the former Deputy Prime Minister of Singapore invited by Mr Deng Xiaoping to advise China on economic development strategy (1985–1989). From June 2002 to June 2005, he was a senior economist at the World Bank office in Beijing where he worked on issues of macro stabilization, integration of the fragmented domestic market, banking reform, international trade and investment as well as regional inequality. In 2004, Professor Tan was a member of the World Bank expert group on the 11th five-year plan (2006–2010) for the State Council in China. The expert group provided analysis and policy recommendations on urbanization, regional inequality, innovation policy, energy and water policy as well as strategy on banking reform to the Chinese government.

Dr Guanie Lim is an Assistant Professor at the National Graduate Institute for Policy Studies, Japan. His main research interests are comparative political economy, value chain analysis, and the Belt and Road Initiative in Southeast Asia. Dr Lim is also interested in broader development issues within Asia, especially those of China, Vietnam, and Malaysia. He has published in several prominent journals such as the *Journal of Contemporary China*, *Marine Policy*, and *World Development.* His latest monograph — *The Political Economy of Growth in Vietnam: Between States and Markets* (published by Routledge) — details the catching-up experience of Vietnam since its 1986 *Doi Moi* (renovation) reforms.

Contents

Foreword

The ancient Silk Road and the more recent Belt and Road Initiative (BRI) will continue to not only inspire but also challenge our minds, going forward.

For someone, who, as the Editor of one of Singapore's major newspapers, covered former Prime Minister Lee Kuan Yew's early visits to China — during the 'Reform and Opening Up' era which began in earnest in late 1978 — and who later served as the Senior Minister of State for Foreign Affairs, I find this collection of articles highly relevant and informative, indeed instructive. The BRI brims with impact on the various economies of the Association of Southeast Asian Nations (ASEAN).

For Singapore, at least, we once primarily facilitated technology and capital transfer to China. As the Chinese learnt from us over the years, they too carved out new niches on their own, ranging from artificial intelligence to renewable energy. Many of the Chinese companies have become global players, forming the backbone of the BRI. As the relevant chapters in this book demonstrate, in the eight years since the launch of the BRI, many Singaporean companies have also benefitted from their Chinese counterparts' expansion in the region.

While each of the ASEAN country's relationship with China is bound to be different, the principles of fostering mutual cooperation and promoting warm ties remain. What is more, cordial ties with China does not mean a downgrading of our relationship with others, as ASEAN has consistently pursued an independent foreign policy based upon the region's own interests. This independent and open attitude is especially important as ASEAN navigates the uncertain decades of the 2020s, facing common issues such as climate change, new geopolitics, ageing and social inequalities.

No doubt many of the issues discussed here have important implications within the region and beyond.

My utmost congratulations to the Editors and contributors for their stellar efforts in curating this volume. The BRI after all presents much in terms of the opportunities and challenges for the future.

Zainul Abidin Rasheed
Member, Board of Trustees,
Nanyang Technological University
Ambassador (Non-Resident) to Kuwait,
and Former Senior Minister of State for Foreign Affairs,
Singapore

Acknowledgments

This edited volume would not have come to fruition without the generous support of our friends and colleagues, who are too numerous to mention. Special thanks must go to Professor Euston Quah and Mr Jackson Teh, both of the *Singapore Economic Review*, for their guidance and advice.

We are especially grateful to the Lien Research Programme on the Belt and Road Initiative at the Nanyang Centre for Public Administration, Nanyang Technological University (NTU), which provided funding for the International Conference on 'Singapore as a Nexus of the Maritime Silk Road: Knowledge Exchanges and Capacity Building' held in December 2018. Hong Liu would also like to acknowledge the funding support from NTU (#04INS000132C430). Some of the articles presented in this conference were subsequently revised and submitted for external reviews for a proposed special issue at *Singapore Economic Review*. These articles were then combined with others that were submitted and reviewed independently, eventually coming together as Volume 66, Issue 01 (March 2021).

When this edited volume was first mooted in the latter half of 2020, the global economy was still coming to terms with the Coronavirus disease (COVID-19) and very fluid US–China relationship. We thus developed the idea to bring in several more articles to bolster the special issue at *Singapore Economic Review*. Our goal is to provide the readership with a richer perspective on the constantly evolving nature of the Belt and

Road Initiative in the region, in addition to updating some of our initial assessment. At World Scientific Publishing, we are grateful to Professor Phua Kok Khoo and Mr Jiang Yulin, who found this project interesting and relevant. While we are indebted to those mentioned here, we remain responsible for any errors, omissions, and opinions.

Introduction

In Pursuit of Regionalism, Trade, and Infrastructure: Southeast Asia, China, and the Belt and Road Initiative in a New Era*

Hong Liu[†], Kong Yam Tan[†] and Guanie Lim[‡]

[†]School of Social Sciences,
Nanyang Technological University, Singapore
[‡]National Graduate Institute for Policy Studies, Japan

1. Belt and Road Initiative and Global Development

Since its launch in late 2013 by Chinese President Xi Jinping, the Belt and Road Initiative (BRI) has become a significant factor in shaping China's economic and diplomatic relations with the rest of the world. The BRI is composed of two key routes — the 'Silk Road Economic Belt' and the '21st Century Maritime Silk Road'. The former was announced in Kazakhstan as a program to connect China to Europe by land, with routes interlinking the relevant countries. In October 2013, the

*This chapter is an updated version of an earlier work by the authors: Liu, H., Tan, K.Y., & Lim, G. (2021). Introduction — Southeast Asia and the Belt and Road Initiative: The Political Economy of Regionalism, Trade, and Infrastructure. *The Singapore Economic Review*, **66**(1), pp. 1–20.

'21st Century Maritime Silk Road', a maritime development initiative targeting the ports of Southeast Asia, South Asia, the Middle East, East Africa, and the Mediterranean, was launched in Indonesia (Liu & Dunford, 2016; Zhao, 2020). The BRI is seemingly solidifying China's already prominent role on the international arena. Chinese firms are renowned for acquiring large, established brand name firms such as IBM (information technology), Club Med (luxury holiday provider), and Volvo (automobile) (Hill & Jongwanich, 2014; Luo, Xue, & Han, 2010).

According to Refinitiv (2020), one of the largest global providers of financial market and infrastructure data, as of July 2019, there were 2,951 projects valued at USD 3.87 trillion already underway across the wider Silk Road region, involving 2,630 companies. In the arena of trade, China's increasing manufacturing sophistication has led to burgeoning trade imbalances with several economies, from wealthy ones such as the United States (US) to less sophisticated ones like Laos. Relatedly, scholars tracking the trade performance of the Association of Southeast Asian Nations (ASEAN) economies have argued that China's economic expansion and integration with global markets have led to a situation in which ASEAN's poorer economies are losing comparative advantage in labor-intensive manufacturing and gaining it in natural resources, ultimately ushering in a new 'resource curse' (Coxhead, 2007; Coxhead & Jayasuriya, 2010). Chinese prowess has also been buttressed by a more assertive stance in global as well as regional economic and financial affairs. At the global stage, Beijing has cooperated with other countries in launching alternative institutions such as the Asian Infrastructure Investment Bank (AIIB) and the New Development Bank (NDB) (Rana & Pacheco Pardo, 2018). Relative to the existing Western-led, Bretton Woods institutions, these Chinese-driven institutions are welcomed by other emerging economies, especially those along the BRI routes.

Increasing Chinese clout is also witnessed in the ASEAN-centric institutions such as the ASEAN+3 Macroeconomic Research Office (AMRO) and Chiang Mai Initiative Multilateralization (CMIM). Driven by discontent with the behaviour of the Western-led organizations during the 1997–1998 Asian Financial Crisis (AFC), the ASEAN states decided to establish these two institutions, with the support of the '+3 partners' (China, Japan, and South Korea), to better address region-specific economic and financial challenges (Kawai, 2010). In infrastructure, Beijing's BRI push has helped several ASEAN states to plug their chronic infrastructure gap. Aware of the benefits of improved connectivity in bolstering trade and investment, they have struck some landmark deals such as Indonesia's Jakarta–Bandung High-Speed Rail (HSR) and the Kyaukphyu–Kunming oil and gas pipelines interlinking Myanmar with China (Andrews-Speed, Qiu, & Len, 2016; Yoshimatsu, 2018). Indeed, over the past decade, infrastructure development has emerged as a new and distinctive policy area in which states are contending for influence in Southeast Asia (Mueller, 2019; ASEAN, 2020a). According to CIMB ASEAN Research Institute (2018: p.15), 'China's investments in BRI projects provide an avenue for ASEAN and its member states to overcome the problem of inadequate infrastructure, which is a major obstacle for both short-term and long-term ASEAN economic growth'.

To foster international trade, the idea of the Regional Comprehensive Economic Partnership (RCEP) has been forwarded. The idea is to place ASEAN at the heart of this bloc, with more liberalized trade and investment flows between the region and the '+6 partners' with which ASEAN has existing free trade agreements (Australia, China, India, Japan, South Korea and New Zealand). Reflecting on the signing of the RCEP by these countries in November 2020, some analysts have argued that these developments reflect a new division between the existing global economic order (led by the US) and China, with smaller states such as ASEAN forced to take sides or risk being alienated (see, for example, Cali, 2020; Bhattacherjee, 2020).[1] Yet, according to Sulaimah Mahmood, Singapore's chief negotiator at the RCEP, it is too simplistic to term the initiative as 'China-led'. If anything, 'it was all driven by ASEAN' (Heng, 2020). Sulaimah revealed that ASEAN was already discussing the idea of an enlarged economic bloc as early as 2006, about 14 years before its recent signing. At that juncture, there were already several 'ASEAN+1' trade agreements, each with different rules, which proved cumbersome. To alleviate this bottleneck, a consolidation of the existing rules was mooted by Sulaimah and her colleagues.

The region's ability to carve out niches also comes through when one takes a more on-the-ground perspective. For instance, despite the vigorous push by the Chinese transnational corporations (TNCs) to expand their production and sales networks in ASEAN, recent research on their operations shows that they have only attained a moderate degree of success. This is especially so in highly regulated industries such as automobile production. To this end, Chinese TNCs are hampered by the competitive and still consolidating marketplace, various national regulations of key ASEAN economies, and the need to dovetail their own corporate goals with those of their ASEAN business partners (Lim, 2017). In Vietnam, the remarkable transformation of the domestic motorcycle manufacturing industry has taken place following a major shock triggered by massive Chinese imports (Fujita, 2013a, 2013b; Ngo, 2017). From a marginal market that produced only about 62,000 units in 1995, it has since grown exponentially (more than 70 times) to one of the largest in the world. For Fujita (2013a), drawing on her observation on Vietnam's decades-long industrial evolution,

[1]India decided to pull out of the RCEP eventually, meaning that the latter now has 15 members (one less than originally planned). The 15 members will have to ratify the agreement in their respective countries before the RCEP comes into force. As of early April 2021, only Singapore has ratified the RCEP.

it is more fruitful to differentiate between the two types of host country's imports from China: imports of capital equipment, components, and materials from China used for *export production*, and imports of Chinese goods for *domestic consumption*. The former type of imports has been responsible for Vietnam's large trade deficits with most East Asian economies like South Korea, Taiwan, and Singapore because the country's export production depends on inputs sourced from these countries. The key question to be asked is if China has also come to play a major role in this picture, and in-depth research into the strategies of TNCs is essential in this regard. Likewise, the latter type of imports, i.e. imports of Chinese goods for domestic consumption, has been perceived as a threat by some Vietnamese economic planners. Although Chinese imports imply competitive threat for domestic producers of equivalent products, such threat may eventually be an opportunity as producers engage in varieties of innovative responses, such as improving product quality and reducing costs. This dynamic has since been borne out in the Vietnamese motorcycle manufacturing industry.

To make sense of these issues, this chapter — and the rest of this edited volume — asks the question: *'Is China's economic ascendancy undermining the ASEAN Economic Community?'* This edited volume answers the question by grounding it along three interlinked themes — *institutions at a regional level*, *industry/sector*, and *particular ASEAN economies' economic relationship with China*. These three themes help to sharpen our conceptualization on how Chinese economic expansion is meshing with ASEAN's increasing regionalism and the specificities of the region's political economy. The breadth and depth of the chapters presented is a key strength in explaining this important regional as well as global trend. We hope that the edited volume will generate insights that can be applied to other economies (within and beyond ASEAN) intending to engage more closely with the BRI.

2. (Southeast) Asian Institutions

Firstly, examining *regional and/or international institutions* will shed light on the convoluted interplay of economic and political factors in shaping the 'rules of the game'. While China's growing economic weight is not to be denied, recent research suggests that ASEAN is simultaneously nudging (and being nudged by) China toward institutional outcomes that are far more unpredictable than commonly predicted (Ravenhill, 2016, 2017). Pitakdumrongkit (2015) shows that ASEAN states (specifically, Indonesia, Malaysia, and Thailand) with little prior experience in dealing with multilateral financial negotiations have employed clever bargaining tactics that help shape the CMIM agreement details in their favour vis-à-vis the much larger economies of the '+3 partners'. Some of their tactics involve the forging of fluid, ad hoc bargaining coalitions amongst themselves and the exploitation of the geopolitical competition between China and Japan in the region. Relatedly, it goes without saying that China has considerably more common goals with its ASEAN peers than what is usually portrayed. This dynamic, albeit competitive, is not necessarily zero-sum.

To this end, one has to examine both pre-existing institutions (e.g. AMRO and CMIM) and emerging ones (e.g. AIIB and RCEP), unfolding how the 'rules of the game' have evolved amidst a rising China. Indeed, one of the oft-cited emerging institutions is the AIIB. Critics (especially those in the field of international relations and security) have alleged it is a vehicle designed to further China's geostrategic goals, while scholars have argued it marks China's adoption of a 'revisionist' foreign policy strategy (e.g. Beeson & Li, 2016; Cai, 2018). However, the AIIB is a radically different institution from that which China initially pitched in 2013. To secure a broad membership and international legitimacy for the AIIB, China compromised with partners during governance negotiations in 2015. To this end, several controversial initial proposals were dropped.[2] In addition, the governance practices of existing multilateral development banks (MDBs) were adopted, and cooperative partnerships were developed with the World Bank and Asian Development Bank (Wilson, 2017).

Analysing the first loans approved by the AIIB, Gabusi (2017) argues that far from representing a China-led challenge to the Western-led liberal order, the AIIB, while promoting Chinese commercial and geopolitical interests, shows the resilience of the Western-centric global financial regime instituted by the Bretton Woods institutions (World Bank, International Monetary Fund (IMF), and World Trade Organization (WTO)) in the post-World War Two era. Put together, the AIIB is now a broad-based multilateral institution with a diverse range of developed and developing country members, adopting policies consistent with international best practices for development financing. Much like Wilson (2017), Liang (2020) shows that the AIIB itself has evolved over the past five years, arguing that Beijing's priority at the initial stage was to exercise precaution, ensuring its acceptance to other countries. More recently, Beijing has adopted a bolder approach to embed a new set of ideas, norms, principles and practices into the AIIB. In project selection and implementation, emphasis has been shifted toward efficiency and flexibility, less formality and legality, and more equal participation of the borrowing developing countries.

Focusing on development within East Asia, Rana and Pacheco Pardo (2018) demonstrate that East Asian countries in general and China in particular are establishing institutions that

[2]The initial proposals were never officially presented, but multiple reports indicated that they involved a focus on attracting member states from within the Asian region, governance arrangements vesting considerable authority in the hands of the AIIB President, with reduced Director oversight relative to other multilateral development banks (MDBs), and a preference for using Chinese construction contractors in AIIB-funded projects. See Wilson (2017) for a fuller elaboration.

complement — rather than compete against — existing Bretton Woods institutions. Even though there is a degree of 'healthy' competition between regional institutions and their global counterparts, the former is essentially complementary to the latter. Global institutions can offer knowledge and capacity building to regional institutions, which in turn can provide access to a larger pool of resources. Analyzing the cases of liquidity provision — in the form of the IMF versus the CMIM — and development financing — with the World Bank on the one hand versus the AIIB and NDB on the other, the prognosis is that the multi-layering of international governance need not lead to unhealthy competition between layers. Indeed, functional overlap can trigger a division of labor process leading to institutional adaptation and, ultimately, cooperation among institutions (see also Ji, 2017).

3. Global Value Chains and Global Production Networks

Secondly, there is a need to analyze the development of industries/sectors in which China is increasingly deepening its competitive advantage such as consumer electronics, artificial intelligence, and HSR. Following years of collaboration and competition with global and regional TNCs, these industries have adopted progressively more transnational characteristics as they diversify from the maturing Chinese domestic market. Some noteworthy issues to be teased out include the business networks forged between the Chinese TNCs and the 'incumbents' such as domestic business groups and Japanese and Western TNCs. Although new technologies and ideas brought in by the Chinese TNCs can theoretically contribute to economic progress, they can also disrupt the pre-existing industrial organization and the wider production networks (Liu & Zhou, 2019). Nevertheless, these disjunctures are manifested differently and unevenly across industries.

One of the best cases to illustrate these dynamics is the semiconductor industry. China's Jiangsu Changjiang Electronics Technology Co., Ltd. (JCET), a private semiconductor manufacturer listed on the Shanghai Stock Exchange, acquired STATS ChipPAC of Singapore for USD 780 million in 2015 in a bid to obtain economies of scale and to secure the core technologies it lacks (Oh & No, 2019). By 2017, JCET's revenue ranked third in the global top 10 providers of outsourced IC packaging and testing services. It also broke into the global top 10 in outsourced semiconductor assembly and test rankings. Although JCET received some funding support from the National Integrated Circuit Industry Investment Fund, set up in 2014 under the Ministry of Industry and Information Technology and the Ministry of Finance, the acquisition did not generate too much controversy. First and foremost, JCET's financing mechanism, while partially supported by the Chinese state, was still relatively transparent and conformed largely to market mechanisms.[3] Relatedly, Temasek (Singapore's sovereign wealth fund), the main shareholder of STATS ChipPAC, had intended to restructure its portfolio, reducing its exposure to the capital- and technology-intensive semiconductor industry. For STATS ChipPAC, it was unable to match the global competition, which saw its market share and profitability decline in the years preceding the acquisition (KINIBIZ, 2014; Thomas, 2014).

In the much-touted HSR industry, the industrial organization is somewhat different. For one, there is a noticeably stronger role for the Chinese state-owned enterprises (SOEs). Because of the projects' exorbitant cost and longer-than-normal payback period, state-backed financing from China's end is, as a norm, a necessity. The confluence of these circumstances inevitably leads to potential politicking on the part of the host economies. In Indonesia, the aforementioned Jakarta–Bandung

[3]Oh and No (2019) detail the instruments by which the Chinese firm utilized in financing this acquisition.

HSR serves as a revealing case for understanding how the growing clout of the BRI and the internationalization of the Chinese TNCs have transformed, if not complicated, the pre-existing industrial organization and production networks of the host economy (Kratz & Pavlićević, 2019). As the highest profile and most capital-intensive BRI project in Indonesia to-date, the HSR represents a key thrust of the Joko Widodo administration (2014 to present) — who is clearly promoting infrastructure development after close to a decade of *laissez-faireism* in the post-AFC period. Perhaps unsurprisingly, the scale and ambition of this project has attracted its fair share of detractors. In particular, Prabowo Subianto, an aspiring Presidential candidate, resorted to China-bashing in his attempt to unseat Widodo during the April 2019 presidential election. However, Prabowo failed to dislodge Widodo as the latter eventually garnered more electoral support (Camba, 2020). More interestingly, Prabowo has been made Minister of Defence during Widodo's second term Presidency, which can be interpreted as an attempt to insulate the Jakarta–Bandung HSR (and by extension, other BRI projects) from further societal pressure (see Lim *et al.*, 2021).

4. Economic Strategies

Lastly, the edited volume aims to unpack *particular ASEAN economies' experience in engaging with China*, especially within the context of the BRI. As discussed previously, China's substantial demand for goods and services and its increasingly integrated status into the global production network of critical industrial products has generated both opportunities and threats for the regional economies (see, for example, Tan, 2007). Put another way, there remains substantial autonomy on the part of the ASEAN countries to capture more benefits from Chinese growth and avoid failing into the new 'resource curse'. Some noteworthy examples include the establishment of reciprocal government-to-government industrial parks in key Chinese and ASEAN cities. For example, China and Malaysia have established industrial parks in each other's territories: China–Malaysia Qinzhou Industrial Park (CMQIP) in Guangxi province and the Malaysia–China Kuantan Industrial Park (MCKIP) in the state of Pahang. Boasting a 51/49 ownership model, with the host country holding 51% of equity and the investing side the remaining 49%, both industrial parks are unprecedented in the world as they represent a new model of 'two countries, twin parks' undertaken jointly by Beijing and Putrajaya. CMQIP and MCKIP are often earmarked as flagship BRI projects in ASEAN, serving as the ideal demonstrative case studies for other countries (within and beyond ASEAN) attempting to tap into the BRI (Kong, 2016). Malaysia's engagement with the BRI is also somewhat bifurcated, with the Chinese SOEs and their private sector counterparts focusing primarily on infrastructure provision and manufacturing respectively. Manufacturing's more integrated linkages to the local industrial ecosystem in turn insulate the latter from political disputes and regime change uncertainties (Zhang, 2020).[4]

At the Greater Mekong Subregion (GMS), Thailand, courtesy of its pro-business 'Thailand Plus One' strategy, has solidified its lead as the gateway economy for TNCs intending to penetrate its less-developed neighbours, namely Cambodia, Laos, Myanmar, and Vietnam. Although the origins of the strategy owe much to Japanese economic planners and TNCs aiming to overcome disruption caused by Thailand's severe flooding of 2011, it has proven popular for even non-Japanese TNCs operating in Thailand to tap the young but increasingly wealthy consumer market, and lower operating costs in the other GMS economies. In Cambodia, the 'Thailand Plus One'

[4]For an alternative perspective on Chinese investment in Malaysia, see de Micheaux (2019).

strategy has created two highly spatialized zones (Kuroiwa, 2016). At the initial phase, TNCs that have mother factories in Thailand prefer to move part of their operations to the Thai–Cambodia frontier region. The proximity to the mother factories is particularly suitable in the early phase, which aims to establish a (usually rather modest) foothold in participating in the existing production network. As the operations mature, in which upgrading is achieved through forming more frequent and denser linkages, a metropolitan area (e.g. Phnom Penh) is preferable to a border region because of market size, local supplier base, human resources, infrastructure facilities, and amenities. Thailand's unique proposition has also appealed to Chinese TNCs eager to deepen their presence in the GMS through their Thai operations. Some of the more notable firms include the Great Wall Motors (automobile), SAIC Motor (automobile), and Hangzhou Zhongce Rubber Company (tire and rubber products) (see Kosaikanont, 2019; Lim, 2017; Maikaew, 2020).

Despite such positive development, recent events suggest that a less-than-careful approach to the BRI by some ASEAN economies have created a dilemma — while they are eager to conclude capital-intensive infrastructure deals with China, improper planning and predatory business practices have reduced the sustainability of such deals. In Malaysia, anti-Chinese sentiment was stirred up by Mahathir Mohamad, the country's longest-serving Prime Minister (1981–2003; May 2018 to March 2020) and then leader of the opposition bloc. Targeting high-end enclaves that are priced out of the local constituents' reach, Mahathir channelled widespread electoral anger toward his political opponents for their perceived role in 'selling out' Malaysian interest to Chinese investors, culminating in the defeat of the long-ruling *Barisan Nasional* (one of Asia's longest-ruling administration since the conclusion of World War Two) in the recently concluded May 2018 general election (see Liu & Lim, 2019).

5. Structure and Themes

Written by authors from a diverse range of professions including academia, government, and the financial sector, the chapters in this edited volume interrogate institutions at a regional level, industry/sector, and economic relationship with China respectively, with the collective aim of unpacking China's economic ascendancy and its impact on the region. In discussing these three inter-related themes, the chapters illustrate the multidimensional manners in which development opportunities (and stumbling blocks) are forged in the wake of the BRI. Yet, the chapters share a set of common assumptions and, through different points of analysis, reach a common understanding that advances our scholarship on Chinese economic development and its relationship with ASEAN. First, international forces matter, especially for highly trade- and foreign direct investment (FDI)-dependent regional economies such as Singapore and Malaysia. If handled improperly, their interaction with domestic factors can complicate domestic growth agenda. Second, as far as engaging with a rising China, the 'rules of the game' are fluid, with ample opportunities for ASEAN economies to leverage Chinese economic prowess and bolster their own positions. Third, related to the previous point, seemingly small states are adept in formulating strategies (at different scales and in different industries) to manage the BRI, creating mutually beneficial outcomes for their stakeholders as well as the Chinese.

In the first chapter, 'Belt and Road Initiative: A Framework to Address Challenges and Unlock Potential for High-Quality and Inclusive Growth', Khor *et al.* (2021) argue that ASEAN is one of the fastest growing regions in the world, and yet practically all accounts it too has underinvested, especially in infrastructure. This suboptimal spending on infrastructure and other types of public investments hampers the ambition of the regional economies in transitioning to the 'new economy'. Addressing chronic underinvestment — especially in infrastructure — should therefore be a top policy priority. In this context, the BRI, led by China, with its offer to work with the regional economies to plug infrastructure gaps, goes to the core of the challenges facing ASEAN. Through its vision of large-scale intra-regional and interregional investments in infrastructure projects to improve connectivity, the BRI is expected to boost cross-border trade and investment and generate economic benefits not only in the BRI region but also globally. Despite disgruntles surrounding some infrastructure projects driven by Chinese TNCs, the BRI remains a worthwhile undertaking. If anything, mismatch of expectations is inevitable but surmountable in any large endeavours. For ASEAN, its own development experience with Japanese-led investment in the economic and infrastructure space following the 1985 Plaza Accord, which steeply appreciated the Japanese Yen and pushed the Japanese TNCs to relocate their facilities abroad (especially Southeast Asia), is encouraging. This oft-forgotten episode suggests that the future prospects of BRI could be bright. To develop and sustain the BRI, Khor *et al.* (2021) propose a three-pronged policy approach. First, there is a need to identify critical issues and challenges which have emerged from past BRI projects. Second, formulate a robust governance framework with well-defined roles for stakeholders to identify needs and difficulties, pool resources, unlock financing, diversify risks, and institute rules of engagement. Third, pursue flagship BRI projects in ASEAN where there is a high degree of integration and complementarities among countries; then use success cases as models for other BRI projects in the region and elsewhere.

In the second chapter, 'The Decentralizing International Trade Architecture: Perspectives from and Role of Asia', Rana *et al.* (2021) trace the evolution of the international trade architecture from the post-World War Two era to the contemporary period. According to Rana *et al.* (2021), the centralized governance architecture established at Bretton Woods has been decentralizing with the co-existence of 'senior' global economic institutions and a plethora of newly established regional institutions, driven in large part by the frustration with difficulties in negotiating global and multilateral agreements. In addition, the increasingly insular, beggar-thy-neighbour policy adopted by the US in recent years have only complicated the situation. At least in Asia, an increasingly confident China is picking up the slack, but with outcome still rather tentative at this stage. The paper ultimately argues that Asian countries, especially those that are members of the G20, should play a greater role in lobbying and driving the needed reforms of the WTO. These countries should also seek to expedite the ratification of the RCEP and eventually institutionalize the complementarity between RCEP, the Comprehensive and Progressive Agreement for Trans-Pacific Partnership and the BRI.

The logics of a closer economic integration, especially that of trade, is also adumbrated by Yong *et al.* (2019). In their spatial panel analysis of the trade ties between China and the more mature Southeast Asian economies (that is, the ASEAN5 of Indonesia, Malaysia, Philippines, Singapore and Thailand), they discover that FDI and difference in gross domestic product are the influential determinants of vertical intra-industry trade (VIIT), although these impacts vary across manufacturing subsectors. Yong *et al.* (2019) also confirm the presence of spatial interaction effects among the ASEAN5 countries in relation to China's trade, suggesting that deeper economic cooperation among themselves is crucial to strengthen bilateral VIIT with China. In a similar vein, Hu *et al.* (2018) show that countries enjoying a strong economic relationship with China have tended to witness rising income levels that are rapid enough to converge to that of the Chinese. Contrarily, countries with relatively weak economic relationships with China tended to display little to no income convergence to the latter. Two interrelated findings could be extrapolated from Hu *et al.*'s (2018) work. For one, China can be said to contribute to a higher degree of income convergence in regional integration. Relatedly, the BRI offers prospective economies a window of opportunity to raise their income levels.

The subsequent chapter focuses on ASEAN electricity market integration, examining the ways by which the BRI can bring investment and technology into ASEAN and its impact on ASEAN's electricity market. Yao *et al.* (2021) provide three scenarios for ASEAN electricity market integration: the Laos–Thailand–Malaysia–Singapore (LTMS) arrangement, a power exchange between heterogeneous grids in the GMS, and a fully competitive electricity market with a fully-developed ASEAN Power Grid (APG). Based on these three scenarios, the authors examine the extent to which the BRI can assist electricity market integration in ASEAN. It is found that Chinese companies can be most helpful under the first scenario and Chinese investments may bring new sources of funding and technology to facilitate the electricity market integration in the LTMS, with more power plants built and more high voltage and ultra-high voltage power grids constructed and connected. Although the third scenario is the most ideal outcome for ASEAN, it is the most difficult arrangement and the least possible situation for the BRI to play a role in. Nevertheless, it remains possible for Chinese TNCs to facilitate the realization of APG. This will require collective efforts from ASEAN to make the region attractive to investors. In other words, how the BRI can play a role in ASEAN electricity market integration depends more on the host countries and on ASEAN as a collective bloc than on the Chinese. At present, ASEAN countries have tended to engage China on a bilateral level. With a more proactive and unified approach, ASEAN countries can make the BRI a truly multilateral and sustainable initiative that promotes win-win cooperation.

It is in this spirit that Tong (2021) examines Chinese FDI entering ASEAN. His chapter takes on a long-term viewpoint as it focuses on three critical period (2004 to 2008, 2009 to 2013, and post-2014) by which FDI from China is analyzed. It shows that the increase in Chinese investment in ASEAN predates the BRI launch of 2013, bearing testimony to the importance of ASEAN economies as destinations for Chinese outward

FDI (OFDI). The changes in sectoral and geographical coverage of Chinese investment in ASEAN (excluding Singapore) reflects evolving motivations and capabilities of Chinese investors. In the early days, resource-seeking motivations were dominant and Chinese investment in ASEAN was more limited to a handful of resource-specific locations. Chinese investment in the region has since become increasingly driven by more complex motivations and spread to a greater number of countries (efficiency-seeking in locations that offer cost and production advantages; market-seeking in all economies particularly sizable ones; and technology-seeking in more advanced, typically higher income economies). Importantly, while Chinese investment became an important source of FDI for ASEAN, it was not above the average China weight in FDI in the developing world. In other words, ASEAN as a region — and most of its economies — has not become 'reliant' on Chinese FDI as some commentators have suggested. Assuming China can sustain the growth momentum in its OFDI flows into ASEAN, the former still has a long way to go before it catches up with the triad of the US, European Union (EU) and Japan (which account for some 70% of world FDI stock in 2017, compared to China's 4.6%). The catch-up will be even slower if the growth momentum in Chinese investment is reversed and becomes a prolonged phenomenon.

Complementing Tong's insights, Yan and Enderwick (2021) unravel the interplay between China's OFDI regulations and enterprise supportive policies, utilizing recent developments in institutional theory. An assessment of the likely impact of Chinese OFDI on the ASEAN members requires understanding of the evolution of Chinese policy, regulations and institutions. For China, institutional reform is a complex and iterative process, constructed through the weaving of diverse interests, while following state-directed development toward a more open, market-based economy. Such investment is not simply the result of FDI liberalization: it is bolstered by a range of supporting policies designed to facilitate Chinese enterprise internationalization. Technological upgrading, access to competitive assets through cross-border acquisitions, closer regional links and funding initiatives are all part of the growing competitive profile of Chinese firms. This perspective is enriched by Shi *et al.* (2021)'s paper, titled 'Does the Belt and Road Initiative Reshape China's Outward Foreign Direct Investment in ASEAN? Shifting Motives of State-Owned and Private-Owned Enterprises'. Utilizing a project-level database from 2010 to 2015, this chapter investigates the changing investment motives of SOEs and private firms before and after the implementation of the BRI in two periods: 2010–2013 and 2014–2015. The rationale behind the comparison of motives between the SOEs and private firms is that the former are often (but not necessarily) conceived as vessels of state power while the latter more sensitive to market forces (thereby, more risk-averse). The conditional logit models show that market-seeking is one of the major motivations for both groups of firms from 2010 to 2015. The models also illustrate that the BRI promotes Chinese FDI in ASEAN through increased senior leader visits and enhanced diplomatic relations. The private firms pursued natural resources in ASEAN based on geographical and relational proximity in the pre-BRI period while SOEs exploited natural resources in ASEAN (in addition to remoter destinations) after the launch of the BRI. Perhaps surprisingly, the models show that private firms are not risk averse before and after the BRI was implemented. According to the authors, this observation is due to the private firms' long history of operating in ASEAN in which socio-economic familiarity are harnessed (such as forming collaboration with the region's ethnic Chinese firms).

In 'The Impact of the Belt and Road Initiative on Firms' Employment Structure and Wage — Evidence from China's Public Listed Firms', Chen and Chen (2021) apply a difference-in-difference analysis together with the propensity score matching approach to estimate the impact of the BRI on China's A-Share listed firms with outbound FDI to the BRI countries. From 2011 to 2017, it is found that Chinese firms investing in the BRI countries, relative to those investing elsewhere, tended to reduce their total employment, increase the share of skilled labor, and increase wages for their employees. However, they note some differences between the SOEs and private firms. SOE parent firms have no adjustment on employment and skill structure after they invest in the BRI nations while private firms tended to hire more workers and proportionally more skilled labor. When it comes to wages, the SOEs hike their payment much more than their private sector counterparts. Chen and Chen (2021)'s observations add nuance to the previous two chapters, illustrating once again that Chinese firms 'Going Out' (and their development impacts on the home and host economies) cannot and should not be homogenized amidst the more 'great game-esque' narrative surrounding the BRI.

Chapter 10, 'Rooting in Nanyang: How Efficient are Chinese Manufacturing Firms in Malaysia?', explores the performance of Chinese TNCs in the manufacturing sector, a relatively under-researched topic. Using a two-stage data envelopment analysis (DEA) approach, Zhang and Mia (2021) deploy variable return to scale output-oriented techniques to estimate efficiency levels of manufacturing firms located in Malaysia. The results illustrate that Chinese-owned manufacturing firms performed better (in most of the cases) than their counterparts (local and other foreign) in terms of efficiency in 2010 and 2015. This finding reflects the growing competitiveness of Chinese manufacturing firms (at least relative to those already operating in Malaysia) over the years. However, the analysis also suggests some cause for concern. More specifically, the efficiency levels of Chinese firms deteriorated from 2010 and 2015, implying that the expansion of production, especially since launching of the BRI, may have been driven by policy distortions provided by the Chinese government rather than the firms' own initiative to sustain or raise efficiency levels.

The remaining chapters discuss the economic strategies of key ASEAN economies. 'Singapore–China Economic Collaboration 2.0' details how — despite its small (population and physical) size — Singapore has forged a close, mutually beneficially economic relationship with China. As a practitioner who has been extensively involved in fostering Singapore's economic linkages with China, Teo (2021) divides this collaboration into two stages. In the first stage, which began in the early 1990s, the focus was on the government's role in foreign investment promotion, urban development, industrial infrastructure development and other related government policies. Platforms of collaboration include the Suzhou Industrial Park, Tianjin Eco-city, Chongqing Connectivity Initiative, the Software Transfer Project, training programs for thousands of Chinese officials, and bilateral economic councils. Singapore's pragmatic leverage on globalization trends and thoughtful application of market forces have been a major factor in the shaping of China's own highly successful economic growth model. The success of the 1.0 model has since laid the foundation for an even more multidimensional collaboration between the two countries. In the 'Singapore-China Economic Collaboration 2.0', which coincided with the BRI's announcement in 2013, there should be a greater emphasis on partnership outside of China, especially along the BRI routes, with the aim of achieving 'win-win-win' objectives for Singapore, China, and the third country. Although governmental support remains vital, there should be a greater emphasis on business-to-business collaboration as we move into a fast-changing world powered by technological advancements. Finally, more sharing and mutual learning can be done on the regulation of various aspects of the business world, be it governance of publicly-listed entities, governance of capital markets, and the competitive landscape between SOEs and private firms.

Putting flesh on Teo's chapter is 'Singapore Engages the Belt and Road Initiative: Perceptions, Policies, and Institutions'. According to Liu *et al.* (2021), Singapore's ability to consistently find avenues to cooperate with the Chinese is primarily due to a strong state which can promote effective polices and coordinate mutually reinforcing institutional mechanisms. Such organizational skills have been evident since Singapore's initial engagement with China during the latter's 'Reform and Opening-Up' era, which began in earnest in late 1978. Mutual cooperation has been embedded through institutions that promote cooperation between the bureaucrats, politicians, TNCs, SOEs, small and medium-sized private firms, and business associations. This chapter builds on the authors' earlier postulation on the 'networked state' (Liu, 2018) and its changing role in a transnational Asia, reinforcing the need to rethink the hitherto dominant nation-state framework in public governance and development studies. In addition to demonstrating the flexibility and autonomy of the 'networked state', it exhorts future researchers to contextualize the chapter's framework and arguments in different settings.

Camba and Magat (2021) train their focus on the economy strategy of the Philippines. Examining the territorial disputes between China and the Philippines over the South China Sea, their thesis revolves around the question: 'How do territorial disputes affect bilateral FDI between claimant states?' Offering statistical backing to the argument that a host country's position in the disputed borders impacts Chinese investments, this chapter plugs a critical gap in the existing scholarship, which either find mixed results or conflate territorial disputes with inter-state conflict (e.g. Olibe Kingsley & Crumbley, 1997; Woodward & Rolfe, 1993). Their difference model shows that a regime's position on the South China Sea has a significant impact on Chinese FDI, meaning that the annual number of new firms with Chinese investment significantly increases when maritime border disputes are stabilized. In contrast, conflictual relations in the maritime borders tend to decrease the annual number of new firms (see also Camba, 2017). More encouragingly, the chapter uses a novel dataset that tracks the annual number of firm registrations, demonstrating a methodological contribution that future projects can emulate. Previous works relied on the World Bank or the host country's FDI inflow-outflow data, which are imprecise because remitted amounts could simply be additional capital to pre-existing firms, making it difficult to match the timing of the investments and the impact of the disputes, if any. Generating original data from the Philippines Security Exchange Commission (SEC) instead, such imprecision has been minimized as firms would only appear in the SEC's system once they have fulfilled the minimum requirements, took the time to file the papers, and invest the minimum capital required. Due to the hefty sunk costs, if disputes appear to trouble investors, they would stop the entire process and their firm would not even enter the records. Therefore, this type of data makes it possible to disentangle the actual impact of the disputes.

In 'The Flying Geese and China's BRI in Indonesia', Negara and Suryadinata (2021) argue that China's rapid growth and the outward expansion of its firms have created opportunities that other Global North countries could not (or hesitate to) offer to aspiring developing economies such as Indonesia. In some emerging industries (such as artificial intelligence and HSR), China is challenging and even eclipsing traditional powerhouses such as Japan and Germany. In other more mature industries, Chinese TNCs might also offer complementarities e.g. mining and motorcycle manufacturing. While Negara and Suryadinata (2021) concede that a concrete assessment of the benefits of BRI project in Indonesia cannot be made at this point, they observe a new type of investment that might in turn transform Indonesian industrial trends, structure, and performance. For instance, in part because of the Widodo administration's efforts to attract Chinese FDI, a new wave of investment into the manufacturing sector (especially in electronics and mineral processing) has occurred. If this change leads to structural improvement in products quality, industrial upgrading, technological transfer, and export, then one may argue that China's investment has brought promised benefits to Indonesia. In addition, Chinese capital is also actively being redirected to the areas outside the key economic hub of Java as Indonesian economic planners promote balanced development in the outer islands that have long suffered from poor infrastructure and low economic activities.

The penultimate chapter sheds light on Malaysia's colorful and longest-serving former Prime Minister, Mahathir Mohamad. Still commanding a large following in Malaysia (and ASEAN), Mahathir remains an august statesman, not least as the last politically active national leader to have emerged from Asia's, particularly Southeast Asia's, anti-colonial generation. Campaigning for the Prime Ministership for the second time in his long career (which he eventually became from May 2018 to March 2020), Mahathir courted widespread controversy as he attacked some projects contracted in the name of the BRI by the Najib Razak-headed administration (2009–2018). However, tracing the speeches, writings, and policy directives of Mahathir from his early days as a medical student to his second stint as Prime Minister, Khoo (2021) finds what Mahathir had championed for decades was not very different from what the BRI envisioned. For one, the BRI's Silk Road-like scenarios of transcontinental rail links to extend trade and investment have a place within a 'Mahathirist imaginary' that opposes inequities in a Western-ruled global order, in addition to fostering the 'rise of Asia'. Mahathir too shares the 'Chinese Dream' of resurrecting ancient land and maritime trade routes as an 'imperative of globalization', despite attempts by others to entangle the BRI in narratives of geopolitics long repugnant to his deep non-aligned convictions.

6. Epilogue: Belt and Road Initiative in Post-Pandemic Southeast Asia

As this edited volume goes into print, the world is still grappling with the fallout of the COVID-19 pandemic, which first reared its ugly head in late 2019 to early 2020. The pandemic has shuttered almost all workplaces, caused massive loss of lives, and crippled the global economy. Although some countries have tentatively reopened borders and resumed economic activities, things are still far from certain. For the guest editors, the pandemic is not merely a public health crisis, but more importantly, it has accelerated a number of socioeconomic trends that were already evident prior to 2020, including deglobalization, growing inequality, economic competition between China and the West, etc. The intensifying US–China tension in the aftermath of the outbreak has further precipitated the possibility of a New Cold War and a remaking of the pre-existing global order (Allison, 2020; Gill, 2020). There are growing worries among ASEAN countries too for the prospect of being forced to take sides in the intensifying US–China confrontation would compromise the region's stability (e.g., Lee, 2020). With Joe Biden becoming US President in January 2021, taking over the reins from the more hawkish Donald Trump (2017–2021), a rapprochement with the Chinese initially seemed to be on the cards. However, high-profile disagreements between the two sides have dampened expectations.[5]

Like many other regions, Southeast Asia has been badly affected by the COVID-19, financially, economically, and socially. Indonesia, the largest economy of the region, saw its output contract by 2.07% in 2020, its first full-year contraction since the 1997–1998 AFC (Suroyo & Nangoy, 2021). The contraction is considerably worse than the 0.5% growth forecasted by the Center for Strategic and International Studies (CSIS), a prominent US-based think tank, in June 2020 (CSIS, 2000). Additionally, political uncertainties in Myanmar, which saw the downfall of a civilian-led government in February 2021, seem to have complicated the region's recovery process. As of 2021, major economies worldwide are still struggling to contain its spread, marking the steepest downturn since the Great Depression of the 1930s (Lawder, 2020).

[5]The most notable exchange of words thus far took place during the March 2021 top-level US–China summit in Alaska, US (see Ignatius, 2021).

Meanwhile, with its focus on investment and infrastructure, the BRI projects are understood to be severely impacted by the pandemic. Wang Xiaolong, Director-General of the Chinese Ministry of Foreign Affairs' International Economic Affairs Department, said in Beijing on June 19, 2020 that about 20% of projects under BRI have been 'seriously affected' by the COVID-19 pandemic. According to a survey by the ministry, about 40% of projects have seen little adverse impact, and another 30–40% have been somewhat affected (*Straits Times*, 2020). While there is no information on the regional and sectoral breakdown of these projects, in view of its proximity to China, it can be assumed that Southeast Asia is unlikely to escape unscathed from the fallout, which includes the non-economic realm.

While it is too early to fully assess the impact of the COVID-19 on the BRI in Southeast Asia, there are green shoots underlining regional cooperation and institutional resilience to aid the region's recovery. For one, at a time of the US's failure to provide global leadership and EU retreating to its own turf, the pandemic has accentuated the significance of regional collaboration in coping with the crisis. For example, the Special ASEAN+3 Summit on the COVID-19 was held on April 14, 2020. Going beyond the politicized rhetoric against China (and the World Health Organization (WHO)) that was common among Western countries (especially the US) of that period, the special summit focused on addressing pressing issues of saving lives, with guidance from the WHO, and revitalizing economy (ASEAN, 2020b). This special summit was followed by ASEAN+3 Ministers of Health and Economy meetings to address more case-specific issues.

Regional cooperation has also been bolstered by growing trade between China and ASEAN during 2020. Data released by the Chinese Customs in January 2021 show that despite the pandemic-induced challenges, China–ASEAN trade volumes in 2020 amounted to USD 732 billion, a 7% growth on a year-to-year basis (*Global Times*, 2021). This hike also elevated ASEAN into China's largest trading partner for the first time, overtaking second-placed EU. Meanwhile, the enhanced trade ties solidify China as ASEAN's largest trading partner for the 12th consecutive year. This development builds on the 'feel good' factor of the RCEP's signing in November 2020, especially if India decides to reverse its decision to pull out of the initiative and when more of the signatory countries ratify the trade agreement. The 'Digital Silk Road', much-lauded after the Second BRI Forum for International Cooperation in April 2019, will be another conducive force to promote regional integration. In view of Chinese advancement in the digital economy, countries such as Malaysia have more tightly integrated their industrial upgrading efforts with the fourth industrial revolution in a bid to graduate into high-income economies (Shen, 2018; Lee *et al.*, 2019).

With regards to institutional resilience, the BRI-related institutions established prior to the global pandemic have not only been intact, but also strengthened to cope with new challenges. In his address to the AIIB annual conference on July 28, 2020, Chinese President Xi Jinping called for efforts to make the AIIB 'a new type of multilateral development bank', 'a new type of development platform' and 'a new paradigm of multilateral cooperation' (Wu, 2020). In their telephone conversation on July 14, 2020, Xi and Singaporean Prime Minister Lee Hsien Loong discussed a number of issues, including ways to facilitate an economic recovery amidst the COVID-19 by 'strengthening cross-border and supply chain connectivity, as well as finance, trade and investment cooperation' and the continued progress in key bilateral projects such as the China–Singapore (Chongqing) Demonstration Initiative on Strategic Connectivity-New International Land-Sea Trade Corridor, as well as cooperation under the Belt and Road Initiative (Ministry of Foreign Affairs, 2020). Subsequently, Singapore Trade and Industry Minister Chan Chun Sing and Vice-Chairman of the National Development and Reform Commission of China Ning Jizhe in a video conference affirmed the deep economic ties that Singapore and China share, namely in government-to-government projects, and the China–Singapore (Chongqing)

Connectivity Initiative-New International Land-Sea Trade Corridor (Aw, 2020). All these are key BRI-centric projects in between China, Singapore, and other ASEAN nations, as demonstrated by Liu *et al.* in their aforementioned chapter.

Therefore, while the COVID-19 pandemic will hamper BRI's progress in the short term, the opportunities it presents to ASEAN remain promising in the long term. This is in line with the historical and continuing trend of intra-regional connectivity. Rapidly growing intra-Asian trade and economic activity had accounted for more than 50% of East Asia's total trade by the early 2010s, recording a substantial increase from the late 1970s when only 20% of their total exports were traded among Asian economies (Das, 2013; Liu, 2018). According to McKinsey Global Institute (2019), 'Asia is becoming more Asian as intra-regional flows expand — moving within the region are 60% of goods traded by Asian economies, 59% of foreign direct investment, 74% of Asian air travellers, and 71% of Asian investment in start-ups'. To tap the growing opportunities while minimizing associated risks, it is imperative for ASEAN, both as a regional grouping aspiring to establish the ASEAN Economic Community in 2025 and individual member states to establish resilient institutions and formulate proactive strategies, to more concretely engage with the BRI while minimizing potential pitfalls.

Acknowledgment

Hong Liu and Guanie Lim express their sincere gratitude to the Lien Research Programme on the Belt and Road Initiative at the Nanyang Centre for Public Administration, Nanyang Technological University (NTU), for funding an international conference in December 2018 when some of the papers in this edited volume were first presented. In addition, Liu thanks NTU Strategic Initiative funding (Plural Co-existence and Sustainable Development: Interdisciplinary and Comparative Perspectives, 04INS000103C430). The authors are responsible for the views and interpretations in this essay.

ORCID

Hong Liu http://orcid.org/0000-0003-3328-8429
Guanie Lim http://orcid.org/0000-0001-9083-8883

References

Allison, G. (2020). The New Spheres of Influence: Sharing the Globe with Other Great Powers. *Foreign Affairs*, *99*(2), 30–40

Andrews-Speed, P., Qiu, M., & Len, C. (2016). Chinese Engagement in Southeast Asian Energy and Mineral Resources: Motivations and Outlook. *Eurasian Geography and Economics*, *57*(3), 316–342.

ASEAN. 2020a. ASEAN Connectivity. Retrieved from https://connectivity.asean.org/

ASEAN. (2020b, 14 April 2020). Joint Statement of the Special ASEAN Plus Three Summit on Coronavirus Disease 2019 (COVID-19). Retrieved from https://asean.org/storage/2020/04/Final-Joint-Statement-of-the-Special-APT-Summit-on-COVID-19.pdf

Aw, C. W. (2020, 28 July 2020). Singapore, China Affirm Deep Economic Ties. Retrieved from https://www.straitstimes.com/business/economy/spore-china-affirm-deep-economic-ties

Beeson, M., & Li, F. (2016). China's Place in Regional and Global Governance: A New World Comes Into View. *Global Policy*, *7*(4), 491–499.

Bhattacherjee, K. (2020, 15 November 2020). China-Led Mega Trade Bloc RCEP Takes Off. November 15, 2020. Retrieved from https://www.thehindu.com/news/national/rcep-signatories-ready-for-negotiations-once-india-gives-written-request-to-join-pact/article33102130.ece

Cai, K. (2018). The One Belt One Road and the Asian Infrastructure Investment Bank: Beijing's New Strategy of Geoeconomics and Geopolitics. *Journal of Contemporary China*, *27*(114), 831–847.

Cali, M. (2020, 20 November 2020). The Significance of the Regional Economic Partnership Agreement. Retrieved from https://www.brookings.edu/blog/future-development/2020/11/20/the-significance-of-the-regional-economic-partnership-agreement/

Camba, A. (2017). Inter-State Relations and State Capacity: The Rise and Fall of Chinese Foreign Direct Investment in the Phillipines. *Palgrave Communications*, *3*(41), 1–19.

Camba, A. (2020). Derailing Development: China's Railway Projects and Financing Coalitions in Indonesia, Malaysia, and the Philippines. *GCI Working Paper*, *008*, 1–22.

Camba, A., & Magat, J. (2021). How Do Investors Respond to Territorial Disputes? Evidence from the South China Sea and Implications on Philippines Economic Strategy. *The Singapore Economic Review*, *66*(1), 243–267.

Chen, B., & Chen, Y. (2020). The Impact of the Belt and Road Initiative on Firms' Employment Structure and Wage — Evidence from China's Public Listed Firms. *The Singapore Economic Review*, doi: 10.1142/ S0217590820490028

CIMB ASEAN Research Institute. (2018). *China's Belt and Road Initiative (BRI) and Southeast Asia.* Kuala Lumpur: CIMB ASEAN Research Institute.

Coxhead, I. (2007). A New Resource Curse? Impacts of China's Boom on Comparative Advantage and Resource Dependence in Southeast Asia. *World Development*, *35*(7), 1099–1119.

Coxhead, I., & Jayasuriya, S. (2010). China, India and the Commodity Boom: Economic and Environmental Implications for Low-income Countries. *The World Economy*, *33*(4), 525–551.

CSIS. (2020, 18 June 2020). The Latest on Covid-19 in Southeast Asia: June 18, 2020. Retrieved from https://www.csis.org/blogs/latest-covid-19-southeast-asia/latest-covid-19-southeast-asia-june-18-2020

Das, D. K. (2013). The Role of China in Asia's Evolution to Global Economic Prominence. *Asia and the Pacific Policy Studies*, *1*(1), 216–229.

de Micheaux, E. L. (2019). Political Economy of China's Investment in Malaysia (2009–2018). *Bandung*, *6*(1), 5–49.

Fujita, M. (2013a). Comment on 'Vietnamese Economy at the Crossroads: New Doi Moi for Sustained Growth'. *Asian Economic Policy Review*, *8*(1), 146–147.

Fujita, M. (2013b). Exploiting Linkages for Building Technological Capabilities: Vietnam's Motorcycle Component Suppliers Under Japanese and Chinese Influence. Tokyo: Springer.

Gabusi, G. (2017). 'Crossing the River by Feeling the Gold': The Asian Infrastructure Investment Bank and the Financial Support to the Belt and Road Initiative. *China & World Economy*, *25*(5), 23–45.

Gill, B. (2020). China's Global Influence: Post-COVID Prospects for Soft Power. *The Washington Quarterly*, *43*(2), 97–115.

Global Times. (2021, 14 January 2021). ASEAN Becomes China's Largest Trading Partner in 2020, with 7% Growth. Retrieved from: https://www.globaltimes.cn/page/202101/1212785.shtml

Heng, J. (2020, 28 November 2020). Hard-Won RCEP Trade Pact Draws Queue of Potential New Partners. Retrieved from: https://

www.businesstimes.com.sg/government-economy/hard-won-rcep-trade-pact-draws-queue-of-potential-new-partners

Hill, H., & Jongwanich, J. (2014). Emerging East Asian Economies as Foreign Investors: An Analytical Survey. *The Singapore Economic Review*, *59*(3), 1450019.

Hu, G. H., Lau, C.-K. M., Lu, Z., & Sheng, X. (2018). Why Participate in the 'One Belt and One Road' Initiative? An Income Convergence Approach. *The Singapore Economic Review*, doi: 10.1142/S0217590818500297

Ignatius, D. (2021, 23 March 2021). Opinion: China is Convinced America is in Decline. Biden Has a Chance to Change that. Retrieved from: https://www.washingtonpost.com/opinions/global-opinions/china-is-convinced-america-is-in-decline-biden-has-a-chance-to-change-that/2021/03/22/675c4cfc-8b48-11eb-a730-1b4ed9656258˙story.html

Ji, X. (2017). Promoting Regional Development Bank Complementarity: Challenges to Asia and Lessons from Europe. *Asia Europe Journal*, *15*, 261–281.

Kawai, M. (2010). Reform of the International Financial Architecture: An Asian Perspective. *The Singapore Economic Review*, *55*(1), 207–242.

Khoo, B. T. (2021). China's Belt and Road Initiative: A View from a Mahathirist Imaginary. *The Singapore Economic Review*, *66*(1), 293–312.

Khor, H.E., Poonpatpibul, C., & Foo, S. Y. (2021). Belt and Road Initiative: A Framework to Address Challenges and Unlock Potential for High-Quality and Inclusive Growth. *The Singapore Economic Review*, *66*(1), 21–58.

KINIBIZ. (2014, 9 September 2014). Possible Temasek Sale of Stats Chippac Stake Rattles Mart. Retrieved from http://www.kinibiz.com/story/singapore/106916/temasek-exit-talks-sap-spore-chip-tester-bonds.html

Kong, T. Y. (2016). China's 21st Century Maritime Silk Road: Malaysian Perspectives. In T. W. Lim, H. Chan, K. Tseng, & W. X. Lim (Eds.), *China's One Belt One Road Initiative* (pp. 289–306). London: Imperial College Press.

Kosaikanont, R. (2019). Chinese Capital Going Global: Thai-Chinese Industrial Zone and Labor Conditions in Thailand. In Y. Santasombat (Ed.), *The Sociology of Chinese Capitalism in Southeast Asia: Challenges and Prospects* (pp. 169–194). Singapore: Palgrave Macmillan.

Kratz, A., & Pavlićević, D. (2019). Norm-Making, Norm-Taking or Norm-Shifting? A Case Study of Sino–Japanese Competition in the Jakarta–Bandung High-Speed Rail Project. *Third World Quarterly, 40*(6), 1107–1126.

Kuroiwa, I. (2016). 'Thailand-Plus-One': A GVC-Led Development Strategy for Cambodia. *Asian-Pacific Economic Literature, 30*(1), 30–41.

Lawder, D. (2020, 14 April 2020). Global Economy in 2020 on Track for Sharpest Downturn since 1930s: IMF. Retrieved from https://www.reuters.com/article/us-imf-worldbank-outlook/global-economy-in-2020-on-track-for-sharpest-downturn-since-1930s-imf-idUSKCN21W1MA

Lee, H. L. (2020). The Endangered Asian Century: America, China, and the Perils of Confrontation. *Foreign Affairs, 99*(4), 52–64.

Lee, K., Wong, C.-Y., Intarakumnerd, P., & Limapornvanich, C. (2019). Is the Fourth Indusrial Revolution a Window of Opportunity for Upgrading or Reinforcing the Middle-Income Trap? Asian Model of Development in Southeast Asia. *Journal of Economic Policy Reform*, 1–18.

Liang, W. (2020). China's Institutional Statecraft Under Xi Jinping: Has the AIIB Served China's Interest? *Journal of Contemporary China*, 1–16.

Lim, G. (2017). China's 'Going Out' Strategy in Southeast Asia: Case Studies of the Automobile and Electronics Sectors. *China: An International Journal, 15*(4), 157–178.

Lim, G., Li, C., & Syailendra, E. A. (2021). Why is It so Hard to Push Chinese Railway Projects in Southeast Asia? The Role of Domestic Politics in Malaysia and Indonesia. *World Development, 138*, 105272.

Liu, H. (2018). Transnational Asia and Regional Networks: Toward a New Political Economy of East Asia. *East Asian Community Review, 1*(1), 33–47.

Liu, H., Fan, X., & Lim, G. (2021). Singapore Engages the Belt and Road Initiative: Perceptions, Policies, and Institutions. *The Singapore Economic Review, 66*(1), 219–241.

Liu, H., & Lim, G. (2019). The Political Economy of a Rising China in Southeast Asia: Malaysia's Response to the Belt and Road Initiative. *Journal of Contemporary China, 28*(116), 216–231.

Liu, H., Tan, K. Y., & Lim, G. (2021). Introduction — Southeast Asia and the Belt and Road Initiative: The Political Economy of

Regionalism, Trade, and Infrastructure. *The Singapore Economic Review, 66*(1), 1–20.
Liu, H., & Zhou, Y. (2019). New Chinese Capitalism and the ASEAN Economic Community. In Y. Santasombat (Ed.), *The Sociology of Chinese Capitalism in Southeast Asia* (pp. 55–73). Singapore: Palgrave Macmillan.
Liu, W., & Dunford, M. (2016). Inclusive Globalization: Unpacking China's Belt and Road Initiative. *Area Development and Policy, 1*(3), 323–340.
Luo, Y., Xue, Q., & Han, B. (2010). How Emerging Market Governments Promote Outward FDI: Experience from China. *Journal of World Business, 45*(1), 68–79.
Maikaew, P. (2020, 18 February 2020). GM Sells Off Factories to Great Wall. Retrieved from https://www.bangkokpost.com/business/1859694/gm-sells-off-factories-to-great-wall
McKinsey Global Institute. (2019). *The Future of Asia: Asian Flows and Networks are Defining the Next Phase of Globalization.* New York: McKinsey Global Institute.
Ministry of Foreign Affairs. (2020, 14 July 2020). Prime Minister Lee Hsien Loong's Telephone Call with President of the People's Republic of China Xi Jinping. Retrieved from https://www.mfa.gov.sg/Newsroom/Press-Statements-Transcripts-and-Photos/2020/07/20200714-P-XJP-Call
Mueller, L. M. (2019, 20 June 2019). ASEAN Connectivity could be Blueprint for World. Retrieved from: https://www.thejakartapost.com/news/2019/06/20/asean-connectivity-could-be-blueprint-world.html
Negara, S. D., & Suryadinata, L. (2021). The Flying Geese and China's BRI in Indonesia. *The Singapore Economic Review, 66*(1), 269–292.
Ngo, C. N. (2017). Local Value Chain Development in Vietnam: Motorcycles, Technical Learning and Rents Management. *Journal of Contemporary Asia, 47*(1), 1–26.
Oh, Y. A., & No, S. (2019). The Patterns of State-Firm Coordination in China's Private Sector Internationalization: China's Mergers and Acquisitions in Southeast Asia. *The Pacific Review*, 1–27.
Olibe Kingsley, O., & Crumbley, C. L. (1997). Determinants of U.S. Private Foreign Direct Investments in OPEC Nations: From Public and Non-Public Policy Perspectives. *Journal of Public Budgeting, Accounting & Financial Management, 9*(2), 331–355.
Pitakdumrongkit, K. (2015). *Negotiating Financial Agreement in East Asia: Surviving the Turbulence.* London: Routledge.

Rana, P. B., Chia, W.-M., & Ji, X. (2021). The Decentralizing International Trade Architecture: Perspectives from and Role of Asia. *The Singapore Economic Review*, *66*(1), 59–84.

Rana, P., & Pacheco Pardo, R. (2018). Rise of Complementarity Between Global and Regional Financial Institutions: Perspectives from Asia. *Global Policy*, *9*(2), 231–243.

Ravenhill, J. (2016). The Political Economy of an 'Asian' Mega-FTA: The Regional Comprehensive Economic Partnership. *Asian Survey*, *56*(6), 1077–1100.

Ravenhill, J. (2017). The Political Economy of the Trans-Pacific Partnership: A '21st Century' Trade Agreement? *New Political Economy*, *22*(5), 573–594.

Refinitiv. (2020). *BRI Connect: An Initiative in Numbers*. New York: Refinitiv.

Shen, H. (2018). Building a Digital Silk Road? Situating the Internet in China's Belt and Road Initiative. *International Journal of Communication*, *12*, 2683–2701.

Shi, J., Hu, X., Li, Y., & Feng, T. (2021). Does the Belt and Road Initiative Reshape China's Outward Foreign Direct Investment in ASEAN? Shifting Motives of State-Owned and Private-Owned Enterprises. *The Singapore Economic Review*, *66*(1), 161–183.

Straits Times (2020, 19 June 2020). China Says One-Fifth of Belt and Road Projects 'Seriously Affected' by Coronavirus Pandemic. Retrieved from https://www.straitstimes.com/asia/east-asia/china-says-one-fifth-of-belt-and-road-projects-seriously-affected-by-coronavirus

Suroyo, G., & Nangoy, F. (2021, 5 February 2021). UPDATE 3-Indonesia's Economy Suffers First Full-Year Slump in over Two Decades in 2020. Retrieved from https://www.reuters.com/article/indonesia-economy-gdp-idUSL4N2K92XC

Tan, K. Y. (2007). China's 11th Five-Year Plan: A Critical Perspective. In J. Wong & W. Liu (Eds.), *China's Surging Economy: Adjusting for More Balanced Development* (pp. 55–132). Singapore: World Scientific.

Teo, E. C. (2021). Singapore–China Economic Collaboration 2.0. *The Singapore Economic Review*, *66*(1), 207–217.

Thomas, D. (2014, 6 November 2014). Temasek to Exit STATS ChipPAC with $1.8 billion Deal with China's JCET. Retrieved from https://www.reuters.com/article/us-stats-jiangsu-m-a/temasek-to-exit-stats-chippac-with-1-8-billion-deal-with-chinas-jcet-idUSKBN0IQ0YY20141106?mod=article_inline

Tong, Y.-S. (2021). China's Outbound Investment in ASEAN Economies in Three Periods: Changing Patterns and Trends. *The Singapore Economic Review*, *66*(1), 105–142.

Wilson, J. (2017). The Evolution of China's Asian Infrastructure Investment Bank: From a Revisionist to Status-Seeking Agenda. *International Relations of the Asia-Pacific*, *19*(1), 147–176.

Woodward, D., & Rolfe, R. (1993). The Location of Export-Oriented Foreign Direct Investment in the Caribbean Basin. *Journal of International Business Studies*, *24*(1), 121–144.

Wu, W. (2020, 28 July 2020). Xi Jinping Uses Annual Conference of Infrastructure Bank to Spell out China's Multilateral and Global Ambitions. Retrieved from https://www.scmp.com/news/china/diplomacy/article/3095048/xi-uses-annual-conference-infrastructure-bank-spell-out-chinas

Yan, T., & Enderwick, P. (2021). Evolution of China's Outward Foreign Direct Investment Regime: Implications for Southeast Asia under the Belt and Road Initiative. *The Singapore Economic Review*, *66*(1), 143–159.

Yao. L, Andrews-Speed, P., & Shi, X. (2021). ASEAN Electricity Market Integration: How Can Belt and Road Initiative Bring New Life to It? *The Singapore Economic Review*, *66*(1), 85–103.

Yong, C.-C., Yew, S.-Y., & Chin, M.-Y. (2019). Spatial Panel Analysis on ASEAN–China Trade Links. *The Singapore Economic Review*, *64*(3), 709–726.

Yoshimatsu, H. (2018). New Dynamics in Sino-Japanese Rivalry: Sustaining Infrastructure Development in Asia. *Journal of Contemporary China*, *27*(113), 1–16.

Zhang, M. (2020). Beyond Infrastructure: Re-Thinking China's Foreign Direct Investment in Malaysia. *Pacific Review*, 1–25.

Zhang, M., & Mia, M. A. (2021). Rooting in Nanyang: How Efficient are Chinese Manufacturing Firms in Malaysia? *The Singapore Economic Review*, *66*(1), 185–206.

Zhao, S. (2020). *China's New Global Strategy: The Belt and Road Initiative (BRI) and Asian Infrastructure Investment Bank (AIIB)*. Volume 1. Oxon: Routledge.

Chapter 1

BELT AND ROAD INITIATIVE: A FRAMEWORK TO ADDRESS CHALLENGES AND UNLOCK POTENTIAL FOR HIGH-QUALITY AND INCLUSIVE GROWTH[¶]

HOE EE KHOR[*], CHAIPAT POONPATPIBUL[†] and SUAN YONG FOO[‡]

ASEAN+3 Macroeconomic Research Office (AMRO)
10 Shenton Way, #15-08 MAS Building, Singapore 079117
[*]Khor.Hoeee@amro-asia.org
[†]Chaipat.Poonpatpibul@amro-asia.org
[‡]Foo.SuanYong@amro-asia.org

Published Online 27 June 2019

Developing economies, especially emerging market economies (EMEs), face complex challenges in investing for growth, including building infrastructure. Many developing economies are trying to sustain the growth catch-up process, and manage disruptions related to transition to the "new economy", as well as headwinds from protectionist tendencies in trade and technology. Investing for the long term — including in infrastructure — has therefore become a critical issue. In this context, the Belt and Road Initiative (BRI) has captured the imagination of the world. An ambitious initiative involving more than 70 countries collaborating through investments in infrastructure, it seeks to improve connectivity for cross-border trade and investment, and generate economic benefits for the countries involved. It seeks to address large infrastructure gaps and build capacities for growth. And it helps countries unable to get affordable financing for plugging savings-investment shortfalls. However, the BRI has drawn criticisms over China's underlying geopolitical motives, and BRI partner countries have been warned of the risk of becoming heavily indebted or getting locked into business platforms created by China. This paper aims to contribute to the policy debate over the BRI from an ASEAN perspective. It analyzes the reasons for the persistent infrastructure investment gaps in EMEs from an ASEAN perspective; assesses whether BRI is more of a development opportunity or a debt trap; outlines a framework to address the risks and concerns in order to unlock the potential benefits; and uses case studies both outside of and within the ASEAN region to distil key themes needing policy attention.

Keywords: Emerging market economies (EMEs); developing economies; trade; investment, growth; development; infrastructure; Belt and Road Initiative (BRI); connectivity; savings-investment; debt.

JEL Classification: B27, E22, F15, F31, F32, F41, F62, H54, H62, H81, H87, N15, O11, O19

1. Introduction

Developing economies, especially emerging market economies (EMEs), face complex challenges in investing for long-term growth, including building infrastructure. Much more

[‡]Corresponding author.

[¶]This article originally appeared in *The Singapore Economic Review*, **66**(1), pp. 21–58 than developed countries, developing economies need high levels of investment over prolonged periods of time to lift potential growth, and move up the income ladder. Starting from low bases, there is a need to accumulate capital rapidly, upskill labor forces, and take measures to boost productivity. Only then can developing economies maintain growth momentum, and stand a realistic chance of escaping the low- and middle-income traps. At the current juncture, many developing economies are trying to sustain the growth catch-up process, cope with disruptions related to the global transition to the "new economy", and use available policy tools to manage headwinds from rising protectionist tendencies in the trade and technology space. Therefore, investing for the long term — including in infrastructure — has arguably taken on even greater importance than before. (See, for example, IMF, 2017; World Bank, 2012; ADB, 2017; UN, 2018).

The remainder of this paper is organized as follows. Section 2 analyzes why there has been a persistent infrastructure investment gap in many EMEs from an ASEAN perspective. Section 3 seeks to take a critical look at the Belt and Road Initiative (BRI), considering both sides of the opinion divide, on whether the Initiative is more of a development opportunity or a debt trap. Section 4 outlines a proposed framework to maximize the benefits of BRI, address risks and concerns, and uses several case studies both outside of and within the ASEAN region to distil several key themes needing policy attention. Section 5 concludes this paper, pulling together the key takeaways.

2. Persistent Infrastructure Gap in EMEs: The Case of ASEAN Countries

ASEAN is one of the most rapidly-growing and dynamic regions in the world, and yet by practically all accounts, it too has underinvested, especially in infrastructure, since the Asian Financial Crisis (AFC). This has been so even through periods when economic growth has picked up pace and income convergence towards advanced economies accelerated. (AMRO, 2017). Yet the importance of investing sufficiently in the right areas is critical for ASEAN countries individually and as a region. The conventional manufacturing-for-exports strategy, which has underpinned many ASEAN economies' growth and development in the past decade, has required large investments year after year, including in infrastructure that support manufacturing exports. And the results have been spectacular. This manufacturing-for-exports strategy has created strong, self-reinforcing dynamics to raise economic growth, productivity, and wages. Looking ahead, ASEAN's transition to the "new economy" will require yet more investments in new types of infrastructure.

2.1. *Coexistence of large developmental needs and massive funding gaps*

Indeed ASEAN's infrastructure needs for the next two decades are so large that they surely exceed the capacity of most countries' individual technical knowhow and financial resources. The Asian Development Bank (ADB) estimates that over the period 2015–2030, climate-adjusted infrastructure investment needs would amount to 5.7% of GDP per annum

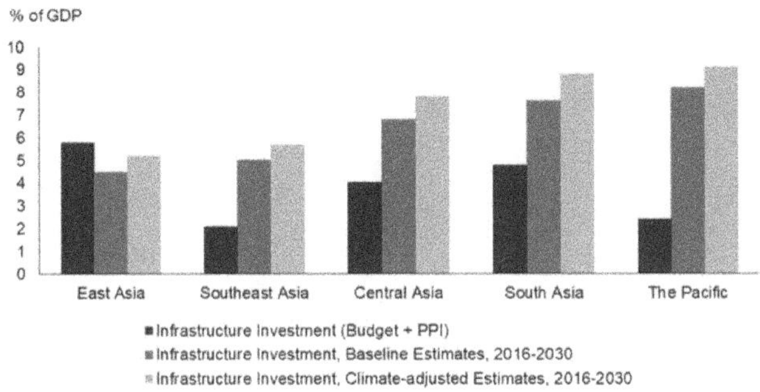

Notes: In this case, East Asia comprises China, Hong Kong, Taipei, China, Korea and Mongolia; Southeast Asia comprises Indonesia, Malaysia, Thailand, the Philippines, Singapore, Brunei, Cambodia, Lao PDR, Myanmar and Vietnam.
Source: ADB (2017).

Figure 1. Infrastructure Development Needs in ASEAN Economies and Comparator Economies

for Southeast Asia and 5.2% per annum for East Asia (Figure 1) (ADB, 2017). An important factor is the continued rapid growth forecasted for the region, which generates new infrastructure demand. Within these estimates, lower-income countries' needs would be much larger as those of high-income countries. Furthermore, the ADB points out that although fiscal reforms could generate additional revenues equivalent to a few percentage points of GDP to help bridge part of the funding gap for some economies, in order for the private sector to fill the remaining gap, it would have to increase investments substantially from current levels, and sustain these levels year after year, which is quite unlikely to happen without external support. These challenges point to the need for countries and multilateral development banks (MDBs) to come together to pool financial resources and share expertize, whether it be in construction, engineering, project management, infrastructure operation, or different types of financing and risk diversification (equity financing, bank lending, debt financing, and even securitization).

ASEAN has a massive infrastructure funding gap. As Figure 1 shows, infrastructure investment using government budgets and public-private partnerships for infrastructure (PPI) is projected to be way below both the baseline and climate-adjusted estimates of the region's needs between 2016 and 2030. The reasons for this chronic underinvestment are manifold, including:

- for the low-income ASEAN countries, a savings-investment gap (Figure 2) and an attendant infrastructure gap;
- for the middle-income ASEAN countries, a lack of supportive ecosystems for infrastructure building, which has translated into sluggish public- and private investments in this space; and
- for many ASEAN countries along the entire income spectrum, significant foreign exchange constraints in the sense that actual or perceived weaknesses in their external positions render them vulnerable to capital flow volatility shocks, which in turn compel

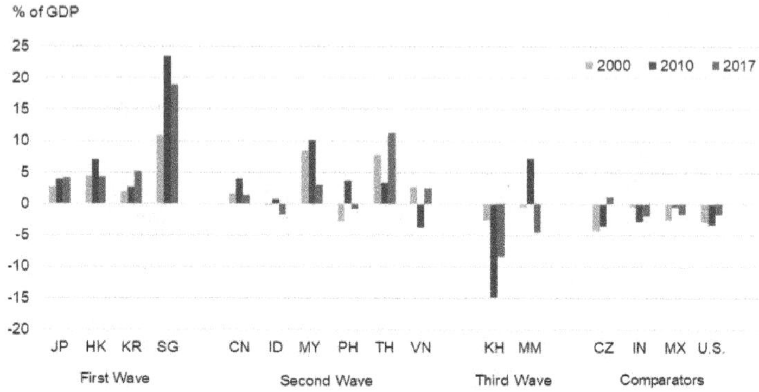

Source: IMF WEO Database, AMRO calculations.

Figure 2. Savings-Investment Gap: ASEAN Economies and Selected Comparators

them to run current account balances that are stronger than optimal, as they should ideally be spending more on infrastructure and other types of investments. In other words, besides an already sizeable savings-investment gap, many ASEAN countries also face a significant foreign exchange gap (Figure 3).

Looking to the future, as ASEAN countries try to make the transition to the "new economy", addressing chronic underinvestment — especially in infrastructure — should be a top policy priority. In this context, the BRI, led by China, with its offer to work with the regional economies to plug the infrastructure gaps, goes to the core of the growth

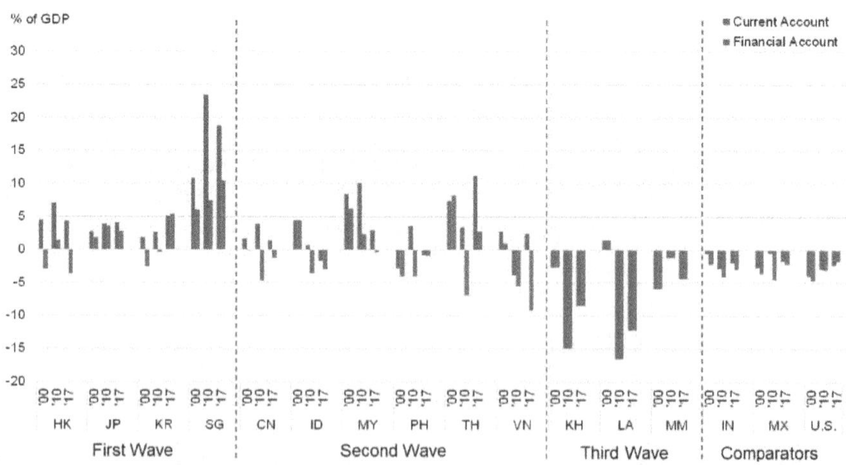

Source: IMF WEO Database.

Figure 3. Foreign Exchange Gap: ASEAN Economies and Comparators

challenges facing the region. It is therefore important to make a rational assessment of the costs and benefits as well as the risks and challenges, which come with this unprecedented initiative — by an EME, for other developing economies globally, to co-invest in infrastructure projects to improve connectivity for boosting cross-border trade and investment; and to address large infrastructure gaps and improve countries' capacities for growth.

2.2. *Broader context: Collapse of investment in ASEAN since the Asian Financial Crisis (AFC)*

The collapse of investment in ASEAN since the AFC (Figure 4) can be found in both the roots of that crisis and in the global economic and financial environment that led to and followed the crisis (AMRO, 2017). Among a myriad of interlinked factors underlying the AFC, overinvestment on the back of optimism that capital inflows would continue indefinitely was the key factor that led to the painful experiences many ASEAN countries went through and still remember vividly today. One consequence of the AFC is the collapse in both public and private investments as governments, banks, and corporates focus on repairing and strengthening their balance sheets to ensure that such a crisis would never happen again. ASEAN countries' policymakers, in particular, have been very mindful of the foreign exchange constraints and have worked hard to build up their foreign reserves as a form of self-insurance against future balance of payments crises. This has led to significant underspending on essential infrastructures, which are critical for enhancing the growth potential of the economies.

More broadly, the global financial environment in the past two decades has been unfavorable for long-term investments in many ways.

First, the rapid growth of the asset management industry, especially the macro hedge funds, implies greater volatility of capital flows as the industry is highly sensitive to yield differentials across asset classes and markets. In particular, EMEs which offer higher yields

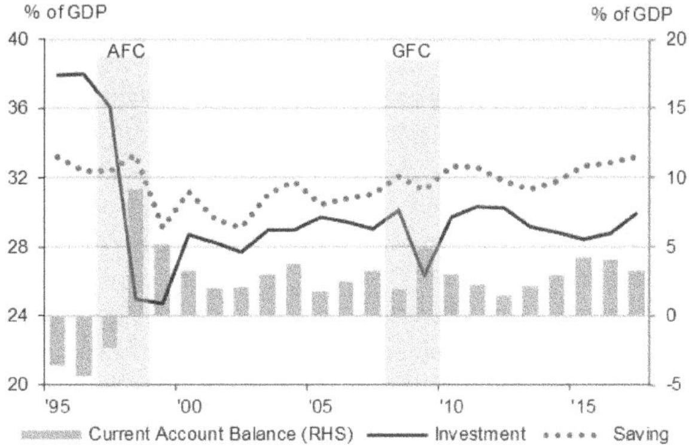

Notes: ASEAN4 in this case refers to Indonesia, Malaysia, Thailand and the Philippines.
Source: IMF, AMRO calculations.

Figure 4. Investment as Percent of GDP: ASEAN4 Economies and Korea

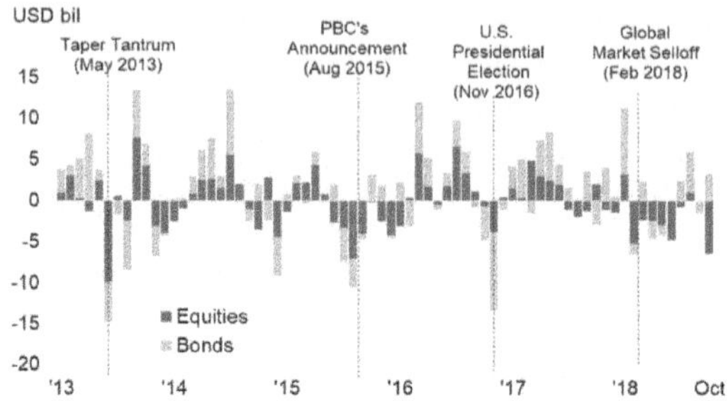

Source: National Authorities.

Figure 5. Capital Flows to ASEAN Economies

are very vulnerable to the risk-on and risk-off behavior of portfolio investors who tend to herd in and out of EMEs' financial markets. As a result, many EMEs are compelled to save and accumulate more foreign reserves than is optimal, from an investment-growth perspective, in order to buffer against capital flow volatility shocks. Hence, global financial markets have required EMEs to maintain relatively strict macroeconomic and financial policies, and allowed them much less leeway in terms of pursuing economic and financial policies supporting growth, before punishing individual countries or entire (sub-) regions by quickly halting or reversing capital flows. In fact, the heightening of general risk aversion globally has often been enough to trigger such "sudden stops" in capital flows to EMEs, including those in the ASEAN region. The past two decades are replete with examples, with some recent ones being: the Taper Tantrum of 2013, the US presidential election of 2016, and the global market sell-off of 2018. Each time, EM regions, including ASEAN, have experienced substantial shifts in capital flows (Figure 5). This has compelled many ASEAN countries to run large current account surpluses and build up foreign reserves even though they should ideally be spending more on infrastructure and other types of investments.

Second, developing economies along the entire income spectrum face daunting challenges to create supportive ecosystems domestically for investments in infrastructure, and combine that with access to affordable financing internationally. Among the key elements needed are: expertise for evaluating and making decisions on the types of projects needed; risk management capability; effective legal framework; access to affordable financing; markets for risk mitigation tools; and capability within the public and private sector to manage projects and ensure environmental protection. In turn, such an ecosystem requires close collaboration among many stakeholders including government, private sector agents, expert advisors, financial institutions (FIs) and MDBs to help overcome the challenges facing developing economies at different stages of economic development and infrastructure building. Most ASEAN countries, like many other EMEs globally, have found it difficult to put in place all the required elements.

Even looking at financing narrowly, the nature of infrastructure projects — long gestation periods, higher uncertainty over economic viability and cash flows compared to

Phase	Economic and Contractual Issues	Financial Characteristics	Potential Investors
Planning	Tight written contracts; Planning 10-30 months; Credit ratings and guarantees needed	Need to find equity investors & debt investors. Debt investors who commit early demand high price	Equity sponsors need to have high level of expertise – often constructors or governments; Debt investors tend to be banks
Construction	Close monitoring req'd; Effective dispute resol mechanism needed	High-risk phase: risk of default and other adverse events	Hard to get refinancing or additional financing if gaps are found
Operational	Ownership structure must be clear; Cash flow mgt is impt	Cash flows need to more than cover debt repayment	Bonds are natural choice for refinancing needs

Source: Ehlers (2014), AMRO.

Figure 6. Financing and Technical Considerations: Different Phases of Infrastructure Projects

other types of investments, and requirements for lenders and investors to possess sufficient technical knowhow — means that the process of securing financing through the planning, building, and operational phases of these projects is unusually challenging. (See, for example, Ehlers, 2014). Some of these considerations are outlined in Figure 6. In the ASEAN+3 region, for private sector participation in infrastructure projects, many countries rely heavily on debt financing relative to equity financing for infrastructure development (Figure 7), reflecting precisely these challenges. Compared to debt investors, equity investors are more demanding and require even higher levels of expertise (ADB, 2017; Ehlers, 2014). Thus debt financing has been the far more predominant mode of infrastructure financing for ASEAN+3 countries.[1]

Third, flaws and deficiencies in the international financial architecture. The financial resources of IFIs are insufficient to meet the bulk of infrastructure building needs of EMEs. Many countries are also wary of contributing more of their own finances to multilateral mechanisms despite recognizing that infrastructure generates shared benefits. More importantly, as the recently released Report of the G20 Eminent Persons Group (EPG) puts it, IFIs can do more to help countries strengthen governance capacity and human capital, as key elements of a strong foundation for an attractive investment climate, job creation, and social stability. The potential for collaboration among the IFIs as well as with other development partners to maximize their contributions as a group, including by convergence around core standards, has been largely untapped. And there needs to be a stronger

[1] Encouragingly, infrastructure investments in ASEAN in particular have become an increasingly attractive asset class for institutional investors, for a few important reasons. (See, for example, PWC, 2018). First, although cash flows from infrastructure projects take some time to be generated, these cash flows do tend to be steady, which means predictable and often high returns for investors. Second, institutional investors hold long-term views, and there can therefore be a good match between them and infrastructure projects. Third, by virtue of being very different from other types of investments, infrastructure as an asset class provides portfolio diversification benefits, and even hedges against inflation risk. Consequently, infrastructure has grown more quickly than other types of asset classes within assets under management for ASEAN, albeit from a low base. For Asian infrastructure projects, sovereign wealth funds (SWFs), pension funds and insurance funds are major investors. But that said, infrastructure constitutes a relatively small share of these entities' total investments, often at less than 10%.

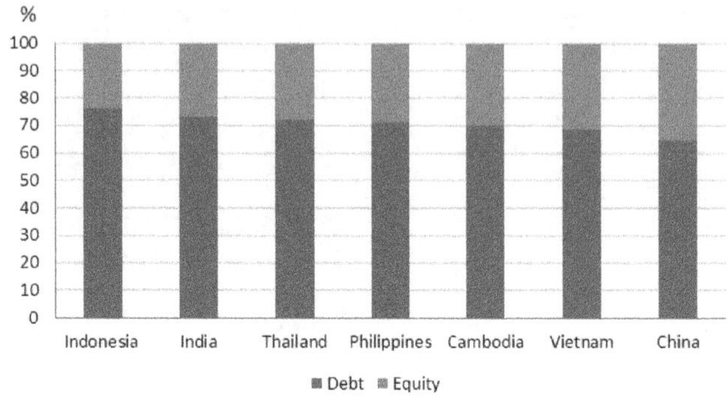

Source: ADB (2017).

Figure 7. Composition of Private Sector Participation in Infrastructure

systematic effort at developing system-wide insurance and diversification of risk, to create a large-scale asset class backed by investment projects, and to mobilize significantly greater private sector participation. (G20 Eminent Persons Group (EPG) Report, 2018).

As a result of these structural factors, investment — especially in infrastructure — having collapsed from probably too high levels following the AFC, has now "undershot" for the past two decades, and, despite efforts by some countries, has yet to show signs of a decisive lift-off in the coming years.

3. Belt and Road Initiative (BRI): Two Sides of the Opinion Divide: Growth Opportunity or Debt Trap

3.1. *BRI: Going to the core of infrastructure-related growth challenges for EMEs*

In this context, the BRI has captured the imagination of the world, and yet drawn a considerable amount of criticism, as well as sparked debate about what is needed for this pan-regional multiyear effort to realize its vision of economic transformation for the global economy.

Going to the core of the perennial infrastructure-related challenges facing developing economies striving to sustain high growth, the BRI is an ambitious initiative led by China and involving more than 70 countries collaborating through investments in infrastructure projects to improve connectivity for boosting cross-border trade and investment. It seeks to address large infrastructure gaps and improve countries' capacities for growth. It helps countries needing to plug savings-investment shortfalls but often unable to do so on affordable financial terms. The coverage is very wide. According to the World Bank, the geographical reach of BRI projects covers about one-third of global GDP, two-thirds of world population, and three-quarters of energy reserves. To this, one should add that this is the first such audacious attempt by an EME for developing countries across different regions of the world, for a very diverse range of projects and financing deals.

3.2. *Prospective benefits for ASEAN*

ASEAN stands to benefit very broadly from the BRI over the long term.

First, as outlined in Section 2 above, ASEAN's infrastructure development needs for the next two decades or so are large, and exceed the capacity of most countries' individual technical knowhow and financial resources. The ADB estimates that over the period 2015–2030, climate-adjusted infrastructure investment needs amount to 5.7% of GDP per annum for Southeast Asia, and points out that the financing gaps are too large to be closed by mobilizing additional fiscal revenue or from the private sector. The BRI, by tapping the financial resources of China as a huge country with surplus savings and bringing together nearly 70 countries worldwide plus several regional financing hubs and IFIs, creates new opportunities for affordable financing.

Second, the crowding-in effects of BRI projects will add impetus to the region's infrastructure development efforts. Simulations by Oxford Economics and AMRO staff suggest that BRI-related public investment will crowd in private investment, especially for countries with large gaps in investments. Assuming, perhaps conservatively, that BRI investment would help fill up 20% of the infrastructure investment gap, the simulations suggest that this could crowd in private investment by as much as 0.3% of GDP within the next two years,[2] with the crowding-in effect most pronounced in the Philippines and in Indonesia, where investment gaps are also the largest among the ASEAN-4 economies[3] (Figure 8) and whose financial sector development lags behind those of more advanced ASEAN+3 economies (Figure 9).

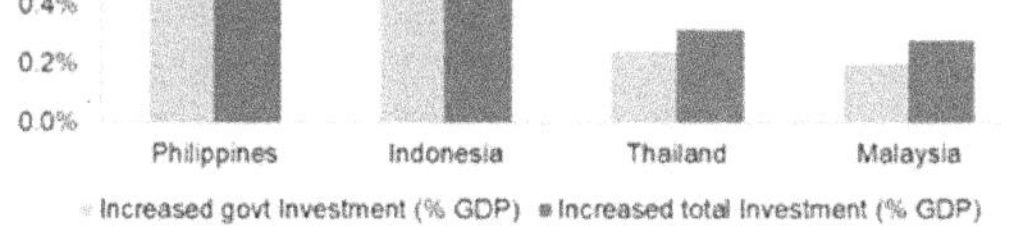

Notes: It is assumed that due to the BRI, government investments in these countries increase, and help to narrow the estimated total investment gaps by 20%. The higher government investment will then push up private investment and GDP in the following period.
Source: Oxford Economics and AMRO staff estimates.

Figure 8. Impact of Total Investment and Crowding-In of Private Investment in ASEAN4, Change 2019–2020

[2] As Oxford Economics' model uses supply-side factors to determine GDP in the long-run, but we only shock the demand-side factors, therefore, we only use the dynamics in the first two years to study the crowding-in effect of BRI investment.
[3] ASEAN-4 economies are: Indonesia, Malaysia, the Philippines, and Thailand.

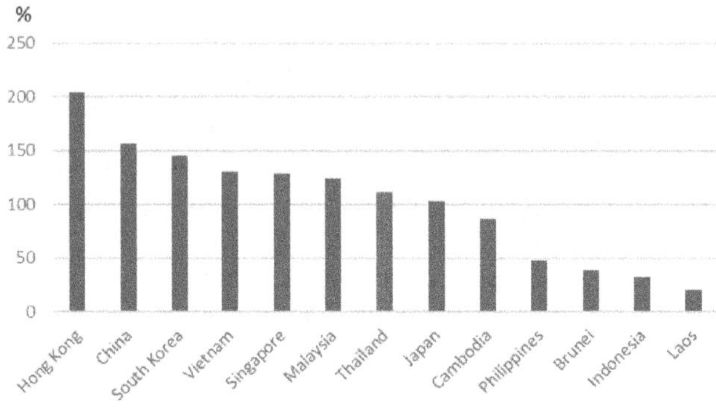

Source: World Economy.

Figure 9. Bank Credit to Private Sector as Percent of GDP: ASEAN Economies and Comparators

Third, once new improved infrastructure generates positive network effects, these effects are likely to create fresh momentum for ASEAN countries' redoubled efforts in recent years to improve capacity across different economic sectors. Studies of different countries' experiences have suggested that new roads, for example, can result in significant movement of surplus labor from agriculture into industries with higher-paying jobs, with the effects most pronounced for villages close to industrializing cities. Creation of new cross-border transport infrastructures can also be expected to generate similar but likely even bigger effects in terms of labor mobility on a regional scale. (see, for example, World Bank, 2012). In this regard, it is pertinent to consider the ADB's observation about the need for countries to collaborate to provide such infrastructure as regional public goods (RPGs). Essentially, such infrastructure creates benefits beyond single countries' boundaries, but narrowly-conceived national interests or the high costs involved are likely to result in undersupply of RPGs. Infrastructure-building at both national and regional levels is needed to take full advantage of the region's stock of human capital, and this is also where the BRI can help to provide a solid lift. (ADB, 2018).

3.3. *Mismatch of expectations between lenders and borrowers: Inevitable but surmountable*

The BRI has drawn a growing amount of criticisms and even scepticism. These criticisms are related to concerns over BRI partner countries investing in projects that are non-viable and becoming over-indebted and losing control over strategic assets with geopolitical implications. There is wariness about the underlying geopolitical motives of China, as well as the risk of many countries becoming heavily indebted to China or getting locked-in to infrastructural or business platforms created by China. Less-developed partner countries, especially, have multiple reservations. First, the fear of falling into debt traps — not by design, but rather by letting high ambition lead to fiscal overstretch, even when loans are on concessional terms. Second, concerns about getting limited local value-add from those BRI projects which are built by Chinese companies using mainly Chinese workers and imported capital equipment. Third, apprehensions about ceding control or ownership of completed projects, in the event that the host country is unable to service its debt. Fourth, concerns about having to bend to China's broader geopolitical interests in bilateral or multilateral deals. These criticisms raise the issue of whether it is possible to create the type of national and supranational ecosystems needed to address the criticisms and to bring about the increased and sustainable infrastructure investment offered by the BRI.

The mismatch of expectations may reflect rising host country aspirations, to move up the regional- and global economic development ladder, while China, as the key investing country, necessarily assesses its returns in the context of its foreign policy and outward investment strategy. History, including that of the ASEAN region's past development experience, suggests that this mismatch of expectations at this early stage of the BRI is not insurmountable. As long as there are substantial economic benefits to be gained over the long term, it is in the interest of both China and the partner countries to work out a framework that addresses the concerns and safeguards the interests of both parties.

The experience of Japan's outward direct investments (ODI) in ASEAN in the 1970s to 1990s, in both the business sectors and the infrastructure space, is illuminating. It suggests that the concerns with the BRI can be addressed in a mutually satisfactory manner, so that the BRI can become a major source of funding and investment for the region.

Japan has been the most advanced and developed country in Asia for the longest time, with the means (financial resources and technological knowhow), as well as the incentives, to invest in the region (boosting the returns on its investments, and spurring its own manufacturing-for-exports strategy through tighter economic linkages with ASEAN countries).

Japan's ODI in ASEAN countries during the 1980s and 1990s was spurred by an alignment of multiple interests on both sides. The rise of Japanese MNCs coincided with a period where production efficiencies were found in the expansion of cross-border production networks. The sharp appreciation of the Japanese Yen following the 1985 Plaza Accord, which impinged on Japanese firms' export competitiveness, was another impetus for Japanese MNCs to outsource the more labor intensive part of the production process to ASEAN countries with abundant labor, in order to lower the unit cost of production and maintain their export competitiveness. This was a win-win proposition for both Japan and the ASEAN countries, many of which had a large pool of workers, and were keen to industrialize in order to move up the manufacturing value chain.

On infrastructure, the Japanese government and its policy banks such as the Japan Bank for International Cooperation (JBIC), have been active since the 1960s in providing concessional loans and grants to help developing countries in the region invest in basic infrastructure. In the early years, Japan's financial aid program was often criticized for being tied to the use of Japanese contractors and procurement of Japanese goods. In response, Japan has changed its policies and practices, and as a result, Japan's financial aid program for infrastructure projects has been well received. In Thailand, the successful development of the Eastern Seaboard in the 1990s is a prime example of significant support by Japan in infrastructure development. Indeed, projects in Asia funded by Japan have included many which help the partner countries in the first instance, without immediate promise of "returns" for Japan. These include poverty-reduction initiative for Vietnam, and sanitation-improvement works for various parts of India. The mode of engagement has included consistent careful efforts to coordinate planning and execution with local governments of partner countries, as well as a strong emphasis on accountability and risk management. For example, impressing upon governments the fact that while guarantees for projects do not automatically constitute liabilities for governments, they can indeed become debt under certain circumstances, and therefore these contingent liabilities should be assessed and managed carefully through debt sustainability analyses and proper risk mitigation measures.

Today, China and its many BRI partners are learning quickly the need to manage the projects in a transparent way and adopt policies and practices to address the criticisms leveled against the BRI. In its recent review of the BRI, the Chinese government has emphasized the importance of sound execution, over and above expanding the scale and scope of BRI projects. It has also set up the Asian Infrastructure Investment Bank (AIIB) as a multilateral investment bank following best practices of corporate governance. The China Development Bank (CDB) and the China Export-Import Bank (EXIM Bank) have refrained from "splashing the cash" in the manner which many sceptics predicted they would. Policymakers and senior officials are also taking great care to base pronouncements of shared benefits on facts and realities. One example is the Chinese ambassador to Sri Lanka's public communication efforts to provide a more balanced "score card" of BRI projects in Sri Lanka.

4. A Proposed Framework to Maximize the Benefits of BRI, Address the Risks and Concerns

Looking ahead, a possible approach for developing and sustaining BRI comprises three key limbs: identifying challenges, shaping sound governance, and using the experiences of successful projects to spur the further development of BRI. First, identify critical issues that have emerged from past BRI projects, including the balance between economic value and debt servicing burden, alignment with countries' broader development plans, and gaps in both high-level governance and ground-level execution. Second, propose key elements of a governance framework based on best practices and considerations which should inform the delineation of roles for China, partner countries, and international organizations (IOs) to identify needs, pool resources, and institute rules of engagement — which could include fostering ownership by participating countries, resolving project-specific conflicts, and perhaps even managing disputes arising from credit–debtor relationships among sovereigns. Third, advocate pursuing some flagship projects in ASEAN where there is a high degree of integration and complementarities among countries. The idea is to achieve good outcomes, and then use these projects as models for other BRI projects in the region and elsewhere.

4.1. *Issues: Projects outside and in ASEAN point to the importance of economic viability, debt sustainability, and prioritization*

A look at several projects outside and within ASEAN suggests the following critical issues: economic viability, debt sustainability, overall policy coherence, ownership and prioritization, and attention to operational issues. [Please see Appendix for more detailed write-ups on all the country case studies.]

Outside of ASEAN, similarities and contrasts between the experiences of Sri Lanka and Bangladesh suggest the following:

- Economic viability and fiscal soundness are a necessary precondition for countries to take on projects of fairly large scale — an approach of starting on projects and hoping that the projects pay for themselves soon enough is too risky and can backfire;
- The overall "score card" for any country should be assessed comprehensively rather than focused narrowly on the impact of any single project;
- Projects which not only improve in-country infrastructure but also strengthen cross-border connectivity are more likely to produce strong economic outcomes.

Turning to ASEAN, the key themes which have emerged from several countries' BRI experiences are as follows:

- It is important for both partner countries to have substantial stakes in projects, as this would incentivize both parties to plan and execute projects soundly, and ensure their economic viability thereafter — a key priority;
- It is equally important to anticipate and then work through operational issues methodically — otherwise, appealing high-level concepts will not translate into economic value-add;
- Countries ought to consider the merit of individual projects in terms of whether they fit coherently into the broader national economic development plans.

4.2. *Governance: Need coherent framework and clearly-defined roles for stakeholders*

4.2.1. *Governance framework*

The proposal is to design a coherent governance framework and clearly-defined roles for countries and IOs (Figure 10) to pinpoint key issues upfront; apply a robust agreed-upon framework to assess whether proposed projects are worth pursuing, and if so, how; and also for lenders and borrowers to each do their due diligence before committing to a collaborative deal.

Several broad categories of issues could be laid out, and each of these should be considered in sufficient depth — including: fiscal soundness of countries, before they take on particular projects; how BRI initiatives could affect countries overall, including goodness of fit with national economic development plans; whether projects will boost cross-border connectivity, or can be adjusted to achieve this effect while also strengthening in-country infrastructure; whether the nature of the project allows both partner countries to

	Project Description			
Country	Name	Project Cost	Collaboration Mode	Status/Assessment
Bangladesh	Dhaka-Jessore Railline: – Length: 172 km – Purpose: The rail line seeks to improve connectivity substantially and boost cross-border trade among the four countries.	US$3.139 billion: – possible partial loan by either the china development Bank or EXIM Bank and part fiscal outlay by the Bangladeshi government	To be handled by Chinese state-owned enterprise SOE China Railway Group Ltd	– Feasibility studies have highlighted some engineering challenges, but at the same time suggest these can be overcome. – The rail line will form part of the Bangladesh-China-India-Myanmar Railway Corridor, as well as potentially part of an even wider "trans-Asian" network
Sri Lanka	Hambantota port – Purpose: be a key node of trade and maritime activity [Concept of this project involves attracting ships to call at Hambantota Port while sailling through the Indian Ocean, benefiting Chinese operators of the port and Sri Lanka's economy.]	US$1 billion, with phase 1 costing US$361 million – due to Sri Lanka having difficulties serving its debts (including but not only for this project), it was agreed that the Chinese take a 70% equity stake and a 99% years lease deal	70% equity stake and 99 year operating lease for China	– Useful projects, but costs should have been recognized by Sri Lankan authorities themselves in the first instance as being too high given the fiscal position. From the outset, Sri Lanka's already-burdened fiscal position imposed constraints on its desire to build infrastructure aggressively, whether through the BRI or other channels. China holds slightly more than 10% of Sri Lanka's public debt, and about two-thirds of this is on concessional terms. The Norocholai Power Plant Projects provides 40% of the national power supply of the country, the Colombo international Container Terminal projects has reportedly become the fastest-growing container terminal in Asia; and the Moragahakanda project is the biggest water reservoir in Sri Lanka.

(*Continued*)

Country	Project Description		Collaboration Mode	Status/Assessment
	Name	Project Cost		
	Other Projects including Norocholai Power Plant, Moragahakanda water reservoir, and Colombo international Container Termial.		Colaborative - China to provide the bulk of the technical expertise and labor for building the infrastruture; operations to be handed to Sri Lanka in phases.	
Cambodia	Expresssway from Phnom Penh to Sihanoukville: – Length: 190 km – Purpose: to improve both goods transportation and traffic along National Road 4, which so far has been frequently afffected by floods leading to road closures	US$2 billion: – BOT Investment Scheme by Cambodia PPSHV Expressway Co. Ltd	Concession period of 54 years	– The project is officially inaugurated on 22 March 2019 and it is expected to be completed in 2023.
	Lower Sesanll Dam: – Capacity: 400 mw – Purpose: to reduce power shortage, lower electricity costs, and promote scoial development	US$800 million: – 51%: China's Hydrolancang international Energy – 39%: Cambodian firm Royal Group – 10%: Vietnam's EVNI	Joint venture	– Offficialy inaugurated on 18 December 2018 – The dam is expected to share around 20 percent of the country's total electricity output, which is believed to help reduce power shortage, lower electricity cost and at the same time promote Cambodia's social development.

(Continued)

	Project Description			
Country	Name	Project Cost	Collaboration Mode	Status/Assessment
Indonesia	Jakarta-Bandung Rail Line: – Length: 140 km – Purpose: to connect Jakarta with Bandung in West Java, which could later be extended to Surabaya in East Java.	US$5.3-6 billion: – 60%: a consortium of Indonesian SOEs – 40: China Railway International	Loan by China Development Bank (CDB): – Maturity 40 years – Fixed interest rates: 75% of the project cost – Grace period: 10 years – No government debt gurantees	– Construction started in 2016, expected to be operational in 2019. – Work progress: delayed because of issues with land acquisition and the need to compensate the land owners. Authorities are working through these issues methodically but in order for these issues to be addressed, the operational start date of the project might be adjusted from 2019 to 2021.
	Kayan hydropower project (Kalimantan): – Purpose: to increase Indonesia's electricity generation capacity	US$17.8 billion	Collaboration between: – PT Indonesia Kayan Hydropower Energy – Power Construction Corporation of China (Power China)	According to North Kalimantan provincial government, the construction of the first phase of the project might start soon, following the signing of a contract between PT Indonesia Kayan Hydropower Energy and a Chinese partner, power Construction Corporation of China (Power China) in April 2018.

(*Continued*)

Country	Project Description		Collaboration Mode	Status/Assessment
	Name	Project Cost		
Lao PDR	Laos-China Railway: – Length: 414 km – Purpose: to connect China with ASEAN, with the Lao section of the railway commencing in Kunming and going through major cities in Lao PDR with a total of 32 stations.	USD 6 billion, of which: – 60 percent (USD 3.6 billion): debt via loans from Chinese banks to the joint venture company established by the Chinese and Lao governments. – 40 percent (USD 2.4 billion): equity, of which: – 70 percent (USD 1.68 billion) contributed by equity from Chinese shareholders – 30 percent (USD 0.72 billion) by Lao government, of which: 65 percent (USD 0.47 billion) loan from China EXIM Bank and 35 percent (USD 0.25 billion) by the government budget (USD 0.05 billion per year during 2017–2021).	A joint venture company established by the Chinese and Lao government (with no guarantee by the Lao government)	– Construction: 20% complete. scheduled launch in December 2021 – The project is expected to break even only after about 20 years, thus, the direct fiscal impact and contingent liabilities need to be carefully managed with a long-term view.

(*Continued*)

Country	Project Description: Name	Project Description: Project Cost	Collaboration Mode	Status/Assessment
	Vientiane-Vang Vieng Expressway: – Length: 113.5 km – Purpose: to significantly cut down the travel time from the capital Vientiane to major tourist destinations in Van Vieng, and so ties in well with Lao PDR's push to develop the country further as a key tourist destination in the ASEAN region.	US$1.3 billion: – 95%: China – 5%: Lao government	A joint venture company called Laos-China joint Expressway Development Company Limited	– Construction of the expressway commenced during the second half of 2018, and is expected to be completed in three years. – A toll charge of between 45,000 to 56,000 kip (US$5.25–6.50) is being proposed for travelling on the Expressway.
Malaysia	Second Penang Bridge: – Length: 24 km (one of the longest briedges in Malaysia and Southeast Asia) – Purpose: built across South Channel of Penang, linking Batu Maung on penang Island with Batu Kawan on the mainland.	US$1.37 billion: – 60%: loans from China EXIM Bank: • Maturity: 20 years • Interest rate: 3% per annum – 40%: Malasian government	Handled by China Highway planning and design Institute (HPDI), AECOM (consultant of China Harbour Engineering Company CHEC)	– In operation: 4 March 2014 – Economic benefits: areas which were primarily plantations became more developed and diversified townships, and more connected to other parts of the country. The upfront and long-term costs were well within Malaysia's fiscal capacity.

(*Continued*)

Country	Project Description: Name	Project Description: Project Cost	Collaboration Mode	Status/Assessment
	ECRL: – Length: 688 km – Purpose: to connect South China Sea in the east coast of Peninsular Malaysia with strategic shipping routes to the west	US$13.1-20 billion (re-estimated)	Owned and operate by Malaysia Rail Link Sdn Bhd (MRL), a special purpose vehicle (SPV) wholly owned by MMOF	– Construction started in August 2017, but suspended in 2018 when a new government came into power and did a critical reassessment of the likely cost of the project-as part of a comprehensive national fiscal analysis which it would have done anyway. – Project currently under review by the two governments.
Myanmar	Gong Hai hydropower station (located on the Pang River): – Capacity:25 MW – Purpose: to increase hydroelectric power generation to meet the much-needed power demand (the government aims to provide electricity to the whole country by 2030.)	Not yet known	To be handled by Shandong Water Conservancy Construction Group	– Construction date: not yet known – In July 2018, Shandong Water Conservancy Construction Group Co., Ltd. was notified of winning the bid for the EPC project of Gong Hai hydropower station in Myanmar. – The economic and social benefits for Myanmar could be very large, as the country has an electrification rate of only 31% and an annual demand growth of 15%.
	Kyaukpyu Port: – Purpose: to connect China to indian ocean	US$ 9-10 billion (50-year term of the project) – 70%: China – 30%: Myanmar	Colloboration between China International Trust and Investment Corporation (CITIC) and Myanmar's Kyaukpyu Special Economic Zone management committee (SEZ)	– Construction date: not yet known – CITIC and SEZ signed an agreement on 18 November 2018. – The project is expected to bring 100,000 jobs to the local community and generate substantial revenue.

(Continued)

Country	Project Description		Collaboration Mode	Status/Assessment
	Name	Project Cost		
Thailand	China-Thailand Railway: – Length: 873 km – Purpose: to provide the missing link in the railway connectivity from Singapore to China, and to shorten the travel time between Bangkok and Nong Khai on the Thai-Lao border from 14 hours to just four hours, and further, to connect to Kunming in Yunnan.	US$12 billion	Chinese state enterprises responsible for the engineering design of the project and the hiring of Chinese technical advisers.	– Construction: after some delays, started in December 2017, with the first phase of the project expected to be operational in 2021. – This project fits well with Thailand's overall economic development, a significant part of which involves deepening sub-regional integration within the Lancang-Mekong area. In addition, Thailand's domestic stakeholders benefit substantialy.
	Eastern Economic Corridor: – Purpose: to transform the area into a thriving economic hub fulfilling multiple roles: a modern metropolitan, a hub of trade and investment, a key center of regional transportation and logistics, a tourist attraction, and even significant source of human resources.	Not yet known	Not yet known	– Thai government is exploring ways to collaborate with China to further develop the Eastern Economic Corridor. This involves improving connectivity between among three of the country's provinces which lie to the East of Bangkok, namely Chacheongsao, Chonburi and Rayong. – Statistics show that there are 259 projects were approved to invest in the ECC directly, worth THB310.337 billion. The government expects to stimulate investment flows to the corridor worth more than THB1.7 trillion by 2021.

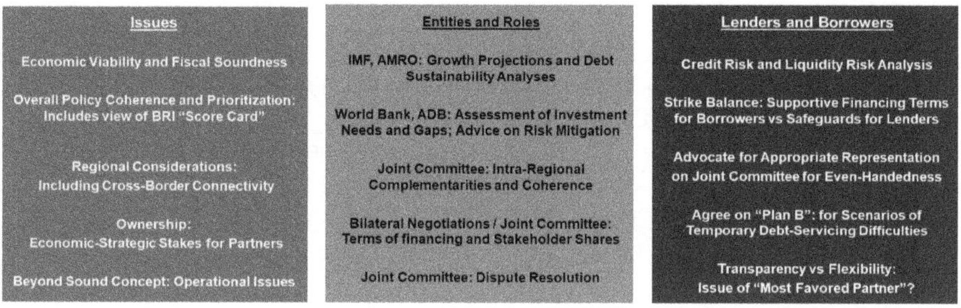

Source: AMRO.

Figure 10. BRI Stakeholders: Clear Distinction of Roles Within a Robust Governance Framework

have meaningful economic stakes which would, in turn, incentivize strong efforts to plan and execute projects well, and to maximize economic value-add thereafter; and finally, whether the nature of operational issues which are likely to arise during the course of the project is surmountable.

A robust governance framework comprising BRI partner countries and relevant IOs — as well as a multilateral governance body or joint committee — could be set up to provide an agreed-on framework to drill down to assessments of key elements including: economic viability of projects, sustainability of public debt (especially for already-stretched countries); balance in terms of financing, i.e., supportive but not imprudent; and measures to mitigate financial and operational risks.

- IOs with mandates for economic-, fiscal- and financial stability — such as the IMF and AMRO – have important roles to play. For instance, in conducting debt sustainability analyses (DSAs) to provide robust comparisons against borrowing countries' own internal assessments. Such analyses will compel all stakeholders to take hardnosed approaches in terms of prioritizing what they would like to undertake, always be practical, and to collaborate with one another in resolving fiscal-related difficulties as they arise. At the current juncture, ASEAN countries generally have sound fiscal positions, although there are a few areas of potential vulnerability (Figures 11 and 12).
- IOs such as the World Bank and ADB can also leverage on their wide membership and overview of countries' development paths and infrastructure-building challenges to provide policy guidance on investment needs and gaps, as well as advice on risk mitigation measures and practices. IOs which have units possessing highly specialized skills in project planning and construction should play leading roles in guiding BRI countries in this respect. Again, the World Bank and the ADB are obvious candidates for BRI projects in ASEAN, and should provide timely advice on the different types of economic- and contractual issues which tend to arise during the planning, construction, and operational phases of projects; advise on financing options given how the characteristics of projects changes during different phases; and perhaps connect potential investors to countries.

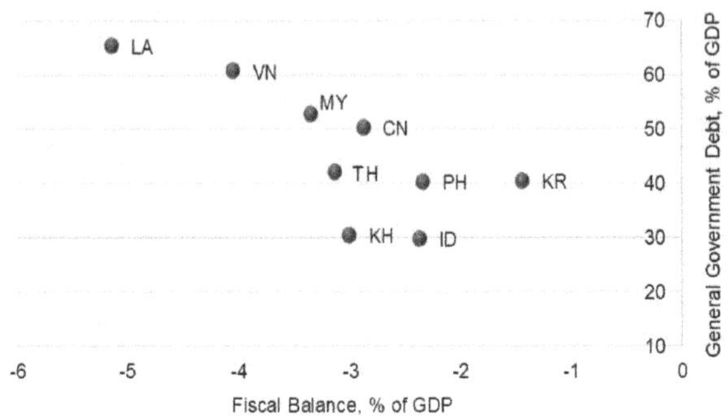

Source: World Bank, AMRO.

Figure 11. ASEAN+3 Economies' Fiscal Management: A Snapshot

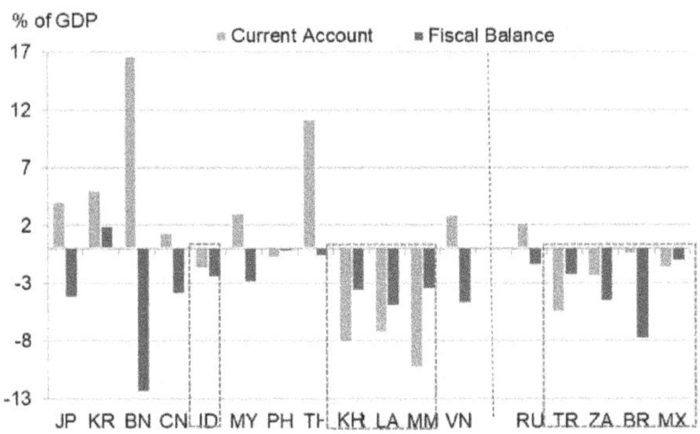

Source: World Bank, AMRO.

Figure 12. Current Account and Fiscal Balance as Percent of GDP: ASEAN Economies and Major EMEs

- Also, as the recently-released G20 EPG Report recommends, it is worthwhile considering shifting the basic business model of MDBs from direct lending towards risk mitigation aimed at mobilizing private capital. The EPG Report also recommends using securitization to a much greater degree in future. It suggests multiplying private capital by adopting system-wide approaches to risk insurance and securitization; developing a standardized, large-scale asset class, that diversifies risk across the development finance system, in order to help mobilize a huge untapped pool of investments by institutional investors.
- Alongside all these, the governance body, as a neutral party, should provide a central platform to help parties iron out terms of financing and the shares which respective stakeholders should take in (eventually completed) projects. This governing body should

also provide a robust dispute resolution mechanism. Experts sitting on panels should be drawn from a good spread of countries and possess recognized expertise and experience in related areas. The selection criteria could be modelled after those found in the dispute resolution clauses of free trade agreements (FTAs).

Lenders and borrowers should manage their risk exposures.

- Lenders should focus on sources and terms of financing, co-opting partners with project-specific technical expertize. Syndicated bank financing is one way for banks in different countries to combine their capital resources, technical knowledge and credit risk management capacity.
- Borrowing partner countries need to assess credit risks and liquidity risks critically. More broadly, they should undertake their own robust economic value assessments and fiscal sustainability analyses, using prudent assumptions about future economic growth, fiscal revenue expansion and spending requirements.
- Indonesia is a good example. Its policymakers have highlighted that part of Indonesia's effort to meet the savings-investment-growth challenge has focused on infrastructure, which has in turn driven other equally important elements of reform. As policymakers stepped up the pace of infrastructure-building in recent years, the realization has set in that Indonesia needs to improve its fiscal strength, in particular revenue generation. Overall, the country's policymakers are confident that Indonesia can sustain annual GDP growth of about 5–6% and the current account deficit at less than 3%, even after factoring in the higher imports that many infrastructure projects would entail. Furthermore, the policymakers are also quite confident that Indonesia can manage capital flows volatility shocks — as experienced recently, when the country saw large capital outflows and downward pressure on the exchange rate, reflecting risk aversion towards EMEs. Indonesian policymakers have shared views along the lines that that Indonesia, as the largest economy in ASEAN, is keen to play a leading role in spurring the region's development and integration as long as this involves a good alignment of national interest with regional interest — and they have pointed to cross-border infrastructure as a key commonality.
- Lenders and borrowers can also advocate for appropriate representation on the joint committee to ensure even-handedness. They can also agree bilaterally on at least the broad outlines of contingency plans for scenarios (such as if borrowers run into temporary debt-servicing difficulties).
- Lenders and borrowers should also provide information to multilateral bodies, as appropriate, to help enhance transparency, while taking into account the usefulness of flexible arrangements between lending and borrowing countries with special relationships, for example.

For regional economic and financial hubs, the value-add can come in various forms, ranging from financial intermediation and risk management, to project engineering capacity enhancement and dispute resolution. (see Box A for an outline of Singapore's role as an infrastructure development hub.)

Box A: How Regional Economic and Financial Hubs Can Help Infrastructure Development in the ASEAN+3 Region: The Case of Singapore

Singapore has played a key role in intermediating financing for infrastructure projects in the region — including but not limited to those pursued under the ambit of the BRI, with many banks and infrastructure-financing firms doing so from their bases in Singapore.

To promote the bankability of infrastructure projects and make them more appealing to investors, Singapore has partnered IOs to establish project development facilities which assist governments in the region with capacity building and project structuring. For example, the World Bank Group Singapore Hub, comprising units from the World Bank the IFC and MIGA, has helped governments in the region (such as Vietnam and Timor-Leste) to prioritize the projects in their pipeline. It also provides advisory and technical assistance to structure projects, and to help match them to Singapore-based investors. Singapore is also a funding partner of the World Bank Group Global Infrastructure Facility (GIF), which provides end-to-end support for preparation and implementation of infrastructure projects. To help institutional investors evaluate infrastructure investment opportunities in the region, Singapore also supported the establishment of the EDHEC Infrastructure Institute-Singapore, which among other things, creates usable performance benchmarks for privately-held infrastructure debt and equity instruments. Singapore's Business Trust framework helps infrastructure sponsors to recycle capital for new projects by injecting infrastructure assets into an equity-type instrument. Infrastructure business trusts listed on the Singapore Exchange (SGX) include: Keppel Infrastructure Trust, Hutchison Port Holdings Trust, and Asian Pay Television Trust.

Beyond financing, the Singapore authorities have highlighted five ways in which Singapore can partner investors in infrastructure in Asia: (i) project development; (ii) risk management (alongside financing); (iii) transaction and legal advisory services; (iv) technical and engineering expertise; and (v) collaboration with multilateral organizations. This comprehensive suite of offerings is made possible by a strong ecosystem of real economy infrastructure development companies, consultancies, law firms, and even speciality insurance firms, which cover many projects in the ASEAN+3 region.

One of the most recent initiatives by Singapore was the establishment of Infrastructure Asia as an office in Enterprise Singapore in 2018, to serve as a one-stop platform for facilitating regional collaboration in infrastructure development. It aims to do so by being a bridge for different industry players across the infrastructure ecosystem, MDBs and the public sector. And a significant part of its efforts will be on capacity building. For example, it will work with partner institutions to organize capacity-building workshops, and also step up engagement with local authorities in regional markets and intensify connections with the regional infrastructure ecosystems.

At the same time, recognizing the growing importance of risk mitigation and its role in enhancing the bankability of infrastructure projects, Singapore's Ministry of Law announced the establishment of the Singapore Infrastructure Dispute Management Protocol, to help parties involved in mega infrastructure projects manage disputes, and minimise the risks of time and cost overruns.

4.3. *ASEAN as testbed*

Finally, it is worthwhile to pursue flagship BRI projects in ASEAN, execute these well, and then use demonstrably good economic- and strategic outcomes to serve as models for other BRI projects in Asia and other EM regions.

There are several aspects to this approach.

One, maximize synergies: leverage on the fact that there is high degree of integration and complementarities among countries in ASEAN, and between ASEAN and China. Trade between China and ASEAN has deepened over the past two decades, prompted by China's accession to the WTO in 2001, and ASEAN countries' exploitation of their competitive advantages through regional production networks. In 2001, goods trade between China and ASEAN was only 6.7% and 4.7% of total trade for China and ASEAN, respectively. By 2017, goods trade between China and ASEAN reached 10.4% and 16.7% of GDP for China and ASEAN, respectively (Figure 13). Measured by share of GDP, most ASEAN countries saw their exports to China rise to high levels in 2017, especially Vietnam (22.5%), Malaysia (17.3%), Thailand (9.1%), Singapore (10.6%), Lao PDR (9.4%). China's exports to ASEAN as a share of GDP stood at 10.1% of ASEAN's GDP in 2017. This reflected China having become the center of regional production networks, and having quickly become a major trading partner of almost all ASEAN countries. In recent years, China has also increased the amount and broadened the sectoral coverage of its investment in ASEAN. While China's ODI into ASEAN has continued to grow significantly, it has diversified from its earlier focus on mining and power sectors, to invest more heavily in wholesale and retail trade, and leasing & commercial services. At the same time, given the rising cost of labor in China, manufacturing companies have begun shifting production activities to lower-cost locations in ASEAN such as the CLMV countries, and ODI in this sector has also risen sharply. Therefore, from both the trade and investment perspectives, it makes good economic sense to have a strong pipeline of infrastructure

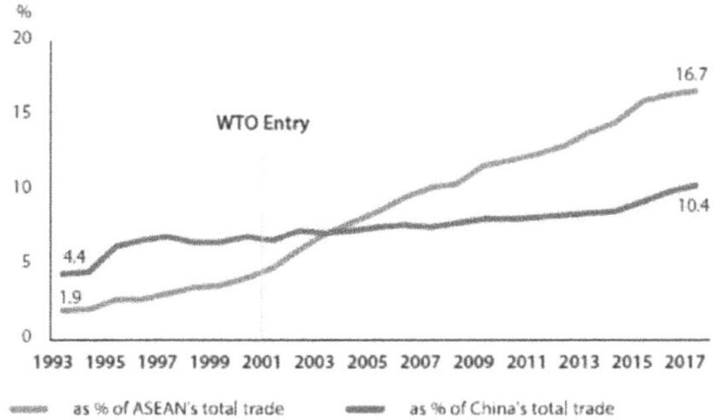

Source: CEIC, AMRO staff calculations.

Figure 13. China-ASEAN Merchandise Trade as Percent of China's Total Trade and ASEAN's Total Trade

projects in ASEAN under the BRI ambit — to connect ASEAN countries better with one another and with China.

Two, find complementarities between the BRI and ongoing development of ASEAN Economic Community (AEC), not least the Master Plan for ASEAN Connectivity (MPAC) 2025. The MPAC has seamless infrastructure as one of five key limbs, the others being digital innovation, seamless logistics, regulatory excellence, and people mobility. Together, the BRI and MPAC — or more broadly, the AEC — can better connect ASEAN countries with one another, and ASEAN as a bloc with China. It would be helpful if policymakers and technical experts steering these initiatives respectively could come together to undertake a close analysis of where the initiatives complement each other, where they duplicate efforts, and where they both stop short of addressing some particular needs of the region. Such collaboration at the policy and technical levels should be on an ongoing basis, rather than a one-off exercise, because the needs of individual countries and the region as a whole change over time.

Three, step up the role of private sector enterprises. As the BRI *is* a national initiative by the largest and most-rapidly developing EME in Asia, with far-reaching implications across all countries in the region, it does make sense for the overarching framework to be designed and overseen at the government-to-government (G-to-G) level. However, private sector feedback, participation and leadership are invaluable. Businesses can contribute to a better understanding of infrastructures and platforms needed, current bottlenecks and potential future pitfalls, and perhaps some solutions to help resolve challenges.

Four, multilateralize the engagement as much as possible. In addition to bilateral cooperation, a framework of collaboration on a multilateral basis between China and partner BRI countries should be set up to maximize the coherence of the region's development and the benefits arising from specific projects. This will increase complementarities, reduce wasteful duplications, and narrow suboptimal gaps.

Five, broaden the scope in due course. i.e., use good outcomes in ASEAN as models for other BRI projects globally. For example, if the rail projects in Malaysia, Thailand and Lao PDR prove to have improved connectivity, boosted trade and other forms of economic activity, and to have come with bearable fiscal costs which are well below the economic benefits generated, then the key characteristics of these infrastructures and the key features of the project management process will be useful reference for similar undertakings in other EME regions.

5. Conclusion: Economic Case Calls for Sound Ecosystem to Produce Sustained Beneficial Outcomes

To conclude, the BRI is a worthwhile initiative, its challenges are tough but surmountable, and close collaboration among stakeholders with clear roles will improve the likelihood of success. Successful flagship projects in ASEAN can serve as useful reference for the BRI in other EM regions.

The economic rationale of the BRI goes to the core of the infrastructure-related growth challenge confronting EMEs including those in ASEAN, and it takes on great relevance as the region's transition to the "new economy" calls for deeper intra-regional *and* inter-regional integration. Through its vision of large-scale cross-regional investments in infrastructure projects to improve connectivity, the BRI is expected to boost cross-border trade and investment and generate economic benefits not only in the BRI region but also globally.

What is also needed is a range of solutions to help ASEAN EMEs at different points along the income spectrum, which face significant savings-investment gaps or forex constraints requiring them to settle for suboptimal spending on infrastructure and other types of investments.

Aside from that, more broadly, there needs to be a sound ecosystem which supports infrastructure investment: a framework for evaluating and making decisions on the types of projects needed; coherent legal framework; access to sustainable financing; markets for risk mitigation tools; and expertise within the public sector and private sector to manage project and ensure environment protection.

This requires close collaboration among many stakeholders including government, private sector, expert advisors, FIs and MDBs to help overcome the challenges facing EMEs at different stages of economic development and infrastructure building. Lessons from China related to the development of the ecosystem for infrastructure investment will also be beneficial for other BRI countries.

For the BRI, some mismatch of expectations is inevitable but surmountable. ASEAN's own development experience with Japanese-led investment in the economic and infrastructure space is encouraging, and suggests that the future prospects of BRI could be bright. BRI stakeholders are learning quickly.

This points to a three-pronged approach for developing and sustaining BRI. First, identify critical issues highlighted by challenges which have emerged from past BRI projects. Second, devise a robust governance framework with well-define roles for stakeholders to identify needs and difficulties, pool resources, unlock financing and diversify risks, and to institute rules of engagement. Third, pursue flagship BRI projects in ASEAN where there is a high degree of integration and complementarities among countries; then use success cases as models for other BRI projects in the region and elsewhere.

Appendix. Selected Brief Case Studies of Asian Countries' BRI Projects

Sri Lanka BRI projects

For Sri Lanka, its already-burdened fiscal position imposes constraints, from the outset, on its desire to build infrastructure aggressively, whether through the BRI or other channels. China, in fact, holds just slightly more than 10% of Sri Lanka's public debt, and about two-thirds of this is on concessional terms. In terms of projects, the Norocholai Power Plant Project which China considers to have been carried out under the BRI initiative provides 40% of the national power supply of the country, while the Colombo International Container Terminal project under the Initiative has become the fastest-growing container terminal in Asia, and the Moragahakanda project is the biggest water reservoir in Sri Lanka. Alongside these, difficulties with the Hambantota Port project has highlighted issues which need to be resolved and to be averted in future. The concept of this project involved attracting ships to call at Hambantota Port while sailing through the Indian Ocean, benefiting Chinese operators of the port and Sri Lanka's economy in various ways. Consultancy firms which did feasibility studies were optimistic. Sri Lanka borrowed from China, at lower-than-commercial rates, but which in the end, still proved too high for the country to service.[4] By 2015, a reported 90% of the Sri Lanka government's revenue was going toward servicing its debt, and the government initiated debt renegotiations with China. The outcome was a 70% equity and 99-year lease deal. The deal invited local criticisms, from both local and foreign commentators, that the Sri Lanka had gotten into a debt trap and been forced to give up a strategic asset to China which will used it for military purpose. Such criticisms have highlighted the political sensitivity of many of the mega projects under the BRI and the need for both China and the recipient countries to select the right projects; decide whether the projects are in line with their development needs; prioritize (i.e., pick the most critical projects to pursue); assess whether the economic benefits outweigh the costs of the projects.

Bangladesh BRI projects

For Bangladesh, there are fairly good assurances about fiscal sustainability, but perhaps less transparency over contracts and the attendant technology transfers for local companies and skills training for local workers. The Dhaka–Jessore Rail line is 172 km long, and in future, will form part of the Bangladesh–China–India–Myanmar Railway Corridor, as well as potentially part of an even wider "trans-Asian" network. It is expected to improve connectivity substantially and boost cross-border trade among the four countries. Feasibility studies have highlighted some engineering challenges, but at the same time suggest these can be overcome. While details of the financing packages are not known, reports suggest a model similar to that used for many other BRI projects, i.e. part loan by either the China Development Bank or EXIM Bank, and part fiscal outlay by the Bangladeshi government. Bangladesh' GDP is about US$250 billion, with its public debt-to-GDP ratio at around 27%, which suggests fiscal sustainability may not be an issue. However, one sticking point for some stakeholders is that a Bangladesh government committee approved a proposal to award the US$3.139 billion contract — without tender — to Chinese state-owned enterprise SOE China Railway Group Ltd (CEREC), with construction to take place between about now and 2022.

Indonesian BRI projects

In the case of Indonesia, fiscal sustainability is sound and the respective stakes of the two countries provide assurances about economic-geopolitical concerns, with the result that attention can be focused on resolving inevitable ground-level operational issues.

The Jakarta–Bandung Rail Line is case in point. This is a US$5.3-6 billion 140 km high-speed rail project connecting Jakarta with Bandung in West Java, which could later be extended to Surabaya in East Java. Construction started in 2016, and the line was expected to be operational in 2019. The contract was awarded to China Railway International — which would hold a 40% stake while a consortium of Indonesian SOEs hold the remaining 60%.

[4] The first phase of the project involved a US$307 million loan at 6.3% interest.

China Development Bank (CDB) was to provide a forty-year loan with fixed interest rates for 75% of the project cost, with an initial grace period of 10 years. [Sources indicate that the CDB has offered a 40-year concessionary loan, without asking for government debt guarantees, to finance 75% of the US$5.29 billion project, with the following features: (i) 10-year grace period; (ii) 60% portion of the loan denominated in US dollars carrying a 2 percent interest rate; and (iii) the remaining 40% in Renminbi, carrying a 3.4% rate.]

Initial concerns about whether the project — for a rail line covering a relatively short distance of 140 km — is economically viable seem to have been addressed by plans to unlock commercial value by having shopping outlets and eateries at each station along the route between Jakarta and Bandung. Work on the project has been held up because of issues with land acquisition and the need to compensate the land owners. Sources suggest that authorities are working through these issues methodically but in order for these issues to be addressed, the operational start date of the project might be adjusted from 2019 to 2021. In terms of governance and financial safeguards, some commentators have wondered whether China ought to have insisted on, rather than waived requirements for the Indonesian government to provide an explicit guarantee for the loan as part of the deal.

Another example is the Kayan hydropower project in Kalimantan, whereby the benefits of increasing Indonesia's electricity generation capacity and the attendant socioeconomic gains are weighed up against the financial costs as well as localized effects on the ecosystem and peoples of affected areas.

The project was first announced in 2013 by Indonesia's Ministry of Energy and Mineral Resources, followed by the signing of a Memorandum of Understanding (MOU) between PT Indonesian Kayan Hydro Energy — the local developer, and Shanghai Electric Power Limited — one of the major listed companies of China Power Investment Corporation (CPI) in 2014.[5] The total cost of the project is up to US$17.8 billion, covering the building of five dams, and generators, power substations and transmission lines along the Kayan river, over a period of 20 years with a combined installed capacity up to 9,000 MW. While some researchers have raised concerns over the impact of the mega project on the ecosystem and people who live in affected areas, these have not escalated.

The project took off recently, quite a few years after the signing of the MOU. The North Kalimantan provincial government then said that that it expected the construction of the first phase of the project[6] might start soon, following the signing of a contract between PT Indonesia Kayan Hydropower Energy and a Chinese partner, Power Construction Corporation of China (PowerChina) in April 2018.

[5] The MOU was one of 12 signed by Indonesian and China's companies in Beijing during a meeting between Indonesian business leaders and their China counterparts in 2014. The signing was witnessed by President Joko Widodo, who visited China to attend the Asia Pacific Economic Cooperation (APEC) Summit during that period.

[6] According to the agreement, the partners plan to build the projects in stages over a period of 20 years, with the first 900 MW plant to be completed within four years. The first plants are principally designed to supply the Tanah Kuning Industrial Park, which is to be built by China Gezhouba Group International Engineering Company and local partner PT Adhidaya Suprakencana. The two companies committed to invest up to US$10 billion in the new industrial estate, under an MoU signed on the same day.

Malaysian BRI projects

The Penang Second Bridge is a 24 km bridge built across the South Channel of Penang, linking Batu Maung on Penang Island with Batu Kawan on the mainland. Opened on 4 March 2014, it is one of the longest bridges in Malaysia and South East Asia. A collaborative project between China and Malaysia, it was the biggest civil engineering work carried out in Malaysia in the past 20 years. The total cost was RM4.5 billion (about US $1.37 billion). RM1.8 billion came from the Malaysian Government. RM2.7 billion was borrowed from China EXIM Bank (with the loan agreement signed in July 2007), to be repaid over 20 years with an interest rate of 3% per annum. The project clinched the Brunel Medal from the Institution of Civil Engineers (ICE) in the UK. The economic benefits were clear — areas which were primarily plantations became more developed and diversified townships, and more connected to other parts of the country. The upfront and long-term costs were well within Malaysia's fiscal capacity.

The ECRL is a more mixed case. The 688 km ECRL is supposed to connect the South China Sea in the east coast of Peninsular Malaysia with strategic shipping routes in the west. It is to be owned and operated by Malaysia Rail Link Sdn Bhd (MRL), a special purpose vehicle (SPV) wholly owned by MMOF. The cost of the ECRL was initially estimated at US$13.1 billion, of which 85% would be loaned from the Export–Import Bank of China on the condition that China Communications Construction Company (CCCC) builds the railway. The loan has a repayment period of 20 years at an annual interest rate of 3.25% and a seven-year payment moratorium. A seven-year project set to be concluded in 2022, construction began in August 2017 but was suspended in 2018 when a new government came into power and felt it had to do a critical reassessment of the likely cost of the project — as part of a comprehensive national fiscal analysis which it would have done anyway. The outcome is that the cost has been re-estimated from about US$13.1 billion to US$20 billion, and the Malaysian government has suggested steep cut in fees paid by Malaysia to CCCC to plug this gap. As of January 2018, MRL and CCCC are currently negotiating the terms for the project to continue, likely on a smaller scale.

The Trans-Sabah Gas Pipeline (TSGP) is a 662 km gas pipeline cutting across the state of Sabah with a total cost of MYR4.06 billion, while the Multi-Product Pipeline (MPP) is a 600 km multi-product petroleum pipeline linking the southwestern coast of Peninsular Malaysia to the north with a total cost of MYR5.35 billion. Both projects — undertaken by Suria Strategic Energy Resources Sdn Bhd, a wholly-owned subsidiary of the Ministry of Finance - would be financed by a soft loan from the Export Import Bank of China and guaranteed by the government. With a total cost of MYR9.4 billion, the two projects were awarded to China Petroleum Pipeline Bureau (CPPN) on November 1, 2016. The projects have been cancelled when the new government took over; it was found that 88% of cost of the two pipelines had been paid to CPPN for work that was only 13% completed.

Thai BRI projects

Thailand's approach to BRI seems to be a sensibly measured one, focused on demonstrable economic benefits and manageable costs. One of the key BRI projects is a US$12 billion — 873 km China–Thailand railway connecting Thailand, Lao PDR and the Chinese province of Yunnan. This project will provide the missing link in the railway connectivity from Singapore to China. The intention is for this high-speed rail to shorten the travel time between Bangkok and Nong Khai on the Thai-Lao border from 14 hours to just 4 hours, and further, to connect to Kunming in Yunnan. It is hoped that the travel time will (eventually) be reduced to such an extent that investments can be drawn to the more remote areas in the northern part of Thailand so that these areas can in turn export more goods and services externally, thereby boosting economic development and local peoples' incomes. More broadly, this project fits well with Thailand's overall economic development, a significant part of which involves deepening sub-regional integration within the Lancang-Mekong area. In addition, Thailand's domestic stakeholders benefit substantially. For example, while Chinese technology will be used for the project,[7] 800 Thai workers will receive training for the project. Construction, after some delays, started in December 2017, with the first phase of the project expected to be operational in 2021.

Apart from the China–Thailand railway project, the Thai government is exploring ways to collaborate with China to further develop the Eastern Economic Corridor. This involves improving connectivity between among three of the country's provinces which lie to the East of Bangkok, namely Chacheongsao, Chonburi and Rayong. The initiative is expected to transform the area into a thriving economic hub fulfilling multiple roles: a modern metropolitan, a hub of trade and investment, a key center of regional transportation and logistics, a tourist attraction, and even significant source of human resources. The Thai–China collaboration will leverage on efforts which Thailand has put in over the past few decades to develop these three provinces, first to support rapidly-growing industries, and more recently, to help the country's transition to the more technology-driven, more innovative "Thailand 4.0" economy. The issues to be addressed include impact on displaced enterprises and families (including some agriculture households), resolution of land rights, and the need for public consultations on the future use of affected areas and the attendant economic rights of stakeholders.

Myanmar BRI projects

In Myanmar's case, the challenge is likewise for the country to fit BRI projects with its long-term economic development plan, but alongside, also to ensure that the costs of these projects can be accommodated within the country's ongoing multiyear fiscal consolidation program.

The Pang River hydro power station project, also considered to be under the ambit of the BRI, is located on the Pang River, a tributary of the Nujiang River, and has a total installed capacity of 25 MW. This is significant because the country's hydro power potential is estimated at more than 100GW, of which only 3GW has been developed so far. Myanmar's government awarded the project to the Shandong Water Conservancy Construction Group. The economic and social benefits for Myanmar could be very large, as the

[7] China conducted a feasibility study and detailed designing for the project. It will provide M&E works, including signalling and telecommunication systems, power supply, train control and track work. Tunnelling and construction of a long span bridge, establishing a new maintenance and training centre, and procuring rolling stock will also be China's responsibility.

country has an electrification rate of only 31% and an annual demand growth of 15%, and the government aims to provide electricity to the whole country by the year 2030. The cost is not yet known. Myanmar will have to assess fiscal sustainability carefully, as it is currently undergoing multiyear fiscal consolidation involving gradual narrowing of annual deficits. Its domestic public debt stands at about 20% of GDP.

Then there is the Kyaukpyu Port project. China International Trust and Investment Corporation (CITIC) and Myanmar's Kyaukpyu Special Economic Zone (SEZ) management committee signed an agreement on November 8, 2018 to build the Kyaukpyu SEZ deep sea port project in Kyaukpyu town after negotiations had been drawn out for a few years to resolve financing- and other issues.

The initial agreement is for a project worth US$ 9-10 billion and the term of the project is to be 50 years. In terms of financing, China will fund 70% of the investment for the project and Myanmar the remaining 30%. The project is expected to generate many jobs and substantial amounts of tax revenue for years to come. Once completed, the port will have an annual gross output of US$3.2 billion.

China has also proposed new highway infrastructure projects in Myanmar, including the construction of Kwanlon Bridge and a Mandalay–Lashio highway, and a railroad connecting Chinshwehaw and Lashio in Shan State. China has proposed a list of infrastructure projects to be implemented along the China–Myanmar economic corridor as part of a wider push to enhance cooperation between the two countries. The connectivity drive aims to link China's Yunnan Province and to Mandalay, Yangon and Rakhine. The two governments have agreed to collaborate on developing the economic corridor, and enhance economic ties more broadly. The authorities are also working towards signing an agreement to build up tourism in Lashio and Lincang, which is located southwest of Yunnan, according to Dr Maung Lay, UMFCCI vice president, who attended the meeting with the Lincang delegation.

Laotian BRI projects

For Lao PDR, a landlock country, the joint railway project with China has the potential to spur Lao's own economic development as well as improve connectivity externally. However, the government needs to undertake careful fiscal management. Lao PDR has the unique geographic advantage of being located at the center of a very dynamic and fast-growing part of the world. However, the land-locked and mountainous geography of the country has held back its development due to high transportation and logistics costs. In this regard, the construction of the China-Laos Railway is an important initiative to transform the country from being landlocked to land-linked. The railway is envisioned to connect China with ASEAN, with the Lao section of the railway commencing in Kunming and going through major cities in Lao PDR with a total of 32 stations. The main freight transport and logistic compound will be located at Vientiane. It is a very large and challenging project, with total route length of 414 km consisting of 75 tunnels and 167 bridges. The total project cost is US$6 billion. Of this, 60% (US$3.6 billion) is financed through debt, via loans from Chinese banks to the joint venture company established by the Chinese and Lao governments — with no guarantee by the Lao government. The remaining 40% (US$2.4 billion) is contributed through equity, by the shareholders of the joint venture company (US$1.67 billion) and Lao government (US$730 million). Of this US$730 million (equivalent to 30% of the equity), US$480 million will come from a China EXIM Bank loan (with the interest rate reportedly set at 2.3%), and US$250 million from the Lao government (provided from the budget at US$50 million each year during the five-year construction period). The fiscal challenge is significant. Although there is no explicit guarantee, the Lao government could be under significant pressure to cover operational losses and debt servicing costs of the Laos-China Railway Company Ltd., particularly in the initial years of operation. The direct burden on the Lao government is about 12% of the project's cost. The estimated additional expenditure from the government budget arising from the project is in the range of 0.4–0.9% of GDP every year between 2017 and 2021. The project is expected to break even only after about 20 years, thus the direct fiscal impact and contingent liabilities need to be carefully managed with a long-term view. Lao PDR's public debt/GDP is on the high side and the government is running annual fiscal deficits of above 5% of GDP, which it needs to progressively cut following a medium-term fiscal consolidation plan. By raising revenue and streamlining expenditure to achieve lower fiscal deficits, it will enable debt to achieve a more sustainable level of 60% of GDP in the medium term.

Another project is the Vientiane–Vang Vieng Expressway. This aims to significantly cut down the travel time from the capital Vientiane to major tourist destinations in Van Vieng, and so ties in well with Lao PDR's push to develop the country further as a key tourist destination in the ASEAN region. The construction and management of the expressway is set-up as a Build-Operate-Transfer (BOT) project, through a joint venture company called Laos-China Joint Expressway Development Company Limited. China will hold 95% of the company through the Yunnan Construction and Investment Holding Group (YCIH), with the Lao government holding the remaining 5%. The Expressway connecting Vientiane and Vang Vieng will be 113 km long, with a total cost of around US$1.3 billion. Construction of the Expressway commenced during the second half of 2018, and is expected to be completed in three years. The Expressway will significantly cut down the travel time from the capital Vientiane to major tourist destinations in Van Vieng, as it is estimated to only take 90 min to cover the length of the expressway, compared to the 3–4 hours it currently takes to drive between the two destinations. A toll charge of between 45,000 to 56,000 kip (US $5.25–6.50) is being proposed for traveling on the Expressway.

Cambodian BRI projects

For Cambodia, the BRI is playing an important role in bridging funding gaps for physical infrastructure investment, not to mention its positive externalities on soft infrastructure development through knowledge and knowhow transfer, investments, among others. However, the challenge for BRI engagement is to think far ahead and decide when to invest, and how much; as well as to manage the concentration of its debt exposures. With successful projects having materialized in the form of the port city of Sihanoukville and several hydroelectric power dams, Cambodia's policymakers have, in consultation with China, decided to develop a national freeway system, the construction of which is anticipated to be completed by the year 2023, with part of the estimated cost of US$26 billion likely to be borne by SOEs and part of it to be financed via concessional loans.

Part of this national freeway system is Cambodia's first-ever expressway from Phnom Penh to Sihanoukville, a new bridge across the Mekong River in Kampong Cham province, as well as a new road connecting Prey Veng province to Kampong Cham province.[8] The 190 km expressway, to be built in parallel with the 232 km long National Road 4, is estimated to cost around US$2 billion and is expected to take 4 years to complete. China has provided concessional loans worth approximately US$2 billion for this. Cambodia is now working with China Road and Bridge Corporation to accelerate the construction of the expressway. The expressway, upon successful completion, will help to improve both goods transportation and traffic along National Road 4, which so far has been frequently affected by floods leading to road closures.

For hydropower dam development, the recent launch of Cambodia's biggest dam "Lower Sesan II"[9] marks a new milestone for the country's power sector development and also represents what the Cambodian authorities consider to be a big achievement under the BRI ambit. With the capacity to generate 400 MW of electricity, the dam is expected to provide around 20% of the country's total electricity output, thus reducing power shortage, lowering electricity costs, and promoting social development. This US$800 million project – a joint venture between China's Hydrolancang International Energy (51% ownership), Cambodian firm Royal Group (39%) and Vietnam's EVNI (10%)[10] — is situated in Sesan district of Steung Treng province, where the "Build-Operate-Transfer" scheme provides for these companies to undertake project construction for five years and then hold operating rights for forty years.

Currently, Cambodia's public debt to GDP ratio is fairly low, with about half of the roughly US$6.95 billion public debt being owed to China. Earlier concerns about spending overrun on infrastructure projects appear overdone, especially considering that the country's economy is expected to grow rapidly in the years ahead, and so its fiscal resources should also become much larger.

Acknowledgments

The authors would like to thank the following colleagues at the ASEAN+3 Macroeconomic Research Office (AMRO): Dr Simon Liu Xinyi for thoughtful insights; Mr Abdurohman, Ms Diana del Rosario, Dr Jerry Huang Xianguo, Ms Laura Grace Gabriella, Mr Justin Lim, Dr Nguyen Thi Kim Cuc, Mr Paolo Hernando, Mr Phanomphone Keovongvichith, Dr Ruperto Majuca, Ms Malichanh Chiemsisoulath, Dr Tanyasorn Ekapirak, and Ms Wanwisa May Vorranikulkij for contributions to the case studies. All mistakes are the responsibility of the authors.

[8] "China Gives $2 Billion for Roads, Bridge", the Khmer Times, October 17, 2016

[9] To date, there are seven hydropower dams, in which the Lower Sesan II Dam is the seventh hydropower project, officially inaugurated on 18 December 2018.

[10] Source: Dam in Sesan begins operations, Khmer Times, 18 December 2018

References

ADB (2017). Meeting Asia's infrastructure needs. Available at: https://www.adb.org/publications/asia-infrastructure-needs.

ADB (2018). Asian Economic Integration Report (AEIR): Towards Optimal Provision of Regional Public Goods in Asia and the Pacific. Available at: https://www.adb.org/sites/default/files/publication/456491/aeir-2018.pdf.

Aquino, C (2015). Challenges and opportunities China faces in 2016. *China Daily*. Available at: http://www.chinadaily.com.cn/opinion/2015-12/28/content_22840536.htm.

ASEAN and China (2017). China-ASEAN joint statement on infrastructure connectivity. Available at: https://asean.org/storage/2017/11/China-and-ASEAN-on-Cooperation-Connectivity-CN-ASEAN_adopted.pdf.

ASEAN and UNCTAD (2017). ASEAN investment report 2017. Available at: https://asean.org/storage/2017/11/ASEAN-Investment-Report-2017.pdf.

ASEAN+3 Macroeconomic Research Office (2017). ASEAN+3 Regional Economic Outlook. Thematic Study: ASEAN+3 Region: 20 Years after the Asian Financial Crisis (AFC). Available at: https://amro-asia.org/wp-content/uploads/2017/05/AREO2017_Full-Text.pdf.

ASEAN+3 Macroeconomic Research Office (2018). ASEAN+3 Regional Economic Outlook. Thematic Study: Resilience and Growth in a Changing World. Available at: https://amro-asia.org/wp-content/uploads/2018/05/AMRO-AREO-Report-2018_Full-Report.pdf.

ASEAN+3 Macroeconomic Research Office (2018). China's Reform and Opening-Up: Experiences, Prospects, and Implications for ASEAN. Available at: https://amro-asia.org/wp-content/uploads/2018/10/China%E2%80%99s-Reform-and-Opening-Up-Experiences-Prospects-and-Implications-for-ASEAN-FINAL.pdf.

Asia Times Staff (2017). China can be a high-income country by 2023: Economist. *Asia Times*. Available at: http://www.atimes.com/article/china-can-high-income-country-2023-economist/.

Baker McKenzie (2017). Belt & Road: Opportunity & Risk. Available at: https://www.bakermckenzie.com/-/media/files/insight/publications/2017/10/belt-road/baker_mckenzie_belt_road_report_2017.pdf.

Belt and Road Advisory (2018). Belt and Road in Malaysia: Make or Break? Available at: https://beltandroad.ventures/beltandroadblog/malaysia.

Bhaskaran, M (2018). Maintaining momentum. *Finance & Development*, 55(3). Available at: https://www.imf.org/external/pubs/ft/fandd/2018/09/future-of-southeast-asia-bhaskaran.htm.

Cai, J and F Tang (2017). Has China really avoided the middle income trap? *South China Morning Post*. Available at: https://www.scmp.com/news/china/economy/article/2116295/has-china-really-avoided-middle-income-trap.

CBBC and Tsinghua University (2016). China-Britain Belt and Road case studies report. Available at: http://www.cbbc.org/cbbc/media/cbbc_media/4.%20Files/China-Britain-Belt-and-Road-Case-Studies-Report.pdf.

Chen, C (2018). The liberalization of FDI policies and the impact of FDI on China's economic development. *China's 40 Years of Reform and Development: 1978–2018*, pp. 595–617, Australia: ANU Press. Available at: http://press-files.anu.edu.au/downloads/press/n4267/pdf/book.pdf?referer=4267.

China Dialogue (2018). Thailand woos Chinese investment for major industrial revamp. Available at: https://www.chinadialogue.net/article/show/single/en/10998-Thailand-woos-Chinese-investment-for-major-industrial-revamp.

Chow, GC (2018). China's economic transformation. *China's 40 Years of Reform and Development: 1978–2018*, pp. 93–115. Australia: ANU Press. Available at: http://press-files.anu.edu.au/downloads/press/n4267/pdf/book.pdf?referer=4267.

Cockburn, J, Y Dissou, J-Y Duclos and L Tiberti (2013). Infrastructure and Economic Growth in Asia. Available at: https://www.researchgate.net/publication/267027599_Infrastructure_and_Economic_Growth_in_Asia/download.

Das, SB (2018). Do the economic ties between ASEAN and China affect their strategic partnership?. *ISEAS*, 32. Available at: https://www.iseas.edu.sg/images/pdf/ISEAS_Perspective_2018_32@50.pdf.

Deloitte (2018). Embracing the BRI Ecosystem in 2018. Available at: https://www2.deloitte.com/cn/en/pages/soe/articles/embracing-the-bri-ecosystem-in-2018.html.

Eastache, A and G Garsous (2012). The impact of infrastructure on growth in developing countries. Available at: https://www.ifc.org/wps/wcm/connect/054be8804db753a6843aa4ab7d7326c0/INR+Note+1+-+The+Impact+of+Infrastructure+on+Growth.pdf?MOD=AJPERES.

Ellis-Petersen, H (2018). 'No Cambodia Left': How Chinese money is changing Sihanoukville. *The Guardian*. Available at: https://www.theguardian.com/cities/2018/jul/31/no-cambodia-left-chinese-money-changing-sihanoukville.

Eminent Persons Group (2018). Making the Global Financial System Work for All. Available at: https://www.globalfinancialgovernance.org/assets/pdf/G20EPG-Full%20Report.pdf.

European Commission (EC) (2014). Infrastructure in the EU: Developments and Impact on Growth. Available at: http://ec.europa.eu/economy_finance/publications/occasional_paper/2014/pdf/ocp203_en.pdf.

Global Security (2018). Thai-China High-Speed Railway. Available at: https://www.globalsecurity.org/military/world/thailand/hsr.htm.

Green, A (2018). The new frontier: Can ASEAN be this decade's China?. *Asia Society*. Available at: https://asiasociety.org/australia/new-frontier-can-asean-be-decades-china.

Huang, Y (2018). China's economy is not normal. It doesn't have to be. *New York Times*. Available at: https://www.nytimes.com/2018/03/13/opinion/china-economy-corruption.html.

Hydrocarbons Technology. (2018). Myanmar-China Pipelines. Available at: https://www.hydrocarbons-technology.com/projects/myanmar-china-pipelines/.

Hydropower-dams.com (2018). Agreement signed to construct Kayan river cascade, Indonesia. Available at: https://www.hydropower-dams.com/news/agreement-signed-to-construct-kayan-river-cascade-indonesia/.

IMF (2017). World Economic Outlook (WEO). Available at: https://www.imf.org/en/Publications/WEO/Issues/2017/04/04/world-economic-outlook-april-2017.

Jakarta P (2018). RI, China sign 12 investment MOUs. Available at: https://www.thejakartapost.com/news/2014/11/11/ri-china-sign-12-investment-mous.html.

Jakarta P (2018). PowerChina to build hydropower plants for $17.8 billion. Available at: https://www.thejakartapost.com/news/2018/04/19/powerchina-to-build-hydropower-plants-for-17-8-billion.html.

Khor, HE and KS Tan (2005). *China's Changing Economic Structure and its Implications for Regional Production, Trade and Integration* (Institutional Knowledge at Singapore Management University Working Paper). Available at: https://ink.library.smu.edu.sg/cgi/viewcontent.cgi?article=2203&context=soe_research.

Kishore, N (2018). Beware of the Chinese dragon: Overcoming the middle income trap. *The Market Mogul*. Available at: https://themarketmogul.com/china-middle-income-trap/.

Lagarde, C (2018). Belt and Road Initiative: Strategies to Deliver in the Next Phase. Available at: https://www.imf.org/en/News/Articles/2018/04/11/sp041218-belt-and-road-initiative-strategies-to-deliver-in-the-next-phase.

Li, W and SL Xinyi (2018). *China's Increasing Economic Linkages with ASEAN and the Potential Spillover Effects* (ASEAN+3 Macroeconomic Research Office Staff Working Paper 03/2018). Available at: https://amro-asia.org/chinas-increasing-economic-linkages-with-asean-and-the-potential-spillover-effects/.

Leung, C (2018). Understanding China: Recalibration of BRI Strategy? *DBS Research*. Available at: https://www.dbs.com/aics/templatedata/article/generic/data/en/GR/072018/180704_insights_understanding_China_recalibration_of_BRI_strategy.xml#.

Lo, C (2017). Hype, Suspicion and Truth of the Belt and Road Initiative. *BNP Research*. Available at: https://docfinder.is.bnpparibas-ip.com/api/files/1E3806D2-6DA7-4FE4-B42A-FF071A566B6D.

Moody's (2017). China's belt and road initiative: BRI report card: Positive factors outweigh negatives for China and recipient countries. Available at: https://www.moodys.com/research/Moodys-Chinas-Belt-and-Road-Initiative-is-credit-positive-overall–PR_372698.

Morgan, S (2017). The next decade of China's transformation. *Forbes*. Available at: https://www.forbes.com/sites/morganstanley/2017/05/23/the-next-decade-of-chinas-transformation/#2041d85356ba.

Normaz Wana Ismail and Jamilah Mohd Mahyideen. (ADBI) (2015). The Impact of Infrastructure on Trade and Economic Growth in Selected Economies in Asia. Available at: https://www.adb.org/sites/default/files/publication/177093/adbi-wp553.pdf.

Perkins, DH (2018). The complex task of evaluating China's economic reforms. *China's 40 Years of Reform and Development: 1978–2018*, pp. 135–154. Australia: ANU Press. Available at: http://press-files.anu.edu.au/downloads/press/n4267/pdf/book.pdf?referer=4267.

Phungtua, W (2017). The Impact of Japanese MNCs and Foreign Direct Investment on Thailand Automotive Industry. Available at: https://www.tci-thaijo.org/index.php/EAUHJSocSci/article/view/90146/74990.

PWC (2017). Transportation and logistics 2030. Available at: https://www.pwc.com/gx/en/transportation-logistics/tl2030/assets/pwc-tl2030-pub.pdf.

PWC (2018). Investing in the ASEAN Infrastructure Asset Class. Available at: https://www.pwc.com/sg/en/publications/assets/cpi-report-3-infrastructure-asset-class.pdf.

PWC (2018). Understanding Infrastructure Opportunities in ASEAN. Available at: https://www.pwc.com/sg/en/publications/assets/cpi-mas-1-infrastructure-opporuntities-in-asean-201709.pdf.

Railway Technology (2018). China-Thailand Railway Project. Available at: https://www.railway-technology.com/projects/china-thailand-railway-project/.

RambuEnergy (2017). Kayan Hydro expected to start construction of hydro power plant in Bulungan in March. Available at: https://www.rambuenergy.com/2017/02/kayan-hydro-expected-to-start-construction-of-hydro-power-plant-in-bulungan-in-march/.

RambuEnergy (2017). CITIC Ltd offered to build mega hydropower plant Kayan in North Kalimantan. Available at: https://www.rambuenergy.com/2017/05/citic-ltd-offered-to-build-mega-hydropower-plant-kayan-in-north-kalimantan/.

RambuEnergy (2018). Kayan hydropower gets major boost after signing deal with China firms (RambuEnergy, April 2018). Available at: https://www.rambuenergy.com/2018/04/kayan-hydropower-gets-major-boost-after-signing-deal-with-china-firms/.

Reuters (2017). After delays, ground broken for Thailand-China railway project. Available at: https://www.reuters.com/article/us-thailand-china-railway/after-delays-ground-broken-for-thailand-china-railway-project-idUSKBN1EF1E6.

Rokon, Z (2017). One Belt One Road in the Context of the Fourth Industrial Revolution. *Financial Express*. Available at: http://www.thefinancialexpress.com.bd/views/one-belt-one-road-in-the-context-of-the-fourth-industrial-revolution.

Royal Thai Embassy in Washington (2019). Eastern Economic Corridor (EEC). Available at: https://thaiembdc.org/eastern-economic-corridor-eec/.

Schellekens, P (2013). *A Changing China: Implications for Developing Countries*. Washington, DC World Bank. Available at: http://documents.worldbank.org/curated/en/212821468214810664/A-changing-China-implications-for-developing-countries.

Sidiropoulos, E (2018). The BRICS in a Multipolar World. *Project Syndicate*. Available at: https://www.project-syndicate.org/commentary/china-brics-south-africa-summit-by-elizabeth-sidiropoulos-2018-07?barrier=accesspaylog.

Standard Chartered (2017). China – Belt and Road is taking shape. Available at: https://av.sc.com/corp-en/content/docs/China-Belt-and-Road-is-taking-shape.pdf.

Sunday Observer (2018). Belt and Road Initiative spurs Sri Lanka's growth. Available at: http://www.sundayobserver.lk/2018/12/02/news-features/belt-and-road-initiative-spurs-sri-lanka%E2%80%99s-growth.

United Nations (UN) (2018). Sustainable Development Goals (SDG) Report 2018. Available at: https://unstats.un.org/sdgs/files/report/2018/TheSustainableDevelopmentGoalsReport2018-EN.pdf.

Viktor, E (2017). The One Belt One Road from Germany's Perspective. *PAGEO*. Available at: http://www.geopolitika.hu/en/2017/08/15/the-one-belt-one-road-from-germanys-perspective/.

World Bank (2010). Post-Crisis Growth in Developing Countries. Available at: http://siteresources.worldbank.org/EXTPREMNET/Resources/489960-1338997241035/Growth_Commission_Special_Report.pdf.

World Bank (2012). Avoiding Middle-Income Traps. Available at: http://documents.worldbank.org/curated/en/422121468155111398/pdf/NonAsciiFileName0.pdf.

Yao, Y (2018). The political economy causes of China's economic success. *China's 40 Years of Reform and Development: 1978–2018*, pp. 75–92. Australia: ANU Press. Available at: http://press-files.anu.edu.au/downloads/press/n4267/pdf/book.pdf?referer=4267.

Yu, Ye (2018). China's Response to Belt and Road Backlash. *East Asia Forum*. Available at: http://www.eastasiaforum.org/2018/12/15/chinas-response-to-belt-and-road-backlash/.

Zhang, J (2017). China's Vision for the Next 30 Years. *Project Syndicate*. Available at: https://www.project-syndicate.org/commentary/china-19th-congress-development-blueprint-by-zhang-jun-2017-11?barrier=accesspaylog.

Zhang, J (2018). Beyond GDP Growth in China. *Project Syndicate*. Available at: https://www.project-syndicate.org/commentary/china-local-government-incentives-gdp-growth-by-zhang-jun-2018-03?barrier=accesspaylog.

Chapter 2

THE DECENTRALIZING INTERNATIONAL TRADE ARCHITECTURE: PERSPECTIVES FROM AND ROLE OF ASIA*,‡

PRADUMNA B. RANA, WAI-MUN CHIA and XIANBAI JI†

Nanyang Technological University, Singapore

†*xji005@e.ntu.edu.sg*

Published Online 23 January 2020

Global economic governance is in flux. The centralized international trade architecture of the post-Bretton Woods era is decentralizing as new regional institutions are being established for various reasons. Decentralization per se is neither good nor bad. It depends on whether there is "healthy" competition and functional complementarity or "unhealthy" competition between global and new regional institutions. This paper has three objectives, to: (i) review the decentralization of the international trade architecture; (ii) identify the benefits and the risks of the decentralization process and its implications for the centrality of the World Trade Organization (WTO), and (iii) recommend policies for the WTO to manage the process. The paper argues that, so far, the benefits of new regional institutions and trade decentralization appear to have outweighed the risks, and as a result global economic governance may have improved. Looking ahead, the paper recommends a number of policy actions that the WTO should take to manage trade decentralization. The paper argues that Asian countries, especially those that are members of the G20, should play a greater role in lobbying and driving the needed reforms of the WTO. They should also seek to expedite the conclusion and ratification of the Regional Comprehensive Economic Partnership (RCEP) and eventually institutionalize the complementarity between RCEP, the Comprehensive and Progressive Agreement for Trans-Pacific Partnership (CPTPP) and the Belt and Road Initiative (BRI).

Keywords: Global trade governance; regionalism; RCEP; CPTPP; BRI.

JEL Classification: F13, F53, F55

1. Introduction

Global economic governance — broadly defined as the act of governing economic relationship that transcends national boundaries in the absence of sovereign authority (Madhur, 2012) — is in flux. The centralized governance architecture established at Bretton Woods is decentralizing with the co-existence of "senior" global economic institutions and a plethora of newly established regional institutions (Rana, 2014). A mere increase in the number of regional institutions per se is neither good nor bad for the delivery of public goods. The outcome is contingent on the nature of the working relationship between new

*The funding support of MOE Tier 1 (RG80/18) is gratefully acknowledged.

‡This article originally appeared in *The Singapore Economic Review*, **66**(1), pp. 59–84

regional and existing global institutions. The quality of global economic governance improves with "healthy" competition and functional complementarity, and deteriorates when "unhealthy" competition that encourages forum shopping, resource duplication and race to the bottom practices prevails between the more established global institutions and their regional counterparts. This inherent indeterminacy leads to an analytical conundrum for academics and policymakers alike. That is, have the benefits of institutional decentralization outweighed the risks across the financial, development and trade pillars of the global economic governance architecture?

In a series of papers, Rana and Pardo (2015, 2018), Pardo and Rana (2015, 2018) and Rana (2019) have argued that, in the realm of financial stability and development finance, the benefits of new regional institutions and decentralization appear to have exceeded the risks. For instance, they find that the relationship between the International Monetary Fund (IMF), the pre-eminent global financial safety net (GFSN), and the Chiang Mai Initiative Multilateralization (CMIM), a major regional financial safety net (RFSN) in East Asia, is characterized by "healthy" competition (and resource additionality) and close inter-institutional functional cooperation and division of labor in various tasks of crisis prevention and crisis management. In the economic development architecture, they argue that the establishment of the Asian Infrastructure Investment Bank (AIIB) and New Development Bank (NDB) has triggered "an infrastructure investment boom" that helps fill the infrastructure financing gaps in developing countries. The memorandums of understanding (MOUs) that have been signed between these institutions and the World Bank and Asian Development Bank (ADB) promote functional cooperation in the areas of knowledge and information sharing, country-specific and sector-specific cooperation, and co-financing. The MOUs also contribute to the ratcheting up of the governance and operational standards of the newly founded AIIB and NDB. Likewise, Wang (2017) also asserts that as long as China refrains from abusing its leading position in the AIIB and NDB, the two regional institutions will "complement the World Bank in supporting different dimensions of development".

Do the above arguments and findings in favor of new institutions and the decentralization process also apply to international trade? In other words, does global trade governance also benefit from the decentralization process whereby regional trade agreements (RTAs) proliferate (Figure 1) in the presence of the World Trade Organization (WTO)? The subject is highly topical given Trump's confrontational trade actions against the multilateral trading system. In this paper, we attempt to provide preliminary answers to the question by employing the "benefit-risk" analysis or the "complementarity-competitiveness" framework as outlined in Kahler *et al.* (2016). This policy-oriented method begins with listing "benefits" or "complementarities" and "risks" or "competitiveness" of the subject matter before proposing policy recommendations geared towards managing the process or "increasing the benefits and decreasing the risks".

More specifically, the analytical framework of the paper is associated with the "contested multilateralism" approach. This approach defines the idea that emerging powers dissatisfied with existing institutions create new institutions to challenge the older ones

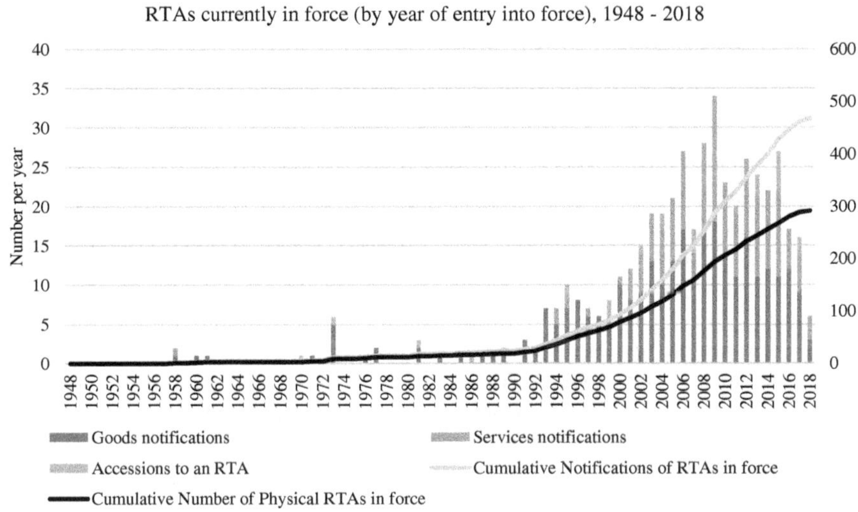

Notes: Notifications of RTAs: goods, services & accessions to an RTA are counted separately. Physical RTAs: goods, services & accessions to an RTA are counted together. The cumulative lines show the number of notifications/physical RTAs currently in force.
Source: WTO Secretariat, as of 30 December 2018.

Figure 1. Rising Popularity of RTAs

leading to a decentralized architecture (Morse and Keohane, 2014).[1] A priori decentralization would have negative connotations because it would lead to forum shopping and race to the bottom (Zürn and Faude, 2013). This is the case where benefits of decentralization are lower than risks. However, decentralization could also have positive impacts on global governance if there is functional complementarity in policy domains and financing between global and regional institutions as noted. This is the case where the benefits of decentralization outweigh the costs. Therefore, "contested multilateralism" is not only related to contestation per se but can also result in improved governance.

The paper is structured as follows. The next section briefly reviews the history of trade regionalism. Section 3 discusses the key "benefits" and "risks" that emerge as the architecture of global trade governance decentralizes. We do so in part by drawing from existing literature on the pros and cons of regionalism. It should also be emphasized that the "benefits" and "risks" to be discussed are framed from a global economic governance point of view. Section 4 proposes policy actions that should be taken by the WTO to manage the decentralization process. The reasons for highlighting the WTO are three-fold. First, the WTO is the incumbent global trade governance body which is ultimately responsible for the coherence of the decentralizing trade "regime complex" (Abbott *et al.*, 2016) should

[1] "Contested multilateralism" could also be regime shifting where states and/or non-stare actors shift their focus from one existing institution to another (Morse and Keohane, 2014).

regionalism come into conflict with multilateralism. Second, the WTO used to adopt a passive stance towards RTAs, assuming them to be expedient interim arrangements that would be obviated by a big-bang multilateral liberalization round. The enduring popularity of RTAs, however, is prompting deep think on the part of the WTO to reposition itself in a new environment where regionalism accounts for an ever growing part of the global trade regime. Third, unlike the IMF and World Bank which have gone through successive phases of institutional reforms, the WTO is in a relatively unreformed state, in view of the continual negotiation deadlocks and the possible dysfunction of the appellate body. Thus, the WTO has a stronger impetus to manage trade decentralization in ways that allow it to stay at the center of international governance. Otherwise, the WTO could be on the path of redundancy.

Asia is at the forefront of trade regionalism. Its role in the decentralizing trade architecture, therefore, warrants special examination in Section 5. We argue that Asian countries, especially the "Asia 5 + 1" countries namely China, Japan, India, South Korea and Indonesia plus Australia, should play a leading role to shape trade decentralization and lobby for WTO reform. This is because "Asia 5 + 1" are currently participating in global governance through the Group of Twenty (G20) and, importantly, because they are leading some of the world's most ambitious regional undertakings like mega-RTAs and the Belt and Road Initiative (BRI). That said, by prescribing a role for a loosely defined "Asia", we do not posit that Asia is a homogenous group free from internal conflicts. For sure, there are and will be conflicts of interest within "Asia 5 + 1" and the group may not have a common "Asian approach" on how the WTO reform ought to proceed. Yet, the countries are structurally similar outward-oriented economies which depend on a robust global trading system for economic prosperity. Meanwhile, they represent a group of predominantly non-Western powers seeking to claim a greater say in global trade governance; therefore, there is sufficient common ground for them to work side by side to make the multilateral trading system more effective and less Western-centric.

2. From Centralized to Decentralizing Trade Architecture

The Bretton Woods conference of 1944 had recognized the need for a comparable institution for trade to complement the IMF and the World Bank. But the United States (US) did not ratify the Havana Charter to establish the proposed International Trade Organization; countries had to fall back to the General Agreement on Tariffs and Trade (GATT) to provide a temporary structure to assist in and regulate the rapid expansion of global trade (Bronz, 1956; Toye, 2003). From the late 1970s, the Group of Seven (G7) of industrialized countries, and in particular the "Quad" consisting of the US, Canada, Japan and Europe, acted as the informal oversight body of GATT. Meeting three to four times a year, the G7 and Quad exercised decisive leadership at GATT via calling for the (re)launch of trade rounds, shaping negotiating agenda, bridging differences in national negotiation positions, setting deadline for conclusion and laying out the rudimentary dispute settlement mechanisms (Ullrich, 2006; Sherifis and Astraldi, 2001). Together, the G7 and GATT made up a two-level global trade governance architecture (Figure 2). Eight rounds of

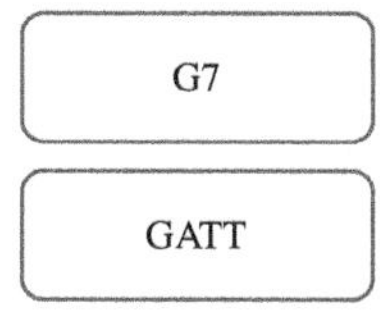

Figure 2. Pre-WTO Centralized International Trade Architecture

multilateral trade liberalization took place under the auspice of GATT between 1947 and 1994, reducing tariffs (on trade in manufactures) from an average level of 40% in 1947 (World Bank, 1987) to around 15% (simple average for all products) in 1995, when the WTO was established. Successful trade liberalization ushered in a sustained period of economic growth and social development across the world. Over the past decades, however, this centralized architecture has also been decentralizing (WTO, 2011).

2.1. *Growing popularity of "new regionalism" in the 1990s*

The first round of regionalism, known as "old regionalism", occurred soon after World War II in the 1950s and 1960s. In Europe, the European Coal and Steel Community (ECSC) and the European Economic Community (EEC) were established in 1952 and 1958, respectively. The EEC prompted several European countries that chose to stay outside of it to form a rival bloc, the European Free Trade Association, in 1960 and served as the template for pursuing regional integration for the then-newly independent countries in Africa, Latin America and the Caribbean. A common feature of the early-stage regional arrangements was that they were formed primarily among geographically neighboring developing countries for the purposes of either supporting import substitution industrialization (ISI) policies or pooling resources to augment collective bargaining power (Langhammer and Hiemenz, 1990) vis-à-vis the developed countries in the North. This "old" model of regionalism quickly fell out of favor by the end of 1970s (de Melo and Panagariya, 1993) in part because of the autarkic nature of ISI policies and the closing power disparity between the developing and the developed countries in conducting international economic relations.

The rise of second wave of regionalism, or "new regionalism" (Ethier, 1998), occurred in the 1990s. In 1991, Argentina, Brazil, Paraguay and Uruguay created the MERCOSUR. In 1992, the Association of Southeast Asian Nations (ASEAN) transformed itself from an anti-communism political-security alliance to an economic community by adopting the ASEAN Free Trade Area. With the 1993 passage of Maastricht Treaty, the EU was officially born. North American countries joined the race by launching the North American Free Trade Agreement (NAFTA, now known as the US-Mexico-Canada Agreement after treaty revision) in 1994. By the end of the same year, the Common Market for Eastern and Southern Africa was founded, marking a step towards the realization of an envisaged African Economic Community.

The first factor that led to this phase of regionalism was the end of the Cold War. On one track, former Soviet republics struck trade agreements with each other and with Russia to cope with trade disruptions arising from the dissolution of the Council for Mutual Economic Assistance in 1991. On the other track, the Baltics edged towards the EU membership by entering into Association Agreements with the EU. Both dynamics led to a large number of RTAs in Eurasia. The second factor that drove "new regionalism" was a shift in the trade policy of the US. For some four decades after World War II, the US was the champion of the multilateral approach to trade governance. This pro-multilateralism policy stance took shape initially because the US believed that it had been the victim of exclusive European colonial blocs and that the absence of globally ordinated trade policy cooperation had aggravated the Great Depression in the 1930s. But as the European integration project steadily enlarged and the frustrations over the long-drawn-out Uruguay Round negotiations mounted, the US turned to regionalism in the mid-1980s to promote free trade while advancing its geopolitical interest (Fiorentino *et al.*, 2007). It signed its first RTA with Israel in 1985. In the early 2000s, the US rolled out a "Competitive Regionalism" strategy, resulting in trade pacts with countries like Peru and Oman. The demonstration effect of the US trade policy paradigm shift was enormous and many countries followed suit to pursue regionalism.

The third factor that led to the popularity of "new regionalism" was the frustration with difficulties in negotiating global agreements. GATT began as a relatively small international institution dominated by the Western countries. As GATT/WTO membership expanded steadily from 23 to 164, the complication of reaching multilateral agreements among an increasingly diverse group on an agenda that was becoming more complex became more difficult. Thus, when the Uruguay Round of GATT negotiations stalled, many governments turned to RTAs under the Article XXIV of GATT (as well as Enabling Clause of the Generalized System of Preference and Article V of General Agreement on Trade in Services). Similarly, the slow progress of the negotiations of the Doha Development Agenda (DDA) has also led to the proliferation of RTAs worldwide (Figure 1).

Gradually, Asia also emerged at the forefront of regionalism (see Table 1). In 1991, there were only five in-effect RTAs involving ADB's regional members. In 2001, the count

Table 1. Rising Regionalism in Asia

Year	Framework Agreement Signed	Negotiations Launched	Signed But Not Yet in Effect	Signed and in Effect	Total	Proposed
1986	0	0	1	3	4	0
1991	0	0	2	5	7	1
1996	0	0	7	31	38	1
2001	0	8	5	42	55	2
2006	15	37	8	80	140	42
2011	12	46	9	118	185	58
2016	5	74	5	148	232	76
2018	4	79	13	156	252	91

Source: Asia Regional Integration Centre, ADB.

grew by more than eight-fold to 42. In 2018, there were 156 RTAs in force, 13 RTAs are pending enactment and 79 RTAs are under negotiations.

Regionalism did not play a central role in East Asia's dynamic growth story until the 1990s.[2] Countries living through colonialism and the Cold War jealously guarded their hard-won sovereignty and found it less desirable to strike transnational economic arrangements like RTAs that might infringe on their commercial policy autonomy. Also, economic interdependence in East Asia was low as countries traded more with developed country markets outside Asia than with each other. Therefore, apart from the Asia Pacific Trade Agreement (APTA) in existence since 1975, there were just a few RTAs in East Asia prior to the 1990s and countries adopted export-oriented development strategies to drive economic growth. In the 1990s, regionalism gradually took hold in East Asia. AFTA was implemented as noted.[3] East Asian countries also became more interwoven on the back of sprawling regional supply chains that held regional countries economically close together (Dent, 2016). Against this backdrop, governments became receptive to RTAs as a policy instrument to facilitate market-led de facto economic integration. Towards the end of the last century, two trajectory-altering economic shocks — one negative, one positive — fully unleashed the regionalism potential of East Asia. The negative shock was the Asian Financial Crisis (AFC) of 1997–1998 which not only exposed the region's interconnectedness and shared vulnerabilities but also laid bare the urgency of regional cooperation on trade and investment (Chia, 2010; ADB, 2008). Therefore, once the AFC subsided, Singapore quickly signed an RTA with New Zealand in 2000 and another one with Japan in 2002. The positive shock, on the other hand, concerned China's entry into the WTO in 2001. To allay ASEAN's fear that China's WTO membership would drain trade and inward investment flows from Southeast Asia, China proposed a China-ASEAN Free Trade Area (CAFTA) in 2000. In the following years, Japan, South Korea, Australia and New Zealand and India all courted ASEAN with similar trade accords. CAFTA set in motion a domino effect.

2.2. *Beginning of mega-FTA negotiations post-global economic crisis*

At the dawn of the 21st century after the global economic crisis, the world's major powers pivoted towards three mega-RTAs. Defined as "deep integration partnerships in the form of RTAs between countries or regions with a major share of world trade and FDI and in which two or more of the parties are in a paramount driver position, or serve as hubs, in global value chains (i.e., the US, the EU, Japan, China)" (Meléndez-Ortiz, 2014), mega-RTAs included the Trans-Pacific Partnership (TPP) comprising 12 Pacific Rim countries (Australia, Brunei, Canada, Chile, Japan, Malaysia, Mexico, New Zealand, Peru, Singapore, Vietnam and the US), the EU-US Transatlantic Trade and Investment Partnership (TTIP) and the Regional Comprehensive Economic Partnership (RCEP) bringing together 16 countries (Brunei, Cambodia, Indonesia, Laos, Malaysia, Myanmar, Philippines,

[2] For reviews of Asian regionalism in the 1990s and 2000s, see Urata (2019).

[3] AFTA was subsumed by a more ambitious ASEAN Trade in Goods Agreement (ATIGA) in 2008.

Singapore, Thailand and Vietnam plus China, Japan, South Korea, Australia, New Zealand and India).

Mega-regionalism can be distinguished from previous waves for three reasons, first of which was the fact that they each drew on a much wider network of participating countries. Barring TTIP which could still be categorized as a "North-North" framework, the TPP and RCEP exhibited great heterogeneity with respect to membership composition, linking together a large number of countries of different sizes, development levels, economic structures, political systems and socio-cultural traditions. Second, mega-RTAs were truly gigantic trading blocs. For instance, RCEP covered 47% of global population, 32% of the global output, 29% of global trade and 32% of global investment flows (2018 figures). Third, the scope (i.e., the number of issue areas covered) and depth (i.e., the degree of market integration) of trade liberalization under the mega-RTAs in the making were remarkably high. The TPP sought to eliminate 75% of tariff lines upon entry into force and 99% at the end of transition period (Freund *et al.*, 2016). The tariff liberalization target for RCEP is to reduce customs duties on around 90% of tradable goods within 15 years of coming into effect. More importantly, unlike conventional RTAs that were mainly tariff-cutting exercises, mega-RTAs were poised to be landmark 21st century trade agreements collectively setting a new high standard for global trade. They were to contain deep commitments governing "behind the border" issues such as rules for protecting investments, intellectual property, environment and labor rights, and regulations on product standards (Table 2). Though also motivated by gains from ambitious tariff reductions as the average tariff levels among its members remained relatively high, RCEP represents the most ambitious trading arrangement that many participants have ever negotiated.

The TPP agreement was signed amidst much fanfare on 4 February 2016. However, as Japan and New Zealand moved swiftly to ratify the agreement, the Trump administration pulled the US out of the pact. Ji and Rana (2019) argue that the failure of the TPP in the US was due to a confluence of "bad timing" (2016 presidential election), "bad politics" (Trump's problematic worldviews and unsympathetic attitudes on trade) and "bad context" (public backlash against US trade policy). But the remaining 11 countries carried on with the deal and signed a trimmed-down agreement, called Comprehensive and Progressive Agreement for Trans-Pacific Partnership (CPTPP), in March 2018 without the US. Starting from 30 December 2018, the CPTPP is taking effect in Australia, Canada, Japan, Mexico, New Zealand, Singapore and Vietnam.

RCEP at this writing is still under negotiation. India's hesitation to open up its economy to the level expected by other RCEP partners has protracted the talks, so much so that a "RCEP-minus-X" formula was proposed allowing India to opt out some of the cooperation and liberalization provisions that it is yet ready to accept (Rana and Ji, 2018). As of August 2019, after 27 formal negotiations rounds and 9 ministerial sessions, 7 chapters and 3 annexes have been concluded. They include chapters on Economic and Technical Co-operation, Small and Medium Enterprises (SMEs), Customs Procedures and Trade Facilitation, Government Procurement, Institutional Provisions, Sanitary and Phytosanitary Measures, and Standards, Technical Regulations and Conformity Assessment Procedures and annexes on all services sectors (Financial Services, Professional Services and

Table 2. Likely Issue Coverage of Mega-RTAs

Policy Areas	TPP	RCEP	TTIP
Market Access	√	√	√
Rules of Origin	√	√	√
Trade Facilitation	√	√	√
Trade Remedies	√	√	
Sanitary & Phytosanitary Measures	√	√	√
Technical Barriers to Trade	√	√	√
Investment	√	√	√
Services	√	√	√
Electronic Commerce	√	√	
Public Procurement	√	√	√
Competition	√	√	√
State-owned Enterprises	√		√
Intellectual Property	√	√	√
Labor	√		√
Environment	√		√
Technical Cooperation & Capacity Building	√	√	
Development	√	√	
Small & Medium-sized Enterprises	√	√	√
Regulatory Coherence	√		√
Transparency & Anti-corruption	√		
Institutional Provisions	√	√	√
Dispute Settlement	√	√	√
Sustainable Development			√
Energy & Raw Materials			√

Notes: The table is based on intended chapter headings of RCEP and TTIP for which final texts are not available. The legal enforceability and depth of commitment of those issues are not necessarily identical across multiple mega-RTAs.
Source: Ji (2019).

Telecommunications Services). Serious sticking points remain on market access offers, e-commerce, investment, etc., but countries are making best efforts towards the goal of delivering on a "technical conclusion" of RCEP negotiations in 2019.

TTIP negotiations were launched in July 2013. The two sides had exchanged offers to eliminate duties on 97% of all tariff lines. But formal negotiations were "suspended" in early 2017 when Trump took office. Despite calls to resume TTIP negotiations not least to form a united North Atlantic front against China's allegedly unfair and predatory trading practices, TTIP was not resuscitated. Prompted by the US' withdrawal from the Paris Agreement, the European Council adopted a decision in April 2019 to terminate the TTIP negotiating directives that it had granted to the European Commission, explaining that "the Union seeks the negotiation of deep and comprehensive free trade agreements only with Parties to that Agreement". Instead, the EU approved a new negotiating mandate on a narrower agreement on (1) the elimination of tariffs for industrial goods and on (2) conformity assessment. Full-fledged negotiations have yet started.

2.3. *Global responses to Trump's protectionist trade agenda*

Lately, in response to Trump's "America First" and his emphasis on "bilateral and reciprocal trade", the rest of the world led by the EU, Japan and China are standing up for open trade and rules-based economic freedom.

Shortly after Trump was sworn in as the 45th US president and promulgated a message in his inauguration address of making trade decisions solely to "to benefit American workers and American families", the European Parliament gave its consent to the Canada-EU Comprehensive Economic and Trade Agreement (CETA) in February 2017, allowing CETA to be implemented provisionally. Four months later, before the G20 summit in Hamburg, the EU announced the conclusion of the Japan-EU Economic Partnership Agreement (JEEPA) at the political level, sending a strong signal in support of economic cooperation and free trade (Jungbluth *et al.*, 2017). JEEPA, which was fast tracked in the face of pressure from Trump protectionism, entered into force on 1 February 2019. It is estimated that the deal would increase the GDP of the EU and Japan by 11 billion and 9 billion per year, respectively (Felbermayr *et al.*, 2017). Elsewhere in the Asia Pacific, the EU approved the EU-Singapore trade pact in February 2019, signed the agreement with Vietnam in June 2019 and is negotiating with Indonesia, Australia and New Zealand. The EU negotiations with China for a bilateral investment treaty are progressing albeit slowly. The EU is also making headway in Latin America. Most notably, an agreement was reached on an EU-MERCOSUR bloc-to-bloc FTA in June 2019.

Once described as an "unlikely pivotal state" in regionalism hampered by "dysfunctional trade politics" (Solís and Katada, 2015), Japan is taking on the leadership mantle as US-led trade liberalization is on the retreat. First, Japan moved ahead with an 11-country CPTPP as noted and is backing the membership bids of Thailand, Colombia and the United Kingdom in an attempt to spread the momentum of anti-protectionism. Second, Japan is working with China and ASEAN for a speedy conclusion of RCEP negotiations. Third, despite internal divisions like the most recent Japan-Korea trade row,[4] economic trilateralism is taking hold in Northeast Asia thanks to Tokyo's persistent push for the realization of a China-Japan-Korea (CJK) trade pact. Last but not least, a Trade Agreement on Goods (TAG) is being finalized between Japan and the US as Trump launches the 2020 reelection campaign. Collectively, the CPTPP, RCEP, CJK and TAG have placed Japan in the linchpin role of Asia-Pacific trade liberalization efforts.

[4] In 2018, the South Korean Supreme Court issued a ruling asking Japanese companies to pay compensation to Koreans over forced wartime labor. The decision drew harsh condemnation from Japan which announced in early July 2019 that it would impose export restrictions of chemicals vital for South Korea's semiconductor industry. South Korea retaliated by fining several Japanese companies. Japan subsequently escalated trade sanctions by removing South Korea from the "white list" of trusted trading partners. In response, South Korea decided to not to renew the bilateral intelligence-sharing pact. The two countries have brought the case to the WTO. This acrimonious episode of trade disputes has deep historical roots and by itself does not signal that Japan is backpedalling on its presently pro-trade liberalization trade policy to embrace protectionism.

China has taken a complimentary approach to regionalism, by focusing on infrastructure development and physical connectivity (i.e., the "hardware" component of the international trade). In this regard, President Xi Jinping's signature scheme, the BRI, inaugurated in 2013, is the main game in town (Rimmer, 2018). China reportedly plans to invest between 1 trillion and 8 trillion dollars (Hillman, 2018) into BRI-related infrastructure projects to connect diverse parts across the Eurasian and African continents.

The developments discussed above have led to a multi-layered and decentralized international trade architecture as depicted in Figure 3. The G20 Finance Ministers process was elevated to the G20 Summits and rose to prominence during the 2008 Global Financial Crisis (GFC) (Schmucker and Gnath, 2011). It took the place of G7 as a macroprudential body overseeing global cooperation issues including international trade. The strength of the decentralizing architecture is that it pulls together the oversight function of the G20, the technical capabilities and legitimacy of the WTO and the rule-making endeavor and agility of RTAs.

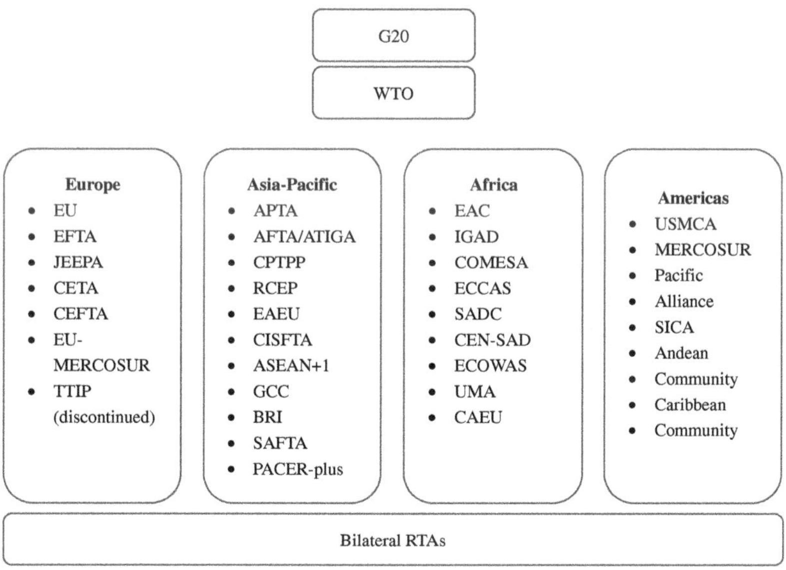

Notes: AFTA = ASEAN Free Trade Area; ATIGA = ASEAN Trade in Goods Agreement; CAEU = Council of Arab Economic Unity; CEFTA = Central European Free Trade Agreement; CEN-SAD = Community of Sahel–Saharan States; CISFTA = Commonwealth of Independent States Free Trade Area; COMESA = Common Market for Eastern and Southern Africa; EAC = East African Community; EAEU = Eurasian Economic Union; ECCAS = Economic Community of Central African States; ECOWAS = Economic Community of West African States; GAFTA = Greater Arab Free Trade Area; GCC = Gulf Cooperation Council; IGAD = Intergovernmental Authority on Development; PACER-plus = Pacific Agreement on Closer Economic Relations Plus; SADC = Southern African Development Community; SAFTA = South Asian Free Trade Area; SICA = Central American Integration System; UMA = Arab Maghreb Union.

Figure 3. The Decentralizing International Trade Architecture Post-GFC

3. Benefits and Risks

The establishment of new regional institutions leading to the decentralizing trade architecture has benefits ("healthy" competition and functional complementarity) as well as risks ("unhealthy" competition).

3.1. *Benefits of decentralization*

A number of benefits of RTAs can be highlighted. First, RTAs provide for an alternative approach to liberalizing trade in addition to multilateralism. In the event of stalling WTO negotiations, as is the case at the present, RTAs lock in existing commitments, permit the continuation of the trade liberalization process and put pressure on the global process. As C. Fred Bergsten's famous "bicycle theory" goes, if you do not pedal forward, you slip backward (Bergsten, 1996). And with fewer countries involved, finding a compromise is relatively more achievable in an RTA context; hence, it is easier to reach a reciprocal agreement to swap trade preferences and concessions. By contrast, the DDA launched in 2001 has been stuck for a long time and sharp North-South divisions over non-agricultural market access, trade in services, intellectual property rights and trade rules remain as key obstacles in the path towards the successful conclusion of the round. After the contentious December 2015 Nairobi WTO ministerial conference, the DDA had been proclaimed dead by analysts (Wilkinson *et al.*, 2016). As such, WTO members have shifted trade negotiating emphasis towards mega-regionals and other RTAs. This trend broadly fits with what Desker (2004) has described as a move "from purity to pragmatism" against the background of multilateralism standstill.

There are tangible economic benefits for countries to do so. Petri and Plummer (2016) estimate that the TPP would promise substantial benefits for Japan, Malaysia and Vietnam; annual real income gains by 2030 would be $492 billion for the world as a whole. Building on their analysis, the World Bank (2016) simulations suggest that the TPP would raise member country GDP by an average of 1.1% and intra-TPP trade by as high as 11% by 2030, although benefits are likely to be back-loaded. With the US withdrawal, the benefits of the CPTPP are comparatively more modest. But it would still generate real GDP gains of about 0.075% or economic welfare benefits of about $13.5 billion by 2035 (Ciuriak *et al.*, 2017). The projected gains from RCEP agreement are high, too. For instance, the latest estimate by Itakura (2019) using a dynamic computable general equilibrium model projects that the agreement's GDP impacts on ASEAN countries are in the range between 0.2% (for tariff liberalization only) and 4.7% (reflecting additional services liberalization and foreign direct investment enhancement effects) by 2035; the agreement could also raise global GDP in a range of 0.1–0.3% over the long run.

Second, modern RTAs typically permit deeper integration as compared to the shallower integration of the WTO which mainly tackles "on-the-border" barriers. The five GATT rounds from the 1940s to the 1960s focused mainly on tariff reductions. Negotiations on reducing non-tariff measures (NTMs) were included in the agenda of Tokyo round (1973–1979) and Uruguay round (1986–1993), but the mandates of negotiation only covered a few issue areas largely of technical nature including customs valuation, import licensing, export restrictions, public procurement, technical barriers to trade, and antidumping and countervailing procedures, among others (Oxley, 1994). In this regard, RTAs play an indispensable positive role in terms of broadening the scope of international trade negotiations via incorporating ground-breaking new disciplines that are known as WTO-plus or WTO-extra provisions (see Table 2). The former deepens commitments already undertaken multilaterally with enhanced import duties liberalization as the best example. Countries agree to a certain maximum upper limit for most-favored-nation (MFN) tariffs, but they extend further tariff cuts through regionalism to selected-free trade partners. WTO-extra commitments, on the other hand, are RTA provisions for which there is no WTO counterpart. Examples include mega-RTA's rules on labor and environmental standards, transparency, competition, state-owned enterprises, SMEs and regulatory coherence. As Table 2 shows, all the three mega-RTAs would provide for commitments that would go well beyond the scope up for discussion at the multilateral front.[5]

Third, the importance of WTO-extra and WTO-plus trade disciplines can be best understood with reference to what Baldwin (2014) calls the "differences between 20th and 21st century trade". The 20th century trade is marked by cross-border flow of finished products (e.g., manufactures and farm produces). Therefore, the basic GATT rules focusing on removing border taxes and limited instances of NTMs liberalization were enough to promote international trade. In the 21st century, however, in part due to advances in information and communications technologies, intermediate and supply chain trade, services trade, international movement of labor, and capital flows come to define interlocking international trade relations and policy agenda (Baldwin, 2014; WEF, 2016). As such, there have been calls for deeper economic integration rules that would reflect the growing complexity of international trade patterns. However, GATT/WTO has been proven slow in responding to such demand (Lester *et al.*, 2008) and the three mega-RTAs and other deep RTAs are filling the gap to craft and experiment with new rules governing many "behind-the-border" issues.

3.2. *Risks of regionalism and decentralization*

Regionalism and the decentralizing trade governance structure also pose a number of risks. The first is that regionalism is seen as "discriminatory" in nature. Granting preferences to some countries effectively discriminates against trade with others which could be more efficient trading partners, resulting in potentially costly trade diversion. That said, problems with trade diversion are more serious at the theoretical level than in practice. Often, the growth impetus from RTAs yields trade creation, positive externality and reversal of trade diversion over time. In comprehensive surveys of the theoretical and empirical regionalism literature, Schott (2008) and Freund and Ornelas (2010) find strong evidence of the primacy of trade creation. Specifically, Freund (2010) investigates the third-country economic impacts of NAFTA, MERCOSUR, Andean Community, and three waves of EU accession, concluding that "there is no evidence of trade diversion" in any of the six cases. In fact, she

[5] While RCEP's coverage of emerging trade issues would be, in comparison, less comprehensive than that of other mega-RTAs, it is still widely regarded as a "high quality" agreement.

goes on to argue that the perceived risk of trade diversion represents a strong incentive for "for external trade liberalisation [by excluded parties] to prevent trade diversion". With particular reference to Asian regionalism, Lee and Shin (2006) find that East Asian RTAs, that are "in effect" and proposed, "create more trade among members without diverting trade from non-members."

The second category of risks conventionally associated with RTAs is the so-called "spaghetti bowl" phenomenon (Bhagwati, 1995). It arises when overlapping RTAs create a web of trade agreements with different documentation rules, inspection procedures, rules of origin (Cadot and Ing, 2019), tariff schedules and institutional arrangements, in effect raising the transaction and compliance costs for the business community in their day-to-day trading activities. Less-than-full utilization of preferential tariff margins is often the symptom of the problem (Gretton, 2017). While there is some element of truth to this argument, this risk also seems to be overstated. First, an ADB Asia-wide, firm-level survey finds that "the view that the Asian noodle bowl has severely harmed the region's business activity over the last eight years [2001–2008] receives little support from the firm surveys" (Kawai and Wignaraja, 2011). A similar survey conducted in Latin American countries by Estevadeordal *et al.* (2009) finds similar results, dismissing the "spaghetti bowl" argument. Second, RTAs are becoming increasingly alike in terms of substance. This is because the process of negotiating an RTA is exceedingly complex and there are obvious benefits of recycling the text from one model agreement to another (Ilott *et al.*, 2017). Over time, the substantive variations across RTAs actually decrease, thereby reducing the trade dampening effect of the "spaghetti bowl". Third, the negative aspects of overlapping RTAs can be mitigated if appropriate public advice and well-designed capacity-building programs are offered to targeted communities. The Asia-Pacific Economic Cooperation (APEC) regularly organizes capacity building workshops on RTA utilizations.

A third and potentially much more critical risk of regionalism is that it could undercut the WTO (Bhagwati, 2008). But the possibility of such risk is not high as regionalism has actually cemented the centrality of the WTO's adjudicational arm. It was feared by the advocates of multilateralism that RTAs would predispose participating countries to litigate trade disputes in venues different to the WTO. This is not happening in actuality. For one, the dispute settlement procedures contained in RTAs have not introduced direct competition with the WTO. The CPTPP, for instance, concedes most traditional, market-access-related issues to the WTO process while focusing on those historically not taken up by the WTO. For another, the WTO has institutional comparative advantage in resolving state-on-state commercial disputes. Bown (2016) notes that "[d]espite many RTAs having their own dispute settlement mechanism provisions, most formal disputes arising since 1995 between RTA partners have been adjudicated at the WTO. Canada, Mexico, and the United States, for example, routinely file disputes against one another in Geneva, even though in-house NAFTA provisions exist to adjudicate their potential grievances. They are not alone: roughly 15% of all WTO disputes have involved members of an existing RTA using WTO to resolve their bilateral disagreements." The reason is that, unlike the WTO, there is no possibility of appeal for any dispute rulings made under RTAs, and there is no RTA secretariat that would provide the same sort of support that are of service to WTO jurists and arbitrators (Bown, 2016). In the WTO, appeals and secretariat staff help contribute to the stability of the system by ensuring that consistent legal decisions are made over time. Dispute settlement mechanisms in RTAs, by contrast, are less transparent, less legitimate, more costly and largely untested.[6] As a result, it remains unclear whether members will adhere to their rulings.

4. Managing Trade Decentralization

The full consequences of trade decentralization remains largely unknown. Yet, from the discussions above, on the whole, it can be argued that the benefits of new regional institutions and the decentralizing trade architecture are likely to outweigh the risks mainly because the risks are overstated. In other words, RTAs could be "stepping stones" rather than "stumbling blocks" to multilateralism. This point is also supported by an opinion survey of Asian policy-makers and experts conducted by the authors with regards to the relationship between mega-RTAs and multilateralism (Ji *et al.*, 2016). The survey found that 62% of the respondents felt that mega-RTAs contributed to global trade liberalization in the long term. Nevertheless, what more should be done to maximize the benefits while minimizing the risks of the decentralizing architecture or, to use the term promoted by Baldwin and Low (2009), "multilateralize regionalism"? The following policy actions could be considered by the WTO. Where possible, we justify the rationale for these recommendations with reference to efforts by other Bretton Woods institution to strengthen engagement with their regional counterparts.

(1) WTO should further enhance its collaboration with RTA member countries by creating a principled multilateralism-regionalism interface. Of particular importance to the functionality of such interaction is transparency. In 2006, the WTO General Council adopted an enhanced transparency mechanism for RTAs (Crawford, 2007). The mechanism requires WTO members to inform the WTO secretariat about the initiation, conclusion, substance and implementation of RTAs on a timely basis so that the WTO's Committee on Regional Trade Agreements (CRTA) can verify the compliance of the notified RTAs with WTO regulations and circulate relevant information to other WTO members. This was a good first step because it signaled the WTO's intention to monitor regional processes from a position of authority. A robust transparency mechanism would also better protect WTO members by allowing them to keep an eye on RTAs from which they are excluded. Developing countries could hone their trade negotiation skills by tapping into the rich technical resources that would be generated by the transparency mechanism (Panezi, 2016). But for it not to be merely symbolic "due diligence", the transparency mechanism needs to be strengthened. The WTO should put in place a right mix of incentives and disincentives to ensure that, as European Commissioner for Trade Cecilia Malmström (2018) has put it, "there should be rewards for following the rules and there should be penalties for breaking them".

[6] Discussion with Pasha Hsieh at the Singapore Trade Policy Forum on 24–25 October 2018.

Making access to a variety of WTO-specific services, WTO-administered global trade infrastructure and confidential institutional memory of GATT/WTO conditional on RTA members' conformity to the regulations put forth by the WTO is one possibility. Such idea is not wholly unprecedented as a similar arrangement can be found in the decentralizing financial architecture. For instance, for Asian countries to apply for short-term liquidity support that goes over 30% of their total allotment under the CMIM, an agreement with the IMF is necessary. This link between IMF consent and CMIM disbursement serves as an effective multilateralism-regionalism interface. Additionally, MOUs between the WTO and RTA members and/or secretariats[7] could also be considered. In the field of development assistance, the World Bank, ADB, AIIB and NDB have also signed formal MOUs with each other (Ji, 2017; Rana and Pardo, 2015).

(2) It is essential for the WTO to have meaningful oversight over the substances of the RTAs being negotiated. This entails the WTO to prepare a high quality "model RTA" for prospective RTA members to work on as their common negotiation baseline. The availability of such a template with WTO-sanctioned provisions has enormous benefits. It allows the WTO to maintain its relevance as the traditional "rule-writer" while creating approvable legal precedents around which potential multilateral disciplines could emerge. The "spaghetti bowl" problem could also be eased as a result. The CPTPP is one such potential template for future RTA to emulate. Alternatively, the WTO may opt to develop one of its own from scratch. The economic research staff from the CRTA and other divisions have undertaken rigorous analytical work to characterize and categorize different kinds of provisions arising from notified RTAs (Bown, 2016) and they should be tasked to come up with an RTA template on the basis of their research.

To maximize the benefits of the WTO as a knowledge center, there is also a case for the WTO to establish regional advisory centers to help countries to design and implement "multilateralizable" and WTO-consistent RTAs. This is a common practice for other Bretton Woods institutions like the IMF which has dedicated Regional Advisory Groups for Asia and Pacific, Caucasus and Central Asia, Europe, Sub-Saharan Africa and Western Hemisphere.

(3) The WTO should also encourage RTA members to make their RTAs more open. Ji *et al.* (2018) empirically find that a hypothetical transition from RCEP to an expanded Free Trade Area of the Asia-Pacific (FTAAP+), one including mega-RTA countries which are currently not party to APEC forum such as India, would significantly

[7] We acknowledge that creating a centralized administrative body to support the implementation of an FTA is not a common practice at the moment, as borne out by the failed attempt to establish a North American Trade Secretariat with permanent location and staff under the NAFTA agreement (Bélanger, 2007). But since new RTAs like the CPTPP and RCEP are typically structured to cover deep integration and highly complex to implement, there is a need for a stronger institutional foundation to strengthen internal management (with respect to periodic amendment, ROOs, dispute settlement mechanism, etc.) and coordinate external relations for example with the WTO and other trading blocs. Establishing secretariats for mega-FTAs in the making should be on the table. For the CPTPP, the potential secretariat could be located in New Zealand, the Depositary of the agreement. As for RCEP, the ASEAN Secretariat could perhaps be in a position to function as an RCEP secretariat.

increase gains from trade. Real GDP gains would be even higher should regional countries implement mega-RTAs and FTAAP + on an "open regionalism" basis. The notion of open regionalism championed by APEC refers to a practice of RTA signatories voluntarily extending negotiated concessions and market opening to non-members. Since the approach is more acceptable politically than unilateral trade liberalization and more rewarding economically than the traditionally "closed" and selective trade deals, the WTO should actively promote this liberalization modality alongside with APEC. Unfortunately, the emphasis of Trump administration on "fair and reciprocal" trade (Gibbon and Vestergaard, 2017) may run counter to the WTO's and regional countries' potential efforts to anchor inter-state trading relationship in an open regional trading system.

(4) In terms of the configuration of RTAs, the WTO should encourage countries to pursue "regional" agreements with as broad country participation as possible instead of signing scattered "bilateral" treaties. As Schott (2017) succinctly argues, when it comes to regional trade arrangements, "bigger is better". For instance, the economic benefits increased as the EU enlarged and the gains from trade reduced as the US withdrew from the TPP. In areas beyond trade such as financial regionalism, the benefits of consolidating smaller arrangements into bigger regional ones are recognized. The evolution of the CMIM illustrates this point particularly well. The CMIM initially emerged as a loose network of bilateral currency swaps and repurchase agreement facilities among members. It was subsequently consolidated into a regional facility in 2010 in the aftermath of the global financial crisis for wider benefits.

(5) Many large developing countries including China, India and South Africa are not willing to abandon the DDA as yet because issues like agriculture trade is still important to them. Hence, it would be difficult to walk away from the Doha agenda and focus on the so-called "WTO 2.0" as proposed by Baldwin (2012). One way out of the impasse is for the WTO to plurilateralize RTAs. Annex 4 of the Agreement Establishing the WTO allows four sectoral "Plurilateral Trade Agreements" (PTAs): the Agreement on Government Procurement and the Agreement on Trade in Civil Aircraft and two others that were terminated in 1997 (the International Dairy Agreement and the International Bovine Meat Agreement). These PTAs are closed agreements in terms of accruing benefits and obligations only for contracting parties. The WTO also recognizes a set of open PTAs, also known as "critical mass" agreements, including Information Technology Agreement (1996) and Trade Facilitation Agreement (2017) that are implemented on an MFN basis. The Trade in Services Agreement is under negotiation. A wider application of such sectoral and plurilateral approaches to trade and services liberalization, once criticized for undermining multilateralism (Oyane, 2001), could open up an escape route for the WTO in the era of (mega)regionalism. As noted in Table 2, the TPP/CPTPP, RCEP and TTIP all strive to write new trade rules on a host of WTO-extra policy areas. If and when the three mega-RTAs' provisions on a certain issue (e.g., SME) converge, the skeleton of a PTA (on SME) involving all TPP/CPTPP, RCEP and TTIP countries could emerge. As the combined share of global trade and GDP covered by mega-RTA participating countries are already large,

the "critical mass" of 80% market share or more to prevent free-riding by non-signatories (Adlung and Mamdouh, 2017) can be relatively easy to achieve for the PTAs. This mega-regionalism-to-plurilateralism (M2P) process may not happen on its own particularly given the difficulties plaguing the negotiations for RCEP and TTIP. The WTO can therefore play an active role to facilitate the process of M2P. Of particular importance for the WTO is to quickly determine which WTO-plus commitments arising from mega-RTAs and other innovative RTAs can be used to update existing PAs and which WTO-extra regional disciplines have the potential to be plurilateralized under the WTO (Bown, 2016).

5. Role of Asia

Since it is the global leader of regionalism and concurrently a fast-growing constituency in the WTO with growing trade shares, Asia should exercise front-line leadership in reforming the WTO. However, it is doubtful whether Asia could act on the proposals sketched out in the preceding section under the presently archaic WTO governance system. To understand the root cause of the WTO stasis and map possible routes for reform, it is useful to bring in the "governance trilemma" conceptualized among others by Kawai *et al.* (2010) and Baldwin (2018). The theory posits that the requirements for international economic institutions to be "democratic" in terms of institutional governance, "universal" in terms of member coverage and policy ownership, and "effective" in timely delivering on the public goods sought after by its member governments, add up to a trilemma (or an "impossible trinity"): achieving any two makes the attainment of the third objective difficult. The WTO as it stands is democratic (consensus-based) and (nearly) universal (in terms of membership), but falling short on the score of effectiveness. Any in-depth analysis of the WTO's governance reform[8] is beyond the scope of the paper and we concede that there are no easy and quick solutions to the WTO's woes, but the trilemma in Figure 4

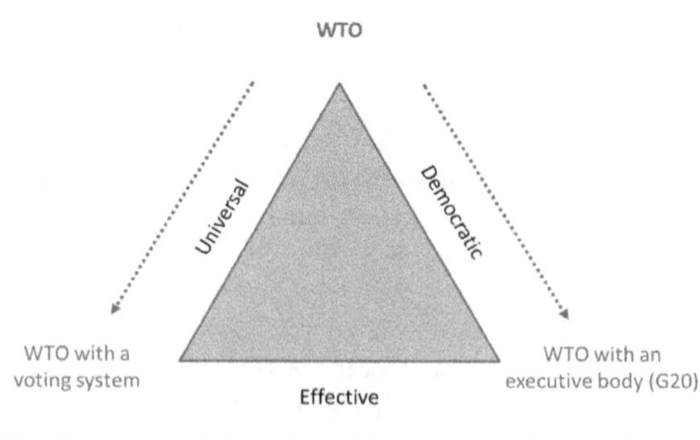

Figure 4. The Governance Trilemma and Two Plausible Ways to Reform the WTO

[8] Interested readers can find useful materials in Jones (2010, 2015).

points to two basic yet meaningful ways to make the WTO more effective, malleable and adaptable to the rapidly changing global economy.

One possible strategy is to move the WTO to the left-hand-side triangle corner to become an institution that is effective and universal but comparatively less democratic. This entails fundamental reforms to the WTO's prevailing consensus-driven legislative tradition for decision making by instituting some majority voting procedures. An useful and balanced proposal of institutionalizing a voting system in the WTO comes from Narlikar (2011) who advocates a two-threshold voting system akin to the EU's "qualified majority" rule.[9] Under such a system, for a WTO-wide decision to go through, a double-majority in an un-weighted vote (i.e., one country, one vote) and a weighted vote must both be reached. The advantage is that a majority in the former honors sovereign equality to protect smaller economies from disenfranchisement, and a majority in the latter secures the buy-in of major stakeholders in the multilateral trading system (who are investing in mega-regional alternatives to the WTO). While the exact threshold for a weighted vote would (and should) be debated and even a blocking minority could be explicitly allowed in exceptional circumstances, the formulae proposed by Cottier and Takenoshita (2003) allocating voting rights based on considerations of trade share, economic size, market openness and population, seem acceptable to many in principle. The Warwick Commission (2007) used to argue against voting for an important reason that the practice violates the institution's consensus principle and egalitarian culture. Yet, voting is a legitimate fall-back option for arriving at decisions under GATT/WTO (Hoekman and Kostecki, 2001). And it should be recalled that voting was a regular legal instrument for decision-making in the early days of GATT (before being phased out in the 1950s) and was resorted to in the case of Ecuador's accession to the WTO. Perhaps, it is time for voting to come back in vogue as the beleaguered WTO fights for self-perseveration.

A second plausible strategy of addressing the WTO's effectiveness deficit is to push the organization to the right-hand-side corner. Retaining its essential democratic characteristics, the WTO could increase flexibility in decision-making by compromising on the principle of universality. Delegating some powers to an executive board where unanimity is the norm could be a viable proposition in this genre of solutions. Proposals centred on forming a "WTO executive committee" are in fact one of the most commonly discussed reform options and have found favor among some members like the EU (Dube, 2012). The precedent for this can be found in the informal "Green Room" format of decision-making in GATT/WTO. A typical Green Room process begins by a small group of self-selected developed countries in consultation with a set of invited developing countries broking breakthroughs before presenting their decisions to the GATT/WTO membership for formal, multilateral adoption. Historically, this inner circle of decision-makers and agenda-setters in the WTO had, depending on the issue at hand and the number of countries involved, taken many forms, such as the "Consultative Group of Eighteen" in the Tokyo Round, the Quad in the Uruguay Round and the Group of 4, Five Interested Parties,

[9] At the EU, a decision is normally adopted if 55% of the EU members, representing at least 65% of the population of the EU, vote in favor.

Group of 6 and Group of 7 in the Doha Round (Vickers, 2012; Dube, 2012). These various "G" groups customarily faced considerable apathy, if not resentment, in the WTO due to their self-serving nature, legitimacy deficit, and the bullying tactics of imposing decisions on the rest of the WTO members on a take-it-or-leave-it basis (VanGrasstek, 2013). Therefore, the WTO is left in a situation where decision-making is proceeding at glacial speed without an executive body but existing and historical intra-GATT/WTO coalitions are not up to the task of facilitating decision-making and building preliminary consensus on global trade matters.

Against this background, the G20, the so-called "premier forum for international economic cooperation" and the de facto global steering committee for macroeconomic coordination, could provide part of the answer. G20 also consists of countries and "guests" invited without transparent and well-established membership rules (Slaughter, 2013), but the grouping's economic size, demographic weight,[10] geographical representativeness and institutional status bestow upon on it a significantly higher degree of legitimacy and influence in comparison with the past and existing country constellations in the GATT/WTO. The G20's greater and more direct participation in the global trade decision-making process should be welcomed by G20 members and cautiously tolerated by countries external to it if the mini-ministerial level forum proves able to get the WTO out of the current deadlock.

The Buenos Aires G20 Summit in 2019 elevated the subject of WTO reforms as an agenda item for the G20 for the first time. With Asia's strong presence in G20 in mind, it would be best if the "Asia 5 + 1" (already defined above) despite their varied positions on specific issues, could follow up by fleshing out concrete Asian ideas and perspectives about the future of multilateralism at relevant G20 meetings such as the G20 Trade and Investment Ministers meetings and the G20 summits.[11] In the area of finance, the G20 had come up with six broad principles for cooperation between the IMF and RFSNs; further to this, the Fund proposed specifically 7 lessons and 4 modalities to operationalize IMF-RFSN cooperation. Based on these activities, encouraging progress is being made in the cooperation between the IMF and CMIM (Rana, 2019). The G20 should also develop similar principles for WTO-RTA cooperation which the WTO could implement.

Apart from seeking to engineer adaptive governance reforms in the WTO, Asia can take actions to improve the decentralizing trading architecture in three other ways. First, with the US abdicating its long-standing leadership role in the liberal, rules-based trade order and Europe being consumed by such domestic policy objectives as Brexit and migration, the leadership task falls to Asia. And, it is incumbent upon Asian policymakers to seize the historic opportunity to play a much bigger role in shaping the evolution of global trade system in an era of great policy uncertainty. Clinching a high-quality RCEP deal soon

[10] Countries participating in 2018 G20 Summit made up 85% of global economic output, 66% of global population, 75% of international trade and 80% of global investment.

[11] For an account of the relationship between the WTO and G20, see Hoekman (2016). Additionally, it should be recalled that the establishment of the global financial safety net and promoting complementarity between the IMF and RFSNs was an agenda item of the Seoul G20 Summit of 2010. This action has resulted in encouraging progress in promoting collaboration between the IMF and RFSNs (Rana and Pardo, 2018).

would be of profound importance to this end. The quality of the final RCEP agreement will be a natural litmus test of the potential, seriousness and credibility of Asia's global trade leadership role. After all, how can Asia play a constructive leading role on trade governance if its own flagship trade initiative is of comparatively lower ambition and if countries continue to cave into protectionist pressures? Encouragingly, RCEP negotiators are aiming to formulate a forward-looking and pro-integration trade treaty which the region has not seen before.

Second, Asian countries should eventually promote the convergence of RCEP and CPTPP (Ji and Rana, 2018). The convergence between the two mega-regional trade undertaking can be realized through a dual-track approach (Ji *et al.*, 2018) or a multi-tier approach (Petri and Abdul-Raheem, 2014; Scollay, 2016). Under the former option, the process starts by Asian countries securing dual membership. CPTPP-only countries should sign up to RCEP when possible (for greater export opportunities for companies to China and India), and RCEP track-only signatories should reciprocate the move by seeking accession into the CPTPP (not least to gain valuable exposure to CPTPP rules). Then there would be impetus to rationalize redundancy arising from the co-existence of the CPTPP and RCEP by merging the two into one agreement. The multi-tier option, for its part, envisages the installation of an "umbrella agreement" from day one. Within this overarching agreement, the CPTPP and RCEP members each adhere to their own rules, and the two groups of countries are glued together by a common set of intermediate obligations achievable in the short term. The expectation is that RCEP countries would voluntarily ratchet up their commitments towards CPTPP standards in the end. A streamlined agreement integrating the RCEP and CPTPP would provide sizable economic gains and a better and more inclusive institutional base for Asian economic integration, fortifying the region's leading position in the global trade landscape.

Third, Asia should promote cooperation between RCEP and China's BRI, considering that the potential for complementarity and functional cooperation between the tariff-cutting RCEP and the infrastructure-enhancing BRI is striking (Intal, 2018). But unlike with the proposed membership convergence between the CPTPP and RCEP, there will not be significant membership overlap between the BRI and RCEP in the medium term. Three key RCEP negotiating parties (Japan, India and Australia) are unlikely to join the BRI in the foreseeable future for geopolitical reasons, and non-RCEP BRI countries like Pakistan, Bangladesh and Mongolia cannot accede to RCEP due to the absence of a separate trade deal with ASEAN. To realize complementarity between the BRI and RCEP, what needs to be done first is to sign a BRI-RCEP MOU to lay the foundation of formal cooperation between the two initiatives. With the MOU, BRI countries currently not participating in RCEP could be allowed to benefit from the trade and investment agenda of the planned RCEP (Vines, 2018) and accorded priority status when RCEP is ready for expansion. On the other hand, the MOU could provide the extra incentive for Japan, India and Australia to take part in the BRI to provide checks and balances from within it given their shared concerns about an unconstrained China allegedly wielding "debt-trap diplomacy" to gain geopolitical advantages.

6. Conclusion

This paper has traced the evolution of the international trade architecture from a centralized to a decentralized one because of the establishment of new regional institutions. We argue that the drivers of this phenomenon include the rising popularity of "new regionalism" in the aftermath of Cold War, the negotiations for mega-RTAs in the post-GFC period, the protectionist trade policies of the Trump administration in recent years, and disappointments with the progress of WTO negotiations. The establishment of new regional institutions that have led to decentralization have a number of benefits such as "healthy" competition and functional cooperation between the WTO and RTAs. At the same time, it also has the risks such as "unhealthy" competition. We argue that the benefits appear to have outweighed the costs and that the global governance of trade has probably improved. Looking ahead, a number of policy actions have to be taken to manage the trade decentralization process or "multilateralize regionalism" and to improve the governance of the WTO. Asian countries, especially the "Asia 5 + 1" countries, whose footprints in the global economic and political system are increasing have an important role to play in this regard.

References

Abbott, KW, JF Green and RO Keohane (2016). Organizational ecology and institutional change in global governance. *International Organization*, 70(2), 247–277.

ADB (2008). Asian regionalism: Context and scope. In *Emerging Asian Regionalism: A Partnership for Shared Prosperity*. Mandaluyong: Asian Development Bank.

Adlung, R and H Mamdouh (2017). Plurilateral trade agreements: An escape route for the WTO? WTO Working Paper ERSD-2017-03. Geneva: World Trade Organization.

Baldwin, R (2012). WTO 2.0: Global governance of supply-chain trade. In *CEPR Policy Insight*. London: Centre for Economic Policy Research.

Baldwin, R (2014). Multilateralising 21st centry regionalism. In *Global Forum on Trade: Reconciling Regionalism and Multilateralism in a Post-Bali World*, Paris.

Baldwin, R (2018). Sources of the WTO's woes: Decision-making's impossible trinity. VoxEU.

Baldwin, R and P Low (2009). *Multilateralizing Regionalism: Challenges for the Global Trading System*. Cambridge: Cambridge University Press.

Bélanger, L (2007). Diverging preferences: The impact of NAFTA on the member states' trade policies. In *Regionalism and the State: NAFTA and Foreign Policy Convergence*, G Mace (ed.) Hampshire: Ashgate.

Bergsten, CF (1996). Globalizing free trade. *Foreign Affairs*, 75(3), 105–120.

Bhagwati, J (1995). US Trade Policy: The infatuation with FT As. In *The Dangerous Obsession with Free Trade Areas*, C Barfield (ed.). Washington, DC: American Enterprise Institute.

Bhagwati, J (2008). *Termites in the Trading System: How Preferential Agreements Undermine Free Trade*. New York: Oxford University Press.

Bown, CP (2016). Mega-regional trade agreements and the future of the WTO. In *Global Order and the New Regionalism*. New York: Council on Foreign Relations.

Bronz, G (1956). An international trade organization: The second attempt. *Harvard Law Review*, 69(3), 440–482.

Cadot, O and LY Ing (2019). How restrictive are ASEANs rules of origin? In *East Asian Integration: Goods, Services and Investment*, LY Ing, M Richardson and S Urata (eds.). Abingdon and New York: Routledge.

Chia, SY (2010). Regional trade policy cooperation and architecture in East Asia. ADBI Working Paper. Tokyo: Asian Development Bank Institute.
Ciuriak, D, J Xiao and A Dadkhah (2017). Quantifying the comprehensive and progressive agreement for Trans-Pacific Partnership. *East Asian Economic Review*, 21(4), 343–384.
Cottier, T and S Takenoshita (2003). The balance of power in WTO decision-making: Towards weighted voting in legislative response. *Aussenwirtschaft*, 58(2), 169–214.
Crawford, J-A (2007). A new transparency mechanism for regional trade agreements. *Singapore Year Book of International Law*, 11, 133–140.
de Melo, J and A Panagariya (eds.) (1993). *New Dimensions in Regional Integration*. London: Centre for Economic Policy Research.
Dent, CM (2016). *East Asian Regionalism*. 2nd ed. Abingdon and New York: Routledge.
Desker, B (2004). In defence of FTAs: From purity to pragmatism in East Asia. *Pacific Review*, 17(1), 3–26.
Dube, M (2012). The way forward for the WTO: Reforming the decision-making process. In *Economic Diplomacy Programme Occasional Paper*. Johannesburg: South African Institute of International Affairs.
Estevadeordal, A, J Harris and K Suominen (2009). Multilateralising preferential rules of origin around the world. *IDB Working Paper*. Washington, DC: Inter-American Development Bank.
Ethier, WJ (1998). The new regionalism. *The Economic Journal*, 108(3), 1149–1161.
Felbermayr, G, F Kimura, T Okubo, M Steininger and E Yalcin (2017). On the economics of an EU-Japan Free Trade Agreement. In *GED Study*. Gütersloh: Bertelsmann Stiftung.
Fiorentino, RV, L Verdeja and C Toqueboeuf (2007). The changing landscape of regional trade agreements: 2006 update. In *WTO Discussion Paper*. Geneva: World Trade Organization.
Freund, C (2010). Third-country effects of regional trade agreements. *World Economy*, 33(11), 1589–1605.
Freund, C, T Moran and S Oliver (2016). Tariff liberalization. In *Trans-Pacific Partnership: An Assessment*, C Cimino-Isaacs and JJ Schott (eds.). Washington, DC: Peterson Institute for International Economics.
Freund, C and E Ornelas (2010). Regional trade agreements. *Annual Review of Economics*, 2, 139–167.
Gibbon, P and J Vestergaard (2017). *US Trade Policy Under Trump: Assessing the Unilateralist Turn*. Copenhagen: Danish Institute for International Studies.
Gretton, P (2017). Bilateral and Regional Trade Agreements: Detangling the Noodle/Spaghetti Bowl. *EABER Working Paper 130*. Canberra: East Asian Bureau of Economic Research.
Hillman, JE (2018). How big is China's Belt and Road? In *CSIS Commentary*. Washington, DC: Center for Strategic and International Studies.
Hoekman, B (2016). Revitalizing the global trading system: What could the G20 do? *China & World Economy*, 24(4), 34–54.
Hoekman, B and M Kostecki (2001). *The Political Economy of the World Trading System: The WTO and Beyond*. Oxford: Oxford University Press.
Ilott, O, I Stelk and J Rutter (2017). *Taking Back Control of Trade Policy*. London: Institute for Government.
Intal, PS (2018). East Asia's transformation and regional architecture. In *Asian Economic Integration in an Era of Global Uncertainty*, S Armstrong and T Westland (eds.) Canberra: ANU Press.
Itakura, K (2019). Economic effects of East Asian integration on Southeast Asia. In *East Asian Integration: Goods, Services and Investment*, LY Ing, M Richardson and S Urata (eds.) Abingdon and New York: Routledge.
Ji, X (2017). Promoting regional development bank complementarity: Challenges to Asia and lessons from Europe. *Asia Europe Journal*, 15(3), 261–281.

Ji, X (2019). Competitive mega-regionalism: The trilateral geo-economic power play by the United States of America, China and the European Union. PhD Thesis, Nanyang Technological University, Singapore.

Ji, X and PB Rana (2018). The United States and the rise, fall and future prospects of the (Comprehensive and Progressive Agreement for) Trans-Pacific Partnership. *12th Berlin Conference on Asian Security*, Berlin.

Ji, X and PB Rana (2019). A deal that does not die: The United States and the rise, fall and future of the (CP)TPP. *Pacific Focus*, 34(2), 230–255.

Ji, X, PB Rana, W-M Chia and C Li (2016). Economic and strategic dimensions of mega-FTAs: A perception survey of Asian Opinion Leaders. RSIS Working Paper.S. Rajaratnam School of International Studies, Singapore.

Ji, X, PB Rana, W-M Chia and C Li (2018). Post-TPP trade policy options for ASEAN and its dialogue partners: "Preference Ordering" Using CGE Analysis. *East Asian Economic Review*, 22 (2), 177–215.

Jones, K (2010). *The Doha Blues: Institutional Crisis and Reform in the WTO*. New York: Oxford University Press.

Jones, K (2015). *Reconstructing the World Trade Organization for the 21st Century: An Institutional Approach*. New York: Oxford University Press.

Jungbluth, C, G Felbermayr, F Kimura, T Okubo, M Steininger and E Yalcin (2017). EU-Japan: Free trade agreement a sign of commitment to economic cooperation. In *Future Social Market Economy Policy Brief*. Gütersloh: Bertelsmann Stiftung.

Kahler, M, CR Henning, CP Bown, H Wang, E Voeten and PD Williams (2016). Global order and the new regionalism. In *Discussion Paper Series on Global and Regional Governance*. New York: Council on Foreign Relations.

Kawai, M, PA Petri and ES Ciamarra (2010). Asia in global economic governance: A case for decentralized institutions. In *Asian Regionalism in the World Economy: Engine for Dynamism and Stability*, M Kawai, J-W Lee, PA Petri and G Capanelli (eds.) Cheltenham: Edward Elgar.

Kawai, M and G Wignaraja (eds.) (2011). *Asia's Free Trade Agreements: How Is Business Responding?* Cheltenham and Northampton: Edward Elgar.

Langhammer, RJ and U Hiemenz (1990). *Regional Integration Among Developing Countries: Opportunities, Obstacles and Options*. Tübingen: JCB Mohr.

Lee, J-W and K Shin (2006). Does regionalism lead to more global trade integration in East Asia? *The North American Journal of Economics and Finance*, 17(3), 283–301.

Lester, S, B Mercurio and A Davies (eds.) (2008). *World Trade Law: Text, Materials and Commentary*. Oxford, UK: Hart Publishing.

Madhur, S (2012). Asia's role in twenty-first-century global economic governance. *Internationl Affairs*, 88(4), 817–833.

Malmström, C (2018). *EU–U.S. Trade and the Future of the WTO: A Conversation with Commissioner Malmstrm*. R Hunter (ed.). Washington, DC: The German Marshall Fund of the United States.

Meléndez-Ortiz, R (2014). Mega-regionals: What is going on? In *Mega-regional Trade Agreements: Game-Changers or Costly Distractions for the World Trading System?*, Global Agenda Council on Trade & Foreign Direct Investment. Geneva: World Economic Forum.

Morse, JC and RO Keohane (2014). Contested multilateralism. *The Review of International Organizations*, 9(4), 385–412.

Narlikar, A (2011). Adapting to new power balances: Institutional reform in the WTO. In *Governing the World Trade Organization: Past, Present and Beyond Doha*, T Cottier and M Elsig (eds.). Cambridge: Cambridge University Press.

Oxley, A (1994). The achievements of the GATT Uruguay Round. *Agenda: A Journal of Policy Analysis and Reform*, 1(1), 45–53.

The Decentralizing International Trade Architecture 83

Oyane, S (2001). Plurilateralism of the United States and its APEC Policies. IDE APEC Study Center Working Paper, Institute of Developing Economies, Chiba.
Panezi, M (2016). The WTO and the Spaghetti bowl of free trade agreements. Policy Brief No. 87, Centre for International Governance Innovation, Waterloo.
Pardo, RP and PB Rana (2015). Complementarity between regional and global financial governance institutions: The case of ASEAN+3 and Global Financial Safety Net. *Global Governance*, 21(3), 413–433.
Pardo, RP and PB Rana (2018). Cooperation not threat: The new multilateral development banks and old. *Global Asia*, 13(1), 72–77.
Petri, PA and A Abdul-Raheem (2014). Can RCEP and the TPP be Pathways to FTAAP? In State of the Region, Pacific Economic Cooperation Council, Singapore.
Petri, PA and MG Plummer (2016). The economic effects of the Trans-Pacific Partnership: New estimates. PIIE Working Paper, Peterson Institute for International Economics, Washington, DC.
Rana, PB (2014). From a centralized to a decentralized global economic architecture: An overview. In *New Global Economic Architecture: The Asian Perspective*, M Kawai, PJ Morgan and PB Rana (eds.). Cheltenham & Northampton: Edward Elgar.
Rana, PB (2019). The ASEAN+3 regional financial safety net 20 years on. In *Financial Cooperation in East Asia*, T Kikuchi and M Sakuragawa (eds.) Singapore: S. Rajaratnam School of International Studies.
Rana, PB and X Ji (2018). The Asia-Pacific's response to rising U.S. protectionism. In *COC Global Memo*. New York: Council on Foreign Relations.
Rana, PB and RP Pardo (2015). ASEAN+3 and the IMF: The need for a marriage of convenience. *Global Asia*, 10(1), 64–71.
Rana, PB and RP Pardo (2018). Rise of complementarity between global and regional financial institutions: Perspectives from Asia. *Global Policy*, 9(2), 231–243.
Rimmer, PJ (2018). China's belt and road initiative: Underlying economic and international relations dimensions. *Asia-Pacific Economic Literature*, 32(2), 3–26.
Schmucker, C and K Gnath (2011). From the G8 to the G-20: Reforming the global economic governance system. In *European Yearbook of International Economic Law 2011*, C Herrmann and JP Terhechte (eds.). Berlin and Heidelberg: Springer.
Schott, J (2008). The future of the multilateral trading system in a multi-polar world. Discussion Paper, German Development Institute, Bonn.
Schott, JJ (2017). US Trade policy options in the Pacific Basin: Bigger is better. Policy Brief, Peterson Institute for International Economics, Washington, DC.
Scollay, R (2016). APEC, TPP, and RCEP: Towards an FTAAP. In *Trade Regionalism in the Asia-Pacific: Developments and Future Challenges*, SB Das and M Kawai (eds.). Singapore: ISEAS–Yusof Ishak Institute.
Sherifis, RF and V Astraldi (2001). *G7/G8: from Rambouillet to Genoa*. Milan: FrancoAngeli.
Slaughter, S (2013). Debating the international legitimacy of the G20: Global policymaking and contemporary international society. *Global Policy*, 4(1), 43–52.
Solís, M and SN Katada (2015). Unlikely pivotal states in competitive free trade agreement diffusion: The effect of Japan's Trans-Pacific Partnership participation on Asia-Pacific Regional Integration. *New Political Economy*, 20(2), 155–177.
Toye, R (2003). Developing multilateralism: The Havana Charter and the Fight for the International Trade Organization, 1947–1948. *International History Review*, 25(2), 282–305.
Ullrich, H (2006). Explaining G7/8 multilateral trade commitments: Is the G7/8 still relevant? *Annual Meeting of the International Studies Association*, San Diego, CA, 22–25 March.
Urata, S (2019). Trends of FTAs in East Asia from the 1990s to the 2010s: Defensive and competitive regionalism. In *East Asian Integration: Goods, Services and Investment*, LY Ing, M Richardson and S Urata (eds.). Abingdon and New York: Routledge.

VanGrasstek, C (2013). The future of the WTO. In *The History and Future of the World Trade Organization*. Geneva: World Trade Organization.

Vickers, B (2012). The role of the B(R)ICS: System supporters or Change agents in the WTO? In *The Oxford Handbook on The World Trade Organization*, A Narlikar, M Daunton and RM Stern (eds.) Oxford: Oxford University Press.

Vines, D (2018). The BRI and RCEP: Ensuring cooperation in the liberalisation of trade in Asia. *Economic and Political Studies*, 6(3), 338–348.

Wang, H (2017). New multilateral development banks: Opportunities and challenges for global governance. *Global Policy*, 8(1), 113–118.

Warwick Commission (2007). The Multilateral Trade Regime: Which Way Forward? Coventry: University of Warwick.

WEF (2016). Will the Trans-Pacific Partnership agreement reshape the global trade and investment system? what's in and what's new: Issues and options. White Paper. Global Agenda Council on Trade & FDI, World Economic Forum, Geneva.

Wilkinson, R, E Hannah and J Scott (2016). The WTO in Nairobi: The demise of the Doha Development Agenda and the Future of the Multilateral Trading System. *Global Policy*, 7(2), 247–255.

World Bank (1987). *World Development Report, 1987*. Washington, DC: World Bank.

World Bank (2016). Potential macroeconomic implications of the Trans-Pacific Partnership. In *Global Economic Prospects*. Washington, DC: World Bank.

WTO (2011). The WTO and preferential trade agreements: From co-existence to coherence. World Trade Report 2011, World Trade Organization, Geneva.

Zürn, M and B Faude (2013). Commentary: On fragmentation, differentiation, and coordination. *Global Environmental Politics*, 13(3), 119–130.

Chapter 3

SPATIAL PANEL ANALYSIS ON ASEAN–CHINA TRADE LINKS[†]

CHEN-CHEN YONG

Department of Economics, Faculty of Economics and Administration
University of Malaya, 50603 Kuala Lumpur, Malaysia
ccyong@um.edu.my

SIEW-YONG YEW

Department of Economics, Faculty of Economics and Administration
University of Malaya, 50603 Kuala Lumpur, Malaysia
yewsy@um.edu.my

MUI-YIN CHIN[*]

Economics and Corporate Administration Department
Faculty of Accountancy, Finance and Business
Tunku Abdul Rahman University College
Jalan Genting Kelang, 53300 Setapak Kuala Lumpur, Malaysia
chinmy@acd.tarc.edu.my

Published Online 23 November 2016

The change of trade structures from the dynamic development of production networks globally had caused processing trade to become more prominent in China. This change drives ASEAN5 to be more aggressive in developing vertical intra-industry trade (VIIT) with China. This study aims to identify the catalysts that strengthened the VIIT relationship between ASEAN5 and China for manufacturing sub-sectors. Both decomposition-type threshold method and spatial panel econometric modelling are used and the results show that foreign direct investment (FDI) and difference in gross domestic products (DGDP) are the influential determinants of VIIT although their impacts vary across manufacturing sub-sectors. The results also confirm the presence of spatial interaction effects among ASEAN5 countries in relation to China's trade. These suggest that deeper economic integration among ASEAN5 countries is vital in strengthening bilateral VIIT with China. Moreover, to foster the value chain between the two regions, emphasis on performing similar tasks with differentiated varieties of products is essential as the two regions have similar comparative advantages.

Keywords: Vertical intra-industry trade; spatial panel model; ASEAN–China bilateral trade; manufacturing sub-sectors.

JEL Classification: C33, F14

[*] Corresponding author.

[†] This article originally appeared in *The Singapore Economic Review*, **64**(3), pp. 709–726

1. Introduction

Association of Southeast Asian Nations (ASEAN) member countries, through the formation of ASEAN–China free trade area in 2010 have attracted many domestic and foreign firms to take advantage of the preferential access to both ASEAN and China markets. The total trade between the five ASEAN5 countries (namely Indonesia, Malaysia, Philippines, Singapore and Thailand) and China which was USD 10,684 million in 1993 had increased moderately to USD 36,095 million in 2000 and further surged to USD 36,236 million in 2014 [United Nations Commodity Trade Statistics Database (UN COMTRADE) database], contributed mainly by the manufacturing sector. The trade shares of the manufacturing sector between the five ASEAN5 countries of Indonesia, Malaysia, Philippines, Singapore and Thailand with China had increased radically from 55.9%, 55.6%, 55.5%, 58.7% and 62.2% in 1993 to 65.6%, 84.3%, 82.9%, 86.3% and 81.4% in 2014, respectively (UN COMTRADE database). This clearly implies that currently, the manufacturing sector plays the leading role in ASEAN5-China bilateral trade. As China's manufacturing sector move up in the value chain, the reduction of imports of parts and components from ASEAN will happen (Shafaeddin, 2004). UN Comtrade Database had shown that most of the ASEAN5 countries are experiencing trade deficit with China in manufacturing sub-sectors except for chemicals and related products [Standard International Trade Classification (SITC) 5]. In addition, the extent of trade deficit is getting larger over time, particularly since 2000. This bias against ASEAN's trade balance, if left unchecked, will be detrimental to ASEAN in the short run and to ASEAN and China bilateral trade in the long run.

ASEAN herself is plagued with problems, which include the wide development gap among member countries and intra-regional competition. Initiatives such as the ASEAN Economic Community (AEC) can narrow down the intra-regional gap and competition through the reduction of the intra-regional trade barriers and future merging of their economies into a single market can create a highly competitive economic block close to the market size of China. The convergence of the market sizes between ASEAN and China can stimulate the bilateral trade relationship and inter-regional integration between ASEAN and China. New initiatives are needed that will encourage more equitable improvements in the aspects of economic development, trade and investment among ASEAN5 countries with China, which will intensify the spatial interaction effect of trade expansion between individual ASEAN5 countries and China as well as between the two regions.

There is also an increasing concern on ASEAN–China bilateral trade arising from China's dynamic structural change from resource-heavy capital spending to consumer-led growth which has the potential to send shocks across ASEAN5. These shocks may be an opportunity as manufacturing sectors globally and regionally realign into industrial clusters that will increasingly determine spending choices. Although the final assemblers still need to source from the vertical production chain, increasing competition and improvement in domestic production capabilities threaten the continuation of IIT. Hence, understanding the determinants of bilateral trade between ASEAN and China is a necessity to achieve the rebalancing of the manufacturing sector arising from dynamic regional integration.

This paper is organized as follows: Section 2 presents the challenges of ASEAN–China bilateral trade; Section 3 describes the methodology used in this study. Section 4 presents the results. Section 5 provides the policy implications. Section 6 concludes the paper and Section 7 describes the limitations of study.

2. The Challenges of ASEAN–China Bilateral Trade

Past literature had documented the determinants of regional trade, which include trade policies (Kandogan, 2008; Baier and Bergstrand, 2007; Carrere, 2006), economic development (Cassim, 2009; Wilson *et al.*, 2003), labor migration (Athukorala, 1993), social cultural factors (Tabellini, 2005; Dziembowska-Kowalska and Funck, 2000) and politics (Vayrynen, 2003; Harris, 1994). However, this study focuses on macroeconomic aspects of fostering ASEAN–China bilateral trade.

China's trade structure has shifted towards products within similar industries, particularly manufactured products as these products involve high degrees of production differentiation (Hu and Ma, 1999). It is also noticeable that China with rich labor endowment has augmented her specialization in labor-intensive production, which in turn induced fundamental changes in China's bilateral trade structure, i.e., changing from horizontal intra-industry trade (HIIT) to vertical intra-industry trade (VIIT).[1] The emergence of VIIT is mainly attributable to the processing trade. From 2000 to 2008, processing exports contributed 50–55% while processing imports contributed 40–45% to China's total trade (Zhang, 2008). Likewise, VIIT has been growing and became crucial in ASEAN (Fukao *et al.*, 2003; Hurley, 2003). Some multinational corporations (MNCs) located in ASEAN, produce and export intermediate goods to China in similar industries for reprocessing purposes. The final goods are then re-exported throughout the world (Thorbecke and Smith, 2010). Hence, arising from the changes in China's trade structure, the VIIT relationship between ASEAN and China has intensified.

In order to promote greater competition, foreign direct investment (FDI) in China has become the platform for technology transfer (Tran, 2010). China's government encourages foreign investors to go into joint ventures or joint production with domestic firms. These policies have given rise to a pool of highly skilled labor in China and the emergence of strong domestic firms (Rodrik, 2006). Hence, the quality of China's exported products had increased over time. Despite being the assembler, China has also emerged as the producer of high-tech intermediate goods (Lemoine and Unal-Kesenci, 2002). As China moves up to high value-added products, her dependency on high value-added imports from ASEAN may decrease over time. Consequently, it may reduce the sustainability of bilateral VIIT between respective ASEAN countries and China.

It is well noted that foreign direct investment plays a vital role in either promoting or reducing the vertical intra-industry trade between ASEAN5 countries and China. FDI is divided into two types. The first type of FDI is known as vertical FDI or efficiency seeking

[1] Based on OECD Glossary of Statistic (2007), HIIT refers to trade in similar products with differentiated varieties; VIIT refers to trade in "vertically differentiated" products distinguished by quality and price.

FDI where the motive of MNCs is to form production linkages and resources network between ASEAN5 countries and China. The foreign firms are assumed to combine the local factors and the firm's technology to produce outputs, which are subsequently re-exported from the host country (Zhang *et al.*, 2005; Yoshida and Ito, 2006). Therefore, based on production fragmentation theory, efficiency seeking FDI will promote vertical intra-industry trade between these two regions. In contrast, the second type of FDI, namely investment-diverting FDI or market seeking FDI will hamper the trade between ASEAN5 countries and China as the motive of MNCs is to expand or supply the domestic markets.

In addition, the production fragmentation theory postulates that the production processes are divided into a few sequential stages. Therefore, if the market size which is proxied by gross domestic product (GDP) between the two trading partners is similar and less divergent, coordination work can be carried out more smoothly, which will reduce the service-linked cost (Kimura and Ando, 2005; Grossman and Helpman, 2005). As such, ASEAN5 countries, under the umbrella of AEC will have created the interaction effect among member countries with China which will narrow the market size between the two regions. Since AEC was launched in 2015, it can be the engine of trade growth for ASEAN5 and China. However, the higher integration of ASEAN5 may increase or reduce the trade flows with China, depending on whether the nature of the trade linkages among ASEAN5 countries is complementary or substitutional, and also the motive of respective ASEAN5 countries' FDI in China.

3. Methodology

ASEAN5 countries' total trade with China constitute more than 70% of ASEAN's total trade with China since 1993 (ASEAN Statistical Yearbooks). Thus, these five ASEAN nations have been selected in this study. This study employs decomposition-type threshold method developed by Fontagne and Freudenberg (1997) to compute VIIT indices. The spatial panel model will then be formed to identify the catalysts that will strengthen and sustain the VIIT relationships between ASEAN5 countries and China in each of the manufacturing sub-sectors, SITC 5, 6 and 7.[2]

3.1. *Decomposition-type threshold method*

The extent of the trade overlap in each product group of SITC 5, SITC 6 and SITC 7 are as follows:

$$\frac{\mathrm{Min}(X_{ACKit}, M_{ACKit})}{\mathrm{Max}(X_{ACKit}, M_{ACKit})}, \tag{1}$$

where

X_{ACKit} = Exports of product K from ASEAN5 country, A, of manufacturing sub-sector, i to China, C, at period t.

[2]Based on UN COMTRADE definition, SITC 6 refers to manufactured goods classified chiefly by material and SITC 7 refers to machinery and transport equipment.

M_{ACKit} = Imports of product K from ASEAN5 country, A, of manufacturing sub-sector i, from China, C, at period t.

Based on the above equation, the trade of the product is considered intra-industry if the above equation holds. It will otherwise be inter-industry trade.

For HIIT trade, there is no substantial gap between the unit values of exports and imports, while VIIT is associated with substantial gaps between unit values of exports and imports (Fontagne and Freudenberg, 1997; Ito and Okubo, 2011). Hence, unit values of exports and imports will be calculated to distinguish VIIT from HIIT. The following equation with a dispersion factor of 25% is used to decompose intra-industry trade. The dispersion factor of 25% is used to distingusih between HIIT and VIIT in order to account for the disparity in China's exports unit value and imports unit value attributable to transportation costs (Hu and Ma, 1999). The intra-industry trade of product K is considered VIIT if the equation below holds.

$$UV^{X}ACkit/UV^{M}Ackit > 1.25 \text{ or } UV^{X}ACkit/UV^{M}Ackit < 1/1.25, \tag{2}$$

where

UV^{X}_{ACkit} = Unit value of product K of manufacturing sub-sector, i exported to China, C, by each ASEAN5 country, A, at time t.
UV^{M}_{ACkit} = Unit value of product K of manufacturing sub-sector, i imported from China, by each ASEAN5 country, A, at time t.

Manufactured goods data of SITC Rev.3 with 4-digit code are derived from UN COMTRADE Database covering a period of 22 years from 1993 to 2014. After calculating the VIIT value for the entire product range in the respective sub-sectors, the yearly aggregate VIIT indices are computed based on Equation (3) below.

$$S^{viit} = \frac{\sum_{i=1}^{n}(X_{ACKit} + M_{ACKit})^{viit}}{\sum_{i=1}^{n}(X_{ACKit} + M_{ACKit})^{iit}}, \tag{3}$$

where

S^{viit} refers to VIIT index.
$(X_{ACKit} + M_{ACKit})^{iit}$ = Intra-industry trade for each manufacturing sub-sector, i in year t.
$(X_{ACKit} + M_{ACKit})^{viit}$ = vertical intra-industry trade for each manufacturing sub-sector, in year t.

3.2. *Spatial panel model*

The spatial econometric model is adopted in this study as the bilateral trade arising from integration among ASEAN5 countries with China is fostered by the spatial interaction effect of macroeconomic factors such as FDI, difference in market size and VIIT among the ASEAN5 countries. Due to the limitation of the consistent availability of data for the period of 1993 to 2014, the number of explanatory variables is limited. As pointed by Elhost (2003) and Anselin (1988) and cited by Porojan (2001), spatial econometrics is able to test and capture the multiple sources of mis-specification in spatial models or other forms of mis-specification as the model consists of spatial specific effect, which control for each space-specific time-invariant variable and time-period specific effect, which control for each time-specific spatial-invariant effects. Besides, fixed effects are used in this model as the estimators of fixed effects are appropriate and produce unbiased estimation if the unobserved variables are correlated with the regressors (Xing, 2007). Arising from the above, the econometric model adopted in this study is the spatial panel fixed effects model. The dependent variable of this model is the computed aggregate VIIT index while the explanatory variables are ASEAN5's direct investment in China (FDI), difference in GDP (DGDP), spatial interaction effect of VIIT, FDI and DGDP (thereafter, SVIIT, SFDI, SGDP).

This model is divided into three types, namely spatial lag, spatial error and spatial Durbin models. Based on Elhorst (2010b), the model that involves spatially lagged dependent variable and/or spatially lagged independent variable is known as spatial lag model while spatial error models contain spatial autoregressive process in the error term. In addition, Elhorst (2010a) also note that the latest type of spatial model, which is advocated after 2007, is known as spatial Durbin models. Spatial Durbin models accounted for both spatially lagged and spatially auto-correlated error term.

Prior to estimation, all of the variables except VIIT and SVIIT are in the form of logarithms as VIIT takes the value from 0 to 1. The specification of the spatial lag, spatial error and spatial Durbin models are formulated respectively as follows:

$$Y_{it} = \delta \sum_{j=1}^{N} S_{ij} Y_{it} + \alpha + \beta X_{it} + U_i + \lambda_t + e_{it}, \tag{4}$$

$$Y_{it} = \alpha + \beta X_{it} + U_i \lambda_t + \gamma_{it}, \gamma = \rho \sum_{j=1}^{N} S_{ij} \gamma_{it} + e_{it}, \tag{5}$$

$$Y_{it} = \delta \sum_{j=1}^{N} S_{ij} Y_{it} + \alpha + \beta X_{it} + \sum_{j=1}^{N} \varphi S_{ij} X_{ijt} + U_i + \lambda t + e_{it}, \tag{6}$$

where

Y_{it} = VIIT for cross-sectional unit i (each ASEAN5 country) at time $t (i = 1 \ldots \text{to}\, 5; t = 1, \ldots, 17)$.
δ = spatial autocorrelation coefficient.
U_i = The spatial specific effect, which control for each space-specific time-invariant variable.
λ_t = The time-period specific effect, which control for each time-specific spatial-invariant effects.
e_{it} = potential heteroskedastic error term.
γ_{it} represents the error term of unit i, which is depends on the error terms of its neighbouring unit j at time, t based on spatial weights matrix S and e_{it}.
ρ = coefficient of spatial autocorrelation.

φ = coefficient of X_{ijt}.
α = constant term parameter.
β = coefficient of X_{it}.
X_{it} = 1xM vector of explanatory variables in the form of X. X is inclusive of Foreign Direct Investment (FDI) and difference in GDP (DGDP) of each ASEAN5 country with China.
$\sum_{j=1}^{N} \varphi S_{\mathrm{ij}} X_{\mathrm{ijt}}$ denotes the spatial interaction effect of each explanatory variable (FDI, DGDP) among ASEAN5 countries with China.
$\sum_{j=1}^{N} S_{\mathrm{ij}} Y_{\mathrm{it}}$ denotes the interaction effect of the dependent variable (VIIT) among ASEAN5 countries with China.

S is the weight matrix, which measures the spatial interaction among ASEAN5 countries and describes the arrangement of the spatial units for the sample of this study. The weight matrix can be specified in different ways. This study adopted row standardized contiguity matrix as ASEAN Free Trade Area (AFTA) treats all member countries equally. In addition, Porojan (2001) pointed out that the row standardized contiguity matrix is the well-recognized formulation. The row standardized contiguity matrix is expressed as follows:

$$S_{ij} = \left(S_{ij}{}^{*} \Big/ \sum_{j} S_{ij} \right), \tag{7}$$

where

$$S_{ij}{}^{*} = 1 \text{ if } i \neq j,$$
$$S_{ij}{}^{*} = 0 \text{ if } i = j,$$

S_{ij} is the i, jth element of a pre-specified non-negative $N \times N$ spatial weights matrix. The diagonal elements are set to zero as $i = j$ while the weight in each row will be summed to one.

To normalize the difference of GDP between each ASEAN5 country and China, the following measurement is adopted:

$$\mathrm{DGDP} = \frac{|\mathrm{GDP}_C - \mathrm{GDP}_A|}{(\mathrm{GDP}_C + \mathrm{GDP}_A)/2}. \tag{8}$$

GDP_c is GDP of China and GDP_A is GDP of each ASEAN5 country.

All data used are the annual statistics covering a period of 22 years from 1993 to 2014 for each ASEAN5 member country. GDP data is extracted from United Nations Conference on Trade and Development (UNCTAD) database while FDI data are extracted from CEIC database.

A selection framework to determine which spatial panel model best describes the data is essential. Based on Elhorst (2010b), the selection framework is divided into two parts, namely specific to general approach and general to specific approach. Specific to general approach will be first adopted to test the non-spatial model against the spatial models. Subsequently, general to specific approach will be employed to ascertain the best model by testing the spatial Durbin model against spatial lag and spatial error models using Wald test and LR test.

4. Results

4.1. *VIIT indices*

The results in Table 1 show that VIIT dominates bilateral IIT between ASEAN5 and China as the VIIT indices were higher than 0.5 in all manufacturing sub-sectors during the study period except for Indonesia in 1995, Malaysia and Thailand in 2011 for SITC 5; Indonesia in 1994 and 1995, Malaysia in 2005 and 2013, Philippines in 2003 and Singapore in 1995, 1997, 2001 and 2002 for SITC 6 and Malaysia in 2005, 2007 and 2013, Philippines in 2009, Singapore in 2014 and Thailand in 1999, 2000, 2004 and 2013 for SITC 7. These findings are consistent with the findings of Fukao *et al.* (2003) and Kang and Lee (2012) as the former revealed that VIIT dominated IIT in Asia while the latter reported that VIIT dominated IIT between South Korea and Taiwan as well as Organization for Economic Co-operation and Development (OECD) countries.

The high VIIT indices signify the IIT between ASEAN5 countries and China in manufacturing sectors is processing trade in nature except that for Indonesia. The consistent high VIIT indices for Indonesia are mainly due to the small number of products involved in IIT trade with China, which lower the denominator value of Equation (3).

The spatial panel estimation is then undertaken to identify the catalyst in strengthening the VIIT relationship between ASEAN5 and China. The panel estimation is divided into two parts, namely specific to general approach and general to specific approach.

4.2. *Specific to general approach*

Specific to general approach is applied to examine whether the non-spatial model or spatial model best describes the data. The test is based on the residuals of the non-spatial model, which are divided into four types, namely pooled OLS, panel model with spatial fixed effects, panel model with time period fixed effects as well as panel model with both spatial and time period fixed effects. The results of the estimation for SITC 5, SITC 6 and SITC 7 are shown in Table 2.

From Table 2, the R^2 values are gradually increased from pooled OLS to spatial and time period fixed effects specification while the adjusted R^2 values are higher under spatial and time period fixed effects specification than that of pooled OLS for all manufacturing sub-sectors. Besides, this model also has the highest value of LogL across manufacturing sub-sectors. Therefore, the model with spatial and time-period fixed effects specification is preferred to the other three models.

Nonetheless, the R^2 and adjusted R^2 value are below 0.5 for all models including the model with spatial and time-period fixed effects. This is due to the spatial interaction effects that are not embedded explicitly in the models as they are not being captured by the explanatory variables. Hence, spatial Durbin model specification with spatial and

Table 1. VIIT Indices between ASEAN5 Countries and China in SITC 5, SITC 6 and SITC 7

	Indonesia			Malaysia			Philippines			Singapore			Thailand		
Year	SITC 5	SITC 6	SITC 7	SITC 5	SITC 6	SITC 7	SITC 5	SITC 6	SITC 7	SITC 5	SITC 6	SITC 7	SITC 5	SITC 6	SITC 7
1993	1.000	0.938	1.000	0.862	0.847	0.984	0.970	0.981	0.879	0.763	0.839	0.860	0.855	0.684	0.949
1994	0.971	0.425	1.000	0.866	0.852	0.668	0.900	0.808	0.564	0.794	0.837	0.740	0.963	0.969	0.950
1995	0.472	0.473	0.923	0.826	0.662	0.700	0.611	0.899	0.938	0.750	0.364	0.661	0.821	0.738	0.943
1996	0.810	0.552	0.844	0.865	0.744	0.733	0.821	0.907	0.929	0.899	0.663	0.833	0.820	0.787	0.996
1997	0.760	0.723	1.000	0.886	0.954	0.631	0.977	0.196	0.793	0.687	0.485	0.987	0.783	0.788	0.964
1998	0.926	0.603	0.934	0.726	0.696	0.884	0.538	0.625	0.992	0.881	0.778	0.658	0.811	0.982	0.206
1999	0.962	0.777	0.953	0.915	0.725	0.779	0.646	1.000	1.000	0.655	0.892	0.851	0.900	0.976	0.461
2000	0.852	0.764	0.927	0.674	0.866	0.536	0.702	0.979	0.991	0.916	0.609	0.814	0.908	0.855	0.465
2001	0.871	0.802	0.988	0.616	0.902	0.924	0.823	1.000	1.000	0.896	0.440	0.915	0.886	0.686	0.926
2002	0.824	0.744	0.979	0.767	0.654	0.811	0.595	1.000	0.997	0.736	0.465	0.876	0.840	0.801	0.979
2003	0.783	0.673	0.956	0.528	0.767	0.941	0.956	0.435	0.730	0.642	0.566	0.850	0.624	0.864	0.673
2004	0.920	0.867	0.965	0.332	0.558	0.914	1.000	0.715	0.988	0.828	0.555	0.870	0.783	0.859	0.448
2005	0.852	0.793	0.951	0.664	0.441	0.384	0.964	0.866	0.983	0.659	0.866	0.816	0.668	0.766	0.830
2006	0.856	0.857	0.932	0.734	0.741	0.957	1.000	0.959	0.818	0.884	0.601	0.945	0.879	0.578	0.577
2007	0.847	0.658	0.975	0.746	0.662	0.248	0.874	0.965	0.968	0.822	0.595	0.955	0.680	0.680	0.697
2008	0.790	0.707	0.797	0.726	0.810	0.599	0.963	1.000	0.993	0.759	0.813	0.845	0.663	0.761	0.726
2009	0.867	0.848	0.996	0.669	0.656	0.947	0.588	0.983	0.418	0.870	0.773	0.845	0.852	0.804	0.858
2010	0.721	0.767	0.651	0.822	0.561	0.821	0.728	0.989	0.559	0.666	0.883	0.561	0.716	0.605	0.644
2011	0.864	0.481	0.912	0.786	0.389	0.617	0.709	0.923	0.504	0.652	0.890	0.737	0.989	0.585	0.614
2012	0.824	0.679	0.685	0.625	0.546	0.862	0.550	0.890	0.460	0.708	0.857	0.718	0.993	0.604	0.616
2013	0.921	0.525	0.863	0.665	0.644	0.806	0.212	0.913	0.592	0.766	0.636	0.242	0.981	0.661	0.497
2014	0.866	0.559	0.833	0.868	0.640	0.528	0.516	0.98	0.673	0.778	0.907	0.781	0.978	0.129	0.635

Source: Authors' compilation.

*The data above have been published by the authors in 2012 at *Wulfenia Journal*, 19(11): 209.

Table 2. Estimation Results of VIIT between ASEAN5 Countries and China in SITC 5, SITC 6 and SITC 7 Using Panel Data Models without Spatial Interaction Effects

SITC	SITC 5				SITC 6				SITC 7			
Determinants	Pooled OLS	Cross Fixed Effects	Time-Period fixed Effects	Cross and Time-Period fixed Effects	Pooled OLS	Cross Fixed Effects	Time-Period Fixed Effects	Cross and Time-Period Fixed Effects	Pooled OLS	Cross Fixed Effects	Time-Period Fixed Effects	Cross and Time-Period Fixed Effects
DGDP	−0.184	−0.173	−0.110	0.271	0.149	−0.023	0.455	0.356	−0.376	−0.424	−0.276	−0.383
	(−1.699)	(−1.391)	(−0.670)	(0.957)	(1.228)	(0.166)	(2.473)*	(1.090)	(2.679)*	(2.787)*	(−1.256)	(−1.057)
FDI	0.004	0.029	0.002	0.048	−0.050	−0.038	−0.005	−0.005	−0.022	−0.055	−0.024	−0.062
	(0.370)	(0.975)	(0.213)	(1.443)	(4.004)	(−1.175)	(−4.236)*	(−0.146)	(−1.539)	(−1.552)	(−1.592)	(−1.496)
intercept	3.164				−0.769				6.474			
	(2.033)				(−0.450)				(3.278)			
R^2	0.124	0.195	0.264	0.354	0.130	0.218	0.301	0.364	0.103	0.273	0.230	0.398
Adjusted R^2	0.098	0.137	0.054	0.127	0.114	0.172	0.114	0.155	0.087	0.231	0.224	0.200
LogL	65.374	69.854	74.502	81.376	44.311	50.140	56.350	68.579	28.280	39.812	36.664	50.236

Note: t-values are provided in parentheses.
Asterisk * denotes level of significance at 5%.
The critical value for LM test at 5% significance level is 5.991.

time-period specific effects will be adopted to carry out the tests based on general to specific approach.

4.3. *General to specific approach*

General to specific approach is applied to examine whether spatial Durbin model can be simplified into spatial lag model or spatial error using Wald test and LR test for each manufacturing sub-sector. The results of the estimation are presented in the following table.

Based on Table 3, although the Wald test infers that the null hypothesis where spatial Durbin model can be simplified to spatial lag model, cannot be rejected for SITC 5. The LR test shows that the null hypothesis can be rejected for all manufacturing sub-sectors. As such, this infers that spatial Durbin model is more appropriate in treating the data. In addition, both Wald and LR tests show that the null hypothesis of spatial Durbin model can be simplified to spatial error model must be rejected for all manufacturing sub-sectors. Hence, the results confirm that spatial Durbin model is more appropriate for the estimation for all manufacturing sub-sectors.

4.3.1. *SITC 5*

Based on the estimation results, the difference in GDP (DGDP), which serves as the proxy of the difference in market size between respective ASEAN5 countries and China, emerges as the most prominent determinant of VIIT between ASEAN5 countries and China in SITC 5. It is negative and statistically significant. This notes that reduction in difference in market size would encourage greater production fragmentation, which in turn stimulates VIIT as Grossman and Helpman (2005) mentioned that firms prefer to trade with trading partners of similar skills that match their requirements. As such, ASEAN5 countries should enlarge their market size for products under SITC 5 to accelerate the bilateral VIIT with China.

On the other hand, FDI is having positive and statistically significant effects on VIIT between ASEAN5 countries and China in SITC 5. The empirical result is consistent with the expectation of production fragmentation theory and in line with the findings of Turkcan and Ates (2011), Zhang and Li (2006), Zhang *et al.* (2005), Fukao *et al.* (2003) and Hu and Ma (1999). The result confirms that the motive of FDI from ASEAN5 countries to China in SITC 5 is efficiency seeking in nature, which aims to form production linkages and resources network.

More to the point, the significance of SGDP and SFDI confirm the presence of spatial interaction effects among ASEAN5 countries in relation to China's trade. Since Falvey and Kierzkowski (1987) cited by Turkcan (2010) argue that difference in GDP which proxy the market sizes reflects the difference between two regions in factor endowment, the positive coefficient of SGDP implies that difference in factor endowment is more important than the low service-linked cost stemming from the similar market size when ASEAN5 countries interact among them in having VIIT with China.

Besides, the positive coefficient of SFDI signifies the presence of positive spatial interaction effects among ASEAN5 countries. The empirical result infers that the increase in

Table 3. Estimation Results of VIIT between ASEAN5 Countries and China in SITC 5, SITC 6 and SITC 7: Spatial Durbin Model Specification with Spatial and Time-Period Specific Effects

SITC 5		SITC 6		SITC 7	
Determinants	Spatial and Time-Period Fixed Effects	Determinants	Spatial and Time-Period Fixed Effects	Determinants	Spatial and Time-Period Fixed Effects
DGDP	−1.475 (−3.850)***	DGDP	−0.881 (−1.187)	DGDP	4.987 (4.594)***
SGDP	0.98 (2.806)**	SGDP	0.542 (0.696)	SGDP	−6.033 (−4.844)***
FDI(−1)	0.212 (3.245)**	FDI	0.135 (1.794)*	FDI	0.206 (2.96)***
SFDI(−2)	0.369 (3.303)**	SFDI(−1)	0.329 (2.103)**	SFDI(−1)	−0.109 (−0.447)
SVIIT	0.242 (0.467)	SVIIT	−0.649 (−1.874)*	SVIIT	−1.713 (−2.586)***
R^2	0.967	R^2	0.934	R^2	0.921
Adjusted R^2	0.906	Adjusted R^2	0.829	Adjusted R^2	0.766
Long Run Variance	0.0006	Long Run Variance	0.002	Long Run Variance	0.002
Wald test spatial lag	0.217 ($p = 0.644$)	Wald test spatial lag	3.513 ($p = 0.068$)*	Wald test spatial lag	6.686 ($p = 0.014$)**
LR test spatial lag	11.15 ($p = 0.000$)***	LR test spatial lag	3.289 ($p = 0.048$)**	LR test spatial lag	13.281 ($p = 0.000$)***
Wald test spatial error	6.634 ($p = 0.014$)**	Wald test spatial error	201.288 ($p = 0.000$)***	Wald test spatial error	9.83 ($p = 0.004$)***
LR test spatial error	51.57 ($p = 0.000$)***	LR test spatial error	119.835 ($p = 0.000$)***	LR test spatial error	44.572 ($p = 0.000$)**

Note: t-values are provided in parentheses.
Lags are chosen based on AIC and SC.
Asterisk ***, ** and * denote level of significance at 1%, 5% and 10%, respectively.
F-statistics for Wald test and LR test.

FDI between each ASEAN5 country with China will stimulate and strengthen the bilateral VIIT between the entire ASEAN region and China in SITC 5. ASEAN5 countries should integrate and collaborate in planning their FDI policies for SITC 5 in order to reap numerous benefits from China's rise as both FDI and SFDI are instrumental in SITC 5. In contrast, SVIIT is statistically insignificant, which indicate that there is no significant spatial interaction effect from VIIT.

4.3.2. *SITC 6*

Based on the estimation results, both DGDP and SGDP are insignificant in SITC 6. The insignificance of DGDP implies that the difference in market size between ASEAN5 and China is not the essential condition for IIT and this is similar to the findings of Xing (2007). Furthermore, the insignificance of SGDP also implies that the spatial interaction effects from DGDP are not present significantly. In a nutshell, the VIIT between any ASEAN5 country and China in SITC 6 is not affected significantly by the changes in DGDP of her neighboring ASEAN5 countries.

Similarly with SITC 5, the coefficients of both FDI and SFDI in SITC 6 are positive and statistically significant. The result is consistent with the expectation of production fragmentation theory and implying that the motive of FDI is efficiency seeking rather than market seeking. As a result, FDI serves as a platform for AEAN5-China to enhance the bilateral VIIT in SITC 6 and therefore should be encouraged.

Nevertheless, the econometric results reveal that SVIIT emerged as the most influential determinant in SITC 6. It is negative and statistically significant. The negative coefficient infers that ASEAN5 countries are competing in a markedly intense approach among each other. When production of goods is sliced into stages, the intermediate inputs are sourced from the most efficient producers among the ASEAN5 countries by China for SITC 6. However, such competition will eventually lead to a heightened efficiency level and a greater extent of product development.

4.3.3. *SITC 7*

The econometric result reveals that all of the explanatory variables except SFDI are significant in SITC 7 (see Table 3). In contrast with SITC 5, the coefficient of DGDP is positive which implies that difference in factor endowment is vital (Falvey and Kierzkowski, 1987) in determining bilateral VIIT between ASEAN5 and China. On the other hand, the negative coefficient of SGDP implies that low service link cost is more crucial (Grossman and Helpman, 2005) than difference in factor endowment when ASEAN5 countries interact among themselves in having VIIT with China in SITC 7. In addition, both DGDP and SGDP serve as the most influential determinant of SITC 7. Hence, the policy makers of ASEAN5 are urged to smoothen the coordination work among them in having VIIT with China.

The coefficient of FDI in SITC 7 is positive and statistically significant. Similar with SITC 5 and SITC 6, the result is consistent with the expectation of production fragmentation theory and implying that the motive of FDI is efficiency seeking rather than market seeking. On the other hand, the coefficient of SFDI is statistically insignificant. This result reveals that there is no significant spatial effect from FDI. Nevertheless, SVIIT is negative and statistically significant. Similar with SITC 6, the significance of SVIIT in SITC 7 confirms the presence of negative spatial interaction effects among ASEAN5 countries in relation to China's bilateral VIIT.

5. Policy Implications

The positive and significant coefficients of FDI for SITC 5, 6 and 7 reflect that FDI is efficiency seeking in nature to enhance the formation of production and resource network between ASEAN5's MNCs and China's domestic firms. The establishment of production bases in China and having export of materials to their China bases ensures a conduit of supply to the final assemblers. This reflects not only profit motivation but also longer term market planning in view of dynamic changes not only in the manufacturing sector but also dynamic changes in China's economy. Nonetheless, the presence of positive spatial interaction effect of respective ASEAN5' FDI with China in SITC 5 implies FDI diversion from ASEAN5 countries to China. The trade statistics show that the trade share of SITC 5 in total manufacturing trade between ASEAN5 countries and China remains approximately 13% during 2000–2014 (UN COMTRADE database). However, the trade deficit for Indonesia-China exhibit increasing trend since 2006, while the trade surplus for Malaysia-China, Philippines–China and Thailand–China are fluctuating from 2000 to 2014 in SITC 5. Singapore with well-endowed capital has been experiencing increasing trade surplus with China since 1997. This implies that there is relatively strong technology progress in China compared with ASEAN4 countries (Indonesia, Malaysia, Philippines and Thailand). This has successfully attracted FDI from ASEAN4 countries to establish their production network in China and re-export the goods back to their home country for SITC 5 manufactured goods.

ASEAN5 countries will also face the challenge of FDI diversion for SITC 6 as the estimated results shows a significant positive spatial interaction effect of FDI in ASEAN5-China bilateral VIIT. From the trade statistics, it is found that the trade share of SITC 6 in total manufacturing trade between ASEAN5 (except Philippines and Singapore) and China has exhibited decreasing trend from 1991 to 2014 (from 30% to 27% for Indonesia; from 20% to 18% for Malaysia from 40% to 20% for Thailand). This evidence further supports the findings of Mckibbin and Woo (2003) who has pointed out that Indonesia, Malaysia, Philippines and Thailand might face the problem of FDI diversion resulting from China's ascension to World Trade Organization (WTO).

Besides, reduction in market size differences and the spatial interaction effect of GDP differences between ASEAN5 countries and China may enhance VIIT trade between the two regions for SITC 5 and 7 either via low service link cost or difference in factor endowment. This findings further provide evidence to support the research work produced by Park (2007), Balassa and Bauwens (1987) and Helpman (1981) where the opportunities of between IIT of ASEAN and China stemmed from the similarity of their income and economic development levels.

However, trade statistics shows that although ASEAN5 have trade deficits with China in both SITC 6 and 7, the growth of the trade share of SITC 7 is at the expense of SITC 6 and vice-versa in total manufacturing trade between ASEAN5 and China from 1993 to 2014 except the case of Singapore. Hence, the economic development policy needs to be approached with caution. For SITC 6, shipping intermediate inputs from ASEAN5 countries to China for final assembly and re-export will crowd out production in ASEAN5 which in turn contribute to higher deficit and reduction in bilateral trade between ASEAN5 and China. Hence, changing from downstream (sending inputs to China for final assembly) to upstream production (sending inputs to neighboring ASEAN member countries for further processing in creating higher embedded value of inputs) would foster production capacity in both ASEAN5 countries and China and thus stimulate greater bilateral trade. It is believed that the upstream activities are well managed among ASEAN5 countries for SITC 7 as they are the important exporter for electronics components and semiconductors to China and the rest of the world. However, policy makers should be cautious and alert as the trade share of SITC 7 exhibits a gradually decreasing trend in all ASEAN5 countries from 2009 to 2014. This is attributable to the failure of one of the member country in performing a specific processing task will result in the collapse of the entire value chain within ASEAN5 countries and hence bilateral trade with China. This has been portrayed by the VIIT indices presented in Table 1 which shows that the unstable trend of VIIT exists from one to another member country which felled from a value greater than 0.5 to less than 0.5 in SITC 6 during 2002–2006 (from Singapore followed by Philippines, Malaysia and Thailand) and SITC 7 during 2006–2009 (from Thailand followed by Malaysia and Philippines). As this occurrence involves more ASEAN5 countries for SITC 6 as compared to SITC 7, it therefore contributes to the contraction of trade share for SITC 6 during 2000s. Besides, the presence of SGDP indicates the interaction between comparative advantage among ASEAN5 and spatial linkages has created additional benefits to distance-related trade costs for SITC 7.

The presence of negative and significant coefficient of SVIIT reflects that ASEAN5 countries are not highly integrated into the same value chain for SITC 6 and 7. This is due to ASEAN5 countries competing with each other to claim more value added profits from their joint output before sending to China for assembly purposes. Hence, harmonizing regulatory policy such as competition policy, movement of capital, foreign ownership and intellectual property rights enforcement might further augment the value chain of ASEAN5 countries.

Given the above challenges and the similarity of comparative advantage between ASEAN5 countries and China, emphasis on competency and skills in performing similar tasks for differentiated varieties of products among ASEAN5 countries and with China should be cultivated in conjunction with the formation of industrial clusters. As such, incentive for retaining highly skilled workers and innovation, retraining programmes for displaced workers and increasing human capital through education are essential.

6. Conclusion

Owing to the changes in trade structures, VIIT has become increasingly important in ASEAN5-China bilateral trade. The results of the econometric estimation confirm that both FDI and DGDP are the determinants of VIIT although their impacts on VIIT vary across manufacturing sub-sectors. As per FDI, the low elasticity for all manufacturing sub-sectors indicates that VIIT between ASEAN5 countries and China is less responsive to the changes of the utilization of ASEAN5's capital in China.

On the other hand, the elasticity of DGDP is relatively high for SITC 5 and SITC 7, which is contradictory to that of FDI. Hence, this implies that VIIT is more responsive to the difference of market size/factor endowment between the two regions.

The econometric estimation also confirms the presence of spatial interaction effects among ASEAN5 countries in relation to China's trade. Thus, deeper economic cooperation and integration among ASEAN5 countries are crucial in strengthening bilateral trade between the two regions. Besides, findings also review that expansion of market size and leveraging of difference in factor endowment in each ASEAN5 country not only brings advantages to the country but the benefits will spill over to other neighboring ASEAN5 countries. As a result, the integration of ASEAN5 countries to fully utilize the difference in factor endowment through intra-ASEAN manufacturing trade should be greatly promoted through the programs under AFTA, ASEAN Investment Area and ASEAN Industrial Cooperation. In addition, the establishment of ASEAN Economic Community in 2015 is another good channel to promote intra-ASEAN manufacturing trade. The implementation of the proposed initiatives above beckons deep commitment by all countries in ASEAN. The industry level planning is not only difficult but the results of the spatial analysis reveal the internal focus of each of the member countries. ASEAN5, like China as a country, is well differentiated by countries and regions respectively and can be matched by economic profiles regionally. While China's focus on economic upgrading, at national level planning is clear and applicable for all regions, the same cannot be said for each of the ASEAN member countries. As a grouping, ASEAN lack cohesiveness in industrial policy and the individual pursuits of each member country will be difficult to ameliorate as a whole. For policy makers at a grouping level, it may become necessary to focus on a single industry for implementation and a detailed and focused study on the identified industry, taking into account the dynamic fluctuations at industry and economic levels, be undertaken as a test of cohesiveness and one pointedness.

7. Limitations of Study

Owing to the limited data availability and the large differences in terms of economic structure between ASEAN5 countries with CMLV and Brunei, this study did not include CMLV and Brunei. However, ASEAN consists of ten countries and representing the 10 countries as a whole.

Furthermore, finely disaggregated trade data on finished goods and intermediate goods or components are not available in this point in time. Besides, there is lack of data concerning domestic value-added on imported intermediate goods. Last but not least, the disaggregated FDI data for each manufacturing sub-sector is also lacking. Hence, the total FDI data in China by each ASEAN5 country is adopted, which limit the precision of this study.

Acknowledgments

This paper has been presented at the International Conference of Business, Accounting, Finance and Economics, Tunku Abdul Rahman University, Malaysia on 4 October 2013.

References

Athukorala, P (1993). International labour migration in the Asian- Pacific region: Patterns, policies and economic implications. *Asian Pacific Economic Literature*, 7(2), 28–57.

Baier, LS and JH Bergstrand (2007). Do free trade agreements actually increase members' international trade? *Journal of International Economics*, 71, 72–95.

Balassa, B and L Bauwens (1997). Intra-Industry specialization in a multi-country and multi-industry framework. *The Economy Journal*, 97(388), 923–939.

Carrere, C (2006). Revisiting the effects of regional trade agreements on trade flows with proper specification of the gravity model. *European Economic Review*, 50(2), 223–247.

Cassim, R (2009). The Determinants of Intra-Regional Trade in Southern Africa with Specific Reference to South African and the Rest of The Region. Working Papers NO01/51. DPRU.

Dziembowska-Kowalska, J and DH Funck (2000). Cultural activities as a location factor in European competition between regions: Concepts and some evidence. *The Annals of Regional Science*, 34, 1–12.

Elhost, JP (2003). Specification and estimation of spatial panel data models. *International Regional Science Review*, 26(3), 244–268.

Elhorst, JP (2010a). Applied spatial econometrics: Raising the bar. *Spatial Economic Analysis*, 5(1), 9–28.

Elhorst, JP (2010b). Matlab software for spatial panels. *Paper Presented at the IVth Conference of the Spatial Econometrics Association* (SEA), Chicago, The United States.

Fontagne, L and M Freudenberg (1997). Intra-Industry Trade: Methodological Issues Reconsidered, Working Paper 97/02. CEPII. Centre d'Etudes Prospectives et d'Informations Internationales.

Fukao, K, I Hikari and K Ito (2003). Vertical Intra-Industry Trade and Foreign Direct Investment in East Asia, Discussion Paper Series A No. 434, The Institute of Economic Research, Hitotsubashi University, Kunitachi, Tokyo.

Grossman, GM and E Helpman (2005). Outsourcing in a global economy. *Review of Economic Studies*, 72, 135–159.

Harris, S (1994). Policy networks and economic cooperation: Policy coordination in the Asia Pacific region. *The Pacific Review*, 7(4), 38–395.

Helpman, E (1981). International trade in the presence of product differentiation, economics of scale and monopolistic competition: A Chamberlin-Heckscher-Ohlin approach. *Journal of International Economics*, 11, 305–340.

Hu, XL and Y Ma (1999). International intra-industry trade of China. *Welwirtchaftiliches Archiv*, 135, 82–101.

Hurley, DT (2003). Horizontal and vertical intra-industry trade: The case of ASEAN trade in manufactures. *International Economic Journal*, 17(4), 1–14.

Ito, T and T Okubo (2011). New Aspects of Intra-Industry Trade: Evidence from EU-15 Countries. Discussion Paper Series RIEB, Kobe University.

Kandogan, Y (2008). Consistent estimates of regional blocks' trade effects. *Review of International Economics*, 16(2), 301–314.

Kang, M and JD Lee (2012). Vertical intra-industry trade and product quality: The case of South Korea, 1996–2003. *Economics and Business Letters*, 1(3), 37–47.

Kimura, F and M Ando (2005). Two-dimensional fragmentation in East Asia: Conceptual framework and empirics. *International Review of Economics and Finance*, 14, 417–348.

Lemoine, F and D Unal-Kesenci (2002). China in the International Segmentation of Production Processes. Working Paper No 2002–02, CEPII.

Park, D (2007). The prospects of the ASEAN-China free trade area (ACFTA : A qualitative overview). *Journal of the Asia Pacific Economy*, 12(3), 485–503.

Porojan, A (2001). Trade flows and spatial effects: The gravity model revisited. *Open Economies Reviewed*, 12(3), 265–280.

Rodrik, D (2006). What's so Special about China's Exports? Working Paper No. 11947, NBER.

Shafaeddin, M (2004). Is China's accession to WTO threatening exports of developing countries? *China Economic Review*, 15, 109–144.

Tabellini, G (2005). Culture and Institutions: Economic Development in the Regions of Europe. Working Paper No. 292, GIER.

Thorbecke, W and G Smith (2010). How would an appreciation of the RMB and other East Asian currencies affect China's exports? *Review of International Economics*, 18, 95–108.

Tran, VH (2010). Impact of the WTO membership, regional economic integration and structural change on China's trade and growth. *Review of Development Economics*, 14(3), 577–591.

Turkcan, K and A Ates (2011). Vertical intra-industry trade and fragmentation: An empirical examination of the US auto-parts industry. *The World Economy*, 34, 154–172.

Vayrynen, R (2003). Regionalism: Old and new. *International Studies Review*, 5, 25–51.

Wilson, JS, CL Mann and T Otsuki (2003). Trade facilitation and economic development: A new approach to quantifying the impact. *The World Bank Economic Review*, 17(3), 367–389.

Xing, Y (2007). Foreign direct investment and China's bilateral intra-industry trade with Japan and the US. *Journal of Asia Economics*, 18, 675–700.

Yong, CC, MY Chin and SY Yew (2012). Resilience to shock and intra-industry trade between ASEAN-5 and China. *Wulfenia Journal*, 19(11), 206–210.

Zhang, J, W Arjen Van and C Zhou (2005). Chinese bilateral intra-industry trade: A panel data study for 50 countries in the 1992–2001 period. *Review of World Economics*, 141(3), 510–540.

Zhang, Z (2008). Can Demand from China Shield East Asian Economies from Global Slowdown? Working Paper: 19, Hong Kong Monetary Authority.

Zhang, Z and C Li (2006). Country-specific factors and the pattern of intra-industry trade in China's manufacturing. *Journal of International Development*, 18, 1137–1149.

Chapter 4

WHY PARTICIPATE IN THE "ONE BELT AND ONE ROAD" INITIATIVE? AN INCOME CONVERGENCE APPROACH[††]

GUO HENG HU[*,§], CHI-KEUNG MARCO LAU[†,¶],
ZHOU LU[‡,||] and XIN SHENG[†,**]

[*]*School of Business*
Henan Normal University, P. R. China

[†]*Department of Accountancy, Finance and Economics*
Huddersfield Business School
University of Huddersfield, Queensgate, HD1 3DH, UK

[‡]*School of Economics*
Tianjin University of Commerce, P. R. China
[§]*guohenghu@163.com*
[¶]*c.lau@hud.ac.uk*
[||]*luzhou59@gmail.com*
[**]*x.sheng@hud.ac.uk*

Published 20 August 2018

This paper seeks to investigate the motivations of countries that participate in the One Belt and One Road (B&R) Initiative, a China-led economic development programme with the intention of enhancing regional economic cooperation. We examine the income convergence hypothesis for B&R countries with both linear and nonlinear unit root tests to detect the presence of economic integration over the periods 1960–2016 and 1979–2016. For the B&R countries that are found to show income convergence to China in our income convergence testing, we argue that they tend to have a strong existing economic relationship with China. By contrast, the countries that have relatively weak economic relationships with China tend to show no convergence to China, and they take advantage of the B&R as an opportunity to catch up. Moreover, we find evidence that more countries converge to China's real per capita income for the years after 1978 when China started its transition to a market economy and initiated the open-door policy to embrace globalization. The results suggest that China contributes to a higher degree of income convergence in regional integration.

Keywords: One Belt and One Road; China; economic integration; income convergence.

JEL Classification: R, C1, C5

1. Introduction

The One Belt and One Road Initiative, also known as the Belt and Road (B&R) Initiative, is a significant development strategy launched by China in 2013. The initiative has been designed to promote free flows of economic factors and to enhance economic cooperation

[||]Corresponding author.

[††]This article originally appeared in *The Singapore Economic Review*, doi: 10.1142/S0217590818500297

among B&R countries. Hence, it can be regarded as a China-led move to improve market integration and create a regional economic cooperation framework. A major focus of the B&R Initiative is the construction of infrastructure facilities including rail and road networks, ports, telecommunications and energy pipelines that promote the connectivity of Asia, Europe and Africa.

Given the significant cross-county disparity between B&R participating counties in terms of income level, geographical location, and particularly the level of economic integration with China, we believe the motivation for participating in the B&R Initiative might vary across countries as well. For the countries that already established solid economic cooperation with China, they regard this initiative as a plan to enhance the existing relationship to a higher level, while the counties with little economic integration with China might want to take advantage of the B&R Initiative as an opportunity to catch up. The central task of this study is to investigate these B&R countries' motivations for greater economic integration with China. More specifically, we want to identify which of those B&R countries are driven by the motivation to enhance existing economic integration and which are driven by the catch-up motivation.

To answer the central question regarding the motivations of B&R participation, we examine the 65 B&R participating counties for income convergence into China. One of the widely held views among mainstream economists is a strong link between economic integration and income convergence. In theory, free capital flow is expected to help poor counties more as the classic economic growth theory suggests that capital tends to flow from high- to low-income economies.[1]

Free trade as a channel of technology spillover gives a poor country access to superior technology embodied in goods and allows greater productivity gains in the poor country (Fan, 2004). Hence, high economic integration between countries in terms of capital and trade flows and technology sharing is supposed to reduce the income gap between the rich and the poor.

In the context of the B&R Initiative, we seek to examine the process of convergence in terms of relative real per capita income of B&R countries towards China. In the milestone year of 1978 in contemporary China, the country began a transition to a market economy and an adoption of open-door policies to embrace globalization. It is widely agreed that China's economic system has experienced a fundamental reform after 1978. Hence, we test for B&R countries with respect to China over 1960–2016 and the post-reform period of 1979–2016. If a country is found to exhibit income convergence to China, then its B&R participation can be explained as being driven by existing strong economic relationship with China. By contrast, if a country shows no convergence to China, then the country participates in the B&R Initiative mostly because of its desire to catch up in economic integration with China.

Our study is aimed to gain a better understanding of the motivations that drove countries to participate in B&R by examining the income convergence hypothesis between China and B&R participating countries. This article contributes to the existing economic

[1] According to the Solow model, the existence of incentives for capital to flow from rich to poor countries is mainly driven by diminishing returns to capital or lower rate of return on capital in rich countries.

integration and income convergence literature in two ways. First, to the best knowledge of the authors, we are the first to apply both linear and nonlinear unit root tests to examine the income convergence hypothesis within the context of the B&R Initiative. Second, this is the first study to examine income convergence among B&R counties in the context of China's economic reform that started in the year 1978.

The remainder of the article is structured as follows: Section 2 provides a brief review of the existing literature on income convergence. Section 3 describes data and methodology; Section 4 presents empirical results and discussion. Section 5 concludes.

2. Literature Review

The study on cross-country income convergence is primarily based on Solow's classic growth theory (1956). This neo-classical growth model predicts that an economy will converge to a balanced growth path and, meanwhile, per capita income in a country will eventually grow to reach that country's steady-state value. The country-specific steady-state value, according to Solow, is determined by that country's structural characteristics including capital accumulation, depreciation of existing capital, population growth, technology, initial endowments and so on. A major implication of the Solow model is that income levels across different countries tend to converge and between-country income disparities tend to decline over time.

There have been a vast amount of empirical studies devoted to the test of the income convergence hypothesis. Many of the existing literature on income convergence are based on the cross-sessional analysis, which regresses per capita gross domestic product (GDP) growth rates on initial income levels. Under the hypothesis of income convergence, poor countries starting with a lower real per capital GDP should have a higher growth rate. Thus, a negative relationship between the per capita income growth and the initial level of income across economies over a given period of time is interpreted as evidence in favour of the income convergence. The income convergence hypothesis implies that, over a long period of time, the per capita income level of a poor country will tend to catch up with the level of a rich country (see e.g., Baumol, 1986). Early studies including Baumol (1986) and Mankiw *et al.* (1992) use cross-section data to test income convergence. Islam (1995) develops a panel-data approach using the same regression and data as Mankiw *et al.* (1992). As Islam (1995) argues, the panel-data approach provides the advantage of accounting for a country's total factor productivity at the initial level of income which should be included in the individual effect. In order to control for cross-country differences in steady state, Barro (1991), Barro and Sala-i-Martin (1992) and Mankiw *et al.* (1992) include the determinants of country-specific steady states (e.g., population growth, rate of capital depreciation, saving rates and technological progress) as conditional variables in their research. While there is little evidence of unconditional convergence among countries with considerable structure difference, these studies find evidence of the conditional income convergence. However, Friedman (1992), Quah (1993), and Evans (1998) point out that the use of cross-sectional methods may generate inconsistent convergence rate estimates and invalid test statistics. In addition, Bernard and Durlauf (1995) suggest that it is possible that a group of divergent countries can exhibit a negative relationship between initial output and income growth (as described by Baumol, 1986) so long as the marginal product of capital is diminishing.

Existing empirical literature also utilizes a time-series approach to test income convergence. The income convergence hypothesis implies that the relative real output per capita should be mean reverting so that income disparities between countries are not persistent over time. This implication leads naturally to the use of unit root tests in examining the hypothesis of income convergence, i.e., relative income per capita between countries should display the stationarity behavior and should not have a unit root. Bernard and Durlauf (1995) suggest that the existence of a common long-run trend in real GDP per capita across countries can be interpreted as evidence for income convergence. The study investigates income convergence by directly examining the univariate dynamics of annual log real output per capita across 15 OECD countries. The unit root tests are employed to detect the presence of integrated processes. However, Bernard and Durlauf (1995) find little evidence of output convergence. Evans (1998) employs unit root tests to examine whether countries revert towards a common trend. The study finds evidence of income convergence for a sample of 13 developed countries and a sample of countries with relatively well-educated populations. In contrast, countries with relatively poorly educated populations display different growth patterns. Cheung and Pascual (2004) study income convergence for the G7 countries using time series unit root tests. This study uses the stationarity properties of real per capita GDP relative to the US to infer income convergence. Cheung and Pascual (2004) also highlight the power issue of using standard unit root procedures in testing output convergence and employ a panel framework to improve the power performance. Lau (2010) examines the regional convergence of the US states. Using both linear and panel nonlinear unit root tests, the study finds evidence in support of income convergence across most US states and suggests that the convergence process follows a nonlinear dynamics because of considerable variation in structure between the US states. Furthermore, Guetat and Serranito (2007) utilize unit root tests to evaluate the income convergence hypothesis for countries in the Middle East and North Africa (MENA) region. The study considers the effect of a possible break in the unit root tests and provides evidence for income convergence among MENA countries. More recently, King and Ramlogan-Dobson (2015) employ unit root tests that accommodate nonlinearities and test 18 Latin American countries for income convergence against the US benchmark. Their results report strong evidence for the income convergence hypothesis, i.e., the relative real output per capita (towards the US) of almost all Latin American economies follows a (nonlinear) trend stationary process. Ceylan and Abiyev (2016) examine the validity of income convergence for 15 European Union countries with respect to the average level of per capita GDP of the group using both linear and nonlinear unit root tests. The linear test results show that only 3 out of 15 countries converge to the group average. By contrast, the number of converging countries increases dramatically to 9 when nonlinear unit root tests are employed.

Regarding economic integration and income convergence, early studies (Baumol, 1986; Barro, 1991; Barro and Sala-i-Martin, 1992; Mankiw *et al.*, 1992) find that the conditions of free factor mobility and free trade are essential and contribute to the acceleration of the convergence process through the equalization of prices of goods and factors of production. More recently, studies on income convergence among countries participating in regional integration began to emerge. Fischer and Stirböck (2006) and Battisti and De Vaio (2008) have studied optimal regional convergence clubs in the European Union. The primary goal of these studies is to define regional clubs sharing the same characteristics in terms of income growth convergence within the European Union. Using a cross-sectional approach, Matkowski and Próchniak (2007) find evidence in support of income convergence within the group of new EU entrants while their convergence process towards existing members seems slower, and trade and FDI are important drivers of high growth dynamics (Ageliki and Ioannis, 2016; Bilgin, Gozgor and Lau, 2017; Percival, 2017; Ucal *et al.*, 2016). Using a time-series approach, Kocenda *et al.* (2006) and Ingianni and Zdarek (2009) also support income convergence among new entrants. Cavenaile and Dubois (2011) test for the existence of two separate groups of convergence within the European Union i.e., 15 Western European countries as opposed to new entrants from Eastern and Central Europe. More recently, Ito (2017) studies growth convergence with a special focus on emerging countries in Asia using panel data. The study establishes three convergence paths among Asian economies and suggests that a country can move from one convergence path to a higher one by implementing economic reforms, such as China's open-door economic reform since 1978. Feng *et al.* (2018) compare the contagious corruption difference between geographic border and distance for B&R countries and find that B&R countries with a common border tend to possess contagious corruption.

3. Data and Methodology

3.1. *Data*

In this paper, we use annual data of the real GDP per capita (in USD) from 1960 to 2016. All data are collected from the World Bank database.[2] This study includes sixty-five B&R countries.[3] In order to test the hypothesis of income convergence towards China's real GDP per capita (GDPA) we construct the relative real GDP per capita for each country towards China, so that the series of interest for a particular country i, at time t, becomes:

$$y_{i,t} = \ln(g_{i,t}/\bar{g}_t) \quad t = 1,\ldots,T, \tag{1}$$

where $y_{i,t}$ is the relative real GDP per capita, $g_{i,t}$ is the real GDP per capita and $\bar{g}_t$ is the China's GDPA across all countries at time t.

[2] GDP per capita is gross domestic product divided by midyear population. GDP is the sum of gross value added by all resident producers in the economy plus any product taxes and minus any subsidies not included in the value of the products. It is calculated without making deductions for depreciation of fabricated assets or for depletion and degradation of natural resources. Data are in constant 2010 U.S. dollars.

[3] These countries are Afghanistan, Albania, Armenia, Azerbaijan, Bangladesh, Bahrain, Belarus, Bhutan, Bosnia, Brunei, Bulgaria, Cambodia, China, Czech, Croatia, Egypt, Estonia, Ethiopia, Georgia, Hungary, Indonesia, India, Iran, Iraq, Israel, Jordan, Kazakhstan, Korea, Kuwait, Kyrgyzstan, Latvia, Laos, Lebanon, Lithuania, Macedonia, Malaysia, Maldives, Moldova, Montenegro, Mongolia, Myanmar, Nepal, New Zealand, Oman, Pakistan, Palestine, Panama, Philippines, Poland, Qatar, Romania, Russia, Saudi, Serbia, Singapore, Slovakia, South Africa, Sri Lanka, Thailand, Turkey, United Arab, Ukraine, Uzbekistan, Vietnam, Yemen.

3.2. *Methodology*

In this subsection, we introduce the test procedures employed to examine the income convergence hypothesis. While the univariate unit root ADF test is a standard econometric tool, there is a growing interest in utilizing nonlinear unit root tests in the literature (e.g., Lau, 2010; Lau *et al.*, 2012; Akhmedjonov and Lau, 2013, among others). Thus, we provide a brief review of these techniques in the following subsections.

3.2.1. *Univariate unit root test*

A formal test regarding income convergence can be carried out through a univariate unit root test. The Augmented Dicky–Fuller (ADF) test is traditionally used to test the stationarity of relative GDPA differential series. Suppose the data generating process (DGP) for relative GDPA differential series for country *i* exhibit the following dynamics:

$$y_{i,t} = \alpha_i + \theta_i y_{i,t-1} + \sum_{j=1}^{K_i} \delta_{i,j} \Delta y_{i,t-j} + \mu_{i,t}, \quad t = 1,\ldots,T, \tag{2}$$

where k_i is the number of augmenting terms and $\{u_i\}$ are white noise series independently distributed across countries, i.e., $u_i \sim id(0, \sigma_i^2)$. Rearranging Equation (2) leads to the following expression:

$$\Delta y_{i,t} = \alpha_i + \beta_i y_{i,t-1} + \sum_{j=1}^{K_i} \delta_{i,j} \Delta y_{i,t-j} + \mu_{i,t}, \quad t = 1,\ldots,T, \tag{3}$$

where Δ is the first difference operator and $\beta = (\theta - 1)$. In applying the ADF test, the null hypothesis and the alternative are

$$H_{0,\mathrm{ADF},i} : \beta_i = 0, \quad H_{1,\mathrm{ADF},i} : \beta_i < 0, \quad (i = 1, 2, \ldots, N).$$

The null hypothesis of non-stationarity (i.e., $H_{0,\mathrm{ADF},i} : \beta_i = 0$) is rejected if the relative GDPA series does not contain a unit root, and it follows the stationary process. A rejection of the null hypothesis provides evidence of income converge of B&R countries to China in the long run.

3.2.2. *Nonlinear unit root test*

The ADF test described in the previous subsection has been criticized for lack of power in rejecting the null hypothesis, especially when the series follows a nonlinear threshold process and contains significant nonlinear components (Lau *et al.*, 2012). Therefore we also use the nonlinear unit root test of Kapetanios *et al.* (2003) (thereafter, the KSS test) to test the hypothesis of income convergence when considering the effect of nonlinear components in relative GDPA differential series. The occurrence of income convergence may start only if the relative output difference reaches a certain threshold level. If this is the case, the time series is assumed to follow a nonlinear exponential smooth transition autoregressive (ESTAR) process. The process allows for the hidden nonlinear components in time series data and provides a theoretical rationale to model the hidden market frictions, such as imperfect market structures and transportation costs. Following Kapetanios *et al.* (2003), we can specify the model as such:

$$\Delta y_t = \xi y_{t-1}[1 - \exp(\theta y_{t-1}^2)] + \mu_t; \quad \mu_t \sim IID(0, \sigma^2), \tag{4}$$

where ξ and θ are the parameters that govern the dynamics of the DGP. Using a first-order Taylor series approximation method, Kapetanios *et al.* (2003) reparametrize Equation (4) as follows:

$$\Delta y_t = \phi y_{t-1}^3 + \mu_t, \tag{5}$$

where ϕ is the KSS test parameter, and the t-statistics could be derived from ϕ that is denoted by

$$t_{\text{KSS}} = \frac{\hat{\phi}}{\text{se}(\hat{\phi})}, \tag{6}$$

where $\hat{\phi}$ is the ordinary least squares (OLS) estimate of ϕ, and $\text{se}(\hat{\phi})$ is the associated standard error.

In absence of a unit root, the null hypothesis of non-stationarity (i.e., $H_{0,\text{KSS}}, i : \phi = 0$) is rejected, and the relative GDPA series follows the nonlinear stationary process. A rejection of the null hypothesis provides evidence of nonlinear long run income converge of B&R countries with respect to China.

4. Results and Discussion

This section provides results of income convergence tests using both the linear and nonlinear unit root methods. We test for the presence of unit root in relative per capita income differential of B&R countries with respect to China using the ADF and KSS tests. First, we use the ADF test in order to examine the convergence hypothesis for B&R countries without the consideration of any nonlinearity in the data. Second, to test nonlinear convergence, we employ the KSS test of Kapetanios *et al.* (2003), which considers the effect of nonlinear components in time series. A rejection of the null hypothesis of non-stationarity in these tests provides evidence for the income convergence hypothesis.

Panel A in Table 1 summarizes the convergence results from univariate unit root tests of relative GDPA series over the full sample period (1960–2016). We find that 24 countries exhibit long-run income convergence towards China over the full sample period. The year 1978 as a milestone in contemporary China marks the beginning of the country's transition to a market economy and adoption of an open-door policy to embrace globalization. It is widely agreed that China experienced a fundamental change in its economic system after 1978. As China moved towards a market system and integrated into the global economy, we should expect some evidence in support of the income convergence hypothesis. Thus, we also employ univariate unit root tests for the post-reform period (1978–2016). Panel B in Table 1 summarizes the convergence results from univariate unit tests for the post-reform period. We report that 22 countries coverage to China during the post-reform period. However, a failure of rejecting the null hypothesis of non-stationarity

Table 1. Summary of Univariate Unit Root Test

Panel A: 1960–2016				
Country				
Armenia	Croatia	Jordan	New Zealand	Saudi
Azerbaijan	Hungary	Kazakhstan	Oman	Serbia
Bosnia	India	Moldova	Pakistan	Ukraine
Brunei	Iran	Maldives	Poland	Vietnam
Bhutan	Israel	Macedonia	Russia	
Number of instances of convergence 24				
Panel B: 1978–2016				
Country				
Armenia	Egypt	Kazakhstan	Oman	Ukraine
Azerbaijan	Croatia	Moldova	Poland	Vietnam
Bosnia	Hungary	Maldives	Russia	
Brunei	Iraq	Macedonia	Saudi	
Bhutan	Jordan	New Zealand	Serbia	
Number of instances of convergence 22				

does not necessarily imply the non-rejection countries are not in the process of converging. Possible nonlinearities in the data of these countries might make the standard ADF unit root test statistics biased. It is well known that the ADF test is not powerful in examining the null hypothesis of a unit root in the presence of nonlinearity in the data (Lau *et al.*, 2012). Thus, the test tends to not reject the null hypothesis of non-convergence while it is false (i.e., there is income convergence). To take into consideration nonlinear convergence among B&R countries, we also employ the nonlinear unit root test in this study.

The summary statistics of the KSS nonlinear unit root test for B&R countries are presented in Table 2. Panels A and B report test statistics for the periods 1960–2016 and 1979–2016, respectively. The results show that 21 countries converge to China over the full sample period (1960–2016). In addition, the number of countries converging to China increases to 24 over the post-reform period (1979–2016). The results show that the relative real output per capita (towards the China benchmark) of these countries follows a (nonlinear) mean reversion process and the underlying (nonlinear) growth paths of these economies are systematically related to that of China. We find evidence supporting the income convergence hypothesis in more B&R countries for the post-reform period than for the full sample period (1960–2016). This finding suggests that China's market transition and open-door orientation contribute to a higher degree of income convergence in regional integration. To gain additional insights in the context of China's B&R Initiatives, we break down the B&R countries into different regions, namely the MENA, Europe, Southeast Asia, South Asia and Central Asia.

Table 2. Summary of KSS Unit Root Test

Europe		MENA		Southeast Asia		South Asia		Central Asia	
Country	Statistics	Country	Statistics	Country	Statistics	Country	Statistics	Country	Statistics
Panel A: 1960–2016									
Albania	−2.069	Bahrain	−2.299	Indonesia	−2.511	Afghanistan	−2.620	Kazakhstan	−2.257
Armenia	−11.962***	Egypt	−1.476	Malaysia	−1.683	Bangladesh	−3.091	Kyrgyzstan	−3.737**
Azerbaijan	−7.487***	Iran	−2.021	Philippines	−1.745	Bhutan	−2.440	Turkmenistan	−2.742
Belarus	−5.509***	Iraq	−3.018	Singapore	−1.904	India	−5.028***	Uzbekistan	−2.976
Bosnia	−18.181***	Israel	−2.002	Thailand	−1.505	Maldives	−12.596***		
Bulgaria	−2.476	Jordan	−1.261	Vietnam	−5.982***	Nepal	−3.233*		
Czech	−2.925	Kuwait	−1.562	Laos	−1.839	Pakistan	−1.448		
Croatia	−1.354	Lebanon	−6.750***	Brunei	−5.629***	Sri Lanka	−3.235*		
Estonia	−1.943	Oman	−7.583***	Myanmar	−0.898				
Georgia	−2.787	Qatar	−2.040	Cambodia	−3.469**				
Hungary	−2.165	Saudi	−4.578***						
Latvia	−2.539	Turkey	−2.529						
Lithuania	−2.271	United Arab	−3.046						
Macedonia	−3.457*	Yemen	0.067						
Moldova	−1.239								
Montenegro	−4.332***								
Poland	−3.312*								
Romania	−3.375*								

Table 2. (*Continued*)

Europe		MENA		Southeast Asia		South Asia		Central Asia	
Country	Statistics	Country	Statistics	Country	Statistics	Country	Statistics	Country	Statistics
Russia	−3.498**								
Serbia	−1.805								
Slovakia	−4.128***								
Ukraine	−1.777								
Number of instances of convergence 21									
Number of instances of convergence in the region	10 countries (45.45%)	3 countries (21.43%)		3 countries (33.33%)		4 countries (50.00%)		1 country (25%)	
Panel B: 1979–2016									
Albania	−2.069	Bahrain	−2.299	Indonesia	−3.746**	Afghanistan	−2.620	Kazakhstan	−2.257
Armenia	−11.962***	Egypt	−4.645**	Malaysia	−3.127	Bangladesh	−0.264	Kyrgyzstan	−3.737**
Azerbaijan	−7.487***	Iran	−3.238*	Philippines	−1.964	Bhutan	−2.440	Turkmenistan	−2.742
Belarus	−5.509***	Iraq	−1.251	Singapore	−3.399*	India	−1.303	Uzbekistan	−2.976
Bosnia	−18.181***	Israel	−2.573	Thailand	−2.262	Maldives	−12.596***		
Bulgaria	−2.476	Jordan	−2.147	Vietnam	−5.982***	Nepal	−3.030		
Czech	−2.925	Kuwait	−1.562	Laos	−1.839	Pakistan	−3.144*		
Croatia	−1.352	Lebanon	−6.750***	Brunei	−6.789***	Sri Lanka	−1.516		
Estonia	−1.943	Oman	−3.568**	Myanmar	−1.599				

Table 2. (*Continued*)

Europe		MENA		Southeast Asia		South Asia		Central Asia	
Country	Statistics	Country	Statistics	Country	Statistics	Country	Statistics	Country	Statistics
Georgia	−2.456	Qatar	−2.040	Cambodia	−3.469**				
Hungary	−2.165	Saudi	−3.533**						
Latvia	−2.539	Turkey	−1.716						
Lithuania	−2.271	United Arab	−3.889**						
Macedonia	−3.457**	Yemen	0.067						
Moldova	−1.239								
Montenegro	−4.332***								
Poland	−3.312*								
Romania	−3.375*								
Russia	−3.498**								
Serbia	−1.805								
Slovakia	−4.128***								
Ukraine	−1.777								
Number of instances of convergence 24									
Number of instances of convergence in the region	10 countries (45.45%)	6 countries (42.86%)		5 countries (50.00%)		2 countries (25.00%)		1 country (25.00%)	

Notes: 1. Asymptotic critical values of t statistics at the 1%, 5% and 10% levels are −3.930, −3.400 and −3.130, respectively.
2. Test results for Mongolia and Korea (East Asia), Panama (Central America), New Zealand (Oceania), Ethiopia (Eastern Africa) and South Africa (Southern Africa) are statistically insignificant at the 10% level and thus not reported in the table.
*, **, *** denote 10 percent, 5 precent, and 1 percent levels of significance respectively.

It is noteworthy that more countries in the MENA converge to China over the post-reform period than the full sample period. The percentage of convergence is 42.86% for MENA countries over the post-reform period while the percentage of convergence for the full sample period is only 21.43%, only half of the region's post-reform percentage.

There are a total of 22 European countries participating in the B&R. These countries previously all belonged to the Eastern Bloc and experienced a transition to a market economy since the collapse of the Soviet Union. In total, 10 European B&R counties, nearly one half (45.45%), are shown to converge to China in both sample periods. This result might reflect the same experience of shifting from a command economy to a market economy that is shared by China and these former Eastern Bloc countries. About 10 out of the 22 European countries in the B&R are members of the European Union. However, only three of these E.U. countries,[4] are shown to converge to China. By contrast, 7 out of the 12 non-E.U. countries in the B&R, a vast majority, are shown to converge to China. These results imply that the E.U. member countries in the B&R are mostly driven by the catch-up motivation while the non-E.U. countries in Europe participate in the B&R mostly because of the existing economic cooperation with China. This implication is consistent with the fact that E.U. membership is associated with economic integration into Western Europe. Cavenaile and Dubois (2011) show that countries within the E.U. including new entrants from the former Soviet Bloc tend to converge.

For the full sample period, there are four counties in South Asia that exhibit income convergence. However, for the post-reform period, the null hypothesis of a unit root cannot be rejected for three of them, namely India, Nepal and Sri Lanka. The Maldives is the only country that exhibits income convergence for both periods in South Asia. This means that the countries in the region, which show convergence to China for the full sample period, tend to show no convergence to China for 1978–2016. This finding is consistent with the work of Ito (2017), which shows a widening of the income gap between Indian and China. Ito (2017) suggests that there has been a divergence between these two countries since China's market-oriented reforms in 1978. Thus, India's participation in B&R is better explained as driven by catch-up motivation. By contrast, Pakistan is the only South Asian country that shows no convergence to China for the full sample period but exhibits convergence to China for the post-reform period. This result is consistent with the strong relationship and increased bilateral economic cooperation between the two countries.

The 10 B&R countries in Southeast Asia are all members of the Association of Southeast Asian Nations (ASEAN). The number of converging countries in the region increased from three for the full sample period to five for the post-reform period. This result implies considerable development in economic integration between China and ASEAN for the post-reform period. The two ASEAN countries that exhibit income convergence for the post-reform period are Singapore and Indonesia, both of which are considered by China as important economic partners. In particular, the concept of the Maritime Silk Road was first proposed by Chinese President Xi, Jinping in his formal visit

[4] Namely Poland, Romania and Slovakia.

to Indonesia in 2013. Hence, the results implied that Singapore and Indonesia participate in the B&R Initiative so as to improve their solid economic relationship with China.

Central Asia is a critical node in the B&R Initiative for China. The result of our study on the region is worth noting. For both sample periods, Kyrgyzstan is the only country in the region that demonstrated convergence to China. However, Kazakhstan has been widely considered as China's most important regional partner in Central Asia.[5] Further study is needed to explore the lack of income convergence between China and Central Asia.

5. Conclusion

We investigate the B&R countries' motivations for greater economic integration with China by examining the per capita real GDP time series from 65 B&R countries. Using both linear and nonlinear unit root tests, we examine the income convergence hypothesis for B&R countries to detect the presence of economic integration for the periods 1960–2016 and 1979–2016. For the B&R countries that show income convergence to China in our testing, we argue that they tend to have strong existing economic relationship with China. Good examples from our income convergence testing include Singapore and Indonesia. By contrast, the B&R countries that show no convergence to China are supposed to have a relatively weak economic relationship with China and they participate in the B&R Initiative to catch up. A good example of our finding is India. In addition, we find evidence of long-run income convergence towards China for around one-third of B&R countries in both periods and evidence that more B&R countries converge to China over the post-reform period of 1978–2016. The results suggest that China contributes to a higher degree of income convergence in regional integration. Our study is based on a widely held view among mainstream economists that there is a strong link between economic integration and income convergence.[6]

References

Akhmedjonov, A and CK Lau (2012). Do energy prices converge across Russian regions? *Economic Modelling*, 29(2), 1623–1631.

Ageliki, A and P Ioannis (2016). Eurasian orientation and global trade integration: The case of Turkey. *Eurasia Economic Review*, 6(2), 275–287.

Barro, RJ (1991). Economic growth in a cross section of countries. *The Quarterly Journal of Economics*, 106(2), 407–443.

Barro, RJ and X Sala-I-Martin (1992). Convergence. *Journal of Political Economy*, 100(2), 223–251.

Baumol, WJ (1986). Productivity growth, convergence, and welfare: What the long-run data show. *The American Economic Review*, 76(5), 1072–1085.

[5] The strategic vision of the B&R Initiative was first formally proposed by President Xi Jinping in a speech delivered at Nazarbayev University during his visit to Kazakhstan in September 2013. Xi suggested that China and Central Asia cooperate to build a Silk Road economic belt.

[6] However, Milanovic (2006) finds out stronger evidence for income convergence during the interwar period than during the first globalization.

Bernard, AB and SN Durlauf (1995). Convergence in international output. *Journal of Applied Econometrics*, 10(2), 97–108. Bilgin, MH, G Gozgor and CK Lau (2017). Institutions and gravity model: The role of political economy and corporate governance. *Eurasian Business Review*, 7(3), 421–436.

Cavenaile, L and D Dubois (2011). An empirical analysis of income convergence in the European Union. *Applied Economics Letters*, 18(17), 1705–1708.

Ceylan, R and V Abiyev (2016). An examination of convergence hypothesis for EU-15 countries. *International Review of Economics & Finance*, 45, 96–105.

Cheung, YW and A García Pascual (2004). Testing for output convergence: A re-examination. *Oxford Economic Papers*, 56(1), 45–63.

Evans, P (1998). Using panel data to evaluate growth theories. *International Economic Review*, 39(2), 295–306.

Fan, CS (2004). Quality, trade, and growth. *Journal of Economic Behavior and Organization*, 55(2), 271–291.

Feng, GF, B Sui, MY Dong, CX Jiang and CP Chang (2018). Border is better than distance? Contagious corruption in one belt one road economies. *Quality and Quantity*, 52(4), 1909–1928.

Fischer, MM and C Stirböck (2006). Pan-European regional income growth and club-convergence. *The Annals of Regional Science*, 40(4), 693–721.

Battisti, M and G De Vaio (2008). A spatially filtered mixture of β-convergence regressions for EU regions, 1980–2002. *Empirical Economics*, 34(1), 105–121.

Friedman, MJ (1992). Do old fallacies ever die? *Journal of Economic Literature*, 30, 2129–2132.

Guetat, I and F Serranito (2007). Income convergence within the MENA countries: A panel unit root approach. *The Quarterly Review of Economics and Finance*, 46(5), 685–706.

Ingianni, A and V Zdarek (2009). Real convergence in the new member states: Myth or reality? *Journal of Economic Integration*, 24, 294–320.

Islam, N (1995). Growth empirics: A panel data approach. *The Quarterly Journal of Economics*, 110(4), 1127–1170.

Ito, T (2017). Growth convergence and the middle-income trap. *Asian Development Review*, 34(1), 1–27.

Kapetanios, G, Y Shin and A Snell (2003). Testing for a unit root in the nonlinear STAR framework. *Journal of Econometrics*, 112(2), 359–379.

King, A and C Ramlogan-Dobson (2015). International income convergence: Is Latin America actually different? *Economic Modelling*, 49, 212–222.

Kocenda, E, A Kutan and T Yigit (2006). Pilgrims to the Eurozone: How far, how fast? *Economic Systems*, 30, 311–327.

Lau, CKM (2010). New evidence about regional income divergence in China. *China Economic Review*, 21(2), 293–309.

Lau, CKM, F Suvankulov, Y Su and F Chau (2012). Some cautions on the use of nonlinear panel unit root tests: Evidence from a modified series-specific non-linear panel unit-root test. *Economic Modelling*, 29(3), 810–816.

Mankiw, NG, D Romer and DN Weil (1992). A contribution to the empirics of economic growth. *The Quarterly Journal of Economics*, 107(2), 407–437.

Matkowski, Z and M Próchniak (2007). Economic convergence between the CEE-8 and the European Union. *Eastern European Economics*, 45(1), 59–76.

Milanovic, B (2006). Economic integration and income convergence: Not such a strong link? *The Review of Economics and Statistics*, 88(4), 659–670.

Percival, P (2017). Financial liberalization and private sector borrowing in ASEAN 4 economies 1990–2012. *Eurasia Economic Review*, 7(2), 277–295.

Romer, D (2012). *The Solow Growth Model. Advanced Macroeconomics*. 4th edn., pp. 1–45. New York: McGraw-Hill Irwin, pp. 1–45.

Quah, D (1993). Galton's fallacy and tests of the convergence hypothesis. *The Scandinavian Journal of Economics*, 95(4), 427–443.

Solow, RM (1956). A contribution to the theory of economic growth. *The Quarterly Journal of Economics*, 70(1), 65–94.

Ucal, M, AA Haug and MH Bilgin (2016). Income inequality and FDI: Evidence with Turkish data. *Applied Economics*, 48(11), 1030–1045.

Chapter 5

ASEAN ELECTRICITY MARKET INTEGRATION: HOW CAN BELT AND ROAD INITIATIVE BRING NEW LIFE TO IT?†

LIXIA YAO* and PHILIP ANDREWS-SPEED

Energy Studies Institute
National University of Singapore, Singapore, 119620
**esiyaol@nus.edu.sg*

XUNPENG SHI

Australia-China Relations Institute
University of Technology Sydney, PO Box 123, Australia

Center of Hubei Cooperative Innovation for Emissions Trading System
Hubei University of Economics
Wuhan 430205, Hubei Province, P. R. China

Published Online 28 August 2019

This paper assesses how China's Belt and Road Initiative (BRI) can bring investment and technology into ASEAN and its impact on ASEAN's electricity market. With the theoretical framework of scenario analysis, this paper provides three scenarios for ASEAN electricity market integration: the Lao PDR–Thailand–Malaysia–Singapore (LTMS) arrangement, a power exchange between heterogeneous grids in the Greater Mekong Sub-region (GMS) region, and a fully competitive electricity market with a fully-developed ASEAN Power Grid (APG). Based on these scenarios, the paper examines the extent to which the BRI can assist electricity market integration in the ASEAN region. It is found that BRI can best fit with and facilitate the first scenario. Given the uncertain outlook for the electricity market integration in the GMS region, how China's BRI can play a role in facilitating the GMS electricity market integration is not clear under the second scenario. Further, BRI may be less helpful in the third scenario in which the region's master plan of APG would be realized. In any sense, how BRI can fit with and facilitate ASEAN's electricity market integration would more depend on the host countries rather than the Chinese side.

Keywords: ASEAN; Belt and Road Initiative; electricity market integration.

1. Introduction

The Association of Southeast Asian States (ASEAN) has a long established plan to connect the national grids of its member states and create an ASEAN power grid (APG). Currently, the interconnection of grids are mostly in the continental Southeast Asia and the electricity trading still remains bilateral and the realization of the ambitious plan needs significant amount of investment in the electricity sector. More recently, ASEAN has announced the intention to promote multilateral power trading and develop an integrated regional power market.

---

* Corresponding author.

†This article originally appeared in *The Singapore Economic Review*, **66**(1), pp. 85–103

Against this backdrop, China has emerged as a major investor in the region's electricity industry. China indeed has a long history of investing in ASEAN's energy sector, but since the 2000s Chinese energy companies have been increasingly active in this region. They have been building coal-fired power plants and hydroelectric dams, and have invested in renewables energy. With regard to Chinese investment in energy connectivity infrastructure, China appears to be very interested in building transmission lines in its neighboring countries so that these lines can be connected with those in China. Therefore, China-built lines are mainly located in mainland Southeast Asia, in Laos, Vietnam, Myanmar and Cambodia.

Since the launch of China's Belt and Road Initiative (BRI), Chinese investment in Southeast Asia has increased. Chinese companies have been particularly active building coal-fired power plants in Indonesia, in direct response to the government's ambitious plans to boost the nation's generating capacity as fast as possible. China continues to be active in hydropower construction in the Greater Mekong Sub-region (GMS) (Lu, 2016). It is also building solar and wind farms and manufacturing facilities for solar panels in Southeast Asia, although the scale is small compared to its investment in the hydropower sector. One BRI power grid project has also been put into operation: the so-called "first Belt & Road power grid cooperation project" in Laos, which is also connected to power grids in Southern China (Xinhuanet, 2015).

The aim of this paper is to examine the extent to which the BRI can assist electricity market integration in the ASEAN region. Using the framework of scenario analysis, this study presents three scenarios of electricity market integration in ASEAN and assesses how China's BRI might fit with each scenario. The three scenarios are: the Lao PDR–Thailand–Malaysia–Singapore (LTMS) arrangement, a power exchange between heterogeneous grids, and a fully competitive electricity market with a fully-developed ASEAN Power Grid. It is found that BRI can best fit with and facilitate the first scenario. Chinese companies, with their existing investments in the power sector in the continental Southeast Asian countries such as Laos and Thailand, can provide indirect support to this scenario; and probably direct support when further down investments in Malaysia and Singapore are made. Yet given the uncertain outlook for the electricity market integration in the GMS region, how China's BRI can play a role in facilitating the GMS electricity market integration is not clear under the second scenario. Further, BRI may be less helpful in the third scenario in which the region's master plan of ASEAN Power Grid would be realized. In any sense, how BRI can fit with and facilitate ASEAN's electricity market integration would more depend on the host countries rather than the Chinese side.

This paper is structured as follows: Section 2 reviews energy situation and the political economy of energy market integration in ASEAN; Section 3 establishes the analytic framework of scenario analysis with a discussion of the rationale for scenario analysis of ASEAN's electricity market integration; Section 4 discusses in detail the current electricity market in ASEAN and each of the three scenarios of its market integration; Section 5 discusses how China's BRI can fit with each scenario; and Section 6 concludes the paper.

2. The Context of Electricity Market Integration in ASEAN

Energy market integration cannot be viewed in isolation from the broader political economy of ASEAN integration. This section reviews the energy situation of ASEAN and examines the political economy of energy market integration in ASEAN in order to build a better understanding of different scenarios of electricity market integration in this region which is discussed in the subsequent sections.

2.1. *Energy situation in ASEAN*

The 10 ASEAN member states are at different stages in their economic development, yet most of them have attained rapid economic growth and are experiencing significant increase in energy demand. Between 2000 and 2016, they collectively experienced economic growth of more than 125%, reaching a combined GDP of US$7.4 trillion in 2016 (in purchasing power parity terms) (OECD/IEA, 2017, p. 34). That year, total primary energy demand in ASEAN reached 643 Mtoe, of which fossil fuel accounted for 74% (OECD/ IEA, 2017). Figure 1 illustrates the fuel mix in ASEAN in 2016.

In terms of electricity supply, ASEAN's installed power generation capacity more than doubled over the same period, reaching around 240 gigawatts in 2016. Fossil fuels continue to dominate the power generation mix. There has been a rapid rise of coal-fired power capacity, although the growth has been slowing down since 2014. The capacity of renewables-based electricity has tripled since 2000, with a rapid expansion of hydropower. In 2016, non-hydro renewables accounted for 6.5% of the total installed electricity capacity. Bioenergy and geothermal capacity contributed to about 70% of the non-hydro renewables (OECD/IEA, 2017, p. 23). Figure 2 shows the power generation mix in Southeast Asia in 2016.

Besides increasing electricity capacity, ASEAN has also been putting efforts to expanding power connectivity. Linkage of power grids across countries has long been

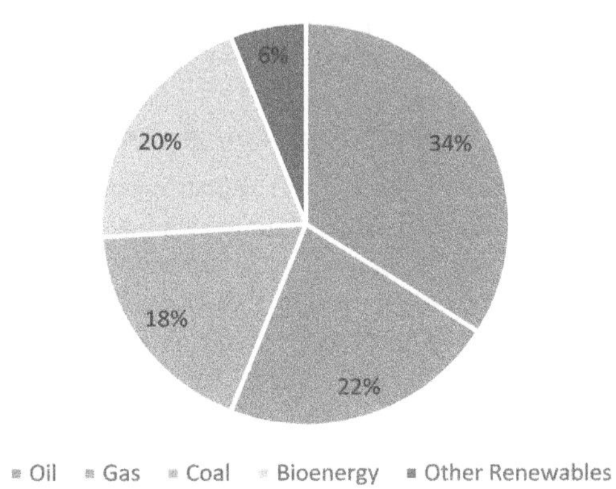

Source: OECD/IEA (2017).

Figure 1. Fuel Mix in ASEAN, 2016

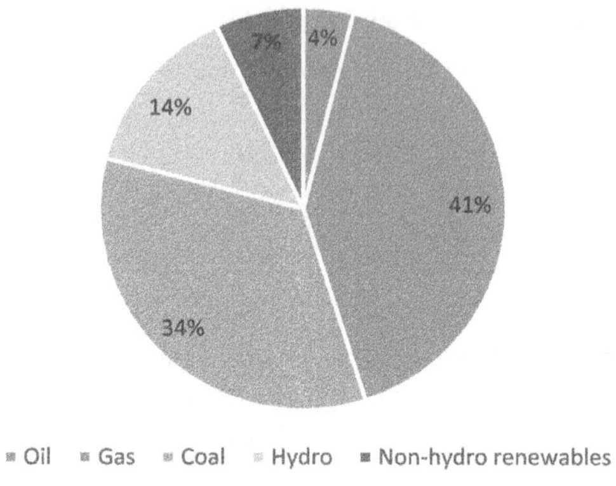

Source: OECD/IEA (2017).

Figure 2. Power Generation Mix in ASEAN, 2016

pursued. Adopted in 1997 at the second ASEAN Informal Summit, the ASEAN 2020 Vision envisioned an energy-interconnected Southeast Asia through two major energy projects: the ASEAN Power Grid (APG) and the Trans-ASEAN Gas Pipeline (TAGP). The APG was proposed for the aim of sharing resources and promoting the efficient utilization of electricity. Through power trading, APG has also been expected to promote a win–win economic relationship between the countries (APAEC, 2004). Therefore, APG is one of the most important elements for electricity market integration in ASEAN. The benefits of an integrated ASEAN electricity market are obvious. Trans-border power grid interconnections and market integration can relieve burdens related to excess power generation capacity, alleviate poverty, reduce energy prices, mitigate supply shortages, and promote development of clean energy and sustainability. Further, economic analysis has identified more benefits such as significant net economic savings via development of cheaper renewable energy resources (Silitonga, 2018).

2.2. *The political economy of electricity market integration in ASEAN*

An applicable approach to understanding the political economy of energy market integration of Southeast Asia is offered by the "Murdoch school", which posits that institutional outcomes (e.g., energy market integration) are inherently determined by rival actors that consistently compete for power and resources (Jones, 2016). Against this backdrop, the member states that demonstrate more enthusiasm for further integration may need to take a proactive approach in understanding the difficulties faced by other member states that are hesitant at best and resistant at worst. Since the benefits accruing from a fully integrated energy market will only be realized in the long term, some member states seem to discount their potential gains right now. This impacts the political will of each member state to act urgently. In any sense, as Andrews-Speed and Hezri (2013) pointed out, the operation of a regional energy grid requires a high degree of collective action, which is likely to require delegation of sovereignty of the participating countries. ASEAN, a region with 10 diversified member states, may be in a complex situation in this regard.

To address the complexities of the underlying political economy, there is a need for clarity on the decision-making mechanism with regard to energy market integration. This pertains to who will make decisions, and how such power will be distributed across different members in this regard. For instance, Nordic energy cooperation relies on consensus among its members (Joergensen, 2016). Thus the Nordic power market, "Nordpool", developed slowly, starting with bilateral exchange between Norway and Sweden, grew to include Denmark and Finland, and eventually integrated with the European Union market (Bredesen and Nilsen, 2013). There is also a need for unambiguous clarity among members as to what kind of public good is aspired to be created, and what benefits are expected to be achieved (Andrews-Speed, 2011). Matters related to benefits and costs cannot have national basis only, as it potentially affects the wellbeing of millions of people living in the member states. Again, as ASEAN member states are quite diverse in terms of economic development, political system, and natural resource endowment, it can be even more difficult for them agree on the benefits, costs and people's wellbeing of an integrated energy market.

Further, trust is an important requirement for collective action and a prerequisite for a high level of energy market integration. However, a lack of political trust is a prominent obstacle that hinders collective action in the ASEAN region. The reasons lie in its history. Most ASEAN member states are young nations that emerged from colonial rule and the Second World War in weak condition. This makes them very sensitive about sovereignty (Andrews-Speed and Len, 2013). To make matters worse, factors such as unresolved disputes over land borders and maritime demarcation and ethnic unrest in border areas make the ASEAN countries tend to look at each other with suspicion. For example, there has still been disputes on the border issue between Vietnam and Cambodia. Their border disputes had led the Vietnamese to invade Cambodia in the late 1970s. Today, still little progress on boundary agreements have been made between the two countries. Further, as one of the most ethnically diverse regions in the world, ethnic unrest frequently happens in the region. In Myanmar, for instance, the escalation of conflict in Kachin state between the army and the Kachin Independence Organisation (KIO) highlights the ethnic issues in the country. The violence has mainly centered on the control of natural resources such as amber mines, jade mines and hydropower plants (Hart, 2018). This can make the investment in Myanmar a complicated issue.

Besides the above obstacles that may hinder the integration of energy markets, some other challenges particularly impede the development of an integrated electricity market in ASEAN, such as the technical, economic, and institutional and market structure challenges and energy security concerns of member states. First, the technical challenge is a major obstacle for the multilateral connections needed to create an ASEAN Power Grid (APG). The power systems of ASEAN member states have different technical standards and their transmission lines may also have different voltages. The existing power grid interconnections serve as a bad example that hinders the progress of the APG. For example, most of the electricity exported from the GMS member states is from generating plants that are independent of the national grids. These electricity transmission lines are built exclusively for exporting electricity, and these electricity flows are small and unidirectional. However, if a large interconnected system is to be developed, it is necessary to coordinate the technical standards and align the standards for electricity-exporting grids with the standards of domestic grids that had not been designed specifically for exports of electricity (Shi and Malik, 2013). To put it simply, harmonization of some technical standard codes is a prerequisite for APG development.

Second, investment constitutes a key uncertainty in the expansion of interconnected power grids across ASEAN. Since the early 2000s, average annual investment in power plants more than doubled, while the average annual investment in transmission and distribution systems remained almost flat (IEA, 2015). Financing cross-border transmission lines will require substantial investment yet it is unclear where the funding is going to come from. Since 2000, about US$365 billion has been invested in the power sector across ASEAN, of which about US$195 billion went to grid expansion and improvement. However, it is estimated that ASEAN would need about US$690 billion invested in its transmission and distribution sectors by 2040 (IEA, 2017). Completion of some interconnections is more realistic than others thanks to the existing funding from development banks and private sector. Yet there is uncertainty about the future of some other interconnections due to lack of funding, although their benefit to the region is undeniable (Finenko *et al.*, 2017).

Another major constraint for APG development is that many interconnection projects are not yet commercially viable which makes it difficult to secure financing (Shi and Malik, 2013). The prevailing subsidies in many ASEAN countries not only discourage investment in clean energy, fossil fuel exploration, and infrastructure, but also prevent greater integration of regional energy markets (Shi and Kimura, 2013). The removal of subsidies, however, is politically challenging, as has been the case of Malaysia (Li *et al.*, 2017). The predominance of 25-year power purchase agreements (PPAs) in the governance of most of the interconnections, is a further commercial factor that prevents the development of multilateral power trading (Antikainen *et al.*, 2011).

Third, institutional challenges further complicate the situation and different modes of power sector regulation can bring about further obstacles. Of the 10 ASEAN member states, only Singapore has a fully liberalized electricity market. Among ASEAN countries, the Philippines comes second to Singapore in terms of having single buyer pools in certain parts of the electricity network. Malaysia and Thailand both have IPPs but they do not have single buyer pools. Other countries such as Cambodia, Myanmar and Laos are served by vertically-integrated state-owned utilities. Price control mechanisms and electricity subsidies in several ASEAN countries are also potential obstacles to the APG development and electricity market integration in ASEAN (Sahid *et al.*, 2013). Another regulatory obstacle is different degrees of liberalization in the transmission sector. For example, private companies in Indonesia are allowed to construct transmission lines, whereas in Malaysia, only the state-owned utility company can build transmission lines (Shi and Malik, 2013). As a result, electricity trading has a lengthy approval process due to the different nature of the leading companies of both countries in the market.

Consequently, the harmonization of regulatory systems will need a lengthy developmental process.

Finally, the prevailing nationally-focused energy security paradigm of ASEAN member states lies behind the continuing fragmentation of the energy markets because the traditional national energy security concept requires maximizing self-sufficiency which undermines potential for regional energy trade (Shi and Kimura, 2010; Wu *et al.*, 2014). In addition, some countries may limit their dependence on other countries to protect their electricity utilities. These energy sector concerns will reduce the electricity trading opportunities (Shi and Malik, 2013). Countries will have to balance the trade-offs between possibly cheaper and cleaner electricity from overseas and national security. If a country becomes reliant on electricity exports, it faces the risk of electricity supply interruption by the exporter. Interruption can be intentional or unintentional. For example, if there is a drought in a big exporting country that relies on hydropower generation, such as Laos, the reliance on such an exporter may also cause serious problem for the importing country.

Further energy market integration will need to be based on projection of different possible forms of integration that may affect the energy market of the individual member state and the region as a whole. To look into the trajectories of energy market integration, this study adopts scenario analysis, focusing on the projection of ASEAN's electricity market integration. Scenario analysis has been developed since the 1960s to produce extrapolations that predict the future. The next section discusses the framework of scenario analysis that is applied to electricity market in ASEAN.

3. The Framework for Understanding Market Integration: Scenario Analysis

Since the 1960s, more sophisticated forecasting techniques which can produce extrapolations to predict the future have been developed. One of these techniques is the scenario analysis. Scenario analysis is a powerful tool to react to future conditions and to develop strategies to address such conditions. Scenarios provide a long-term macro view which serves as a backdrop for more traditional forecasting approaches. The methodology of scenario analysis has been extensively used for policy analysis, social forecasting, and decision making in 1960s. In the late 1980s, it matured as a well-developed planning and forecasting technique. Scenario analysis provides a powerful tool to react to future conditions and to develop strategies to address such conditions. This methodology is best in use when scenarios are suited in "long-term, macro, uncertain environments which are typified by a scarcity of data and a large number of non-quantifiable factors" (Huss, 1988, p. 380). In this section, we review the state of the art associated with scenario analysis and provide the rationale for scenario analysis in electricity market integration in ASEAN.

3.1. *State of the art of scenario analysis*

Scenarios provide a long-term macro view which serves as a backdrop for more traditional forecasting approaches. The methodology of scenario analysis has been extensively used for policy analysis, social forecasting, and decision making in 1960s. Helping the decision-makers to be prepared for the future, scenario analysis deals with uncertainty and the usefulness of overall decision-making process (Heijden, 2005; Varum and Melo, 2010).

It provides an overall picture of the future and highlights the interactions among several trends and events in the future (Martino, 2003). Moreover, it integrates all complex elements to describe a future situation and the course of events which allows the decision-makers to move forward from the actual to the future situation. Therefore, scenario analysis is considered a valuable tool that helps decision-makers to prepare for possible eventualities. Until now the most popular definition of scenario is that scenarios are alternative futures resulting from a combination of trends and of the policies of agents (Fontela and Hingel, 1993, p. 139).[1]

On different basis, scenarios can be classified into different types. They can be grouped and classified on the basis of topic, perspective (Porter *et al.*, 2011), scope, focus of action, level of aggregation (Mietzner and Reger, 2005), and methods of building (van Notten *et al.*, 2003). Particularly, perspective and methods of building are most relevant to the study in this paper. On the basis of perspective, scenarios can be classified into descriptive and normative scenarios. According to Porter *et al.* (2011), descriptive scenarios are extrapolative in nature and present a range of events that describe alternative futures whereas normative scenarios are goal-directed and passively react to policy planning concerns for the achievement of desired targets. On the basis of methods of building, scenarios can be qualitative and quantitative. Georgoff and Murdick (1986) published a paper in *Harvard Business Review* that explicitly specifies scenario analysis as a qualitative technique designed as "smoothly unfolding narratives that describe an assumed future expressed through a sequence of time frames or snapshots" (p. 114), while as of the past decade, many have been making extensive use of quantitative tool and techniques (Vecchiato and Roveda, 2010). This study adopts the descriptive scenario with a qualitative technique to forecast the future of electricity market in Southeast Asia.

3.2. *Rationale for scenario analysis in electricity market integration in ASEAN*

Despite of these perceived benefits, the progress of ASEAN electricity market integration still remains slow given the obstacles discussed in Section 2. These obstacles are difficult to overcome. Of all the obstacles, the technical incompatibility of transmission lines between some ASEAN countries need to be addressed before other problems can be solved. Further, technically if connected, the unstable voltage and frequent power outages in some poorest countries in the region such as Cambodia, Laos and Myanmar can seriously affect the overall performance of the regional power grid (Zhang and Zha, 2014). Political distrust between some of the ASEAN countries involved in the integration can hinder the interconnection of power grids across their borders (Wu *et al.*, 2012; Shi and Kimura, 2013). As a result, some governments would boost their own electricity capacity rather than save costs by connecting to their neighbors' grids (Olchondra, 2016) while some other

[1] For a comprehensive literature review of scenario analysis, see Amer *et al.* (2013).

governments are less keen to support APG due to the need to protect their own energy sectors (Kumar, 2015).

National energy market regulations have delayed the development of APG as well. Electricity is often the most regulated energy product of a country. To break up monopolies and attract investment, electricity sector liberalization has been implemented across ASEAN to varying degrees since the 1980s. Many targets, however, have not been achieved yet (Sharma, 2005). Regulation gaps of mismatches have impeded cross-border power trading, including issues such as taxation, transmission tariffs, and third-party access (Andrews-Speed, 2016). Another major obstacle is the lack of capital. The investment requirement of eventual realization of APG is estimated to be US$5.9 billion (Zhang and Zha, 2014, p. 92). However, as Andrews-Speed (2016) mentioned, "[n]ational governments and state-owned enterprises have been unable, unwilling or slow to invest and, at the same time, many interconnection projects remain commercially unattractive to private investors" (p. 11).

The difficulty of removing these obstacles produces a lot of uncertainties for the evolving of APG and electricity market integration. With this said, our study evaluates what are the likely trajectories of the evolving electricity market integration. For such evaluation, scenarios offer a powerful approach to glimpsing into the future. The following section constructs three scenarios for ASEAN electricity market integration.

4. Scenarios for ASEAN Electricity Market Integration

This section reviews the current situation of ASEAN power grid connection and forecasts the ASEAN electricity market integration scenarios.

4.1. *Current situation of ASEAN power grid connectivity*

Linkage of power grids across countries has long been pursued in ASEAN. Adopted in 1997 at the 2nd ASEAN Informal Summit, the ASEAN 2020 Vision proposed an energy-interconnected Southeast Asia through two major energy projects: the ASEAN Power Grid (APG) and the Trans-ASEAN Gas Pipeline (TAGP). The APG was proposed for the aim of sharing resources and promoting the efficient utilization of electricity (ASEAN, 2008; Shi, 2014). Through power trading, the APG has also been expected to promote a win–win economic relationship between the countries. Therefore, APG is one of the most important elements for electricity market integration in ASEAN. Yet, the development of APG has encountered technical, political, institutional, and financial obstacles. These factors, among others, also affect ASEAN electricity market integration (Shi, 2014; Halawa *et al.*, 2018). Nevertheless, the basic foundation and also the most important prerequisite is the physical cross-border interconnection of national power grids across ASEAN. ASEAN has been endeavoring to construct the ASEAN Power Grid (APG) since 1997 when HAPUA (Heads of ASEAN Power Utilities/Authorities) was tasked to ensure regional energy security by sharing energy resources via APG (ACE, 2017a). Currently, there are totally 16 planned APG projects, 8 of which have been completed. APG is still at the stage of physical interconnection development between individual member states (ACE, 2017b, p. 9).

However, even if all these interconnections are realized as planned, APG does not by itself bring about an integrated ASEAN electricity market (Shi and Malik, 2013; Shi, 2014).

4.2. *ASEAN electricity market integration scenarios*

Nonetheless, the integration of the market has to start in a gradual and incremental way, and the bottom-up approach is more suitable for ASEAN than the top-down one. ASEAN does not have any institution that represents a strong supranational authority, nor does it have an overall regional governance to facilitate the development of regional power connectivity. Therefore, a bottom-up and incremental approach is practical to advance regional power connectivity in the absence of an overall regional integration architecture. In order to pursue the APG programme, Heads of ASEAN Power Utilities/Authorities (HAPUA) adopted a strategy that encourages the gradual development of the identified interconnection projects. First on cross-border bilateral terms, then gradually expanding to a sub-regional basis and finally to a totally integrated Southeast Asian power grid system (Shi and Malik, 2013). This sub-section constructs three scenarios of ASEAN electricity market integration with a discussion of how China's BRI can play a role under each scenario.

4.2.1. *Scenario 1: LTMS interconnection*

Currently, all power trading within ASEAN is bilateral between individual member states. ASEAN is yet to develop its first multilateral connection so as to initiate multilateral electricity trade by 2018. Using existing interconnections, the pilot project "Lao PDR–Thailand–Malaysia–Singapore (LTMS) Power Integration Project (PIP)" was intended to start multilateral electricity trade from Laos to Singapore, through Malaysia and Thailand. This pilot project was expected to be a pathfinder to realize multilateral electricity trade in the ASEAN (ACE, 2017b). Under the first phase of the LTMS Project, 100 MW of electrical power would be delivered to Malaysia via Thailand's national grid by 1 August 2018. Under the second phase, it is expected that Laos will export another 100 MW of power to Singapore via Thailand and Malaysia's network by 2020 (Lao News Agency, 2017; The Laotian Times, 2017). However, the involvement of Singapore is more complex on account of the specific context of its power sector. In principle, the availability of hydropower from Laos would diversify Singapore's fuel mix, enhance security of supply and reduce carbon emissions. However, Singapore not only hosts the only fully liberalized power market in ASEAN, but this market has massive generation overcapacity. If the power available via LTMS was truly competitive in this market, the existing generating companies might be driven out of business. Conversely, if the transmission tariffs charged by Thailand and Malaysia were high, the power from Laos would not be able to enter the Singapore market without special dispensation. Therefore, Singapore has withdrawn from the LTMS project for the moment.

From the perspective of energy security concerns, Malaysia and Thailand have the motivation to meet their rapidly growing electricity demand without increasing their dependence on natural gas imports for power generation. On the exporter side, Laos is keen to be the battery of Southeast Asia. It has large hydropower potential and it expects to operate 100 hydropower plants with combined installed generation capacity of 28 GW by 2020 (Phomnuny, 2017).

4.2.2. *Scenario 2: Multilateral power exchange*

Although ASEAN has already established some institutions to develop APG, such as ASEAN Centre for Energy (ACE) and HAPUA, none of them have binding authority. There is still a long way to go before ASEAN can uniformly make rules to create a truly competitive ASEAN-wide electricity market due to the big differences in the national conditions of the individual countries. Therefore, at the current stage, due to technical, regulatory and other barriers, it may only be possible initially to create a multilateral power exchange platform involving willing participants. But as more countries join and as market actors realise the advantage of trading power, investment in interconnection will grow and the sophistication of trading mechanisms will increase. That is to say, to first establish the market can bring in investment and expansion of power grids. Such an approach was taken by the Nordic countries in developing the Nordpool and is currently being pursued in other regions, notably in the Southern African Power Pool (Bredesen and Nilsen, 2013).

The GMS could be a good place to test such an exchange due to the relatively high level of interconnection. Currently, electricity trade in GMS is only conducted through PPAs between utilities. The ideal condition of the electricity market integration in the region would be the establishment of a regional electricity exchange center with multiple buyers and sellers within the GMS countries that could then expand across the rest of ASEAN. Countries with huge hydropower potential such as Laos, Myanmar and Cambodia can be electricity exporters while countries with large electricity demand such as Thailand, Malaysia and Vietnam would be the importers. Under such scenario, according to a study done by ADB (2009), Thailand would be the dominant importer of electricity, which primarily comes from Myanmar through Laos. Located in the center of the continental Southeast Asia, Thailand can be a trading hub of electricity.

The GMS power market integration was planned to be progressed into several stages from bilateral cross-border connection and grid-to-grid power trading between any pair of GMS countries to transmission links for cross-border trading using third party's transmission facilities and a fully integrated GMS regional competitive power market. GMS countries are now moving from the stage of bilateral electricity trading to trading between any pair of GMS countries with access to third country's transmission facilities (ADB, 2018).

4.2.3. *Scenario 3: A fully competitive electricity market with a fully-developed APG*

Under this scenario, there will be comprehensive regulatory, institutional and market arrangements based on the ASEAN countries' high-level cooperation and trust. This scenario, a fully-developed APG, is a major energy infrastructure project mandated in 1997 by the ASEAN Heads of States/Governments under the ASEAN Vision 2020. Motivations for a full APG are to complement different load shape among ASEAN countries and to make ASEAN less dependent on fuel imports from non-ASEAN countries. Further, energy resources sharing and potential total cost savings from interconnection are beneficial to the ASEAN region as well (Shi and Malik, 2013). The ultimate goal of APG is to interconnect the grids of all the 10 ASEAN member states to optimize the use of energy resources in the region by sharing the benefits and to reduce capital required for the expansion of generation capacity. In such a fully competitive power market, there will be vertical unbundling of state-owned utilities. There will also be full independence of transmission system operators from electricity production. More importantly, a fully competitive power market has unrestricted and non-discriminatory third-party grid access to all participants (Finenko *et al.*, 2017), which would be one of the key characteristics in the fully competitive power market. Against this condition, comprehensive institutional arrangement including summits, ministerial meetings and senior official meetings are needed.

5. The Role of BRI under ASEAN Electricity Market Integration

With these scenarios in mind, this section discusses how China's BRI can bring new source of technology and funding to the electricity market integration of ASEAN under each scenario.

5.1. *BRI under Scenario 1*

We find that of the three scenarios, BRI can play the most important role under Scenario 1, the LTMS interconnection. China has long invested in the power sector in the continental Southeast Asia. These investments are in projects that increase power capacity or expand power connectivity within the borders of the host country. In its neighboring countries Laos, Vietnam and Myanmar, Chinese companies have also built national power transmission lines that can be connected to China's power grid to enable electricity trading. Although these connections operate on a bilateral basis, they are beneficial to the power grid building of these continental Southeast Asian countries. Since BRI was initiated, one "BRI power grid project" has been put into operation — the "first Belt & Road power grid cooperation project" located in Laos. Constructed by China Southern Power Grid, this power grid project links four northern Lao provinces and is supposed to enhance regional connectivity (Xinhuanet, 2015). It seems that Chinese companies are very interested in constructing transmission lines that connect China with its neighboring countries such as Laos and Myanmar, which are also willing to exchange electricity with China. By the year 2035, it is hoped that the power grid system in some of these continental Southeast Asian countries could be connected to China's power grid through bilateral, multilateral and regional arrangements (GEIDCO, 2018).

It is also planned that a synchronous power interconnection will be established within Southern China, Laos, Myanmar and Thailand. Currently, in terms of voltage level, only seven of the existing cross-border transmission lines (one between China and Myanmar, six between Laos and Thailand) are 500 kV. The other transmission lines are 230 kV, 110 kV and below. By 2035, the power grids in these countries will need to be reinforced.

A 500 kV alternating current (AC) synchronous interconnection covering Myanmar, Laos, Thailand and Vietnam has also been recommended. By 2050, the cross-border power exchange will reach 16 GW between Thailand and Laos. Therefore, further upgrading of the voltage will be required possibly, by deploying ultra-high voltage (UHV) interconnection technology based on the existing 500 kV AC synchronization grids (GEIDCO, 2018). All these projects will require a large amount of investment and Chinese companies, with their rich experiences in power grid building in the continental Southeast Asian region, would play a key role under this scenario. In addition, there is also an urgent need to construct additional power generation capacity to serve a region with more than 60 million people without access to electricity.

Under the BRI, Chinese companies can invest in countries rich in non-fossil energy resources. They have already been very active in the hydropower sector in Laos and Myanmar. BRI has also brought new opportunities for investment in other forms of renewable power capacity. Chinese companies have already exported some US$8 billion of solar equipment exports from China, making the country the number one exporter of environmental goods and services (Timperley, 2018). These continental Southeast Asian countries remain an attractive destination for new and renewable energy investment. For example, Laos' energy sector is dominated by hydropower projects along the Mekong river basin. The Power Construction Corporation of China has been constructing one of the largest hydropower projects in the region with a proposed installed capacity of more than 1,000 MW. Thailand has the highest installed solar capacity in the ASEAN region (IRENA, 2017). Since BRI started, Chinese investors have moved rapidly into Thailand's solar power sector to build solar panel factories and solar power projects, making Thailand a country with a fast increasing solar power capacity and a construction center of solar PV equipment. Malaysia is one of the top three global destinations for renewable energy (BMI Research, 2017). With its positive macro-economic outlook and supportive energy policies, it has attracted several Chinese investments especially in solar and hydropower. One key example is the Sarawak Corridor of Renewable Energy, which covers 70,000 sq. km. of the central Sarawak region. From 2008 until 2015, 3.3% of all FDI in Sarawak was from China (Chia and Ten, 2015). In 2016, the largest investment in renewables in Malaysia was made by one of the largest Chinese solar manufacturers, LONGi, which is expected to spend about US$269 million in the country on solar panel manufacturing (Pim, 2017).

Chinese companies, with their existing investments in the power sector in the continental Southeast Asian countries such as Laos and Thailand, can provide indirect support to LTMS scenario; and probably direct support to this scenario when further down investments in Malaysia and Singapore are made. Further, through the construction of power generation transmission capacity, Chinese companies, through the BRI, are continuing to contribute to the development of the APG in continental Southeast Asia. If this continues, a foundation will have been built for ASEAN to develop an integrated power market. Nevertheless, progress may still be hampered by some of the political and policy obstacles identified above, in Section 2.

5.2. *BRI under Scenario 2*

What Chinese investment can do for ASEAN electricity market integration under Scenario 2 is basically the same as described in Scenario 1. Yet under Scenario 2, it is needed for the GMS region to get China involved in its market integration process. As above mentioned, a 500 kV alternating current (AC) synchronous interconnection covering Myanmar, Laos, Thailand and Vietnam is recommended and therefore synchronous power interconnection could be established throughout Southern China, Laos, Myanmar, Thailand and Vietnam. The GMS region use BRI as an opportunity to realize such interconnection, which is highly possible because Chinese companies have rich experience in power grid construction in these countries.

In addition to the investment in Laos, Thailand and Malaysia, Chinese companies have also constructed power plants and power grids in GMS countries such as Vietnam and Cambodia. In Cambodia, a country not bordering China, Chinese companies such as China National Heavy Machinery Corporation (CHMC) has been very active in the Cambodian electricity market. Together with the Cambodia's state-owned Electricite du Cambodge (EDC), CHMC has committed to constructing the national grid in Cambodia and the renovating of its rural power system. Between 2009 and 2012, CHMC signed several contracts for power grid construction and expansion, including the Phnom Penh Loop Line Transmission System Project, the Cambodian Rural Power Grid Expansion Project (Phase I), and the Phnom Penh-Bavet Transmission Line Project (Industrial Headlines, 2016). The Phnom Penh Loop Line Transmission System connects to transmission lines bringing electricity from all over Cambodia, including several hydroelectric dams within the borders of the country and other lines that bring electricity from coal and gas power plants in Vietnam (Chun, 2009). The Phnom Penh Loop Line Transmission System not only improves the electricity supply in Phnom Penh but also enhance the supply stability of the entire country. Since the BRI was proposed in 2013, more project contracts have been signed by CHMC with relevant Cambodian counterparts. Some contracts are follow-up projects of those already existing before the BRI. For example, the Cambodian Rural Power Grid Expansion Project (Phases II, III and IV) committed in 2014 and the Cambodian Rural Power Grid Expansion Project (Phases V and VI) committed in 2016 (Industrial Headlines, 2016). When completed, these projects will hopefully transmit electricity to each village of Cambodia.

Based on the existing power grids and bilateral power trading, Chinese investment may be positively engaged in and continue to facilitate grid connection within the GMS. Yet how the GMS multi-lateral power trading can bring more transmission lines and how Chinese investment can contribute to GMS electricity market integration remains to be seen. The reason is, under Scenario 2, the uncertain outlook for the GMS electricity market integration blurs the prospect of what and how lines will be built. With this said, how the Chinese companies can bring in more lines into this region is also unclear.

5.3. *BRI under Scenario 3*

In the third scenario, a competitive electricity market with a fully-developed APG is ASEAN's ambitious plan yet difficult to be realized in the near future. Under this scenario, the fully-established APG will require the establishment of power grid interconnection across Brunei, Indonesia, Malaysia, the Philippines and Singapore (BIMPS), which will consist of three synchronous grids given the geographical condition. They are the Western Malaysia–Singapore–Indonesia (Sumatra-Java), Eastern Malaysia–Brunei–Indonesia (Kalimantan), and the Philippines grids. Given archipelagic nature of this region, there will only be limited power exchange in the near future. Interconnections between these islands have not yet been established and the cross-border electricity trading in Eastern Malaysia, Indonesia and the Philippines will remain relatively small. It is expected that by 2050, 400/500 kV transmission lines as backbone grids would be constructed in each of the aforementioned countries. In Indonesia's Sumatra and Java Islands, the voltage level of the existing grid could be upgraded to 1,000 kV considering the land-saving and capacity issues (GEIDCO, 2018).

All these grids require huge investment. However, until now it seems that China is more interested in constructing and investing in the lines in continental Southeast Asia. The transmission projects undertaken by Chinese companies are nearly all in the GMS region and bilateral in nature. There is no evidence to suggest that China's BRI would strongly support ASEAN's ambition of region-wide APG or full power market integration. The archipelagic characteristics may hinder not only the integration of the entire ASEAN electricity market, but also the investment interests of Chinese companies. It seems that the BRI may not fit well with this scenario, which requires not only power grids interconnection within ASEAN but also third-party electricity flowing through power grids all around ASEAN.

6. Conclusion

Using the framework of scenario analysis, this study identifies three possible scenarios of electricity market integration in ASEAN. The first scenario is LTMS interconnection. This is probably a relatively easy start-up of the eventual ASEAN Power Grid. Given the difficulty of getting Singapore involved in the LTMS arrangement, it may be easier to have the "LTM" in place first. The second scenario is the interconnection of several heterogeneous power grids and markets. This is the most likely scenario to be achieved after the LTMS or the "LTM" power trading is realized. Such a scenario will possibly take place in the GMS region, which has already had power trading on bilateral basis across countries in this region. The third scenario would be a competitive electricity market with a fully-developed APG, which requires high-level cooperation and trust among ASEAN countries. Under such a scenario, all electricity utilities will have unrestricted and non-discriminatory grid access to the ASEAN electricity market.

This study examines how China's Belt and Road Initiative can facilitate electricity market integration under each scenario. It is found that Chinese companies can be most helpful under the first scenario and Chinese investments may bring new sources of funding and technology to facilitate the electricity market integration in the LTMS, or LTM countries, with more power plants built and more high voltage and ultra-high voltage power grids constructed and connected. Under the second scenario, given the existing power plants and power grids that they have built, Chinese companies can still be helpful in facilitating the interconnection of several heterogeneous grids in the GMS region. However, given the indistinctness of the progress of GMS electricity market integration, it remains to be seen that to what extent the Chinese investment can help electricity market integration in the region. Compared to the contribution the Chinese companies can do under the first scenario, their contribution is not quite clear under the second one. Under the third scenario, Chinese investment may play a less important role, because it seems that Chinese investment in ASEAN's power transmission is concentrated in the continental Southeast Asian region.

Further, given the characteristics of archipelago of maritime Southeast Asia, it is projected that there will only be limited power exchange in the near future. This may also deter Chinese companies from entering into this region. The third scenario is the most difficult arrangement for ASEAN to achieve and the least possible situation for BRI to play a role. Despite the difficulty, however, it is still possible for China to engage in the third scenario and facilitate the realization of APG. Yet this needs ASEAN as a whole to take collective action to make maritime Southeast Asia a region attractive to power sector investors. In any sense, how China's BRI can play a role in the ASEAN electricity market integration depends more on the host countries and on ASEAN rather than on the Chinese side. Against the BRI background, the ability for ASEAN countries to manage investments to finance high profile projects has become increasingly crucial. At present, ASEAN countries have tended to engage China on a bilateral level. In the future, ASEAN governments can collectively play a bigger role in attracting high quality projects from China. With a proactive approach, ASEAN countries can make the BRI a truly multilateral and sustainable initiative that promotes win–win cooperation, which can lead to a sustainable partnership between ASEAN and China. ASEAN and its member states should have their own plans as to how to make best use of China's BRI to encourage it to contribute to the region's electricity sector and electricity market integration.

References

ACE (2017b). *ASEAN Energy Cooperation Report 2017.* Jakarta: ASEAN Centre for Energy.

ACE (2017a). ASEAN Power Grid. *ASEAN Centre for Energy.* http://www.aseanenergy.org/programme-area/apg/ [accessed 18 April, 2018].

ADB (2009). *Building a Sustainable Energy Future: The Greater Mekong Subregion.* Manila: Asian Development Bank.

ADB (2018). *The Ha Noi Action Plan 2018–2022.* Manila: Asian Development Bank.

Amer, M, TU Daim and A Jetter (2013). A review of scenario planning. *Futures*, 46, 23–40.

Andrews-Speed, P (2011). *Energy Market Integration in East Asia: A Regional Public Goods Approach*, ERIA Discussion Paper Series. Jakarta: Economic Research Institute for ASEAN and East Asia.

Andrews-Speed, P (2016). Energy security and energy connectivity in the context of ASEAN energy market integration. *Energy Security and Connectivity: The Nordic and European Union Approaches.* Singapore: Energy Studies Institute, National University of Singapore, February.

Andrews-Speed, P and A Hezri (2013). Institutional and governance dimensions of AEMI. In *ASEAN Energy Market Integration (AEMI): From Coordination to Integration*, by AEMI Group (eds.), pp. 149–173. Bangkok: ASEAN Studies Center, Chulalongkorn University.

Andrews-Speed, P and C Len (2013). The political economy of AEMI. In *ASEAN Energy Market Integration (AEMI): From Coordination to Integration*, by AEMI Group (eds.), pp. 197–214. Bangkok: ASEAN Studies Center, Chulalongkorn University.

Antikainen, J, R Gebert and U Moller (2011). Review of the Greater Mekong SubRegion Regional Power Trade. Stockholm.

APAEC (2004). ASEAN Plan of Actions for Energy Cooperation 2004–2009. https://www.asean.org/wp-content/uploads/images/archive/pdf/APAEC0409.pdf.

Bhattacharyay, BN (2009). *Infrastructure Development for ASEAN Economic Integration.* ADBI Working Paper 138, Asian Development Bank Institute, Tokyo.

BMI Research (2017). BMI Research: Malaysia in world's top three for renewable energy investment. http://bradmanrecruitment.com/bmi-research-malaysia-worlds-top-three-renewable-energy-investment/.

Bredesen, H-A and T Nilsen (2013). *Power to the People: The First 20 Years of Nordic Power-Market Integration.* Oslo: Nord Pool Spot/Nasdaq OMX.

Chia, J and M Ten (2015). Sarawak needs more investments from China. http://www.theborneopost.com/2015/12/03/sarawak-needs-more-investments-from-china/.

Chun, S (2009). EdC signs electricity line deal with China. *The Phnom Penh Post.* September 4. http://www.phnompenhpost.com/business/edc-signs-electricity-line-deal-china [accessed June 8, 2017].

Finenko, A, AD Owen and J Tao (2017). Power interconnection in the ASEAN region: Lessons learnt from international experience. *ESI Policy Brief.* Singapore: Energy Studies Institute, March 10.

Fontela, E and A Hingel (1993). Scenarios on economic and social cohesion in Europe. *Futures*, 25, 139–154.

GEIDCO (2018). *Research Report of Southeast Asian Energy Interconnection Planning.* Beijing: Global Energy Interconnection Development and Cooperation Organization.

Georgoff, DM and RG Murdick (1986). Manager's guide to forecasting. *Harvard Business Review*, 110–120.

Halawa, E, G James, X Shi, N Sari and R Nepal (2018). The prospect for an Australian–Asian power grid: A critical appraisal. Energies. https://doi.org/10.3390/en11010200.

Hart, M (2018). Myanmar's ethnic conflicts have multiple fronts, and high barriers to peace. *World Politics Review.* 24 May. https://www.worldpoliticsreview.com/articles/24782/myanmar-s-ethnic-conflicts-have-multiple-fronts-and-high-barriers-to-peace [accessed 19 June, 2019].

Heijden, K (2005). *Scenarios: The Art of Strategic Conversation*, 2nd edn. Chichester, England: Wiley.

Huss, WR (1988). A move toward scenario analysis. *International Journal of Forecasting*, 4, 377–388.

IEA (2015). *Southeast Asia Energy Outlook 2015.* World Energy Outlook Special Report, Paris: OECD/IEA.

IEA (2017). *Southeast Asia Energy Outlook 2017.* World Energy Outlook Special Report, Paris: OECD/IEA.

Industrial Headlines (2016). President Xi and the Prime Minister Hun Sen are all concerned the Cambodian project (in Chinese). *Industrial Headlines (Gongye Toutiao).* October 19. http://www.gongyetoutiao.com/xw/html/5526.shtml [accessed June 8, 2017].

IRENA (2017). *Renewable Energy Outlook — Thailand.* https://www.irena.org/-/media/Files/IRENA/Agency/Publication/2017/Nov/IRENA_Outlook_Thailand_2017.pdf.

Joergensen, BH (2016). Asean energy market integration (AEMI) Energy Security and Connectivity: The Nordic and European Union Approaches. ASEAN Studies Centre, ESI, NIAA.
Jones, L (2016). Explaining the failure of the ASEAN economic community: The primacy of domestic political economy. *The Pacific Review*, 29, 647–670.
Kumar, PP (2015). Malaysia: ASEAN power grid needed to develop region. *Anadolu Agency*, 5 October. https://aa.com.tr/en/economy/malaysia-asean-power-grid-needed-to-develop-region/431995 [accessed 13 April, 2018].
Kunmakara, M (2014). China power plant open. *The Phnom Penh Post.* August 15. http://www.phnompenhpost.com/business/china-power-plant-open [accessed June 8, 2017].
Li, Y, X Shi and B Su (2017). Economic, social and environmental impacts of fuel subsidies: A revisit of Malaysia. *Energy Policy.* https://doi.org/10.1016/j.enpol.2017.08.015.
Lu, G (2016). China seeks to improve Mekong Sub-Regional Cooperation: Causes and Policies. Policy Report, S. Rajaratnam School of International Studies, Singapore.
Martino, JP (2003). A review of selected recent advances in technological forecasting. *Technological Forecasting and Social Change*, 70, 719–733.
Mietzner, D and G Reger (2005). Advantages and disadvantages of scenario approaches for strategic foresight. *International Journal of Technology Intelligence and Planning*, 1, 220–239.
OECD/IEA (2017). *Southeast Asia Energy Outlook 2017.* Paris: OECD/IEA.
Olchondra, RT (2016). NGCP aligns plan with Asean power interconnection vision. *Philippine Daily Inquirer.* 4 March. http://technology.inquirer.net/47042/ngcp-aligns-plan-with-asean-power-interconnection-vision [accessed 13 April, 2018].
Phomnuny, P (2017). Laos expects to have 100 hydropower plants by 2020. *Lao News Agency.* 6 July. http://kpl.gov.la/En/Detail.aspx?id=25944 [accessed 26 April, 2018].
Pim, LH (2017). *Borneo Online.* http://www.theborneopost.com/2016/03/25/chinese-firm-invests-rm1-bln-in-sama-jaya/.
Porter, AL, SW Cunningham, J Banks, T Roper, TW Mason and FA Rossini (2011). *Forecasting and Management of Technology*, 2nd edn. New York: Wiley.
Sahid, EJM, IM Aishah, YP Leong and X Shi (2013). Rationale for AEMI. *ASEAN Energy Market Integration (AEMI) Initiative*. September. http://www.asean-aemi.org/aemi-working-papers/ [accessed 19 April, 2018].
Sharma, D (2005). Electricity reforms in the ASEAN: A panoramic discourse. *Economic and Political Weekly*, 40(50), 5318–5326.
Shi, X (2014). ASEAN power grid, trans-ASEAN Gas pipeline and ASEAN economic community: Vision, plan and the reality. *Global Review*, 3, 116–131.
Shi, X (2016). The future of ASEAN energy mix: A SWOT analysis. *Renewable & Sustainable Energy Review*, 53, 672–680. https://doi.org/10.1016/j.rser.2015.09.010.
Shi, X and F Kimura (2010). Energy market integration in the East Asia Summit region: Review of initiatives and estimation of benefits. *ERIA Research Project Report*, No. 13.
Shi, X and F Kimura (2013). The status and prospects of energy market integration in East Asia. In *Energy Market Integration in East Asia: Deepen Understanding and Move Forward*, Y Wu and F Kimura (eds.), pp. 9–24. London: Rutledge.
Shi, X and C Malik (2013). *Assessment of ASEAN Energy Cooperation within the ASEAN Economic Community.* ERIA Discussion Paper Series, Economic Research Institute for ASEAN and East Asia, Jakarta.
Silitonga, RJP (2018). Trading renewable energy through the ASEAN power grid. *ASEAN Centre for Energy.* August 7. http://www.aseanenergy.org/blog/trading-renewable-energy-through-the-asean-power-grid/ [accessed December 17, 2018].
Timperley, J (2018). China leading on world's clean energy investment, says report. *EcoWatch.* January 10. https://www.ecowatch.com/china-clean-energy-investment-2524206487.html [accessed July 4, 2018].

van Notten, PWF, J Rotmans, MBA van Asselt and DS Rothman (2003). An updated scenario typology. *Futures*, 35(5), 423–443.

Varum, CA and C Melo (2010). Directions in scenario planning literature — A review of the past decades. *Futures*, 42(4), 355–369.

Vecchiato, R and C Roveda (2010). Strategic foresight in corporate organizations: Handling the effect and response uncertainty of technology and social drivers of change. *Technological Forecasting and Social Change*, 77(9), 1527–1539.

Wu, Y, F Kimura and X Shi (2014). Energy market integration in East Asia: Deepening understanding and moving forward. Routledge, London.

Wu, Y, X Shi and F Kimura (2012). Energy market integration in East Asia: Theories, electricity sector and subsidies. ERIA Res. Proj. Rep. 2011, No. 17.

Xinhuanet (2015). Laos' northern 230 KV power grid put into operation. *Xinhuanet*. November 30. http://www.xinhuanet.com/english/2015-11/30/c_134866617.htm [accessed January 23, 2018].

Zhang, J and D Zha (2014). Promoting energy market integration between China and the Association of Southeast Asian Nations through trade facilitation. In *Energy Market Integration in East Asia: Deepening Understanding and Moving Forward*, Y Wu, F Kimura and X Shi (eds.), pp. 76–98. Oxon: Routledge and Economic Research Institute for ASEAN and East Asia.

Chapter 6

CHINA'S OUTBOUND INVESTMENT IN ASEAN ECONOMIES IN THREE PERIODS: CHANGING PATTERNS AND TRENDS*

YEE-SIONG TONG

Institute for Manufacturing Education and Consultancy Services (IfM ECS)
Department of Engineering, University of Cambridge
Alan Reece Building, 17 Charles Babbage Rd
Cambridge CB3 0FS, UK
yst26@cam.ac.uk; yst26@cantab.net

Published Online 9 July 2020

Southeast Asian economic sentiments toward China tend to dither between competitive and cooperative instincts. Initial warmth among the Association of Southeast Asian Nations (ASEAN) members toward the China-led Belt and Road Initiative (BRI) is slowly giving way to project-related concerns as well as fears that "China is buying the world". This paper examines Chinese outward foreign direct investment (OFDI) in global and ASEAN contexts shortly after the start of the country's "going out" strategy. The analysis draws on country- and firm-level investment data. It shows that a handful of ASEAN economies have become more important to Chinese investors as their motivations, capabilities and needs evolve. Nonetheless, with the exception of three (Cambodia, Laos and Myanmar), ASEAN economies have not become "reliant" on Chinese investment post-BRI launch, once one considers the increased weight China carries as a foreign investor in the developing world. This is either because these countries generally do not rely on FDI, or because traditional foreign investors from industrialized economies and more advanced ASEAN member states are far more entrenched than Chinese investors in the host economies.

Keywords: Foreign direct investment; Belt and Road Initiative; regional integration; China; Southeast Asia.

JEL Classification: F21, F23, F50

1. Introduction

The rise of China is the singular unfolding phenomenon with deep implications for the global economy. China surpassed the US to become the world's largest economy in international dollar or purchasing power parity terms since 2014, and overtook Japan as the world's second largest economy in current US dollar terms since 2010 (World Bank, 2019). As China opens to the global economy, it has become an important international actor. Southeast Asian countries view China both as a promising opportunity and a potential threat. On the one hand, with a population of 1.4 billion, China presents sizable market opportunities and has become an important partner in trade and investment. On the other

*This article originally appeared in *The Singapore Economic Review*, **66**(1), pp. 105–142 © 2021 World Scientific Publishing Company.

hand, its growing economic influence — seen against the backdrop of increased military presence in the South China Sea — is seen as cementing China's political "domination" of the rest.

China introduced a formal policy to encourage its firms to invest abroad, in anticipation of its accession to the World Trade Organization (WTO), to sustain economic reform and promote global industry champions. Outbound investment was meant to equip Chinese firms and their management with international experience so that they could compete better in domestic markets and, in time, take the competition to home markets of foreign competitors (Wang and Gao, 2018). The "going out" policy has since initiated a steady flow of outbound investment, accompanied by loans from Chinese policy banks, aid and other forms of development assistance, to mostly developing countries.

Across a number of Association of Southeast Asian Nations (ASEAN) economies,[1] emotive rumblings have surfaced more recently that Chinese investment has grown powerful and will overrun domestic economies and threaten sovereign rights. In Viet Nam, Prime Minister Nguyen Xuan Phuc pledged to "protect our own legitimate interests and sovereignty" amid enhanced economic ties with China (*Nikkei Asian Review*, 24 January 2019). A pending legislative enactment to create three special economic zones for foreign investors was deferred to after 2020, following large-scale anti-China protests nationwide that denounced the measure as "selling out the country to China" (*Asia Times*, 30 May 2019). Such views were not limited to the policymakers and general public. One Viet Namese academic argued that "Chinese FDI activities in Viet Nam generally tends to take advantage of the cheap Viet Namese labor, exploit mineral resources, pollute the environment, consume much energy, and increase the trade deficit" (Ha, 2019).

In Indonesia, Chinese foreign investment was associated with imports of Chinese workers and machinery. Reports circulating on social media claimed that millions of Chinese workers had flooded Indonesia. Those reports had since been discredited by official statistics on foreign labor, but the belief that Chinese investment displaced Indonesian unskilled labor persisted and led to hostile actions at times. In one incident in Sulawesi Island, a group of college students stopped vehicles suspected of ferrying illegal Chinese workers to Chinese-owned smelters, and handed the passengers to the authorities. Chinese investment was also featured as a prominent issue in the 2017 Jakarta gubernatorial election, ostensibly to fan anti-Chinese sentiments (the incumbent governor who sought reelection against two other candidates was of Chinese descent) (Reuters, 2017). Even in Malaysia which historically enjoyed close ties with China (Malaysia was the first Southeast Asian country to establish diplomatic relations with China, in 1974), the attitude toward Chinese investment has turned negative. In the run-up to the 14th general election of Malaysia in May 2018, the manifestos of the opposition coalition (which later won the

[1] Southeast Asia refers to the geographic region comprising 11 economies, according to the United Nations Statistics Division's Standard Country or Area Codes for Statistical Use (commonly referred to as the M49 standard). Analysis of Southeast Asia in this article does not include Timor Lester and covers the other 10: Brunei, Cambodia, Indonesia, Laos, Malaysia, Myanmar, Philippines, Singapore, Thailand and Viet Nam. Also, the use of the term "ASEAN" refers to the 10 economies as an aggregate statistical unit, not the regional intergovernmental organisation which counts all Southeast Asian economies except Timor Leste as its members.

polls and formed the government) contained a pledge to scrutinize Chinese investment if it came into power, hinting that the rights and interests of the country were under threat.[2] A 2017 survey of Malaysian companies' showed that half the respondents had "mixed perceptions" about Chinese investors, associating investment from Chinese firms with a "direct threat to local companies", "crowding out of domestic SMEs", "less employment", "reduced market share" and "a potential threat to national sovereignty" (Socio-Economic Research Centre, 2017).

While actions in Southeast Asian countries against Chinese investment appear sporadic thus far, left unchecked, myths that Chinese investment is flooding ASEAN economies to their detriment could take on a life of their own and lead to misguided perception and policy. This paper seeks to clarify the scale and scope of Chinese investment in ASEAN economies over time. It asks three inter-related questions. First, where does China stand in the global investment landscape in comparative perspectives with regard to the positions held by developed and developing countries? Second, on what basis can one determine whether ASEAN economies as a whole and individually have become "reliant" on Chinese investment and what explains the reliance or the lack thereof? Third, on what basis can one determine whether ASEAN economies as a whole and individually have become "important" as a destination for Chinese investment and if so, what explains the change?

The paper shows that China's historically weak international investment position has improved with increased outward investment, in line with the trends among developing countries (especially those from East and Southeast Asia). It further observes that many ASEAN economies have become ever more reliant on foreign investment, but they are far from being reliant on China as a source of foreign investment. Only Cambodia, Myanmar and Laos — three lower middle income Indo-China countries which joined ASEAN and which opened up their once centrally planned economies relatively late — can be considered as being reliant on Chinese FDI. Others rely more on FDI from ASEAN sources as well as the "Triad" which provide and receive most of global FDI: the US, the European Union and Japan. At the time, while a number of ASEAN economies generally assumed greater importance to Chinese investors, China's outbound investment remains largely concentrated in a handful of territories outside Southeast Asia. Section 2 outlines the extant literature and contextualizes China-ASEAN investments relations for the discussions that follow. Section 3 presents the main findings and discussions emerging from analysis of various investment data at the global, regional, country and firm levels. Section 4 offers some concluding remarks.

2. Contextualizing Investment Relations between China and ASEAN Economies

There are two views on how FDI affects the economic development of the host country (Moran, 1998; Peng, 2012). The benign view holds that in the case of a host country being

[2] In one interview with the media prior to the election, Dr Mahathir Mohamad, chairman of the then opposition coalition, said that "lots of people do not like Chinese investments. We are for Malaysians. We want to defend the rights of Malaysians. We do not want to sell chunks of this country to foreign companies who will develop whole towns." (*Bloomberg*, April 8, 2018). The coalition went on to win the election and Mahathir was appointed as the Prime Minister. Consequently, his statements towards foreign investors, including Chinese firms, became noticeably more measured.

mired in a vicious cycle of low productivity due to insufficient investment, FDI may complement local savings and such capital inflows can improve the host country's balance of payments. Furthermore, technological and managerial inputs as well as transfers and spillovers to local firms may cause the national production to shift outward. FDI creates direct employment when foreign investors employ individuals locally. The additional demand for labor should bid up the wages of workers, improving their income and quite possibly health and education throughout the society. FDI also creates indirect employment when local suppliers increase hiring and when better paid workers spend money locally resulting in more jobs. Thus, FDI should raise efficiency, expand output, and lead to greater economic and social development in the host country.

In contrast, the less than sanguine view on FDI centers on the possibility that multinational enterprises (MNEs) of extraordinary size and strength may drive domestic firms out of business, increase barriers to entry, and monopolize local markets in the industries in which MNEs operate. Another concern is associated with capital outflow when foreign investors make profits in host countries and repatriate such earnings to headquarters in home countries. Local affiliates of MNEs may also spend a lot of money importing components and services abroad, which also results in capital outflow. Through the use of new, capital-intensive technologies that have higher skill, technical and organizational demands, FDI may produce a small labor elite and a small oligarchy of indigenous partners, generating an unfavorable impact on income distribution and social development (Moran, 1998). MNEs' tight control over technology, higher management functions, and export channels may also prevent the beneficial spillovers and externalities hoped for in the more sanguine scenarios. The production of MNEs is more footloose and can be moved across national borders more easily than that of domestic firms. The presence of FDI in the host economy thus tends to increase the volatility of the local economy. Importantly, there are concerns over the loss of some (though not all) economic sovereignty and national autonomy in which the state loses some of its authority and power in decision-making out of considerations to attract and retain foreign investment. Thus, reliance on FDI stunts development of indigenous firms, increases risks of economic shocks, and harms economic and social development in the long run.

The debates on the impact of FDI on growth and development are not fully resolved; more recent empirical work has cast some doubt on the early findings (see, for example, Balasubramanyam *et al.*, 1996; de Mello, 1997; Carkovic and Levine, 2002). Notwithstanding this, developing-country governments became considerably more receptive to MNEs and acclaimed FDI as good news since the 1980s. The change in their attitudes partly reflected the triumph of neoliberal economic ideology and the resort to neoliberal economic policies by most governments (O'Brien and Williams, 2016). But it also signaled the rise of a more pragmatic approach which viewed FDI as having both pros and cons, and which only approved FDI when its benefits outweighed costs. Governments recognized that technology and other intangible assets were becoming more mobile across national boundaries but were also increasingly housed within MNE systems. The successful industrialization of a number of East Asian countries — which shifted toward a blend of export orientation and FDI attraction — validated arguments that the impact of FDI was likely to vary depending on the local context, and that FDI presence in the economy could contribute positively to development when accompanied by suitable government policies (Lall and Narula, 2004). Furthermore, countries learnt that there were ways to regulate the behavior of FDI to ensure it promotes their social and economic goals.

Since 1997, ASEAN economies have been among the most active FDI reformers. They significantly liberalized their investment regimes and moved toward those observed in more advanced economies (OECD, 2018). As ASEAN economies compete intensely for FDI coming into the region, it seems rather puzzling that some begin to question the desirability of Chinese investment. If the criticisms did not single out FDI of a particular nationality (which was not the case), one could argue that they showed concerns about the negative impact of FDI at large to the host economy. Alternatively, one could make an argument against Chinese investment, based on a novel strand of work which suggests that the nationality of foreign investors matters for the developmental impact of FDI due to different technology endowments of firms across source (Havranek and Irsova, 2011).[3] Yet, no FDI from developing countries has attracted the same levels of public disapproval and attention as Chinese investment has, despite that the major foreign investors in a number of ASEAN economies include other ASEAN economies — all of which are developing countries. It thus seems plausible that the stance against Chinese investment extends behind the rise of nationalism and reflects at least in part two important factors: (i) the heightened perceptions of threat in what the historically fluid economic dynamics between China and ASEAN economies, and (ii) increased international discourse that has been highly alarmist in tone about Chinese investment.

Viewed through the prisms of trade and investment, ASEAN economies' attitudes toward China are dynamic and continuous, instead of static and dichotomous. Their attitudes tend to oscillate across a spectrum of competitive and complementary/cooperative stances. These dynamic and continuous shifts in part extend from endogenous differences as well as historical and geographical contexts of their relations with China.[4] For example, the mainland states have been historically more anxious of China compared to maritime states due to geographic proximity (Goh, 2007). Viet Nam's policy toward China has changed several times in the past decades as a result of altering conditions and the legacy of nearly 2,000 years of Chinese domination on the Viet Namese psyche (Storey, 2011).

Shifts in ASEAN economies' position on China also reflect changes in the prevailing circumstances. In the aftermath of the 1997–1998 Asian financial crisis, amid currency devaluation and economic recession in Southeast Asia, China won itself much goodwill in

[3] One view emerging from this strand of work suggests that investment originating from and going to developing countries (South-South FDI) may be less beneficial for spillovers than investment flowing from industrialized to developing countries (North-South FDI) because developing-country firms tend to be in more labor-intensive industries with less advanced technology (see, e.g., Lin *et al.*, 2009; Du *et al.*, 2011). Others argue that the converse is true: South-South investments contribute more than North-South investments to productivity, especially in less dynamic and more labor-intensive sectors, presumably because the technology gaps are not so large that foreign technology cannot be absorbed by domestic firms in the host economy (see, e.g., Takii, 2011; Pfeiffer *et al.*, 2014).

[4] Notable endogenous differences include ASEAN economies' varied stages of economic and human development (in 2017, Singapore had the third highest gross national income per capita in the world while Myanmar's income level was marginally higher than that of Zimbabwe), and diverse political systems ranging from Communist and military rule to parliamentary and presidential democracies.

the region through some specific actions. The first was China's decision not to devalue the renminbi as a measure to boost its export competitiveness (Wang, 1999). The second was the country's support for the Chiang Mai Initiative, which started as a series of bilateral currency swap arrangements but has since evolved into a multilateral effort to protect the region against short-term liquidity problems.

New concerns soon arose that ASEAN economies would be dwarfed by China or "under sold" by China's comparative cost and size advantages as they compete to produce and supply goods to Western markets (Jarvis and Welch, 2011). This was subsequently disproved by a number of studies. Eichengreen *et al.* (2007) observe that ASEAN economies' exports to third markets were in fact crowded out by Chinese exports but these were mostly in consumer goods. The effect of Chinese growth was thus negative for low-income countries that exported mainly consumer goods, but positive for high-income countries that exported mainly capital goods due to China's growing appetite for imported machinery and equipment. Similarly, Ravenhill (2006) finds that while ASEAN economies lost market shares to China in specific key manufactured exports in finished goods, their growing trade with China possibly offset the losses that they suffered in the traditional markets. Recalibration of regional production networks of large MNEs led to dynamic economic complementarities between China and ASEAN economies. As a result, much of ASEAN manufactures trade with China was intra-industry in nature, with ASEAN economies supplying intermediate manufactured goods for assembly and processing in China into finished goods destined for industrialized countries' markets (Ravenhill, 2006).

These days, China is ASEAN's largest trading partner, accounting for 17% of the region's total merchandise trade in 2017. After the 2008–2009 global financial crisis, amid slowdown in trade, there were expectations that strong growth in intra-Asia trade will ease reliance of Asian exporters on the traditional markets. Yet, China's sustained ascent as a world economic power — while still being a developing country — complicated the nature of its relations with others. Not only did the Western nations grow suspicious of China's intentions and the impact of its rise on an international order of their design; developing countries as a global bloc also turned wary about the potential adverse effects arising from China's geopolitical and economic competition (Freeman, 2015). In Southeast Asia, the rise of China, which was previously celebrated as evidence of the emergence of the "Pacific century", has been met increasingly with trepidation about the implications for national economies and ways of life (Jarvis and Welch, 2011).

Conflicting instincts and sentiments were evident in the case of investment. A remarkable increase in China's receipts of FDI since the late 1990s occurred at a time when many Southeast Asian countries were experiencing a downturn in FDI inflows. This led to concerns that Southeast Asia would come off second best, with FDI heading toward the eastern seaboard of China at the expense of ASEAN economies (see, e.g., Wong and Chan, 2003). It was further suggested that increased FDI flows to China meant hollowing out of industries and job losses in ASEAN economies. However, there was no clear evidence that increased FDI flows to China resulted in relocation of manufacturing operations and unemployment in Southeast Asia (Ravenhill, 2006).

Since the mid-2000s, FDI flows into ASEAN economies (as a whole, not necessarily for every individual economy) recovered. Southeast Asia's position as a key destination for FDI strengthened when viewed in stock terms (see Section 3). Several econometric studies suggested that increased FDI flows into China actually had a positive effect on ASEAN's FDI receipts (Eichengreen and Tong, 2005; Zhou and Lall, 2005). At the same time, as China began to invest more actively abroad, the ASEAN region was well located to receive such flows. Initially, ASEAN economies' reactions to Chinese investment ranged from neutral and supportive. Such level of support and receptiveness continued well into the early 2010s. In fact, most ASEAN economies signed some form of agreements of cooperation with China soon after President Xi Jinping announced the Belt and Road Initiative (BRI) which targets infrastructure development in transport, energy, and information and communication technology across more than 60 countries in Asia, Europe and Africa.[5] Before long, the more positive reactions gave way to reservations and opposition in relation to Chinese investment in a number of countries, fuelled by project-specific concerns that such investment benefits Chinese enterprises at the expense of local economy and that it leads to other problems such as "debt trap diplomacy".

Importantly, the critical stance toward Chinese investment in a number of ASEAN economies came on the heels of increasingly unfavorable portrayals of Chinese investment in international publications and discourse. These portrayals arguably contributed to negative perceptions about Chinese investment in two mutually reinforcing ways. First, the scale and scope of China's outward FDI (OFDI) was said to be huge. For example, popular magazines have run eye-catching cover stories with headlines such as "China Goes Shopping" (*BusinessWeek*, 20 December 2004), "China Buys the World" (*Fortune*, 26 October 2009), and "Buying up the World: The Coming Wave of Chinese Takeovers" (*Economist*, 11 November 2010). This was despite that the high-income countries' stock of FDI in China was almost 20 times as large as China's FDI stock in the high-income countries. In other words, the Chinese economy had a huge presence of foreign firms from high-income economies but Chinese firms had a negligible presence in high-income economies ("I have you within me but you do not have me within you") (Nolan, 2012). Chinese firms had been conspicuously absent from major international mergers and acquisitions because these firms were entering the "global level playing field" at a point at which business power has never been more concentrated in the hands of powerful firms from high-income economies that occupy the commanding heights in almost every segment of global supply chains (Nolan, 2012). Furthermore, the efforts of Chinese large firms to acquire businesses in the high-income countries mostly ended in failure due to an increasingly hostile international political environment.

In addition to the purportedly huge scale and scope, Chinese investment may serve as a channel through which Chinese regime is exported to threaten international norms and rules. For some, such "threats" are real and possible because China has purportedly achieved hypergrowth by unfairly manipulating markets at other countries' expense. In addition, many Chinese MNEs are state-owned enterprises which "emerged and grew in a

[5] All ASEAN countries are considered BRI economies by China, given their adjacency to the Maritime Silk Road from Fuzhou, China to Venice, Italy, which goes through South China Sea and the Malacca Strait.

markedly different economic and political system (that is) characterized by state capitalism, wide-ranging industrial policies and strong government intervention. The political system in China is authoritarian and dominated by the Communist Party of China" (Knoerich and Miedtank, 2018). Through various legal measures and institutional frameworks, Chinese MNEs cultivate strong links to the Chinese government or may even be ultimately owned by the state. Their investment approaches are thus not only driven by profits but also other considerations that have economic, political and security implications for the host economies. Meunier (2019) argues that China is not a security ally (though not an enemy) of the US and European countries, and has avowed geopolitical ambitions and foreign policy goals that are at odds with those of the Western countries. Technology acquired by Chinese FDI in the West could make it way in the hands of countries that are on friendly terms with China but are considered rogue states in the West. Furthermore, China could potentially use its ownership of foreign assets as political leverage to pressure host-country governments into falling in line on issues that are important to the Chinese government. However, others note that the rise of China has not been about rewriting the global economic order but tying itself to foreign rules and rule-making authorities. As one scholar puts it:

> The bottom line is that China today is growing not by writing its own rules but instead by internalizing the rules of the advanced industrial West. It has grown not by conjuring up its own unique political economic institutions but instead by increasingly harmonizing with our own. In essence, China today — a country at the peak of its modernization revolution — is doing something it historically never really did before. It is playing our game (Steinfeld, 2010).

The three questions outlined at the beginning of this paper aim to contribute to a better understanding of the scale and scope of Chinese investment specifically in ASEAN economies, which is little understood and discussed. The questions are addressed primarily through analysis of: (i) data published by China's Ministry of Commerce (MOFCOM) in its annual publication *The Statistical Bulletin of China's Outward Foreign Direct Investment*, (ii) foreign direct investment (FDI) data by the United Nations Conference on Trade and Development (UNCTAD) and (iii) a firm-level dataset on Chinese mergers and acquisitions in ASEAN economies. Since 2003, MOFCOM's annual publication of Chinese OFDI statistics has incorporated the definitions, statistical principles and methodology based on *OECD Benchmark Definition of Foreign Direct Investment (Third Edition)* and *IMF Balance of Payment Manual (First Edition)* — both of which formed the basis of international definitions and standards of FDI concepts and statistics (OECD, 2008; UNCTAD, 2009). To ensure accuracy and comparability of FDI statistics, the three periods considered in this paper span from 2004 to 2017.

3. Chinese Outbound Investment

3.1. *China in global investment landscape 1970–2017*

Notwithstanding intermittent periods of decline, FDI in both flows and stock terms has grown steadily over the years. In current price terms, between 1970 and 2017, on average

FDI flows increased by 13% per year from USD13.3 billion to USD1.5 trillion while FDI stock increased by 11% per year from USD 2.2 trillion to USD 32.6 trillion. The sources and destinations of FDI changed dramatically over the years (Table 1). In the immediate post-World War II period, global FDI mostly flowed from one developed economy to another. After the commodity-price boom in the 1970s, developing countries took up an increasing share of global FDI flows as large MNEs from developed economies invested heavily in the developing world to access the latter's consumer and factor markets for marketing and production purposes (Ramamurti, 2009). Growth in developing countries' share of global inward FDI flows was briefly interrupted by restrictive domestic policy stance toward foreign investment, but it soon resumed and continued well into the next three decades. For the 2010–2017 period, developing (including transition) countries received more than 50% of the cumulative global FDI flows — compared to 25% of the total in the 1970–1979 period. Just as developing countries received larger shares of global FDI, many of their firms also began to invest more actively abroad.[6] This was underpinned by rising internationalization of domestic firms, otherwise known as emerging multinational enterprises (EMNEs). For the 2010–2017 period, developing (including transition) countries contributed to more than 30% of cumulative global FDI flows, in contrast to a paltry 1% share in the 1970–1979 period.

China was a major laggard compared to other developing countries initially (China attracted almost no FDI when ASEAN economies accounted for 5% of global FDI flows). Its subsequent evolution from an economy with almost no foreign investors (through the 1970s and 1980s), to a key host economy to FDI (during the 1990s), and to a visible investing economy (since the 2000s) fits the broad trajectory shown by developing countries. What distinguished China from other developing countries was the astonishing pace at which it caught up as a recipient and sender of FDI globally. The change in China's international investment position captured one of the many aspects of the country's very rapid integration into the global economy. In particular, China's increased OFDI can be traced to the country's "inviting in, going out" (*qing jin lai, zou chuqu*) strategy, which was noted for its emphasis to encourage outward FDI early on instead of focusing only on attraction of inward FDI.

Early Chinese OFDI was driven by state-owned enterprises (SOEs); private firms were legally prohibited from investing abroad prior to 2003 (Buckley *et al.*, 2007a). This prompted debates over the applicability of the mainstream theories in explaining outward FDI from developing countries and, specifically, from China. There were two points of contention. The first was that developing-country including Chinese firms lacked ownership advantages (Moon and Roehl, 2001; Rugman, 2009). The general theory of FDI, as encapsulated in Dunning's eclectic paradigm (Dunning and Lundan, 2008), suggests that FDI occurs when firms of a particular nationality: (i) possess some firm-specific advantages (trademarks, production techniques, etc.) over firms of another nationality

[6] The progress made by developing countries as international investors was uneven. Countries in East and Southeast Asia (excluding Japan) and Latin America and the Caribbean made the strongest advances while others — Middle East and North Africa, Oceania (excluding Australia and New Zealand), South Asia and Sub-Saharan Africa — made modest gains.

Table 1. Shares of FDI Flows by Development Status and Region, 1970–2017 (%)

	As Recipient of FDI Flows (Inbound)					As Sender of FDI Flows (Outbound)				
Development Status/Region	1970–1979	1980–1989	1990–1999	2000–2009	2010–2017	1970–1979	1980–1989	1990–1999	2000–2009	2010–2017
World flows (current USD billions)	240	931	4,018	11,208	13,198	282	937	4,181	11,296	12,196
Developed	**75.0**	**77.6**	**69.0**	**62.6**	**49.7**	**98.9**	**93.8**	**89.0**	**81.6**	**64.5**
ANZ and Japan	5.7	4.7	2.6	2.7	3.2	6.5	18.2	6.7	5.5	8.3
Europe	42.8	32.8	41.6	40.7	26.9	43.6	52.1	58.4	54.0	32.0
North America	26.5	40.2	24.8	19.2	19.5	48.8	23.5	23.9	22.0	24.2
Developing	**25.0**	**22.4**	**30.0**	**33.5**	**46.6**	**1.1**	**6.2**	**10.7**	**16.4**	**32.3**
East and Southeast Asia	7.0	9.4	16.2	14.5	22.0	0.2	4.0	8.0	8.9	20.2
China	0.0	1.7	7.2	6.1	7.7	0.0	0.4	0.6	1.7	7.6
East Asia (Exc. China)	1.8	3.4	3.4	4.7	7.3	0.0	3.0	5.5	4.9	8.4
ASEAN	5.1	4.3	5.6	3.6	7.1	0.2	0.6	1.9	2.3	4.1
Latin America and the Caribbean	11.8	7.1	10.5	10.2	15.7	0.4	0.9	2.1	4.7	8.2
Middle East and North Africa	0.5	4.1	1.5	5.1	3.9	0.2	0.9	0.2	1.8	2.6
Oceania (Exc. ANZ)	0.3	0.2	0.1	0.1	0.1	0.0	0.0	0.0	0.0	0.1
South Asia	1.5	0.2	0.6	1.9	2.6	0.0	0.0	0.0	0.7	0.6
Sub-Saharan Africa	3.9	1.4	1.1	1.7	2.3	0.3	0.5	0.4	0.2	0.6
Transition (South-Eastern Europe and CIS)	**0.0**	**0.0**	**1.0**	**3.8**	**3.8**	**0.0**	**0.0**	**0.3**	**2.0**	**3.2**

Source: Calculations from UNCTAD.

(Ownership), (ii) decide to exploit these advantages outside of their national boundaries (Location) and (iii) perceive it to be in their interest to internalize the markets for the exploitation of such advantages (Internalization). The second was that Chinese OFDI was driven by government involvement; whereas the general theory, built on the experience of largely private-owned industrialized-country investors, posits that FDI is driven by economic considerations to minimize costs and maximize benefits (including profits), which can be broken down into motivations to seek resources, efficiency, strategic assets and markets.[7]

Chinese OFDI became less dominated by SOEs over time. In 2006, SOEs accounted for 81% of Chinese OFDI stock but the share decreased to 49% by 2017 (MOFCOM, 2017). Notwithstanding political objectives to strengthen China's position on the stage of world affairs, it was argued that Chinese OFDI was largely driven by and could be explained by FDI motivations in the literature (Shen and Mantzopoulos, 2013). Furthermore, a number of studies showed that developing-country including Chinese firms had special ownership advantages derived from their home country-embeddedness, which enabled them to exploit culturally-dependent relational assets and to operate in locations unattractive to developed-country firms, as well their abilities to customize particular technology and products appropriately for other developing-country markets (Erdener and Shapiro, 2005; Ramamurti, 2012).

As China increasingly invested more abroad, it progressively narrowed the gaps between its inward and outward flows. Historically, Chinese — and most developing countries — received more foreign investment than they invested abroad in a given year (in contrast to developed countries which invested more abroad than they received investment from outside their countries). This can be observed in a comparison of the ratio of outward to inward FDI flows. A ratio of more than 1 indicates that a country or region receives more foreign investment than it invests abroad and is considered a net investor in flows terms for a given period. Conversely, a ratio of lower than 1 indicates that a country or region invests more abroad than it receives foreign investment and is therefore a net recipient of foreign investment for a given period. Between 1970 and 2017, developed regions had a ratio of more than 1 and retained largely their position as net investors. Developing regions inched toward a balance in their flows (a ratio of 1), with East and Southeast Asia making the most progress (Panel A, Figure 1). Within East and Southeast Asia, East Asia in particular (led by Hong Kong, South Korea and Taiwan) has been a net investor since the 1980s. Both China and ASEAN economies remained net recipients of FDI. They improved their respective positions, the momentum of change accelerated in China but slowed in ASEAN economies as a whole since the 2000s (Panel B, Figure 1).

[7] Investor motivations as well as factor endowments and other conditions of host economies determine the choice of location for FDI. Resource-seeking refers to acquisition of physical resources (particularly natural resources) at lower comparative costs, or which do not exist in the home country. Efficiency-seeking refers to rationalization of production structures to gain from the differences of costs, culture, institutional arrangements and economic systems across locations. It usually involves the transfer of mature, labor-intensive activities to low-cost locations. Market-seeking investment is to supply products through a direct presence in specific markets abroad identified as important. Asset-seeking investment is for accessing intangible assets (e.g. brand equity, technology, patents, and distribution networks) to strengthen the investing firm's competitive position or to weaken that of its competitors.

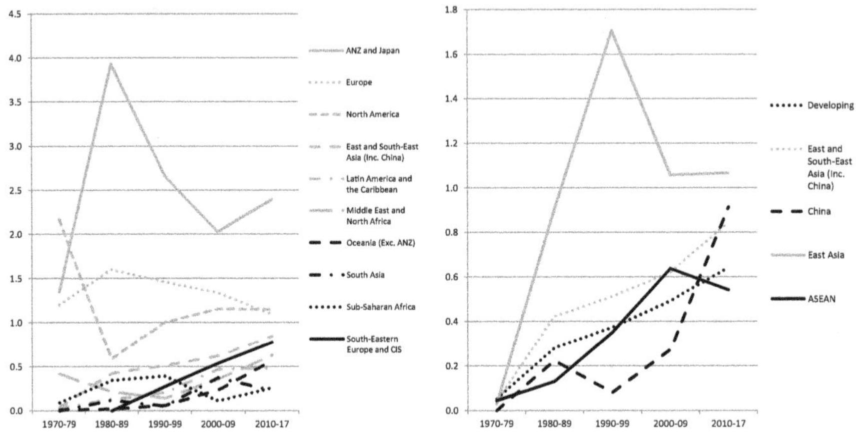

(a) World Regions

(b) Within East Southeast Asia

Source: Calculations from UNCTAD.

Figure 1. Ratio of Outward to Inward FDI Flows by Region, 1970–2017

Despite the progress shown by China, East and Southeast Asia, and the developing world at large as outward investors in flows terms, a more nuanced picture emerges when their FDI performance is considered in stock terms. FDI flows are records of capital transactions (in the form of equity capital injections, reinvested earnings or intra-company loans) made during a given period, typically a quarter or a year. In comparison, FDI stock captures cumulative foreign investment made in the past (at book value or historical price when the investment was made). Thus, stock more accurately depicts the actual investment position of an economy.

The deeply entrenched position of the developed world as a destination for global FDI is reflected by the fact that developed countries, home to 14% of the world's population, hosted 62% of global FDI stock in 2017 (compared to 76% in 1990) despite the purported rise of developing countries (Table 1). Developed countries also remain the dominant source of global FDI stock, contributing to 73% of the world total in 2017 (compared to 94% in 1990). In comparison, developing countries, home to 86% of the world's population in 2017, accounted for 38% of global inward FDI stock and 27% of outward stock. Within East and Southeast Asia, China's share of global inward FDI stock came third after East Asia (led by Hong Kong, South Korea and Taiwan) and ASEAN economies. China's share of global outward FDI stock was lower than that of East Asia but higher than that of ASEAN economies. To put it into perspective, China accounted for 4.6% of global outward FDI stock — which was not an insignificant share — and was the eighth largest investor after, among others, the US (24% of global outward stock); Germany, Netherlands and the UK (15% in total), Japan (4.8%) and Canada (4.7%).

Table 2. Shares of FDI Stock by Development Status and Region, 1990–2017 (%)

	As Host of FDI Stock (Inbound)				As Holder of FDI Stock (Outbound)			
Development Status/Region	1990	2000	2010	2017	1990	2000	2010	2017
World stock (current USD billions)	2,199	7,442	20,717	32,601	2,256	7,502	21,457	31,963
Developed	**76.4**	**77.4**	**64.8**	**62.0**	**93.6**	**89.2**	**81.5**	**73.2**
ANZ and Japan	4.5	2.6	3.9	2.9	10.8	5.1	6.0	6.3
Europe	42.3	33.0	39.6	31.8	46.7	42.3	48.4	37.9
North America	29.7	41.8	21.3	27.3	36.2	41.8	27.1	29.1
Developing	**23.5**	**21.9**	**32.0**	**35.5**	**6.3**	**10.6**	**16.8**	**25.4**
East and Southeast Asia	13.7	12.8	14.6	18.4	2.6	7.7	10.3	16.2
China	0.9	2.6	2.8	4.6	0.2	0.4	1.5	4.6
East Asia (Exc. China)	10.0	6.7	6.2	7.2	2.0	6.2	6.0	7.8
ASEAN	2.8	3.5	5.5	6.6	0.4	1.1	2.8	3.8
Latin America and the Caribbean	5.0	5.4	10.0	10.0	2.4	1.9	4.3	6.1
Middle East and North Africa	2.7	1.8	4.1	3.6	0.5	0.4	1.2	1.6
Oceania (Exc. ANZ)	0.1	0.0	0.1	0.1	0.0	0.0	0.0	0.0
South Asia	0.3	0.4	1.3	1.6	0.0	0.0	0.5	0.5
Sub-Saharan Africa	1.6	1.4	1.9	1.8	0.9	0.5	0.5	1.0
Transition (South-Eastern Europe and CIS)	**0.1**	**0.7**	**3.3**	**2.6**	**0.0**	**0.3**	**1.7**	**1.4**

Source: Calculations from UNCTAD. 1990 is chosen as the first year due to data availability and quality considerations

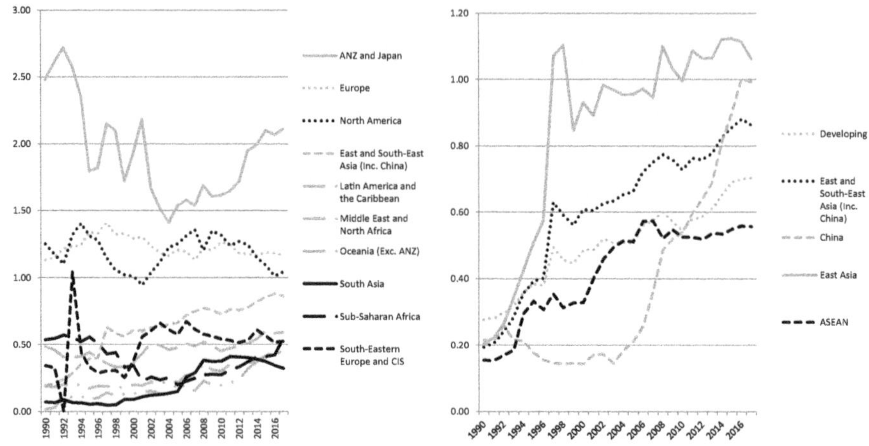

(a) World Regions

(b) Within East Southeast Asia

Source: Calculations from UNCTAD. 1990 is chosen as the first year due to data availability and quality considerations.

Figure 2. Ratio of Outward to Inward FDI Stock by Region, 1970–2017

Furthermore, developing countries continue to hold less FDI stock abroad than foreign economies' investment holdings in them. The reverse is true for developed regions, which hold more FDI stock in foreign economies than foreign economies own investment stock in them (Panel A, Figure 2). This can be observed through the ratio of outward to inward FDI stock. A ratio of more than 1 indicates that the economy has positive net FDI stock while a ratio of lower than 1 indicates that the economy has negative FDI stock. This is not without implications. From the international investment position perspective, an economy's FDI stock abroad is an asset to the economy because its resident direct investors have claims on foreign-based affiliated enterprises. Conversely, the FDI stock hosted by an economy is considered its liability because foreign-based direct investors have claims on locally-based affiliated enterprises. In other words, since 1990, developed regions have had more assets than liabilities for most if not all years while developing regions have had liabilities in excess of assets. Among the developing regions, East and Southeast Asia improved its international investment position the most. Within East and Southeast Asia, China made impressive gains in narrowing its gap to its East Asian counterparts and achieved an almost balanced net FDI stock position by 2017 (Panel B, Figure 2).

3.2. *Chinese OFDI in Southeast Asia 2004–2017*

China's OFDI development in ASEAN since 2004 can be divided into three broad periods. The "high growth period" from 2004 to 2008 was characterized by weak initial OFDI position, at a time when the Chinese economy expanded at a breakneck pace of 11.6% on average per year. During this period, China's OFDI flows grew by an average of 65.6% per year. China entered into the "post-crisis period" from 2009 to 2013. China's GDP growth slowed to 9.0% as its exports were affected by collapsed consumer demand in key developed economies in the aftermath of the global financial crisis. China had by now been building its OFDI stock to almost 5% of its GDP. The average annual growth rates in China's OFDI flows declined substantially to 16.1%, in tandem with slowing GDP growth. In the BRI period starting 2014 (a year after the initiative was launched), growth rates in China's GDP further decelerated to an average of 6.9% per year up to 2017, while its OFDI flows increased by an average of 8.4% annually. In the process, outbound investment became important to the Chinese economy. In 2004, China had an OFDI stock worth USD45 billion or 2.5% of its GDP in current prices. By 2017, China's OFDI stock grew to USD1.9 trillion or 12.3% of its GDP. ASEAN economies were more positive toward Chinese OFDI in the first and second periods, but the sentiments turned more negative in the third period (see Section 2).

Since China published its OFDI data in a format that is consistent with the OECD and IMF standards for the first time in 2003, it became increasingly visible as a foreign investor on the world stage. The country's share of world OFDI flows increased from less than 2% in the high growth period to almost 10% in the BRI period. Between 2004 and 2017, China's contribution to world OFDI stock increased from less than 1% to almost 6%. In 2004, China ranked 27th in the world by the value of its yearly OFDI flows (about USD6 billion). By 2017, it was the world's third largest economy in outward investment flows terms — after the US and Japan — with OFDI flows totaling USD124 billion that year. In stock terms, China accounted for some 13% of the FDI stock in developing countries in 2017, compared to less than 2% in 2004.

The increased prominence of China's outbound investment in ASEAN needs to be seen within the larger context of a rapidly growing *large* developing economy that attempts to tackle its weak initial international investment position, amid closer integration with its regional neighbors that have been historically *FDI-reliant*. Given the context, Chinese investment, with its increased weight in the global FDI scene, is bound to play a greater role in ASEAN's FDI scene. Put differently, if Chinese investment became a more important source of FDI globally but not as a more important of FDI for Southeast Asia, it would mean the latter fell behind in global competition for FDI (unless it attracted more investment from other, non-Chinese sources).

The total FDI flows and stock of developing and transition countries as a share of their total current GDP for a given period is used as a benchmark against which ASEAN as a whole or an ASEAN country is judged (Table 3). Tellingly, ASEAN has relied on foreign investment far more than the developing world as a whole in all three periods under consideration. For example, in the 2014–2017 period, inward FDI flows represented 4.6% of ASEAN total current GDP. In comparison, inward FDI flows represented 3.5% of developing countries' current GDP. In inward flows terms, ASEAN as a whole has become increasingly reliant on FDI over three periods, just as the world as well as developing countries as a whole relied less on FDI. ASEAN's reliance on FDI also holds in stock terms: the ratio of FDI stock hosted by ASEAN economies to the size of their economies was greater than what was observed for the developing countries as a whole, and the gap

Table 3. Inward FDI as a Share of GDP for ASEAN, 2004–2017 (%)

	Inward FDI Flows as % of Country Current GDP			Inward FDI Stock as % of Country Current GDP	
	2004–2008	2009–2013	2014–2017	2004	2017
World	2.5	2.2	2.2	24.3	40.6
Developing/transition countries (benchmark)	**3.5**	**2.9**	**2.6**	**25.2**	**36.0**
ASEAN	4.6	4.4	4.9	43.7	78.7
Brunei	2.5	3.9	1.0	21.0	48.4
Cambodia	7.2	12.5	11.6	39.2	93.7
Indonesia	1.6	1.9	1.8	5.8	24.5
Laos	4.0	3.4	6.1	25.3	39.2
Malaysia	3.6	3.2	3.4	34.5	44.4
Myanmar	2.7	3.5	4.2	62.1	41.1
Philippines	1.5	0.9	2.2	13.9	25.1
Singapore	17.3	18.0	22.7	189.1	413.9
Thailand	3.4	2.5	1.2	31.2	48.7
Viet Nam	6.4	5.9	5.9	41.4	57.9

Source: Calculations from UNCTAD and MOFCOM. Light grey cells denote higher reliance on FDI than what is observed for developing countries as a whole.

continued to widen as ASEAN's level of reliance on FDI increased much faster that of the developing world. With Southeast Asia, with the exception of Indonesia and the Philippines, all countries were reliant on FDI (in the sense that FDI *stock* as a share of economic output was higher than what was observed for all developing countries for a given year).

Reliance on FDI partly reflects history. Much of Southeast Asia has been a key destination for foreign investment since colonial days. Major MNEs such as Coca-Cola, General Electric, Citibank and Unilever invested and operated in the region since long before the establishment of modern-day ASEAN states. Reliance on FDI also reflects industrial policy post-independence which did not pursue autonomous strategies (as was the case with South Korea and Taiwan) and which leaned more toward FDI-assisted development. Among these countries, some relied on FDI in a more active manner — Singapore for example used a more targeted approach to screen and direct FDI into high value-added activities, and focused on development of the relevant skills, capabilities and institutions to ensure continuous transfers of new technologies and functions by MNEs. Others including Malaysia practiced more passive reliance on FDI, in that their aim was FDI attraction using factors such as low wages for unskilled and semi-skilled labor, good infrastructure, a conducive macroenvironment, and incentives. They had little post-FDI strategy to induce capability development and upgrading from simple to more advanced activities (Lall, 1996). Other drivers of FDI growth in ASEAN include economic considerations (the afore-mentioned investor motivations), geopolitical considerations and proximity. After the yen appreciated following the Plaza Accord, Japan shifted labor-intensive activities (such as assembly for re-exports) to Southeast Asia. This cemented Japan's position as a key foreign investor within Southeast Asia, and increased the region's reliance on FDI (Thorbecke and Salike, 2011).

3.2.1. *Importance of Chinese FDI to ASEAN (or ASEAN reliance on Chinese FDI)*

Reliance on global FDI (first order) and reliance on Chinese FDI (second order) are two interrelated yet distinct aspects. There are three possibilities: being reliant on global FDI but not being reliant on Chinese FDI, being reliant on both global and Chinese FDI, and not being reliant on both global and Chinese FDI. It is logically impossible to have a region or a country reliant on Chinese FDI but not reliant on FDI in general, because Chinese FDI is a subset of global FDI. With China's increased importance as a foreign investor and ASEAN's continued reliance on FDI, the question is not whether ASEAN as a whole received more FDI flows from China in absolute values — it most definitely did. Rather, one needs to ask whether ASEAN relied more on Chinese FDI relative to other, non-Chinese FDI than what one would expect of developing countries. For this, the weight of Chinese investment in inward FDI of all developing countries is determined and used as a benchmark to which ASEAN as a whole or an ASEAN country is subsequently compared (Table 4). If the Chinese share of inward FDI in ASEAN or its constituent economy

Table 4. Share of China in Total Inward FDI of World, Developing Countries and ASEAN, 2004–2017 (%)

	China Weight in Inward FDI Flows			China Weight in Inward FDI Stock	
	High Growth Period	Post-crisis Period	BRI Period	2004	2017
World	1.9	5.7	9.8	0.4	5.7
Developing/transition countries (benchmark)	**4.1**	**8.6**	**15.5**	**1.6**	**12.8**
ASEAN	1.5	5.6	9.3	0.3	4.1
Brunei	0.3	1.6	39.3	0.0	3.6
Cambodia	11.4	28.9	24.9	4.3	26.2
Indonesia	1.3	5.2	9.0	0.8	4.2
Laos	40.0	172.2	84.7	2.4	100.0
Malaysia	0.2	2.6	10.9	0.3	3.5
Myanmar	16.3	30.3	12.5	0.3	19.9
Philippines	0.5	6.8	1.3	0.1	1.0
Singapore	1.6	4.0	8.3	0.1	3.5
Thailand	0.4	4.8	17.0	0.3	2.4
Viet Nam	1.4	3.6	6.2	0.8	3.8

Source: Calculations from UNCTAD and MOFCOM. Light grey cells denote higher reliance of ASEAN and its constituent economies on China FDI using the level of reliance on China FDI by developing countries as a benchmark (provided that the first order reliance (on global FDI) was established).

exceeds Chinese share of inward FDI in developing countries, China is clearly more important as a foreign investor in the region or economy than it is in developing countries. On this basis, it can be argued that ASEAN or the particular economy is "reliant" on Chinese FDI.

As said, China has become an increasingly important foreign investor at the global level and within the developing world. While China has also become more important as a source of foreign investment in ASEAN, it is difficult to argue that the region has become reliant on Chinese FDI. China's shares of FDI flows in developing countries in the three periods under consideration were 4.1%, 8.6% and 15.5%, respectively. By contrast, China's shares of FDI flows in ASEAN for the same periods (at 1.5%, 5.6% and 9.3%, respectively) were significantly lower than those observed for the developing world, and even marginally lower than China's shares of FDI flows at the global level. In stock terms, similar observations can be made that China was becoming a more important foreign investor in ASEAN, but nowhere near China's level of importance as a foreign investor in the developing world. China accounted for 4% of FDI stock in ASEAN in 2017, which meant 96% of the FDI stock in ASEAN was owned by countries other than China.

At the country-level in flows terms, four economies — Brunei, Cambodia, Laos and Thailand — can be categorized as reliant on Chinese FDI in the latest BRI period. Brunei and Thailand's reliance on Chinese FDI is less of an issue because the phenomenon seems more cyclical than structural (both countries were not reliant on Chinese FDI in the two preceding periods) and because, importantly, in stock terms they cannot be considered reliant on Chinese FDI (although they are reliant on FDI).

Once historical flow patterns and current stock patterns are taken into consideration, seven out of 10 ASEAN economies can be classified as either reliant on FDI but not reliant on Chinese FDI (Brunei, Malaysia, Singapore, Thailand and Viet Nam) or not reliant on FDI — Chinese or otherwise — at all (Indonesia and the Philippines). Only three ASEAN economies — Cambodia, Laos and Myanmar — can be considered reliant on FDI and, specifically, Chinese FDI. The situation of Laos was particularly worrisome as almost all of its inward FDI stock originated from one single source: China. The trio of Cambodia, Laos and Myanmar has been reliant on Chinese FDI flows since 2004–2008, even before China became a major outward investing economy. Geographical and political considerations played a part — all three Indo-China countries are close to the borders of China and have been courted to be China's allies. But economics also played a part. While these countries initiated market reforms in the late 1990s, the economies remained beset with obstacles for business and struggled to attract foreign investors. Being resource-rich and eager to improve their infrastructure, they nonetheless caught the interest of Chinese firms which were seeking natural resources including fuel and timber, and which were looking to invest in large-scale regional infrastructure (e.g., hydropower facilities in the Mekong River Basin).

Comparing flows between the 2004–2008 and 2014–2017 periods, Myanmar stood out as the only ASEAN country in which China became a less — not more important foreign investor. In other words, Myanmar became less reliant on Chinese investment in spite of Myanmar receiving more Chinese investment in absolute value. The reduced reliance on

Chinese investment was possible because Myanmar managed to diversify its FDI portfolio and attract more capital from sources other than China, following a series of political, economic and administrative reforms initiated in 2011 which sought to move the country toward liberal democracy and mixed economy.

The experience of Myanmar leads to a pertinent fact that a country's level of reliance on Chinese FDI is not contingent upon whether it receives more FDI flows from China per se. It also depends on whether the country can maintain and grow FDI flows from other sources. FDI performance of ASEAN economies has always been highly uneven given their disparate characteristics.[8] On the one hand, there is the highly FDI-reliant Singapore, which has consistently accounted for up to half (and more) of the foreign investment flowing into ASEAN, due to the island city-state's position as a hub for regional headquarters and offices by MNEs that use it as a gateway to penetrate emerging markets and to perform coordination functions that are geographically distant to be managed by the global headquarters (Yeung *et al.*, 2001). On the other hand, there is the resource-rich and moderately FDI-reliant Brunei, which accounts for a negligible share of FDI in ASEAN. All ASEAN economies received more FDI flows from China in absolute monetary value and as a share of total FDI coming to ASEAN (Table 5). For example, Chinese investment to Singapore accounted for 0.8% of total FDI flows into ASEAN in the 2004–2008 period, which further increased to 4.5% in the 2014–2017 period. During the same periods, FDI from other, non-Chinese sources to Singapore increased from 47.6% to 50.5% of total FDI flows into ASEAN, suggesting Singapore was becoming more attractive to the wider international investor community. As a result, China accounted for 8.3% of FDI flows into Singapore in the 2014–2017 period and the latter did not become reliant on Chinese FDI (using the level for developing countries as benchmark).

In fact, six out of 10 ASEAN economies successfully attracted more FDI flows from other, non-Chinese sources, judging by the change in non-Chinese FDI them received as a share of total FDI flows into ASEAN between the 2004–2008 and 2014–2017 periods. The four economies which bucked the trend were Brunei, Laos, Malaysia and Thailand. The collapse in non-Chinese FDI flows was particularly acute for Thailand, whose share of non-Chinese FDI flows into ASEAN decreased from 14.3% in the 2004–2008 period to 3.3% in the 2014–2017 period. This coincided with a tumultuous time in Thailand, which experienced continuous political unrest and violence since 2006 following a military-backed coup. Brunei demonstrated a similar trend in its receipt of FDI flows from sources other than China, likely due to a decline in foreign investment in its oil and gas sector amid softening commodity prices around 2015. Malaysia and Laos also received less FDI flows from sources other than China. This negatively affected their levels of reliance on Chinese FDI in flows terms in the 2014–2017 period. Brunei, Laos and Thailand were reliant on Chinese FDI. In the case of Malaysia, the weight of Chinese investment in its total inward

[8] Most studies suggest that demand characteristics such as host country GDP, GDP per capita and GDP growth have a significant positive impact on FDI inflows at large, and other economic variables related to infrastructure, production conditions, macroeconomic stability, institutions and investment incentives are also important (for surveys, see Blonigen, 2005; Faeth, 2009; Koepke, 2019).

Table 5. Distribution of ASEAN Inward FDI by Source and Destination, 2004–2017 (%)

		ASEAN Inward FDI Flows			ASEAN Inward FDI Stock	
Source	Destination	High Growth Period	Post-crisis Period	BRI Period	2004	2017
World	**ASEAN**	**100.00**	**100.00**	**100.00**	**100.00**	**100.00**
China	**ASEAN**	**1.52**	**5.60**	**9.34**	**0.26**	**4.12**
	Brunei	0.00	0.01	0.04	0.00	0.01
	Cambodia	0.11	0.49	0.44	0.02	0.25
	Indonesia	0.15	0.84	1.17	0.03	0.49
	Laos	0.11	0.54	0.62	0.00	0.31
	Malaysia	0.03	0.24	0.91	0.03	0.23
	Myanmar	0.13	0.57	0.28	0.01	0.26
	Philippines	0.02	0.14	0.07	0.00	0.04
	Singapore	0.79	1.99	4.54	0.06	2.06
	Thailand	0.06	0.47	0.68	0.05	0.25
	Viet Nam	0.11	0.30	0.59	0.04	0.23
Others (Non-China)	**ASEAN**	**98.48**	**94.40**	**90.66**	**99.74**	**95.88**
	Brunei	0.55	0.66	0.07	0.49	0.27
	Cambodia	0.89	1.21	1.34	0.54	0.71
	Indonesia	11.36	15.26	11.89	4.22	11.01
	Laos	0.17	−0.23	0.11	0.17	0.00
	Malaysia	11.16	9.11	7.44	11.51	6.23
	Myanmar	0.67	1.32	1.94	1.70	1.03
	Philippines	3.59	1.99	5.15	3.41	3.61
	Singapore	47.60	47.53	50.46	57.85	57.37
	Thailand	14.34	9.28	3.33	14.39	9.90
	Viet Nam	8.14	8.27	8.93	5.45	5.76

Source: Calculations from UNCTAD and MOFCOM.

FDI flows was the highest (at 10.9%) among all ASEAN economies that were considered not reliant on Chinese FDI.

3.2.2. *Importance of ASEAN to Chinese FDI*

As a region, ASEAN has become more important to Chinese FDI. The region's share of Chinese OFDI flows more than doubled to 7.5% in the BRI period. This is unusual considering China was rebalancing its investment toward developed economies (Table A.1). During the high growth period, only 6% of China's OFDI flows were destined for developed economies while 94% headed for developing economies. In the BRI period, 17% of China's OFDI flows headed for the developed world — most notably North America and Europe — while 83% was for the developing world. Within the developing regions, all regions within the developing world — with the sole exception of East and Southeast Asia — saw the shares of Chinese investment in their total inward FDI flows decrease through the three periods. For Latin America and the Caribbean as well as

Sub-Saharan Africa — two traditional key regions for Chinese investment — the decreases were significant.

At the country level, the lion's share of Chinese outbound investment throughout the periods flowed to just three economies: Hong Kong, the Cayman Islands, and the British Virgin Islands (a combined share of approximately 70%). A special administrative region of China, Hong Kong's share of Chinese OFDI flows increased from 56% to 59% between the high growth and BRI periods. Much of the Chinese capital absorbed by Hong Kong was possibly re-routed back into China as part of a 'round tripping' exercise, as domestic Chinese firms sought to access generous tax and fiscal incentives that were accorded only to 'foreign' firms (China treats Hong Kong-domiciled firms as foreign firms), and to take advantage of Hong Kong's position as an international financial center for financing purposes (Xiao, 2004). Between the two widely used Caribbean tax havens, the British Virgin Islands' share of Chinese OFDI flows increased marginally over the periods while that of the Cayman Islands declined rapidly.

Within the developed world, the US, Australia and a handful of European countries (the Netherlands, Switzerland, Germany and the UK) were important destinations for Chinese investment. During the BRI period, the US became the second largest magnet (after Hong Kong) for Chinese capital, a spot that previously belonged to the Cayman Islands. Resource-rich developing countries such as Algeria, Pakistan, Kazakhstan, Nigeria, South Africa and Zambia — which Chinese investors targeted during the high growth period — had disappeared from the list of major country destinations for Chinese OFDI flows during the BRI period.

The importance of ASEAN to Chinese FDI is skewed by the special case of Singapore.[9] The island city-state was the top sixth recipient of Chinese OFDI flows in the high growth period, and rose to the top fourth recipient in the BRI period. Singapore consistently accounted for about half of Chinese FDI flows into ASEAN through all three periods, its share of Chinese OFDI flows globally more than doubled to almost 4% in the BRI period.

Apart from Singapore, seven other ASEAN economies appeared on the list of top 20 country recipients in at least one of the three periods. They were Cambodia, Indonesia, Laos, Malaysia, Myanmar, Thailand and Viet Nam. In particular, Indonesia and Laos received substantial Chinese investment flows in all the three periods, and could be considered as being consistently and increasingly important to Chinese investors. The performances by others were more erratic. Nonetheless, most economies became more important to Chinese investors, as reflected by increases in their shares of Chinese OFDI flows globally between the high growth and BRI periods. In the latest BRI period, Malaysia, Thailand and Viet Nam appeared among the top 20 country recipients (ranked 14th, 16th and 19th, respectively) for the first time. In contrast, Brunei and the Philippines consistently attracted little Chinese investment and were never once made it to top 20, a sign that they were relatively unimportant to Chinese investors.

[9] In practice, Chinese investment in Hong Kong and Singapore can be diverted to other ASEAN economies (to an indeterminate extent) and will be therefore considered Hong Kong and Singaporean investment if it does occur (based on residency of the investing firm for tax purposes).

Reflecting the changes in flows, Chinese OFDI stock showed signs of 'deconcentration' at first, before 'reconcentrating' more recently. In 2004, the Chinese OFDI stock held by the top five country hosts represented 87% of the total. It decreased progressively to 75% in 2013, respectively, before climbing again to 81% in 2017. Hong Kong remained the key host for China's outbound investment; its share of Chinese OFDI stock however decreased to 54% in 2017 from 68% in 2004. Of the 20 major countries that hosted the most Chinese OFDI stock in 2004, 10 (8 developing and 2 developed) had disappeared from the top 20 list by 2017. The new entrants on the top 20 list for 2017 consisted mostly of developed economies, including the UK, the Netherlands, Luxembourg, Canada and Switzerland.

In stock terms, ASEAN as a region clearly became more important to China (it accounted for 4.9% of Chinese OFDI stock in the BRI period, compared with 2.1% in the high-growth period). This, however, was again mainly due to Singapore. In 2017, Singapore accounted for 2.5% of Chinese OFDI stock globally (making it the top fifth holder of Chinese OFDI stock globally, after Hong Kong, the Cayman Islands, the British Virgin Islands and the US) and more than 50% of Chinese OFDI stock in ASEAN. Besides Singapore, four other ASEAN economies also increased their shares of Chinese OFDI stock globally between 2004 and 2017: Cambodia, Indonesia, Laos and Myanmar. In 2017, Indonesia and Laos together accounted for 1% of Chinese OFDI stock globally (making them among the top 20 hosts of China's global OFDI stock).[10] On that basis, Singapore, Indonesia and Laos have become more important to Chinese investors.

3.2.3. *Chinese M&As in ASEAN by country by sector*

Why have some ASEAN economies become more important investment destinations for China while others have not? Some possible explanations include host-country conditions and bilateral investment treaties. Part of the explanations can also be found in the changing needs and capabilities of Chinese investors as the economy goes through different stages of development, as reflected by the sectoral profile of Chinese investment in individual countries. With respect to this, published officials statistics by China and ASEAN economies offer very limited information. Given the constraints with official data, this paper uses a specialized dataset on mergers and acquisitions (M&As) by Chinese firms in ASEAN which was compiled by Dealogic. The principal weakness of the dataset is that it lacks comprehensiveness and representativeness — it excludes greenfield investment and is biased toward brownfield investment with high transaction value by large firms. However, given that cross-border M&As accounted for substantial shares of annual Chinese OFDI flows, ranging from 21% to 55% of annual flows between 2004 and 2017 (MOFCOM, 2017), the dataset is still useful for providing broad indication of the evolving contours of Chinese investment in ASEAN.

In the high growth period, a total of 70 Chinese M&As in ASEAN were recorded, with a combined value of some USD8 billion. In the post-crisis period, the number of Chinese M&As in ASEAN rose to 126 but the total value decreased slightly to USD7.5 billion.

[10] Thailand and Viet Nam, which were previously top 11th and 13th holders of Chinese OFDI stock globally in 2004, experienced erosion in their shares to eventually fall off the top 20 list in 2017.

In the BRI period, there were 111 Chinese M&As in ASEAN with a significantly higher total value at USD19 billion. It suggests that the average deal size had increased.

In each of the three periods, a substantial portion of Chinese M&As in ASEAN (by share of total value, between 26% and 78%) was concentrated in Singapore's services sector, reflecting China's imports from Singapore's service trade (Gao and Zhang, 2016). Of the 20 largest Chinese M&As in ASEAN in all three periods, half were in Singapore's services sector, including: (i) the USD3.1 billion acquisition of Tuas Power Ltd (power generation) in 2008 by China Huaneng Group Co. Ltd. from Temasek Holdings (Pte) Ltd., (ii) the USD1.3 billion acquisition of SeaCo SRL (sales and lease of maritime containers) in 2014 by Bohai Leasing Co. Ltd. from Hainan Traffic Control Holding Co. Ltd., (iii) the USD1.1 billion acquisition of St James Holdings Ltd. (night entertainment services) in 2015 by Perennial Real Estate Holdings Pte Ltd., (iv) the USD1 billion acquisition of Lazada Southeast Asia Pte Ltd. (online market operator and retailer) in 2016 by Alibaba Group Holding Ltd from Rocket Internet SE, Tesco plc, and Investment AB Kinnevik and (v) the USD965 million acquisition of Singapore Aircraft Leasing Enterprise Pte Ltd. (commercial aircraft sales and leasing) in 2006 by Bank of China Ltd from Singapore Airlines Ltd, GIC Special Investments Pte Ltd., WestLB AG and Temasek Holdings (Pte) Ltd.

Once the Chinese M&As in Singapore's services sector are excluded, the changing patterns of Chinese investment by country and by sector emerged. In the high growth period, rapid export-oriented industrialization meant that the needs for natural resources were high while the capabilities of Chinese investors were relatively low (in that they were more inclined to invest in "less advanced" developing countries in ASEAN) (Table A.2). Chinese OFDI was resource-seeking and investment flows to resource-rich countries increased. Thus, mining and quarrying in Indonesia and agriculture in Cambodia were important for Chinese M&As, as investors sought to secure access location-specific raw materials and resources (resource-seeking). Notable Chinese M&As in Indonesia's primary sector during this period included: (i) the USD452 million acquisition of PetroChina International Ltd (oil and gas exploration) in 2006 by China National Petroleum Corp from PetroChina Co Ltd., (ii) the USD350 million acquisition of SEA Mineral Ltd (iron and nickel ores mining and trading) in 2007 by China Special Steel Holdings Co Ltd from Easyman Assets Management Ltd and Morgan Corp and (iii) the USD125 million acquisition of Madura BD gas fields in 2008 by CNOOC Ltd from Husky Energy Inc. Notable deals in Cambodia's primary sector included: (i) the USD35 million acquisition of Agri-Industrial Crop Development (Cambodia) Co. Ltd. (forest exploitation) in 2008 by China Asean Resources Ltd. and (ii) the USD5 million acquisition of China Zhen Rong Cambodia Energy Co. Ltd. (offshore oil exploration) in 2006 by China Petrotech Holdings Ltd. from Power Unicorn Investments Ltd.

There was also some investment interest in the manufacturing sector but this was limited to Singapore, and to a much lesser extent, Thailand and Viet Nam. Overall, manufacturing deals accounted for less than 6% of Chinese M&As in ASEAN. Notable M&As in Singapore's manufacturing sector included: (i) the USD201 million acquisition of GMG Global Ltd (natural rubber supply chain operations) in 2008 by Sinochem International

Corp and (ii) the USD115 million acquisition of Evanton Pte Ltd. (manufacturing of animal pharmaceuticals) in 2007 by Colorland Animation Ltd.

During the post-crisis period, the resource needs had somewhat moderated. China enhanced its manufacturing capabilities and extended its lead as a global manufacturing power house. Other needs began to emerge, notably the impetus to exploit emerging markets in developing countries due to the deterioration of traditional markets in advanced economies. Successful exporters also felt compelled to set up foreign affiliates to provide services for distribution, final assembly or maintenance to support their exports. This fits what the FDI literature describes as market-seeking motivation. Increased production costs in China also caused Chinese firms to relocate part of their operations to ASEAN countries that have a cost advantage, or what is considered efficiency-seeking motivation in which foreign investment is made to take advantage of lower costs and policy incentives and to improve or maintain firm competitiveness. In tandem with these developments, Chinese OFDI in ASEAN shifted to countries offering production efficiencies, which became more integrated with China's production chains.

The primary sector remained important and accounted for 20% of total Chinese M&As in ASEAN in the post-crisis period (Table A.3). Apart from Indonesia and Cambodia, Viet Nam and Malaysia became important for Chinese M&As in the primary sector. Notable deals in Indonesia included: (i) the USD680 million acquisition of Gendalo-Gehem deepwater natural gas assets in 2011 by China Petrochemical Corp from Chevron Corp, (ii) the USD87 million acquisition of PT Servindo Jaya Utama (iron ore mining) in 2011 by Shanghai Wanye Enterprises Co. Ltd. from Salim Wanye (Shanghai) Co. Ltd. and (iii) the USD50 million acquisition of PT Ironman Royale Indonesia (coal mining) in 2012 by Qingdao Evercontaining Electric Co Ltd. Thailand's services sector also attracted substantial Chinese investment interest. Notable Chinese M&As in Thailand's services sector included: (i) the USD529 million acquisition of ACL Bank pcl (financial services) in 2010 by Industrial & Commercial Bank of China (ICBC) from Bangkok Bank pcl, (ii) the USD28 million acquisition of Mweb Holdings (Thailand) Ltd. (Internet solutions and services) in 2013 by Tencent Holdings Ltd from Naspers Ltd. and (iii) the USD9 million acquisition of Thai Vegetable Oil International Ltd (distribution of vegetable oil products) in 2011 by Shengfeng Investment Management Co Ltd from Thai Vegetable Oil pcl.

Significantly, the manufacturing sector overtook both primary and services sectors, accounting for 45% of Chinese M&As in ASEAN. The bulk of the M&As in manufacturing took place in Singapore, including: (i) the USD2.4 billion acquisition of Singapore Petroleum Co. Ltd. (refining and trading of petroleum products) in 2009 by PetroChina Co. Ltd. from Keppel Corp Ltd, (ii) the USD120 million acquisition of Biosensors International Group Ltd (medical device manufacturing) in 2011 by Shandong Weigao Group Medical Polymer Co Ltd. and (iii) the USD85 million acquisition of New Lakeside Holdings (animal feed manufacturing) in 2012 by SDIC Zhonglu Fruit Juice Co Ltd. Despite Singapore's dominance, there was also substantial M&A interest in the manufacturing sector of Malaysia and Indonesia (and to a lesser extent, Viet Nam and Thailand).

Notable Chinese M&As in Malaysia's manufacturing sector included: (i) the USD313 million acquisition of Nam Cheong Dockyard Sdn Bhd (construction of offshore support vessels) in 2011 by Eagle Brand Holdings Ltd, (ii) the USD38 million acquisition of Ogawa World Bhd (small electrical appliance manufacturing) in 2013 by Xiamen Comfort Science & Technology Group Co Ltd. and (iii) the USD16 million acquisition of Pelikan International Corp Bhd (stationery manufacturing) by China Stationery Ltd from Persada Bina Sdn Bhd and Mahir Agresif (M) Sdn Bhd. Meanwhile, among prominent Chinese M&As in Indonesia's manufacturing sector were: (i) the USD39 million acquisition of PT Budi Dharma (steel product manufacturing) in 2009 by an undisclosed investor, (ii) the USD30 million acquisition of PT Semen Kupang (Persero) in 2009 by Guangshou Co Ltd. and (iii) the USD6 million acquisition of PT Star Comgistic Indonesia (household appliance manufacturing) by Tsann Kuen (China) Enterprise Co Ltd.

During the BRI period, China increasingly moved from investment-led to consumption-driven growth and the demand for final goods and technologies increased. Chinese OFDI became more technology-seeking in nature. The resource needs had largely subsided while Chinese investors' capabilities improved. In addition to supplying innovative and competitively priced products particularly suited to emerging markets (thus exploiting their home advantages abroad), Chinese firms were acquiring strategic assets such as marketing skills in order to enhance their competitiveness back at home. Such strategic asset-seeking motivation is also known as technology-seeking motivation, in which foreign investment is made for the purpose of accessing knowledge and acquiring key capabilities in fields such as technology, design, management and marketing. This has been shown to be important for Chinese OFDI in countries such as the UK (Buckley *et al.*, 2007b), Italy (Pietrobelli *et al.*, 2011) and Germany (Schüler-Zhou and Schüller, 2009).

In addition, rising levels of protectionism in the international trade and investment environment since the global financial crisis resulted in sustained relocation and expansion of manufacturing operations of Chinese firms elsewhere for risk mitigation purposes (*South China Morning Post*, 22 May 2019). For example, Malaysia received substantial Chinese investments in solar cells manufacturing for the purpose of exporting to the US and to circumvent US anti-dumping duties on imports of solar panels from China since 2016 (Tham, 2018).

In the BRI period, Chinese investment in ASEAN primary sector slowed significantly and contributed to only 7% of total Chinese M&As within the region, largely reflecting falling international commodity prices since the start of the period (Table A.4). The services sector was again the prime target for Chinese M&As but the geographical coverage expanded beyond Singapore to cover other countries. These included countries that were previously attractive to Chinese investors in the primary sector (Cambodia, Indonesia, Myanmar and Viet Nam) and the manufacturing sector (Malaysia). Chinese M&As in Malaysia's services sector were dominated by one mega utilities deal: the USD3.8 billion acquisition of Edra Global Energy Bhd (power generation) in 2016 by China General Nuclear Power Corp from 1Malaysia Development Bhd (1MDB). The deal was so large that it represented a fifth of the value of total Chinese M&As in ASEAN in the BRI period. It was the also largest single Chinese M&A in ASEAN by value to date. Other prominent

Chinese M&As in Malaysia's services sector included: (i) the USD185 million acquisition of land plots in 2014 by Greenland Holding Group Co Ltd from Iskandar Waterfront Holdings Sdn Bhd, (ii) the USD108 million acquisition of a 40% stake in Kuantan Port Consortium Sdn Bhd (container port) in 2014 by Guangxi Beibu Gulf International Port Group Co Ltd from IJM Corp Bhd and (iii) the USD35 million acquisition of Secret Recipe Cakes and Café Sdn Bhd in 2014 by Fosun International Ltd.

Notable M&As elsewhere included: (i) in Thailand, the USD880 million acquisition of True Corp pcl (telecommunications carrier) in 2014 by China Mobile Ltd, (ii) in Myanmar, the USD206 million acquisition of Golden Land Real Estate Development Co Ltd (property development) in 2016 by Cedar Strategic Holdings Ltd, (iii) in Cambodia, the USD179 million acquisition of Sino-Cambodia Phnom Penh Special Economic Zone Co Ltd. (industrial park operations) in 2017 by Beijing Properties (Holdings) Ltd, (iv) in Indonesia, the USD150 million acquisition of Lester Listrik Pte Ltd. (power generation) in 2016 by SDIC Power Holdings Co Ltd from Genting Bhd and (v) in Viet Nam, the USD140 million acquisition of JAKS Pacific Power Ltd (power plant development) in 2015 by China Power Engineering Consulting Group Corp.

Chinese M&As in ASEAN manufacturing sector mostly took place in Singapore, with deals such as: (i) the USD1.75 billion acquisition of STATS ChipPAC Ltd (semiconductor manufacturing) in 2015 by Jiangsu Changjiang Electronics Technology Co Ltd. and (ii) the USD625 million acquisition of Halycon Agri Corp Ltd. (rubber product manufacturing) in 2106 by Sinochem International Corp from Credence Partners Pte Ltd.

Malaysia, along with countries which previously attracted investment interest in their primary sectors (Indonesia, Cambodia and Viet Nam), also became a target for Chinese M&As in ASEAN manufacturing. Among the largest deals were: (i) in Malaysia, the USD370 million acquisition of Shell Refining Co (FOM) Bhd (oil refinery) in 2016 by Shandong Hengyuan Petrochemical Co Ltd from Royal Dutch Shell plc, (ii) in Malaysia, the USD175 million acquisition of SCA Hygiene Malaysia Sdn Bhd (hygiene product manufacturing) in 2016 by Vinda International Holdings Ltd from Svenska Cellulosa AB SCA, (iii) in Indonesia, the USD114 million acquisition of PT Dua Kuda Indonesia (oleochemicals manufacturing) in 2016 by Zhejiang Zanyu Technology Co Ltd from Rugao Shuangma Chemical Industry Co Ltd, (iv) in Viet Nam, the USD39 million acquisition of Integral Materials Investment Vietnam Co Ltd (metal smelting) in 2016 by Shenghe Resources Holding Co Ltd from Peaceful Art International Ltd. and (v) in Cambodia, the USD33 million acquisition of Cement Chakrey Ting Factory Co Ltd (cement manufacturing) in 2015 by Huaxin Cement Co Ltd from Cement Construction Resources Co Ltd.

With faster growth in flows into the manufacturing sector than other sectors, the manufacturing share of China's FDI stock in ASEAN increased from 12% to 18%, while the primary and services sectors' share decreased (Table 6). Overall, Chinese FDI stock remained concentrated in the services sector, primarily in the leasing and business activities, wholesale and retail trade, and utilities. The changes in the distribution of Chinese FDI stock in ASEAN were broadly in line with the changes in the distribution of Chinese FDI stock globally — in that the primary sector gave way to manufacturing while services

Table 6. Distribution of China FDI Stock in ASEAN and World by Industry, 2012 and 2017 (%)

	% of China FDI Stock in ASEAN		% of China FDI Stock in the World	
	2012	2017	2012	2017
All Sectors	**100.0**	**100.0**	**100.0**	**100.0**
Primary	**17.8**	**16.7**	**15.0**	**9.6**
Agriculture	3.5	5.1	0.9	0.9
Mining and quarrying	14.3	11.6	14.1	8.7
Manufacturing	**11.9**	**17.5**	**6.4**	**7.8**
Services	**70.3**	**65.8**	**78.6**	**82.6**
Construction	7.8	7.4	2.4	2.1
Finance	9.1	5.9	18.1	11.2
Health and social work	0.1	0.4	0.0	0.1
Hotels and restaurants	0.1	0.1	0.1	0.2
Information and communication technology	0.4	1.1	0.9	12.1
Leasing and business activities	12.0	19.6	33.0	34.0
Other services	0.3	0.9	0.7	1.4
Professional, scientific and technical services	1.6	0.9	1.3	1.2
Real estate	0.6	2.5	1.8	3.0
Recreational, cultural and sporting activities	0.1	0.1	0.1	0.4
Transport and storage	7.4	2.8	5.5	3.0
Utilities	18.1	10.8	1.7	1.4
Wholesale and retail	12.6	13.3	12.8	12.5

Source: Calculations from MOFCOM. 2012 was the first year when a sectoral overview was provided for Chinese FDI in ASEAN.

remained important — with two significant differences. One, manufacturing is more important to Chinese investors in ASEAN than to Chinese investors at the global level, pointing to China's integration into regional production networks. Two, while the services sector is less important to Chinese investors in ASEAN than to Chinese investors at the global level, within the services sector, utilities and construction are far more important to Chinese investors in ASEAN than to Chinese investors at the global level, even before the BRI was launched.

4. Conclusions

The paper provides some clarity on the scope and scale of China's investment in ASEAN, an issue that has attracted considerable attention since the launch of the BRI. It shows that the increase in Chinese investment in ASEAN pre-dates the BRI launch, bearing testimony to the importance of ASEAN economies as destinations for Chinese OFDI. The changes in sectoral and geographical coverage of Chinese investment in ASEAN excluding Singapore reflect evolving motivations and capabilities of Chinese investors. In the early days, resource-seeking motivations were dominant and Chinese investment in ASEAN was more limited to a handful of resource-specific locations. Chinese investment in the region has since become increasingly driven by more complex motivations and spread to a greater number of countries (efficiency-seeking in locations that offer cost and production advantages; market-seeking in all economies particularly sizable ones and technology-seeking in more advanced, typically higher income economies).

Importantly, while Chinese investment became an important source of FDI for ASEAN, it was not above the average China weight in FDI in the developing world. In other words, ASEAN as a region — and most of its economies — has not become "reliant" on Chinese FDI as some commentators or analysts have suggested. Assuming China can sustain the growth momentum in its OFDI flows into ASEAN, the country still has a long way to go before it catches up with the Triad of the US, European Union and Japan (which account for some 70% of world FDI stock in 2017, compared to China's 4.6%). The catch up will be even slower if the growth momentum in Chinese investment is reversed and becomes a prolonged phenomenon. Since 2016, Beijing has introduced stringent capital control measures with regard to foreign investment. With guidelines classifying OFDI as "encouraged", "restricted" and "prohibited", Chinese OFDI policy entered into a more regulated stage and its annual OFDI flows declined for the first time in value, by almost 30%, the following year. This was heralded by Chinese officials as a positive sign that "market entities have become mature and returned to rationality". Slowing Chinese OFDI comes at a time of increased geopolitical risks, rising tensions in global trade, and technological shifts — all of which contribute to slowing expansion in international production sharing, which has always been inextricably intertwined with investment. In 2017, global FDI flows fell by a quarter, led by declining flows to developed economies. The UNCTAD projections are that global FDI will experience weaker growth going forward, well below the average over the past decade.

A handful of ASEAN economies need to diversify their sources of FDI. Relying on a single source of FDI creates risks to the host countries as sudden shifts from a big investor could have potential macro implications. Most other ASEAN economies will be wise not to be overanxious about a country that is far from dominant in their investment landscape. Given slowing global and Chinese FDI, their main policy approach should focus on improving FDI attraction and leveraging FDI for social and economic development, should they indeed opt to continue with FDI-assisted development. Foreign investment is not preordained, and its benefits are no more potential. In respect to this, they should be concerned about the absorptive capacity of their economies and firms as well as the quality and technology content — not nationality — of FDI.

Appendix A

Table A.1. Geographical Distribution of China OFDI Flows and Stock by Region and Major Country, 2004–2017 (%)

Development Status/ Region/Country	% of China OFDI Flows			Top 20 Country Ranking			% of China OFDI Stock		Top 20 Country Ranking	
	High Growth Period	Post-crisis Period	BRI Period	High Growth Period	Post-crisis Period	BRI Period	2004	2017	2004	2017
World	**100.0**	**100.0**	**100.0**				**100.00**	**100.0**		
Developed	**6.0**	**14.8**	**17.1**				**4.7**	**12.4**		
ANZ and Japan	2.6	3.7	3.1				1.5	2.3		
Australia	2.4	3.3	2.5	5	4	6	1.1	2.0	7	6
Japan	0.1	0.3	0.2				0.3	0.2	15	
Europe	1.6	7.0	6.5				1.2	5.3		
France	0.1	1.0	0.5		11	17	0.0	0.3		
Germany	0.6	0.7	1.1	16	14	9	0.3	0.7	16	11
Luxembourg	0.0	2.3	-0.6		7		0.0	0.3		9
Netherlands	0.2	0.3	2.5			7	0.0	1.0		8
Spain	0.0	0.0	0.1				0.3	0.0	17	
Sweden	0.1	0.5	0.3				0.0	0.4		19
Switzerland	0.0	0.1	1.3			8	0.0	0.4		16
UK	0.6	1.6	1.1	15	8	10	0.2	1.1		7
North America	1.9	4.1	7.5				2.0	4.3		
Bermuda	-0.1	0.1	0.3				0.4	0.5	10	15
Canada	0.9	1.0	0.9	10	10	13	0.1	0.6		12
USA	1.0	3.0	6.3	8	5	2	1.5	3.7	4	4
Developing/Transition	**94.0**	**85.2**	**82.9**				**95.3**	**87.6**		
East and Southeast Asia	60.9	64.5	67.3				72.9	60.3		
ASEAN	3.5	6.7	7.5				2.1	4.9		
Brunei	*0.0*	*0.0*	*0.0*				*0.0*	*0.0*		

Table A.1. (*Continued*)

Development Status/ Region/Country	% of China OFDI Flows			Top 20 Country Ranking			% of China OFDI Stock		Top 20 Country Ranking	
	High Growth Period	Post-crisis Period	BRI Period	High Growth Period	Post-crisis Period	BRI Period	2004	2017	2004	2017
Cambodia	*0.3*	*0.6*	*0.4*		*18*		*0.2*	*0.3*		
Indonesia	*0.3*	*1.0*	*0.9*	*19*	*12*	*12*	*0.3*	*0.6*		*13*
Laos	*0.3*	*0.6*	*0.5*		*17*	*18*	*0.0*	*0.4*		*20*
Malaysia	*0.1*	*0.3*	*0.7*			*14*	*0.3*	*0.3*		
Myanmar	*0.3*	*0.7*	*0.2*		*16*		*0.0*	*0.3*		
Philippines	*0.0*	*0.2*	*0.1*				*0.0*	*0.0*		
Singapore	*1.8*	*2.4*	*3.7*	*6*	*6*	*4*	*0.5*	*2.5*	*9*	*5*
Thailand	*0.1*	*0.6*	*0.5*			*16*	*0.4*	*0.3*	*11*	
Viet Nam	*0.3*	*0.4*	*0.5*			*19*	*0.4*	*0.3*	*13*	
Hong Kong	55.5	56.6	58.7	1	1	1	67.9	54.2	1	1
Macao	0.6	0.3	0.2	14			1.4	0.5	5	14
Mongolia	0.5	0.6	0.1	17	20		0.2	0.2		
North Korea	0.7	0.3	0.6	12		15	1.3	0.0	6	
Latin America and the Caribbean	21.5	12.7	10.3				18.5	21.4		
BVI	5.2	4.9	6.1	3	3	3	2.4	6.7	3	3
Cayman Islands	15.6	6.0	3.4	2	2	5	14.9	13.8	2	2
Mexico	0.0	0.1	0.1				0.3	0.0	19	
Peru	0.0	0.1	0.0				0.3	0.0	18	
Venezuela	0.1	0.6	0.1		19		0.1	0.2		
Middle East and North Africa	1.3	1.6	1.1				1.7	1.1		
Algeria	0.3	0.2	0.1	20			0.1	0.1		
Iraq	0.0	0.1	0.0				1.0	0.0	8	

Table A.1. (*Continued*)

Development Status/ Region/Country	% of China OFDI Flows			Top 20 Country Ranking			% of China OFDI Stock		Top 20 Country Ranking	
	High Growth Period	Post-crisis Period	BRI Period	High Growth Period	Post-crisis Period	BRI Period	2004	2017	2004	2017
Sudan	0.2	0.3	0.0				0.4	0.1	12	
Oceania	0.3	0.1	0.1				0.0	0.2		
South Asia	1.3	1.3	0.7				0.2	0.9		
Iran	0.1	0.7	0.0		15		0.1	0.2		
Pakistan	1.0	0.3	0.4	9		20	0.1	0.3		
South-Eastern Europe and CIS	2.5	2.4	1.4				0.5	1.5		
Kazakhstan	0.8	1.1	0.0	11	9		0.1	0.4		17
Russia	1.4	0.9	1.0	7	13	11	0.3	0.8	20	10
Sub-Saharan Africa	6.4	2.6	1.9				1.5	2.1		
Nigeria	0.6	0.3	0.1	13			0.2	0.2		
South Africa	4.6	-0.1	0.2	4			0.1	0.4		18
Zambia	0.4	0.3	0.2	18			0.3	0.2	14	

Source: Calculations from MOFCOM. Only countries that are top 20 recipients of Chinese OFDI flows or top 20 hosts of Chinese OFDI stock in at least one of the time periods are shown.

Table A.2. Distribution of Chinese M&As in ASEAN by Country by Sector, 2004–2008 (%)

	Cambodia	Indonesia	Malaysia	Philippines	Singapore	Thailand	Viet Nam	**Subtotal**
Primary	**0.53**	**14.44**		**0.05**				**15.02**
Agriculture	0.45							**0.45**
Mining and quarrying	0.08	14.44		0.05				**14.57**
Manufacturing		**0.07**			**4.39**	**0.79**	**0.46**	**5.71**
Services		**1.21**	**0.04**		**77.97**	**0.04**		**79.26**
Construction		0.96			0.20			**1.16**
Education					0.01			**0.01**
Finance		0.26			0.06	0.04		**0.35**
Hotels and restaurants					0.01			**0.01**
Information and communication technology			0.01		0.08			**0.08**
Leasing and business activities					11.21			**11.21**
Professional, scientific and technical services					0.10			**0.10**
Real estate					13.20			**13.20**
Transport and storage					2.22			**2.22**
Utilities			0.02		47.28			**47.29**
Wholesale and retail			0.01		3.61			**3.63**
Subtotal	**0.53**	**15.73**	**0.04**	**0.05**	**82.36**	**0.83**	**0.46**	**100.00**
Subtotal (current USD millions)	**40**	**1,203**	**3**	**4**	**6,301**	**64**	**35**	**7,650**

Source: Calculations from Dealogic. The data are by no means comprehensive and should be taken as indicative at best.

Table A.3. Distribution of Chinese M&As in ASEAN by Country by Sector, 2009–2013 (%)

	Brunei	Cambodia	Indonesia	Laos	Malaysia	Philippines	Singapore	Thailand	Viet Nam	**Subtotal**
Primary		**0.57**	**13.45**		**1.84**	**0.02**	**0.60**		**2.92**	**19.40**
Agriculture		0.57							2.92	**3.49**
Mining and quarrying			13.45		1.84	0.02	0.60			**15.91**
Manufacturing	**0.00**		**1.06**	**0.00**	**5.15**		**37.74**	**0.23**	**0.64**	**44.82**
Services		**0.67**	**0.03**	**0.16**	**0.14**		**25.90**	**7.72**	**1.15**	**35.77**
Construction			0.01				2.64			**2.65**
Education										**0.00**
Finance							0.18	7.24	0.05	**7.46**
Health and social work							0.02			**0.02**
Hotels and restaurants							0.18			**0.18**
Information and communication technology					0.02		0.59	0.49		**1.10**
Leasing and business activities		0.67			0.07					**0.74**
Other services									0.03	**0.03**
Professional, scientific and technical services					0.04		6.96			**7.00**
Real estate							11.69			**11.69**
Transport and storage					0.01		0.08		1.07	**1.16**
Utilities				0.16			1.36			**1.52**
Water and environment management							1.61			**1.61**
Wholesale and retail			0.03		0.00		0.60			**0.64**
Subtotal	**0.00**	**1.24**	**14.55**	**0.16**	**7.14**	**0.02**	**64.24**	**7.96**	**4.71**	**100.00**
Subtotal (current USD millions)	**0**	**92**	**1,086**	**12**	**533**	**1**	**4,795**	**594**	**351**	**7,465**

Source: Calculations from Dealogic. The data are by no means comprehensive and should be taken as indicative at best.

Table A.4. Distribution of China M&As in ASEAN by Country by Sector, 2014–2017 (%)

	Cambodia	Indonesia	Laos	Malaysia	Myanmar	Philippines	Singapore	Thailand	Viet Nam	**Subtotal**
Primary		**7.01**	**0.16**		**0.18**				**0.00**	**7.35**
Agriculture										**0.00**
Mining and quarrying		7.01	0.16		0.18				0.00	**7.35**
Manufacturing	**0.31**	**0.87**		**2.97**		**0.02**	**21.14**	**0.04**	**0.23**	**25.58**
Services	**1.08**	**2.50**		**22.55**	**1.10**	**0.03**	**32.87**	**6.18**	**0.75**	**67.07**
Construction	0.96			0.13	1.10		1.21		0.75	**4.15**
Finance		0.26								**0.26**
Health and social work							0.21			**0.21**
Hotels and restaurants				0.21			0.78			**0.99**
Information and communication technology	0.12	0.50		0.01		0.03	7.31	4.82	0.00	**12.80**
Other services							0.01			**0.01**
Professional, scientific and technical services				0.05			3.18	0.00		**3.23**
Real estate				0.99			7.32			**8.31**
Recreational, cultural and sporting activities							5.82			**5.82**
Transport and storage				0.58			2.87			**3.45**
Utilities		1.75		20.57				0.77		**23.09**
Water and environment management							1.04	0.24		**1.28**
Wholesale and retail				0.01			3.11	0.34		**3.46**
Subtotal	**1.39**	**10.37**	**0.16**	**25.53**	**1.28**	**0.06**	**54.01**	**6.21**	**0.99**	**100.00**
Subtotal (current USD millions)	**260**	**1,939**	**29**	**4,772**	**240**	**11**	**10,098**	**1,162**	**184**	**18,695**

Source: Calculations from Dealogic, 2017 is up to March. The data are by no means comprehensive and should be taken as indicative at best.

References

Asia Times (2019). *Vietnam Seeks to Slow China Inflows*. https://asiatimes.com/2019/05/vietnam-seeks-to-slow-china-inflows/

Balasubramanyam, VN, M Salisu and D Sapsford (1996). *Foreign Direct Investment and Growth: New Hypotheses and Evidence* (Working Paper Ec7/96). Department of Economics, University of Lancaster.

Blonigen, BA (2005). A review of the empirical literature on FDI determinants. *Atlantic Economic Journal*, 33(4), 383–403, doi: 10.1007/s11293-005-2868-9.

Bloomberg (2018). *Malaysia's Mahathir Pledges to Review China Investment If Re-Elected*. https://www.bloomberg.com/news/articles/2018-04-08/mahathir-pledges-to-review-china-investment-after-malaysia-vote

Buckley, PJ, LJ Clegg, AR Cross, X Liu, H Voss and P Zheng (2007a). The determinants of Chinese outward foreign direct investment. *Journal of International Business Studies*, 38(4), 499–518.

Buckley, PJ, C Wang and J Clegg (2007b). The impact of foreign ownership, local ownership and industry characteristics on spillover benefits from foreign direct investment in China. *International Business Review*, 16(2), 142–158, doi: 10.1016/j.ibusrev.2006.12.006.

BusinessWeek (2004). *China Goes Shopping*. https://www.bloomberg.com/news/articles/2004-12-19/china-goes-shopping

Carkovic, M and RE Levine (2002). Does foreign direct investment accelerate economic growth? *SSRN Electronic Journal*, doi: 10.2139/ssrn.314924.

de Mello, LR (1997). Foreign direct investment in developing countries and growth: A selective survey. *Journal of Development Studies*, 34(1), 1–34, doi: 10.1080/00220389708422501.

Du, L, A Harrison and G Jefferson (2011). *Do Institutions Matter for FDI Spillovers? The Implications of China's 'Special Characteristics'* (Policy Research Working Paper No. 5757). World Bank, doi:10.1596/1813-9450-5757.

Dunning, JH and SM Lundan (2008). *Multinational Enterprises and the Global Economy*, 2nd Edition. Cheltenham, UK: Edward Elgar.

Economist (2010). *Buying up the World: The Coming Wave of Chinese Takeovers*. https://www.economist.com/leaders/2010/11/11/china-buys-up-the-world

Eichengreen, B, Y Rhee and H Tong (2007). China and the exports of other Asian countries. *Review of World Economics*, 143(2), 201–226, doi: 10.1007/s10290-007-0105-0.

Eichengreen, B and H Tong (2005). *Is China's FDI Coming at the Expense of Other Countries?* NBER Working Paper 11335, National Bureau for Economic Research.

Erdener, C and DM Shapiro (2005). The internationalization of Chinese family enterprises and Dunning's Eclectic Mne paradigm. *Management and Organization Review*, 1(3), 411–436, doi: 10.1111/j.1740-8784.2005.00021.x.

Faeth, I (2009). Determinants of foreign direct investment—A tale of nine theoretical models. *Journal of Economic Surveys*, 23(1), 165–196, doi: 10.1111/j.1467-6419.2008.00560.x.

Fortune (2009). *China Buys the World*. https://archive.fortune.com/galleries/2009/fortune/0910/gallery.china_shopping_list.fortune/index.html

Freeman, CP (Ed.). (2015). *Handbook on China and Developing Countries*. Edward Elgar Publishing.

Gao, Y and J Zhang (2016). Emerging China and its interaction with ASEAN economies. In Y.-C. Kim (Ed.), *Chinese Global Production Networks in ASEAN*. Springer International Publishing.

Goh, E (2007). Southeast Asian perspectives on the China challenge. *Journal of Strategic Studies*, 30(4–5), 809–832, doi: 10.1080/01402390701431915.

Ha, LT (2019). *Chinese FDI in Vietnam: Trends, Status and Challenges*. ISEAS–Yusof Ishak Institute.

Havranek, T and Z Irsova (2011). Estimating vertical spillovers from FDI: Why results vary and what the true effect is. *Journal of International Economics*, 85(2), 234–244.

Jarvis, DSL and AR Welch (2011). Introduction: structural changes, economic challenges and political accommodation: managing the rise of China in Southeast Asia. In *ASEAN Industries and the Challenge from China*, DSL Jarvis and AR Welch (eds.), Basingstoke, Hampshire: Palgrave Macmillan.

Knoerich, J and T Miedtank (2018). Chinese foreign direct investment in the EU. *CESifo Forum*, 19(4), 3–8.

Koepke, R (2019). What drives capital flows to emerging markets? A survey of the empirical literature: What drives capital flows to emerging markets? *Journal of Economic Surveys*, 33(2), 516–540, doi: 10.1111/joes.12273.

Lall, S (1996). *Learning from the Asian Tigers: Studies in Technology and Industrial Policy*. Basingstoke, Hampshire: MacMillan.

Lall, S and R Narula (2004). Foreign direct investment and its role in economic development: Do we need a new agenda? *The European Journal of Development Research*, 16(3), 447–464, doi: 10.1080/0957881042000266589.

Lin, P, Z Liu and Y Zhang (2009). Do Chinese Domestic firms benefit from FDI inflow? Evidence of horizontal and vertical spillovers. *China Economic Review*, 20(4), 677–691. https://doi.org/10.1016/j.chieco.2009.05.010.

Meunier, S (2019). Beware of Chinese bearing gifts: Why China's direct investment poses political challenges in Europe and the United States. In *China's International Investment Strategy: Bilateral, Regional, and Global Law and Policy*, J Chaisse (ed.), Oxford: Oxford University Press.

MOFCOM (2017). *2017 Statistical Bulletin of China's Outward Foreign Direct Investment*. Beijing: Ministry of Commerce of the People's Republic of China.

Moon, H-C and TW Roehl (2001). Unconventional foreign direct investment and the imbalance theory. *International Business Review*, 10(2), 197–215, doi: 10.1016/S0969-5931(00)00046-9.

Moran, TH (1998). *Foreign Direct Investment and Development: The New Policy Agenda for Developing Countries and Economies in Transition*. Washington, DC: Institute for International Economics.

Nikkei Asian Review (2019). *Vietnam Seeks More Trade with China but Will Defend Interests: PM*. https://asia.nikkei.com/Politics/International-relations/Vietnam-seeks-more-trade-with-China-but-will-defend-interests-PM

Nolan, PH (2012). *Is China Buying the World?* Polity Press.

O'Brien, R and M Williams (2016). *Global Political Economy: Evolution & Dynamics*, 5th Edition. MacMillan Education.

OECD (2008). *OECD Investment Policy Reviews: China 2008: Encouraging Responsible Business Conduct*. Paris: Organisation for Economic Co-operation and Development, doi:10.1787/9789264053717-en.

OECD (2018). *OECD Investment Policy Reviews: Southeast Asia*. Paris: Organisation for Economic Co-operation and Development.

Peng, MW (2012). *Global Business*, 3rd Edition. Eagan, MN: Cengage Learning.

Pfeiffer, B, H Görg and L Perez-Villar (2014). *The Heterogeneity of FDI in Sub-Saharan Africa: How Do the Horizontal Productivity Effects of Emerging Investors Differ from Those of Traditional Players?* (GIGA Working Papers No. 262; p. 35). German Institute of Global and Area Studies.

Pietrobelli, C, R Rabellotti and M Sanfilippo (2011). Chinese FDI strategy in Italy: The 'Marco Polo' effect. *International Journal of Technological Learning, Innovation and Development*, 4(4), 277, doi: 10.1504/IJTLID.2011.044138.

Ramamurti, R (2009). Why study emerging-market multinationals? In *Emerging Multinationals in Emerging Markets*, R Ramamurti and JV Singh (eds.), Cambridge University Press.

Ramamurti, R (2012). What is really different about emerging market multinationals? *Global Strategy Journal*, 2(1), 41–47, doi: 10.1002/gsj.1025.

Ravenhill, J (2006). Is China an economic threat to Southeast Asia? *Asian Survey*, 46(5), 653–674, doi: 10.1525/as.2006.46.5.653.

Reuters (2017). *In Indonesia, Labour Friction and Politics Fan Anti-Chinese Sentiment.* https://www.reuters.com/article/us-indonesia-election-china/in-indonesia-labor-friction-and-politics-fan-anti-chinese-sentiment-idUSKBN17K0YG

Rugman, AM (2009). Theoretical aspects of MNEs from emerging economies. In *Emerging Multinationals in Emerging Markets*, R Ramamurti and JV Singh (eds.), New York: Cambridge University Press.

Schüler-Zhou, Y and M Schüller (2009). The internationalization of Chinese companies: What do official statistics tell us about Chinese outward foreign direct investment? *Chinese Management Studies*, 3(1), 25–42, doi: 10.1108/17506140910946124.

Shen, RSJ and V Mantzopoulos (2013). China's "going out" policy: Inception, evolution, implication. *Journal of Business and Behavioral Sciences*, 25(2), 121–136.

Socio-Economic Research Centre (2017). *China's Investment in Malaysia: Perceptions, Issues and Prescriptions*. Kuala Lumpur: SERC.

South China Morning Post (2019). *US-China Trade War Manufacturing Exodus Creating Boom Times for Chinese Logistics Companies*. https://www.scmp.com/economy/china-economy/article/3011178/us-china-trade-war-manufacturing-exodus-creating-boom-times

Steinfeld, ES (2010). *Playing Our Game: Why China's Economic Rise Doesn't Threaten the West.* Oxford: Oxford University Press.

Storey, I (2011). *Southeast Asia and the Rise of China: The Search for Security*, 1st Edition. Abingdon, Oxon: Routledge.

Takii, S (2011). Do FDI spillovers vary among home economies?: Evidence from Indonesian manufacturing. *Journal of Asian Economics*, 22(2), 152–163, doi: 10.1016/j.asieco.2010.12.002.

Tham, SY (2018). Chinese investment in Malaysia: Five years into the BRI. *ISEAS-Yusof Ishak Institute Perspective*, 11.

Thorbecke, W and N Salike (2011). Understanding Foreign Direct Investment in East Asia. ADBI Working Papers 290, Asian Development Bank Institute.

UNCTAD (2009). *UNCTAD Training Manual on Statistics for FDI and the Operations of TNCs Volume 1: FDI Flows and Stocks*. Division on Investment and Enterprise, Geneva: United Nations Conference on Trade and Development.

Wang, B and K Gao (2018). Outward direct investment: Restricted, relaxed and regulated stages of development. In *China's 40 Years of Reform and Development: 1978–2018*, R Garnaut, L Song and F. Cai (eds.), pp. 619–636. Canberra: ANU Press.

Wang, H (1999). The Asian financial crisis and financial reforms in China. *The Pacific Review*, 12(4), 537–556, doi: 10.1080/09512749908719305.

Wong, J and S Chan (2003). China-Asean free trade agreement: shaping future economic relations. *Asian Survey*, 43(3), 507–526, doi: 10.1525/as.2003.43.3.507.

World Bank (2019). *World Bank Open Data*. Washington, DC: World Bank, https://data.worldbank.org/.

Xiao, G (2004). *Round-Tripping Foreign Direct Investment in the People's Republic of China.* ADBI Research Policy Brief 10, Asian Development Bank Institute.

Yeung, HW, J Poon and M Perry (2001). Towards a regional strategy: The role of regional headquarters of foreign firms in Singapore. *Urban Studies*, 38(1), 157–183, doi: 10.1080/00420980124278.

Zhou, Y and S Lall (2005). The impact of China's FDI surge on FDI in South-East Asia: Panel data analysis for 1986–2001. *Transnational Corporations*, 14(1), https://unctad.org/en/Docs/iteiit20051a2_en.pdf.

Chapter 7

EVOLUTION OF CHINA'S OUTWARD FOREIGN DIRECT INVESTMENT REGIME: IMPLICATIONS FOR SOUTHEAST ASIA UNDER THE BELT AND ROAD INITIATIVE[‡]

THERESA YAN[*] and PETER ENDERWICK[†]

Faculty of Business, Economics and Law
Auckland University of Technology
Private Bag 92006, Auckland, New Zealand
[*]chenxiyant@163.com
[†]peter.enderwick@aut.ac.nz

Published Online 17 July 2019

Assessment of the likely impact of Chinese OFDI on the ASEAN members of the Belt and Road Initiative (BRI) requires understanding of the evolution of Chinese policy, regulations and institutions. Utilizing recent developments in institutional theory, this paper examines the interplay between China's OFDI regulations and enterprise supportive policies. Liberalization of FDI regulations complements policies of technological catch-up and the development of regionally focused multilateral institutions. Evidence of an increasing level of Chinese OFDI since 2003, and of a larger share attracted to the BRI group, particularly the ASEAN countries, is consistent with the theorizing.

Keywords: BRI; OFDI; China; institutions; ASEAN.

JEL Classification: O19, O25, P33.

1. Introduction

Over the past several decades China has evolved to become an important source country for outward foreign direct investment (OFDI) in the world economy (United Nations, 2018). The process of internationalization of latecomer firms from emerging economies is not easy due to their relative lack of capital and of global operational experience (Mathews, 2002; Li, 2007; Luo and Tung, 2007, 2018). In such situations, home country governments and institutions may serve an important role in supporting the internationalization of their enterprises (Li, 2007; Luo *et al.*, 2010; Gaur *et al.*, 2018). This is particularly true for China, with extant literature stressing the crucial role that the Chinese government plays in shaping the structure and pattern of Chinese overseas investment through ownership and regulatory policies (Deng, 2003; Child and Rodrigues, 2005; Buckley *et al.*, 2007; Luo *et al.*, 2010; Wang *et al.*, 2012).

The economic development model of China is shaped by "Chinese characteristics", a state-led capitalist, authoritarian regime that sustains strong government power, uses

[†]Corresponding author.

[‡]This article originally appeared in *The Singapore Economic Review*, **66**(1), pp. 143–159

significant influence, and enforces an administrative bureaucratic system at the national level (Luo *et al.*, 2010). The Chinese government is able to use its considerable influence as a powerful 'visible hand' to quickly enact and amend OFDI policies to direct Chinese firms' internationalization decisions in support of the country's economic imperatives (Scott, 2002; Li, 2007). An important implication of this is the likelihood that as China's policies on international engagement evolve, their impact on host economies also changes. The most recent manifestation of this evolving international engagement is the BRI, announced in 2013.

The internationalization processes of Chinese firms are substantially affected by the country's unique institutional factors (Morck *et al.*, 2008; Luo *et al.*, 2010). The institution-based view argues that a home country government's regulatory policies can accelerate firm internationalization if they are supportive and transparent, especially for a home country with close government-business ties (Deng, 2003; Gaur *et al.*, 2018). This is evidenced by findings that China's regulatory policies can significantly advantage firms enabling them to overcome resource constraints, leverage their economic and political positions against competitors, and aid success in overseas markets (Rugman, 1990; Scott, 2002; Sauvant, 2005).

The aim of this paper is to conceptualize the challenges and opportunities that South-East Asia is likely to experience with the implementation of the BRI initiative, the most recent stage in China's embryonic internationalization model, utilizing an institutional perspective. The key argument is that as a state-influenced economy a primary determinant of China's OFDI is government policy exercised through evolving institutional arrangements (del Sol and Kogan, 2007; Dau, 2012; Luo and Wang, 2012; Sun *et al.*, 2015). Effective assessment of the likely impacts of the BRI initiative necessitates understanding the evolution of underlying institutional pressures and government directives that Chinese enterprises experience. That is, analysis of changes in the country's OFDI policy present only a partial picture of the forces that firms respond to. Simultaneously, we may expect the authorities to also implement or sanction a range of supportive policies in complementary areas that contribute to the competitiveness, or reduce the liabilities of foreignness (Gaur *et al.*, 2011), that domestic firms face. An example is provided by technological upgrading facilitated by the rapid growth of Chinese asset-seeking acquisitions that targeted United States and European companies after 2010 (Meunier *et al.*, 2014; Rosen and Hanemann, 2014).

The discussion draws on institutional theory (North, 1990; Scott, 1995) and more recent analyzes encompassing dynamic sources of home country advantage (Cuervo-Cazurra *et al.*, 2018), 'institutional work' (Yan *et al.*, 2018), and institutional open access (Sun *et al.*, 2015) to provide a conceptually grounded framework for examining the likely impacts of the BRI on the ASEAN nations.

The paper makes three main contributions. First, it highlights the evolutionary nature of institutional arrangements in an emerging economy like China, and how such changes are likely to affect the volume and location of OFDI. The evolution of China's OFDI regime also makes clear the wide range of supportive activities that the state undertakes to facilitate firm internationalization. We identify and develop four key areas of government-led support and how these have facilitated internationalization. Second, the discussion enables the derivation of several simple propositions regarding the changing nature of Chinese OFDI under the BRI. Finally, we use the conceptual underpinning offered by institutional theory to identify the key challenges and opportunities that South–East Asian economies are likely to experience under the BRI initiative.

The paper is organized around five main sections. Following this introduction, we set out the underlying institutional theory and its value in understanding China's evolving OFDI regime. We then provide a brief overview of the changes that have occurred in China's OFDI policy since the opening of the economy in 1978. This discussion also allows us to develop propositions on trends in Chinese OFDI. The fourth section offers a discussion of the key challenges and opportunities that South–East Asia is likely to face as the BRI becomes the central component in China's international engagement. Concluding thoughts and suggestions for further research are provided in the final section.

2. Institutional Theory and a Framework for Understanding the Impact of OFDI

It is now accepted that market exchange does not occur in isolation: it is underpinned by a variety of institutional arrangements that both constrain and encourage human interactions. Such institutions can be informal (sanctions, customs and traditions), or formal (laws, regulations, property rights). Formal institutions at the level of the nation state issue or enforce laws and regulations consistent with the economic system they support. Key to China's OFDI policy are regulative institutions that control the behavior of agents (firms) through largely coercive mechanisms. Traditionally, research has focused on the influence of firm-, industry- and host market conditions on firm internationalization, with, until recently, less consideration given to home country considerations (but see *Journal of World Business* Special Section 2018). The institutional perspective suggests that it is simplistic to believe that OFDI activities are influenced only by regulative agencies charged with the oversight of OFDI. Rather, the Chinese state has strengthened the international competitiveness of its firms in a variety of ways (Ramamurti and Hillemann, 2018).

Three strands of recent work in institution theory are relevant for our discussion. The first is the notion of institutional open access. This is based on the idea that institutional reform serves to increase the relative importance of formal over informal institutions through a consolidation of formal rules emphasizing market-driven decisions (Sun *et al.*, 2015). Crucial to institutional open access is liberalization of legal and financial markets. Reform of legal rules provides emerging market firms with experience of operating in more advanced economies, reducing the uncertainty they face (Wu and Chen, 2014). Regulatory freedom needs to be coupled with financial market opening if firms are to have the resources to pursue autonomous internationalization strategies. For example, capital was limited in China by onerous approval processes that favored state-owned enterprises (SOEs), and constrained the use of initial public offerings (IPOs) by private firms. Many private firms were forced to turn to overseas exchanges to raise funds. The value of institutional open access thinking is that it recognizes that irrespective of the level of state pressures for firm internationalization, this will require the enactment of complementary institutional changes. It also offers guidance on the direction of policy and institutional reform, suggesting greater convergence with advanced market economies.

A second important concept is provided by 'institutional work', the idea that institutional reform is neither a smooth, nor simply a top-down, process. Rather, a complex interplay exists whereby regulatory innovation, such as the BRI, is inspired from the top, but interpreted at national and provisional levels, challenged by firms seeking to ensure their legitimacy, maintained by relevant agencies, and continually refined in the light of experience (Yan *et al.*, 2018). Such a view helps explain the success of complex institutional reform on a 'trial and error' basis as well as why Chinese firms have been willing to embrace often quite radical institutional change. These concepts illustrate that firm 'support' within China is multifaceted, enabling clear state-direction, but ensuring agent buy-in through an assurance of both involvement, and acceptance, of the direction of change.

The third strand examines the diversity of supportive policies from the perspective of firm competitiveness. A useful framework for analysing the sources of internationally supportive policies is provided by Cuervo-Cazurra *et al.* (2018). We build on this to explore four key ways in which the state helps its firms to augment ownership advantages, or to overcome uncertainty and the liabilities of foreignness.

The framework is summarized in Table 1 and identifies four principal sources of advantage influenced by government policy. These relate to country of origin advantages and liabilities, competitive advantage and institutional advantage. State policies in these areas impact firm internationalization in two key ways: by increasing ownership advantages; and/or by reducing uncertainty. Both are positively associated with firm internationalization (Hilmersson and Jansson, 2012; Ramamurti, 2012; Williamson and Wan, 2018). We explore each of these in more detail.

Table 1. Government Policies Supporting Chinese Firm Internationalization

Nature of Advantage	Influence on Firm Internationalization	Form of Government Influence	Impact on Firm Internationalization
Country of origin advantages	Reducing uncertainty	Government promotion of key sectors e.g., infrastructure. Development of new technologies. Prestigious investments showcasing technology e.g., smart cities. Provision of an alternative development model.	Creates positive perception in host markets. Expectation of positive spillovers. Facilitates host market acceptance and legitimacy. Contributes to ownership advantages (OAs).

Table 1. (*Continued*)

Nature of Advantage	Influence on Firm Internationalization	Form of Government Influence	Impact on Firm Internationalization
Competitive advantage	Increasing efficiency	Contribution to the creation of OAs through policies encouraging upgrading. Learning from IFDI. Public investment in innovation. Firm level initiatives to overcome market and institutional voids. Permissive competitive policy to facilitate scale. Creation of national champions.	Contributes to the upgrading of OAs. Upgrading and expansion of OAs. Upgrading and expansion of OAs. Private capture of internationally transferable IPRs. Advantages of scale, resources and experience. Benefits of state support.
Institutional advantage	Increasing efficiency	Variety of institutional arrangements Allowing 'institutional work' that optimises OFDI policies. Institutional advantage resulting from variety of arrangements and pace of reform. Focus on pro-market reforms offering an internationally transferable template.	Institutional knowledge as an OA. Enables optimization of OFDI and supporting policies. Enables entry into a variety of markets. Geographical focus on markets at diverse stages of reform.
Country of origin liabilities	Reducing uncertainty	Reform of SOEs. Campaigns to deny close government/firm links and strong diplomatic responses. Overcoming claims of excessive value extraction. Perception of obtaining 'assets in crisis'	Reducing negative perceptions. Targeting institutionally similar economies. Encouraging use of PPPs, JVs, and soft funding. Pressures to increase greenfield FDI.

Source: Based on Cuervo-Cazurra *et al.* (2018).

2.1. *Country of origin advantages*

In the case of country of origin advantages, policies are used to buttress a perception in overseas markets of economic capability and performance in the home market (China). This can be achieved in a number of ways including government funding of prestigious projects such as smart cities, key investments in areas of interest to potential host markets such as advanced infrastructure (high speed rail for example), and the creation of a world leading capability in new technologies such as artificial intelligence and alternative energies. China has been highly successful in all of these areas and is now a dominant producer of a number of products including wind and solar technologies, electric vehicles, and personal mobility devices. As industry has moved up the value chain the perception of China as an assembler and exporter of labor-intensive manufactured products has declined. As a result of rapid growth the country has made massive investments in infrastructure that have contributed to an overseas image of modernization. Also of relevance is the promotion of the BRI package as an alternative development model. The creation of the Shanghai Cooperation Organization in 2001 provided an initial institutional framework for facilitating cross-border interactions between China and a number of its Eurasian neighbors. While originally designed to resolve border and security issues, recently the SCO intensified its focus on regional economic initiatives (Albert, 2015). More recently, the creation of the Asian Infrastructure Investment Bank (AIIB) has provided an important funding mechanism for an infrastructure-driven development model. Part of the appeal of the BRI is that it targets areas of the world that have not greatly benefitted from the recent globalization wave, particularly parts of West Asia and Central Europe. Furthermore, the BRI model offers an alternative to the Western view of globalization that emphasizes privatization and liberalization underpinning an export-led or consumer-driven development model. The Chinese view of development based on infrastructure and trading assets may hold considerable appeal for a number of BRI participant nations.

The effect of these policies is to reduce investor uncertainty and increase likely acceptance of investing firms in host economies. Source country prestige could increase firm acceptance and legitimacy, facilitating a positive perception amongst local stakeholders. Such perceptions could also be reinforced by the likelihood that investing firms enjoy stronger ownership advantages as a result of their involvement in domestic upgrading. In turn, this could offer higher levels of positive spillovers in the host market as investing firms could contribute technological and marketing capability (Gorodnichenko *et al.*, 2014; Lu *et al.*, 2017).

2.2. *Competitive advantages*

A second area of policy influence occurs through home market economic development and the augmentation of firm-level ownership advantages. Much of the literature on emerging market multinationals focuses on the competitive weaknesses of these firms and their need to augment advantages (Narula, 2012; Hennart, 2018), often through asset-seeking internationalization (Mathews, 2002; Luo and Tung, 2018). While this belief of the need for catch-up is widespread, the reality is that China's rapid development and supporting industrialization policies have created a number of sectors where Chinese firms already enjoy a strong competitive position. In some of these sectors highly targeted policies are used to ensure rapid upgrading of firm capabilities. For example, in the electric vehicle industry subsidies are provided to manufacturers and consumers by both central and local governments. In 2017, at an average vehicle cost of US $10,000 the total value of subsidies exceeded US $7.7 billion (Perkowski, 2018). Support for the industry goes beyond direct subsidy. For example, a number of cities guarantee licenses to electric vehicles and preferential use of carpool lanes. An indication of 'institutional work' is offered by recent announcements to shift the costs of supportive policies to vehicle producers. The new policy focus offers a combination of credits and disincentives through a credit trading scheme based on vehicle efficiency and battery density, effectively rewarding the most efficient and innovative producers, while eliminating marginal competitors.

Chinese producers also enjoy opportunities for competitive upgrading as a result of the significant amount of inward investment that China has enjoyed over the last forty years, and the positive spillovers that local firms have captured from this (Lin *et al.*, 2009). The government insistence in the early years on joint ventures and other collaborative forms, facilitated knowledge transfer accelerating domestic upgrading (Buckley *et al.*, 2004). This is readily apparent in the automotive industry for example (Zhao *et al.*, 2005).

Chinese firms have also benefited from the growing level of public investment in innovation that complements expenditure by private firms. China is now the second largest spender on R&D and has increased R&D spending from 0.72% of GDP in 1991 to 2.13 in 2017. This compares with 2.7% for the United States. Almost three-quarters of China's spending on innovation is undertaken by business (CSIS, 2019). Chinese enterprises are able to upgrade their competitive advantages both directly through their own expenditures, both domestically and through targeted M&As, and indirectly, as beneficiaries of public investments.

Advantages have also been created through the responses of Chinese firms to widespread market and institutional failures that are characteristic of emerging markets (Khanna and Palepu, 1997). For example, China's social media giants Alibaba and Tencent have both used private data they have compiled to create credit scoring businesses, services that did not previously exist in China. They have also been successful in overcoming the lack of trust in e-commerce transactions through the use of escrow payment facilities.

The formation of ownership advantages by Chinese firms has also benefitted from lax competition policy which has allowed the creation of dominant market positions in a number of sectors including banking, social media, and telecommunications. This has enabled a number of enterprises to profit from advantages of scale and rapid growth, while enjoying protection from foreign competition. Research has indicated the considerable benefits of creating national champions that are associated with above average growth rates in emerging economies (MGI, 2018).

These policies contribute to the creation and upgrading of competitive advantages possessed by Chinese firms facilitating internationalization (Ramamurti, 2012). In some cases (technology, cost advantages, brands) these advantages are similar to those employed by most MNEs, in other cases (propriety advantages based on exploiting institutional voids for example), they are quite distinct, supporting calls for widening the search for sources of ownership advantages within emerging market firms (Hennart, 2012; Contractor, 2013).

2.3. *Institutional advantage*

A third area of government support occurs through the diverse institutional arrangements, and their rapid evolution, characteristic of many emerging economies. Exposure to a variety of institutions, with formal institutions often weaker than those found in developed economies, provides a valuable learning opportunity for emerging market firms given the tremendous differences in institutional patterns across the world (Jackson and Deeg, 2008). Knowledge of institutional diversity and evolution provides a novel source of advantage, institutional advantage (Martin, 2014). Knowledge of a diverse set of institutions increases the likelihood of successful entry into a variety of overseas markets (Cuervo-Cazurra *et al.*, 2018), as exemplified by the BRI participants.

The direction of China's institutional development is also noteworthy. The move towards a more market-based economic system (open access) offers a template that has considerable value elsewhere, particularly, in later reforming economies, again characteristic of a number of the BRI nations. This enhances the international transferability of institutional knowledge as a proprietary asset.

Recognition that 'institutional work', that is the development of regulations and policies through a constructive interaction of institutions, government departments, and firms, facilitates accommodative policy that meets the needs of potential investors, increases both the likelihood of internationalization, as well as success following establishment (Luo and Rui, 2009; Duanmu, 2014). Where policies are vague, ambiguous or rapidly evolving (Luo and Zhang, 2016), the opportunity to influence their final form can be highly valuable. Policies that encourage institutional learning increase the likelihood of internationalization through the development of novel sources of advantage, as well as locational preference by increasing capability to prosper in a wide range of institutional settings.

2.4. *Country of origin liabilities*

The distinctive characteristics of Chinese OFDI can also be a liability in overseas markets. The three enduring traits, state-directed investment, a significant role for SOEs, and a high incidence of entry through mergers and acquisitions, have all raised concerns in overseas markets (Wang *et al.*, 2012; Dobson, 2014; Tingley *et al.*, 2015; Cuervo-Cazurra, 2018). Firms suspected of close government links have been perceived as a threat to host nation security and have been targeted in a number of cases, most notably Huawei, which has been denied telecommunications contracts in countries including the United States, Australia, and New Zealand, with Japan likely to follow.

Chinese firms also suffer from a perception that they fail to share value creation when undertaking overseas projects, with a disproportionate share of materials and even labor, sourced from China. This criticism has been most strongly expressed in Africa (Adisu *et al.*, 2010). A preference for acquisitions has also seen Chinese firms accused of underpaying for assets, particularly when targeting distressed firms and industries in a downturn.

The Chinese authorities have begun to step up their campaign to reduce such perceptions. One strategy has been to provide development loans to potential host countries, reducing risk, increasing access to resources, and lowering the likelihood of political conflict (Shapiro *et al.*, 2018). The AIIB plays a central role within this strategy. A second strategy has been reform of SOEs and the introduction of incentives to encourage their innovativeness (Ralston *et al.*, 2006). Third, following a sharp increase in OFDI into North America and Europe, the Chinese authorities in 2018 restricted investment into what were termed 'sensitive' sectors including real estate, hotels, sport clubs and entertainment (Baker McKenzie, 2018). The BRI increases the likelihood that Chinese investors will be entering economies that have similar economic ideologies and structure, particularly the transition economies of Central Asia. Involvement in infrastructure projects also encourages the use of greenfield entry and the sharing of value through public–private partnerships and joint ventures with local firms. Overall, the BRI nations represent a group that is likely to have fewer negative perceptions of Chinese investment either as a result of familiarity due to diaspora and the representation of overseas Chinese in business and trading activities (South and East Asia), the opportunity to attract much needed funds (Central Asia), or because of anticipated trade stimulus (Europe).

3. The Evolution of OFDI Policy

As a result of these diverse policies China's economy and international engagement have evolved, gradually reducing direct command and control of the economy and creating new institutions to manage and guide economic development while retaining a regulatory state logic (Bach *et al.*, 2006). Despite the increasing adoption of a market system, China remains a political economy characterized by active government involvement in business, both through ownership and through regulation (Davies, 2013). In the same way, China's OFDI policies continue to reflect the government's continuing pursuit of national interests (Voss, 2011).

Since China's reform and opening up in 1970s, the overall strategy for OFDI has gradually shifted from strict limits to the current policy of encouragement (Luo *et al.*, 2010). China's initial response to globalization was mostly passive: from the 1970s to the beginning of this century, China adopted a strict examination and approval system for foreign direct investment; from 1999 onward, with the gradual improvement of China's comprehensive economic strength and the deepening of reform and opening up, the restrictive OFDI policy changed, and the government begun to encourage OFDI. Since the Belt and Road Initiative (BRI) was announced in 2013, China has further loosened controls on OFDI and simplified the OFDI approval process to stimulate enterprise internationalization.

In 1999, the Chinese government instigated the 'Go Global' ('zou chu qu') policy. The policy sought to encourage internationalization with the aim of improving the international competitiveness of domestic companies through OFDI, as well as supporting the country's economic development (Sauvant, 2005; Voss, 2011). Furthermore, the 'Go Global' policy set a strong institutional environment with national public endorsement that fostered OFDI (Child and Rodrigues, 2005). The 'Go Global' policy contributed to the rising trend of Chinese OFDI subsequently (Luo *et al.*, 2010; Wang and Zhao, 2017). In compliance with accession of the WTO in 2001, China gradually opened its once protected markets (Qin, 2007). The business environment for Chinese firms changed dramatically; domestic markets experienced stronger competition forcing Chinese firms to seek new markets both within China and abroad (Taylor, 2002; Von Keller and Zhou, 2003).

This discussion allows us to put forward the first proposition:

P1: Increasing liberalization of China's OFDI regime has resulted in an increase in both the volume of Chinese OFDI and OFDI as a percent of China's GDP.

In 2012, the eighteenth National Congress of the Communist Party of China proposed accelerating the 'Going Global' process to enhance Chinese enterprises' ability to operate internationally, and to create a group of successful global companies. The 2013, BRI announcement provided strategic support for Chinese enterprises going global, and opened up vast new opportunities for overseas investment. Since the announcement of BRI, the Chinese government has introduced a series of supportive policies to promote investment in infrastructure in participating countries (Zhai, 2018) and the AIIB to provide funds for BRI projects. The third session of the Twelfth National People's Congress in 2015 sought to integrate the BRI into regional development and China's opening up (Zhai, 2018).

China is adopting a different growth model for the next stage of its economic development, undertaking structural adjustment processes that will also alter the country's international investment position (Lardy, 2012). New markets are needed for the export of commodities such as glass, steel and cement which suffer from overcapacity. Increased investment into the BRI markets, particularly in the short-term, will facilitate domestic economic restructuring by reducing adverse adjustment pressures on these declining industries. There is some evidence that China's OFDI is shifting in ways consistent with these arguments. China's average annual OFDI flows increased from under US$7 billion in 2003–2005, to more than $155 billion in 2015–2017, a more than twenty-two fold increase over the period. OFDI also increased as a percentage of GDP from 0.35% in 2003–2005 to 1.35% in 2015–2017. Also notable is that the share of Chinese OFDI targeting BRI countries doubled over the period to reach almost 12% by 2015–2017 (National Bureau of Statistics of China [various]).

In the light of this discussion we offer two further propositions:

P2: The growing emphasis placed by the Chinese authorities on the BRI countries means that OFDI to these countries will increase in both monetary terms and as a percent of total Chinese OFDI.

P3: Because of established economic links between mainland China and the BRI economies of South and East Asia, these two areas will dominate Chinese OFDI to BRI nations.

4. Opportunities and Challenges of the BRI for South-East Asia

Given that the BRI is still at a very early stage, and that its full effects may take 50 years to realize, any discussion of benefits and challenges for a particular region must be considered tentative (Enderwick, 2018). However, it is possible to identify a number of areas that present both opportunities and challenges for the economies of South-East Asia.

4.1. *Opportunities*

In terms of opportunities the BRI participant economies of South–East Asia appear to enjoy a number of advantages. They benefit from geographical proximity, strong existing economic links with China, and in many cases, historical and cultural ties. Rapid growth in global value chains, even those controlled from outside the region, have deepened economic links between China and its ASEAN neighbors (ASEAN-Japan Centre, 2017). Not surprisingly, due to the high level of regional integration, simulations of the impact of the BRI suggest that South-East Asia is likely to be a principal beneficiary (Villafuerte *et al.*, 2016). This expectation is reinforced by other work suggesting that the ASEAN nations will benefit from the current US-China trade war (EIU, 2018).

The region is also likely to benefit from its location, and in particular, it centrality to a number of new transport links that China would like to expand. This suggests that South–East Asia may be an early beneficiary of OFDI as new ports and transport hubs are developed. For example, huge sums have been attracted to port development in Singapore.

Complementarity of competitive advantage between China and other parts of South–East Asia will ensure that both upstream and downstream trade and production linkages are likely to be strengthened under the BRI. China's domestic restructuring will see continuing demand for high-tech intermediate parts and services from Korea, Taiwan and Singapore as output increasingly targets the home market. Industries that are losing their advantage in resource and labor cost arbitrage, such as footwear and clothing and garments, are likely to be increasingly relocated to emerging economies such as Vietnam, Cambodia and Myanmar. In the longer term, a number of ASEAN economies including Indonesia, Malaysia, Vietnam and the Philippines have the scale and growth potential to be major markets of the future.

A further area of mutual economic stimulation, and one that receives little attention in discussions of the BRI, is the need for complementary investments in 'soft' infrastructure. While the early stages of the BRI emphasize hard infrastructure such as roads, ports and railways, this must be integrated and coordinated through digital capabilities in finance, telecommunications and e-commerce, and is likely to drive a second wave of BRI related investment. China is well placed to take the lead in this area with some of the world's leading banks, major telecoms equipment (Huawei and ZTE) and service providers (China Mobile, China Telecom and China Unicom) and e-commerce and social media giants (Baidu, Alibaba and Tencent). However, investments in these areas will raise concerns regarding dependency, data privacy, and national security. It is likely that the leading Chinese enterprises may wish to pioneer investments into economies where they already enjoy recognition and legitimacy.

Investments into the South–East Asian region may also benefit from more effective governance. As China liberalizes, its investors will become more familiar with undertaking market transactions and an early focus on the ASEAN region will enable them to design, monitor and enforce contracts in economies with which they have some familiarity. In contrast, they are likely to experience much higher levels of corruption, opacity and government intervention in other regions of the BRI. In addition, Chinese enterprises improved their management of overseas investments during the 'Go Global' phase and are now less likely to overpay for assets or to invest in poor performing activities (Zhang and Ebbers, 2010).

4.2. *Challenges*

While the BRI brings huge economic opportunities, it also carries significant challenges. Its sheer scale and massive time scale are obvious characteristics that could result in delays, disputes and derailments. Our discussion also highlights that the political and economic context is continually developing. While the BRI may be the key external initiative, China is also managing complex domestic restructuring on a scale that no other country has ever experienced before. Key domestic challenges include growing regional disparities, increasing debt levels, the restructuring of heavy industry, and the need to tackle environmental concerns. While the BRI may contribute to tackling some of these issues, they could still divert significant policy resources.

China will need to address the considerable diversity of the constituent countries to the BRI initiative. They vary in terms of income levels, in terms of infrastructure potential as measured by land mass, population, road, and rail density and in levels of trade links, with China having much lower trade rates with South, Central, and Western Asia, when compared with South–East Asia. Obstacles to doing business also vary across the region with problems arising from administrative delays and poor quality infrastructure (World Economic Forum, 2016).

Policy coordination is also likely to be adversely affected by differences in policy approaches and institutional quality between BRI participants. A number of participant countries are prone to economic and political instability and widespread corruption. The financing model of private-public partnerships will also be affected by the credit worthiness and sovereign risks found in member countries. However, any move by Chinese investors towards more market based transactions and to market-seeking motives, will disproportionately favor South-East Asia.

The impact of the BRI initiative will depend on the effective governance of the proposed projects. Funding misdirected to wasteful projects renders any assessment based on plausible multiplier effects futile, so that ensuring sound governance is critical. This is particularly true for a funding model based on private-public partnerships that require transparency, effective cross-border regulation, and adherence to something close to market principles. Participant nations within the BRI scheme also vary in terms of effective governance. Cross-national governance is further complicated by the reality of difficult political relationships between China and a number of BRI countries resulting from territorial disputes. These may need to be resolved at a fairly early stage.

A fourth challenge is the fact that the monetary cost and value of projects may be misleading when significant productivity or efficiency effects occur. The heavy involvement of the private sector in infrastructure projects is likely to reduce the public debt burden, encourage knowledge sharing, and the adoption of best practice. Efficiency is also subject to synergistic integration of the many constituent projects proposed, since interdependency is a key characteristic of the BRI scheme. In other words, the routes, and their transaction costs, are only as effective as the weakest link. We might anticipate significant productivity enhancing effects when experienced Chinese contractors take on the majority of the work because of weaknesses within the private sector of many participant economies.

However, the scale and interdependency of the BRI scheme also raises fears within a number of nations of Chinese domination and growing dependency on Chinese controlled resources. Chinese firms have undoubtedly learned from their experiences in parts of Africa where their practices and a perception that the benefits of investments were not being shared, creating significant opposition (Klaver and Treblicock, 2011). Optimizing the benefits of the scheme will entail effective and transparent governance.

5. Conclusions

This paper has argued the need to understand the evolution of China's OFDI policy when evaluating the likely impacts of the BRI on ASEAN nations. Recent theory has provided insights that reveal regulatory and institutional reform as a complex and multifaceted process. For China it is an iterative process, constructed through the interplay of diverse interests, while following state-directed development towards a more open, market-based economy. The internationalization of Chinese firms will likely follow this evolution with an increasing proportion of OFDI attracted to the BRI nations. Within this group, South–East Asian economies offer particular attractions and are the target for a rising proportion of foreign investment.

Such investment is not simply the result of FDI liberalization: it is bolstered by a range of supporting policies designed to facilitate Chinese enterprise internationalization. Technological upgrading, access to competitive assets through cross-border acquisitions, closer regional links and funding initiatives are all part of the growing competitive profile of Chinese enterprises. Exposure to a template of 'institutional open access' is equipping Chinese firms to compete in sophisticated economies in Europe for example. At the same time, past institutional knowledge is not 'unlearned', enabling these firms to compete successfully in a range of institutional arrangements as exemplified by the BRI group. Their growing competitiveness has important implications for host nations that will face strong competitive pressure from the growing presence of Chinese investors. The ASEAN nations may benefit from Chinese domestic restructuring as areas of declining comparative advantage are relocated, and industries suffering overcapacity seek to shift capacity. At the same time the BRI presents significant challenges in areas such as transparency, effective governance and financing. Our arguments highlight the need to interpret Chinese OFDI flows in a dynamic context, with recognition that such firms are being strongly supported by a determined and increasingly well-resourced state. In theoretical terms, they also offer a possible integration of resource- and institutional perspectives, two approaches to explaining emerging market firm internationalization that have, to date, been largely separated. China's involvement in a number of regionally focused multilateral institutions including the SCO, AIIB, Asian Regional Forum and the ASEAN-China Free Trade Agreement, are consistent with the view that China will increasingly direct its influence through such institutional arrangements, a reflection of what Ikenberry and Lim (2017) term "China's emerging institutional statecraft".

The paper has examined an important consideration in the evaluation of FDI impacts, but must be seen as simply a starting point. More analysis will be required as the BRI unfolds: its geographical spread, time scale, and interdependency mean that assessments need to be continually updated.

Conceptually, our ideas would benefit from further refinement, examining the changing profile of Chinese FDI by location, industry and firm type, for example, and case studies of the internationalization of specific enterprises. Institutional theory also has application at a provincial or regional level (Li *et al.*, 2018) and could explain differential rates of OFDI from different regions with the expectation that higher rates or levels of investment might be expected from more open regions. There is also the interesting question of whether all facets of OFDI are impacted in the same way by supportive policies, or whether there might be differences in terms of location, entry mode, number, or scale of investment. These are all questions worthy of further research effort.

References

Albert, E (2015). *The Shanghai Cooperation Organization.* Council on Foreign Relations, 14 October, New York.

Adisu, K, T Sharkey and SC Okoroafo (2010). The impact of Chinese investment in Africa. *International Journal of Business and Management*, 5(9), 3–9.

ASEAN-Japan Centre (2017). *Global value chains in ASEAN: A regional perspective.* ASEAN-Japan Centre, Paper 1, September, Tokyo.

Bach, D, AL Newman and S Weber (2006). The international implications of china's fledgling regulatory state: From product maker to rule maker. *New Political Economy*, 11(4), 499–518.

Baker McKenzie (2018). *Rising Tensions: Assessing China's FDI Drop in Europe and North America*, Chicago, Illinois: Baker McKenzie/Rhodium Group.

Buckley, PJ, J Clegg and H Tan (2004). Knowledge transfer to China: Lessons from foreign affiliates. *Transnational Corporations*, 13(1), 31–72.

Buckley, PJ, LJ Clegg, AR Cross, X Liu, H Voss and P Zheng (2007). The determinants of Chinese outward foreign direct investment. *Journal of International Business Studies*, 38(4), 499–518.

Child, J and SB Rodrigues (2005). The internationalization of Chinese firms: A case for theoretical extension?, *Management and Organization Review*, 1(3), 381–410.

Contractor, FJ (2013). "Punching above their weight" the sources of competitive advantage for emerging market multinationals. *International Journal of Emerging Markets*, 8(4), 304–328.

CSIS (2019). Is China a global leader in research and development? Center for Strategic and International Studies, Washington.

Cuervo-Cazurra, A (2018). Thanks but no thanks: State-owned multinationals from emerging markets and host-country policies. *Journal of International Business Policy*, 1(3), 128–156.

Cuervo-Cazurra, A, Y Luo, R Ramamurti and SH Ang (2018). The impact of the home country on internationalization. *Journal of World Business*, 53(5), 593–604.

Dau, LA (2012). Pro-market Reforms and Developing Country Multinationals. *Global Strategy Journal* 2(3), pp. 262–276.

Davies, K (2013). *China Investment Policy: An Update. OECD Working Papers on International Investment*, Paris: OECD Publishing.

del Sol, P and J Kogan (2007). Regional competitive advantage based on pioneering economic reforms: The case of chilean FDI. *Journal of International Business Studies*, 38(6), 901–927.

Deng, P (2003). Foreign investment by multinationals from emerging countries: The case of China. *Journal of Leadership and Organizational Studies*, 10(2), 113–124.

Dobson, W (2014). China's state-owned enterprises and Canada's FDI policy. *Canadian Public Policy*, 43(S2), 29–44.

Duanmu, J (2014). State-owned MNCs and host country expropriation risk: The Role of home state soft power and economic gunboat diplomacy. *Journal of International Business Studies*, 45(8), 1044–1060.

EIU (2018). Creative disruption: Asia's winners in the US-China trade war. Economist Intelligence Unit, London.

Enderwick, P (2018). The economic growth and development effects of china's one belt, one road initiative. *Strategic Change*, 27(5), 447–454.

Gaur, AS, V Kumar and R Sarathy (2011). Liability of foreignness and internationalization of emerging market firms. In *Dynamics of Globalization: Location-Specific Advantages or Liabilities of Foreignness? (Advances in International Management)*, CG Asmussen, T Pedersen, TM Devinney and L Tihanyi (eds.), Vol. 24, pp. 211–233, Bingley: Emerald Group Publishing Limited.

Gaur, AS, X Ma and Z Ding (2018). Home country supportiveness/unfavourableness and outward foreign direct investment from China. *Journal of International Business Studies*, 49(3), 324–345.

Gorodnichenko, Y, J Svejnar and K Terrell (2014). When does FDI have positive spillovers? evidence from 17 transition market economies. *Journal of Comparative Economics*, 43(4), 954–969.

Hennart, JF (2012). Emerging market multinationals and the theory of the multinational enterprise. *Global Strategy Journal*, 2(3), 168–187.

Hennart, JF (2018). Springing from where? how emerging market firms become multinational enterprises. *International Journal of Emerging Markets*, 13(3), 568–585.

Hilmersson, M and H Jansson (2012). Reducing uncertainty in the emerging market entry process: On the relationship among international experiential knowledge, institutional distance, and uncertainty. *Journal of International Marketing*, 20(4), 96–110.

Ikenberry, GJ and DJ Lim (2017). *China's Emerging Institutional Statecraft: The Asian Infrastructure Investment Bank and the Prospects for Counter-Hegemony. Project on International Order and Strategy*, Washington: Brookings Institute.

Jackson, G and R Deeg (2008). Comparing capitalisms: Understanding institutional diversity and its implications for international business. *Journal of International Business Studies*, 39(4), 540–561.

Khanna, T and KG Palepu (1997). Why focused strategies may be wrong for emerging markets. *Harvard Business Review*, 75(4), 41–51.

Klaver, M and M Treblicock (2011). Chinese investment in Africa. *Law and Development Review*, 4(1), 168–217.

Lardy, NR (2012). *Sustaining China's Economic Growth After the Global Financial Crisis*, Washington: Peterson Institute for International Economics.

Li, PP (2007). Toward an integrated theory of multinational evolution: The evidence of Chinese multinational enterprises as latecomers. *Journal of International Management*, 13(3), 296–318.

Li, J, J Xia, D Shapiro and Z Lin (2018). Institutional compatibility and the internationalization of Chinese SOEs: The moderating role of home subnational institutions. *Journal of World Business*, 53(5), 641–652.

Lin, P, Z Liu and Y Zhang (2009). Do Chinese domestic firms benefit from FDI inflow? Evidence of horizontal and vertical spillovers. *China Economic Review*, 20(4), 677–691.

Lu, Y, Z Tao and L Zhu (2017). Identifying FDI spillovers. *Journal of International Economics*, 107(C), 75–90.

Luo, Y and H Rui (2009). An ambidexterity perspective toward multinational enterprises from emerging economies. *Academy of Management Perspectives*, 23(4), 49–70.

Luo, Y and RL Tung (2007). International expansion of emerging market enterprises: A springboard perspective. *Journal of International Business Studies*, 38(4), 481–498.

Luo, Y and RL Tung (2018). A general theory of springboard MNEs. *Journal of International Business Studies*, 49(2), 129–152.

Luo, Y and SL Wang (2012). Foreign direct investment strategies by developing country multinationals: A diagnostic model for home country effects. *Global Strategy Journal*, 2(3), 244–261.

Luo, Y, Q Xue and B Han (2010). How emerging market governments promote outward FDI: Evidence from China. *Journal of World Business*, 45(1), 68–79.

Luo, Y and H Zhang (2016). Emerging market MNEs: Qualitative review and theoretical directions. *Journal of International Management*, 22(4), 333–350.

Martin, X (2014). Institutional advantage. *Global Strategy Journal*, 4(1), 55–69.

Mathews, JA (2002). Competitive advantages of latecomer firms: A resource-based account of industrial catch-up strategies. *Asia-Pacific Journal of Management*, 19(4), 467–488.

Meunier, S, B Burgoon and W Jacoby (2014). The politics of hosting Chinese investment in Europe — an introduction. *Asia Europe Journal*, 12(1), 109–126.

MGI (2018). Outperformers: High-growth emerging economies and the companies that propel them, San Francisco: McKinsey Global Institute.

Morck, R, B Yeung and M Zhao (2008). Perspectives on China's outward foreign direct investment. *Journal of International Business Studies*, 39(3), 337–350.

Narula, R (2012). Do we need different frameworks to explain infant MNEs from developing countries? *Global Strategy Journal*, 2(3), 188–204.

National Bureau of Statistics available from: http://www.stats.gov.cn/was5/web/search?channelid=250710&andsen=+foreign+direct+investment&x=31&y=9.

North, DC (1990). *Institutions, Institutional Change and Economic Performance*, Cambridge: Cambridge University Press.

Perkowski, J (2018). *What China's Shifting Subsidies Could Mean for its Electric Vehicle Industry.* Forbes.

Qin, JY (2007). Trade, investment and beyond: The impact of WTO accession on China's legal system. *The China Quarterly*, 191, 720–741.

Ralston, DA, J Terpstra-Tong, RH Terpstra, X Wang and C Egri (2006). Today's state-owned enterprises of China: Are they dying dinosaurs or dynamic dynamos? *Strategic Management Journal*, 27(9), 825–843.

Ramamurti, R (2012). What is really different about emerging market multinationals? *Global Strategy Journal*, 2(1), 41–47.

Ramamurti, R and J Hillemann (2018). What is "Chinese" about Chinese multinationals? *Journal of International Business Studies*, 49(1), 1–15.

Rosen, DH and T Hanemann (2014). The changing US-China investment relationship. *China Economic Journal*, 7(1), 84–102.

Rugman, AM (1990). *Global Corporate Strategy and Trade Policy*, London and New York: Routledge.

Sauvant, KP (2005). New sources of FDI: The BRICs-outward FDI from Brazil, Russia, India and China. *Journal of World Investment and Trade*, 6(5), 639–710.

Scott, WR (1995). *Institutions and Organizations Sage*, Thousand Oaks.

Scott, WR (2002). The changing world of chinese enterprise: An institutional perspective. In *The Management of Enterprises in the People's Republic of China*, AS Tsui and CM Lau (eds.), pp. 59–78, Boston, MA: Springer.

Shapiro, DM, C Vecino and J Li (2018). Exploring China's state-led FDI model: Evidence from the extractive sectors in latin America. *Asia Pacific Journal of Management*, 35(1), 11–37.

Sun, SL, MW Peng, RP Lee and W Tan (2015). Institutional open access at home and outward internationalization. *Journal of World Business*, 50(1), 234–246.

Taylor, R (2002). Globalization strategies of chinese companies: Current developments and future prospects. *Asian Business and Management*, 1(2), 209–225.

Tingley, D, C Xu, A Chilton and HV Milner (2015). The political economy of inward FDI: Opposition to Chinese mergers and acquisitions. *The Chinese Journal of International Politics*, 8(1), 27–57.

United Nations (2018). World Investment Report 2018: Investment and New Industrial Policies, New York and Geneva: UNCTAD.

Villafuerte, J, E Corong and J Zhuang (2016). The one road one belt initiative: Impact on trade and growth. Paper presented at the *19th Annual Conf. Global Economic Analysis*, The World Bank, pp. 15–17, Washington.

Von Keller, E and W Zhou (2003). *From Middle Kingdom to Global Market: Expansion Strategies and Success Factors For China's Emerging Multinationals*, Munich: Roland Berger Strategy Consultants.

Voss, H (2011). *The Determinants of Chinese Outward Direct Investment.* Cheltenham: Edward Elgar.

Wang, C, J Hong, M Kafouros and M Wright (2012). Exploring the role of government involvement in outward fdi from emerging economies. *Journal of International Business Studies*, 43(7), 655–676.

Wang, Y and L Zhao (2017). Outward foreign direct investment from China: Recent trend and development. *The Chinese Economy*, 50(5), 356–365.

Williamson, P and F Wan (2018). Emerging market multinationals and the concept of ownership advantages. *International Journal of Emerging Markets*, 13(3), 557–567.

World Economic Forum (2016). The Global Enabling Trade Report 2016. WEF, Geneva.

Wu, J and X Chen (2014). Home country institutional environments and foreign expansion of emerging market firms. *International Business Review*, 23(5), 862–872.

Yan, ZJ, JC Zhu, D Fan and P Kalfadellis (2018). An institutional work view toward the internationalization of emerging market firms. *Journal of World Business*, 53(5), 682–694.

Zhai, F (2018). China's belt and road initiative: A preliminary quantitative assessment. *Journal of Asian Economics*, 55(C), 84–92.

Zhao, Z, J Anand and W Mitchell (2005). A dual networks perspective on inter-organizational transfer of R&D capabilities: International joint ventures in the chinese automotive industry. *Journal of Management Studies*, 42(1), 127–160.

Zhang, J and H Ebbers (2010). Why half of china's overseas acquisitions could not be completed. *Journal of Current Chinese Affairs*, 39(2), 101–131.

Chapter 8

DOES THE BELT AND ROAD INITIATIVE RESHAPE CHINA'S OUTWARD FOREIGN DIRECT INVESTMENT IN ASEAN? SHIFTING MOTIVES OF STATE-OWNED AND PRIVATE-OWNED ENTERPRISES[¶]

JIN SHI[*], XIAOHUI HU[†,§], YUNXIONG LI[‡] and TAO FENG[†]

[*]*School of Economics, Zhejiang University of Technology, China*

[†]*School of Public Administration*
Zhejiang University of Finance and Economics, China

[‡]*Department of Geography and Environment*
London School of Economics and Political Science, United Kingdom
[§]*xhhugeo@gmail.com*

Published Online 23 July 2020

In recent years, China has been increasingly witnessed as a major global outward investor, especially since the launch of the Belt and Road Initiative (BRI) in 2013. The question of whether and if yes how the BRI reshapes firm outward investment motives remains under-researched. Using a project-level database of China's Outward Direct Investment from the Ministry of Commerce from 2010 to 2015, this paper investigates the changing investment motives of state-owned and private-owned enterprises (SOEs and POEs) before and after the implementation of the BRI in two periods, namely 2010–2013 and 2014–2015. Our conditional logit models show that (1) market-seeking is one of the key motives for both POEs and SOEs; (2) POEs pursued natural resources in ASEAN based on geographical and relational proximity in the pre-BRI period while SOEs are directed to exploit natural resources in ASEAN besides remoter destinations after the launch of the BRI; (3) POEs are risk-taking in both periods, which runs counter to conventional expectations. This can be explained by the long-term investment tradition of POEs in ASEAN in which POEs are attracted predominantly by socio-economic factors and often less sensitive to variegated host institutions among ASEAN countries and (4) the BRI promotes Chinese OFDI in ASEAN through increased senior leader visits and enhanced diplomatic relations.

Keywords: The Belt and Road Initiative; ASEAN; outward foreign direct investment (OFDI); firm ownership; motive change.

JEL Classification: C35, F21, F23

1. Introduction

The emergence of China in the global political economy can be well witnessed by its consistently growing volume and rapidly expanding geographical reach of outward foreign direct investment (OFDI, hereafter) from the reform and opening-up from 1979 onwards. It has been recognized that China's OFDI is very much policy-driven, involved with a vast

---

[§] Corresponding author.

[¶]This article originally appeared in *The Singapore Economic Review*, **66**(1), pp. 161–183

number of state-owned enterprises (SOEs), and strongly influenced by changing home policies (Deng, 2009; Zhang and Daly, 2011; Stoian, 2013; Buckley *et al.*, 2018). Since the "Going Global" policy in 2000, WTO accession in 2001, liberalization for firm internationalization in 2003, and arguably, the recent Belt and Road Initiative (BRI, hereafter) in 2013, China has experienced a dramatic shift in OFDI. From a stock of only US$28 billion in 2000, at out of the 20th largest, behind Portugal, China's OFDI rocketed to US$1357.4 billion in 2016, reached as the second-largest global investor, behind the US (OECD, 2008; UNCTAD, 2016).

In particular, the BRI is a national strategy aiming at promoting regional economic integration (covering 65 countries in Asia, Europe and Africa) and sustaining China's peaceful rise and growth. It is implemented in a state capitalism model in which massive SOEs are designated to bring (more) investment and constructions in the BRI countries (Du and Zhang, 2018). The BRI has significantly influenced the spatial pattern of Chinese OFDI. During 2014 and 2015, the Chinese OFDI increase in the BRI countries was about 40% higher than that of non-BRI countries (Kang *et al.*, 2018). In 2017, Chinese OFDI has encountered a big recession due to the policy change. Its flow decreased by 25% compared to 2016 while in the BRI regions the investment flow still increased by 15% (Ministry of Commerce of China, 2017). In this regard, the BRI primarily functions as an economic policy that can generate a long-last positive impact on the BRI countries via OFDI (Li *et al.*, 2019). However, many commentators show skepticism on BRI's motivation, arguing that despite considerable OFDI in the foreseeable future it is *de facto* a geopolitical means that can hardly generate significant long-term economic benefits to the world, and that may rather bring about more global conflicts (Blanchard, 2018).

Much scholarly work on Chinese OFDI has been done, with a particular focus on its nation-specific motives — exploring why China as an emerging economy conducts OFDI and what specificities the Chinese OFDI has that differ from OFDI of developed economies (Buckley *et al.*, 2007; Huang and Wang, 2011). Despite the use of various theories and methods, the existing literature on the topic consists of three main yet interrelated research stances. First, by taking an inward-looking perspective highlighting China's peculiarity of home institutions, the overall motives of Chinese OFDI are identified. It is evident that the key motive of Chinese OFDI is strongly captured by government strategies aiming at fulfilling national development objectives and agendas in a broader sense (Wang *et al.*, 2012). It thus goes beyond the conventional firm-centric/specific model that is often applicable to OFDI from developed economies (Dunning, 1977). In particular, Chinese OFDI is both market and resource-seeking (Buckley *et al.*, 2007, 2018). Chinese global investors are more risk-taking, characterized by investing host countries with poor institutions (Ramasamy *et al.*, 2012). In many cases, Chinese OFDI bears more political and diplomatic missions regardless of economic efficiency and returns (Lv *et al.*, 2018). Moreover, public policies such as liberalization promote OFDI in certain locations and with certain sectors (Buckley *et al.*, 2018). Second, a growing literature addresses that the Chinese OFDI motives have become more heterogeneous as firm ownership significantly matters. The pro-SOEs national institutional environment has led to distinctive differences in the motives of OFDI between SOEs and private-owned enterprises (POEs, hereafter)

(Amighini *et al.*, 2013; Buckley *et al.*, 2018). Compared to SOEs, POEs are more market-oriented, risk-averse, and capital-sensitive (e.g., investing in tax havens) (Lu *et al.*, 2011; Huang and Chi, 2014). Their behaviors are path dependent, often oriented to "round tripping" and/or investing in their previous export destinations (Sutherland and Ning, 2011). Third, from political economy and international relation perspectives, studies have highlighted that geographical proximity, trade and diplomatic relationship (or political/institutional distance), ethnic networks (e.g., the size of Chinese diaspora in host countries) and cultural proximity (e.g., shared language and values) which all refer to certain host countries and regions, play pivotal roles in explaining why Chinese OFDI goes to certain places (Buckley *et al.*, 2007; Song *et al.*, 2011).

Despite the useful contributions, some research questions deserve more thorough investigation. On the one hand, most quantitative studies whose findings are based on country-level OFDI flow data prior to 2010 may lose explanatory power to capture the very recent dynamism of the heterogeneous Chinese Multinationals in ownership types and motives (Ramamurti and Hillemann, 2018). Little research has been done on the motivation shift of Chinese OFDI. On the other hand, as suggested by Buckley *et al.* (2018), Chinese OFDI has been more in line with government policies. This calls for more evidence on how and to what extent certain national-level policies, such as the recent BRI, (re) shape Chinese OFDI motives (Liu *et al.*, 2018). More importantly, despite the recognized differences in the OFDI motive between SOEs and POEs, most studies have focused either on SOEs or POEs on a global scale involving highly diversified host contexts (Duanmu, 2012; Lu *et al.*, 2011; Ramasamy *et al.*, 2012). It lacks nuanced work on the divergent motives of SOEs and POEs' OFDI in one specific host destination.

Given that, by focusing on ASEAN (the Association of Southeast Asian Nations) region — one of the largest Chinese OFDI receivers and the frontline of the BRI (particularly referring to the Maritime Silk Road), this paper explores the role of the BRI in affecting Chinese OFDI. It examines what determinants of Chinese OFDI in ASEAN are before and after the BRI launch, respectively. It also comparatively scrutinizes how the OFDI motives of Chinese SOEs and POEs in ASEAN may differ under the BRI. This study not only enriches the existing literature on Chinese OFDI in ASEAN but also provides important evidence to a better understanding of the economic-side value of the BRI.

The paper is organized into five sections. In Section 2, we review the literature on Chinese OFDI in terms of determinants and motives. After addressing the Chinese OFDI in ASEAN under the BRI, four hypotheses served to our research aims are constructed. Section 3 clarifies our dataset and model for hypothesis tests. Results are presented and discussed in Section 4. Section 5 concludes.

2. Literature Review and Hypotheses

2.1. *Changing determinants and motives of Chinese OFDI*

Why do firms conduct OFDI? This question has been extensively researched since the 1960s and has remained highly intriguing even in current times (Buckley *et al.*, 2018). In the 1970s and 1980s, multinational corporations (MNCs) from developed economies played a dominant role in promoting OFDI. They engaged OFDI mainly because of their oligopolistic advantages that endowed them with sufficient capabilities to go global for reaping external benefits and reducing transaction costs (Bain, 1956; Hymer, 1960; Buckley and Casson, 1976).

Firms do not invest abroad randomly, but often in certain geographic locations on purpose. Dunning (1977) stated that countries with locational advantages (including endowments such as abundant natural resources, large size of labor and markets, high density of technologies and knowledge, and transparent legislation environment) have a greater attraction for FDI. Dunning (2001) further put forward the Ownership-Location-International (OLI) model by incorporating ownership advantage with location advantage and international theory. Based on the model, firm OFDI motives include market-seeking, efficiency-seeking and resource-seeking. The OLI model is particularly applicable to OFDI motives from developed economies (Huang and Chi, 2014).

However, the OLI model which overemphasizes firm characteristics has increasingly lost explanatory power to OFDI behavior of MNCs from emerging economies who lack adequate firm-specific ownership advantages but still significantly invest abroad since the late 1980s. For emerging MNCs, OFDI works as a "spring board" for exploring new Ownership Advantages to catch up with their western counterparts quickly rather than exploiting their existing advantages (Luo and Tung, 2007). Moreover, it is evident that many MNCs' OFDI from China, India and Brazil, is not merely for acquiring firm-specific benefits but also for broader strategic assets of home country (Stoian, 2013). Particularly, Chinese OFDI is widely regarded as "institutionally embedded" in its unique party-centered authoritarian institutional system (Buckley *et al.*, 2007). Its motives may not be merely economic benefit-seeking, due to the strong influence of government policies (Cheung and Qian, 2009).

Since the 2000s, Chinese OFDI has skyrocketed. Many have argued that the Chinese OFDI has its own model owing to the peculiarity of home institutions (Wang *et al.*, 2012; Buckley *et al.*, 2018). Such peculiarity, featured by the ubiquitous involvement of the government in the economy, has created a favorable financial and political environment to SOEs (Song *et al.*, 2011). Buckley *et al.* (2007) find prior to 2001 Chinese OFDI — mainly driven by SOEs — was significantly oriented to natural resource — rich but low-income countries where poor institutional systems often existed. Zhang and Daly (2011) reveal that the primary sector accounted for 18.7% of Chinese total OFDI flow between 2006 and 2008, much higher than that of other countries. It shows that Chinese OFDI was strongly directed by the government to fulfill national resource needs. On the contrary, POEs face more constraints compared with the SOEs in securing low-interest loans (Morck *et al.*, 2008; Voss *et al.*, 2010) and approving process (Luo *et al.*, 2010).

However, more scholars argue that Chinese OFDI, for instance, in African countries, is not merely natural resource seeking but also market seeking (Cheung *et al.*, 2012). Indeed, Chinese OFDI is not simply attracted by poor institutions *per se*, but rather by available natural resources, large market sizes, high export/trade records and good cultural/political relations that are often positively correlated with poor governance (Quer *et al.*, 2012; Amighini *et al.*, 2013). Moreover, Chinese OFDI is risk-taking, but not necessarily sticking to natural resource-rich countries (Buckley *et al.*, 2018). It may also venture for acquiring strategic assets in developed economies or exploiting relational assets in politically risky destinations (Deng, 2009).

Recently, the motives of Chinese OFDI seem to shift. First, geographically, it is expanding globally into new host countries, covering culturally, economically and institutionally more diversified economies. In this regard, Chinese OFDI tends to exhibit multi-dimensional motives across different host countries (partially) due to a wider variation in host institutions and endowments (Cheung and Qian, 2009). Besides, the implementation of new national policy interventions such as the BRI, and the rise of new domestic and international challenges (e.g., manufacturing overcapacity and emerging geopolitical tensions with the US), may also reshape the past motives of Chinese OFDI (Buckley *et al.*, 2018; Liu *et al.*, 2018).

Second, POEs started to go global aggressively since 2003 whose investment amount surpassed that of SOEs in 2017 (Ministry of Commerce of China, 2017). Motives of Chinese OFDI become increasingly difficult to generalize (Huang and Chi, 2014; Buckley *et al.*, 2018; Lv *et al.*, 2018). Ramasamy *et al.* (2012) find that the locational directions of Chinese OFDI differ based on firm ownership. Generally, SOEs become more aggressive in locational choice while POEs remain cautious. First, the former maintains a strong natural resource seeking motivation and also shows an increasing strategic-assets seeking desire (Song *et al.*, 2011). In comparison, POEs are more heterogeneous in motive. Some are market and efficiency-seeking in order to facilitate trade relations and to deal with rising labor costs at home (Lu *et al.*, 2011). Others, in particular, giant POEs, such as Huawei, Lenovo and Geely have a strong asset-seeking tendency (Deng, 2007; Rui and Yip, 2008). Second, SOEs and POEs apply different methods to control investment uncertainties. Backed by the central government, central SOEs use the friendly diplomatic relationship to obtain legitimacy in host countries (Cui and Jiang, 2012). Therefore, they are less sensitive to the institutional voids and investment risks. On the contrary, being risk-averse, POEs depend more on geographic proximity, overseas Chinese as well as stable business environment in host countries (Amighini *et al.*, 2013).

Nevertheless, in reality, the recent OFDI motives of Chinese SOEs and POEs are more complex. On the one hand, they may vary from region to region, and even in some cases, are not crystal clear in difference. In Africa, for instance, POEs' OFDI is evident as significantly natural resource seeking in host countries with poor governance (Ramasamy *et al.*, 2012). That is, POEs are not necessarily market seeking, and they resemble SOEs in some particular contexts (Duanmu, 2012). As argued by Milhaupt and Zheng (2015), giant POEs in China are likely to be influenced by the state, "exhibiting substantial similarities in areas commonly thought to distinguish SOEs from POEs".[1] However, the number of those large and successful POEs is quite limited. Therefore, firm ownership still matters in the study of China's OFDI, especially when our econometric model is based on project-level entry rather than investment value.

On the other hand, Chinese OFDI motives evolve over time. Buckley *et al.* (2007) point out that the determinants of overall Chinese OFDI between 1984 and 1991 were positively

[1] We thank one of the reviewers to point out this argument.

related to host market size, political stability, cultural and geographical proximity, while they significantly shifted to host natural resources endowments between 1991 and 2001. Similarly, the strategic asset seeking motivation was not significant before 2001 (Buckley *et al.*, 2007), but it has become popular both for SOEs and POEs since 2010 (Huang and Chi, 2014). Such motivation shifts seem to be apparent in host countries that have been relevant to China's national development policies such as the 2003 Going Global strategy and the 2013 BRI (Lv *et al.*, 2018).

In sum, based on our review of the literature above, we raise several key research questions that have remained unclear so far: Do conventional determinants still matter now for Chinese OFDI in any context? What's the impact of new national policy interventions such as the BRI on Chinese OFDI motives? Do SOEs and POEs differ in OFDI motivation and how their motives might evolve in a certain host context? More specifically, does OFDI of POEs positively associated with large markets everywhere? Why are POEs interested in seeking natural resources or strategic assets in here but not there? With these questions, the paper focuses on China's most important investment host — ASEAN under the recent BRI for further addressing our research rationales.

2.2. *BRI and Chinese OFDI in ASEAN*

The BRI, literally, refers to the "Silk Road Economic Belt" (mainly covering Continental Asia and Europe) and "21st Century Maritime Silk Road" (mainly involving Southeast Asia) initiatives. The two initiatives were first proposed by the Chinese President Xi Jinping in 2013 during his visits to Kazakhstan and Indonesia. In an official statement, the BRI is defined as an economic policy in a clear attempt to promote "facilities connectivity, unimpeded trade, and financial integration" (NDRC, MFA and MOC, 2015). The launch of the Asian Infrastructure Investment Bank (AIIB) supporting FDI in Asia verifies the statement. It also has led to more scholarly attention on the role of the Maritime Silk Road Initiative in Asia (particularly in ASEAN), rather than the Belt (Kiik, 2016; Blanchard, 2018; Dunford and Liu, 2019; Liu and Lim, 2019).

One emerging research stream highlights the economic value of the BRI by focusing on the relationship between the initiative and Chinese OFDI in ASEAN. Yu (2017) argues that the BRI is at base a national economic development policy as it is explicitly derived from the need for transforming the domestic economic model. Kang *et al.* (2018) find that Chinese OFDI and the BRI are positively correlated, given that the Chinese OFDI increased by 46.2% in the post-BRI period of 2014–2015. Du and Zhang (2018) note that Chinese OFDI in infrastructure increased significantly in ASEAN after the announcement, supporting the claim that the BRI is an infrastructure-led OFDI policy (Liu *et al.*, 2018). However, some scholars critically argue that it is nature that the BRI can facilitates OFDI in ASEAN, as it encompassing government support, political trust building, specific locational focus, trade and investment is conducive to reinforce the existing favorable determinants of OFDI in ASEAN, including well established political and economic relations, cultural and geographical proximity, open market and rich natural resources (Li *et al.*, 2019; Liao, 2019).

More importantly, Liu *et al.* (2018) pinpoint that the BRI does matter in OFDI locational decisions, with aligning more firms to invest the BRI countries. Previous Chinese

OFDI in ASEAN, for instance, was mainly market-seeking. It is strongly associated with three key host countries that are endowed with open and large market and cultural proximity (given a large group of ethnic Chinese), namely Singapore, Malaysia and Indonesia (Liu and Lim, 2019). After the launch of the BRI, Chinese OFDI expands to all Southeast Asian countries, involving more mergers and acquisitions by SOEs for natural resources and strategic assets in less marketized and institutionally risky countries, such as Myanmar, Vietnam and Laos (Kang *et al.*, 2018). It is further argued that the BRI provides an added impulse to SOEs by implementing large construction projects and may also reshape the existing motives of POEs' OFDI in ASEAN as well (Dunford and Liu, 2019).

Despite the BRI impact on Chinese OFDI in ASEAN, it remains unclear on how the BRI would affect the OFDI motives of both SOEs and POEs in ASEAN (Fu *et al.*, 2018). Moreover, skepticism on the true motivation of the BRI particularly in ASEAN persists. By overlooking BRI's economic value, scholars regard it as a geopolitical means fully enacted by the anti-market authoritarian government for shifting domestic crises onto other countries and for enhancing its leadership position in Asia (Kiik, 2016; Blanchard, 2018). In this regard, it is worthy to examine the impact of the BRI on Chinese OFDI to shed light on the real value of the BRI.

2.3. *Hypotheses*

Drawing upon the literature review and the development trends and characteristics of Chinese OFDI in ASEAN under the BRI, four key hypotheses are introduced in the following.

2.3.1. *Market-seeking*

The market-seeking motivation is prevailing for Chinese OFDI as a whole (Buckley *et al.*, 2007). In general, POEs are recognized as market seekers, whereas SOEs may not particularly when investing low-income and natural resource-rich countries (Amighini *et al.*, 2013). However, when it comes to host countries with a large size of the Chinese diaspora, SOEs' OFDI is also market seeking (Ramasamy *et al.*, 2012). Thus, ASEAN with a large size of the Chinese population and GDP may be positively attractive both to SOEs and POEs. Moreover, the BRI on ASEAN has its economic logic, as seeking new markets can help to alleviate domestic overcapacity and excessive foreign exchange reserve. Chinese firms may thus relocate their labor-intensive and low-tech sectors in ASEAN (Liu and Dunford, 2016). We hypothesize:

H1: China's OFDI of SOEs and POEs are both attracted to ASEAN countries with large markets, especially after the BRI announcement.

2.3.2. *Resource-seeking*

In the 2000s, Chinese SOEs' OFDI drive for natural resources was evident in Southeast Asia (Morck *et al.*, 2008). BRI thus seems to be highly relevant to SOEs, because in addition to the market seeking intention, it is infrastructure-led and oriented to acquiring imported natural resources for securing China's sustainable growth (Liu and Dunford, 2016). Moreover, it is documented that many SOEs have invested large flagship infrastructure projects in natural resource-rich countries in ASEAN (Liu *et al.*, 2018). We assume that with infrastructure improvement the BRI facilitates SOEs to seek more natural resources in ASEAN. However, the resource-seeking motivation is often not applicable to Chinese POEs in the existing literature. POEs' OFDI in ASEAN is market seeking, often attracted by strong export/trade relations and large markets (Buckley *et al.*, 2007). BRI may hardly promote POEs' resource-seeking OFDI. We thus hypothesize:

H2: SOEs are more attracted to countries with abundant natural resources, especially after the BRI announcement.

2.3.3. *Institution: Rule of law*

One important feature of Chinese OFDI, compared to others, is more risk-taking, namely preferring host countries with weak rule of law (Buckley *et al.*, 2007). This is particularly the case for OFDI from SOEs. Liao (2019) argues that the past Chinese national policies in ASEAN, namely *Going Out and Good Neighbor*, have largely stimulated Chinese SOEs (mainly from mining and energy industries) to invest in host countries with weak rule-of-law institutions. SOEs have tended to take advantage of the national policy agendas — often under the banner of diplomacy — to pursue strategic and/or natural resources. Since the BRI can be also regarded as a policy promoting better diplomatic relations in ASEAN, we expect that countries with lower-level rule of law may significantly attract more OFDI from SOEs. In contrast, POEs is more rational and risk-averse. They are more inclined to invest in host countries with transparent governments and sophisticated rule of law (Ramasamy *et al.*, 2012). Given the SOE-favored BRI, host institutions may have limited impact on the shift of POEs' OFDI after 2013. We thus hypothesize:

H3: SOEs are more attracted to countries with poor institutions, especially after the BRI announcement.

2.3.4. *Politics: Diplomatic relations and senior leader's visits*

A good diplomatic relation between home and host countries promotes OFDI, for both SOEs and POEs (Fornes and Butt-Philip, 2011; Amighini *et al.*, 2013). In the context of the BRI, Zhang *et al.* (2014) reveal that Chinese senior leader's visits can efficiently lead to large projects of investment in host countries, because bilateral senior leader's visits facilitate political trust-building and enhance diplomatic relations that can further lower institutional distance and risks for OFDI both from SOEs and POEs. It is assumed that the higher level of diplomatic relations China and a host country have, the more willingness of Chinese firms to invest in that country. Moreover, the BRI, as a top-down and national government-led policy priority, has brought about an increase of bilateral senior leader's visits since 2013 particularly in ASEAN (Dunford and Liu, 2019). We thus hypothesize:

H4: Closeness of diplomatic relations between China and a host country encourages Chinese OFDI of both SOEs and POEs to that country after the launch of the BRI. Specifically, bilateral senior leader's visits would enhance diplomatic relations and facilitate Chinese OFDI inflow. This is particularly the case after the launch of the BRI.

3. Data and Model

3.1. *Chinese OFDI in ASEAN*

We use a project-level database of China's OFDI toward all 10 members of ASEAN from the Ministry of Commerce between 2010 and 2015. The total number of approved records is 3,838. It is a disaggregated dataset that contains the following attributes of the investment project: a unique ID of approval, the destination, the name of domestic establishment and its foreign counterpart, the affiliation (i.e., central or local government), a description of business abroad, and the date of approval.[2] Amighini *et al.* (2014) argue that number of transactions is better than value of investment as a unit of analysis if one investigates the location strategy and investment motives of multinational enterprises, because choice of the host country and investment value are, to a larger extent, independent, and the latter varies with sectors. The ownership of the domestic establishment is of a particular concern. The database from the Ministry of Commerce, however, does not provide such information. We thus turn to the Publicity System of Enterprise Credit Information (http://www.gsxt.gov.cn), maintained by the State Administration for Market Regulation of China. By matching the records in the Publicity System, we are able to acquire the registration type, as well as the registered capital of the domestic establishment. We then build a concordance table that maps registration types into ownership types.[3] However, those registration types, such as limited liability corporations and limited shareholding corporations, do not refer to their ownerships. Given that, we further look up shareholding structures of those establishments in a commercial database which are created by a private company in China[4] similar to Dun & Bradstreet. We then classify them according to majority ownership.

Table 1 shows the number of investment projects and average registered capital by ownership types during 2010–2015. OFDI projects increased considerably after the launch of the BRI, which started from 388 in 2010 to 599 in 2013, then jumped to 705 in 2014, and skyrocketed to 1,147 in 2015. While the number of POEs was nearly three times more than that of SOEs, the average registered capital of POEs was less than one-tenth of that of SOEs. Giant POEs are conspicuous and case studies reveal that some of them might be captured by

[2] Most recent data in 2016 and 2017 are not available in the disaggregated form with the same attributes. Only the destination, the name of domestic establishment and its foreign counterpart are publicly accessible. The date of approval is hidden on the official website of China's Ministry of Commerce of to our dismay.

[3] See Table A.1 in the Appendix for details.

[4] The name of the company is *tianyancha* (in pinyin, or 天眼查 in Chinese), whose website is https://www.tianyancha.com/. It collects information about business establishments and institutions in China from the Publicity System of Enterprise Credit Information and many other publicly accessible sources.

Table 1. Investments Projects by Different Firm Ownerships, 2010–2015

	2010	2011	2012	2013	2014	2015	Total	Avg. Registered Capital (Millions of RMB)
POEs	259	308	368	366	465	804	2,570	317.20
SOEs	95	115	122	176	157	225	890	4630.84
HMT*	18	16	23	24	48	43	172	251.64
Foreign	16	20	27	33	35	75	206	794.46
Total	388	459	540	599	705	1,147	3,838	1185.28

Note: *HMT stands for enterprises with investment from Hong Kong, Macau and Taiwan.

the state (Milhaupt and Zheng, 2015), but their numbers are limited. Most POEs in our data are small and median-sized and their investment motives tend to be different from those of SOEs. In terms of the number of projects, Figure 1 reveals that Singapore and Indonesia ranked first and second, respectively, as the largest destination within ASEAN for both private and state-owned projects of China's OFDI. Vietnam turned out the third attractive host country for POEs and Malaysia for their state-owned counterparts.

It is worth noting that 172 and 206 projects are implemented by establishments from Hong Kong, Macau and Taiwan of China (HMT), and those from foreign countries, respectively. Owing to preferential treatments in mainland China towards enterprises from HMT and abroad, the practice of 'roundtripping investment' through Hong Kong and tax havens (such as British Virgin and Cayman Islands) is well documented in the literature (see, e.g., Amighini *et al.*, 2014). As a result, it is rather difficult to distinguish between *de facto* HMT or foreign-invested enterprises and those in disguise by utilizing roundtripping, and to classify them into SOEs or POEs in the latter case. Besides, their numbers are quite small. Therefore, we exclude them in the econometric analysis.

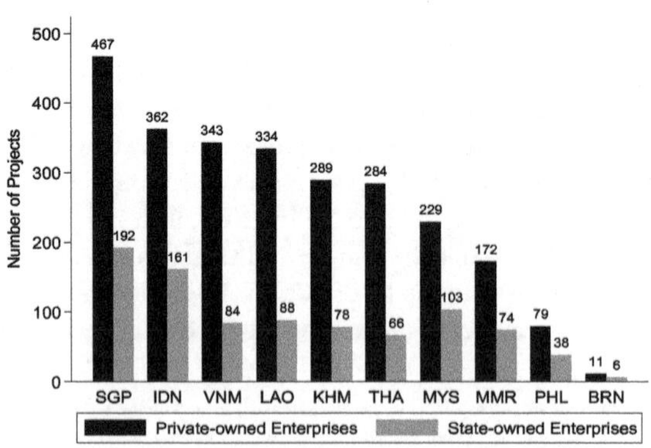

Notes: SGP = Singapore, IDN = Indonesia, VNM = Vietnam, LAO = Lao PDR, KHM = Cambodia, THA = Thailand, MYS = Malaysia, MMR = Myanmar, PHL = Philippines and BRN = Brunei Darussalam.

Figure 1. Number of China's OFDI Projects in ASEAN, 2010–2015

Table 2. The Determinants of China's OFDI in ASEAN

Variable	Explanation	Expected Sign				Data Source
		POE 2010–2013	POE 2014–2015	SOE 2010–2013	SOE 2014–2015	
GDP	Market-seeking: Host country GDP (in billions)	+	+	+	+	World Bank Development Indicator
resource	Resource-seeking: Ratio of fuel, ore and metal exports to merchandise exports of host country (in percentages)	NS	NS	+	+	World Bank Development Indicator
rule_of_law	Institution: Host country's rule of law rating (ranges from −2.5 to +2.5 with higher values indicating better rule of law)	NS	NS	–	–	World Bank Governance Indicator
dipl_level	Politics: China's diplomatic relationship with the host country (1 for simply diplomatic relation, 2 for cooperative partnership, 3 for strategic cooperative partnership, and 4 for comprehensive strategic cooperative partnership)	NS	+	NS	+	Ministry of Foreign Affairs of China
visit	Politics: weighted number of senior leader's visit (two for a visit by top national leaders, and one for a visit by other leaders)	NS	+	NS	+	Ministry of Foreign Affairs of China
bit_length	Control: length of time (in years) that the host country and China have signed a bilateral investment treaty	+	+	+	+	Ministry of Commerce of China
gGDP	Control: Annual percentage increase in host GDP	+	+	+	+	World Bank Development Indicator
CPI	Control: Host country annual consumer price index	–	–	–	–	World Bank Development Indicator
FDIGDP	Control: Ratio of inward FDI stock to host GDP	+	+	+	+	World Bank Development Indicator

Notes: All monetary values are in constant (2010) US prices; POE = private-owned enterprises, SOE = state-owned enterprises; NS = not significant.

3.2. Characteristics of host countries

In line with our hypotheses, we collect data of characteristics of host countries from economic, institutional and political perspectives. We also include other control variables. Details of variables, including names, proxies, expected signs as well as data sources are shown in Table 2.

We first build proxies for the market- and resource-seeking motives according to Dunning's eclectic paradigm. We use GDP (in constant year 2010 US dollar) of the host country as the indicator for the market-seeking motive. Following Kolstad and Wiig (2012), we add up fuel exports and ore and metal exports together to better capture various resources that China's OFDI aims to secure for supporting its phenomenal economic growth. For instance, Lao PDR is a major supplier of ores and metals, and Brunei Darussalam relies on its fuel endowment.

For the institutional view of OFDI, we choose the rule of law ratings from "World Bank Governance Indicator", instead of the much-used similar index provided by the PRS group. This is because values for Lao PDR and Cambodia are available only in the former database. By rule of law, we mean "perceptions of the extent to which agents have confidence in and abide by the rules of society, and in particular the quality of contract enforcement, property rights, the police, and the courts, as well as the likelihood of crime and violence". It is more specific than the general political stability index since it measures directly the institution that is related to business operation. It ranges from −2.5 to +2.5 with higher values indicating better rule of law.

As with political factors, we construct one variable for diplomatic relationships and another for senior leader's visits. First, we code four types of diplomatic relationships between China and a host country according to their relative closeness in the "dipl_level" variable: (1) for simply diplomatic relation, (2) for cooperative partnership, (3) for strategic cooperative partnership, and (4) for comprehensive strategic cooperative partnership. This data source is the same as the "visit" variable. Second, following Zhang *et al.* (2014), "visit" is calculated as the weighted number of bilateral visits of senior leaders between China and a host country in a certain year. A visit by top national leaders (president and premier) are weighted "two", and a visit by other leaders are weighted "one". The visits are collected from the news on the official website of the Ministry of Foreign Affairs of China.[5]

We control for the length of time during which the host country and China had signed a bilateral investment treaty ("bit_length") as well as several conventional variables. From 1985 to 2001, China signed bilateral investment treaties with all 10 members of ASEAN.[6] We, therefore, calculate the length of time since the agreements were signed because the longer the agreement has taken effect, the more likely that China will invest in that country.

As for conventional variables, growth rate of GDP reflects the market potential while the consumer price index captures the macroeconomic condition of the host country. A high growth economy with a low rate of inflation is expected to attract inward FDI.

[5] https://www.fmprc.gov.cn/web/gjhdq_676201/gj_676203/yz_676205/ (in Chinese, accessed on Jan 2, 2019).

[6] See Page 84 in "A guide to OFDI and economic cooperation: ASEAN (2017)" compiled by Ministry of Commerce of China, available at http://fec.mofcom.gov.cn/article/gbdqzn/ (in Chinese, accessed on Jan 2, 2019).

The ratio of inward FDI stock to GDP measures the openness to FDI in the host country, and a higher ratio increases the likelihood of inward FDI. China's exports to and imports from the host country are excluded here because they are highly correlated with the variable "bit_length". In addition, the China-ASEAN Free Trade Area (CAFTA) has been established since 2010 which is just the year when our data starts. As strategic asset is not a major concern for China's OFDI in ASEAN except for a few projects, mostly in Singapore, number of patents by residents of the host country is not included in the control variables. Moreover, similarities and differences in leadership styles across all 10 members of ASEAN vis a vis China are important qualitative factors. While such labels as "hierarchical", "paternalistic" and "autocratic" are attached to countries like Malaysia, Indonesia and Philipines, respectively, Singapore is best positioned to bridge the gap between the East and the West as a cosmopolitan city with a global outlook (Human Capital Leadership Institute, 2016). Those interesting nuances of leadership characteristics, however, can hardly be quantified and put into econometric models. Last but not least, overseas Chinese populate all ASEAN members, notably Indonesia, Thailand and Malaysia in absolute numbers and Singapore in proportion. Their ethnic networks play pivotal roles in explaining the location choice of China's OFDI.[7] Unfortunately, we are not able to collect data of overseas Chinese in ASEAN for the research period.

Before econometric modeling, Table 3 examines pair-wise correlations among both explanatory and control variables reflecting characteristics of host countries. It turns out that no serious multicollinearity is identified.

3.3. *The conditional logit models*

The limited number of investment destinations within ASEAN (i.e., 10) makes the conditional logit model the most suitable choice in the econometric toolkit. It models the probability of an investment project from China to choose a particular country conditioned on a number of host-country-specific variables (Cameron and Trivedi, 2005).

Let us suppose that the random utility of project i choosing host country j can be written as

$$U_{ij} = x_j'\beta + \varepsilon_{ij} \quad (i = 1,\ldots,n;\ j = 1,\ldots,J),$$

where x_j is a vector of characteristics of host countries (irrespective of project i), β is a vector of coefficients which determines the effects of x_j on U_{ij} (irrespective of host country j) and ε_{ij} is IID and follows the type I extreme value distribution. It can then be deduced that the conditional probability of project i choosing host country j equals

$$P(y_i = j|x_j) = \frac{\exp(x_j'\beta)}{\sum_{k=1}^{J} \exp(x_k'\beta)}.$$

[7] We thank one of the reviewers to point out this argument, but data of overseas Chinese since 2014 are unavaible in the series of 'Overseas Chinese Economy Year Book', which are published by their editorial committee in Taiwan with the most reliable estimates.

Table 3. Correlation Analysis of Independent Variables

	GDP	Resource	Rule_of_Law	Visit	Dipl_Level	Bit_Length	gGDP	CPI	FDIGDP
GDP	1								
Resource	−0.177	1							
Rule_of_Law	0.126	0.164	1						
Dipl_Level	−0.21	0.313**	−0.543***	1					
Visit	−0.292**	−0.265**	0.029	0.1	1				
Bit_Length	0.355***	−0.542***	0.510***	0.251*	−0.424***	1			
gGDP	−0.026	−0.275**	−0.348***	0.054	−0.022	−0.016	1		
CPI	0.099	−0.221*	−0.340***	0.063	0.17	−0.005	0.398***	1	
FDIGDP	−0.188	−0.209	0.472***	0.293**	−0.442***	0.305**	0.211	−0.033	1

Note: ***$p < 0.01$, **$p < 0.05$ and *$p < 0.1$.

The coefficients can be estimated by the maximum likelihood method. It should be noted that the conditional logit model depends on the assumption of independence of irrelevant alternatives (IIA). Given the considerable differences among countries in ASEAN in terms of economic development, political regimes, peoples, languages and religious beliefs, etc., the IIA assumption probably holds.

To investigate the effects of the BRI launch in 2013, we employ a structural break framework by dividing the 2010–2015 period into two phases, namely, 2010–2013 and 2014–2015. To compare the different motives and determinants between POEs and SOEs, we further split the data into two sub-samples according to ownership. Last but not least, we lag the independent variables one year to address endogeneity or reverse causality problems.

4. Results

The estimation results of the conditional logit models are presented in Table 4. Model 1 covers the whole 2010–2015 period with the full sample. Models 2 and 3 divide the whole period into two phases. Models 4–7 further split the subsample in each period into POEs and SOEs. Model 1 is to assess the overall effect of explanatory variables on China's OFDI. Models 2 and 3 are used to examine the structural break due to the launch of the BRI in 2013. Models 4–7 are designed to contrast the differences in determinants based on ownership in each phase.

First of all, we find that GDP and resources of the host country are all significant and correctly signed in Models 1–3. A further look at Models 4–7 verifies Hypothesis 1, but partially supports Hypothesis 2 for the 2014–2015 period.

The absolute host market size has a positive effect on Chinese OFDI. A rise in GDP by 100 billion constant (2010) US dollars would increase the odds ratio of a particular host country in attracting an investment project from China by 13.3%.[8] That positive effect holds for all sub-models with little variation in its value, indicating that market seeking was a key motive for China's OFDI in ASEAN from 2010 to 2015 for both POEs and SOEs, which is in line with the previous literature (Cheung and Qian, 2008; Ramasamy, 2012).

Natural resources in the host country also have a positive effect on Chinese OFDI. An increase in the ratio of fuel, ore and metal exports to merchandise exports by 10% would raise the odds ratio of a particular host country in attracting an investment project from China by 6.28%.[9] However, its coefficients are significant for POEs in 2010–2013 and SOEs in 2014–2015. It might be argued that in the 2010–2013 pre-BRI period ASEAN was not targeted as a key destination by the Chinese government for resource seeking OFDI. SOEs thus were designated by the government to exploit natural resources in remoter destinations such as Mideast, Africa, Australia and Latin America. This geographical distribution is supported by the project-level database of China's OFDI from the Ministry of Commerce in 2010–2013, which listed all the countries/regions in which

[8] Calculated as $\exp(0.00125 \times 100)$, based on coefficients in Model 1, for GDP is measured in constant (2010) US dollars in billions.

[9] Calculated as $\exp(0.00609 \times 10)$, based on coefficients in Model 1.

Table 4. Estimates of China's OFDI in ASEAN

	(1) ALL 2010–2015	(2) ALL 2010–2013	(3) ALL 2014–2015	(4) POE 2010–2013	(5) POE 2014–2015	(6) SOE 2010–2013	(7) SOE 2014–2015
GDP	0.00125***	0.00138***	0.00145***	0.00128***	0.00141***	0.00174***	0.00160***
	(8.32e-05)	(0.000130)	(0.000160)	(0.000159)	(0.000185)	(0.000233)	(0.000332)
resource	0.00609***	0.00882***	0.00378**	0.0113***	0.00277	0.000997	0.00735**
	(0.00112)	(0.00158)	(0.00172)	(0.00181)	(0.00195)	(0.00344)	(0.00374)
rule_of_law	−0.491***	−0.629***	−0.276***	−0.738***	−0.379***	−0.282*	0.0842
	(0.0546)	(0.0764)	(0.0918)	(0.0895)	(0.105)	(0.153)	(0.197)
dipl_level	0.0621*	0.0625	0.225***	0.132**	0.228***	−0.0873	0.207*
	(0.0324)	(0.0479)	(0.0525)	(0.0580)	(0.0601)	(0.0873)	(0.110)
visit	0.0136***	0.00293	0.0197***	0.000345	0.0197***	0.0107	0.0206**
	(0.00317)	(0.00523)	(0.00443)	(0.00608)	(0.00508)	(0.0105)	(0.00926)
bit_length	0.0877***	0.112***	0.0837***	0.136***	0.0945***	0.0420*	0.0489**
	(0.00694)	(0.0106)	(0.0113)	(0.0124)	(0.0131)	(0.0216)	(0.0233)
gGDP	0.0301***	−0.0133	0.139***	−0.0258*	0.131***	0.0162	0.180***
	(0.00868)	(0.0121)	(0.0220)	(0.0145)	(0.0256)	(0.0223)	(0.0446)
CPI	0.0538***	0.0600***	0.0129	0.0644***	0.0116	0.0462***	0.0217
	(0.00695)	(0.00761)	(0.0294)	(0.00875)	(0.0334)	(0.0158)	(0.0629)
FDIGDP	0.0850***	0.0999***	0.0896***	0.114***	0.0944***	0.0631***	0.0722***
	(0.00516)	(0.00847)	(0.00746)	(0.0102)	(0.00851)	(0.0158)	(0.0158)
Log Likelihood	−7183.16	−3596.04	−3551.44	−2581.11	−2731.26	−994.479	−810.327
LR χ^2	972.57***	543.68***	500.26***	426.41***	381.44***	158.16***	138.52***
Pseudo R^2	0.0634	0.0703	0.0658	0.0763	0.0653	0.0737	0.0787
Obs.	32,922	16,412	16,510	11,841	12,690	4,571	3,820

Notes: Standard errors in parentheses; POE = private-owned enterprises; SOE = state-owned enterprises; $^{***}p < 0.01$, $^{**}p < 0.05$ and $^{*}p < 0.1$.

centrally administered SOEs invested to explore natural resources. This also suggests that POEs seeking resources in ASEAN during that time were mainly based on geographical and relational proximity with their own interests. This result indeed well supports the argument that Chinese OFDI is significantly influenced by national government policies in terms of locational choice and underlying motives (Cheung and Qian, 2009; Buckley *et al.*, 2018). During 2014–2015, the launch of the BRI directed SOEs to tap into handy resources in ASEAN, such as oil and natural gases in Indonesia and Malaysia, and ores and metals in Lao PDR and Myanmar. Moreover, POEs were more inclined to exploring emerging markets and exploiting cheap labor in ASEAN, largely pressured by increased costs of manufacturing and overcapacity in China. To sum up, we find that the BRI does reshape the resource-seeking motives of POEs and SOEs.

Second, we find that the rule of law, which represents the quality of host institutions, is significant and correctly signed in Model 6, partially supporting Hypothesis 3 (expecting the risk-taking SOEs in the 2010–2013 period only). Nevertheless, the coefficients are negative in Models 4 and 5, indicating that POEs are risk-taking, which strongly deviates from theoretical expectations. While the result echoes the outcome of Ramasamy *et al.* (2012) that SOEs are attracted to countries with abundant natural resources and risky political environments, the reason why POEs are not risk-averse requires discussion.

Several explanations might be useful to answer the question: (1) Southeast Asia has been the most invested region for Chinese POEs since the 1980s or even earlier. As a long-term tradition, POEs have been attracted predominantly by socio-economic factors such as the market size, GDP per capita, cultural and geographical proximity, often being less sensitive to the variegated host institutions among ASEAN countries (Buckley *et al.*, 2007; Ismail, 2009). This tradition or investment history allows POEs to have no fear to invest in risky environments in ASEAN. (2) Investment intentions are more affected by similarities in institutions between home and host country than the quality of institutions *per se* (Kolstad and Wiig, 2012). In this sense, POEs from emerging economies like China have comparative advantages when operating in most countries in ASEAN with similarly weak institutions (e.g., regulated economies with massive government intervention) compared to their counterparts from the developed world. That ownership advantage generated by home country embeddedness helps to mitigate the adverse impact of poor institutions. (3) POEs' OFDI might prefer to invest in communist countries. In ASEAN, Vietnam and Lao PDR are countries with similar ideologies to China, but their institutions are poor with average ratings of rule of law being −0.52 and −0.91, respectively. (4) The abnormal finding might reflect shortcomings in the indicators of institutions provided by the World Bank and other think tanks as they are typically calculated from the perspective of developed countries. Put alternatively, MNCs from emerging economies like China might perceive the quality of institutions in a different manner (Buckley *et al.*, 2007).

Third, we find that the closeness of diplomatic relations and bilateral senior visits between China and a host country is significant and correctly signed in Models 1, 3, 5 and 7, confirming Hypothesis 4.

The launch of the BRI has improved China's diplomatic relations with members of ASEAN. During the 2014–2015 period, more close diplomatic relations and more frequent senior leader's visits sent strong signals of business opportunities and political confidence for Chinese SOEs and POEs. BRI promotes Chinese OFDI in ASEAN through increased senior leader visits and enhanced diplomatic relations. Those findings indicate that after the BRI, bilateral diplomatic relationship, no matter how it is measured, played a more vital role in Chinese OFDI. Good political relationships attract Chinese OFDI, which are very common in the economic cooperation between China and ASEAN countries. The Vice Premier of Thailand, Mr. Somkid visited China in 2018, which attracted 2.3 billion RMB of investment from Alibaba and ZTE under the BRI framework. Moreover, after investment, good bilateral political relationships also help Chinese firms to conquer the liability of foreignness in host ASEAN countries. For example, in 2012, the Letpadaung mining project invested by China North Industries Corporation in Myanmar was interrupted by local protests. As the implementation of the BRI and improvement of Sino-Myanmar relations, Myanmar officials stepped in to resolve this conflict. People's court of Myanmar set up a federal commission chaired by Aung San Suu Kyi, which finally ended the conflict and restarted the mining project (Tang-Lee, 2016).

We now turn to the results of our four control variables. The coefficients of "bit_length" and "FDIGDP" are positive and significant in all the models, suggesting that the length of time that China has signed a bilateral investment treaty with the country, and the openness of the country to FDI would encourage China's OFDI towards it. The coefficients of "CPI" and "gGDP" are positive and significant in 2010–2013 and 2014–2015, respectively, indicating that China's OFDI was attracted to countries with a moderate level of inflation in the first phase, and with greater growth potentials in the second phase.

5. Concluding Remarks

This paper investigates the determinants of Chinese OFDI in ASEAN before and after the launch of BRI using a project-level database in 2010–2015 and explicitly comparing the OFDI motives of POEs and SOEs from economic, institutional and political perspectives. Our conditional logit models show that (1) market-seeking is one of the key motives for both POEs and SOEs; (2) POEs pursued natural resources in ASEAN based on geographical and relational proximity in the pre-BRI period while SOEs are directed to exploit natural resources in ASEAN besides remoter destinations after the launch of the BRI; (3) POEs are risk-taking in both periods, which runs counter to conventional expectations but could be explained by the long-term investment tradition of POEs in ASEAN attracted predominantly by socio-economic factors and often less sensitive to variegated host institutions among ASEAN countries and; (4) the BRI promotes Chinese OFDI in ASEAN through increased senior leader visits and enhanced diplomatic relations.

This paper has made three contributions to the existing literature on China's OFDI. First, it provides an updated period of time up to 2015 to account for the rapidly evolving Chinese MNCs and their changing investment motives. Second, it compares the motives between SOEs and POEs from economic, institutional and political perspectives, demonstrating how firm ownership further complicates the motives of China's OFDI. Third, it enriches the discussion on how home institutions influence China's OFDI by examining the role played by the BRI, the most recent national-level policy of China, in (re)shaping the motives and location choice of Chinese MNCs in ASEAN. The ASEAN is a case in point as it is one of the largest Chinese OFDI receivers and the frontline of the BRI (particularly referring to the Maritime Silk Road). The economic-side value of the BRI is underscored as it enhances diplomatic relations rather than escalate geopolitical conflicts between China and ASEAN, which in turn promotes regional economic integration and facilitates China's OFDI towards countries with greater growth potentials.

Nevertheless, a few questions remain to be answered. For one thing, a considerable proportion of Chinese OFDI in many countries in ASEAN is attracted by its abundant low-cost labor, but this efficiency-seeking motive is not analyzed in the conditional logit model because of too many missing values in the wage data provided by the International Labor Organization in its ILOSTAT database. Moreover, the complex labor relations between Chinese OFDI and local workforces could better be revealed by in-depth qualitative studies. For another, some Chinese MNCs which shift their production bases to many countries in ASEAN are not targeting for the market of the hosting country *per se* (Yang, 2016). They indeed use them (such as Vietnam) as springboards to gain easier access to markets of the United States, the EU, and other developed economies. This motive might be better understood by case studies using frameworks such as global value chains and global production networks (Yeung, 2016). Another important aspect of OFDI is the entry mode (greenfield, joint venture or acquisition). However, because it is not available in our OFDI dataset, this research does not discuss the entry model change before and after the BRI. The choice of entry mode or the degree of equity control is determined by the balance between investment benefits and uncertainties. On the one hand, if the resources of host country are strategic assets, Chinese MNCs may be more likely to have a fully owned mode such as via acquisitions for internalization, which can be widely seen in technology investment (Guo, 2008). On the other hand, if the investments are of high risks and cost, Chinese firms may choose lower equity control degree or find a local partner by joint venture to avoid the institutional voids (Meyer *et al.*, 2009), which can be seen by some OFDI in politically unstable regions. For example, in the Letpadaung mining project case, the investor, China North Industries Corporation needs to establish a joint company with the military government of Myanmar. Finally, the peculiarities of ASEAN, such as diversified styles and capabilities of national leadership and the role of overseas Chinese, are not well covered in this study, partly because they are qualitative factors that are difficult to incorporate into econometric models. All the above limitations should be acknowledged and studied in the future.

Appendix A

Table A.1. The Concordance Table between Registration Types and Ownership Types

Name of Registration Types	Code	Ownership Types
Domestic enterprises		
State-owned enterprises	110	state
Collectively owned enterprises	120	private*
Shareholding cooperative enterprises	130	private
Joint ownership enterprises		
Joint state-owned enterprises	141	state
Joint collectively owned enterprises	142	private*
Joint state-collective enterprises	143	state
Other joint ownership enterprises	149	private
Limited liability corporations		
Solely state-funded limited liability Corporations	151	state
Other limited liability corporations	159	to be classified according to majority ownership
Limited shareholding corporations	160	to be classified according to majority ownership
Private enterprises		
Private sole proprietorships	171	private
Private partnership enterprises	172	private
Private limited liability corporations	173	private
Private limited shareholding corporations	174	private
Other domestic enterprises	190	private
Enterprises with investment from Hong Kong, Macau, and Taiwan (HMT)		
Joint ventures	210	HMT
Cooperative enterprises	220	HMT
Wholly owned enterprises	230	HMT
Limited shareholding corporations	240	HMT
Other enterprises	290	HMT
Foreign-invested enterprises		
Joint ventures	310	foreign
Cooperative enterprises	320	foreign
Wholly owned enterprises	330	foreign
Limited shareholding corporations	340	foreign
Other enterprises	390	foreign

Note: *Collectively owned enterprises are for the most part *de facto* private enterprises in disguise (i.e., "wearing red hats", in Chinese), especially when private ownership is not politically encouraged.
Source: based on Lin and Hu (2011).

References

Amighini, AA, R Rabellotti and M Sanfilippo (2013). Do Chinese state-owned and private enterprises differ in their internationalization strategies? *China Economic Review*, 27, 312–325.

Amighini, A, C Cozza, R Rabellotti and M Sanfilippo (2014). Investigating Chinese outward foreign direct investments: How can firm-level data help? *China & World Economy*, 22, 44–63.

Bain, JS (1956). Barriers to new competition, their character and consequences in manufacturing industries (No. HB771 B23).

Blanchard, JF (2018). China's Maritime Silk Road Initiative (MSRI) and Southeast Asia: A Chinese 'pond' not 'lake' in the works. *Journal of Contemporary China*, 27(111), 329–343.

Buckley, PJ and M Casson (1976). *The Future of the Multinational Enterprise*. London: Macmillan.

Buckley, PJ, LJ Clegg, AR Cross, X Liu, H Voss and P Zheng (2007). 'The determinants of Chinese outward foreign direct investment'. *Journal of International Business Studies*, 38, 499–518.

Buckley, PJ, LJ Clegg, H Voss, AR Cross, X Liu and P Zheng (2018). A retrospective and agenda for future research on Chinese outward foreign direct investment. *Journal of International Business Studies*, 49(1), 4–23.

Cameron, AC and PK Trivedi (2005). *Microeconometrics: Methods and Applications*. Cambridge, MA: Cambridge University Press.

Cheung, YW and X Qian (2009). Empirics of China's outward direct investment. *Pacific Economic Review*, 14(3), 312–341.

Cheung, YW, J De Haan, X Qian and S Yu (2012). China's outward direct investment in Africa. *Review of International Economics*, 20(2), 201–220.

Cui, L and F Jiang (2012). State ownership effect on firms' FDI ownership decisions under institutional pressure: A study of Chinese outward-investing firms. *Journal of International Business Studies*, 43(3), 264–284.

Deng, P (2007). Investing for strategic resources and its rationale: The case of outward FDI from Chinese companies. *Business Horizons*, 50(1), 71–81.

Deng, P (2009). Why do Chinese firms tend to acquire strategic assets in international expansion? *Journal of World Business*, 44(1), 74–84.

Du, J and Y Zhang (2018). Does one belt one road initiative promote Chinese overseas direct investment?. *China Economic Review*, 47, 189–205.

Duanmu, JL (2012). Firm heterogeneity and location choice of Chinese multinational enterprises (MNEs). *Journal of World Business*, 47(1), 64–72.

Dunford, M and W Liu (2019). Chinese perspectives on the Belt and Road Initiative. *Cambridge Journal of Regions, Economy and Society*, 12(1), 145–167.

Dunning, JH (1977). 'Trade, location of economic activity and the MNE: A search for an eclectic approach'. In *The International Location of Economic Activity*, B Ohlin, PO Hesselborn and PM Wijkmon (eds.). London: Macmillan, pp. 395–418.

Dunning, JH (2001). The eclectic (OLI) paradigm of international production: past, present and future, *International Journal of the Economics of Business* 8(2), 173–190.

Fornes, G and A Butt-Philip (2011). Chinese MNEs and Latin America: A review, *International Journal of Emerging Markets*, 6(2), 98–117.

Fu, Y, A Supriyadi and T Wang (2018). China's Outward FDI in Indonesia: Spatial patterns and determinants. *Sustainability*, 10(12), 4632.

Guo, B (2008). Technology acquisition channels and industry performance: An industry-level analysis of Chinese large- and medium-size manufacturing enterprises. *Research Policy*, 37(2), 194–209.

Human Capital Leadership Institute (2016). *Leadership Mosaics Across Asia*. Singapore. https://www.hcli.org/research/leadership-mosaics-across-asia (accessed on July 31, 2019).

Huang, X and R Chi (2014). Chinese private firms' outward foreign direct investment: Does firm ownership and size matter? *Thunderbird International Business Review*, 56(5), 393–406.

Huang, Y and B Wang (2011). Chinese outward direct investment: Is there a China model?. *China & World Economy*, 19(4), 1–21.

Hymer, SH (1960). The international operations of national firms: A study of direct foreign investment. Ph.D. Thesis, Dept. of Economics, Massachusetts Institute of Technology.

Ismail, NW (2009). The determinant of foreign direct investment in ASEAN: A semi-gravity approach. *Transition Studies Review*, 16(3), 710.

Kang, L, F Peng, Y Zhu and A Pan (2018). Harmony in diversity: Can the One Belt One Road Initiative promote China's outward foreign direct investment? *Sustainability*, 10(9), 3264.

Kiik, L (2016). Nationalism and anti-ethno-politics: Why 'Chinese Development' failed at Myanmar's Myitsone Dam. *Eurasian Geography and Economics*, 57(3), 374–402.

Kolstad, I and A Wiig (2012). What determines Chinese outward FDI? *Journal of World Business*, 47, 26–34.

Li, Z, Z Huang and H Dong (2019). The Influential Factors on Outward Foreign Direct Investment: Evidence from the "The Belt and Road". *Emerging Markets Finance and Trade*, 55(14), 3211–3226.

Liao, JC (2019). A good neighbor of bad governance? China's energy and mining development in Southeast Asia. *Journal of Contemporary China*, 28(118), 575–591.

Lin, GCS and FZY Hu (2011). Getting the China story right: Insights from national economic censuses. *Eurasian Geography and Economics*, 52, 712–746.

Liu, W and M Dunford (2016). Inclusive globalization: Unpacking China's belt and road initiative. *Area Development and Policy*, 1(3), 323–340.

Liu, X and X Hu (2018). Are 'Sister Cities' from 'Sister Provinces'? An Exploratory Study of Sister City Relations (SCRs) in China. *Networks and Spatial Economics*, 18(3), 473–491.

Liu, H, J Jiang, L Zhang and X Chen (2018). OFDI agglomeration and Chinese firm location decisions under the "Belt and Road" initiative. *Sustainability*, 10(11), 4060.

Liu, H and G Lim (2019). The political economy of a rising China in Southeast Asia: Malaysia's response to the Belt and Road Initiative. *Journal of Contemporary China*, 116(28), 216–231.

Lu, J, X Liu and H Wang (2011). Motives for outward FDI of Chinese private firms: Firm resources, industry dynamics, and government policies. *Management and Organization Review*, 7(2), 223–248.

Luo, Y and R Tung (2007). International expansion of emerging market enterprises: a springboard perspective. *Journal of International Business Studies*, 38(4), 481–498.

Luo, Y, Q Xue and B Han (2010). How emerging market governments promote outward FDI: Experience from China. *Journal of World Business*, 45(1), 68–79.

Lv, P, C Guo and X Chen (2018). 'How the Belt and Road Initiative affects China's outward FDI: Comparing Chinese independent firms and business group affiliates'. In *China's Belt and Road Initiative*, W Zhang, I Alon and C Lattemann (eds.). Palgrave Macmillan, Cham, pp. 243–263.

Meyer, KE, S Estrin, SK Bhaumik and MW Peng (2009). Institutions, resources, and entry strategies in emerging economies. *Strategic Management Journal*, 30(1), 61–80.

Milhaupt, CJ and W Zheng (2015). Beyond ownership: State capitalism and the Chinese firm. *The Georgetown Law Journal*, 103, 665–722.

Ministry of Commerce of China (2017). Statistical bulletin of China's outward foreign direct investment.

Morck, R, B Yeung and M Zhao (2008). Perspectives on China's outward foreign direct investment. *Journal of International Business Studies*, 39(3), 337–350.

NDRC, MFA and MOC (2015). Vision and actions on jointly building the Silk Road Economic Belt and the 21st-Century Maritime Silk Road. http://en.ndrc.gov.cn/newsrelease/201503/t20150330_669367.html.

OECD (2008). *OECD Investment Policy Reviews-China 2008: Encouraging Responsible Business Conduct*. Paris: OECD Publisher.

Quer, D, E Claver and L Rienda (2012). Political risk, cultural distance, and outward foreign direct investment: Empirical evidence from large Chinese firms. *Asia Pacific Journal of Management*, 29(4), 1089–1104.

Ramamurti, R and J Hillemann (2018). What is "Chinese" about Chinese multinationals? *Journal of International Business Studies*, 49(1), 34–48.

Ramasamy, B, M Yeung and S Laforet (2012). China's outward foreign direct investment: Location choice and firm ownership. *Journal of World Business*, 47, 17–25.

Rui, H and GS Yip (2008). Foreign acquisitions by Chinese firms: A strategic intent perspective. *Journal of World Business*, 43(2), 213–226.

Stoian, C (2013). Extending Dunning's investment development path: The role of home country institutional determinants in explaining outward foreign direct investment. *International Business Review*, 22(3), 615–637.

Song, L, J Yang and Y Zhang (2011). State-owned enterprises' outward investment and the structural reform in China. *China & World Economy*, 19(4), 38–53.

Sutherland, D and L Ning (2011). Exploring 'onward-journey' ODI strategies in China's private sector businesses. *Journal of Chinese Economic and Business Studies*, 9(1), 43–65.

Tang-Lee, D (2016). Corporate social responsibility (CSR) and public engagement for a Chinese state-backed mining project in Myanmar — Challenges and prospects. *Resources Policy*, 47, 28–37.

UNCTAD (2016). *World Investment Report 2016 — Investor Nationality: Policy Challenges*. New York: UN.

Voss, H, PJ Buckley and AR Cross (2010). The impact of home country institutional effects on the internationalization strategy of Chinese firms. *Multinational Business Review*, 18(3), 25–48.

Wang, C, J Hong, M Kafouros and A Boateng (2012). What drives outward FDI of Chinese firms? Testing the explanatory power of three theoretical frameworks. *International Business Review*, 21(3), 425–438.

Yang, C (2016). Relocating labour-intensive manufacturing firms from China to Southeast Asia: a preliminary investigation. *Bandung: Journal of the Global South*, 3(1), 3.

Yeung, HWC (2016). *Strategic Coupling: East Asian Industrial Transformation in the New Global Economy*. Ithaca, NY: Cornell University Press.

Yu, H (2017). Motivation behind China's 'One Belt, One Road' initiatives and establishment of the Asian infrastructure investment bank. *Journal of Contemporary China*, 26(105), 353–368.

Zhang, X and K Daly (2011). The determinants of China's outward foreign direct investment. *Emerging Markets Review*, 12(4), 389–398.

Zhang, J, J Jiang and C Zhou (2014). Diplomacy and investment — the case of China. *International Journal of Emerging Markets*, 9(2), 216–235.

Chapter 9

THE IMPACT OF THE BELT AND ROAD INITIATIVE ON FIRMS' EMPLOYMENT STRUCTURE AND WAGE — EVIDENCE FROM CHINA'S PUBLIC LISTED FIRMS[‡]

BO CHEN* and YUE CHEN†

School of Economics
Huazhong University of Science and Technology
1037 Luoyu Rd., Wuhan, Hubei 430074, P. R. China
**chenbo1947@gmail.com*
†893484567@qq.com

Published Online 8 August 2020

In this paper, we use the Belt and Road Initiative (B&R) as a semi-natural experiment and apply a difference-in-difference analysis together with the propensity score matching approach to estimate the impact of the B&R on China's A-Share listed firms with outbound FDI to the B&R countries during 2011–2017. We find that China's firms investing in B&R countries, compared to those investing elsewhere in the world, tend to reduce their total employment, increase the share of skilled labor, and increase wages. Various tests show that the key results of B&R impacts remain robust. We also find that the adjustment after investing in B&R countries is mainly found in non-SOEs, the firms in key provinces that enjoy pilot B&R policies. Both vertical and horizontal FDI firms are found to significantly adjust their employment, skill structure, and wage payment, with the former as more responsive.

Keywords: Belt and Road Initiative; difference-in-difference; employment; wage.

JEL Classifications: F12, F14, F16.

1. Introduction

In September and October, 2013, China's President Xi Jinping announced, respectively, his ambitious initiatives on the Silkroad Economic Belt and the 21st century Maritime Silkroad when he visited Central Asia and Southeast Asia. Later, these two initiatives merged as the integrated one which is now officially named as the Belt and Road Initiative (hereafter, B&R). So far, more than 60 countries have signed cooperation agreements or memorandums with China for their participation in the B&R. During 2014–2018, the B&R led to fast growth on both trade and FDI between China and the participating countries. According to the Ministry of Commerce of China (MOFCOM), the aggregate bilateral trade between China and the other B&R participants amounted to almost USD $6.5 Trillion, with its share in China's global trade increasing from 23.9% in 2011 to 27.4% in 2018. China's non-financial outbound FDI to the B&R participants exceeded USD$90

* Corresponding author.

‡This article originally appeared in *The Singapore Economic Review*, doi: 10.1142/S0217590820490028

Billion during the same period. Particularly, due to the escalated trade war between the U.S. and China, China's multinational firms became more active in investing B&R countries for the security purpose for supply chain and the detour of trade barriers. In 2018, the non-financial OFDI to B&R countries exceeded USD 15.6 Billion, with a growth rate of 8.9% compared to its 2017 level, which is in sharp comparison with the 0.3% China's overall OFDI growth rate to the world.

With the emergence of MNEs, FDI has become a research focus since 1970s (Frank and Freeman, 1978). Though agreed on the importance on FDI, the existing literature differs in their findings on how FDI affects the employment at home (Baldwin, 1995). Helpman (2006) surveyed FDI literature and summarized the relevant research based on three types of FDI purposes. That is, horizontal FDI produces products directly at the local markets to detour tariff and nontariff barriers; vertical FDI aims at building supply chain with all the production procedures that do not have comparative advantages being outsourced to other countries; and the mixed FDI is a hybrid type of horizontal and vertical FDI. Given the different types of FDI, it is not surprising to find that FDI results in different impacts on employment at home. Some studies provide evidence that outbound FDI increases home countries' job loss (McCarthy, 2002; Hatzichronoglou, 2006), while others argue that FDI by may help reduce unemployment rate in the home countries (Egger and Kreickemeier, 2008; Mitra and Ranjan, 2010).

As different types of FDI can influence the employment structure at home, it could therefore impact the wage level as well. Helpman (2014) reviewed the literature on trade and FDI which discusses the link between FDI and wages. Harrison and McMillan (2007) found that for US firms that perform the same tasks in foreign affiliates and at home (i.e., horizontal FDI), foreign and domestic employees appear to be substitutes and hence lower employment and lower wages at home; for those which do significantly different tasks at home and abroad (i.e., vertical FDI), foreign and domestic employment are complements and thus higher wages and higher U.S. manufacturing employment are more possible. Similar to the trade liberalization and wage argument (Chen *et al.*, 2017), FDI might result in more efficient allocation of its production and hence higher profits, which in turn benefits workers in parent firms thanks to the fair wage mechanism.

The effect of FDI due to the B&R to China's MNEs has also received well attention recently. Yu *et al.* (2019) studied the impacts B&R on China's OFDI and found that the B&R does significantly promote China's OFDI to the participating countries. Du and Zhang (2018) documented the preferred destinations and sectors of investment of China's OFDI according to the MNEs' ownership structure. Liu and Mandzoor (2019) assess the impacts of OFDI in B&R countries from China's MNEs and find that they seem receive slightly negative impacts in terms of both productivity and profitability.

However, it is still silent about whether the fast growing OFDI from China's MNEs to the B&R nations has significant impacts to those MNEs' performance. Based on the data of China's A-share listed firms from 2011 to 2017,[1] we investigate how the B&R affects

[1] All the China's domestically listed firms are included in the so-called A-Share markets which are in Shanghai and Shenzhen.

China's A-share listed firms' employment and its employment structure as well as the wages. We treat B&R as a semi-natural experiment and use the difference-in-difference (DID) approach to estimate these impacts. We find that the OFDI to B&R countries, compared to the OFDI to the rest of the world, results the firms in reducing their employment, increasing their employment share of skilled labor and increasing their wage payment. We further analyze the impacts of B&R to firms with different ownership, locations, and FDI types. Our results show that though both SOEs and non SOEs tend to increase their share of skilled labor after OFDI to B&R countries, the former significantly increases their wage payment while the latter is more prominent in reducing domestic employment. Furthermore, we find that the wage effect is significant in those firms in provinces with B&R promotion policies while the effects on home employment reduction and increased share of skilled labor exist in all the OFDI firms engaging in B&R. Finally, we find that the magnitudes of the impacts on employment and skill labor share are larger in the firms engaging in vertical OFDI whilst firms with horizontal OFDI tend to pay higher wages.

Compared to the existing literature, this paper contributes at least in the following two folds. First, this is the first paper that assesses the impact of OFDI to B&R on firm's employment, skill structure, and wage. Second, with propensity score matching for the data and a difference-in-difference approach, we avoid the endogeneity problem caused by wage driven OFDI.[2]

The rest of the paper is organized as follows. Section 2 describes the empirical strategies and data. Section 3 conducts the empirical tests. Section 4 provides investigations on B&Rs impacts on firms with different ownership, locations, and types of OFDI. Section 5 concludes.

2. Measures and Data

2.1. *Estimation specification and variables*

Based on the data of the China's A-share listed firms during 2011–2017, we investigate the impact of the B&R on OFDI firms' employment and wage. Treating the B&R as an exogenous shock, we use a Difference in Difference (DID) approach to conduct the estimation. The B&R emphasizes on cooperation with countries mainly across Asia-Europe continent, including infrastructure development, reducing trade barriers, improvement of business environment, etc. Therefore, it is expected that China's firms with OFDI to B&R countries are more likely to be benefited. Hence, we put the OFDI firms to B&R countries in the treatment group and the rest of China's OFDI firms in the control group to examine the B&R effect on employment and wage.

The validity of DID estimation relies on the assumption that the control group and the treatment group should satisfy the common trend with no systematic difference before B&R. However, whether a firm invests in B&R countries is not completely exogenous, it took time for B&R policies to be gradually added so that to some extent firms can

[2]The endogeneity issue of wage and OFDI for China's MNEs are well discussed in Fan *et al.* (2018).

anticipate the change. Moreover, there is vast heterogeneity among listed firms in terms of their age, size, ownership, etc. The heterogeneity might lead to sample selection bias. For example, larger firms, firms that rely on natural resources, cheap labor, or firms with closer relationship to government (mostly SOEs) would be more likely to participate in the B&R in the first place. In order to solve the problem, we introduce the propensity score matching method (PSM) proposed by Rosenbaum and Rubin (1983) and select the matching control group firms through PSM to mitigate sample selection bias. The main idea of PSM is to find the firm j of the control group as similar as possible in the observable variables to the firm i of treatment group. Therefore, after matching firm j of control group, firm i is similar in terms of their characteristics, i.e., $X_i \cong X_j$. Here, we choose the variables as matching variables including firm size, age, labor productivity, capital intensity and export status. We match the samples by the nearest neighbor matching method.

Specifically, we construct the following specification for our DID estimation after matching:

$$Y_{it} = \alpha_0 + \beta \times \text{treat}_i \times \text{post}_t + \gamma \times X_{it} + \lambda_i + \mu_i + \varepsilon_{it}, \quad (1)$$

where Y_{it} is a vector of dependent variables, includes employment, the skill structure, and the average wage of the firm i in year t. Employment is the logarithm of total employment (at home), skill structure is measured by the ratio of employees with college education or above in total workforce, and average wage is the logarithm of the aggregate salary plus cash (i.e., net payroll) paid to the employees divided by total number of employees. The variable "treat" is an indicator of firm group, which is equal to unity if a firm is in the treatment group, and zero otherwise; "post" is a dummy equal to unity if $t \geq 2014$, and zero otherwise.[3] X_{it} is a vector of firm i's characteristics at time t. As mentioned, these variables include firm's size (measured by the logarithm of total assets), age (the difference between the current year and the founding year), labor productivity (the logarithm of the value-added divided by the number of employees),[4] capital intensity (defined as the log value of fixed capital over employment), profit ratio (the ratio of profit over sales revenue) and the export status "EX" (a dummy variable with the value of unity if a firm exports or zero otherwise); λ_t is the year fixed effect, used to control for all yearly shocks common to all firms; μ_i is firm fixed effect, used to control for all time-invariant characteristics of firms and ε_{it} is the error term.

Our main interest focuses on parameter β, which identifies the difference of the changes in employment structure and wage between the treatment group and the control group. A positive sign of β indicates that investing in OBOR countries increases the firm's employment, average wage and promotes the firm's skill structure, while a negative sign indicates the opposite effect.

In addition, the coefficient of the interaction term, treat × post, estimates the average treatment effect between the control group and the treatment group after 2014. We then use

[3] We select the year 2014 as the shocking time as in Sun and Qin (2018). Although the B&R was proposed in September and October 2013, the real promotion was started in March 2014 when it was written in the government work report.

[4] Value-added is derived from the total sales' revenue minus the expenses on intermediate goods and services.

the following specification to estimate the dynamic effect of B&R on employment and wage:

$$Y_{it} = a_0 + \sum_{t=2012}^{2017} \beta_t \times \text{treat}_i \times \text{year}_t + \gamma \times X_{it} + \lambda_i + \mu_i + \varepsilon_{it}, \quad (2)$$

where year_t is the year dummy variable, with 2011 as the base year; the interaction coefficient β_t here captures to the dynamic effect from 2012 to 2017; other variables are defined the same as model (1).

2.2. *Data*

Our empirical analysis relies on several sets of data which include information on firm-level operation and the status of outbound foreign direct investment. The first data source is the WIND database, which provides the information about A-share listed firms' accounting, financial data as well as their employees' information. Our second dataset is a compilation of outbound FDI projects by Chinese firms, which is reported by MOFCOM. MOFCOM reports all the outbound FDI projects approved by the ministry from 1988 to 2017. The dataset from 1988 to 2015 records detailed information of each outbound FDI project, including the starting year, firm registration information both at home and overseas, investment destination, firm locations, types of business of their investment. However, MOFCOM only reports the information on firm name and destination for OFDI in 2016 and 2017.

To identify the OFDI status of listed companies, we first match these two data by firm names; and then we can distinguish whether the firms are in the control group based on the information on the investment country (region). In particular, we select those firms with OFDI to B&R countries before 2015 into the treatment group for the following two reasons. First, to investigate the impacts of B&R policies (typically in 2014 and after), firms are supposed to be operating and benefited for a while. That is, the firms investing in B&R in 2016 and 2017 are too new to enjoy the policies. Second, the data in 2016 and 2017 misses some important information. For instance, lack of detailed types of investment makes it impossible for the discussion on the different impact of horizontal and vertical FDI.[5] Following a common practice of existing literature (i.e., Choi *et al.* (2011), Cao *et al.* (2017)), we exclude the firms in financial sectors, since their investment purposes and behavior are much different from non-financial firms (which are our research focus). Moreover, we drop the firms with leverage ratios greater than 100, or in special treatment marked by the regulatory committee as "ST" and "ST*".[6] Firms with missing financial data and employment information are also excluded. Furthermore, we winsor the top and bottom 1% quantile of observations to avoid the disturbance by extreme values usually caused by misreporting. Following the above-mentioned criteria, we obtain a sample of 975 firms with 3,668 firm-year observations, of which 280 firms are in the treatment group.

[5] For robustness check, we also conduct the DID analysis putting all the OFDI firms before 2017 into the treatment group and the qualitative results remain the same. The report is available upon request to the authors.

[6] "ST" refers to those firms reporting negative profit in two consecutive years and "ST*" refers to those firms with negative profit for three consecutive years and have the risk of being removed from the A-share list.

Table 1. The Result of Balance Test

Variable	Types	Mean Treated	Mean Control	% Bias	Bias Reduction	t-test t-values	t-test $p > \|t\|$
lnkl	Unmatched	12.474	12.368	10.0		3.54	0.000
	Matched	12.484	12.483	0.1	99.2	0.02	0.983
lnlp	Unmatched	13.973	13.69	32.6		11.70	0.000
	Matched	13.958	13.987	−3.3	89.9	−0.92	0.360
age	Unmatched	17.674	17.742	−1.2		−0.41	0.682
	Matched	17.795	17.803	−0.1	88.3	−0.04	0.968
size	Unmatched	22.82	22.166	45.2		16.36	0.000
	Matched	22.763	22.768	−0.3	99.2	−0.09	0.925
EX	Unmatched	0.87478	0.72139	38.9		12.91	0.000
	Matched	0.87293	0.86673	1.6	96.0	0.54	0.592
Profit ratio	Unmatched	0.07565	0.09543	−17.2		−5.73	0.000
	Matched	0.07625	0.07886	−2.3	86.8	−0.71	0.479
Sample | Ps R^2	LR chi2	$p >$ chi2	Mean Bias	Med Bias	B	R	% Var
Unmatched | 0.074	547.71	0.000	24.2	24.9	67.1*	1.04	60
Matched | 0.000	1.66	0.948	1.3	1.0	4.4	0.78	40

Notes: if variance ratio outside [0.91; 1.10] for U and [0.91; 1.10] for M
*if $B > 25\%$, R outside [0.5; 2].

As shown in Table 1, the normalized errors of the variables are significantly reduced after matching, all lower than 10%. And t-value of the variables cannot reject the null hypothesis that the treatment group and the control group have no significant difference. Moreover, Figures 1 and 2 are the kernel density distribution graphs before and after matching. It is clear that the matched control group are more analogous to the treatment group than

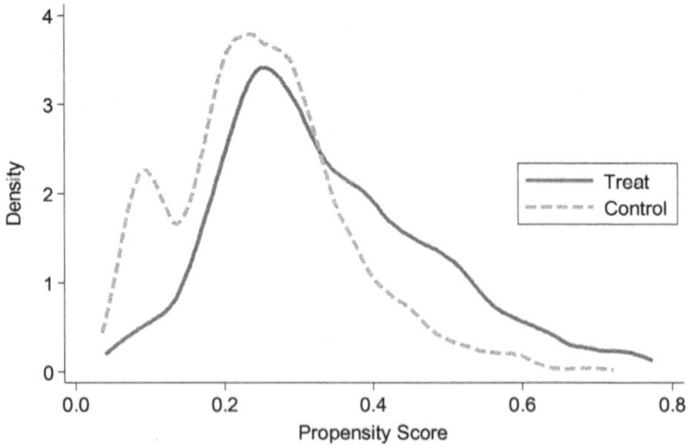

Figure 1. Before Matching

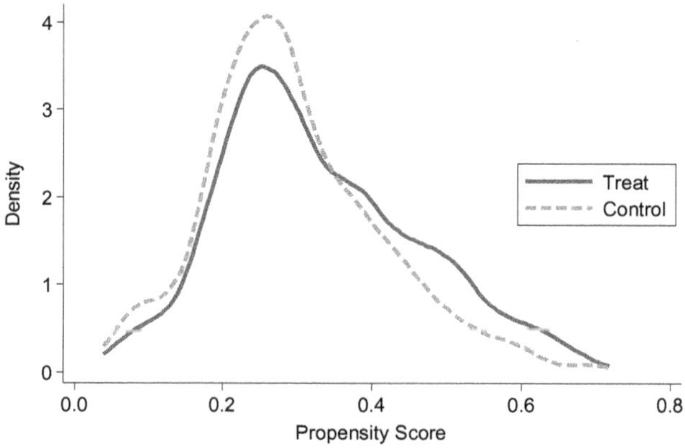

Figure 2. After Matching

Table 2. Summary Statistics of Variables

Variables	N	Mean	SD	Minimum	Maximum
average wage	3668	11.49	0.511	10.41	12.97
theta	3668	0.453	0.243	0	0.986
lnL	3668	8.171	1.358	5.017	11.70
lnkl	3668	12.47	1.074	9.589	15.06
lnlp	3668	13.90	0.890	12.13	16.44
Profit ratio	3668	0.0816	0.111	−0.396	0.502
age	3668	17.81	5.768	3	63
size	3668	22.61	1.471	19.82	26.77
EX	3668	0.847	0.360	0	1
year	3668	2014	2.005	2011	2017

unmatched ones. Overall, both the table and figures show that the matched samples are more appropriate for our regression. Table 2 reports the descriptive statistics of the variables used in our basic empirical analysis.

3. Empirical Analysis

3.1. *Baseline results*

Table 3 presents the basic regression results based on our DID specification (1), using the year 2014 as the critical year.[7] Estimates for the unmatched sample are presented in columns (1)–(3), while columns (4)–(6) contain the matched sample regressions.

[7] As the B&R initiative was proposed on October, 2013, the corresponding policies were mainly implemented after 2014.

Table 3. Baseline Results

	Unmatched Sample			Matched Sample		
Variables	(1) Employment	(2) Skill Structure	(3) Wage	(4) Employment	(5) Skill Structure	(6) Wage
treat × post	−0.0592***	0.0238***	0.0289***	−0.0644***	0.0229***	0.0415***
	(−5.16)	(3.66)	(2.95)	(−4.59)	(2.77)	(3.37)
Profit ratio	0.0355	−0.0156	−0.339***	0.110**	0.00542	−0.251***
	(1.04)	(−0.80)	(−11.63)	(2.19)	(0.18)	(−5.67)
Lnkl	−0.172***	0.00368	0.0846***	−0.185***	−0.00229	0.0969***
	(−25.61)	(0.96)	(14.76)	(−19.77)	(−0.42)	(11.79)
Lnlp	−0.529***	0.0439***	0.419***	−0.521***	0.0426***	0.413***
	(−56.42)	(8.25)	(52.42)	(−39.56)	(5.48)	(35.73)
Age	0.00630***	0.0180***	0.0601***	0.00840***	0.0164***	0.0544***
	(2.94)	(14.79)	(32.91)	(2.77)	(9.16)	(20.44)
Size	0.752***	−0.00485	−0.0549***	0.747***	0.00970	−0.0495***
	(85.18)	(−0.97)	(−7.29)	(59.60)	(1.31)	(−4.49)
EX	0.0340**	−0.0180**	0.0219*	0.00459	−0.00797	0.0515***
	(2.44)	(−2.27)	(1.85)	(0.22)	(−0.64)	(2.79)
Firm FE	Yes	Yes	Yes	Yes	Yes	Yes
Year FE	Yes	Yes	Yes	Yes	Yes	Yes
N	6261	6261	6261	3668	3668	3668
R^2	0.737	0.156	0.648	0.722	0.168	0.635

Notes: Robust t-values corrected for clustering at the firm level are in parentheses.
*, ** and *** indicate significance at the 10%, 5% and 1% levels, respectively.

The dependent variable of columns (1) and (4) is employment, that of columns (2) and (5) is skill structure, and that of columns (3) and (6) is workers' average wage, respectively. All regressions control for the firm-fixed effect and year-fixed effect. Table 3 shows that firms in treatment group with higher profit ratio tend to pay higher wages in based on both unmatched and matched data. Results from matched data also suggest that firms with higher profit ratio also tend to employ more. Results also show that firms with higher capital intensity tend to employ less but pay more compared to the firms in the control group. The treatment group with higher (labor) productivity also tends to employ less and pay more and they prefer to hire skilled labor. Furthermore, the treatment group with longer history (i.e., higher value in age) tends to have more employment, higher skilled labor proportion and higher average wage. Table 3 shows that bigger firms in treatment group tend to hire more but pay less (average) wages yet whether they prefer to hire skilled labor is not clear as the result in unmatched data suggests no while the matched data suggests yes. Though it shows in columns (1) and (2) that the treatment group with export activities tends to hire more and prefer to unskilled labor, it is not supported in columns (4) and (5) when the data is arranged by PSM. However, columns (3) and (6) show that the treatment group would pay more to its employees if it exports. Our main interest is the coefficient β, the coefficient of interaction term of treat and post, which measures the influence of the B&R on firms' employment and wage. In columns (1) and (4), when the dependent variable is employment, we find β is negative and significant, indicating that after the introduction of B&R firms investing in B&R countries tend to employ less at home compared to other OFDI firms. In columns (2) and (5), β is significantly positive, indicating that firms engaging in B&R tend to increase its proportion of skilled labor than the control group. In columns (3) and (6), β is also positive and significant, indicating that the firms investing in B&R tend to pay higher to their employees at home compared to the control group.

3.2. *Validity of DID specifications*

Since the supportive B&R policies were implemented in and after 2014, our baseline results might be sensitive to the choice of critical year. In this subsection, rather than using the interaction term treat $\times$ post in model (1) for the year 2014, we use a series of interaction terms between "treat" and the year dummies from 2012–2017. We run the specification (2) and report the results in Table 4. The estimated coefficients that we focus are β_t, which measure the yearly changes (compared to 2011) of the treatment group thanks to their investment in B&R countries relative to the control group. Table 4 shows that all the estimated coefficients are insignificant before 2014 yet all of them become statistically significant in and after 2014. The results imply that the control group and the treatment group satisfy the common trend before the implementation of the B&R. The matched samples passed the common trend test. Further, we can also derive the dynamic impact of the B&R policies on the related firms' employment and wage. For the B&R related firms' employment, the coefficients of the interaction terms are persistently increased (in absolute terms). For the skill intensity, the magnitude of the coefficients increases in 2016 and 2017

Table 4. Validity of the Specifications

Variables	(1) Employment	(2) Skill Structure	(3) Average Wage
treat × Year2012	−0.0392	0.0130	0.0101
	(−1.48)	(0.83)	(0.43)
treat × Year2013	−0.0327	0.00775	0.0144
	(−1.22)	(0.49)	(0.61)
treat × Year2014	−0.0577**	0.0265*	0.0428*
	(−2.24)	(1.74)	(1.89)
treat × Year2015	−0.0764***	0.0252*	0.0489**
	(−2.97)	(1.66)	(2.16)
treat × Year2016	−0.107***	0.0340**	0.0468**
	(−4.17)	(2.25)	(2.08)
treat × Year2017	−0.115***	0.0342**	0.0609***
	(−4.51)	(2.27)	(2.71)
Firm controls	Yes	Yes	Yes
Firm FE	Yes	Yes	Yes
Year FE	Yes	Yes	Yes
N	3668	3668	3668
R^2	0.723	0.168	0.635

Notes: Robust *t*-values corrected for clustering at the firm level are in parentheses. *, **, and *** indicate significance at the 10%, 5%, and 1% levels, respectively.

compared to 2014 and 2015, indicating that B&R effect became more influential in later years. For wage payment, the coefficients become more significant after 2014 and the magnitude of the B&R influence turned much stronger in 2017.

3.3. *Placebo test*

If there are some other unobservable factors around the time of B&R proposal which might also affect our treatment and control groups differently, then the effect of those factors may also be captured in the DID estimates and mistakenly attributed to B&R effect. We conduct a placebo test by assigning China's OFDI firms in the sample to treatment and control group randomly. Specifically, we randomly select 280 firms from the sample to form a treatment group and the others to form the control group. By repeating this process 1,000 times, we obtain 1,000 estimated coefficients of B&R policy shock. Most of the 1,000 coefficients should be insignificant if our basic results are convincing, otherwise there might be other latent factors that drive for our previous results. Figure 3 shows the coefficients distribution of placebo test. When the dependent variable is average wage, the mean of the estimated coefficients is 0.000111, the standard deviation is 0.02017; for the skill structure, the mean of the estimated coefficients is –0.00045, the standard deviation 0.01349; for employment, the mean of estimated coefficient is 0.000160 and the standard deviation is 0.0234159. None of the results above can reject the null hypotheses that the

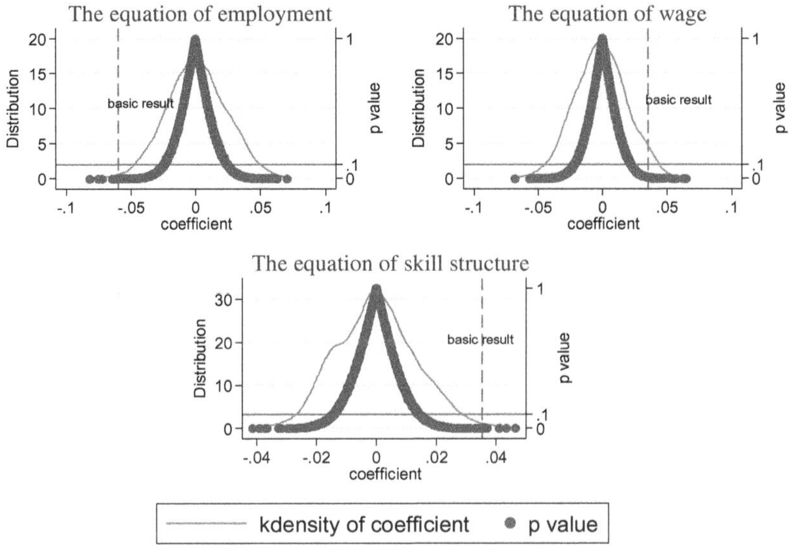

Figure 3. Placebo Test

key coefficient is 0. We also graph the nuclear density distribution of coefficients. Among them, the red line is the nuclear density distribution of the 1000 estimated coefficients, and the blue is the corresponding p-value distribution. We find that the estimated coefficient distribution is concentrated near the zero point, and the most of p-values are greater than 0.1. Therefore, our basic results are not due to other unobservable factors, it is because the proposal of the B&R.

3.4. *Alternative matching approach and measurement of dependent variables*

We further check the robustness of our results for other concerns such as the matching method, the measurement of skill structure and wage payment. The results are presented in Table 5. Columns (1)–(3) show the results based on the nonparametric kernel matching method, and the dependent variables are the same as before. We find the results of the treatment effect are similar to the baseline results in columns (4)–(6) of Table 3. Then we check our results using alternative dependent variables. In column (4), the worker's accrued payroll is used to replace the payment to the employee and the cash paid for the employee.[8] It shows again that firms investing in B&R countries tend to pay higher to their employee at home.

[8] Compared to the net payroll, accrued payroll also includes income taxes and voluntary deductions.

Table 5. Alternative Matching Approach and Measurement of Dependent Variables

	(1) Employment	(2) Skill Structure	(3) Wage	(4) Wage
treat × post	−0.0623***	0.0245***	0.0297***	0.0613*
	(−5.39)	(3.73)	(3.02)	(1.84)
profit ratio	0.0542	−0.0171	−0.358***	0.0979
	(1.56)	(−0.87)	(−12.12)	(0.82)
lnkl	−0.171***	0.00336	0.0835***	0.0920***
	(−25.42)	(0.88)	(14.55)	(4.13)
lnlp	−0.533***	0.0435***	0.423***	0.394***
	(−56.46)	(8.11)	(52.62)	(12.55)
age	0.00632***	0.0183***	0.0600***	0.0699***
	(2.93)	(14.94)	(32.62)	(9.69)
size	0.753***	−0.00779	−0.0556***	0.0831***
	(84.24)	(−1.54)	(−7.31)	(2.78)
EX	0.0327**	−0.0176**	0.0243**	0.0857*
	(2.33)	(−2.20)	(2.03)	(1.71)
Firm FE	Yes	Yes	Yes	Yes
Year FE	Yes	Yes	Yes	Yes
N	6221	6221	6221	3668
R^2	0.737	0.154	0.649	0.300

Notes: Robust *t*-values corrected for clustering at the firm level are in parentheses. *, **, and *** indicate significance at the 10%, 5%, and 1% levels, respectively.

4. Explorations on the B&R Effect

In this session, we explore the different effects of B&R on firms with different characteristics with respect to their ownership, location, and types of OFDI. Ownership is important because it is widely believed that B&R is highly risky to average firms and only those SOEs are strong enough to face the risk given their ties with China's government or they are simply forced to participate as is demanded by China's government. Locations of the firms might also be important due to the fact that China imposed province-specific "pilot" policies at the start as one of the B&R promotion measures. Finally, it is also interesting to investigate the B&R effects on vertical and horizontal investment as the theories on this regard suggest that vertical and horizontal FDI might generate fairly different effect to parent firms.

4.1. *Ownership*

Given the high risk and political concerns, it is widely suspected that the B&R would mainly affect SOEs, especially at the beginning. Therefore, in this section, we separate firms as SOEs and non-SOEs, and examine the impacts of the B&R on OFDI firms with different ownership. The results are reported in Table 6. Columns (1)–(3) show the results for SOEs, and columns (4)–(6) for non-SOEs. Table 6 shows clear difference due to

Table 6. The Types of Ownership

	(1)	(2)	(3)	(4)	(5)	(6)
	SOEs			Non-SOEs		
Variables	Employment	Skill Structure	Average Wage	Employment	Skill Structure	Average Wage
treat × post	−0.0234	0.00887	0.0693***	−0.0822***	0.0272***	0.0253*
	(−1.03)	(0.59)	(3.36)	(−4.75)	(2.73)	(1.66)
Profit ratio	0.281***	−0.0282	−0.408***	0.0806	−0.00172	−0.223***
	(2.74)	(−0.41)	(−4.36)	(1.41)	(−0.05)	(−4.43)
lnkl	−0.344***	0.0138	0.158***	−0.138***	−0.00619	0.0705***
	(−17.65)	(1.06)	(8.86)	(−13.03)	(−1.01)	(7.52)
lnlp	−0.524***	0.0546***	0.442***	−0.485***	0.0339***	0.382***
	(−22.20)	(3.45)	(20.46)	(−29.89)	(3.62)	(26.59)
age	−0.000599	0.0219***	0.0329***	0.0113***	0.0122***	0.0703***
	(−0.13)	(7.17)	(7.89)	(2.88)	(5.42)	(20.32)
size	0.835***	−0.00555	0.0119	0.708***	0.0217**	−0.0736***
	(34.48)	(−0.34)	(0.54)	(47.68)	(2.54)	(−5.61)
EX	0.0121	0.0121	0.106***	0.00241	−0.0191	0.0270
	(0.35)	(0.52)	(3.38)	(0.10)	(−1.31)	(1.21)
Firm FE	Yes	Yes	Yes	Yes	Yes	Yes
Year FE	Yes	Yes	Yes	Yes	Yes	Yes
N	1176	1176	1176	2492	2492	2492
R^2	0.775	0.193	0.657	0.712	0.157	0.643

Notes: Robust t-values corrected for clustering at the firm level are in parentheses. *, **, and *** indicate significance at the 10%, 5%, and 1% levels, respectively.

Table 7. Key Provinces and General Province

	(1)	(2)	(3)	(4)	(5)	(6)
	Key Provinces			Other Provinces		
Variables	Employment	Skill Structure	Average Wage	Employment	Skill Structure	Average Wage
treat × post	−0.0807***	0.0280**	0.0600***	−0.0466**	0.0178	0.0201
	(−3.92)	(2.29)	(3.43)	(−2.50)	(1.59)	(1.15)
Profit ratio	0.0917	0.0782*	−0.153**	0.139**	−0.0786**	−0.357***
	(1.25)	(1.79)	(−2.46)	(2.08)	(−1.97)	(−5.71)
lnkl	−0.165***	−0.00115	0.101***	−0.232***	−0.00200	0.0981***
	(−12.72)	(−0.15)	(9.21)	(−17.25)	(−0.25)	(7.79)
lnlp	−0.566***	0.0199*	0.427***	−0.460***	0.0606***	0.399***
	(−28.88)	(1.71)	(25.64)	(−26.34)	(5.81)	(24.42)
age	0.0246***	0.0148***	0.0470***	−0.00438	0.0176***	0.0604***
	(5.36)	(5.43)	(12.05)	(−1.12)	(7.52)	(16.44)
size	0.661***	0.0330***	−0.0215	0.826***	−0.0108	−0.0717***
	(33.75)	(2.84)	(−1.29)	(52.45)	(−1.15)	(−4.86)
EX	−0.0000738	−0.000272	0.0817***	−0.00110	−0.0168	0.0228
	(0.00)	(−0.02)	(3.19)	(−0.04)	(−0.99)	(0.86)
Firm FE	Yes	Yes	Yes	Yes	Yes	Yes
Year FE	Yes	Yes	Yes	Yes	Yes	Yes
N	1920	1920	1920	1748	1748	1748
R^2	0.678	0.175	0.628	0.779	0.178	0.650

Notes: Robust t-values corrected for clustering at the firm level are in parentheses. *, **, and *** indicate significance at the 10%, 5%, and 1% levels, respectively.

Table 8. Vertical OFDI and Horizontal OFDI

	(1)	(2)	(3)	(4)	(5)	(6)
	Vertical OFDI			Horizontal OFDI		
Variables	Employment	Skill Structure	Average Wage	Employment	Skill Structure	Average Wage
treat × post	−0.0921***	0.0344**	0.0642***	−0.0680***	0.0204*	0.0600***
	(−3.78)	(2.53)	(3.02)	(−3.76)	(1.81)	(3.43)
Profit ratio	0.0617	0.0606	−0.166**	0.132**	−0.0362	−0.153**
	(0.79)	(1.38)	(−2.42)	(2.03)	(−0.90)	(−2.46)
lnkl	−0.146***	−0.00929	0.0877***	−0.224***	0.00824	0.101***
	(−9.96)	(−1.13)	(6.86)	(−18.27)	(1.09)	(9.21)
lnlp	−0.512***	0.0667***	0.421***	−0.509***	0.0173	0.427***
	(−25.36)	(5.92)	(23.97)	(−29.13)	(1.59)	(25.64)
age	0.00635	0.0170***	0.0512***	0.0107***	0.0160***	0.0470***
	(1.39)	(6.68)	(12.89)	(2.58)	(6.26)	(12.05)
size	0.717***	0.00640	−0.0290*	0.773***	0.00975	−0.0215
	(36.88)	(0.59)	(−1.71)	(47.12)	(0.96)	(−1.29)
EX	−0.00970	−0.0265	0.0111	0.0368	0.00725	0.0817***
	(−0.32)	(−1.56)	(0.42)	(1.26)	(0.40)	(3.19)
Firm FE	Yes	Yes	Yes	Yes	Yes	Yes
Year FE	Yes	Yes	Yes	Yes	Yes	Yes
N	1555	1555	1555	2113	2113	1920
R^2	0.683	0.204	0.625	0.756	0.154	0.628

Notes: Robust t-values corrected for clustering at the firm level are in parentheses. *, **, and *** indicate significance at the 10%, 5%, and 1% levels, respectively.

ownership. SOE parent firms have no adjustment on employment and skill structure after they invest in B&R nations while non SOEs tend to hire more workers and proportionally more skilled labor. However, even though both SOEs and non-SOEs tend to pay higher in their parent firms, the former exhibits much stronger effect.

4.2. *The location of listed firm*

Although one of the B&R purposes is to promote China's firms' investment to the participating countries, the initiative may also affect firms differently due to their geographical locations: firms in the provinces which enjoy "pilot" policies of B&R are supposed to benefit earlier and more from the initiative.[9] To investigate the influence of geography, we categorize the matched sample into two groups. One group is the firms in key provinces which have specific B&R promotion policies, and the other is the firm group in other provinces. The results are shown in Table 7. Columns (1)–(3) show the results for firms in the key provinces, and columns (4)–(6) for firms in the non-key provinces. Table 7 shows that the skill structure and wage effects indeed are mainly driven by the firms in key provinces. It is also interesting to find that firms in both groups reduce their home employment in response to their investment in B&R countries.

4.3. *Types of OFDI*

As discussed in the introduction, the FDI literature has well noticed that different types of FDI might cause different impacts on employment and wage payment. We classify the OFDI according to the projects' business scopes reported by a compilation of outward FDI projects of MOFCOM. Following the classification of OFDI by Antràs and Yeaple (2014), treating the products in their parent firms are the final goods, the OFDI projects engaged in part of the value chains of those final goods are deemed as vertical OFDI while the others engaged in the whole value chains are deemed as horizontal OFDI. The first three columns (1)–(3) in Table 8 are the effects of vertical OFDI, and columns (4)–(6) are the effects of horizontal OFDI. Table 8 shows that the general impacts of the B&R on employment, skill structure and average wage remain the same as the baseline regression regardless of the investment types. The magnitudes of the impacts are larger in the firms engaging in vertical OFDI than the counterparts engaged in horizontal OFDI.

5. Concluding Remarks

The B&R is considered as one of the most important cross-continent economic cooperations in the 21st century. However, due to its short history since promotion and lack of data, the impacts of B&R are still hard to assess comprehensively.

[9] In May 2015, China's National Development and Reform Committee, Ministry of Commerce and Ministry of Foreign Affairs jointly publish "Vision and Actions on Energy Cooperation in Jointly Building Silk Road Economic Belt and 21st-Century Maritime Silk Road". The document lists 18 key provinces in promoting B&R: Xinjiang, Shanxi, Gansu, Ningxia, Qinghai, Inner Mongolia, Heilongjiang, Jilin, Liaoning, Guangxi, Yunnan, Xizang, Shanghai, Fujian, Guangdong, Zhejiang, Hainan, Chongqing.

Given the abundant production and accounting data of the China's A-share listed firms from 2011 to 2017, we treat the B&R as a semi-natural experiment and apply a difference-in-difference analysis together with propensity score matching approach to estimate the impacts of the B&R on firm employment, skill structure, and wage. Our baseline results show that firms investing in B&R countries tend to reduce their total employment, increase the share of skilled labor, and increase wage relative to the other OFDI firms. Then we apply for different matching method and use alternative measurement for the key variables. The results for B&R impacts remain robust.

It is also interesting to investigate whether the important characteristics, such as ownership, locations, and types of FDI, could significantly affect the performance of firms with OFDI to B&R countries. Our study shows that SOE parent firms are indeed not responsive to their OFDI to B&R countries while the non-SOEs are. Furthermore, both types of firms pay higher after their investment to B&R countries with the SOE adjust their payment much more than the non-SOEs. In addition, we find that the skill structure and wage effects wage effect are significant only to firms in the key provinces that enjoy B&R pilot policies. And all firms significantly reduce their home employment regardless of their locations. Finally, we also find that though both vertical OFDI and horizontal OFDI firms have significant impacts on employment, skill structure, and wage, the magnitudes of the former are bigger than the latter.

Acknowledgments

We are grateful for the valuable suggestions from seminar participants in University of Macau, Sun Yat-sen University, and Jinan University. Bo Chen also thanks the National Social Science Foundation of China (Grant Nos. 20AZD052 and 17BJL094) and the Key Fund on Interdisciplinary Social Science of HUST for financial support. All errors are ours.

References

Antràs, P and S R Yeaple (2014). Multinational firms and the structure of international trade. In *Handbook of International Economics*, Gita Gopinath, Elhanan Helpman, Kenneth Rogoff (ed.), Vol. 4, Elsevier, pp. 55–130.

Baldwin, R (1995). The effects of trade and foreign direct investment on employment and relative wages. NBER Working Papers No. 5037.

Cao, X, X Pan, M Qian and GG Tian (2017). Political capital and CEO entrenchment: Evidence from CEO turnover in Chinese non-SOEs. *Journal of Corporate Finance*, 42, 1–14.

Chen, B, M Yu and Z Yu (2017). Measured skill premia and input trade liberalization: Evidence from Chinese firms. *Journal of International Economics*, 109, 31–42.

Choi, SB, SH Lee and C Williams (2011). Ownership and firm innovation in a transition economy: Evidence from China. *Research Policy*, 40(3), 441–452.

Du, J and Y Zhang (2018). Does one belt one road initiative promote Chinese overseas direct investment? *China Economic Review*, 47, 189–205.

Egger, H and U Kreickemeier (2008). International fragmentation: Boon or bane for domestic employment. *European Economic Review*, 52(1), 116–132.

Frank, RH and RT Freeman (1978). Chapter V – The Employment Impact of Direct Foreign Investment. *Distributional Consequences of Direct Foreign Investment*, RH Frank and RT Freeman (eds.), pp. 49–63. Academic Press.

Harrison, A and M McMillan (2007). Outsourcing jobs? Multinationals and US Employment, NBER Working Papers No. 12372.

Hatzichronoglou, T (2006). The impact of offshoring on employment: Measurement issues and implications. Organisation for Economic Co-operation and Development, Paris. www.oecd.org/dataoecd/33/60/35644921.pdf.

Helpman, E (2006). Trade, FDI, and the organization of firms. *Journal of Economic Literature*, 44(3), 589–630.

Helpman, E (2014). Foreign trade and investment: Firm-level perspectives. *Economica*, 81(321), 1–14.

Liu, H and A Manzoor (2019). The impact of OFDI on the performance of Chinese firms along the 'belt and road'. Forthcoming in *Applied Economics*, 52(11), 1219–1239.

McCarthy, JC (2002). 3.3 million U.S. Services Jobs to Go Offshore. TechStrategy Research, Forrester Research, November, Cambridge, Mass., Forrester Research.

Mitra, D and P Ranjan (2010). Offshoring and unemployment: The role of search frictions and labor mobility. *Journal of International Economics*, 81(2), 219–229.

Rosenbaum, PR and DB Rubin (1983). The central role of the propensity score in observational studies for causal effects. *Biometrika*, 70(1), 41–55.

Sun, Y and Q Fei (2018). Does "belt and road" initiative reduce firm-level foreign direct investment risk. *Journal of International Trade*, 8, 66–79.

Yu, S, X Qian and T Liu (2019). Belt and road initiative and Chinese firms' outward foreign direct investment. Forthcoming in *Emerging Markets Review*, 41, 100629.

Chapter 10

ROOTING IN NANYANG: HOW EFFICIENT ARE CHINESE MANUFACTURING FIRMS IN MALAYSIA?[†]

MIAO ZHANG

The Center for Southeast Asian Studies
& Institute of Malaysia Studies, Xiamen University
Xiamen University, Xiamen 361005
Fujian Province, P. R. China
miaozhang@xmu.edu.cn

MD ASLAM MIA*

School of Management
Universiti Sains Malaysia (USM)
11800 Pulau Pinang, Malaysia
aslammia@usm.my

Published Online 11 October 2019

While China's Belt and Road Initiative (BRI) is widely considered as an attempt to reshape the global geo-political landscape through its massive investment/engagement in capital-intensive infrastructure, an often-neglected topic is the performance of Chinese-funded firms in manufacturing sector. Therefore, this paper sought to examine the efficiency levels of Chinese manufacturing firms in Malaysia. By using firm-level data supplied by Malaysia's Department of Statistics, this study employs Data Envelopment Analysis to examine the efficiency levels of Chinese manufacturing firms in comparison with local and other foreign firms in 2010 and 2015. The results show that Chinese manufacturing firms show higher efficiency levels than local and foreign firms in 2010 and 2015, implying that these firms have the potential to transfer technology and share managerial skills to local firms. However, the efficiency levels of Chinese firms deteriorated from 2010 to 2015, suggesting that firms' relocations decision may have been driven by distortions created by incentives and other supports provided by the Chinese government rather than by firms' efforts to sustain or raise efficiency levels. The findings suggest that Chinese firms have to be careful in making strategic decision to relocate operations abroad to ensure that government initiatives are in sync with firm-level performance.

Keywords: Chinese outward foreign direct investment; manufacturing; data envelopment analysis; Malaysia.

JEL Classification: C1, F2, L6

1. Introduction

After several decades of miraculous growth since economic reforms were launched in 1978, China's economy has shown signs of slowing down from 2008 (Rasiah *et al.*, 2013).

---

* Corresponding author.

[†]This article originally appeared in *The Singapore Economic Review*, **66**(1), pp. 185–206

While the growth deceleration is unlikely to cause a hard landing, China has developed a new momentum to sustain its economy through a massive increase in outward foreign direct investment (OFDI) since the 2010s. Part of OFDI has been sailing to Nanyang, the Chinese name for the geographical region of Southeast Asia (Wang, 1978). The sheer magnitude of Chinese investment inflow has wielded considerable economic influence on Southeast Asia (Kawai and Naknoi, 2017). Accounting for 12.8% of total Chinese OFDI in Asia, Chinese investment in ASEAN recorded a significant annual growth of 37% in 2017 (Statistical Bulletin of China's Outward Foreign Direct Investment, 2017, p. 31).

As China's biggest trade partner in ASEAN over the period 2009 to 2017 (with exception of 2016), Malaysia has become one of the hottest destinations for Chinese investment (Liu and Lim, 2018). Attracting USD 1.7 billion investment in the year 2017, Malaysia became the second largest Chinese OFDI recipient after Singapore among the ASEAN members. Overall, investment-friendly Malaysia became China's third largest foreign direct investor with a cumulative FDI stock of RM69.5 billion by 2018Q1. Notably, China has become the biggest foreign investor in Malaysia's manufacturing sector, accounting for 25% and 46% of total approved FDI in 2017 and the first half of 2018 respectively (Table 1).

The huge increase in capital flows has certainly generated interest and concerns among the public and policy makers on how Malaysia can appropriate economic synergies from Chinese investment, and whether Chinese manufacturers in Malaysia are more efficient than local and other foreign manufacturers. These questions are pertinent as only if China's firms are more efficient than local firms can one expect positive spillover to the latter through demonstration effects, competition, and technology transfer. Although Chinese multinational corporations (MNCs) have relocated extensive operations in Malaysia, there remains a number of issues that have been argued to have restricted the appropriation of economic synergies by both Chinese and local firms (Lim, 2016; Zhang *et al.*, 2018).

Prior to Malaysia's 14th General Elections, alarm bells were rung by the then-opposition leader Tun Dr. Mahathir Mohammad who claimed that Chinese investment into Malaysia brought little economic benefits to local economy, while crowding out local small and medium enterprises (SMEs). Shortly after Tun Dr Mahathir's coalition government were elected on 9th May 2018, the new government undertook a rigorous review of China-backed mega infrastructure projects, which threatened to cause friction in China–Malaysia diplomatic ties. Nevertheless, the rescaled costing of railway projects i.e. East Coast Rail Link (ECRL) was finally agreed to in April 2019. In addition to the mega-sized infrastructure project, such as RM44 billion worth of projects that was sealed at the government-to-government (G-G) level, there is wide existence of smaller-scale investments from Chinese investors (henceforth Chinese-owned or Chinese-funded) that are looking to explore Malaysia's market potential, and through Malaysia to tap the entire ASEAN market. Being an essential component of Chinese outward FDI, the investment by non-state actors in non-infrastructure sector, such as manufacturing sector, shall not be overshadowed by geo-political narratives that is largely drawn from mega-sized infrastructure projects.

In view of the scale of Chinese investment in Malaysia and its implications, it is worth examining the efficiency of Chinese manufacturers compared to local and other foreign

Table 1. Approved Investment from China to Malaysia's Manufacturing Sector, 2006–2018, in RM

Year	No. of Projects Approved			Investment Amount Approved			Total FDI in Manufacturing	China's Share in Total FDI in Manufacturing
	From Mainland China	From Hong Kong	From China in Total	From Mainland China	From Hong Kong	From China in Total		
2006	19	9	28	134,052,932	84,460,615	218,513,547	20,227,884,033	1.08%
2007	13	14	27	1,883,191,954	59,781,174	1,942,973,128	33,425,889,050	5.81%
2008	17	7	24	35,655,186	83,557,592	119,212,778	46,098,774,530	0.26%
2009	17	7	24	162,221,544	5,315,671,056	5,477,892,600	22,144,676,912	24.74%
2010	20	11	31	639,534,090	2,766,457,013	3,405,991,103	29,056,604,806	11.72%
2011	20	10	30	1,194,224,823	394,929,855	1,589,154,678	34,148,867,413	4.65%
2012	23	7	30	1,977,802,063	90,888,472	2,068,690,535	20,919,008,512	9.89%
2013	22	9	31	3,017,650,478	453,483,541	3,471,134,019	30,536,400,000	11.37%
2014	24	5	29	4,751,700,000	70,400,000	4,822,100,000	39,592,700,000	12.18%
2015	17	9	26	1,872,000,000	3,180,900,000	5,052,900,000	21,941,600,000	23.03%
2016	33	12	45	4,774,800,000	265,200,000	5,040,000,000	27,417,500,000	18.38%
2017	21	10	31	3,854,500,000	1,494,500,000	5,349,000,000	21,543,000,000	24.83%
2018*	17	5	22	6,557,600,000	467,400,000	7,025,000,000	15,237,800,000	46.10%

Note: *the first half of the year.
Source: Malaysia Investment Development Agency (various years).

manufacturers in Malaysia. In short, we seek to answer the question of whether Chinese firms are more efficient than local and other foreign firms in Malaysia. By answering these questions, we aim to contribute to a better understanding of how Chinese investment contributes to economic progress in Malaysia. The rest of the paper is organized as follows. Following this introduction, Section 2 profiles recent developments of Chinese investment in Malaysia as the context of this study. Section 3 introduces the methodology and data. Section 4 analyses the results, while Section 5 presents the conclusions.

2. Chinese Investment in Malaysia

Following China's shift in policy to promote OFDI and the introduction of the Belt and Road Initiative (BRI) in 2013, Malaysia has become one of the biggest destinations for Chinese investment (Tham, 2018; Zhang *et al.*, 2017). The volume of Chinese investment into Malaysia rose from RM7.3 billion in 2008 to RM69 billion in 2017. China surpassed the U.S. and Netherlands as the third largest foreign direct investor in Malaysia after Singapore and Japan since 2016 (Figure 1).

The buoyance of China's investment stock is attributable to the continuous influx of investment inflows (Figure 2). After its peak in 2016Q1 when RM11.4 billion worth of Chinese OFDI entered the Malaysian economy in a single quarter, China's investment into Malaysia has become relatively steady. The exceptional bumper year of 2016 was caused by China General Nuclear's (CGN) purchase of power assets, which is known as Edra Global Energy Bhd. from 1Malaysia Development Bhd (1MDB) with cash amounting to RM9.8 billion. The acquisition of Edra resulted in CGN becoming the biggest foreign direct investor in Malaysia.

A disaggregation of investments by sector[1] shows that Chinese FDI are largely concentrated in energy-related activities (US$ 6.9 billion, 36%), real estate sector (US$4.0

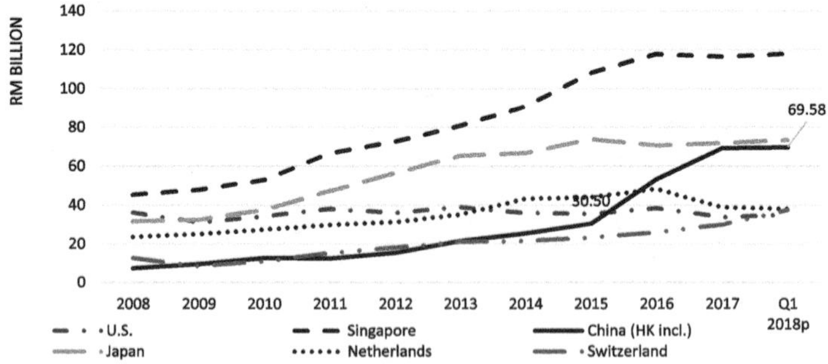

Source: Bank Negara Malaysia and Department of Statistics Malaysia (2018).

Figure 1. FDI Stock in Malaysia, by Selected Country, 2008–2018 (RM Billion)

[1] The analysis of this section is based on date from 31 mega projects in Malaysia with Chinese investments of over USD 100 million from 2008 to 2018. Data was obtained from China Global Investment Tracker via http://www.aei.org/china-global-investment-tracker/

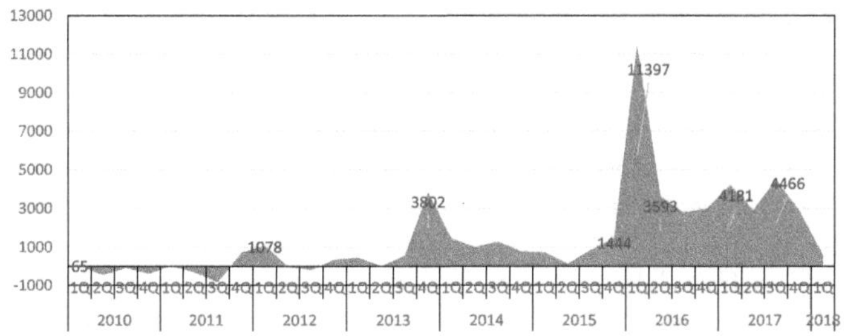

Source: Bank Negara Malaysia (2018).

Figure 2. FDI Flow, from China to Malaysia, 2010–2018, (RM Million)

billion, 21%), and transport-related sector (US$3.1 billion, 16%), which together accounted for two-thirds of Chinese investments from 2005 to 2018. The structural target of Chinese investment into Malaysia seems not much different from what others have documented where investment into energy resources is hedged against future increases in commodity prices (Kolstad and Wiig, 2009).

While energy, real estate and transport accounted for the bulk of Chinese investment in Malaysia over the period 2015 till 2018, the share going to manufacturing rose from 25% in 2017 to 46% in the first half of 2018. Approved Chinese FDI inflows into Malaysian manufacturing surged by 410% from RM3.9 billion in 2017 to RM19.7 billion in 2018 (Ministry of Finance Malaysia, 2019). Another characteristic is that it is primarily invested by state-owned enterprises or publicly-owned enterprises (Dong and Guo, 2013) with only 28% of cumulative investment were accounted by private firms up to 2017. By sectors, China's State-Owned Enterprises (SOEs)[2] have monopolized the infrastructure sector, thereby leaving the non-strategic sectors, such as textile and photovoltaics manufacturing, to non-state firms. State-owned investors are undoubtedly beneficiaries of government policies, such as financial assistance from state-owned banks and subsidies in early stage of business start-ups, but state intervention hardly extends to day-to-day operations of these firms. Therefore, though in the long run the governance of enterprises can be different owing to the composition of state officials in corporate boards of SOEs, managers of Chinese company, regardless of ownership structures, still have to meet similar targets to enhance efficiency and maximize profit in the short run (Li and Cheong, 2018).

3. Methodology and Data

We discuss the methodology and data used in this section. Given the question we seek to answer, a quantitative methodology is preferred as it provides the rigor for interpretation.

[2] State-owned Enterprises (SOE) is a legal entity created and owned by the government to undertake commercial activities on its behalf. Since the economic reforms, SOEs have evolved from work units before reforms to the state's sole or partial agent to serve the dual role of meeting both business and public interests. In this study, we refer SOE as legal entities engaged in business affairs, which are under the supervision of the regulatory authorities of the State-owned Assets Supervision and Administration Commission (SASAC) at different levels (Zhang and Rasiah, 2015, p. 10).

3.1. *Estimation method*

3.1.1. *Evaluating efficiency by Data Envelopment Analysis (DEA)*

Efficiency is widely defined as how well resources (inputs) are used to produce output. To evaluate the efficiency of decision-making units (DMUs), data envelopment analysis (DEA) is used in this study. Technical efficiency refers to the physical relationship between inputs (resources) and output. According to Palmer and Torgerson (1999), a technically efficient level is achieved when the maximum possible output improvement is obtained from a set of resource inputs. In contrast, a technically inefficient position means the same output is produced with more inputs than in the technically efficient position (Thanassoulis, 2001; Baumol, 1965; Reinhardt, 1992).

Originally developed by Charnes *et al.* (1978), DEA remains one of the most popular techniques to assess DMU's efficiency level in a single year or over a certain of period (Miranda *et al.*, 2012). Wide acceptance of DEA demonstrates its advantages as a non-parametric method, which considers linear programming techniques without a need of prerequisites or prior functional form (Ali and Lerme, 1997; Stolp, 1990). DEA takes multiple inputs and outputs simultaneously to estimate firms' efficiency. As a unit invariance, DEA has no disturbance on the estimated efficiency, and therefore the output and input do not have to be in same units. By using DEA, the efficiency index can be decomposed into a few factors, such as scale efficiency, and for this reason, it becomes attractive to management and policy makers.[3] It worth mentioning that although stochastic frontier analysis (SFA) increasingly gained popularity as alternative method to evaluate efficiency, one of the drawbacks is that the correlation of inefficiency terms with the firm's attributes may result in biased estimates of efficiency scores (Tybout, 1992). Therefore, considering the limitations of SFA in addition to the nature of our dataset of being relatively small in sample size, DEA is chosen as estimation method (Mok *et al.*, 2010; Mutz *et al.*, 2017). Variable return to scale (VRS)-output-oriented techniques is employed to estimate efficiency scores of manufacturing firms (Banker *et al.*, 1984). By constructing an output oriented production function in assessing efficiency, we are able to capture the amount of output produced from a given amount of input if the firm attains technical efficiency (Mok *et al.*, 2007). Efficiency scores range from 0 to 1, with 1 being the most efficient and 0 as the least. A user written command in STATA was deployed to estimate technical efficiency of manufacturing firms in this study (Ji and Lee, 2010).

As DEA is sensitive to the number of variables, the selection of input and output variables are vital in efficiency estimations. On the one hand, *total income* (Totalincome) was chosen as the main output, which refers to the income of a firm in a given year that derives from sale of products and other associated income-generating activities (Cheruiyot, 2017; Barasa *et al.*, 2019). On the other hand, *cost of raw materials* (Costofraw) was taken as input since manufacturing industry uses a large amount of raw material in the production process (Le *et al.*, 2018). In addition, *administrative expense* (Costofadmin) was selected

[3] DEA allows us to use a smaller sample, though a smaller sample size may result in higher average efficiency scores as reported in Alirezaee *et al.* (1998).

as a second input variable. Administrative expenses include salaries of employees, rental and other related costs incurred in the production process (Leibenstein and Maital, 1992; Mia and Chandra, 2016).

3.1.2. *Determinants of Chinese manufacturing firms efficiency*

Firms' efficiency is often influenced by external/environmental factors. To determine the variable that influences firms' efficiency, we chose firm's age, size and export as independent variables to regress against firm's efficiency scores in the second stage analysis (Coelli and Rao, 2005). While the three independent variables were selected as they are related to firm's characteristics, the selection is also constrained by the availability of the dataset. The regression equation is constructed as follows:

$$\text{Efficiency}_{\text{it}} = \alpha_0 + \beta_1 \text{LNAGE}_{\text{it}} + \beta_2 \text{LNSIZE}_{\text{it}} + \beta_3 \text{LNEXPORT}_{\text{it}} + \varepsilon_{\text{it}}, \quad (1)$$

where subscripts *i* represents a Chinese firm and *t* represents the respective time period or year. ε_{it} is the error term.

Firms' age is measured by the commencement year of firm's operation (Cheruiyot, 2017), and firms' size uses yearend book value as a proxy. Since Malaysia is the country where the selected manufacturing firms are located, both book value and export earnings are measured in Malaysian Ringgit (MYR). Natural logarithm of age, size and export are used in final estimation in order to better interpret the coefficient and minimize data skewness.

3.2. *Data source*

The data this study employed is unpublished firm-level data of Malaysia's manufacturing industry in 2010 and 2015. They were collected by Department of Statistics Malaysia (DoS). The data was obtained directly from DoS. About 30% of the total establishments were picked up for our use. National Economic Census data is well suited to examine efficiency of Chinese investment, as it contains key financial information that are commonly used to estimate firm-level efficiency, including input and output, ownership, employment and skills, exports, expenditure and turnover by regional location and sector.

In total, the dataset finally captured 11,887 and 14,705 businesses establishments, which were formally registered in manufacturing industry of Malaysia over the years of 2010 and 2015 respectively. Using a filter based on ownership, 21 firms were identified as Chinese-funded firms with operations in Malaysia. For comparative purposes, we have chosen 100 Malaysian and foreign firms each for the analysis. Given the fact that Chinese investment in Malaysia only gained momentum after 2013, a sample size of 21 is a reflection that investment by Chinese investors stayed at a relatively low level. For confidential reasons, firms' identification was represented by dummy code.

4. Results and Discussion

The results using DEA approach produced interesting findings. We discuss them in this section first by comparing the efficiency levels of Chinese firms with Malaysian and other foreign firms, followed by a detailed assessment of efficiency levels of Chinese firm over time. By reporting the results from the second stage regression, we subsequently discuss the factors that contribute to Chinese manufacturers' efficiency performance.

4.1. *Chinese firms' efficiency in comparison*

The first part of Table 2 displays the descriptive statistics of selected input and output variables of Chinese owned,[4] Malaysian owned, and other foreign manufacturing firms in Malaysia. In general, despite of differences in growth, we observe that the mean values of output and input increased from 2010 to 2015 in all three categories, which is to be expected in an economy undergoing expansion. Recognizing the importance of firms, especially in the manufacturing industry, for generating jobs and revenue, the Malaysian government undertook reforms of business regulations and smoothen integration with the global economy (Baharudin and Yap, 2017). Indeed, the World Bank (2010, 2015) considered these reforms to have raised Malaysia's ranking on the ease of doing business from 23rd in 2010 to 18th in 2015 in the world.

When input and output are compared across ownerships, foreign firms (including Chinese-owned firms) outweighed Malaysian firms in generating total income, suggesting that foreign firms tend to operate on a bigger scale, which is understandable as foreign firms are largely MNCs with headquarters in their own country whereas Malaysian firms are largely small and medium enterprises (Rasiah *et al.*, 2011).

The standard deviations (Std. Dev.) of input and output are several times bigger than the mean value in both years, indicating a large dispersion among the manufacturing firms in the sample. It reflects big differences in firm-level income with the income of the biggest Chinese-owned firm (RM1.5 billion) amounting to 643 times higher than the smallest firm (RM 2.3 million) in 2015. The huge output variance suggests that not only big firms were keen, but also small ones were attracted to relocate production in Malaysia. From capital-intensive steel fabrication to light clothing manufacturing, there is a wide existence of Chinese manufacturing in Malaysia seeking to use the country as either a tariff circumventing harbor or a gateway to Southeast Asia (Malaysia Investment Development Authority, 2019; Tham and Kam, 2019).

A general efficiency comparison between Chinese-owned firm, Malaysian and foreign firms shows that Chinese manufacturing firms demonstrated relatively higher efficiency levels than Malaysian and other foreign firms in both years in all segments (Figures 3 and 4). Among the three, Malaysian firms showed the lowest efficiency levels in 2010, while they performed slightly better than foreign firms (VRS_TE and NIRS_TE) in 2015. In order to verify the robustness of this finding, we attempted another comparison by re-examining Chinese firms with a re-sampled Malaysian firms and other foreign firms (100 for each category). The changing sample selections give us quite a similar result, which is

[4] Chinese-owned firms refer to firms from both mainland China and Hong Kong, unless stated otherwise.

Table 2. Descriptive Statistics (2010 and 2015)

Variable*	Obs.		Mean		Std Dev		Min		Max	
	2015	2010	2015	2010	2015	2010	2015	2010	2015	2010
Chinese Firm										
Total income ('000)	21	21	234606.100	71886.390	403388.400	125714.000	2327.000	144.000	1498018.000	562715
Cost of raw ('000)	21	21	160169.000	49650.440	335770.700	93382.600	711.000	0.000	1318666.000	413004.900
Cost of admin ('000)	21	21	53613.140	16768.870	87158.680	21287.390	207.500	138.200	321140.100	86025.400
Other Foreign Firm										
Total income ('000)	100	100	317220.700	254719.8	558343.200	443995.800	518.700	146.200	2838968.000	2569567
Cost of raw ('000)	100	100	183088.900	158707.9	336446.600	288201.700	42.900	28.900	1795842.000	1735665
Cost of admin ('000)	100	100	88746.560	63433.86	207463.500	124465	138.900	37.900	1381601.000	756187.900
Malaysian Firm										
Total income ('000)	100	100	21903.520	2677.064	91673.790	15793.090	8.400	1.500	606648.100	118933.300
Cost of raw ('000)	100	100	9305.497	1734.252	34887.170	11426.940	0.000	0.000	235881.700	102272.600
Cost of admin ('000)	100	100	6702.428	522.471	36233.510	2857.975	0.600	1.400	325016.700	27781.300

Source: Authors estimation based on DOS data.
Note: *measured in thousand ('000) of Malaysian Ringgit (MYR).

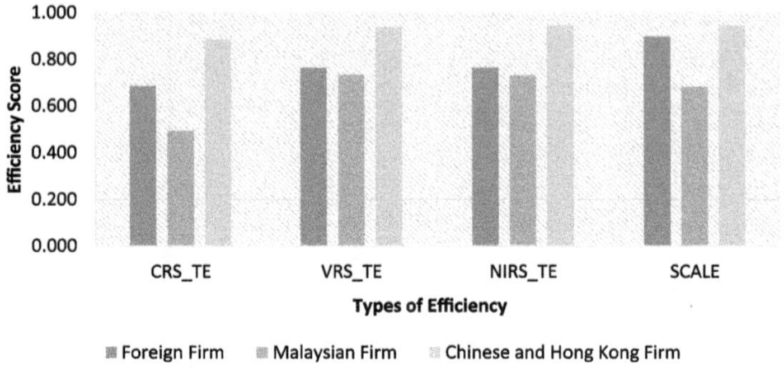

Note: The efficiency of individual foreign and Malaysian firm is available upon request. Efficiency reported shown in the figure is the average.
Source: Authors' estimation based on DOS data.

Figure 3. Efficiency of Manufacturing Firms Based on Ownership in Malaysia (2010)

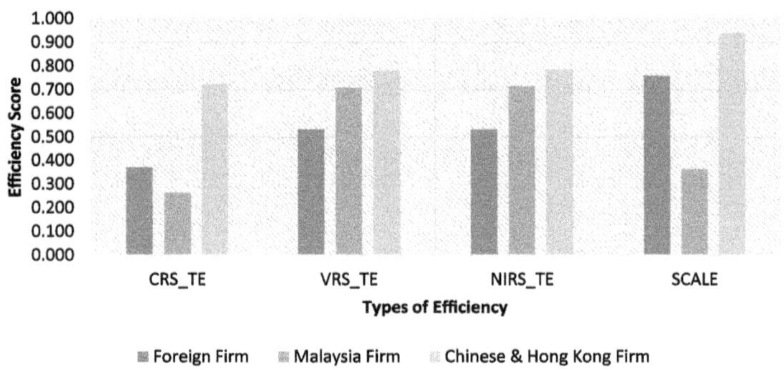

Note: The efficiency of individual foreign and Malaysian firm is available upon request. Efficiency reported shown in the figure is the average.
Source: Authors' estimation based on DOS data.

Figure 4. Efficiency of Manufacturing Firms Based on Ownership in Malaysia (2015)

Chinese firm is more efficient than Malaysian firms in 2010 and 2015 and other foreign firms in 2010 (with an exception in 2015).[5]

The better performance of Chinese-funded firms over its counterpart reflects the optimal use of technology cost-wise to offer them competitive advantage over other firms in manufacturing. As an integrated part of global supply chains, Chinese manufacturing' development provides evidence that efficiency is positively correlated with technological intensity and export-oriented production. Since China's accession to WTO, China's manufacturing has rapidly moving up global value chain, thanks to the

[5] Please see Appendix A for the final comparison results (after resampling). The raw results in details based on re-sampling is available upon request.

government's supportive policies, such as preferential loans, tax credits, and non-financial incentives (see also Lin *et al.*, 2014; Hong *et al.*, 2016; Wang *et al.*, 2017). The introduction of market mechanism provides Chinese firm great motivation to develop capabilities of technology commercialization and manufacturing-related innovation that has helped them to enhance firm performance (Nahm and Steinfeld, 2014). When cost keeps rising and market becomes increasingly competitive in domestic China, producers who monopolizing income-generating assets i.e. cutting-edge technology tend to engage in foreign production, as it is in their best interests to combine spatially transferable intermediate products with immobile factor endowments, e.g. technology in order to optimize resource allocation for profits maximization (Dunning, 1988, p. 4). Connecting to global value chain by locating production in business-friendly Malaysia enables technology-advanced Chinese firms higher efficiency levels than other firms in Malaysian manufacturing sector.

The finding that Chinese manufacturers deliver the highest efficiency level among the three ownership-based categories of firms is vital. What this means is that Chinese firms carry the potential to transmit best practices to Malaysian and other firms through demonstration effect and technology transfer. However, whether this potential can be fully realized depends very much on efforts by the Malaysian government and local organizations to stimulate technology spillover to local firms through better institutions, connectivity and coordination and the establishment of backward linkages (Hirschman, 1970; Rasiah, 2011). Government policy should also encourage the formation of production networks to stimulate interactions between Chinese firms, and Malaysian and other firms, in customization and upgrading of technology and quality control.

4.2. *Chinese firms' efficiency over time*

The disaggregated results of firm's efficiency levels in Table 3 suggest that the efficiency levels of Chinese-owned firms could be further improved despite the average efficiency level of the 21 firms was fairly high at 0.939 in 2010. Looking at efficiency scores, only 8 out of 21 firms achieved an efficient level equal to 1, which means that 13 Chinese firms did not operate at the optimal efficiency level.

Notably, 18 of the 21 Chinese firms experienced decreasing RTS in 2010 indicating that increase inputs would not bring a proportional increase in output. Therefore, attempts to increase their inputs would be counterproductive. We found that DMU 7 (textiles) and DMU 18 (wearing apparel) could only be made more efficient if their input1 (*Costofraw*) and input2 (*Costofadmin*) are reduced by 3213 units and 4686 units respectively.

Although the composition firms can be different, Tables 3 and 4 suggest that the average efficiency of Chinese-owned manufacturing firms declined from 0.939 in 2010 to 0.779 in 2015. Only 7 firms are found to be efficient in 2015 compared to 8 firm in 2010. However, 12 firms show a positive RTS in 2015 though no firms reported increasing return to scale in 2010. Notably, the majority of the firms whose efficiency level was less than 1 recorded a positive RTS, which implies that if inputs are increased by a certain percentage, output will be higher than the increase in inputs for these DMUs. In other words, input

Table 3. Efficiency of Selected Chinese-Owned Manufacturing Firms in Malaysia (2010)

DMU	Rank	Efficiency	CRS_TE	NIRS_TE	SCALE	RTS	Input1-slack	Input2-slack	Output-slack
dmu:1	16	0.887	0.811	0.887	0.914	−1	—	—	0.00
dmu:2	19	0.843	0.827	0.843	0.981	−1	—	—	0.00
dmu:3	20	0.818	0.813	0.818	0.993	−1	—	0.00	—
dmu:4	1	1.000	1.000	1.000	1.000	0	0.00	—	—
dmu:5	14	0.928	0.917	0.928	0.989	−1	—	0.00	—
dmu:6	1	1.000	0.869	1.000	0.869	−1	—	0.00	—
dmu:7	10	0.973	0.889	1.000	0.914	−1	3213.00	—	—
dmu:8	21	0.738	0.701	0.738	0.950	−1	—	0.00	—
dmu:9	1	1.000	0.974	1.000	0.974	−1	—	0.00	—
dmu:10	12	0.958	0.863	0.958	0.901	−1	—	—	0.00
dmu:11	13	0.955	0.945	0.955	0.989	−1	—	0.00	—
dmu:12	1	1.000	0.900	1.000	0.900	−1	—	—	0.00
dmu:13	18	0.856	0.754	0.856	0.880	−1	—	—	0.01
dmu:14	1	1.000	0.945	1.000	0.945	−1	—	0.00	—
dmu:15	1	1.000	1.000	1.000	1.000	0	—	—	0.00
dmu:16	15	0.914	0.876	0.914	0.959	−1	—	0.00	—
dmu:17	1	1.000	1.000	1.000	1.000	0	—	—	0.00
dmu:18	17	0.886	0.756	1.000	0.853	−1	—	4685.84	—
dmu:19	9	1.000	0.913	1.000	0.913	−1	—	0.00	0.00
dmu:20	1	1.000	0.937	1.000	0.937	−1	—	0.00	—
dmu:21	11	0.964	0.923	0.964	0.957	−1	—	0.00	—
Average		0.939	0.886	0.946	0.944				

Note: CRS_TE = Constant Return to Scale_ Technical Efficiency; NIRS_TE = Non-Increasing Returns to Scale_ Technical Efficiency; SCALE = Scale Efficiency; RTS = Return to Scale. −1, 0 and 1 represent decreasing return to scale, constant return to scale and increasing return to scale, respectively.

Source: Authors estimation. Variable Return to Scale (VRS) - Output oriented two-stage DEA is used to estimate efficiency of firms.

Table 4. Efficiency of Selected Chinese-Owned Manufacturing Firms in Malaysia (2015)

DMU	Rank	Efficiency	CRS_TE	NIRS_TE	SCALE	RTS	Input1-slack	Input2-slack	Output-slack
dmu:1	15	0.626	0.613	0.626	0.980	−1.000	0.010	—	—
dmu:2	6	1.000	0.735	1.000	0.735	−1.000	0.000	144562	—
dmu:3	20	0.485	0.484	0.484	0.999	1.000	—	—	18.602
dmu:4	1	1.000	1.000	1.000	1.000	0.000	—	—	0.000
dmu:5	4	1.000	0.914	0.914	0.914	1.000	—	—	217.705
dmu:6	18	0.561	0.550	0.550	0.982	1.000	—	—	116.913
dmu:7	9	0.903	0.897	0.903	0.993	−1.000	3075.890	—	0.000
dmu:8	21	0.325	0.323	0.323	0.994	1.000	—	—	55.262
dmu:9	12	0.768	0.767	0.767	0.999	1.000	—	—	15.800
dmu:10	17	0.595	0.595	0.595	1.000	1.000	—	—	0.440
dmu:11	10	0.816	0.816	0.816	1.000	1.000	200.185	—	0.000
dmu:12	8	0.923	0.921	0.921	0.998	1.000	—	—	94.795
dmu:13	16	0.610	0.609	0.610	0.999	1.000	0.000	—	—
dmu:14	11	0.800	0.796	0.796	0.995	1.000	—	—	65.339
dmu:15	7	1.000	0.934	1.000	0.934	−1.000	1267893.000	—	0.000
dmu:16	13	0.747	0.480	1.000	0.642	−1.000	—	88236	—
dmu:17	14	0.683	0.671	0.683	0.982	−1.000	0.011	—	—
dmu:18	19	0.515	0.513	0.513	0.995	1.000	—	—	92.149
dmu:19	1	1.000	0.992	1.000	0.992	−1.000	0.000	—	—
dmu:20	1	1.000	1.000	1.000	1.000	0.000	—	—	0.000
dmu:21	5	1.000	0.590	1.000	0.590	1.000	—	200.851	1835.690
Average		0.779	0.724	0.786	0.939				

Note: CRS_TE = Constant Return to Scale_ Technical Efficiency; NIRS_TE = Non-Increasing Returns to Scale_ Technical Efficiency; SCALE = Scale Efficiency; RTS = Return to Scale. −1, 0 and 1 represent decreasing return to scale, constant return to scale and increasing return to scale, respectively.

Source: Authors estimation. Variable Return to Scale (VRS) - Output oriented two-stage DEA is used to estimate efficiency of firms.

Table 5. Parametric and Non-Parametric Mean Efficiency Test by Ownership of Firm (2015 and 2010)

	Year = 2015		Year = 2010	
Ownership	t-test	Kruskal–Wallis	t-test	Kruskal–Wallis
Malaysian	−1.514*	2.496	−5.343***	24.965***
Chinese	−4.532***	16.635***	−5.671***	24.393***
Foreign				

Source: Authors estimate based on efficiency result. *significant at 10%, ***significant at 1%. We have used STATA 12 software to create random sample of 100 Malaysian and Foreign firms from the full dataset. Re-sampling results are reported in Appendix A. Except between the Chinese and Foreign firms in 2015, the significance level almost remain the same.

Table 6. Parametric and Non-Parametric Mean Efficiency Test by Year (2015–2010)

Efficiency		t-test	Kruskal–Wallis
Year = 2010	0.939	3.284***	5.186**
Year = 2015	0.778		

Source: Authors estimate based on efficiency result. **significant at 5%. ***significant at 1%.

increase may improve production efficiency of these firms with a positive RTS though their efficiency levels are less than 1.

The results offer policy implications to raise efficiency levels of selected manufacturing firms as resource utilization in a number of DMUs have not been optimal. For example, input1 (*Costofraw*) could be reduced to raise efficiency levels of DMU 7, 11, and 15, while input2 (*Costofadmin*) could be lessen to raise efficiency levels in DMU 2, 16 and 21 in 2015. Furthermore, output-slack represents that the efficiency could be improved by increasing the output of DMU 3, 5, 6, 8, 9, 10, 12, 14, 18 and 21 without altering the inputs in 2015.

In short, while Chinese firms show higher efficiency levels than Malaysian and other foreign firms (see Table 5), efficiency levels of China's manufacturing firms in Malaysia has deteriorated in 2015 compared to 2010 (see Table 6). To empirically check whether Chinese firms outperform their counterparts, parametric (t-test) and non-parametric (Kruskal–Wallis) mean efficiency test (Malaysian and Chinese; Chinese and Foreign) were performed. With an only exception of Kruskal–Wallis test in 2015 between Malaysian and Chinese, significant differences between the efficiency of Chinese-owned firms and their counterparts are statistically proved (significant at 10% and 1%). Thus, we confirmed Chinese-owned manufacturing firms outperformed local (Malaysian) and foreign-owned firms in Malaysia in terms of efficiency. In addition, same statistical treatment was exercised to test whether there is significant difference between the efficiency level of year 2010 and 2015 (only for Chinese-owned firms). The result confirmed that the efficiency level was higher in 2010 compared to 2015 and they are proved to be statistically significant in both tests at 5% (Kruskal- Wallis) and 1% (*t*-test) levels.

Deterioration of efficiency level of Chinese-owned firm requires special attention from business managers and policy makers. While the optimization of profit is one goal of business managers, firms and policy makers could be alerted to the importance of technical efficiency. It is pertinent for governments not to push for production expansion when it will only undermine technical efficiency. In this sense, the Chines government's efforts to provide incentive to firms for overseas expansion since 2013 could have been not always productive. This is especially true for those SOEs that have top management members who are politically appointed (Cheong *et al.*, 2014). Albeit the efficiency level of Chinese firms in this study is still higher than those operating in cost-rising China (e.g. toy has average efficiency level of only 0.54 in China) (Mok *et al.*, 2007), simply going overseas without proper production planning may not be economically wise. Although China's BRI has played an important role in guiding Chinese firms to Malaysia, our findings suggest that when relocating operations abroad, Chinese firms have to be careful in making strategic decisions to dovetail their own corporate goals with national policy initiative (Lim, 2017; Zhang *et al.*, 2017).

4.3. *Determinants of Chinese firms' efficiency*

To better understand determinants of firm's efficiency, we applied Tobit regression (Phan *et al.*, 2016), ordinary least square (OLS) (McDonald, 2009), and truncated bootstrapping (Simar and Wilson, 2007) respectively on Equation (1) in the second stage analysis.

As the results shown in Table 7, the model fitness is relatively good as witnessed by F-statistics and Wald Chi2 being statistically significant at all conventional levels. With R^2 of OLS being 0.386, it shows a reasonable explanatory power of the model, as it suggests that 38% of the variations in the dependent variables could be explained by the included independent variables.[6] Nevertheless, although regression results based 42 firms (21 in 2010 and 21 in 2015) may not generate perfectly concise and robust result in statistical sense, this study provides an indication of relationship between firm's efficiency and the three independent variables as our practice indicates.[7]

The three techniques present similar results (same sign of coefficient) with a slight variations of coefficient values, and significant levels remain almost same across the different models. While the coefficient values are almost identical under OLS and Truncated bootstrapping, the coefficient value is slightly higher under Tobit regression approach. Overall, we argue that the estimated coefficient sign and significance levels are reliable and consistent, as it did not vary significantly in different models.

The results show that firms' age has a negative effect on efficiency which means that old firm would have low level of technical efficiency. It seems relatively difficult for an aging

[6] We have observed higher Pseudo R^2 under the Tobit regression. However, they are not equivalent to normal R^2 that we get from OLS.

[7] We opted to use only Chinese firm's data in the second stage analysis.

Table 7. Determinants of Efficiency in Chinese Manufacturing Firms

Dependent Variable: Efficiency						
	Tobit Regression	OLS	Truncated Regression	Mean	Minimum	Maximum
LNAGE	−0.144***	−0.099***	−0.099**			
	(0.044)	(0.025)	(0.047)	2.752	0.0000	3.951
LNSIZE	−0.067**	−0.056**	−0.056***			
	(0.028)	(0.021)	(0.022)	8.868	1.610	12.533
LNEXPORT	0.098***	0.076***	0.076***			
	(0.028)	(0.023)	(0.024)	9.921	6.301	14.219
Cons	0.956***	0.888***	0.888***			
	(0.255)	(0.149)	(0.191)			
Number of Firms	42	42	42			
Pseudo R^2	0.478					
R^2		0.386				
Adj. R^2		0.312				
F Statistics	6.195***	6.140***				
Wald chi2			11.910***			

Source: Authors' estimation. Robust standard errors in parentheses. *$p < 0.10$, **$p < 0.05$, ***$p < 0.01$. The minimum number of age for a firm was 1 year. When we log transform age, it becomes 0, hence the minimum value of LNAGE is 0.000.

firm to adopt new technologies and managerial skills that are required for an efficient production. Our findings based on Chinese-funded manufacturing firms in Malaysia is echoed by Tingum and Ofeh's research (2017) where the duo found that the older firms tend to become less efficient in Cameroonian manufacturing industry. An old firm may experience low level of efficiency if they fail to respond to new market conditions and do not adapt latest innovations and technologies in their operation (Little *et al.*, 1987). If a firm fails to upgrade industrial capacity through learning and innovation, the archaic and outdated technology used in production process often leads to production inefficiency. Nevertheless, if firm growth is accompanied by continuous gain in experience and capacity to modify production methods, it is not impossible to reverse the negative relations between age and efficiency (Rasiah, 1994).

Meanwhile, the empirical studies suggest a negative relation between firms' size and efficiency. It is understandable that big firms tend to be inefficient due to coordination problems or complexities in decision-making process (Yang and Chen, 2009). This finding is consistent with Tingum and Ofeh (2017) where a negative relationship between size and efficiency is observed in the manufacturing sector of Uganda, Tanzania and Cameroon. Although the past literature presents a mixed result where positive relations may also be possible, small firms tend to be more efficient as they are exposed to greater competition, while big firm often suffers coordination problems in the course of production and operation scaling-up (Söderbom and Teal, 2004).

Not surprisingly, we found a positive relationship between firm's exports and efficiency, as firms with exports behavior enjoy better opportunities of exposing themselves through learning-by-doing, sub-contracting and production coordination (Rasiah, 1994; Granér and Isaksson, 2009). A large extent of past literature reported that efficiency of exports-oriented firms is higher than non-exporters (Chen and Tang, 1987; Granér and Isaksson, 2009; Moral-Pajares *et al.*, 2015; Vn *et al.*, 2016). Mok *et al.* (2010) identified internationalization, economies of scale and technological progress as the driving forces of manufacturers' higher efficiency. Apart from this, export earnings allow firms more spending on upgrading, and to provide incentives and many other fringe benefits to employees that lead to a better efficiency performance. By being a member of regional trading agreements, such as ASEAN-China Free Trade Agreement (ACFTA), business-friendly Malaysia has offered foreign firms policy privileges to export locally produced products to other markets with low tariff and non-tariff barriers. For example, under the Rule of Origin condition, firms can enjoy preferential tariffs throughout ASEAN so long as 40% of the cumulative value are added within ASEAN region. The expected free flow of labor and capital over the regions will help Chinese manufacturers in globalizing its production network. Therefore, export has offered Chinese firms not only scales, but also policy privileges to enhance competitiveness through cost reduction.

5. Conclusion

Given the massive outflow of FDI from China to Southeast Asia in general and Malaysia in particular, this paper examined if the technical efficiency levels of Chinese manufacturing firms were comparable to national and other foreign firms in Malaysia. Using a two-stage DEA approach, we deployed variable return to scale (VRS)-output-oriented techniques to estimate efficiency levels of selected firms. To do so, we employed unpublished firm-level data of Malaysia's manufacturing industry in 2010 and 2015. The data is directly obtained from the Department of Statistics Malaysia (DoS).

The results suggest that Chinese manufacturing firms performed better (in most of the cases) than their counterparts (local and other foreign) in terms of efficiency in 2010 and 2015. While this finding reflects the growing competitiveness of Chinese manufacturing firms over the years, it also implies that the much-debated technology transfer and managerial skill sharing could be meaningful for local economic upgrading if the right institutions and organizations are installed, and effective connection and coordination between firms are in place. To foster a collaborative and mutually beneficial economic partnership with Chinese firms, Malaysian government should focus on positive economic spin-offs that intertwine with domestic and regional producers and stakeholders (Lim, 2016; Pavlićević and Kratz, 2017).

The euphoria over China's investment abroad took on a global dimension following China's launching of the BRI. However, the efficiency levels of Chinese firms deteriorated over the years 2010 and 2015 suggesting that the expansion of production, especially since launching of the Belt and Road Initiative, may have been driven by policy distortions created by incentives and other supports provided by the Chinese government rather than firms' own initiative to sustain or raise efficiency levels. Albeit one cannot exclude the undesirable consequences of inserting abruptly into the ever-challenging external environment globally, it suggests that production expansion without efficiency improvements may also be a consequence of hastily organized policy push strategy by the Chinese government, for example the BRI from the government at different levels. As the second-stage results imply, older and bigger firms have higher possibilities of suffering production inefficiency due to coordination problem and decision-making complexities. It becomes especially true when a firm decides to extend their production overseas. Therefore, a simple production expansion without carefully-crafted business strategy may not necessarily bring in efficiency improvement and business gains for a firm's long-term development. Therefore, Chinese firms have to be very careful in making strategic decisions to relocate operations abroad to ensure that government policy initiatives are in sync with firm-level performance.

Interestingly, unlike the turbulence and uncertainties facing Chinese-funded mega-sized infrastructure projects since early 2018 in Malaysia, Chinese investment in manufacturing has encountered little political upheaval (Liu and Lim, 2019). While a number of Chinese-initiated BRI projects, such as East Coast Rail Link, that were suspended or reviewed by the newly elected Pakatan Harapan government caught much public attention, a comprehensive assessment of Chinese investment in Malaysia shall look beyond infrastructure sectors. As our study shows, Chinese investment in Malaysia manufacturing sector could be made mutually beneficial, as high efficiency level enjoyed by Chinese firms implies potential to transmit best practices to local firms through demonstration effect and technology transfer. To do this, government policies shall be introduced to stimulate technology spillover through better institutions, connectivity and coordination (Hirschman, 1970; Rasiah, 2012). One way to make Chinese investment beneficial to local economy could be the formation of production networks, in which the interactions between Chinese firms, and Malaysian and other firms help to create economic synergies in upgrading of technology capacity and efficiency levels.

The results of this study could be strengthened through an expansion of the sample size used. As 100 Malaysian and foreign firms each chosen arbitrarily may not be perfectly representative of the whole sector, the findings should be treated with caution and should not be over-generalized. Also, as argued by evolutionary economists, location, timing, and sectors matters (Nelson, 2008), an analysis based on aggregate data may not be able to broach the intricacies and on-the-ground complexities. To further study how technology spillover has evolved over the years, a snowballing research methodology or industry-specific case studies targeted at an extensive mapping of a wider set of institutional relationships with Chinese, national and other foreign firms will be necessary to formulate clear policies.

Acknowledgments

The authors would like to thank the two anonymous reviewers for their valuable comments and constructive suggestions. We would like to extend our deep appreciation to Dato Prof.

Majid Khan, Prof. Rajah Rasiah, Mr. Risal Hussin, Ms. Maizatul Akma Mat Eil @Ismail and the colleagues from Department of Statistics Malaysia for their generous support to acquire the data used in this paper. No potential conflict of interest was reported by the authors. The authors are responsible for all interpretations and any remaining errors in this article.

The research is supported by the Fundamental Research Funds for the Central Universities, China (Project No. 20720191034) and the MOE Project of Key Research Institute of Humanities and Social Sciences.

Appendix A. Parametric and Non-Parametric Mean Efficiency Test by Ownership of Firm, Based on Resampling, 2015 and 2010

	Year = 2015		Year = 2010	
Ownership	t-test	Kruskal–Wallis	t-test	Kruskal–Wallis
Malaysian	−3.687***	11.546***	−5.305***	21.089***
Chinese	−0.634	0.652	−4.420***	16.750***
Foreign				

Source: Authors estimate based on efficiency result. ***significant at 1%. We have used STATA 12 software to create random sample of 100 Malaysian and Foreign firms from the full dataset.

References

Ali, AI and CS Lerme (1997). Comparative advantage and disadvantage in DEA. *Annals of Operations Research*, 73, 215–232.

Baharudin, AH and SF Yap (2017). A contemporary re-examination of Malaysia's economic growth: The issues of equity, efficiency and liberalization. *Singapore Economic Review*, 62(2), 509–530, doi: 10.1142/S0217590815501167.

Banker, RD, A Charnes and WW Cooper (1984). Some models for estimating technical and scale inefficiencies in data envelopment analysis. *Management Science*, 30(9), 1078–1092.

Barasa, L, P Vermeulen, J Knoben, B Kinyanjui and P Kimuyu (2019). Innovation inputs and efficiency: Manufacturing firms in Sub-Saharan Africa. *European Journal of Innovation Management*, 22(1), 59–83, doi: 10.1108/EJIM-11-2017-0176.

Baumol, WJ (1965). *Economic Theory and Operations Analysis*, Prentice Hall International Series in Management, 2nd edn. Englewood Cliffs, N.J.: Prentice-Hall.

Charnes, A, WW Cooper and E Rhodes (1978). Measuring the efficiency of decision making units. *European Journal of Operational Research*, 2(6), 429–444.

Chen, TJ and DP Tang (1987). Comparing technical efficiency between import-substitution-oriented and export-oriented foreign firms in a developing economy. *Journal of Development Economics*, 26(2), 277–289.

Cheong, KC, R Li, EC Tan and M Zhang (2014). China's state enterprises, economic growth and distribution: A revisionist view. *China: An International Journal*, 12(1), 132–152.

Cheruiyot, KJ (2017). Determinants of technical efficiency in Kenyan manufacturing sector. *African Development Review*, 29(1), 44–55, doi: 10.1111/1467-8268.12237.

Coelli, TJ and D Rao (2005). Total factor productivity growth in agriculture: A Malmquist index analysis of 93 countries, 1980–2000. *Agricultural Economics*, 32(s1), 115–134.

Dong, B and G Guo (2013). A model of China's export strengthening outward FDI. *China Economic Review*, 27, 208–226, doi: https://doi.org/10.1016/j.chieco.2012.07.003.

Dunning J (1988). The eclectic paradigm of international production: A restatement and some possible extensions, *Journal of International Business Studies*, 19(1), 1–31, http://www.jstor.org/stable/154984.

Granér, M and A Isaksson (2009). Firm efficiency and the destination ff exports: Evidence from Kenyan plant-level data. *The Developing Economies*, 47(3), 279–306.

Hirschman, A (1970). *Exit, Voice and Loyalty: Responses to Decline in Firms, Organizations and States*. Cambridge: Harvard University Press.

Hong, J, B Feng, Y Wu and L Wang (2016). Do government grants promote innovation efficiency in China's high-tech industries? *Technovation*, 57–58, 4–13, doi: https://doi.org/10.1016/j.technovation.2016.06.001.

Ji, Y and C Lee (2010). Data envelopment analysis. *Stata Journal*, 10(2), 267–280.

Kawai, M and K Naknoi (2017). Asean's trade and foreign direct investment: Long-term challenges for economic integration. *Singapore Economic Review*, 62(3), 643–680, doi: 10.1142/S021759 0818400040.

Kolstad, I and A Wiig (2009) What determines chinese outward FDI? CMI Working Paper WP 2009, doi: https://www.cmi.no/publications/3332-what-determines-chinese-outward-fdi.

Le, V, XBB Vu and S Nghiem (2018). Technical efficiency of small and medium manufacturing firms in Vietnam: A stochastic meta-frontier analysis. *Economic Analysis and Policy*, 59, 84–91.

Leibenstein, H and S Maital (1992). Empirical estimation and partitioning of x-inefficiency: A data-envelopment approach. *The American Economic Review*, 82(2), 428–433.

Li, R and KC Cheong (2018). *China's State Enterprises: Changing Role in a Rapidly Transforming Economy (1978–2018)*. Singapore: Palgrave Macmillan.

Lim, G (2016). China's investments in Malaysia: Choosing the "right" partners. *International Journal of China Studies*, 6(1), 1–30.

Lim, G (2017). China's 'going out' strategy in Southeast Asia: Case studies of the automobile and electronics sectors. *China: An International Journal*, 15(4), 157–178.

Lin, H, SX Zeng, HY Ma, GY Qi and VWY Tam (2014). Can political capital drive corporate green innovation? Lessons from China. *Journal of Cleaner Production*, 64, 63–72, doi: https://doi.org/10.1016/j.jclepro.2013.07.046.

Little, IMD, JM Page and D Mazumdar (1987). *Small Manufacturing Enterprises: A Comparative Study of India and Other Economies*. New York: Oxford University Press.

Liu, H and G Lim (2018). The political economy of a rising China in Southeast Asia: Malaysia's response to the 'belt and road initiative'. *Journal of Contemporary China*, doi: 10.1080/10670564.2018.1511393.

Malaysia Investment Development Authority (2019). What's up with Manufacturing? published online on 10 May 2019, accessed 22 July 2019, doi: http://www.mida.gov.my/home/8885/news/what%E2%80%99s-up-with-manufacturing-/.

McDonald, J (2009). Using least squares and tobit in second stage DEA efficiency analyses. *European Journal of Operational Research*, 197(2), 792–798.

Mia, MA and BIB Soltane (2016). Productivity and its determinants in microfinance institutions (MFIs): Evidence from South Asian countries. *Economic Analysis and Policy*, 51, 32–45.

Ministry of Finance Malaysia (2019). Press release: The 48% increase in 2018 approved FDI to RM80.5 billion and the 3.2% rise in the industrial production index (IPI) for January 2019, published 16 March 2019, accessed 22 July 2019, doi: https://www.treasury.gov.my/index.php/en/gallery-activities/press-release/item/5034-press-release-the-48-increase-in-2018-approved-fdi-to-rm80-5-billion-and-the-3-2-rise-in-the-industrial-production-index-ipi-for-january-2019.html.

Miranda, R, MC Gramani and E Andrade (2012). Technical efficiency of business administration courses: A simultaneous analysis using DEA and SFA. *International Transactions in Operational Research*, 19(6), 847–862, doi: 10.1111/j.1475-3995.2012.00857.x.

Mok, V, G Yeung, Z Han and Z Li (2007). Leverage, technical efficiency and profitability: An application of DEA to foreign-invested toy manufacturing firms in China. *Journal of Contemporary China*, 16(51), 259–274.

Mok, V, G Yeung, Z Han and Z Li (2010). Export orientation and technical efficiency: Clothing firms in China. *Managerial and Decision Economics*, 31(7), 453–463.

Moral-Pajares, E, A Mozas-Moral, E Bernal-Jurado and MJ Medina-Viruel (2015). Efficiency and exports: Evidence from Southern European companies. *Journal of Business Research*, 68(7), 1506–1511.

Mutz, R, L Bornmann and HD Daniel (2017). Are there any frontiers of research performance? Efficiency measurement of funded research projects with the Bayesian stochastic frontier analysis for count data. *Journal of Informetrics*, 11(3), 613–628.

Nahm, J and ES Steinfeld (2014). Scale-up Nation: China's specialization in innovative manufacturing. *World Development*, 54, 288–300, doi: https://doi.org/10.1016/j.worlddev.2013.09.003.

Nelson, R (2008). Economic development from the perspective of evolutionary economic theory, *Oxford Development Studies*, 36(1), 9–22.

Palmer, S and DJ Torgerson (1999). Economic notes: Definitions of efficiency. *BMJ (Clinical Research Edition)*, 318(7191), 1136–1136.

Pavlićević, D and A Kratz (2017). Testing the China threat paradigm: China's high-speed railway diplomacy in Southeast Asia. *The Pacific Review*, 1–18.

Phan, HTM, K Daly and S Akhter (2016). Bank efficiency in emerging Asian countries. *Research in International Business and Finance*, 38, 517–530.

Rasiah, R (1994). Flexible production systems and local machine-tool subcontracting: Electronics components transnationals in Malaysia. *Cambridge Journal of Economics*, 18, 279–298.

Rasiah, R, M Rosli and P Sanjivee (2011). Production linkages, technological intensities and economic performance: Small and medium enterprises in Malaysian manufacturing. *Asian Journal of Technology Innovation*, 19(2), 279–296, doi: 10.1080/19761597.2011.630504.

Rasiah, R, M Zhang and XX Kong (2013). Can China's miraculous growth continue? *Journal of Contemporary Asia*, 43(2), 295–313.

Reinhardt, UE (1992). Reflections on the meaning of efficiency: Can efficiency be separated from equity. *Yale L. and Pol'y Rev.*, 10, 302.

Söderbom, M and F Teal (2004). Size and efficiency in African manufacturing firms: Evidence from firm-level panel data. *Journal of Development Economics*, 73(1), 369–394.

Simar, L and PW Wilson (2007). Estimation and inference in two-stage, semi-parametric models of production processes. *Journal of Econometrics*, 136(1), 31–64.

Statistical Bulletin of China's Outward Foreign Direct Investment (2017), doi: http://img.project.fdi.gov.cn//21/1800000121/File/201810/201810301102234656885.pdf, accessed 22 July 2019.

Tham, SY (2018). Chinese Investment in Malaysia: Five Years into the BRI, Perspective, Yusof Ishak Institute, https://www.iseas.edu.sg/images/pdf/ISEAS_Perspective_2018_11@50.pdf, accessed on 9 August 2018.

Tham, SY and AJY Kam (2019) Exploring the Trade Potential of The DFTZ for Malaysian SMEs, Trends in Southeast Asia, 2019(3), Yusof Ishak Institute, Retrieved from https://www.iseas.edu.sg/images/pdf/TRS3_19%20(002).pdf.

Thanassoulis, E (2001). *Definitions of Efficiency and Related Measures. In Introduction to the Theory and Application of Data Envelopment Analysis*, pp. 21–35. Springer.

Tingum, EN and MA Ofeh (2017). Technical efficiency of manufacturing firms in cameroon: Sources and determinants. *International Journal of Financial Research*, 8(3), 172–186.
Tybout, JR (1992). Making noisy data sing: Estimating production technologies in developing countries. *Journal of Econometrics*, 53(1–3), 25–44.
Vu, HV, M Holmes, TQ Tran and S Lim (2016). Firm exporting and productivity: What if productivity is no longer a black box. *Baltic Journal of Economics*, 16(2), 95–113.
Wang, W, B Yu, X Yan, X Yao and Y Liu (2017). Estimation of innovation's green performance: A range-adjusted measure approach to assess the unified efficiency of China's manufacturing industry. *Journal of Cleaner Production*, 149, 919–924, doi: https://doi.org/10.1016/j.jclepro.2017.02.174.
Wang, GW (1978). *The Chinese Minority in Southeast Asia.* Singapore: Chopmen.
The World Bank (2010). Doing Business, http://www.doingbusiness.org/en/doingbusiness.
The World Bank (2015). Doing Business, http://www.doingbusiness.org/en/doingbusiness.
Yang, C and K Chen (2009). Are small firms less efficient?, *Small Business Economics*, 32(4), 375–395, http://www.jstor.org/stable/40344559.
Zhang, M and R Rasiah (2015). Institutionalization of state policy: Evolving urban housing reforms in china, springer, ISBN: 978-981-287-569-3, doi: http://www.springer.com/gp/book/97898 12875693 2.
Zhang, M, R Rasiah and JKY Lee (2017). Navigating a highly protected market: China's chery automobile in Malaysia. *Journal of Contemporary Asia*, 47(5), 774–791, doi: 10.1080/ 00472336.2017.1345000.00.

Chapter 11

SINGAPORE–CHINA ECONOMIC COLLABORATION 2.0*

ENG CHEONG TEO

CEO, International (Singapore, Southeast Asia, North Asia)
Surbana Jurong Group
engcheong.teo@surbanajurong.com

Published Online 21 May 2019

Singapore and China started their close economic collaboration in the early 1990s. The collaboration model in the first 25 years focused mainly on the government's role in foreign investment promotion, urban development, industrial infrastructure development and other related government policies. Platforms of collaboration included the Suzhou Industrial Park, Tianjin Eco-city, Chongqing Connectivity Initiative, the Software Transfer Project, training programs for thousands of Chinese officials and bilateral economic councils. Singapore's pragmatic leverage on globalization trends and thoughtful application of market forces have been a major factor in the shaping of China's own highly successful economic growth model.

Singapore–China economic collaboration model 2.0 will be different. China is now the second largest economy in the world and is expected to establish its global leadership in the world. Singapore has developed successfully into a leading global business hub complete with trading, manufacturing, financing and professional services as the engines of the business hub. Model 2.0 will be about mutual sharing and partnership. We should see more collaboration outside of China, driven by the private sector and in new technologies. If collaboration model 2.0 is successful, we will see both China and Singapore emerging stronger, in a more sustainable way. Major companies in both countries will be more tightly coupled in projects and joint ventures in China and elsewhere.

Keywords: Made in China 2025; economic reforms; China–Singapore bilateral relations; Suzhou Industrial Park; Belt and Road Initiative.

JEL Classification: F02, F63, O32

1. Singapore–China Economic Collaboration 1.0

In 1990, Singapore and China formally established a diplomatic relationship and started a journey of economic collaboration that is truly unique. Despite the differences in size and political system, both countries have relied on strong governments and pragmatic policies to create economic miracles within short periods. There is much mutual respect among the leaders, stemming from a deep understanding of one another and years of collaboration.

Over this period from 1990 to 2015, Singapore transformed from a Newly Industrialized Economy among the four Asian Little Dragons (Singapore, Hong Kong, Taiwan and South Korea) to a knowledge-intensive Global Business Hub with world-class capabilities in manufacturing, trading, financial and other professional services. In the same period, China

*This article originally appeared in *The Singapore Economic Review*, **66**(1), pp. 207–217

embarked boldly on its economic reforms by opening up to foreign trade and investments. It stepped up on infrastructure development, encouraged urbanization and undertook a series of policy reforms. China joined the WTO in 2001 and fully embraced globalization, setting the stage for years of impressive growth through the tumultuous events of SARS, Global Financial Crisis, Arab Spring, Euro crisis, etc. By 2015, China was already the world's second largest economy, one of the largest foreign investors globally and the largest trader with many countries, deeply immersed in the development of new technologies and well-positioned to take on a global leadership role.

From 1990 to 2015, China was very much in the learning mode in its relationship with Singapore, especially in the earlier years. The subject matters that were of most interest to China were: (a) How Singapore attracted and managed foreign investments; (b) How Singapore planned and managed townships; and (c) How Singapore managed the state-owned enterprises among other topics. In this regard, various platforms were created. First, there were the three Government-to-Government (G-to-G) projects in Suzhou, Tianjin and Chongqing, which served as the vehicles for the pilot implementation of "Singapore-styled" policies. Even today, the Suzhou Industrial Park project remains one of the most impactful projects in China that is studied by many as a highly successful township model. Second, there were high level G-to-G councils such as the Joint Council for Bilateral Cooperation and other Provincial level business councils, whereby officials and businessmen from both countries meet regularly to discuss opportunities for collaboration. Third, there was a constant stream of Chinese government officials and private sector representatives trained in Singapore by various tertiary institutions and government bodies. The result of all these initiatives is a very good appreciation among top Chinese officials of how Singapore has succeeded as a cohesive, stable and prosperous nation punching above its weight. More importantly, because of the sharing of experience by Singapore, China has picked up lessons which have served it well. The Chinese leaders remain highly appreciative of this support from Singapore.

2. Singapore–China Economic Collaboration 2.0

The circumstances in both Singapore and China are now different and this sets the context for the next phase of Singapore–China economic collaboration.

Singapore's founding Prime Minister Lee Kuan Yew was a key pillar in the first 25 years of collaboration. His great achievements, strong personality, deep understanding of geopolitics won him much respect in China and globally. His willingness to share his pragmatic wisdom with China and his relationship with older Chinese leaders like Deng Xiaoping and Jiang Zemin made him an elderly figure that subsequent Chinese leaders respect and were prepared to learn from. In China's celebration of 40 years of reform and opening up in December 2018, Mr. Lee was among the 10 foreigners honored with the China Reform Friendship Medal for helping China open up to the world. In PM Lee Hsien Loong's words, "Mr. Lee Kuan Yew laid the foundation for China–Singapore ties".[1]

[1] Straits Times, 30 Dec 2018.

Unfortunately, Mr. Lee passed on in 2015. Singapore–China collaboration 2.0 will depend crucially on the chemistry between the younger leaders on both sides.

Secondly, the emergence of Artificial Intelligence as a General Purpose Technology will fundamentally change the world in ways that no countries and no one are able to fully appreciate yet. While Singapore was ahead of China in the first 25 years of collaboration in terms of recognizing and leveraging on the effects of globalization, China is likely to have many advantages in the years ahead when it comes to developing AI technologies and applications. As noted by Dr. Lee Kai Fu, China has huge amount of data, aggressive entrepreneurs, good AI engineers and a pro-AI business environment.[2] All these factors will support China in its race to be the global AI industry leader. China, with its well-oiled government machinery, will be able to move fast to establish its leadership. Singapore, with its usual nimble and cohesive government, can also decide and act fast. How each country adapts and carves out a role for itself in the new technological world, will also determine the nature of their collaboration.

Third, the US-China rivalry will continue and likely become more intense. The US-China trade war and the various investigations involving Huawei, ZTE, etc., are the beginning of more confrontations to come. As China continues in its strategy of Manufacturing 2025 and Belt and Road Initiative, US will become more and more concerned about losing its global influence. Even without Trump, future US leaders will be compelled to address a rising China and its threats to US global leadership. How Singapore navigates in this environment between the two superpowers will also be key to our collaboration.

The strong foundation of Singapore–China economic collaboration 1.0 was built on the basis that China was getting out of its centrally-planned economic model into a more market-driven economy, and Singapore was there to provide useful lessons, being a successful market economy with strong government influence.

What then is the foundation of Singapore–China economic collaboration 2.0?

At the risk of over-simplification, China's economic strategies in the next few decades, may be described as:

(a) Looking outward — where China will seek to establish its economic influence and markets overseas through trade and direct investments abroad. This is best represented by the Belt and Road Initiative (BRI) as well as its predecessor initiative, "Going Out" (走出去);
(b) Looking forward — where China will seek to establish its industrial leadership in selected strategic industries in preparation for Industrial Revolution 4.0 and the world of AI in the future. This is best represented by the initiative that is known as Made in China 2025 (MIC2025);
(c) Looking inward — where China will have to undertake Economic Restructuring measures to address structural challenges in the Chinese economy. Economic Restructuring measures include SOE reforms, financial sector reforms and debt

[2] 李开复,"AI.未来"。

deleveraging to address various imbalances in the Chinese economy. In implementing these reforms, China may experiment with new policies in contained environment such as the Free Trade Zone (FTZ) and Free Trade Port (FTP) initiatives.

3. Looking Outward — Belt and Road Initiative

A key feature of Singapore–China economic collaboration 2.0 will be partnership outside of China. China has embarked on its ambitious Belt and Road Initiative (BRI) in 2013. To date, China's companies have invested billions of dollars into BRI projects and some 80 over countries and international organizations have signed MOUs with China to come on board the BRI.[3]

China has expressed its interest to work with Singapore for the BRI because of our familiarity with some countries in the BRI, Singapore's track record in developing infrastructure and urbanization, and the acknowledged neutrality of Singapore. As a result, in the last 5 years, many Singapore companies have worked with Chinese SOEs on various projects along the BRI.

While the BRI is positioned as an initiative to help countries build infrastructure, it has recently attracted some resistance and negative publicity. In August 2018, the new Malaysian Government under PM Mahathir, cancelled the East Coast Rail Link and two pipeline projects, which were part of the BRI. One of the reasons given was that Malaysia would not be able to repay the debts from these projects if they were to go ahead.

To better understand how the BRI will turn out, we use a 2 × 2 matrix framework as shown below. On the vertical axis is the impact on China from BRI and on the horizontal axis, we have the impact on BRI countries. In this instance, we use South-east Asia (SEA), which is a key target region of the BRI, as a specific case. The 2 × 2 matrix shows the different possible scenarios.

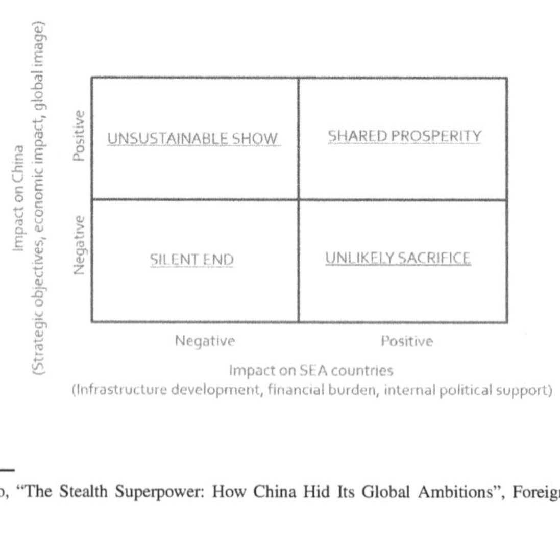

[3]Oriana Skylar Mastro, "The Stealth Superpower: How China Hid Its Global Ambitions", Foreign Affairs Jan/Feb 2019 issue.

On the vertical axis, we look at the possible impact on China from BRI, which may be strategic, economic or publicity-related. First, the impact may be strategic in nature. The impact will be positive for China if it is able to develop physical access points for its manufactured exports and its imports of strategic resources. For instance, the development of Gwadar Port in Pakistan and Kyaukpyu Port in Myanmar would allow Chinese manufactured goods to have access to the Indian Ocean and for import of strategic goods to reach the western part of China. Second, the impact may be economic. If the BRI allows China's state-owned enterprises (SOEs) to establish their market presence in SEA or utilize their excess capacity which resulted from the 2008 stimulus package, the economic impact would be positive. However, if the projects turn out to be commercially unviable, the economic benefits of BRI for SOEs will be in doubt. Finally, the impact can also be related to China's public image. If the BRI leads to a positive global image and greater acceptance of China as a global superpower, it will be positive for China. However, if the BRI generates negative media for China, it will lead to a negative image for China.

On the horizontal axis, we look at the impact on SEA countries which may be economic, financial or political in nature. First, if the BRI leads to sustainable infrastructure development, it may have a positive impact by stimulating immediate demand for various products and services, build a long term competitive edge for the country and create good jobs. Second, if the project is financed responsibly without incurring too much financial burden, it would be viewed positively. Finally, if there is widespread internal political support for the project, the political impact will also be positive. Conversely, if it leads to infrastructure projects that are not well-utilized, too much government debt and too much opposition internally, the BRI will have a negative impact on SEA.

How China and the SEA countries go about securing their own interests and how they react to one another's actions will be key to how the BRI plays out. Another group of players in the BRI comprises other countries which may have their own geopolitical considerations regarding the rise of China. How the BRI is portrayed in various international media will also affect the perception of BRI in various countries.

The current backlash against BRI in some countries suggest that the impact for SEA countries may be perceived to be negative today, rightly or wrongly. This is not sustainable. If China is perceived to benefit from the BRI while the SEA countries do not benefit much, then the SEA countries will stop participating. Similarly, if SEA benefits from the BRI while China does not, it is also not sustainable.

In the longer term, the two more likely scenarios are

(a) Silent End — if the impact on China and on the SEA countries turn out to be more negative than positive, both sides will slowly disengage themselves from the BRI and the initiative will fizzle out over time.
(b) Shared Prosperity — However, if there are effective efforts by both China and the SEA countries to develop win-win solutions, the BRI may enter a golden phase where both sides enjoy many years of mutual benefits.

The BRI creates the opportunity to build much-needed infrastructure in SEA and for strong economic development in these countries. If we do not take advantage of the BRI, and it ends up in the "Silent End" scenario, it would be an unfortunate loss of opportunity for the entire region. If Singapore can help move the scenario to that of "Shared Prosperity", it would be a good outcome for both China and SEA.

Singapore enjoys good relations with China and many countries along BRI, especially in ASEAN. It is more familiar with the culture and business norms in ASEAN. The BRI represents a good opportunity for Singapore and China to continue their collaboration. Singapore can play a role to support the BRI so that it leads to a win–win outcome for all. The Singapore Government and companies can actively partner the Chinese Government and SOEs in the BRI projects. To move towards the scenario of "Shared prosperity", the Singapore entities should advocate the following:

(a) Pragmatic Infrastructure Roadmaps. First, the SEA countries should each develop a pragmatic Infrastructure Roadmap. Such a roadmap should have a clear vision of what infrastructure projects are important and should be given priority within the next 10 years. It should estimate the costs of these projects, identify those that are commercially viable and those that require government support. It should examine how these can be financed without creating a budget deficit crisis for the country, including whether private sector companies can be involved in the financing, ownership and operation of such projects. It should also address social and environmental concerns in the community. In this way, the SEA countries would be able to leverage on the funds made available by the BRI to advance its infrastructure development plans, rather than take on projects that turn out to be ineffective or too costly. In this regard, glamorous large-scale projects may not always be the most impactful projects.
(b) Principles of Market Forces. Second, principles of market forces should be adopted as much as possible. Feasibility studies should have realistic commercial projections, robust technical evaluation, and reviewed carefully to determine if projects should be pursued. For instance, users of the infrastructure should be made to pay for the services they consume, at full operating costs if possible. Commercial operators of the infrastructure should be engaged on a Private Public Partnership basis if suitable. SEA Governments must be politically well-supported and could help overcome political and social obstacles when the projects are beneficial to the countries in the long term.
(c) High Standards of Governance. Third, more emphasis needs to be placed on the governance of the BRI projects by the Chinese SOEs, the SEA governments and other companies involved. If BRI projects are associated with improper use of funds, budget overruns or technical incompetence, the global image of China, the Chinese SOEs and the SEA governments will be negatively impacted. To prevent this, a strong code of governance should be put in place and strictly adhered to by the Chinese SOEs and the SEA governments for BRI projects.
(d) Strong Project Leadership. Finally, each major infrastructure project must be supervised by a competent leader. A leader with a clear vision, good management skills, integrity and strong political support will be able to deliver the infrastructure project on

time and on budget. Conversely, without good project leadership, even structurally sound projects will be badly implemented and end up as failures.

4. Looking Forward — Made in China 2025

The MIC2025 strategy is a comprehensive manufacturing and technology roadmap issued by the State Council in 2015.[4] It clearly identified manufacturing as a key pillar for a powerful China. It recognized that while manufacturing in China had grown big, it is not strong technologically and structurally. As China enters into a period of "new normal", with constraints on resources and the environment, and with the impending new Industrial Revolution, it is imperative that China fundamentally re-energises its manufacturing sector.

The Chinese Government issues thousands of documents every year. And many other countries have similarly formulated industry policies to boost their manufacturing capabilities. So why did the MIC2025 document caused so much concern among other countries, especially the US?

Clearly, it reflects the US' recognition that China is rapidly developing as a superpower with potential to equal the US. More importantly, the US recognizes the strategic importance of MIC2025. In a White House document, the US expresses concern about "economic aggression" of China, specifically China's systematic effort to "acquire key technologies and intellectual property from other countries…" and to "capture the emerging high-technology industries that will drive future economic growth and many advancements in the defense industry".[5]

MIC2025's emphasis on civilian and military technological exchanges, government support for selected enterprises and its intent to achieve self-reliance,[6] has raised alarm bells in Washington. More importantly, the US is indirectly agreeing that the sectors and technologies identified in MIC2025 are indeed the driving forces of the future economy and leading in in these sectors is a strategic geopolitical advantage.

The 10 priority sectors identified by MIC2025 are as follows:

Sector	Examples of key technologies, products or processes
InfoComm Technologies	Advanced integrated circuits, 5G technologies, IoT and big data
Digital machine tools and robotics	Robotics for automobiles, defence, healthcare
Aerospace	Aircraft manufacturing, unmanned aviation vehicles, space & rocket technologies
Marine and shipbuilding	Deep sea monitoring, cruise ship design and fabrication
Railway transport	Green, smart railway transport
Energy-saving and new energy vehicles	Electric cars and batteries

[4] ≪中国制造2025≫, 国务院, 2015 年 5 月 8 日。

[5] "How China's economic aggression threatens the technologies and intellectual property of the United States and the world", White House Office of Trade and Manufacturing Policy, June 2018.

[6] China plans to be self-reliant in 70% of core components and materials by 2025.

(*Continued*)

Sector	Examples of key technologies, products or processes
Clean energy	Large-scale power stations, renewables
Agriculture	Agricultural equipment
New materials	Military-civilian dual-use materials, nanotechnology, graphene
Biomedical sciences and biotechnology	3D printing of biomedical products, medical devices

China's approach in MIC2025 will be heavily government-led.[7] However, it may also leverage on the entrepreneurial spirit of the private sector, as it has done in the internet economy. In the arena of e-commerce, e-payment, bike sharing, cab-sharing, online chats, online videos, and others, it is clear that given the room to compete, the entrepreneur in the Chinese business community will spring into action and compete rigorously. Only the toughest, fastest and most innovative wins in China's internet economy, resulting in strong companies like Baidu, Alibaba, Tencent, Xiaomi, SenseTime, iFlytek and powerful apps like WeChat, Jinritoutiao and Tik Tok.

China acknowledges that it lacks significantly behind the US in many of these core technologies. For instance, China is painfully aware that it is far behind in terms of semiconductor technologies. China still imports most of its semiconductor chips. Its biggest player, Semiconductor Manufacturing International Corporation (SMIC), lags behind its Korea and US competitors technologically. More starkly, when American companies were banned from selling to Chinese telecommunications equipment manufacturer, ZTE, the latter was almost put out of business.

At the same time, China knows that many companies depend on its huge market. Hence it has leveraged on its huge market to engage technology leaders, learn from them while injecting large sums of subsidies for R&D in parallel. It will aim to leapfrog the current technology, support selected enterprises and move into the next wave. For instance, China sold 770,000 units of New Energy Vehicles last year, half the world's demand. Shenzhen's BYD makes an Electric Vehicle every 90 sec. But yet it is well-recognised that China's battery technology lacks far behind the US. China is therefore working with companies like BYD and Baidu to produce intelligent electric cars. The same can be said of China's aviation industry.[8]

Many of the sectors identified are strategic to Artificial Intelligence (AI), which will be the key driver of the future economy. In this future economy, data will be the new oil and 5G telecommunication network the new pipelines.[9] New semiconductor chips for sensors,

[7] In 2017, the Chinese government's investment in R&D amounted to 2.2% of the GDP. MIC2025 has called for the establishment of 40 Manufacturing Innovation Centers by 2025. Some of these Centers have already been set up to look into R&D and incubation for specific areas such as electric car batteries.

[8] According to the South China Morning Post, China's jet engine technology is 20–30 years behind its competitors and only 50% of the key components are produced domestically.

[9] 5G networks will be the basic infrastructure for the industrial internet because it offers much faster data rates compared to 4G, allowing for smooth connectivity for new mobile applications, such as the internet of things, autonomous cars and smart cities. It will be able to support 1 million devices per sq km, according to International Telecommunication Union.

drones will be needed to power the processes to source for data and to eventually transform data into intelligent applications. Robotics will translate these applications into actual work on the factory floor or households.[10]

In the competition for leadership in AI, China has the advantage of data from 1.2 billion people, a greater tolerance of loss of privacy, a large pool of good engineers, a competitive pool of internet companies and entrepreneurs as well as a history of cooperation between the government and companies. However, it lacks cutting edge R&D and top scientists. Hence, China is putting in much effort in this area. Last year, China was the largest contributor to the equity funding of AI start-ups globally (48%), followed by the US (38%).

This is already showing results. Today, one of the most valuable AI start-ups is SenseTime, a Chinese AI in facial recognition. China is now moving into biological and genomic data as it combines AI and biotech capabilities. Shenzhen-based BGI (formerly known as Beijing Genomics Institute) already holds DNA samples of 40 million people.[11]

Singapore has also done much in R&D in new technologies as well. It has successfully developed a cluster of high-tech companies in the One-North location. It has a strong stable of companies, including the government-linked companies (GLCs). In the rapidly changing world of internet and AI, the private sector would be better positioned to make quick decisions. It is in the interest of each country to support the development of a strong, nimble and well-governed private sector and mutually beneficial collaboration between the two private sectors.

China's economy is now highly complex and large. While it will still rely heavily on government-led initiatives, China will have to increasingly build up a large pool of well-run companies and depend on these companies to drive its economy. China has been keen to learn how the Singapore Government manages its Government-Linked Companies (GLCs), such that they remain a key part of the Singapore Government and yet are driven by market forces to innovate and perform. This should be a key feature of Singapore-China economic collaboration model 2.0.

Two aspects of such collaboration can be promoted:

(a) B-to-B collaboration and
(b) Collaboration on government's regulation of businesses.

The G-to-G relationship and mechanism have been well-established. In comparison, the B-to-B collaboration is more ad hoc and less impactful. There are already many government efforts to help the private sector work together, e.g., the various business councils, programmes by government agencies such as Enterprise Singapore. This should continue. More importantly, Singapore companies must aggressively pursue lasting partnership with good Chinese companies and help strengthen the bilateral relationship between the two

[10] China's level of automation at 68 robots per 10,000 industrial workers, is lower compared with 631 robots for every 10,000 manufacturing staff in South Korea, the global leader in automation. Singapore, Germany and Japan all have higher densities of automation than China.
[11] South China Morning Post.

countries. This requires business leaders who believe in China, understand how Chinese companies work and who can add value to the latter in and outside China.

The Singapore Government can also share with China more on how it regulates the private sector, including areas such as governance for publicly-listed entities, relationship between the government and government-linked companies, competition laws, IP protection, etc. In the last 25 years, China has liberalized many of its policies as it allows market forces to work. However, there are instances whereby businesses leverage on regulation loopholes or personal connections to make commercial gains, at the expense of the general public. The various episodes of wild swings in the stock market, Ponzi schemes and cryptocurrency speculation suggest that a more thoughtful regulation regime and stronger rule of law are necessary. These are areas which the Singapore Government has done well generally. More systematic sharing of Singapore's approaches can be useful.

5. Looking Inward — Economic Restructuring

China fully recognizes the flaws in its economy today and has called for economic reforms in various areas such as SOE management, market competition, revenue distribution between the Central and local governments, financial regulations and national debt. These are complex issues which are beyond the scope of this paper.

While Singapore also may not have experience in some of these areas, eg, revenue distribution between the federal and the local governments, there are other areas which we may be able to offer more insights. One area is the relationship between the government and the government-linked companies. As China reviews its SOE policies and weighs the balance between SOEs vs POEs, it will continue to study the Singapore model. How much of this can be applied in China is of course a much more complex issue.

Regulation of the capital market is another potential area for strengthened collaboration, as China seeks to develop its capital markets as a support mechanism for the growth of companies while minimising the harm from excessive speculation. This is already one of the 4 pillars identified in the Chongqing G-to-G project.

A more systematic approach towards identifying the key areas whereby Singapore and China can share and learn from one another will be useful as China undertakes its economic restructuring.

6. Conclusion

Singapore and China enjoy a unique partnership, starting from the early days when Deng Xiaoping visited Singapore 1978. The collaboration intensified from 1990 when diplomatic relations were established. The various G-to-G projects, especially the Suzhou Industrial Park, have captured the imagination of many leaders, officials and companies. This foundation is a strong basis for the next era of collaboration between the two countries.

In Singapore–China economic collaboration 2.0, there should be a greater emphasis on partnership outside of China, especially along the BRI, with the aim of achieving win–win–win objectives for Singapore, China and the third country. There should also be a greater emphasis on B-to-B collaboration as we move into a fast-changing world powered by technological advancements and decisive, nimble private sector responses will be increasingly important. Finally, more sharing and mutual learning can be done on the regulation of various aspects of the business world, be it governance of publicly-listed entities, governance of capital markets, relationship between the government and government-owned enterprises or the competitive landscape between SOEs and POEs.

The future of Singapore–China relations continues to be bright. With careful planning and creativity, we can elevate this to yet another level and strengthen the bilateral relations for many years to come.

Acknowledgment

The opinion expressed in this paper is entirely the author's and does not reflect that of any organizations that he is associated with.

Chapter 12

SINGAPORE ENGAGES THE BELT AND ROAD INITIATIVE: PERCEPTIONS, POLICIES, AND INSTITUTIONS[†]

HONG LIU

School of Social Sciences
Nanyang Technological University, Singapore

XIN FAN

School of Humanities
Nanyang Technological University, Singapore

GUANIE LIM [*]

Nanyang Centre for Public Administration
Nanyang Technological University, Singapore
guanie.lim@ntu.edu.sg

Published Online 21 August 2020

This article argues that Singapore, courtesy of its strong state capacity and long-standing connections with China, has promoted effective polices and coordinated mutually reinforcing institutional mechanisms in engaging with the Belt and Road Initiative (BRI). While some of these institutions predate the BRI, they have been continuously enhanced or modified to meaningfully foster Singapore-China cooperation. In certain cases, new institutions have been created to fulfill specific demands the existing institutions cannot adequately serve. These two types of institutions not only complement each other but also promote cooperation between the bureaucrats, politicians, transnational corporations, government-linked corporations, small- and medium-sized private firms and business associations. The article also illustrates the flexibility of the 'networked state' in formulating collaborative ties linking key international and domestic actors, demonstrating how a small state like Singapore can partner China effectively and deepen its strategic importance to the BRI to enhance its own strategic and economic interests. Lastly, the article highlights the two key conditions in BRI-related nations for their successful engagement: the existence of mutual interests between China and a counterpart nation bolstered by conducive perceptions and policies, and the institutionalization of competent mechanisms to materialize and operationalize these interests.

Keywords: Belt and Road Initiative; state-business relations; transnational state; state capacity; China; Singapore.

JEL Classification: F02, F60, P16

[*]Corresponding author.

[†]This article originally appeared in *The Singapore Economic Review*, **66**(1), pp. 219–241

1. Introduction

Since its 'Reform and Opening-up' policies in 1978, China has experienced rapid growth, emerging as a prominent player in the global economy. It not only boasts of a large domestic consumer market but also has become a key foreign direct investment (FDI) contributor in the international arena since the early 2000s (Lim, 2017). Its stature has been elevated even further after the Belt and Road Initiative (BRI) was announced by Chinese President Xi Jinping in late 2013. Revolving around five major priorities, infrastructure connectivity, unimpeded trade, financial integration, policy coordination and connecting people, the BRI has become China's foremost diplomatic and economic strategy in engaging with neighboring countries and beyond since 2013 (Xi, 2014; Zhao, 2020).

Six years after the BRI's promulgation, there remains relatively little research on how (small- to medium-sized) states, such as those from Southeast Asia which occupies a key place in the 21st Century Maritime Silk Road, engages with the BRI in advancing their own national interests (cf. Liu and Lim, 2019; Tong and Kong, 2018; Kratz and Pavlićević, 2019; Khoo, 2019; Teo, EC, 2019; Ba, 2019). Much of the existing analysis has focused almost exclusively on the interests and strategies of Chinese political and economic actors (see Liou, 2014; Yoshimatsu, 2018; Beeson, 2016). Extending Liu and Lim's (2019) as well as Kratz and Pavlićević's (2019) work on Malaysia and Indonesia, respectively, this article studies how a small (yet important) state such as Singapore manages its interactions with China as well as the BRI by skilfully incorporating domestic political economy factors with China's growing presence in the region. Going beyond a macro-level analysis, it adopts a mesoscale perspective to take into account diverse economic, political, societal interests, and more importantly, the fluid interplay among these factors. From a theoretical point of view, this article adds depth to the concept of the 'networked state'. Capturing the experience of Singapore, it reframes the hitherto dominant nation-state framework in the existing literature, moving the scholarship toward one which recognizes the multiple poles of power (beyond the nation-state) that have emerged since the liberalization of the 1980s.

With the above as a backdrop, this article addresses the following questions: how does Singapore — both the government and business groups — perceive the BRI and its opportunities (as well as challenges)? What are their respective policies and stances toward the BRI? What are the (pre-existing and new) institutions established to facilitate their objectives and what are the outcomes of these engagements? What are the implications of the Singapore experience in engaging the BRI for a broader understanding of the complex and varied reactions to this ambitious initiative that is reshaping the regional and global orders?

We argue that Singapore's strong state has allowed it to promote effective policies and to create and coordinate mutually reinforcing institutional mechanisms in engaging with China. Some of these institutions predate the BRI but have been continuously enhanced to more meaningfully foster Singapore-China cooperation. In certain cases, new institutions have been created to fulfill specific demands the existing institutions cannot adequately serve. These two forms of (transnational) institutions complement each other, coordinating resources among the bureaucrats, politicians, transnational corporations (TNCs), government-linked corporations (GLCs), small- and medium-sized private firms and business associations.[1] The Singaporean approach sheds light on a potentially new model of transnational governance as well as economic strategy. With a cohesive, strong 'networked state' at its core, key actors can be mobilized to formulate effective, broad-based and sustainable partnerships. Although this form of governance is occasionally interpreted as top-down and rigid, the reality is far more multidimensional. As the rest of the article shall demonstrate, Singapore's closely coordinated and highly integrated governance style is especially useful in mediating cross-border resource exchange vis-à-vis other economies (in our case, China).

The next section unpacks the literature on Singapore's capitalist development and state-society relations. It underscores the need to be sensitive to the city-state's politics, in which a strong, efficient state has governed since its independence in 1965. The longevity of the incumbent administration has in turn allowed it to foster collaboration (rather than confrontation), especially in dealing with a prominent economy such as China. The article then puts forth a conceptual framework to make sense of how major domestic players interact with each other and how they contribute to exchanges of resources between Singapore and China. This is followed by an analysis of the perceptions of these key players toward the BRI and how they have engaged the initiative. Subsequently, the article presents the main institutions responsible for fostering Singapore-China collaboration, particularly since the BRI's inception. The penultimate section concludes with a discussion of the main findings and suggests avenues for future research.

2. Literature Survey

As a city-state with limited natural resources, Singapore has to rely on international trade and investment to power its economy. The loss of the enlarged Malaysian market during Singapore's separation from the former in 1965 only heightened the reliance on the international environment. However, what is generally less well-understood of this account is the institutional features with which Singapore manages its economy in navigating the peaks and troughs of the global economy. Singapore's engagement with the international economy (and by extension, that of China) can be conceptualized under three interrelated spheres — *economy, politics* and *state-society relations.*

Singapore has witnessed continued governance from a single party, the People's Action Party, since 1959, even before its Independence. The longevity of the incumbent has allowed it to shape state-society relations to one which is pro-growth and long term in nature (Low, 2005; Tan and Bhaskaran, 2015). Coupled with its small size, this feature provides the state the advantage of quick, centralized policy implementation. In addition, the state's 'two-legged' policy of attracting foreign TNCs and cultivating its own GLCs has reduced its reliance on the domestic private sector during the immediate post-Independence decades (Tsui-Auch, 2004). Unlike the capital- and technology-intensive TNCs and GLCs,

[1] Within the context of this article, small- and medium-sized private firms are defined as those with annual sales not exceeding S$100 million and/or with employment not exceeding 200 people.

these firms were perceived to be 'dragging the economy down in terms of low productivity and intensive use of labor resources in the wake of severe labor shortage at that time' (Chan and Ng, 2000, 294). Consequently, these firms were either displaced or had to subcontract their services to the foreign TNCs and/or the GLCs (Low, 1990). The relative weakness of the domestic private firms has in turn lead to an unusual outcome — they possess little power to influence public dialogue and policymaking, allowing the state to push policies that are beneficial for the entire society but which require a longer-than-normal horizon. The two-legged policy worked well as Singapore enjoyed robust growth in its post-Independence decades, joining the ranks of Korea, Taiwan and Hong Kong as Asia's first-tier tiger economies (Shin, 2005).

However, this model was interrupted by a worldwide recession in the mid-1980s. To counter the impasse, the state came up with a regionalization strategy, in which firms are encouraged to venture into markets adjacent to Singapore, including but not limited to China. The goal is to develop a second market to augment Singapore's small domestic market (Tan and Yeung, 2000; Saw, 2014). Both marking a break from and building on its hitherto two-legged policy, the state began to more actively drawing in the (small- and medium-sized) domestic private firms to complement the TNCs and GLCs in its regionalization efforts (Dahles, 2008; Tan and Bhaskaran, 2015).

This strategy has also been bolstered by concrete state support. One of the landmark projects of this sort is the Government-to-Government (G-to-G) Suzhou Industrial Park, China. This project was conceptualized in 1992 to attract foreign firms (including those from Singapore) into Suzhou to spearhead industrialization, as part of Singapore's effort in sharing its experience in industrial development with China.[2] Encompassing 70 km^2 and covering industrial, commerce and residential components, Suzhou Industrial Park is designed to attract a total investment of US$20 billion. The township is to support a population of 600,000 and employ 300,000 people upon completion (Lye, 2014; Zeng, 2019).

The success of the Suzhou Industrial Park has since deepened bilateral cooperation. In November 2003, Singapore-China cooperation was put on an institutionalized basis when the high-level Joint Council for Bilateral Cooperation (JCBC) was launched by then Prime Minister Goh Chok Tong and then Premier Wen Jiabao (Saw, 2014). The JCBC, co-chaired by the Deputy Prime Ministers of China and Singapore, allows the two countries to review annually the state of existing relations and to identify new areas of collaboration. Its inception has provided a regular and systematic platform for political leaders, bureaucrats and businessmen from both countries to network and cooperate on ventures.

In addition, Singapore's (ethnic Chinese) business associations function as important non-governmental resources in promoting Singapore-China ties, supplementing the top-down approach of the state (Liu *et al.*, 2016). These business associations play an integral role in the following aspects: collecting business information, protecting commercial

[2] In its effort to reintegrate into the global economy, China launched its 'Reform and Opening-up' policies in 1978. The Chinese political leadership found in Singapore a useful reference to bolster its then backward economy (Lye, 2014; Liu and Wang, 2018; Teo EC, 2019).

credit, organizing relevant trade activities, providing collective bargaining ability and reducing transaction costs. Liu *et al.* (2016) also illustrate that these organizations — by deploying their social capital and knowledge of the Southeast Asian market — can become suitable conduits in promoting the BRI in the region, not least in deepening the understanding of the public about the effectiveness of the BRI. This 'whole-of-nation' approach has retained its relevance since, playing an equally (if not more) important role after the launching of the BRI.[3]

Notwithstanding its good relationship with China, Singapore has managed to maintain neutrality in its ties with other countries, sometimes serving as an effective intermediary between China and the West. Even in view of the escalating tension between the United States and China, Singaporean Prime Minister Lee Hsien Loong announced that the city-state would resolutely stick to its policy of maintaining good ties with both countries (Sim, 2019). His stance is ultimately centered on economic reasoning rather than zero-sum state-state contestation, which can potentially be ruinous. Enriching this perspective is Ba's (2019) research on the strategic narratives deployed by Singapore's policymaking community. She demonstrates the adept construction of a historical narrative of a 'special relationship' and underlined by Singapore's support for key Chinese priorities and critical moments in China's historical development. This narrative has provided Singapore an important foreign policy tool with which to manage its bilateral relations with China. Singapore's position is also buttressed by its adherence to the Association of Southeast Asian Nations (ASEAN). For example, in dealing with the geopolitical tension arising from the South China Sea disputes, Singapore has always maintained that the disputes be resolved based on international law. And it has consistently reiterated that freedom of navigation in the South China Sea and a united ASEAN are the country's national interest (Tong and Kong, 2018).

3. Conceptual Framework: Institutionalization of the Networked State

Synthesizing and going beyond the above literature, this article aims to account simultaneously for the agency of several key actors by presenting a conceptual framework to analyze how they interact with the external world (see Figure 1). Figure 1 illustrates seven of the most critical players in Singapore, and how they simultaneously contribute to the exchange and allocation of resources between Singapore and the international economy (in this article, China). Marking a break from the predominant nation-state framework, which remains important in its own right, Figure 1 recognizes the heightened pace of cross-border movements of people, ideas and capital, especially since the rise of neoliberalism after the 1980s (Aalbers, 2013; Castells, 2000; Wolf, 2004; Carroll and Jarvis, 2017). According to Ohmae (1995), this means that the controlling mechanisms over society are no longer the exclusive purview of the state. In other words, there exist substantially more poles of power in shaping economic transformation.

[3] See the subsequent sections for a more detailed elaboration of the JCBC and its functions.

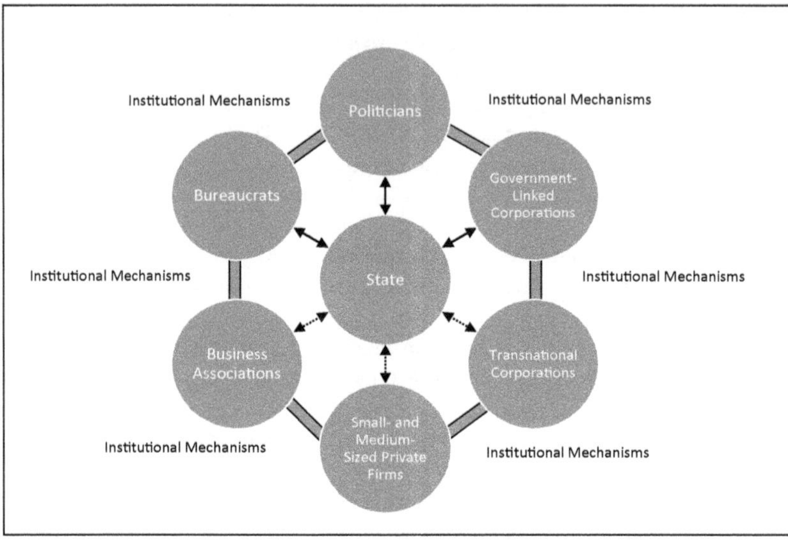

= National Borders of Singapore

*: Solid arrows indicate more direct influence while dotted ones indicate indirect influence

Source: By the authors.

Figure 1. Institutionalization of the Networked State: The Case of Singapore

However, Singapore's unique development experience (i.e., the uninterrupted governance of a single dominant party and the initial ambivalence toward its small- and medium-sized domestic private firms) suggests that the state is likely to play a larger-than-usual role in governance affairs.[4] What is more important here is to recognize, in addition to the continued prevalence of the Singaporean state, the three dimensions of network — as a relational entity; an interconnected node and a collective layer of spatially constructed ties (Liu, 2018). Here the state is to be conceptualized as a 'networked state', communicating with various key players through existing and new institutional mechanisms. These institutions are important because they can coordinate and manage the often diverse interests and agendas of key stakeholders, establishing an effective and broad-based partnership (Liu, 2018). This highly coordinated governance style is critical in mediating policy diffusion and cross-border resources (e.g., FDI and trade of goods and services) exchange vis-à-vis other economies.

[4] Unlike the other Northeast Asian developmental states and economies (i.e., Japan, Korea and Taiwan), Singapore has continued to enjoy uninterrupted governance by a single party since the post-World War Two era. See Low (2003), Johnson (1982), Wade (2003), Amsden (2003), Carroll and Jarvis (2017), and Rahim and Barr (2019) for a critical review of the concept of the developmental state.

4. Perceptions, Policies and Strategies: State-Society Collaboration

4.1. *Politicians, bureaucrats and GLCs*

Singapore is one of the first countries to publicly express support for the BRI. During the 11th China-ASEAN EXPO Opening Ceremony, held in Guangxi on 16 September 2014, Prime Minister Lee Hsien Loong affirmed China's efforts in playing a bigger role in the international as well as regional setting. Some of the initiatives he explicitly supported were the upgrading of the ASEAN-China Free Trade Agreement (FTA), establishment of the Asian Infrastructure Investment Bank (AIIB) and promotion of the 21st Century Maritime Silk Road (Prime Minister's Office Singapore, 2014).[5]

To foster cooperation through multilateral channels, Singapore, as early as 24 October 2014, signed in Beijing an intergovernmental memorandum of understanding (MOU) with 20 other countries, earmarking itself as a first-mover in establishing the AIIB, a new multilateral development bank commonly viewed as the financing arm of the BRI (Tan, 2014).[6] The signatories of the MOU then took part in negotiations for the AIIB's Articles of Agreement. The countries which subsequently signed and ratified the Articles of Agreement will then officially become founding members of the AIIB. On 29 June 2015, less than a year after the signing of the MOU, the AIIB took a crucial step forward with 50 countries, including Singapore, signing off on its charter (Kor, 2015). Contributing US$250 million toward the US$100 billion capital of the AIIB, Singapore enjoys a 0.2585% stake in the bank, giving it 0.4365% voting rights. According to Singapore's representative, the then Senior Minister of State for Finance and Transport Josephine Teo, this move was 'to support further economic development in the region, by working with all founding members to build up the AIIB as a first-class multilateral financial institution' (Kor, 2015).

Building on its efforts on the multilateral front, Singapore has also implemented several bilateral policies to strengthen bilateral cooperation. During the First Belt and Road Forum for International Cooperation, held on 14 and 15 May 2017 in Beijing, Singapore and China signed another MOU (Ministry of National Development, 2017; Koh, 2017). The MOU subsequently was fine-tuned, pinpointing to and promoting collaboration in three areas: *infrastructure connectivity*, *project financing* and *joint undertaking of projects in third countries*.

Firstly, in promoting infrastructure connectivity, both sides shall reinforce existing efforts to deepen the Chongqing Connectivity Initiative, a G-to-G project launched by Xi Jinping during a state visit to Singapore in November 2015.[7] The Chongqing Connectivity Initiative is conceptualized as an important part of China's drive to reduce the income disparity between its wealthy coastal and poor inland and Western regions, promoting greater trade and investment in the regions and provinces of Guizhou, Guangxi, Ningxia and Gansu

[5] The BRI is composed of two main components: the Silk Road Economic Belt (connecting China to Europe by land through Central Asia) and the 21st Century Maritime Silk Road (connecting China to Europe by sea through Southeast Asia).

[6] This view is not entirely true as its purpose is to support infrastructure financing in Asia. Although China is the AIIB's largest shareholder with a 30.79% stake that will give it 26.56% voting rights and veto powers over major decisions, it is noticeably more egalitarian compared to the US-led World Bank and the Europe-led International Monetary Fund (Wilson, 2017; Asian Infrastructure Investment Bank, 2019; Zhao, 2020).

[7] The Chongqing Connectivity Initiative and its broader relevance to Singapore-China economic ties shall be elaborated in the subsequent sections.

via Chongqing. At a broader level, the initiative is to more thoroughly connect the overland Silk Road Economic Belt with the 21st Century Maritime Silk Road. This will offer a shorter and more direct trade route between Western China and Southeast Asia. Potentially, it can enhance cross-border trade flows and help to catalyze the economic development of both regions, thud directly benefiting Singapore as a key transport and logistics hub in the Asia-Pacific. Departing from conventional approaches in which investment and trade effort is targeted at a specific location such as an industrial park or a city, the Chongqing Connectivity Initiative is an open platform, encouraging more users (regardless of nationality) to build up economies of scale, ultimately reducing per unit cost (Lim, 2018).

Secondly, in the financing of BRI projects, both sides view the infrastructure-oriented outlook of the BRI as an opportunity to bridge Asia's persistent infrastructure shortfall, with the ADB projecting in 2017 that Asia needs to invest $26tn by 2030 to resolve a serious infrastructure shortage (Pell and Mitchell, 2017). The overarching objective is to make currently unfeasible projects more bankable, thereby attracting funding from the private sector. This is an area where Singapore is not a direct beneficiary of housing an infrastructure project, but plays an important role in partnering Chinese stakeholders (e.g., banks and construction firms) intending to internationalize their operations. As a major center of global and regional finance, approximately 60% of infrastructure projects in Southeast Asia obtain their finance and advisory services from Singapore-based financial institutions. Beyond financing, Singapore also houses a full suite of professional service provides that are necessary to bring infrastructure projects to fruition. This ecosystem is equally conducive for Chinese banks intending to raise credit and debt for their clients. For example, risk management solutions (e.g., risk pooling, especially for larger and more complex infrastructure projects) pertaining to the needs of Chinese insurers and reinsurers are in the process of being formulated. Some of the noteworthy success stories are the Bank of China (Singapore branch) and the China Construction Bank (Singapore branch). In 2017 alone, they issued US$600 million and RMB 1 billion worth of BRI-themed bonds respectively (Ministry of National Development, 2017).

Thirdly, Singaporean and Chinese firms are encouraged to forge partnerships to undertake joint projects, in addition to collaborating on human resource development in third countries. Tapping into the growing ambitions of Chinese firms 'Going Out' of their home economy, Singapore offers strong, mature linkages for the former to venture into Southeast Asia and beyond. For Singapore, this move dovetails with its goal of developing markets adjacent to it, augmenting its small domestic economy. Although this initiative started in the mid-1980s, it has continued to receive attention from policymakers. Singapore's capital-intensive GLCs are examples of how potentially win-win partnerships can be forged. Surbana Jurong — one of the top GLCs in design, engineering and consultancy services — has set up a joint venture with China Highway Engineering Consulting Corporation in 2017.[8] The latter specializes in the construction of complex, large-scale transport infrastructure (often in challenging landscapes), but has only entered

[8] Their joint venture, China Highway-Surbana Jurong Transportation Design and Research Co Ltd, is 51% owned by China Highway Engineering Consulting Corporation and 49% held by Surbana Jurong (Williams, 2017).

the Southeast Asian market relatively recently. This partnership essentially promotes a division of labor — China Highway Engineering Consulting Corporation brings to the table its technical expertise while Surbana Jurong (through itself and/or its affiliates) offers tacit knowledge of the different Southeast Asian economies. Despite its size, Surbana Jurong appears to network fairly frequently with key business associations/federations in Singapore, suggesting that there is likely to be some degree of cooperation between them.[9]

4.2. *Small- and medium-sized private firms, TNCs and business associations*

Although generally lacking capital and technology (relative to the GLCs and TNCs), Singapore's small- and medium-sized private firms are important players in Singapore's dovetailing with the BRI. As a result of their decades-long experience operating in China *and* Southeast Asia, they have developed some innovative capabilities and place-specific cultural nuances, competitive advantages that are difficult to replicate. In addition, they are often able to match (or even usurp) the GLCs and TNCs in reacting to market opportunities primarily because of their small size and shorter chain of command. Such features make them 'natural partners' for Chinese firms entering the region (especially those lacking experience outside China) as well as Western and Japanese TNCs eager to tap into the opportunities opened up by the BRI.

Their proactiveness can be witnessed in how swiftly the business associations/federations are in associating their major events and forums with the BRI to create greater awareness, generate discussions and build mindshare of the BRI with its members. Examples of such Singapore associations are Business China (a semi-official organization established in 2007 by the Singapore government and business sector in engaging China), Singapore Chinese Chamber of Commerce (SCCCI) and Singapore Business Federation (SBF), among others.[10] Beyond business-related discussion, these business associations have also played a significant role in strengthening cultural and people-to-people exchanges with China's business chambers (Enterprise Singapore, 2017). To this end, the SBF's actions are particularly noteworthy.[11] The SBF and *Lianhe Zaobao*, the Chinese language flagship newspaper of Singapore Press Holdings, jointly launched a BRI-themed portal on 8 March 2016 (Singapore Business Federation, 2016). The portal is Southeast Asia's first bilingual (Chinese and English) comprehensive website to focus on the BRI, offering a Southeast Asian perspective and promoting BRI-related business activities between Singapore, Southeast Asia and China. It presents an overview of the BRI, its latest development, news, business opportunities, analyses, commentaries and a calendar showcasing activities related to the BRI within the region.

[9] Most of the members of these associations are small- and medium-sized private firms. See BizQ (2019) and Surbana Jurong (2019a) on some of the avenues in which Surbana Jurong engages with the small- and medium-sized private firms.

[10] As mentioned previously, small- and medium-sized private firms make up the bulk of the membership of these associations. See Business China (2018), Liu *et al.* (2016) for an elaboration on the roles of Business China and SCCI, respectively, in promoting Singapore-China ties.

[11] The SBF is the city-state's leading business chamber representing as many as 25,800 firms (mostly small- and medium-sized). It also represents smaller local and foreign business chambers.

The tentative sentiment of the small- and medium-sized private firms can be gauged from the National Business Survey 2017/2018 (Singapore Business Federation, 2018).[12] The survey shows that about two in five firms feel positive about BRI. More than half of the firms surveyed are also looking for updates on the latest development on the BRI (62%) as well as market intelligence and research (54%). About two in five of these firms are interested to embark on or are already involved in BRI projects in Thailand (40%), Vietnam (40%) and Singapore (38%). When polled on the industrial activities that they are most interested in to participate under the BRI, as many as 34% selected industrials, transportation and logistics. The second most popular activity is technology (29%), followed by professional services (26%), financial services (19%) and others (18%).

For the TNCs, their perception and overtures to Singapore's stance toward the BRI are harder to determine as they tend to be driven by firm- and industry-specific logic, in addition to unexpected events such as natural disasters.[13] However, the early 2019 decision by British appliance maker Dyson to relocate its headquarters to Singapore can shed some light on how a brand name TNC is responding to the city-state's actions in managing the BRI. According to Jim Rowan, Dyson's Chief Executive Officer, the move underlines the importance of the Asian market, where the firm sees the biggest opportunities for growth in the future (BBC, 2019). Moreover, analysts point to Dyson's preference to operate closer to its suppliers (most of whom are Asia-based) and Singapore's multiple FTAs with major economies, in addition to 'policy clarity which will not see manufacturing operations being disrupted by policy flip-flop' (Ng, 2019).[14]

5. Institutional Mechanisms: Continuity and Change

Singapore's engagement with the BRI can be broken into two broad institutional mechanisms: existing ones and new ones. Utilizing existing institutions, the former has been enhanced and updated to more effectively engage with the challenges and opportunities arising from the BRI. For the latter, they have been established to fill a specific niche, which the existing institutions cannot adequately serve. These two forms of institutions complement each other, collectively coordinating resources among the bureaucrats, politicians, TNCs, GLCs, small- and medium-sized private firms and business associations (see Figure 1).

[12] Conducted by SBF, this annual survey collected views from over 1,000 (1,019) SBF members across all major industries from 11 October 2017 to 13 December 2017. All members were invited to participate via email and encouraged to complete the questions via phone reminders. For each firm, a maximum of one response was collected via an online survey platform. The survey covered a wide range of topics including manpower challenges, business transformation, and international expansion. Of the 1,019 firms polled, 84% were classified as small- and medium-sized private firms.

[13] One of the most commonly cited natural disasters that impacted the Southeast Asian manufacturing industry is the 2011 Thailand floods which severely disrupted the operations of Japanese manufacturers based in the Kingdom. Since then, Japanese manufacturing firms are more aware of the need to better manage (or at least spread out the risk of) their supply chain in the region.

[14] Dyson's two principle supply chain partners are Meiban and Flex. Singaporean-owned Meiban started as a small firm supplying services to TNCs but has since expanded operations across China, Singapore, and Malaysia. Flex, founded in the US, has three sites in Singapore and a presence in a further 30 countries. Both firms work with Dyson in supplying parts for products like its famed vacuum cleaners and bladeless fans (see Ng, 2019).

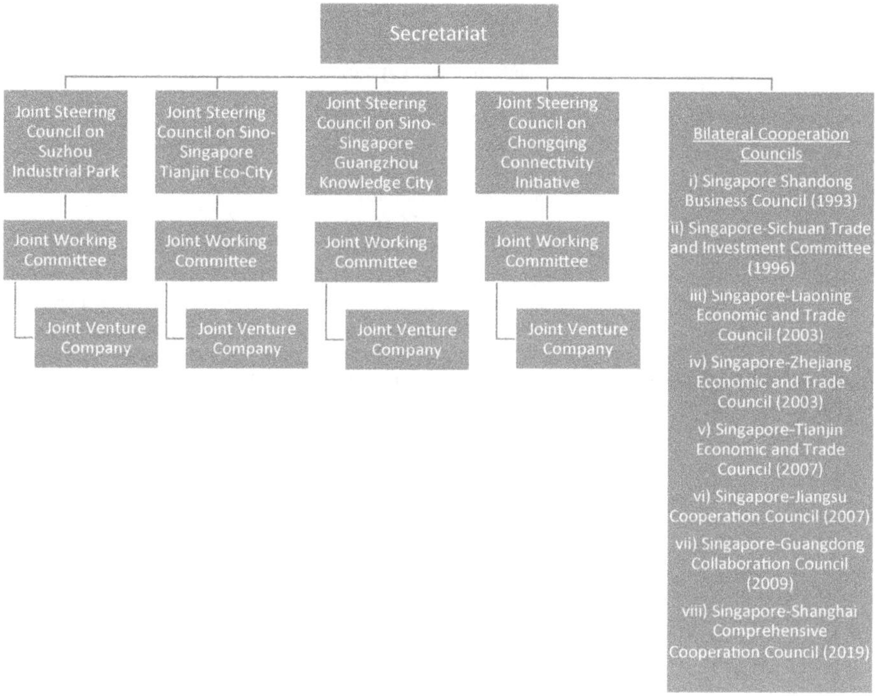

Source: Compiled by the authors based on publicly available data.

Figure 2. Organizational Structure of the Joint Council for Bilateral Cooperation

Singapore's deep experience in dealing with China means that it has developed critical institutional mechanisms to foster cooperation with the Chinese, even prior to the BRI's announcement. The aforementioned JCBC ranks as the most prominent and overarching institution in managing Singapore-China relations in the economic and social arenas (see Figure 2). Conceptualized in 2003, it has continually been revitalized to reflect the latest development between the two economies. This is reflected in the ways through which key bilateral cooperation councils linked to eight municipals and provinces are integrated under the JCBC. Seven of these councils have been formed prior to the BRI, with the earliest one established in 1993. In May 2019, the Singapore-Shanghai Comprehensive Cooperative Council was formed and parked under the JCBC.

Taking a 'whole-of-nation' approach, these councils are co-chaired by top officials of both Singapore and China. Reflecting on the renewal of Singapore's political leadership, it is fitting that its next crop of politicians in Singapore (known commonly as the fourth-generation leaders) is co-chairing several of these bilateral cooperation councils (Au-Yong, 2018). Some of the top names include Deputy Prime Minister and Minister for Finance Heng Swee Keat, Minister for Trade and Industry and Minister-in-Charge of the

Table 1. Co-Chairmen of Singapore-China Bilateral Cooperation Councils

Bilateral Cooperation Councils	Co-Chairmen (Singapore)	Co-Chairmen (China)
Singapore Shandong Business Council	Chee Hong Tat, Senior Minister of State for Trade and Industry and Senior Minister of State for Education	Ren Airong, Deputy Governor of Shandong Province
Singapore-Sichuan Trade and Investment Committee	Ng Chee Meng, Minister in the Prime Minister's Office	Li Yunze, Deputy Governor of Sichuan Province
Singapore-Liaoning Economic and Trade Council	Masagos Zulkifli, Minister for the Environment and Water Resources	Tang Yijun, Deputy Secretary of the Provincial Party Committee and Governor of Liaoning Province
Singapore-Zhejiang Economic and Trade Council	Sim Ann, Senior Minister of State for Communications and Information and Senior Minister of State for Culture, Community and Youth	Zhu Congqi, Deputy Governor of Zhejiang Province
Singapore-Tianjin Economic and Trade Council	Lawrence Wong Shyun Tsai, Minister for National Development and Second Minister for Finance	Zhang Guoqing, Mayor of Tianjin City
Singapore-Jiangsu Cooperation Council	Indranee Rajah, Minister in the Prime Minister's Office and Second Minister for Finance and Second Minister for Education	Wu Zhenglong, Governor of Jiangsu Province
Singapore-Guangdong Collaboration Council	Ong Ye Kung, Minister for Education	Ma Xingrui, Governor of Guangdong Province
Singapore-Shanghai Comprehensive Cooperation Council	Heng Swee Keat, Deputy Prime Minister and Minister for Finance	Ying Yong, Deputy Secretary of the Municipal Party Committee and Mayor of Shanghai Municipal Government

Public Service Chan Chun Sing, Minister for Education Ong Ye Kung, Minister for the Environment and Water Resources Masagos Zulkifli, Minister for Manpower and Second Minister for Home Affairs Josephine Teo and Minister in the Prime Minister's Office Ng Chee Meng (see Table 1). These sub-national councils provide additional avenues to bureaucrats, politicians and businessmen from both sides to cooperate on a more intimate level, moving beyond the strategy set at the national level.[15]

[15] One of the authors of this paper took part in a Collaboration Council meeting in 2017 and observed that the participants of both sides were those in charge of respective agencies involved in Singapore-China cooperation and the discussions were candid and productive, aiming at resolving specific issues and moving forward.

The evolving nature of these councils is exemplified by the Singapore-Shandong Business Council (SSBC). Formed in 1993, it remains the oldest bilateral business council interlinking Singapore and China. Its original function was primarily to assist Singaporean and Chinese firms in locating business opportunities, exploring joint areas of cooperation and promoting the investment of Singaporean companies into Shandong. In the early years, the businesses targeted were mostly labor-intensive, ranging from real estate to logistics management.

As the Chinese economy grew more sophisticated, the SSBC has expanded to cover more high value-added activities. In 2014, Li Qun, then Party Secretary of the Qingdao Municipal Party Committee, proposed to former Prime Minister Goh Chok Tong, during the latter's visit to Qingdao (a municipal under Shandong), to deepen cooperation with Singapore in the financial industry (Ruiji Touzi, 2014). Such a proposal, while reflecting on the domestic politics and economic logics of the subnational Chinese governments' engagement in the BRI (Ye, 2019), resonates with Singapore's ambition to play a bigger role in the BRI, especially in coordinating financial exchange between China and other BRI recipient states. To this end, Qingdao established a pilot zone in the same year to more effectively foster its goal of deepening financial cooperation with Singapore. In 2018, the 'Qingdao Wealth and Financial Management Comprehensive Reform Pilot Zone Overall Plan' was formally legislated by the State Council of China.

The SSBC's evolution suggests that it is keeping pace with the development of both the Singaporean and Chinese economies. Providing business information about Shandong (and the rest of China), its goals during the 1990s and early 2000s were tailored to meet Singapore's regionalization strategy and China's urgent need for investment during its opening-up phase. In recent times, the SSBC has rejuvenated itself to better support the ambitions of Chinese firms internationalizing their operations, and the Singaporean firms eager to play a part in the BRI. In addition to providing trade and investment information, the SSBC has deepened its expertise to provide more targeted support to the aspirations of Shandong-based firms (e.g., Qingdao's desire to shore up its expertise in financial management) and the competitive advantage of Singaporean firms (e.g., expertise in high value-added manufacturing and financial services).[16]

Apart from the eight bilateral councils, the JCBC also directly monitors key G-to-G projects such as the aforementioned Suzhou Industrial Park through the setting up of project-specific joint steering councils (see Figure 2). These joint steering councils are co-chaired by top politicians of Singapore and China, respectively. It also brings together various ministries and agencies from both sides to facilitate and coordinate development. Below the joint steering committees are the joint working committees that focus more on operational issues (Lye, 2014). They in turn monitor progress of the Singapore-China joint venture companies, which are responsible for the physical development of the project and their commercial viability. One of the joint steering committees' unique feature is the manners in which GLCs are mobilized by the Singaporean state in the establishment of

[16]During one of the authors' business trips to Qingdao in 2016 and 2017, the city's leaders were very keen on attracting business schools from Singapore to set up a branch campus in Qingdao to further promote the establishment of the financial hub in the area of wealth management.

joint venture companies in these large G-to-G undertakings. A legacy of Singapore's two-legged economic policy, the GLCs are mobilized to partake in deals entailing a long gestation period and huge capital outlay (at least at the outset), thereby overcoming potential lack of investment from the private sector. The longer-than-usual horizon of the GLCs, coupled with the political continuity of both the Singapore and Chinese states, creates a stable, predictable environment for which accompanying investment from other TNCs and small- and medium-sized private firms can be attracted.

More importantly, the streamlined, tri-level structure of these joint steering councils promotes frequent interactions — both at the institutional and individual levels — among bureaucrats, politicians, TNCs, GLCs, small- and medium-sized private firms and business associations, enhancing Singapore-China bilateral ties. This can be seen in the continuity by which G-to-G industrial parks/urban centers are constructed. For the Suzhou Industrial Park, it was conceptualized in the early 1990s, an era in which China sought to learn from Singapore in attracting FDI to develop its then backward economy. The Tianjin Eco-City was launched in 2008. Following three decades of rapid growth, several Chinese cities were beginning to suffer severe cases of pollution. Both Singapore and China decided to use this project as a model for sustainable, green development for other Chinese cities, with the main focus on environmental conservation, resource and energy conservation and sustainable development (Flynn *et al.*, 2016; Caprotti, 2014). In 2010, the Sino-Singapore Guangzhou Knowledge City was launched. This project represented both countries' increasing awareness of the need to tap into the highly competitive and globalized knowledge economy. If executed well, it can further the progress of China's emerging niche in highly knowledge-intensive industries such as artificial intelligence and high-technology manufacturing, with Singapore reaping the rewards as a facilitator.

In November 2015, the aforementioned Chongqing Connectivity Initiative was launched. This project is the highest profile collaboration between Singapore and China since the BRI was announced in 2013. Unlike the previous G-to-G collaboration, this project is not geographically bound. Epitomizing the ideals of the BRI, this project is also more ambitious than the other Singapore-China projects thus far, aiming to enhance the connectivity of Chongqing within China itself and with the rest of the world (Chong, 2019). Singapore's expertise in infrastructure planning and logistics development would be useful for this project. During the 14th JCBC, held in Singapore on 20 September 2018, the then Deputy Prime Minister Teo Chee Hean announced that Singapore and Chongqing companies have formed joint ventures — the Sino-Singapore Chongqing Connectivity Solutions (SSCCS) and the Sino-Singapore (Chongqing) DC Multimodal Logistics (SSDCML) — to drive the new trade route's development (Prime Minister's Office Singapore, 2018).

One of the most important new institutions with regards to the BRI is the establishment of Infrastructure Asia in October 2018. This new government agency, set up by Enterprise Singapore and the Monetary Authority of Singapore, serves as a one-stop platform to facilitate regional infrastructure collaboration. Given the central role of infrastructure provision in the BRI and the broader need to address infrastructure demand in the region,

Infrastructure Asia's establishment is timely. In particular, it tackles the issue of financing by making large, long-term infrastructure projects more bankable and investible.

According to Seth Tan Keng Hwee, Executive Director of Infrastructure Asia, the savings rate of (Southeast) Asia in relation to the demand for investment in infrastructure is sufficient to meet its demand (see also Khor *et al.*, 2019). However, one of the prime reasons infrastructure in the region remains undersupplied is because projects are not bankable or they do not fit the needs and expectations of investors (Oxford Business Group, 2018). For Infrastructure Asia, it offers solutions to make projects more bankable and investible such as tweaking the financing structure and standardizing contracts to shorten the preparation and negotiation phases of a project. In addition, Infrastructure Asia leverages on Singapore's diplomatic neutrality, familiarity with the other regional economies, connectivity to world-class firms as well as institutions and successful development experience (Oxford Business Group, 2018).

Some of the more prominent partners Infrastructure Asia has signed MOU with are the aforementioned SBF and the World Bank Group (Infrastructure Asia, 2019a). With the MOU, Infrastructure Asia is slated to hold quarterly briefings with the SBF to market and match its members to relevant business opportunities. For the World Bank Group, it will leverage its own and Infrastructure Asia's networks and expertise to drive knowledge building and exchange within Asia and to help countries strengthen capacities for infrastructure project structuring, financing, implementation and operation (Infrastructure Asia, 2019b).

Despite its recent establishment, Infrastructure Asia has initiated and facilitated the formation of the China-Singapore Co-Investment Platform, bringing together the aforementioned Surbana Jurong and Silk Road Fund (a medium- to long-term investment fund set up by China's central government in 2014 in financing the BRI projects). Under the agreement, both partners will set up a co-investment platform worth US$500 million that is primarily focused on greenfield infrastructure projects in Southeast Asia. The partners expect to invest about US$500 million over the next few years, with each partner investing in principle equal amounts in the projects (Surbana Jurong, 2019b). Investments of the platform could take various forms, including equity and debt. For Infrastructure Asia, it not only brought Surbana Jurong and Silk Road Fund together due to their complementary capabilities and common intent of investing in Southeast Asia but also facilitated Singapore's ambition of cooperating with China in projects in third countries (in this case, other Southeast Asian economies).

At an on-the-ground level, there is a growing perception that both old and new institutions have interacted to forward Singaporean interests, especially in third countries (with the support of the Chinese). Owned and managed by the Teo family, Pacific International Lines has invested an initial 1 billion yuan (S$206 million) to build an integrated logistics park in Nanning, the capital city of Guangxi Zhuang Autonomous Region in 2017 (Straits Times, 2017). Present at the launching ceremony was Minister for Trade and Industry and Minister-in-Charge of the Public Service Chan Chun Sing. In a short opening address, he noted that the park could play a key role in supporting the Southern Transport Corridor, part of the Chongqing Connectivity Initiative. When ready, the Southern Transport

Corridor could offer a more cost-effective way for companies in Southeast Asia to go into western China and *vice versa* (The New Paper, 2017). This sentiment is shared by Pacific International Lines managing director Teo Siong Seng who declared: 'Guangxi does a lot of border trade with Vietnam, and many of the imported goods are sent to Guangzhou for processing. With this park, we hope to attract businesses to do some of the processing and packaging here' (The New Paper, 2017).[17] This project builds on and reinforces another Singaporean undertaking in Qinzhou City, Guangxi province, i.e., the new container terminal called Beibu Gulf-PSA International Container Terminal Co. Conceptualized in June 2015, this venture is spearheaded by a Singapore-China consortium. For Singapore, the project is pushed by PSA International (a GLC), supported by Pacific International Lines. On China's side is the state-owned Beibu Gulf Port Group. When completed, the terminal will support the container trade growth in the region and serve the vast hinterlands of Guangxi, Sichuan, Chongqing and Hunan. It will also connect the region to key shipping routes linking China to Southeast Asian countries, East Africa and the Mediterranean (Lee, 2015).

At a broader scale, this 'whole-of-nation' approach has yielded substantial tangible economic outcomes for both countries. This can be interpreted from Singapore's continued relevance to Chinese firms, relative to the other regional economies. Table 2 shows that from 2010 to 2018, Singapore has maintained (and even extended its lead in some years) its number one position in Southeast Asia for the attraction of Chinese FDI. Although there were fluctuations on a yearly basis, the general trend is for Singapore to garner about 50% of the total FDI inflow entering the region. However, the impact is less noticeable in

Table 2. Flow of Chinese Foreign Direct Investment into Various ASEAN Economies, 2010–2018 (Billion USD)

Host Country	2010	2011	2012	2013	2014	2015	2016	2017	2018	Total
Singapore	0.7	5.5	6.0	2.5	4.2	4.0	4.4	6.7	3.8	37.8
Brunei	0	—	—	—	—	—	—	—	0	0
Cambodia	0.1	0.2	0.4	0.3	0.6	0.5	0.5	0.6	0.8	4.0
Indonesia	0.4	0.2	0.3	0.6	1.1	0.3	0.4	1.8	2.1	7.2
Laos	0	0.3	—	—	0.6	0.7	0.7	1.3	1.0	4.6
Malaysia	0	0	0	0.1	0.3	0.3	1.4	1.6	0.2	3.9
Myanmar	1.5	0.7	0.5	0.8	0.1	0.1	0.2	0.6	0.5	5.0
Philippines	0	0	0	0	0	0.1	0	0	0.2	0.3
Thailand	0.6	0	0.6	0.9	−0.2	0.2	1.1	0.1	0.5	3.8
Vietnam	0.1	0.4	0.2	1.0	0.2	0.4	1.0	0.9	1.1	5.3

Source: ASEANstats.

[17] Teo Siong Seng is widely known as a proponent of the BRI and a supporter of stronger Singapore-China ties. He is also the Chairman of the SBF, which provides him with considerable clout in the domestic business community. See Teo, SS (2019) for his open call for Singaporean small- and medium-sized private firms to more aggressively tapping into commercial avenues opened up by the BRI.

Table 3. ASEAN and Selected Economies' Trade with China, 2009–2019 (Billion USD)

	Singapore	Vietnam	Malaysia	Indonesia	Philippines	ASEAN
2009	5.9	2.6	6.5	3.6	2.4	26.0
2010	5.3	3.7	7.1	4.9	2.5	29.8
2011	5.5	4.5	8.3	5.9	3.1	33.9
2012	7.0	5.4	10.1	6.9	3.1	40.3
2013	7.2	6.8	10.6	6.7	3.6	44.4
2014	8.5	9.6	10.5	5.8	3.9	47.7
2015	7.5	9.4	9.2	4.9	4.2	45.3
2016	7.5	10.7	9.9	5.9	4.4	48.0
2017	7.7	14.1	9.7	6.5	4.7	52.5
2018	7.5	13.1	9.4	6.3	4.2	50.1
2019	9.8	16.6	12.6	7.3	5.4	64.1

Source: CEIC Database.

bilateral trade promotion. Originally the second largest trade partner for China, Singapore began to move down one spot in 2014 following Vietnam's aggressive push to promote trade ties with the Chinese (see Table 3). In 2015, Vietnam even became China's largest trade partner in the region, usurping Malaysia (the hitherto incumbent). Nevertheless, when one accounts for Singaporean performance over the entire period surveyed, the trend is for it to mirror the movement of ASEAN's bilateral trade. This implies that it is not losing out too much to its fellow regional economies. Put together, Singapore still is China's largest source of FDI and third largest trade partner, maintaining its lead over far bigger economies such as Indonesia and the Philippines.

6. Conclusion

By taking a step further of Liu's (2018) postulation of the 'networked state' and its changing role in a transnational Asia, this article has underscored the need to reconsider the hitherto dominant nation-state framework in public governance and development studies. Admittedly, the greatly intensified pace of cross-border exchange of resources since the 1980s has meant the mushrooming of multiple poles of power in shaping governance and economic transformation. Nevertheless, Singapore's unique development experience (i.e., the uninterrupted governance of a single dominant party and the initial ambivalence toward its small- and medium-sized domestic private firms) suggests that the state is to play a larger-than-usual role in governance affairs, not least in engaging with China. This can be witnessed in the more concerted attempt of mobilizing its cohort of small- and medium-sized private firms to counter the mid-1980s global economic downturn. A masterstroke in economic strategy, this move helped bolster Singapore's presence in the economies adjacent to Singapore, especially China. It also enhanced Singapore's previously dominant two-legged policy by injecting entrepreneurship of the small- and medium-sized private firms into the commercial power of the TNCs and GLCs, a point raised by Dahles (2008) and Tsui-Auch (2004).

More importantly, the above transformation demonstrates the flexibility of the 'networked state'. From an initial ambivalence toward the small- and medium-sized private firms, the state has since formulated collaborative, broad-based ties among key domestic actors to engage the Chinese economy effectively. Singapore's highly coordinated and closely integrated governance style can be witnessed in the institutions that were created before (such as the JCBC) as well as after the BRI's inception (such as Infrastructure Asia). These two types of institutions not only complement each other but also promote cooperation between the bureaucrats, politicians, TNCs, GLCs, small- and medium-sized private firms and business associations. These institutions have been conceptualized at different stages of China's economic growth. Although the Chinese economy has advanced considerably since its economic reforms started in 1978, Singapore — deploying its highly networked and mutually reinforcing governance model — has come in and partnered China at critical junctures of the latter's progress. This approach is likely to maintain, if not deepen, Singapore's strategic importance to the BRI (and by extension, China).

What then are the region-wide implications of this article? In a recent survey of Southeast Asian elites conducted by the Institute of Southeast Asian Studies ISEAS (2019), titled *The State of Southeast Asia: 2019 Survey Report*, a rising China has received mixed responses from the region. Most respondents (45.4%) think 'China will become a revisionist power with an intent to turn Southeast Asia into its sphere of influence', with the second most prevalent view regionally (35.3%) being 'China will provide alternative regional leadership in the wake of perceived US disengagement'. Less than one in ten respondents (8.9%) sees China as 'a benign and benevolent power'. With respect to the BRI, close to half of the respondents (47%) think it 'will bring ASEAN member states closer into China's orbit', and 35% acknowledges China's for giving loans to provide 'much needed infrastructure funding for countries in the region'. The overwhelming majority of the respondents (70%), however, opine that their government 'should be cautious in negotiating BRI projects, to avoid getting into unsustainable financial debts with China'.

Our findings suggest that such fears are perhaps overblown. From its initial engagement with China during the 'Reform and Opening-up' era to the contemporary period, Singapore has consistently found avenues to cooperate with the Chinese, showing that mutual benefits can be gained through joint projects and bilateral tie-ups while preserving its sovereign interests. These interests, in the meantime, have been embedded through institutions including the governmental (e.g., JCBC), semi-official (e.g., Business China) and business associations (e.g., SBF and SCCCI), thus providing multiple avenues for exchanges of ideas, resources and effective implantation at both the national and local levels. The revitalization of existing mechanisms and establishment of new ones have provided impetus for both continuity and change. Through these shared interests and mutually reinforcing institutions, the states of both China and Singapore are essentially networked under the framework of the BRI. More critically, Singapore's success thus far demonstrates that small states possess sufficient autonomy to manage the opportunities and challenges resulting from the BRI. Our article has also demonstrated how state-society collaboration (rather than confrontation) can be fostered in critical matters related to a rising China.

It is hoped that the framework put forth in this article as well as its arguments will stimulate future research, contextualizing this article's framework and arguments in different settings. For example, Brunei — Singapore's 'twin' in Southeast Asia — and its engagement with the BRI can be explored. Much like Singapore, Brunei boasts a small population size and promotes relatively open economic policies. Facing a slowing global economy, the Sultanate has also been actively courting Chinese capital to stimulate its economy. Another relevant economy to be studied is Malaysia, Singapore's northern neighbot. Sharing similar colonial heritage with Singapore and boasting a similar level of economic output, Malaysia too has been attemping to forge closer economic ties with the Chinese, not least in recent years. We believe that such a study will contribute to the further exploration of the ways through which other Southeast Asian states have formulated their respective economic strategies in response to the BRI.

Acknowledgment

Research for this article has been supported by the MOE Tier-2 AcRf "Transnational Knowledge Transfer & Dynamic Governance in Comparative Perspective" (MOE2016-T2-2-087) and an SUG from Nanyang Technological University (Integrating through Mobility: Cross-border Migration and Transnational Networks between China, Japan and Singapore, M4081383). The authors are solely responsible for the views and any remaining errors in this article.

ORCID

Hong Liu http://orcid.org/0000-0003-3328-8429

Guanie Lim http://orcid.org/0000-0001-9083-8883

References

Aalbers, M (2013). Neoliberalism is dead … Long live neoliberalism! *International Journal of Urban and Regional Research*, 37(3), 1083–1090.

Amsden, A (2003). *The Rise of 'The Rest': Challenges to the West from Late-Industrializing Economies*. New York: Oxford University Press.

Asian Infrastructure Investment Bank (2019). *Members and Prospective Members of the Bank*. Asian Infrastructure Investment Bank.

Au-Yong, R (2018). *PAP Unveils New Party Leadership with 4G Leaders at Helm; Tharman, Teo Chee Hean Among Heavyweights Who Step Down*. Singapore: Straits Times. https://www.straitstimes.com/politics/pap-unveils-new-party-leadership-with-4g-leaders-at-helm-tharman-teo-chee-hean-among.

Ba, AD (2019). China's 'Belt and Road' in Southeast Asia: Constructing the strategic narrative in Singapore. *Asian Perspective*, 43(2), 249–272.

BBC (2019). Dyson to move head office to Singapore. BBC, Accessed 23 September 2019, https://www.bbc.com/news/business-46962093.

Beeson, M (2016). Can ASEAN cope with China? *Journal of Current Southeast Asian Affairs*, 35(1), 5–28.

BizQ (2019). Singapore: Regional infrastructure summit: Plugging the financial gap. BizQ, Accessed 18 February 2020, https://bizq.sbf.org.sg/singapore-regional-infrastructure-summit-plugging-the-financial-gap/.

Business China (2018). Mission and vision. Business China, Accessed 19 August 2019, https://www.businesschina.org.sg/en/about-us/mission-and-vision/.

Caprotti, F (2014). Critical research on eco-cities? A walk through the Sino-Singapore Tianjin Eco-City, China. *Cities*, 36, 10–17.

Carroll, T and DSL Jarvis (2017). *Asia after the Developmental State: Disembedding Autonomy.* Cambridge: Cambridge University Press.

Castells, M (2000). *The Rise of the Network Society: The Information Age: Economy, Society and Culture*. Oxford: Blackwell.

Chan, KB and BK Ng (2000). Myths and misperceptions of ethnic Chinese capitalism. In *Chinese Business Networks: State, Economy and Culture*, KB Chan (ed.), pp. 285–302. Singapore: Prentice Hall & Nordic Institute of Asian Studies.

Chong, KP (2019). Singapore and China deepen cooperation to expand Chongqing's transport connectivity. Straits Times, Accessed 19 August, https://ie.enterprisesg.gov.sg/Media-Centre/News/2017/2/Singapore-and-China-deepen-cooperation-to-expand-Chongqing-s-transport-connectivity.

Dahles, H (2008). Entrepreneurship and the legacies of a developmental state: Singapore enterprises venturing across national borders. *Journal of Developmental Entrepreneurship*, 13(4), 485–508.

Enterprise Singapore (2017). China's belt and road initiative (BRI): What it means for Singapore companies. *Insighs*, 31, 1–28.

Flynn, A, L Yu, P Feindt and C Chen (2016). Eco-cities, governance and sustainable lifestyles: The case of the Sino-Singapore Tianjin Eco-City. *Habitat International*, 53, 78–86.

Infrastructure Asia (2019a). IA chats: 5 questions with Seth Tan, Executive Director of Infrastructure Asia, Accessed 6 September, https://www.infrastructureasia.org/Insights/IA-Chat-5-questions-interview-with-Seth-Tan.

Infrastructure Asia (2019b). *Making Infrastructure Happen*. Singapore: Infrastructure Asia.

ISEAS (2019). *The State of Southeast Asia: 2019 Survey Report*. Singapore: ISEAS-Yusof Ishak Institute.

Johnson, C (1982). *MITI and the Japanese Miracle: The Growth of Industrial Policy, 1925–1975*. Palo Alto, California: Stanford University Press.

Khoo, BT (2019). China's belt and road initiative: A view from a Mahathirist imaginary. *The Singapore Economic Review*, 1–20.

Khor, HE, C Poonpatpibul and SY Foo (2019). Belt and road initiative: A framework to address challenges and unlock potential for high-quality and inclusive growth. *The Singapore Economic Review*, 1–38.

Koh, J (2017). Singapore ready to work with China on belt and road: Lawrence Wong. Channel NewsAsia, Accessed 23 September 2019, https://www.channelnewsasia.com/news/singapore/singapore-ready-to-work-with-china-on-belt-and-road-lawrence-8854738.

Kor, KB (2015). Singapore among 50 nations signing AIIB charter. Straits Times, Accessed 23 September 2019, https://www.straitstimes.com/business/banking/singapore-among-50-nations-signing-aiib-charter.

Kratz, A and D Pavlićević (2019). Norm-making, norm-taking or norm-shifting? A case study of Sino–Japanese competition in the Jakarta–Bandung high-speed rail project. *Third World Quarterly*, 40(6), 1107–1126.

Lee, PC (2015). PSA expands port network in China with new project in Guangxi Beibu Gulf Region. The Edge Singapore, Accessed 20 February 2020, https://www.theedgesingapore.com/psa-expands-port-network-china-new-project-guangxi-beibu-gulf-region.

Lim, G (2017). China's 'Going Out' strategy in Southeast Asia: Case studies of the automobile and electronics sectors. *China: An International Journal*, 15(4), 157–178.

Lim, L (2018). ASEAN-China trade to receive a boost with southern transport corridor: Chan Chun Sing. Channel NewsAsia, Accessed 23 September 2019, https://www.channelnewsasia.com/news/business/asean-china-trade-to-receive-a-boost-with-southern-transport-10661022.

Liou, C-S (2014). Rent-seeking at home, capturing market share abroad: The domestic determinants of the transnationalization of China State Construction Engineering Corporation. *World Development*, 54, 220–231.

Liu, H (2018). Transnational Asia and regional networks: Toward a new political economy of East Asia. *East Asian Community Review*, 1(1), 33–47.

Liu, H, H Zhang and X Fan (2016). Overseas Chinese Business Associations in Southeast Asia and the construction of the belt and road initiative. *Southeast Asian Affairs*, 4, 1–10.

Liu, H and T Wang (2018). China and the Singapore model: Perspectives from the mid-level cadres and implications for transnational knowledge transfer. *The China Quarterly*, 236, 988–1011.

Liu, H and G Lim (2019). The political economy of a rising China in Southeast Asia: Malaysia's response to the belt and road initiative. *Journal of Contemporary China*, 28(116), 216–231.

Low, L (1990). State entrepreneurship. In *Local Entrepreneurship in Singapore: Private and State*, TY Lee and L Low (eds.), pp. 150–175. Singapore: Institute of Policy Studies.

Low, L (2003). Singapore Inc: A success story. *South African Journal of International Affairs*, 10(1), 49–63.

Low, L (2005). Entrepreneurship development in Ireland and Singapore. *Journal of the Asia Pacific Economy*, 10(1), 116–138.

Lye, LF (2014). Suzhou industrial park: Going beyond a commercial project. In *Advancing Singapore-China Economic Relations*, S-H Saw and J Wong (eds.), pp. 62–93. Singapore: Institute of Southeast Asian Studies.

Ministry of National Development (2017). Keynote address by Minister Lawrence Wong at the Singapore Regional Business Forum. Ministry of National Development, Accessed 23 September 2019, https://www.mnd.gov.sg/newsroom/speeches/view/keynote-address-by-minister-lawrence-wong-at-the-singapore-regional-business-forum.

Ng, JY (2019). The real reason Dyson is swapping Brexit Britain for Singapore. *South China Morning Post*, 23 September 2019.

Ohmae, K (1995). *The End of the Nation State: The Rise of Regional Economies*. New York: The Free Press.

Oxford Business Group (2018). Seth Tan Keng Hwee, Executive Director of Infrastructure Asia, Accessed 6 September, https://oxfordbusinessgroup.com/views/seth-tan-keng-hwee-executive-director-infrastructure-asia.

Pell, M and T Mitchell (2017). Asia's $26tn infrastructure gap threatens growth, ADB warns. *Financial Times*, February 27.

Prime Minister's Office Singapore (2014). Transcript of Prime Minister Lee Hsien Loong's speech at the 11th China-ASEAN EXPO Opening Ceremony on 16 September 2014. Prime Minister's Office, Accessed 23 September 2019, https://www.pmo.gov.sg/Newsroom/transcript-prime-minister-lee-hsien-loongs-speech-11th-china-asean-expo-opening.

Prime Minister's Office Singapore (2018). 14th Joint Council for Bilateral Cooperation (JCBC) and related meetings in Singapore, Accessed 19 August, https://www.pmo.gov.sg/Newsroom/14th-joint-council-bilateral-cooperation-jcbc-and-related-meetings-singapore.

Rahim, LZ and MD Barr (2019). *The Limits of Authoritarian Governance in Singapore's Developmental State*. Petaling Jaya: Strategic Information and Research Development Centre and Palgrave Macmillan.

Ruiji Touzi (2014). Wu Zuodong: Xinjiapo Touzi Qingdao Zouxiang Gao Zengzhi Xiangmu [Goh Chok Tong: Singapore invests in Qingdao to promote high value-added projects]. Shenzhen: Ruiji Touzi.

Saw, S-H (2014). Evolution of Singapore-China economic relations. In *Advancing Singapore-China Economic Relations*, S-H Saw and J Wong (eds.), pp. 1–30. Singapore: Institute of Southeast Asian Studies.

Shin, J-S (2005). The role of the state in the increasingly globalized economy: Implications for Singapore. *The Singapore Economic Review*, 50(1), 103–116.

Sim, D (2019). Singapore will continue not to take sides between US and China, says PM Lee Hsien Loong. *South China Morning Post*, 19 August.

Singapore Business Federation (2016). Lianhe Zaobao and SBF jointly launch 'One Belt, One Road' Portal. Singapore Business Federation, Accessed 23 September 2019, https://www.sbf.org.sg/lianhe-zaobao-and-singapore-business-federation-jointly-launch-one-belt-one-road-portal.

Singapore Business Federation (2018). *National Business Survey 2017/2018 Summary Report: The Changing Face of Singapore Businesses*. Singapore: Singapore Business Federation.

Straits Times (2017). Singapore firm investing $206m to build Guangxi Logistics Park. Straits Times, Accessed 24 February 2020, https://www.straitstimes.com/asia/east-asia/spore-firm-investing-206m-to-build-guangxi-logistics-park.

Surbana Jurong (2019a). Surbana Jurong and REDAS to collaborate on enhancing developer's knowledge in digitalisation and smart sustainability solutions, Accessed 18 February 2020, https://surbanajurong.com/resources/news-press-releases/surbana-jurong-and-redas-to-collaborate-on-enhancing-developers-knowledge-in-digitalisation-and-smart-sustainability-solutions/.

Surbana Jurong (2019b). Singapore's Surbana Jurong and China's Silk Road Fund form co-investment platform for infrastructure projects in Southeast Asia, Accessed 6 September, https://surbanajurong.com/resources/news-press-releases/singapores-surbana-jurong-and-chinas-silk-road-fund-form-co-investment-platform-for-infrastructure-projects-in-southeast-asia/.

Tan, C-Z and HW-C Yeung (2000). The regionalization of Chinese business networks: A study of Singaporean firms in Hainan, China. *The Professional Geographer*, 52(3), 437–454.

Tan, KS and M Bhaskaran (2015). The role of the state in Singapore: Pragmatism in pursuit of growth. *The Singapore Economic Review*, 60(3), 1550030.

Tan, M (2014). 21 Countries sign MOU to set up Asian Infrastructure Investment Bank. *Business Times*, 23 September.

Teo, EC (2019). Singapore-China Economic Collaboration 2.0. *The Singapore Economic Review*, 1–11.

Teo, SS (2019). Zhang Songshen: Bendizhongxiaoqiye Yingzhuazhu Yidaiyilujudajiyu Xinjiapo Touzi Qingdao Zouxiang Gao Zengzhi Xiangmu [Teo Siong Seng: Local small- and medium-sized firms should grasp opportunities from the belt and road], Accessed 19 February 2020, https://www.zaobao.com.sg/sme/finance/story20190628-967996.

The New Paper (2017). Singapore firm investing $206m to build Guangxi Logistics Park. The New Paper, Accessed 24 February 2020, https://www.straitstimes.com/asia/east-asia/spore-firm-investing-206m-to-build-guangxi-logistics-park.

Tong, S and TY Kong (2018). Singapore's role in the belt and road initiative. In *Securing the Belt and Road Initiative: Risk Assessment, Private Security and Special Insurances Along the New Wave of Chinese Outbound Investments*, A Arduino and X Gong (eds.), pp. 63–80. Singapore: Springer.

Tsui-Auch, LS (2004). The professionally managed family-ruled enterprise: Ethnic Chinese business in Singapore. *Journal of Management Studies*, 41(4), 693–723.

Wade, R (2003). *Governing the Market: Economic Theory and the Role of Government in East Asian Industrialization*. Princeton: Princeton University Press.

Williams, A (2017). Surbana Jurong sets up joint venture with china highway in design, consultancy services. *Straits Times*, 23 September.

Wilson, J (2017). The evolution of China's Asian Infrastructure Investment Bank: From a revisionist to status-seeking agenda. *International Relations of the Asia-Pacific*, 19(1), 147–176.

Wolf, M (2004). *Why Globalization Works*. Yale: Yale University Press.

Xi, J (2014). *The Governance of China*. Beijing: Foreign Languages Press.

Ye, M (2019). Fragmentation and mobilization: Domestic politics of the belt and road in China. *Journal of Contemporary China*, 28(119), 696–711.

Yoshimatsu, H (2018). New dynamics in Sino-Japanese Rivalry: Sustaining infrastructure development in Asia. *Journal of Contemporary China*, 27(113), 719–734.

Zeng, DZ (2019). Building a competitive city through integrating into global value chains: The case of the Sino–Singapore Suzhou Industrial Park. *China: An International Journal*, 17(2), 164–180.

Zhao, S (2020). *China's New Global Strategy: The Belt and Road Initiative (BRI) and Asian Infrastructure Investment Bank (AIIB)*. Volume 1. Oxon: Routledge.

Chapter 13

HOW DO INVESTORS RESPOND TO TERRITORIAL DISPUTES? EVIDENCE FROM THE SOUTH CHINA SEA AND IMPLICATIONS ON PHILIPPINES ECONOMIC STRATEGY†

ALVIN CAMBA*

Korbel School of International Studies
University of Denver
Denver, Colorado
alvin.camba@du.edu

JANICA MAGAT

Department of Political Science
Texas A&M University
College Station, Texas
janicamagat@tamu.edu

Published Online 24 March 2020

How do territorial disputes affect bilateral foreign direct investment (FDI) between claimant states? Using a difference model, we find that a regime's position on the South China Sea (SCS) significantly impacts Chinese FDI. We used a novel dataset on firm registrations in the Philippines, finding that the annual number of new firm entrants with Chinese investment significantly increases when maritime border disputes are stabilized. In contrast, we observe that conflictual relations in the maritime borders tend to decrease the number of new firms. We also notice that disputes do not influence FDI from non-claimant states.

Keywords: Foreign Direct Investment; Territorial Disputes; South China Sea; Philippines; Development.

JEL Classification Codes: F00, O10, Z00

1. Introduction

How do territorial disputes affect bilateral foreign direct investment (FDI) between claimant states? Territorial disputes, defined as inter-state conflict over the allocation of sovereignty over a territory or the distribution of resources in a common resource pool, are still frequent occurrences in global politics. Most of the literature on the political economy of conflict has focused on the effect of FDI on the onset and management of disputes and the adverse impact of militarized conflict on economic integration (e.g., Schultz, 2015). However, the impact of inter-state conflict on FDI has received far less attention. Existing works on the subject either find mixed results or conflate territorial disputes with inter-state

*Corresponding author.

†This article originally appeared in *The Singapore Economic Review*, **66**(1), pp. 243–267

conflict (e.g., Woodward and Rolfe, 1993; Olibe and Crumbley, 1997). The key question that these studies ultimately overlook is the impact of territorial disputes on the FDI, specifically on the firms of the claimant state and other investors. As such, our paper sets out to address the following questions. First, does the end of the dispute or the consensus on relatively well-defined borders or boundaries lead to an uptick in FDI? Second, how does the onset of disputes affect FDI between the claimant states? Finally, what is the impact of the disputes or the stabilization of borders on the FDI of other states? Alongside these questions, we also assess the importance of other political and economic factors that impact FDI and their attending implications on Philippine economic strategy.

Our paper examines the effects of the People's Republic of China's (PRC) increasingly assertive territorial assertions on their FDI. China's disputes, ranging from Senkaku Islands, a group of small islets under Japanese suzerainty since 1972, to the South China Sea (SCS), accompany the massive surge of Chinese capital exports to the global economy (Camba and Hung, 2018). The Chinese Communist Party (CCP) has resolved most of their disputes during the Cold War era. However, in recent decades, China's increasing political and military power along with its rapidly accumulating FDI, which surged to a total of $US 1.2 trillion in 2015 alongside Hong Kong's own $1.3 trillion, has become a cause of concern for policy makers, political elites and social movements in the developing world. Many of these actors now feel that they must choose between sovereignty and economic development.

Our paper specifically examines the territorial disputes between China and the Philippines over the SCS or the West Philippine Sea. To do so, we generated an original dataset on the annual number of newly registered firms with foreign investors since the 1990s until 2018. We used the Philippines Security Exchange Commission's (SEC) company registration system, which houses the records of millions of firms since the 1930s, to count the number of newly established firms with Chinese investors from 1990 to 2018. We also acquired comparable data on the number of new firms with Japanese, American, Taiwanese and Singaporean investors. Since firms only enter the SEC registration system once they undergo the registration process, which entails hiring lawyers, filing documents and paying initial capital requirements, the database records real time firm behavior.[1] The SEC system's trackability bypasses the problems of conventional FDI inflow-outflow data. The annual inflow and outflow of investments measure is noisy as it includes remitted payments to prior commitment, making it difficult to disentangle the impact of the disputes or other political processes.

The Philippines is a functioning democracy with an electoral system that mandates electoral turnover every six years and bans Presidential re-election. Each election brings a new leader with potentially different coalitions and attitudes toward the SCS. A new regime every six years places a quasi-randomized test on the relationship between territorial disputes and FDI. This relationship would be much more difficult to capture in non-democratic states like Vietnam and Malaysia, where leaders and parties stay in power for decades. Furthermore, the size of the territorial claims of Malaysia, Indonesia and Brunei are far smaller than that of the Philippines. Vietnam, whose claim would be

[1] The SEC database includes not only the name of the firms, nationality of the investors, and the size of the board, but also numerous other firm-level characteristics. One crucial datapoint is the firm's monetary deposits in the Philippines, which assure the firm's minimum level of investment in the country, making the database robust.

comparable in size, suffers from the problem of limited electoral turnover. Choosing the Philippines, with data that spans 28 years, controls for the same size of the claim and the likely resource at stake.

We find that the position of the Philippines towards the SCS significantly affects Chinese FDI. We use the SEC dataset alongside comparable data from other foreign investors in concert with variables that control for economic growth, political risks and institutional strength to assess the impact of disputes on Chinese FDI. We draw from Max Weber's work on calculability to develop a framework that highlights the role of uncertainty on territorial disputes and investment decisions. Using a difference model, we estimate the effect of a regime's position on the annual number of new firm entrants. We observe that the regime's position on the SCS has a significant impact on Chinese FDI. We find that the annual number of new firms with Chinese investment significantly increases when maritime border disputes are stabilized. In contrast, we observe that conflictual relations in the maritime borders tend to decrease the annual number of new firms. We note that the disputes do not influence FDI from other states, specifically the United States, Japan, Singapore and Taiwan. By finding that a regime's SCS position affects Chinese FDI, this paper provides statistical backing to the argument that a host country's position in the disputed borders impacts Chinese investments.

2. The South China Sea Disputes and Key Empirical Questions

The Philippines has vacillated over the SCS towards the PRC since the 1970s. As a result, the Philippine economic strategy towards the PRC, ranging from FDI acquisition and aid to people-to-people ties, has also been widely inconsistent. Ferdinand Marcos' administration (1965–1985) firstly recognized the PRC over Taiwan, holding talks with Deng Xiaoping to temporarily avoid any discussion of the disputed areas. However, Filipino leaders have always believed their rightful claim over the disputed areas.[2] During the post-Marcos era, President Fidel V. Ramos (1992–1998) fervently defended Mischief Reef from PRC encroachment (Meyer, 1996), leading to a weeklong maritime standoff. After the interrupted regime of Joseph Estrada (1998–2001), that of Gloria Macapagal-Arroyo (2001–2010) became the first Philippine administration to proactively recognize China's inevitable role in the Asia-Pacific Region. Arroyo set aside her country's territorial claims in the SCS in order to strengthen bilateral ties, culminating in more than 20 major investments from Chinese state-oriented enterprises (SOE) and private firms. A number of these major commitments included anomalous procedures rife with rent seeking opportunities. Due to elite and social mobilization, all but one of these major projects were canceled by the end of Arroyo's term (Camba, 2018). However, the number of state and private investments increased despite domestic political conflict.

In contrast to the Arroyo administration, the Aquino government maintained a hardline, anti-China approach in the disputes. In April 2012, a Philippine Navy plane spotted eight Chinese fishing vessels near the Scarborough Shoal, prompting Aquino to order the BRN Gregorio del Pilar to move in the vicinity. The initial encounter snowballed into a foreign policy

[2] Interviews with PDP-Laban, Liberal Party, and Nationalist Party members between 2016–2018.

issue that impacted the entirety of Aquino's presidency. In response to the naval standoff, Aquino bitterly defied the PRC territorial claims over the seas, leading to a reaffirmation of the Philippines' stake in the SCS and the strengthened role of the United States in Southeast Asian affairs (De Castro, 2014). The Philippines took the disputes to international arbitration, which China rejected. In 2016, The Hague Arbitration declared that the disputed areas between the Philippines and China should be recognized under the jurisdiction of the Philippines. Despite the verdict, Beijing unilaterally refused to recognize the ruling.

When Rodrigo Duterte (2016) became president, he gave up the arbitration claim of the Philippines and insisted on maintaining "the SCS" name over that of "the West Philippines Sea," placating the PRC. In October 2016, his state visit acquired an earmarked $24 billion worth of Chinese FDI and official development assistance (ODA) for the Philippines. Both governments signed multiple memoranda of understanding (MOUs), leading to an expectation of increasing Chinese capital — FDI, development finance, and aid — in the Philippines through Chinese SOE and major private firms. In 2017, Duterte and China agreed on the Sino-Philippines joint energy cooperation, an offshoot of Arroyo's own Joint Maritime Seismic Undertaking (JMSU). On their part, China lifted the ban on Philippine banana exports, committed to increasing tourist travels to the Philippines, and began to encourage state-to-state business matching to induce investments (Ramirez, 2017).

The vacillating position of Philippine administrations on the SCS brings up several important empirical and conceptual questions. First, to what degree does the stabilization of the maritime borders, as exemplified by the Arroyo (2001–2010) and Duterte (2016) regimes, induce Chinese FDI? Second, what is the impact of the disputes, which occurred during the pre-Arroyo (1990–2001) and Aquino (2010–2016) regimes, on Chinese FDI? Third, how are other major investors across these administrations affected by the disputes? Alongside these questions, two other issues linger: how important is a regime's position towards the disputed seas relative to other factors, such as the Philippine macroeconomic fundamentals, trade, and bureaucratic strength? Furthermore, what are the policy implications from our paper's findings on the Philippine economic strategy towards China?

The first three questions are vital because of a broader literature on the varieties of Chinese capital, which argues that Chinese state firms have encompassing political, social and economic motivations (Lee, 2018). If Chinese firms have multiple goals, how important are the disputes? Firms that rely heavily on subsidies and political support from the Chinese state — central, provincial, or city governments — may be discouraged from investing if the disputes encourage the Chinese state to limit subsidies and political support. However, there are firms that will continue to invest regardless of state support because of other factors such as strong host country linkages and expected profits. In other words, while firm response will vary greatly, what remains unanswered is how, on average, do Chinese firms respond to the disputes. In addition, does the dispute affect the firms of non-claimant states? Previous literature finds that even if firms of the claimant states withdraw (Schultz, 2015), firms of non-claimant states can compensate. In other words, is there a surge of non-Chinese foreign firms in the Philippines during the disputes?

The fourth question is crucial because, as seen in the descriptive data, Chinese FDI continued to increase despite the Philippines' stances on the disputes. As Camba (2017) shows, the amount of FDI during the Aquino administration surpassed that of Arroyo despite the territorial issues. While major SOE investments, development finance and construction contracts decreased (Camba, 2019a), the number of firms and amount of FDI increased, partly due to the marginal improvement of Philippine administrative-legal capacity. How important were the disputes during Aquino in addition to these other governance and economic factors to Chinese FDI? Put in another way, can the surge of Chinese FDI during Duterte's administration be attributed to his reconciliatory approach towards China, especially when controlling for a robust economic environment that the Aquino regime left? The final question brings up the issue of the opportunity cost of missing out on Chinese capital. Our interviews with several security analysts over the years reflect the widespread skepticism on the development potential of Chinese FDI and aid, despite initial statistical evidence suggesting otherwise (Bluhm *et al.*, 2018).

3. Literature Review

3.1. *The political economy of conflict*

The relationship between conflict and FDI inflows forms a major literature. For instance, Schneider and Frey (1985) find that political instability, which includes inter-state conflict, decreases the likelihood for FDI, trade and other economic engagements. Similarly, Globerman and Shapiro (2003) examined US FDI in 143 countries across three years, finding that political violence decreases the amount of FDI inflows that a country receives. Nigh (1986, p. 104) also posits that whether companies invest or not depends largely upon the sending country's general perception of "conflictive inter-nation events" in the host country. His findings show that territorial conflict decreases US FDI while cooperation increases it. Other scholars have contested these findings. Olibe and Crumbley (1997, p. 346) argue that there is no consistent correlation between political instability and FDI inflows. Overall, works that focus on the impact of disputes on FDI have led to mixed results across a wide variety of tests, pooled datasets and periods (e.g., Woodward and Rolfe, 1993; Sethi *et al.*, 2003).

Li's (2006, 2008) intervention advances the literature by identifying that the measure for conflict relies on a broader political stability index, which conflates different types of international and domestic factors. Here, Li categorizes political instability into three different types: civil war, inter-state wars and transnational terrorism. He also uses a variable that measures anticipated and unanticipated political violence. Afterwards, Li divided the outcome into investment location and overall FDI inflow. While there are interesting observations on civil war and terrorism, more relevant to the paper is Li's findings that unanticipated definition of inter-state war reduces the likelihood that the disputing countries will be chosen as an investment location. However, Li finds that there is no effect on the overall amount of investment that goes into the country.

Nonetheless, Li's inter-state conflict ignores territorial disputes. While disputes over land and maritime borders can easily escalate into inter-state wars (Olibe and Crumbley, 1997), they are two distinct concepts that deserve their own analysis. Here, scholars have generated a territorial dispute dataset (Huth and Allee, 2002), which has recently been merged with spatial data (Schultz, 2015). In recent years, the most relevant work is Lee and

Mitchell's (2012) examination of FDI's effects on territorial disputes, arguing that increasing levels of monadic, bilateral and global FDI inflows reduce the likelihood of disputes or militarized conflict over the borders. The authors point to two mechanisms that reduce conflict, specifically the costs of violence on FDI inflows and the signaling effect of FDI, which would increase the chances for peace agreements to be struck. While their findings are convincing, the question of the impact of disputes on FDI remains unanswered.

3.2. *Economic statecraft and South China Sea*

Economic statecraft, defined as the use of economic tools to achieve foreign policy goals, has been the foundation of the SCS literature. Scholars focus on Beijing's grand strategy (Norris, 2016), which international relations scholars often extend to the "Going Out" Policy in 1999 and the Belt and Road Initiative (BRI). More recent works on China's SCS disputes explore why and when states pursue coercion. In that vein, Zhang (2019) argues that states pursue economic coercion when (1) the existing cost for military coercion is high; (2) it deters other states from bandwagoning; and (3) it corrects existing imbalances.

There are other approaches to understanding the SCS disputes, ranging from the historical disagreements, regional ramifications, and the perspectives of various countries. Kaplan (2015) compares China's quest for hegemony to the American imperialism in the Caribbean. Hayton (2014) examines China's SCS historical claim, arguing that it rests on carefully manufactured fictions about China's history. Situating the SCS and China's *Charm Offensive*, Kurlantzick (2006) examines how trade, aid and investment forward China's interests in the developing world. With a distinct focus on Southeast Asia, the three authors implicitly or explicitly point out that Chinese state bodies are willingly engaging in rent-seeking and corruption to forward China's geopolitical goals.

There is a subliterature on China and the Philippines over the SCS. For example, comparing the impact of Chinese economic sanctions in the Philippines and Vietnam, Ravindran (2012, p. 111) points out that the "importance to the Philippines of an economic relationship with China, especially in the case of FDI from China, at a time of slow GDP growth cannot be overstated." He concludes that while the Philippines is less vulnerable to import and export restrictions, Vietnam is less likely to give into Chinese demands because of the anti-China sentiments of the population. As a response to the $24 billion commitment that Duterte acquired, De Castro (2019) argues that Duterte's conciliatory turn demonstrated a simple reasoning for Southeast Asian political elites: play nice with Beijing, gain investment and aid. Despite their contributions, these works suffer from two problems: (1) they assume that Chinese FDI is directly controlled by the CCP, ignoring the variation and complexity of China's capital exports; and (2) they tend to descriptively point out what China has done and can do, but do little to systematically test the effect of territorial disputes on Chinese FDI.

4. Conceptual Framework

Before discussing the framework, it is crucial to point out alternative explanations. We do not explicitly disagree with previous explanations, but rather our work aims to nuance these specific arguments, accounting for outcome, timing and variation. First, drawing from the literature on economic statecraft and the impact of inter-state conflict on FDI (Li, 2008), there is an alternative mechanism that the Chinese government limited FDI in the Philippines (e.g., De Castro, 2019). At the height of the SCS dispute, the PRC decided to cut government-to-government (G2G) financing to the Aquino's Philippines, sanctioned banana imports and limited tourism. All of which were lifted when Duterte won the presidency. However, there were no explicit policies from Beijing that stopped their firms from investing. A key reason is China's decentralized mode of economic governance (Hung, 2008), which limits the ability of the Chinese government to rein in the behavior of firms and investors. Chinese state and private firms also have existing investments in the Philippines, which would make banning subsequent investments harmful to China as well. During the Aquino administration, China also continued to import massive amounts of nickel and iron inputs (Camba, 2015), which would make the two states interdependent despite the political disagreements. All these make a direct ban empirically false in the Philippine case.

Another alternative mechanism is that the Philippine government limited Chinese FDI. At the height of the disputes, Aquino refused to renew the visas of engineers from the State Grid Corporation of China (SGCC) and politicians were grandstanding against China.[3] However, there were no overt or direct policies that limited or targeted Chinese investments during the disputes. Some economic sectors were protected against foreign capital, such as infrastructure projects, which were monopolized by Philippine firms, and the banning of new mining applications, which protected incumbent firms. However, these policies targeted all foreign firms, Chinese or otherwise. The mechanism's alternative explanation is that because Chinese deals involved rent-seeking practices (O'Neill, 2018; Wong, 2019), Philippine democratic institutions or level of public accountability caused the cancellation of major Chinese construction contracts. However, this assumes the effectiveness of Philippine institutions. Area studies scholars and country-level indicators show that the Philippines suffer from low-levels of public accountability and the selective use of institutions. For foreign aid and investments, many controversial non-Chinese projects continued, and Philippines democratic institutions largely serve the rich and the powerful.[4]

[3] To our knowledge, no one has made this claim. However, this is a possible argument, which draws from Wellhausen's work (2015). She argues that governments break contracts with foreign firms under several political conditions: (1) absence of a supply chain to organizes collective action; (2) the limited power of the firm's national government; and (3) the ability of the government to replace the firm.

[4] These explanations suffer from selection bias and an idealistic understanding of Philippine politics. While there are datasets that capture the Philippines' marginally higher accountability rate than that of other non-democratic states, the accuracy of these data needs to be questioned. Area specialists have documented patronage politics and democratic deficit in the country for decades (Bello *et al.*, 2004; Hutchcroft and Rocamora, 2012). There are widely documented cases on non-Chinese foreign mining firms that promote environmental degradation, hire paramilitary organizations, and subvert public institutions (see Camba, 2015; Nem Singh and Camba, 2016). In another broader dataset, non-Chinese foreign firms were responsible for 57 unfair trade, labor, and land practices (Temper *et al.*, 2015). All these works make the characterization of the Philippines' high level of accountability or democratic checks problematic. (Bello *et al.*, 2014) In other words, why were these non-Chinese foreign firms relatively immune from democratic institutions or public accountability? Alternatively Camba (2018), shows that elites in the Philippines banded together and used the democratic institutions to derail Chinese investments, whereas non-Chinese investments have been left unscathed. This brings up the alternative argument that non-Chinese firms are socially embedded and know how to maneuver Philippine institutions. Indeed, this point links up well with the literature on "socially acceptable" corruption by Western firms (Hoang, 2018).

As such, the alternative explanation that the host government limited foreign investments for accountability reasons is not applicable in this context.

We suggest that rather than resulting from the Chinese government's imposition, or the Philippine government's unilateral decision, or democratic institutional effects on investments, disputes generated uncertainty that diminished the incentives of would-be Chinese investors.[5] We argue that Chinese investors, like all other investors, depend on the predictability and calculability of the economy.[6] To understand this further, we draw from Max Weber's *Social Categories of Economic Action*, where he connects bureaucracies, rationalization and actions of the capital holders. Weber (1978) argues that predictability and calculability are necessary for modern capitalism to succeed. He speaks about the need for firms to quantify and predict the net worth of their enterprises and assets. In other words, firms need to know whether or not a venture is worth investing in to generate profit. This presumes some degree of calculability, wherein the firm needs to "control" the area of economic production as much as they can.

To maximize calculability, firms impose ruthless, impersonal and modern organizational rules. However, an even more important aspect is the relationship between firms and politics. Here, Weber addresses the interdependence of the modern economy and a legal order of the state, as well the state's dependence on the modern economy. Weber argues that the security of the property through the rule of law and the predictability of the state through its rules and procedures make politics calculable for firms. Indeed, state laws are crucial because of how they universalize spheres of life into specific standards and procedures. The protection of private property excludes value-laden reasoning of sentiments and nationalism in favor of formal rationality, which describes investments and decisions based upon possible economic returns.

Weber's insights apply to the SCS disputes in two ways. First, the disputes may cause the Chinese state authorities — central, provincial, or local — to reverse the subsidies or political support to invest in the Philippines. While some firms can still invest regardless of the state's support, the political and financial support are important considerations for less wealthy and smaller Chinese firms. Major private and state firms need political support in case property expropriation or politicization occurs. As Weber argues, the calculability of investments is crucial for firms to predict profitability and losses. If the host country disrespects the rights of Chinese firms, subsidies can offset the monetary losses while political support accords the firms some leverage over the host state. If there are no disputes, the Chinese state authorities can freely accord political and financial support to

[5] Major national SOEs, often located in strategic sectors, are partly funded by the Chinese policy banks, and respond largely to the Central Politburo (CP). The biggest private firms are also reliant on the CP. While these firms are massive and have enormous capital, they only comprise 1 to 2 percent of the overall number of Chinese firms (Ang, 2016). Research has revealed that China has relied on decentralized authoritarianism, featuring competing Chinese provincial, local, and city governments (Hung, 2008; Ang, 2016). Chinese firms compete further when it comes to investing outside, relying on subsidy from various government bodies or private funding from various sources. As a result, provincial governments and offshore financial centers affect investment behavior, which would sometimes be indifferent or contradictory to the Central Government (Gu *et al.*, 2016).

[6] Similarly, the political economy of conflict has observed uncertainty's similar effects. For instance, Simmons (2005: 827) argues that territorial conflict, as a form of conflictual relationship, limit property rights, derail jurisdictional control, and create policy uncertainty, thereby generating a decrease in bilateral trade and FDI opportunities.

firms. The Central Government generates funding and subsidies for major construction contracts and investment ventures, often taken up by centralized SOE and major private firms in the host country's strategic sectors. Smaller state and private firms acquire subsidies and support at the provincial and city levels. These smaller firms would not only follow the direction of major firms, becoming suppliers of, or participating firms in, forward- and backward- industries, but also use their own political and economic networks to expand in the Philippines.[7]

The second source of uncertainty comes from the host country actors, such as the Philippine state, regional governments, or private actors. Should disputes erupt, host country actors may have a reason not to enforce contracts, honor agreements and accord protection to the investor. As Weber argues, the host state's willingness to secure and apply private property protection to firms create a sense of predictability. If the host country is unwilling to apply these laws because of the disputes, firms would not be able to predict the worth and profitability of their assets. The risk of property expropriation increases as politics and conflict intensify. As a result, uncertainty makes it difficult to sell the project to investors and to calculate the overall amount of potential returns to the project. Without the disputes, state and private actors in both the sending and host countries have incentives to credibly work together for mutual gain. Following Weber, certainty makes it easier for firms to acquire investors and plan their capital allocation accordingly.[8] The above theoretical discussion leads us to two main hypotheses that will be tested using a novel dataset on the annual number of new firms with Chinese FDI.

Hypothesis #1. *Stabilizing the maritime borders increases the likelihood for Chinese investors to invest in the Philippines.*

Hypothesis #2. *Maritime border disputes with China decrease the likelihood for Chinese firms to invest in the Philippines.*

We also examine the impact of disputes on firms from non-claimant states. The literature states three possible outcomes. First, competing investors might increase their FDI inflows in order to compensate for the hypothetical loss of the claimant state's FDI. As Schultz (2015) finds, there is no relationship between disputes and FDI because monadic FDI decreases tend to be compensated by global FDI increases. Second, disputes can also lead to capital flight or the mass exodus of foreign capital out of the disputed country. However, this impact depends on whether disputes lead to militarized conflict. Finally, disputes generate improved market signaling, which would mean that FDI from other states are careful not to over or underinvest, allowing market drivers to decide. We expect that territorial disputes only affect the FDI of other states if and only if the host country is

[7] For example, in anticipation of the major construction contracts in Duterte's Philippines, smaller state and private firms in the adjacent sectors of steel, real estate, and wholesale-retail were also established (Camba, 2018).

[8] The sending and host country governments may give subsidies to state owned and private companies to invest or knit together aid packages to finance projects in the host country (Moravcsik, 2013).

engaged in a militarized conflict.[9] According to Weber, there is no extenuating reason for the host country to exclude the firms of non-claimant states from private property protection. As there are no militarized disputes between the Philippines and China, we do not expect firms from non-claimant states to be affected by the SCS disputes. Firms from non-claimant states have no reason to expect their sending country's support to stop or be potentially targeted by the host state.

Hypothesis #3. *Maritime border disputes with China have no effect on the FDI of other states in the Philippines.*

5. Research Design

5.1. *Annual number of newly registered firms from the SEC*

If a firm or a group of investors wants to creates a corporation in the Philippines, they must register with the SEC, which has held records of millions of firms since the 1930s. We drew from the SEC company registrations system to count the number of firms with Chinese, American, Japanese, Taiwanese and Singaporean investments. The SEC data only tracks actualized investments because of the initial capital registration and bank deposit requirements. Firms are required to transfer money from their own accounts to a Philippine bank and acquire Philippines-based assets, assuring the transfer of capital from foreign entities to the Philippines. There is the share-commitments category, which means that the investors are required to pay a minimum 20% of the total worth of the firm during the registration. Bigger or more liquid corporations can pay more than 20% or fulfill the full amount. Though firms do not invest or pay for the entire commitment category at the start, the yearly amounts that foreign citizens or firms invest are remitted to the Philippine government.[10] In the subsequent years after forming the firm, the board of directors can require the investors to fulfill the entire worth of the commitment. Put simply, the initial capital requirements and the arduous registration process make the annual registration an imperfect but the best proxy for the interests of foreign investors who want to establish their businesses in the Philippines.

We opted to use the annual number of new firms to indicate the increasing number of partnerships between the Philippines and foreign businesses. Unlike FDI inflow-outflow data from the Bangko Sentral ng Pilipinas (BSP, 2018), the annual number of newly established firms is a better measure for whether or not territorial disputes affected the investment decision. Aggregate FDI inflow or stock data could increase regardless of the disputes because of preexisting investors, whose preexisting assets and projects could simply require further financing, which would register as investment increases in the data. Furthermore, the sudden surge of inflow or lack of FDI could simply be explained by the sudden need to infuse capital, or the lack of necessity to remit capital at that stage because

[9] Militarized disputes block off trade routes, damages property, and take human lives. In contrast, overt posturing and gradual buildup characterize non-militarized disputes.

[10] The minimum amount of capital that needs to be invested varies across different sectors.

of previous decisions.[11] Here, the better proxy is the annual number of new firms with FDI. If territorial disputes generate enough uncertainty, firms planning to acquire new assets, or a minority share can still reverse their decision. Should investors decide to cancel their plans, their names and shares would not appear in the SEC data. In other words, the annual number of newly established firms' best captures whether or not territorial disputes affect investment decisions.[12]

While not all firms that register in the SEC become businesses, most of them eventually do. While the SEC registration process would take about two weeks to an entire month, preparing the SEC documents and requirements alone tends to be a gruesome ordeal, requiring at least a few months for a law firm to complete. After obtaining the SEC registration, corporations need to attain local-, city- and regional-level business permits, which would also take a month or two. Some sectors need national-level approval, which would add several weeks to a month onto the process, depending on the policy issue. Put simply, a business can begin operations in four months to a year. In sum, the substantial initial capital requirements and the laborious registration process make the annual registration the best measure of investor intent.

A big issue for the SEC database, and any other similar database is the inability to track nominees. Investors or firms can hide their names with host country nominees. As a result of masking foreign investors or firms under local ones, the amount of FDI in the country is underestimated These firms can be dummy corporations, absorbing tons of capital to get in the country in order to avoid money laundering or other issues. While there is no way to detect the nominees, we argue that firms with foreign investors are likely the same firms that use the nominees too, hiding the amount of capital they invested by using their Filipino partners. The use of nominees is also widespread among foreign investors. As such, it will not bias the results since it's an opportunity to open all foreign investors. If anything, this data limitation will make it more difficult to find any effect as the measure underestimates FDI activity in a given year.[13]

[11] In the appendix, we tested the sum of FDI inflow-outflows from the Central Bank of the Philippines (CPB). Unfortunately, there are several problems. One is that the dataset comprised a limited number of years, which led to lower statistical power. The other is it is difficult to detect whether or not conflict affected investments because recurring patterns of capital inflows can simply be explained by previous physical assets.

[12] There is an alternative yet far less robust database. The DTI Sole Proprietorship (SP), the other government database, contains the names of all single person owners of firms in the country. However, most of the names in the DTI's list tend to be extremely small entrepreneurs, shop owners, or vendors. The firms in the DTI SP database are likely to be smaller since bigger corporations need multiple investors to commit. As such, it is unlikely that foreign firms go through the hurdles of investing just to own extremely small businesses that typically target the poor. Furthermore, there are foreign investment negative lists, such that the foreign investor cannot fully own the corporation and needs Filipino partners, making it a requirement to register in the SEC. In several sectors, the foreign investor can fully own the company, but these sectors tend to be worth billions and thus are often shared with other conglomerates, which would make these firms appear in the SEC list as well. Moreover, the SEC created the Only Person Corporation (OPC) to capture most firms in the DTI's SP list.

[13] Another issue in our dataset is that it includes firms that have closed, overestimating the number of currently operating companies. In our discussion with SEC officials, they said that their bureaucracy prioritizes making new registrations for firms rather than updating or closing old records. While they have closure records for some, they do not have for others. We chose to bypass this problem by taking the database as it is. Since overestimation is a problem for firms with Chinese and non-Chinese FDI alike, this problem will not bias the results. More importantly, as the registration process is costly, we expect that the number of closures for each year is trivial. Furthermore, our dataset coded the shares of foreign investors during the first year of investing. As such, we are unable to capture whether or not these firms divested or chose to reduce their investments to equity

5.2. *Analytical strategy*

Our dependent variable is the first difference of the annual number of newly registered firms in the Philippines, which comprise more than 10 percent of the ownership or the asset. We counted firms with Chinese, American, Japanese, Singaporean and Taiwanese investors. Respectively, there are two reasons for this operationalization. First, we expect maritime stabilization to generate certainty that impact the incentives of investors. As such, the quantity of interest is changes in investment behavior as a result of non-disputes. Conversely, we expect that territorial disputes to magnify uncertainty, limiting the incentives of investors. As Figures 1 and 2 show, the number of firms created in the Philippines continues to increase over time except during the period of the global economic recession from 2008–2009. However, Figures 3 and 4 show a 150% increase in newly registered firms with Chinese investors during Arroyo's second year in office (2002) and a sharp decline during Aquino's first full year. Second, the annual number of new firms is a

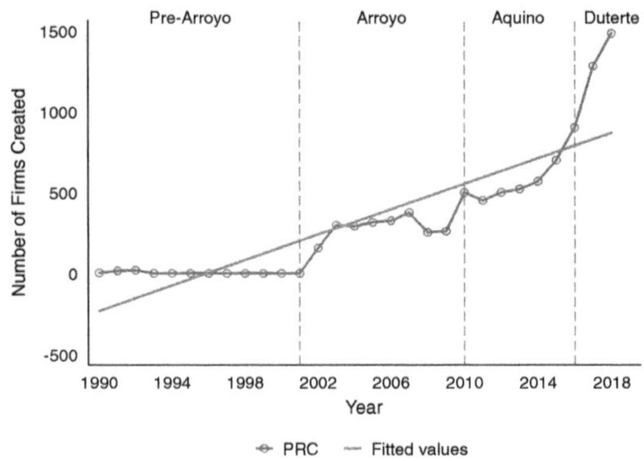

Figure 1. Annual Number of Registered Firms with Chinese FDI, 1990–2018

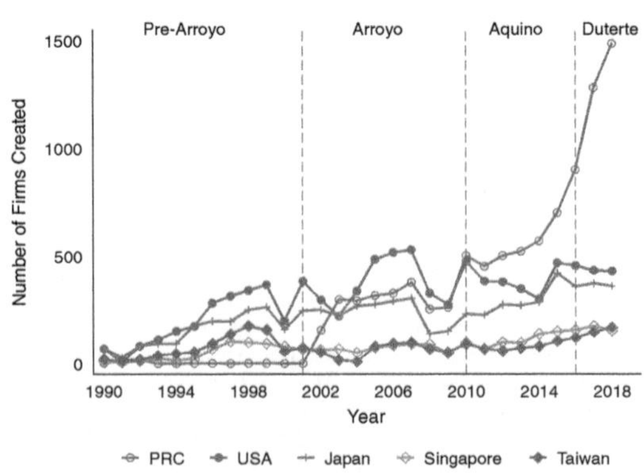

Figure 2. Annual Number of Registered Firms with FDI from Foreign States, 1990–2018

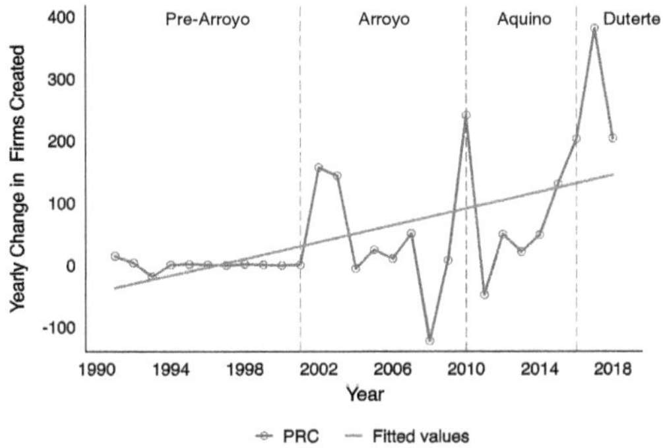

Figure 3. Annual Change in Registration of Firms with Chinese FDI, 1990–2018

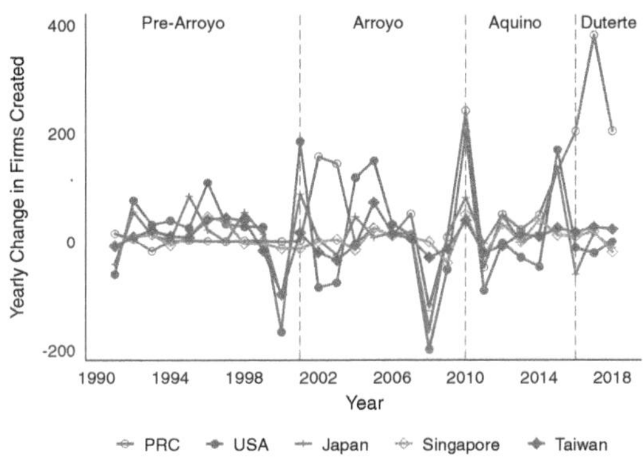

Figure 4. Annual Change in Registration of Firms with FDI from Foreign States, 1990–2018

non-stationary series and is integrated of order 1. Here, taking the first difference of the dependent variable is the most appropriate modeling strategy.

To measure territorial disputes, scholars often use the ICOW Territorial Claims dataset (Hensel and Mitchell, 2015; Wiegand, 2011). Since our paper is specific to China, there is currently no existing dataset specific to Chinese territorial disputes. The ICOW dataset only records information up to 2002, which is just at the start of China's massive capital exports, making it difficult to ascertain the relationship between FDI and territorial disputes. As such, we opted to choose a specific case wherein the relationship between FDI and disputes could be examined across time. Here, we chose four "administrations," which vacillated in their position in the SCS. The pre-Arroyo and Aquino years experienced some territorial disputes with China while the Arroyo and Duterte regimes stabilized the maritime borders. A limitation of this measure is its inability to capture multiple cases of disputes or encounters within a regime. However, we argue that given the nature of territorial disputes between the Philippines and China, which is static and primarily over the SCS, this categorical measure is the best available proxy. We code the independent variable "regime" to equal 1 if the president at time t is Arroyo, 2 if Aquino, 3 if Duterte and 0 otherwise. The reference category is the pre-Arroyo regime, which is from 1990 to 2001. Since presidential elections occur mid-year, we code an election year as the outgoing regime, such that 2016, the year Duterte won, is coded 2 (Aquino) and 2010 is 1 (Arroyo).

To control for other factors that are correlated with both disputes and investment, we include a set of covariates relating to the economic and political characteristics of the Philippines. Using data from the Quality of Government, we add World Development Indicators (WDI) measures of per capita GDP growth, imports (as % GDP), exports (as % GDP) and inflation rate. We also add the International Country Risk Guide measure for the quality of government. As we do not expect the effects of these time-varying confounders to be contemporaneous, we lag them by one year.

To estimate the impact on other investors, we analyzed the change in American, Japanese, Singaporean and Taiwanese investments in the Philippines. The US and Japan have been the biggest investors in the Philippines since the 1950s while Singapore and Taiwan rank at the top 7 since the early 2000s. The Netherlands, which has been a major investor in the Philippines and Southeast Asia since 2008, is known to be a major offshore financial center for many other investors. Meanwhile, other European investors have lagged behind Singapore and Taiwan in the past 10 years.

Our estimation strategy is as follows:

$$\Delta\text{FDI} = \beta_0 + \beta_1 \text{regime} + \gamma_m z_{mt-1} + \varepsilon,$$

where β_0 is the intercept and β_1 is the coefficient of our main independent variable of interest, regime. z_{mt-1} are time-varying covariates, lagged by one year and γ_m are the coefficients of these control variables. The dependent variable, ΔFDI, is the change in newly registered firms with FDI from one year to the next. We estimate five models, each corresponding to Chinese, American, Japanese, Taiwanese and Singaporean FDI, respectively. For robustness, we also estimate the models using the change in FDI inflow-outflow as the dependent variable. Due to data availability, we only estimate the model for Chinese FDI. We report the results of these analyses in Appendix (see Figures A.1 to A.3).

Based on our theoretical argument, we expect that, compared to a conflictual regime, being in a regime where the president supports stabilization of maritime disputes will

Table 1. Theoretical Expectations

Firms with Chinese FDI	Firms with Non-Chinese FDI
Pre-Arroyo < Arroyo	Pre-Arroyo = Arroyo
Pre-Arroyo = Aquino	Pre-Arroyo = Aquino
Pre-Arroyo < Duterte	Pre-Arroyo = Duterte
Arroyo > Aquino	Arroyo = Aquino
Arroyo = Duterte	Arroyo = Duterte
Aquino < Duterte	Aquino = Duterte

increase Chinese investments in the Philippines. As such, compared to the Pre-Arroyo years, Chinese firms register at a higher rate during the Arroyo presidency. We expect the same pattern during Duterte's administration. Conversely, compared to the pre-Arroyo regime, we expect that having Aquino as a president to yield similar rates of registration. Finally, we expect that, compared to a conflictual regime, having an administration that support policies to stabilize maritime disputes has no effect on non-Chinese foreign investments. We summarize our hypotheses in Table 1.

6. Results

As reported in Table 2, we find evidence to support our hypotheses. The results in Column 1 illustrate that in times of maritime stability, Chinese investors are more likely to invest in businesses in the Philippines (Hypothesis 1). The stabilization of the maritime borders increases certainty, which opened the floodgates of Chinese investments in the Philippines. In terms of magnitude, the Duterte regime, relative to the pre-Arroyo administrations, has

Table 2. OLS Regression Results, Effect of Disputes on FDI

	(1) PRC	(2) USA	(3) Japan	(4) Singapore	(5) Taiwan
Pre-Arroyo	–	–	–	–	–
Arroyo	168.339**	91.800	80.183	5.729	22.989
	(57.259)	(94.678)	(53.004)	(20.753)	(28.561)
Aquino	107.326	38.066	95.036	–11.356	–9.464
	(65.263)	(107.912)	(60.413)	(23.654)	(32.553)
Duterte	247.764**	–13.539	46.064	–34.745	–20.160
	(82.231)	(135.969)	(76.120)	(29.804)	(41.018)
GDP pc growth (t-1)	–15.583	–6.605	–4.243	0.378	6.293
	(8.569)	(14.170)	(7.933)	(3.106)	(4.274)
Imports (t-1)	14.418*	8.748	7.878	1.438	4.812
	(6.664)	(11.019)	(6.169)	(2.415)	(3.324)
Exports (t-1)	–22.176*	–11.834	–9.376	–3.100	–6.708
	(8.636)	(14.279)	(7.994)	(3.130)	(4.307)
Inflation (t-1)	–0.698	4.462	10.217	–0.860	1.978
	(7.400)	(12.235)	(6.850)	(2.682)	(3.691)
Quality of Government (t-1)	252.362	107.466	153.859	27.718	–9.064
	(194.783)	(322.073)	(180.308)	(70.598)	(97.159)
Constant	85.294	–20.329	–151.628	53.504	24.021
	(144.735)	(239.318)	(133.979)	(52.459)	(72.195)
Observations	28	28	28	28	28
R^2	0.706	0.084	0.193	0.130	0.224
Adjusted R^2	0.582	–0.302	–0.147	–0.237	–0.103

Note: Standard errors in parentheses, $^{*}p < 0.05$, $^{**}p < 0.01$, $^{***}p < 0.001$.

the biggest effect on Chinese foreign investment. All else equal, there are approximately 168 more firms with Chinese FDI created during the Arroyo regime (compared to pre-Arroyo). Meanwhile, the Duterte presidency has 248 more registered firms with Chinese FDI than the pre-Arroyo era. This should be unsurprising given that Duterte opened the Philippines to the BRI, recalibrated infrastructure construction to tap development finance, and explicitly given directives to work with the Chinese state. In addition, ongoing attempts of the CCP to reign in private capital embolden capital holders to invest and launder their money outside China.

Our results imply that involvement in the territorial dispute decreases the likelihood of investment from China. Indeed, as shown in Table 3, Chinese investment in the pre-Arroyo and Aquino administrations, regimes that had conflictual relationships with PRC, are statistically indistinguishable from each other ($p = 0.117$). This is notwithstanding the fact that Chinese investment was close to zero prior to Arroyo becoming president.[14] Moreover, we find that registration of firms with Chinese FDI are significantly higher in the Duterte administration than in Aquino's. Wald tests confirm that there is a statistically significant difference between Chinese investments during Aquino and during Duterte (p-value $= 0.048$), lending support to Hypothesis 2 that conflictual relations hinder investors. Taken together, our results confirm that stable maritime borders are conducive for investments, while maritime disputes produce uncertainty that weakens the incentives for investment.

We also find support that FDI from non-claimant states would not be affected by the disputes (Columns 3 to 6). There are no statistically significant changes in non-Chinese foreign investments which suggests that non-militarized territorial disputes only introduce uncertainty to the parties involved in the conflict. These findings lend credence to the

Table 3. Results of Pairwise Comparisons

Firms with Chinese FDI	Firms with Non-Chinese FDI
Pre-Arroyo < Arroyo✓	Pre-Arroyo = Arroyo✓
Pre-Arroyo = Aquino✓	Pre-Arroyo = Aquino✓
Pre-Arroyo < Duterte✓	Pre-Arroyo = Duterte✓
Arroyo > Aquino	Arroyo = Aquino✓
Arroyo = Duterte✓	Arroyo = Duterte✓
Aquino < Duterte✓	Aquino = Duterte✓

Note: Checkmark (✓) indicates that we find statistical support for our theoretical expectations.

[14] Note that while the coefficient is positive, compared to times of stability, the change in registration rates of firms with Chinese FDI is statistically indistinguishable from zero. However, Chinese investments during the Arroyo administration are not statistically different from that of the Aquino regime (p-value $= 0.367$). We interpret this as a result of an open investment channel. Specifically, Chinese firms have already invested in the Philippines during the Arroyo administration, which would increase the available amount of information to would-be Chinese investors. In other words, the uncertainty of territorial disputes has weaker effects on a portion of Chinese firms.

existing argument that unless conflict occurs in the disputed territories and spillover in the location of the investments, other countries will continue to invest. Indeed, while the model explains 71% of the variation in Chinese FDI, it only explains at most 25% of the variation in investments of other foreign states. Lastly, while we have no explicit theoretical expectations for the control variables, the results, unsurprisingly, show that political and economic conditions matter. While bureaucratic and business conditions have marginally improved over the years,[15] none of these changes have been significant or important to affect the relationship between disputes and FDI. The full results are presented in graphical format in Figures 5 and 6.

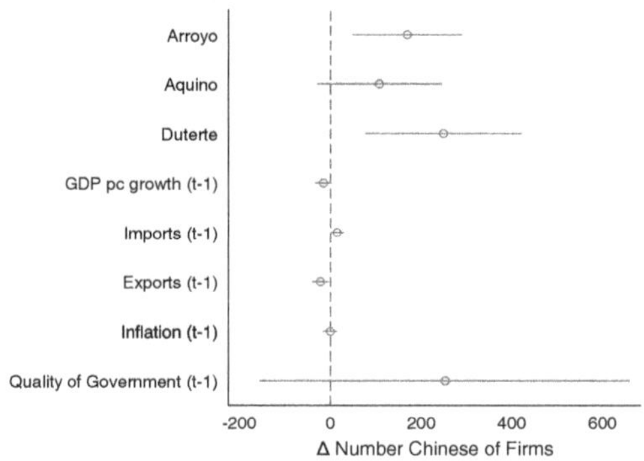

Figure 5. OLS Regression Results, Effect of Disputes on Chinese FDI

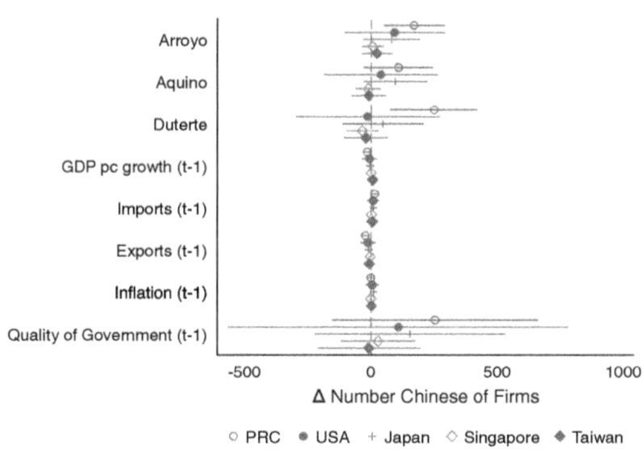

Figure 6. OLS Regression Results, Effect of Disputes on FDI

[15] There is broader literature on the relationship between weak institutions and Chinese FDI (e.g. Duanmu, 2014). However, we do not find the political and economic factors to covary. While the worldwide amount of Chinese FDI surged in 1999 and in 2013, the economic and political strength of the Philippine regimes barely changed (1999–2018). This is unsurprising given that institutions tend to be sticky.

Lastly, we contend that these results are robust. Indeed, the data limitations bias against us finding any effects. The firm registration process, which allows the use of nominees, underestimates the amount of FDI in the Philippines by masking foreign capital under local ones. As such, having the full universe of cases should only strengthen our findings. We included a pairwise comparison in Table 3 to simplify our results.

7. Implications on Philippine Economic Strategy

The results point to the Philippines' economic and political strategy towards China. First, we argue that future Philippine governments should pursue a China strategy not simply built on geopolitics, but also on the lessons provided by our Southeast Asian neighbors. Vietnam, Malaysia and Indonesia have pursued a middle-ground approach that rejects the extreme vacillation of previous regimes in the Philippines, which were either anti-China Pre-Arroyo and Aquino or pro-China Arroyo and Duterte regimes. In the early 1990s, the Philippines was recovering from the Marcos era dictatorship and, therefore, more concerned with internal politics. The Ramos regime pursued liberalization policies that led to an increase in FDI. In addition, the relative insularity of the Philippine economy limited the impact of the Asian Financial Crisis (AFC) on the country. Both conditions could have attracted Chinese firms and bolstered the Philippine economy since Chinese firms started to invest in Southeast Asia in the early 1990s.[16] However, uncertainty brought about by the disputes contributed to the dismal number of firms with Chinese FDI in the country.[17]

By no means are we arguing that the Philippines gives up its territorial claim. As other Southeast Asian states have shown, there can be cordial relations with China despite disagreements about fishing rights or maritime domains. During the Aquino administration, an even-keeled solution with China about the dispute could have acquired Chinese FDI at a higher rate and given the Philippines stronger economic footing in 2016.[18] Similarly, we argue that the Duterte government's current stance appears to be unnecessary: there was no need to immediately and informally give up the claim.[19] Opening the dialogue would have been enough to stabilize the maritime borders and decrease uncertainty.[20] Indeed, Duterte could have leveraged his "newfound" friendship with China to acquire better investment and loan deals. As President Joko Widodo's Jakarta-Bandung

[16]There were Chinese firms that wanted to invest during the Ramos administration, but the disputes generated concern on likely political targeting. Interview with a former Chinese embassy official in the Philippines, Singapore. August 25, 2017.

[17]Works on comparative politics have already documented the expansion of Chinese foreign investments in sub-Saharan Africa and other parts of Southeast Asia in the 1990s (Bräutigam, 2009, Doner and Ramsay, 1997).

[18]During the Arroyo administration, our interviews show that major Chinese SOEs wanted to invest in the Philippines, which led to an initial commitment of $15 billion. Most of these amounts did not push through because of elite conflict during the Arroyo administration. Our fieldwork indicates that during the Arroyo administration, thousands of firms considered the possibility of investing in the Philippines. Most of them were discouraged by elite conflict.

[19]Vietnam's pushback against China and Indonesia's drive to protect their waters show that economic relations can still be pursued while protecting the maritime domains.

[20]Ideally, the Association of Southeast Asian Nations (ASEAN) can collectively mediate the conflict. However, as shown during the Aquino administration, the lack of unity among ASEAN countries and their own desire for economic development make a unified stance extremely unlikely.

High-Speed Railway Project and IMIP have shown, China is willing to offer better terms for critical, growth-enhancing projects (Tritto and Camba, 2019).[21]

Second, while Chinese FDI has been increasing since the Arroyo administration, the sectoral targets and growth-enhancing aspects of these investments also need to be questioned. Our recent fieldwork in Malaysia's Pahang province and Central Sulawesi in Indonesia reveals that both these countries have been able to strategically channel Chinese FDI toward the least-developed provinces, generating jobs for thousands and spurring economic growth in these left behind regions. The post-Marcos Philippine governments could have used Chinese FDI to supplement conventional Japanese and Western financial sources in order to target critical and strategic economic sectors that can raise the quality of life in the Philippines. Unlike Japanese and Western investors, which have been the biggest investors of the Philippines since the 1960s, Chinese foreign investors can put their money in critical sectors that conventional foreign investors see as too costly.

Third, these issues root back to the lack of a workable and a long-term Philippine economic strategy apart from relying on remittances, an oligarchic-centered consumption economy, and call center investments. Recent decreases in call center investments due to automation made the Philippine real estate and construction sectors pivot to Chinese online gambling, which has generated mixed economic and social effects across the country, ranging from rent-seeking officials and opportunistic local businesses to unlicensed businesses and Chinese sex workers (Camba, 2019b). The inability of the current administration to manage these inflows point to the need to further diversify the Philippine economy away from domestic consumption, services and export labor toward industrial manufacturing and upgrading.[22] For the Philippines to accomplish these policy goals, it needs to commit to a clear development strategy, and perhaps a long-term industrial policy. Here, if properly managed and guided, Chinese state and private capital can play critical roles in positively redirecting the Philippine economy. These actions involve forming and empowering new administrative units, employing Philippine academics with legitimate expertise, and recalibrating existing strategy to match research on the development strategies.[23]

Now, the role of the Philippine government, domestic firms and Chinese investors are discussing the possibility of establishing industrial parks in the country, such as the Ayala Corporation's joint venture with Chinese firms in Central Luzon (Rivas, 2019). These types of investments, which would generate employment for thousands and spur domestic

[21] Recent reports on the Philippines' contractual obligations on the approved deals, such as commodity-based payments and China-driven arbitration, have spurred intense domestic opposition. In addition, the Duterte government could be more transparent when it comes to Chinese FDI and loans. Released documents, which took immense public pressure to acquire, had omitted appendixes.

[22] Different socio-economic determinants and factors of endowment explain the different types of Chinese and non-Chinese FDI in ASEAN. The limited capacity of the Philippine state and strength of regional-local elites explain the slow infrastructure growth and the difficulties of acquiring land, which make manufacturing more expensive. In Malaysia, Indonesia, and Thailand, Japan's infrastructure and manufacturing bolstered industrial capacity that attract Chinese manufacturing investments.

[23] Malaysia and Indonesia created new administrative units to deal with China and the Belt and Road. These units allow both states to coherently pursue Chinese capital and foreign policy interests (Liu and Lim, 2019). While the Philippines' *Build Build Build* Commission exists, it seems to be an administration-specific sub-agency that lacks the teeth to implement infrastructure projects. Furthermore, it does not deal with FDI, but focuses on infrastructure projects.

upgrading, should have been the primary focus rather than simply investments for capital's sake. The government should mandate these investments to train Filipino workers to learn some level of Chinese, increasing the local labor workforce, alongside crucial technical skills. There should be streamlined regulations to handle these investments properly, such as ensuring the appropriate national and local taxation regimes.

8. Conclusion

Our paper makes three contributions. First, our paper adds to the literature on the political economy of conflict. Previous research shows mixed effects due to the reliance on a broader political stability index, or the conflation of disputes with other types of inter-state conflict. In contrast, our empirical analysis shows that territorial disputes between two states affect firms from the sending country through the conflict-generated uncertainty. Drawing from Weber's proposition that investors rely on calculability, our results show: (a) there was a significant increase in the number of new firms with Chinese investments between the pre-Arroyo and the Arroyo regimes; (b) no statistically significant increase in the annual number of new firms between the Arroyo and the Aquino administrations; (c) a significant increase between Aquino and the Duterte regimes; (d) finally, rather than divestment or increased investments, we show that disputes on firms from non-claimant states have null effects.

Our argument nuances previous works on the Chinese economic statecraft in the Philippines. While previous works point to the possibility of the Chinese state discouraging their investors, the Philippine government's deliberate targeting of Chinese firms, or the "democratic" safeguards that kept selected Chinese projects out, our paper presents and defends an argument that highlights how disputes generate uncertain investment environments. It describes how territorial disputes impact the predictability of sending state subsidies and political support in addition to host country behavior which, in turn, affect investor decisions. We argue that in order to show the impact of disputes, it is crucial to look at the effect on the broader population of firms with Chinese and non-Chinese FDI. Examining the number of newly registered firms in the Philippines, their yearly increases or decreases, and overall regime-level aggregation, we demonstrated that maritime border disputes diminish the incentives of firms with FDI from the claimant state to invest. We subsequently examined the impact of disputes on the firms with FDI from non-claimant states, showing that these firms are unaffected by the eruption of the disputes or stabilization of the maritime borders. We arrived at this conclusion while controlling for various political and economic factors in the Philippines.

Second, we used a novel dataset that tracks the annual number of firm registrations, demonstrating a methodological contribution that future projects can emulate. Previous works relied on the World Bank or the host country's FDI inflow-outflow data, which are imprecise because remitted amounts could simply be additional capital to preexisting firms, wherein we do not expect any divestment or decrease in financing. Put simply, the nature of the inflow-outflow data makes it extremely difficult to match the timing of the investments and the impact of the disputes, if any. For the SEC dataset, firms would only appear in the registration once they have fulfilled the minimum requirements, took the time to file the papers, and invest the minimum capital required. Due to the hefty sunk costs, if disputes appear to be trouble to investors, they would stop the entire process and their firm would not even enter the records. Thus this type of data makes it possible to disentangle the actual impact of the disputes. Future research on China's disputes with the Philippines can examine the sectoral and regional effects of the disputes. In addition, similar types of research can be done in Vietnam, Malaysia and Brunei. The SEC data can also be combined with other types of global and host country processes.

Third, our paper contributes statistical evidence to resolve several empirical debates that Philippine analysts have brought up over the years. Despite smaller actualized investments to the announced commitments, we statistically show that Duterte's China pivot contributed to the surge of Chinese investments in the Philippines. Some analysts repeatedly pointed out that China has fooled the Philippines into giving up the SCS in exchange for unrealized government to government loans and investments. Others have similarly questioned the impact of Duterte's China Pivot. While these authors have valid concerns, their analysis relies on aggregate data that does not capture the investment decisions of foreign firms. The Philippines Statistics Authority (PSA) data comprise commitments that usually get canceled, while the BSP data document the sum of FDI inflows and outflows. Unlike the partial pictures offered by these other data sources, our results instead show that territorial disputes discourage Chinese FDI, while stabilizing the maritime borders encourage it. Our analysis also features a significant increase in Chinese FDI despite only including two years of Duterte's term in our dataset, making the finding even more surprising because of the limited time horizons.

Furthermore, our paper systematically traced the impact of the disputes during the widely publicized Aquino administration. While China limited development finance, banana imports and tourist inflows, other political and business relations continued between the two states: consistent FDI inflows, massive nickel imports and China grants to the Philippines. Looking at the descriptive data, there is no reason to believe that the rate of investment from Chinese firms or nationals diminished since institutional reforms and the steady growth of the Philippine economy point to profitable conditions. However, we show that these institutional factors do not reach statistical significance, suggesting that the strongest predictor of the change in the number of investors in new entrants is the regime's position on the SCS. This lends evidence to the argument that had Aquino and Beijing stabilized the maritime borders despite their disagreements, Chinese FDI could have been higher.

Acknowledgment

During the research and writing process, one of the authors spent time as a China Initiative Fellow at the Global Development Policy (GDP) in Boston University. The authors would like to thank Shirley Lung, Guanie Lim, Kevin Gallagher, Rebecca Ray, and Xinyue Ma for their comments. The authors also acknowledge the two anonymous reviewers for their feedback.

Appendix A

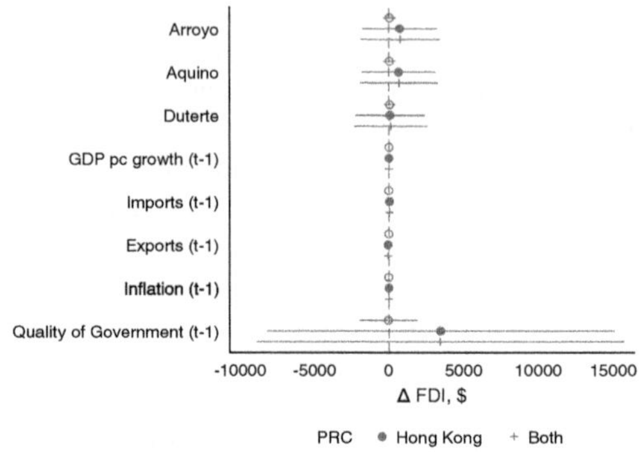

Figure A.1. OLS Regression Results, Effect of Disputes on FDI Inflow-Outflow

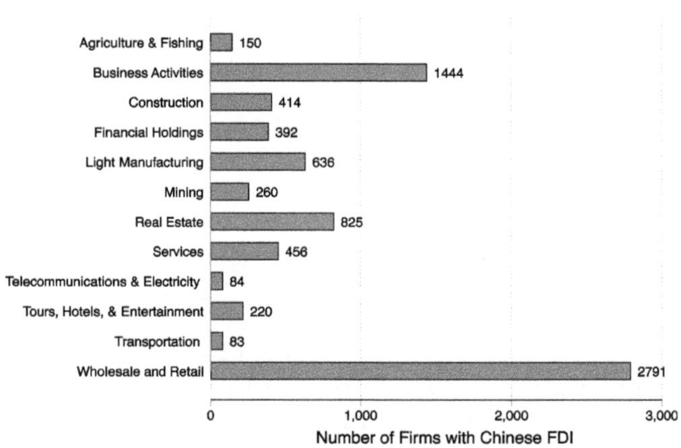

Figure A.2. Total Number of Firms with Chinese FDI from 1990–2017, by Sector

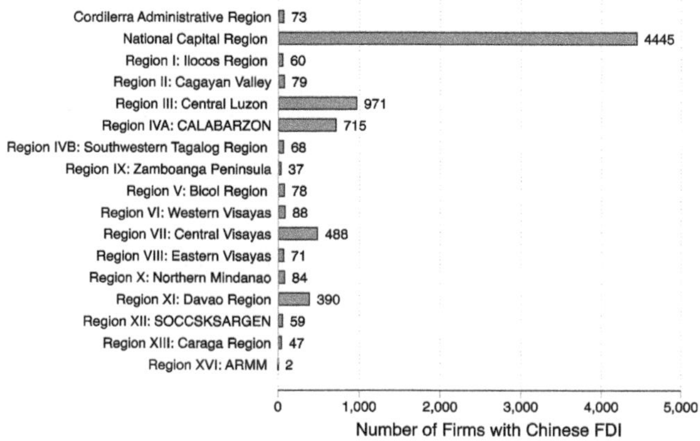

Figure A.3. Total Number of Firms with Chinese FDI from 1990–2017, by Region

References

Ang, YY (2016). *How China Escaped the Poverty Trap*. Cornell University Press.

Bangko Sentral ng Pilipinas (BSP) (2018). Based on BPM6 concept, 2005-Present (May 2016), http://www.bsp.gov.ph/statistics/excel/fdi-country2.xls.

Bello, W, WF Bello, M De Guzman, ML Malig and H Docena (2005). *The Anti-Development State: The Political Economy of Permanent Crisis in the Philippines*.

Bello, W, K Cardenas, JP Cruz, A Fabros, MA Manahan, C Militante and JJ Chavez (2014). *State of Fragmentation: The Philippines in Transition*. Focus on the Global South.

Bluhm, R, D Axel, F Andreas, P Bradley, S Austin and T Michael (2018). Connective financing: Chinese infrastructure projects and the diffusion of economic activity in developing countries. AidData Working Paper #64. Williamsburg, VA: AidData at William and Mary.

Bräutigam, D (2009). *The Dragon's Gift: The Real Story of China in Africa*. Oxford University Press.

Camba, A (2015). From colonialism to neoliberalism: Critical reflections on Philippine mining in the long twentieth century. *The Extractive Industries and Society*, 2(2), 287–301.

Camba, A (2017). Inter-state relations and state capacity: The rise and fall of Chinese foreign direct investment in the Philippines. *Palgrave Communications*, 3(1), 41.

Camba, A (2018). The Philippines' Chinese FDI Boom: More Politics than Geopolitics. *New Mandala (blog)*.

Camba, A (2019a). China Money: How the numbers differ, philippine center for investigative journalism. May 9, 2019.

Camba, A (2019b). Inside a Chinese gambling entity: What happens, who works, how, Philippine Center for Investigative Journalism. May 9, 2019.

Camba, A and HF Hung (2018). China, Africa, and global economic transformation. In *New Directions in Africa–China Studies*, pp. 318–331. Routledge.

De Castro, RC (2014). The 21st century Philippine-US Enhanced Defense Cooperation Agreement (EDCA): The Philippines' policy in facilitating the Obama administration's strategic pivot to Asia. *Korean Journal of Defense Analysis*, 26(4), 427–446.

De Castro, RC (2019). East Asia, 1–23, https://doi.org/10.1007/s12140-019-09315-9.

Doner, RF and A Ramsay (1997). Competitive clientelism and economic governance: The case of Thailand, in *Business and the State in Developing Countries*, Sylvia Maxfield and BR Schneider, pp. 237–276. Ithaca: Cornell University Press.
Duanmu, JL (2014). State-owned MNCs and host country expropriation risk: The role of home state soft power and economic gunboat diplomacy. *Journal of International Business Studies*, 45(8), 1044–1060.
Globerman, S and D Shapiro (2003). Governance infrastructure and US foreign direct investment. *Journal of International Business Studies*, 34(1), 19–39.
Gu, J, C Zhang, A Vaz and L Mukwereza (2016). Chinese state capitalism? Rethinking the role of the state and business in Chinese development cooperation in Africa. *World Development*, 81, 24–34.
Hayton, B (2014). *The South China Sea: The Struggle for Power in Asia*. Yale University Press.
Hutchcroft, P and J Rocamora (2012). Patronage-based parties and the democratic deficit in the philippines: Origins, evolution, and the imperatives of Reform. In *Routledge Handbook of Southeast Asian Politics*, Richard Robison (ed.), Routledge: Taylor and Francis Group, New York USA, pp. 97–119.
Hensel, PR and SM Mitchell (2015). Lessons from the Issue Correlates of War (ICOW) project. *Journal of Peace Research*, 52(1), 116–119.
Hung, HF (2008). Rise of China and the global overaccumulation crisis. *Review of International Political Economy*, 15(2), 149–179.
Huth, P and T Allee (2002). *The Democratic Peace and Territorial Conflict in the Twentieth Century*, Vol. 82, Cambridge University Press.
Kaplan, RD (2015). *Asia's cauldron: The South China Sea and the End of a Stable Pacific*. Random House Trade Paperbacks.
Kurlantzick, J (2006). China's charm offensive in Southeast Asia. *Current History*, 105(692), 270–276.
Lee, CK (2018). *The Specter of Global China: Politics, Labor, and Foreign Investment in Africa*. University of Chicago Press.
Lee, H and Mitchell, SM (2012). Foreign direct investment and territorial disputes. *Journal of Conflict Resolution*, 56(4), 675–703.
Li, Q (2006). Political Violence and Foreign Direct Investment. In *Regional Economic Integration*, pp. 225–249, Emerald Group Publishing Limited.
Li, Q (2008). Foreign direct investment and interstate military conflict. *Journal of International Affairs*, 62(1), 53–66.
Liu, H and G Lim (2019). The political economy of a rising China in Southeast Asia: Malaysia's response to the belt and road initiative. *Journal of Contemporary China*, 28(116), 216–231.
Meyer, S (1996). Incident at Mischief Reef: Implications for the Philippines, China, and the United States. US Army War College.
Moravcsik, A (2013). *The Choice for Europe: Social Purpose and State Power from Messina to Maastricht*. Routledge.
Nem Singh, JT and AA Camba (2016). Neoliberalism, resource governance and the everyday politics of protests in the Philippines. *Everyday Political Economy of Southeast Asia*, 49–71.
Nigh, D (1986). Political events and the foreign direct investment decision: An empirical examination. *Manage and Decision Economics*, 7(2), 99–106.
Norris, WJ (2016). *Chinese Economic Statecraft: Commercial Actors, Grand Strategy, and State Control*. Cornell University Press.
Olibe, KO and CL Crumbley (1997). Determinants of US private foreign direct investments in OPEC nations: From public and non-public policy perspectives. *Journal of Public Budgeting Account Financial Management*, 9(2), 331.
O'Neill, D (2018). *Dividing ASEAN and Conquering the South China Sea*. Hong Kong: Hong Kong University Press.

Ramirez, R (2017). Philippines expects 2 M Chinese tourists this year. Philippine Star, 19 March, http://www.philstar.com/headlines/2017/03/19/1682570/philippines-expects-2-m-chinese-tourists-year.

Ravindran, MS (2012). China's potential for economic coercion in the South China Sea disputes: A comparative study of the Philippines and Vietnam. *Journal of Current Southeast Asian Affairs*, 31(3), 105–132.

Rivas, R (2019). Ayala to build first Philippine-China industrial park in Pampanga. Rappler, 26 April, https://www.rappler.com/business/229082-ayala-to-build-first-philippine-china-industrial-park-pampanga.

Schultz, KA (2015). Borders, conflict, and trade. *Annual Review of Political Science*, 18, 125–145.

Schneider, F and BS Frey (1985). Economic and political determinants of foreign direct investment. *World Development*, 13, 161–175.

Sethi, D, SE Guisinger, SE Phelan and DM Berg (2003). Trends in foreign direct investment flows: A theoretical and empirical analysis. *Journal of International Business Studies*, 34, 315–326.

Simmons, BA (2005). Rules over real estate: Trade, territorial conflict, and international borders as institution. *Journal of Conflict Resolution*, 49(6), 823–848.

Temper, L, D Del Bene and J Martinez-Alier (2015). Mapping the frontiers and front lines of global environmental justice: The EJAtlas. *Journal of Political Ecology*, 22, 255–278.

Tritto, A. and Camba, A. (2019). The belt and road: The good, the bad, and the mixed, *The Diplomat*, April 15, https://thediplomat.com/2019/04/the-belt-and-road-the-good-the-bad-and-the-mixed/.

Wiegand, KE (2011). *Enduring Territorial Disputes: Strategies of Bargaining, Coercive Diplomacy, and Settlement*. University of Georgia Press.

Weber, M (1978). *Max Weber on Law in Economy and Society*, 20th century legal philosophy series, Vol. 6, Berkeley: University of California Press.

Wellhausen, RL (2014). *The Shield of Nationality: When Governments Break Contracts with Foreign Firms*. Cambridge University Press.

Wong, A (2019). Reaping What you sow: Public accountability and the effectiveness of China's economic statecraft, Working Paper. https://ndisc.nd.edu/assets/320488/wong_audrye_emerging_scholars_051019.pdf .

Woodward, D and R Rolfe (1993). The location of export-oriented foreign direct investment in the Caribbean Basin. *Journal of International Business Studies*, 24, 121–144.

Zhang, K (2019). Cautious bully: Reputation, resolve, and beijing's use of coercion in the South China sea. *International Security*, 44(1), 117–159.

Chapter 14

THE FLYING GEESE AND CHINA'S BRI IN INDONESIA†

SIWAGE DHARMA NEGARA* and LEO SURYADINATA
ISEAS-Yusof Ishak Institute
**siwage_dharma_negara@iseas.edu.sg*

Published Online 30 December 2019

In recent years, China has been catching-up with other advanced economies and become one of the "leading geese" in the Asian economy. China not only plays a leading role in regional production network but also in various regional economic cooperation. Indonesia, being one of the following geese, needs to adjust its position to benefit from this change in global and regional order. While other more advanced economies have less to offer, Indonesia has gradually moved closer toward China in terms of economic cooperation. Using the flying geese model, this paper argues that China's BRI might change trade and investment trends in Indonesia. China BRI might complement the role of Japan as a catalyst for economic development in the Asian region in general and in Indonesia in particular. There is no official BRI project agreed by Indonesia so far. However, there are a number of completed and ongoing China–Indonesia projects, which arguably might pave the way for future BRI investment. Currently, apart from the Jakarta–Bandung high speed railways, most of the projects are concentrated in resource-exploitation needed by China and the fulfilment of Indonesian development needs, such as power generation, mineral smelters and industrial parks. From the Beijing's perspective, these projects are perceived as part of BRI. Since these so-called BRI projects have not been completed, it is therefore impossible to assess their impacts on Indonesia's industrialization at this point. However, we can still argue that BRI might have initiated a new type of investment that might in turn change the industrial trends, structure and performance in Indonesia. If this change leads to improvement in products quality or value added, industrial upgrading, technological transfer and export boost, then one may argue that BRI has brought promised benefits to the host economy (i.e., Indonesia). Otherwise, the benefits would be negligible.

Keywords: China; Indonesia; Belt and Road Initiative (BRI); flying geese; trade; investment.

1. Introduction

China's Belt and Road Initiative (BRI) has been received with mixed responses in different parts of the world. One can argue that China's BRI has a global strategic significance as it has been actively promoted in various economic-non-economic aspects, such as finances, trade, investment and cultural/international diplomacy. Nevertheless, for many "participating" countries, mainly developing countries, BRI has been seen as an opportunity for them to improve their infrastructure and connectivity with the region or the world (Rimmer, 2018; Shen and Chan, 2018; Negara and Suryadinata, 2018b; Damuri *et al.*, 2018). Many

* Corresponding author.

† This article originally appeared in *The Singapore Economic Review*, **66**(1), pp. 269–292

of the countries along the BRI routes are in dire need of promoting infrastructure to boost their domestic production, promote manufacturing export capacity and to create large pool of skilled workers. This raises question as to what extent BRI can support developing economies, like Indonesia, in terms of achieving their development goals.

While China has proclaimed that BRI is a win-win deal for China and the partnering countries, however, there are also growing concerns with regard to rising dependence on China and adverse implications of the initiative. The scepticism appears because the Chinese government has not (purposely) articulated its initiative clearly (Rimmer, 2018; Shen and Chan, 2018). As a result, there are many speculations on multiple domestic drivers and external factors, with economic, financial, security, political, diplomatic, socioeconomic, geo-economic and geopolitical elements (Hallgren and Ghiasy, 2017; Rimmer, 2018; Liu and Lim, 2019). These speculations might be attributed to the absence of a clear official plan, target and timetable for the BRI (Rimmer, 2018; Damuri *et al.*, 2018).

Nevertheless, Indonesia seems to welcome BRI positively, though not without reservation (Negara and Suryadinata, 2018b; Damuri *et al.*, 2018). On the one hand, BRI is perceived as a strategic opportunity for promoting infrastructure development; revitalizing domestic industry and improving connectivity. Those priorities are stated in the nine-national-priority agenda (Nawa Cita) of the Joko "Jokowi" Widodo government (Damuri *et al.*, 2018). As such, BRI offers an opportunity for Indonesia to support one or several points in Nawa Cita. This would be welcome by Indonesia.

On the contrary, there are also concerns over potential adverse effects of BRI projects, ranging from worsening trade deficit, increasing government's debt burden and fiscal sustainability, job losses due to foreign workers, lack of spill-over effects to local industries and so on. All of these concerns can be easily intertwined with domestic political dynamics, which might in turn hinder the implementation of BRI projects in the country.

It is important to note, however, that there is no official BRI project implemented in Indonesia. Therefore, it is unlikely to make any concrete assessment of the benefits and costs of BRI project at this juncture. While there is no official BRI project, there are a number of past and current China–Indonesia projects, which relate to infrastructure projects such as power plants, dams, roads and the Jakarta–Bandung high speed railway (Negara and Suryadinata, 2018b; Salim and Negara 2016). These infrastructure projects, which might be seen by China as part of BRI, are likely to contribute either directly or indirectly to Indonesia's economic growth. What is more interesting is that, in recent years there has been some Chinese investment that comes to manufacturing sectors, including the electronics, electrical equipment, automotive, machineries and smelters. These investments are likely to increase domestic production of particular goods, increase exports and local jobs. From China's view point, this investment can be perceived as part of BRI.

For Indonesia, it does not matter if it is considered as BRI or not as it is more interested in seeking economic benefit, stemming from capital inflow, technology transfer and jobs creation. This paper aims to analyze how China's BRI fits or may not fit into Indonesia's development plan, in particular with respect to its ambition to revitalize its industry and move up the value chain. For that, we adopt a flying geese framework developed by Akamatsu (1962) to illustrate a model for international division of labor in East Asia based on dynamic comparative advantage. While long-range statistical data are limited, however, the model might provide some insight into possible benefits that China's BRI could bring to the host economy.

The paper is organized as follows. The next section discusses the relevance of the flying geese theory to understand industrial development trajectory in the region. The third section examines some stylized facts related to China–Indonesia economic relations and its relative importance for Indonesia. The fourth section discusses some Chinese projects in Indonesia and their implications on the industrial and sub-national development in the country. The fifth section discusses some issues and criticism related to growing economic relations with China. The last section concludes and provides some insights on the prospects of Indonesia being benefited by China's BRI.

2. The Flying Geese Pattern of Industrial Development

One of the most inspiring concepts among numerous theories of stages of economic development would certainly be the "flying geese" development model, introduced by Kaname Akamatsu (1962). The theory postulates that different stages of development determine countries' comparative advantage in regional value chain; this in turn creates a pattern of regional production network, in which production of tradable goods would constantly move from the more developed countries to the less developed ones (Akamatsu, 1962). Following a geese-flying pattern, therefore the less developed countries in the region position themselves to be lined up successively behind the more technologically advanced economies. In this development pattern, there is a successive process of catching up of economic progress with Japan as the leading goose, followed by the newly industrializing economies (South Korea, Singapore, Taiwan and Hong Kong), then ASEAN and finally China chasing from behind (Nakagane, 2013).

In the last decades, we see the formation of the flying geese has changed. China has experienced over three decades of rapid economic growth and development since its economic reform started in 1978. There have been a great number of literatures analyzing China's remarkable development pattern and implication to other regions or economies (Wong, 2007; Lin, 2011; Qu *et al.*, 2012; McKay and Song, 2012; Nakagane, 2013, among others). What is notable is the way China catch-up to advanced countries (Japan and NIEs) and to become one of the leading geese, if not the leading goose, in certain industries, such as artificial intelligence and 5G technology.[1] The flying geese theory implies that as China continues its rapid development, it may surpass Japan as the leading goose. And along the process, it opens up opportunities for other developing countries in the region to ride along China's technological advancement. These countries may potentially become the host of China's companies that seek to relocate as their comparative advantage shifts to higher-value added, less labor-intensive industries (Ahearne *et al.*, 2006; McKay and Song, 2012).

[1] https://www.economist.com/books-and-arts/2018/09/27/in-the-struggle-for-ai-supremacy-china-will-prevail (accessed on May 31, 2019).

In its original formulation, the flying geese analogy was used to illustrate historical trends of industrialization within Japan. The model reflected an idea of the potential of reverse engineering and the nation's aspiration to catch up and then to overtake the world's technological leaders. Akamatsu's theory has been widely applied to explain the catching-up process of industrialization of latecomer economies from the following characteristics: (1) intra-industry aspect: product development within a particular industry; (2) inter-industry aspect: sequential development of industries, with industries being diversified and upgraded from simple to more sophisticated products; (3) international aspect: subsequent relocation process of industries from advanced to developing countries during the latter's catching-up process (Akamatsu, 1962). Within the regional industrialization process, the flying geese model focusses on the role of Japanese FDI and MNCs as a catalyst for Asian development. It conceives Japan as the leading player, shutting the possibility of other goose to take over her role (Yamazawa, 1990). This model accentuates the dynamism of FDI as well as focussing on the spatial distribution of MNC operations in Asia-Pacific (Edgington and Hayter, 2000; Hayter and Edgington, 2004).

The flying geese concept also presumes a certain political economy and geopolitical model of development (Hatch and Yamamura, 1996; Edgington and Hayter, 2000). Japan's industrialization in the late 19th century had been associated with political and economic "imperialism" towards Asia (Steven, 1996). After the World War 2, Japan has successfully reconstructed its economy and developed a more benign form of political economy relationships with Asia.

Bernard and Ravenhill (1995) associated the flying geese model with the product-cycle model of international investment. The latter model conjectures the relocation of "mature" products to low-wage regions. As such, the flying geese model envisages a dynamic sequence of development for any given industry, beginning with mature products, from Japan to the Newly Industrialized Economies (NIEs), followed by ASEAN, China, Vietnam and India (Edgington and Hayter, 2000; Hayter and Edgington, 2004). The flying geese model also allows for FDI in capital goods, components and business services.

The flying geese model is quite generalized and simplistic. Chen and Kwan (1997) argued that innovations no longer emerge only in core countries. Innovations now occur in a wider number of countries and generate more complex divisions of labor. This is very different from the orderly diffusion of technology from country to country in a hierarchical manner as predicted by the flying geese model. As a result, we observe continuously change position and roles of leading geese, and no clearly defined tier or hierarchy emerges. Despite its limitation, the framework remains relevant to capture the changes in industrial hence technological development in the region.

In this paper, we apply the flying geese theory, and position China's BRI as another catalyst for development, which to some extent competing or complementing the role of Japanese and NIEs FDI in the region. Specifically, we attempt to guesstimate the benefits and costs of BRI on industrial development in Indonesia.

There are two opposing views on this. One view is that the BRI will create more benefits for the host economy, through improvement in production (both quantity and quality), industrial upgrading, technological transfer and merchandise exports boost. In this case, the

BRI investment might help the host economy to level up its share of high-tech export. Moreover, the BRI projects might further the integration of product lines between China and the host economy, hence strengthening bilateral economic relations.

The other view sees China's BRI may not bring much benefits for the host economy. This is because the projects may only lead to small improvement in product quality and industrial upgrading, while there is no significant transfer in innovative capability and technology. This is partly because of the weak capacity and inability of the host economy to absorb the knowledge and technology. As a result, it will lead to further dependency on the imported technology from China.

Moreover, there might be some costs related to BRI projects. Initially, the projects might worsen trade deficit in the host economy. This is because the projects might need a lot of imported materials as the capacity of the local suppliers may not be sufficient or may not exist. Trade deficit will not only arise in goods but also in services, given that the projects might use foreign engineers, managers and other types of professional workers to make it run. Also, the projects may also adversely affect the environment and may disrupt some communities, which are affected due to relocation. All these costs must be taken into consideration. And as time goes by, the costs related to the project can be lowered only if the local suppliers and local workers can gradually step up to fill in the demand and the benefits can be trickled to community.

In this case, there are a number of scenarios that potentially happen after BRI projects are commenced, among others:

(1) China's BRI might open new wave of investment in the new manufacturing sectors. This will increase manufacturing production of some specific goods (commodities), including raw materials and consumer goods, mostly cater for domestic market.
(2) As production of the specific manufacturing goods increases, consequently, import of these goods will decrease. However, some important inputs need to be imported. There is also possibility that the BRI will induce higher import for capital goods and intermediate inputs that are not available in the host economy.
(3) Some of China's BRI might also increase production of higher value-added products. This might bring higher export revenue for the host economy.
(4) China's BRI might also open access to knowledge and technology transfer, through training and learning process. As Chinese companies start training the local workers, we expect that this will enlarge the pool of skilled workers in the host country.
(5) China's BRI might also bring along their suppliers and supply chain to the host country. This will create not only new jobs but also possibility of joint venture (JV) with local entrepreneurs.

It is important to note that both country-specific and firm-specific variables are important in determining the impact of BRI on the host economy. Some key country-specific factors include the quality of institutions, regulations and rules enforcement, human resources and infrastructure, among others. Firm-specific factors include capital, labor, technology, strategic and managerial-related variables. All those factors are closely intertwined and it is the capacity of the host economy in managing those factors that will determine the likely benefits of the BRI projects.

To understand Indonesia's capacity in benefiting from BRI, one needs to examine the country's historical trade and investment pattern with respect to its major economic partners. Specifically, trade and investment patterns with China might indicate whether or not China's BRI would bring changes to export and import composition, e.g., from heavy reliance on commodity exports to higher value-added manufacturing exports and from heavy reliance on capital goods and intermediate inputs to a more diversified import.

To assess the causal impact of BRI on the trade and investment structure, one may need to use the longest possible time series data related to importation, production and exportation of a number of industrial goods (covering a substantial period after BRI projects are completed). With such statistical data, one can determine whether or not BRI might have changed the host country's position in the flying geese formation. One can also examine how industrial production and trade of the country is being transformed after the BRI. Unfortunately, to date, such long time series is not available to use. The available statistical data can only show how much does Indonesia rely on China in terms of trade, investment and development financing. Nevertheless, the trend might give some indication on how they would change in the future if BRI projects' benefits are real. On this, one may ask how far it is possible for Indonesia to tap the maximum benefits from BRI. Answers to these questions may shed light on the extent to which Indonesia sees the strategic value of BRI and its overall fit into Indonesia's development plan.

3. Stylized Facts: China–Indonesia Economic Relations

After the normalization of ties in 1999, economic relations between China and Indonesia intensified. As the two countries gradually opened up their economies, bilateral trade and investment grew rapidly (Negara and Suryadinata, 2018b). In fact, in the last decades, due to rising labor costs in China, many enterprises have moved their operations and capital to Southeast Asia.[2]

In recent years, we have observed rapidly evolving trade and investment relationships between the two economies. Below, we present data that at the aggregate level, China's economic growth and that of Indonesia move in tandem, indicating that both depend on common shocks, such as global booms and busts. Moreover, we show that to some extent, the two economies appear to have complementary.

For Indonesia, China's rapid economic growth has contributed to its own growth (Figure 1). This means that China's economic dynamics may have significant direct association with Indonesia's economic situation more than any other countries. Moreover, China's rapid growth itself represents a significant opportunity for Indonesia. This is because China's imports have grown in parallel with its exports, and China is thus an important source of demand for goods from Indonesia. To see China's growing economic

[2] https://asia.nikkei.com/Economy/Southeast-Asia-s-production-gains-speed-as-China-slows (accessed on March 14, 2019).

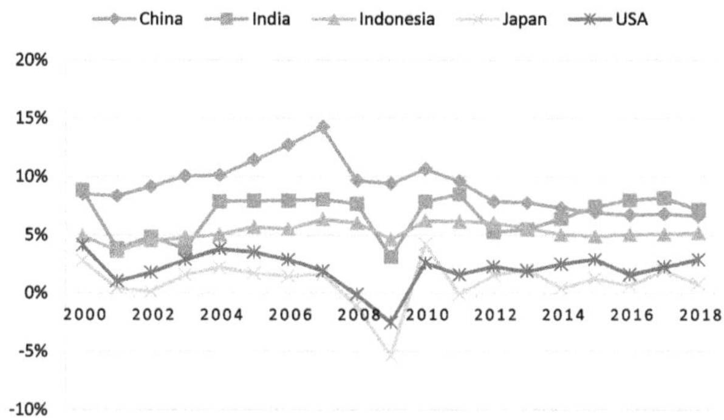

Source: CEIC.

Figure 1. GDP Growth for Select Countries, 2000–2018 (%, Year-on-Year)

influence in Indonesia, one can start by looking at the trade share of China and compared that with other key trading partners (Figure 2).

After the signing of 2005 strategic partnership, Indonesia's trade with China surged to overtake that of the USA (Figure 2). By 2009, China has surpassed Singapore as Indonesia's main trading partner. Subsequently, in 2012, China took over Japan as the most important trading partner for Indonesia. In fact, as China has become a "global factory," Indonesia's economy seems getting more and more integrated with China's production network. In 2005, the share of bilateral trade with China was still only around 8.7% of Indonesia's total trade value of $143.4 billion. By 2018, the share rose to almost 20% of total trade value of $369 billion. Interestingly, the "leading geese," Japan, has shown a declining trade share with Indonesia, from 21% in 2000 to about 10% by 2018.

After the 2008–2009 global financial crisis (GFC), Indonesia started to have trade deficit with China. From then on, China's trade surplus has grown as bilateral trade between the two countries rose from $8.7 billion in 2004 to $72 billion in 2018, an increase by 700%. Consequently, Indonesia's trade balance with China has changed from a surplus of $2.4 billion in 2007 to a deficit of $16 billion in 2018 (Figure 3). It might be noted that Indonesia's trade surplus with Japan has also been declining especially after the GFC.

If one looks at the trade pattern, Indonesia's trade with China relies heavily on commodity exports. In fact, China has become the biggest market for Indonesia's commodities exports, such as coal, natural gas, palm oil and rubber (Figure 4). Tan (2007) argues that as a result of substantial expansion in demand from China, there has been a major rise in commodities and oil prices around the world. During the period of 2008–2013, Indonesia's coal export benefited from the rise of China's coal demand. After 2013, China reduced its coal demand, given increased in domestic concern of the adverse environmental impact of coal usage.[3] From 2013 onwards, China has gradually replaced coal with cleaner energy

[3] https://www.wri.org/blog/2017/01/china-s-decline-coal-consumption-drives-global-slowdown-emissions (accessed on March 14, 2019).

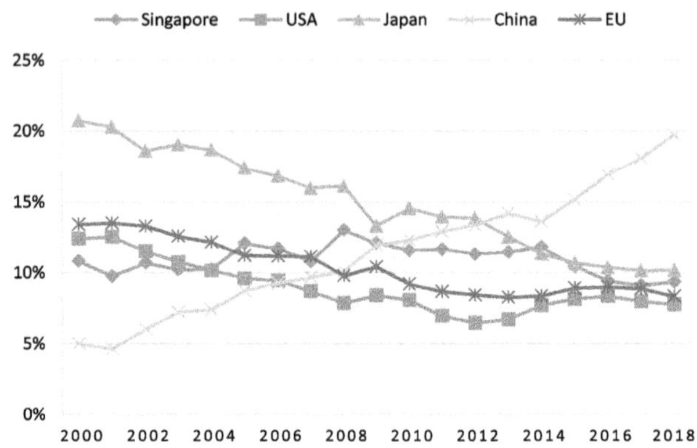

Note: Trade share is defined as total exports and imports value between Indonesia and specific country divided by total exports and imports value that Indonesia recorded with the world in that particular year.
Source: BPS.

Figure 2. Indonesia's Trade with Key Trading Partners, 2000–2018 (Percentage Share of Total Trade Value)

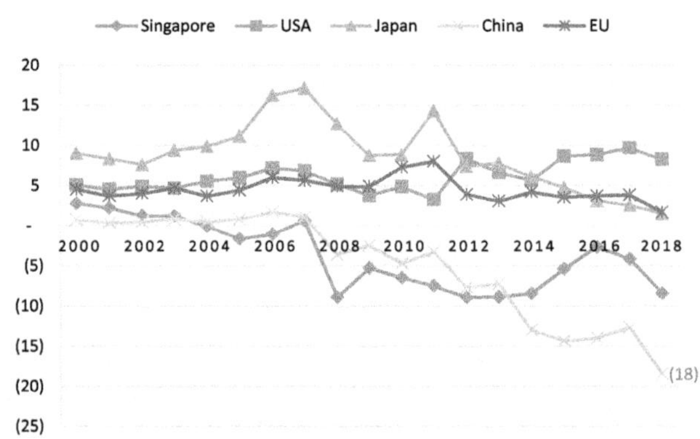

Note: Net trade balance is defined as exports minus imports value that Indonesia has with specific country.
Source: BPS via CEIC.

Figure 3. Indonesia's Trade Balance with Key Trading Partners, 2000–2018 ($ Billion)

sources, such as natural gas. As a result, export of natural gas from Indonesia to China has increased significantly. In 2013, China's share of Indonesia's natural gas export was only around 2.5%, by 2018, the share has jumped to 22%. While EU has put restriction on Indonesia's palm oil exports, China, on the other hand, keeps buying the commodity from Indonesia. As a consequence, its share has gradually increased in recent years, and the trend is expected to continue in the near future. This trend shows how China's economic policies have significant impact on Indonesia's economy.

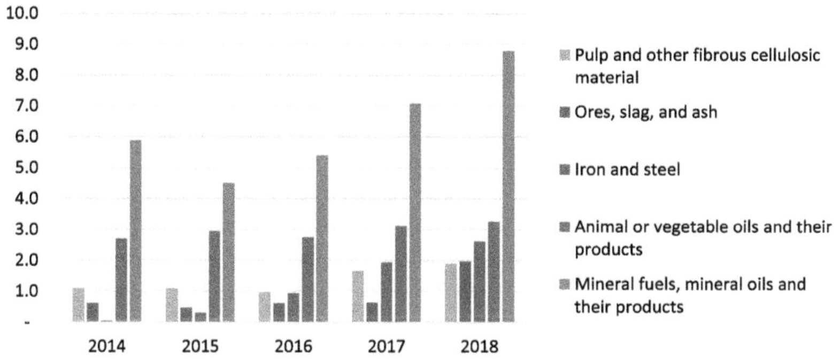

Source: BPS via CEIC.

Figure 4. Indonesia's Top Five Exports Categories to China, 2014–2018 ($ Billion)

It is useful to examine what are Indonesia's key imports from China. Figure 5 shows that Indonesia imported a great number of electrical machinery and mechanical equipment from China. Most of this importation is related to a number of infrastructure projects, which have been accelerated since 2014 (coincided with the start of BRI but these projects are not BRI projects). In addition, significant portion of import from China is in the form of intermediate inputs/materials needed for local industries. What is interesting, in Indonesia, around 60% of telecommunication equipment import is from China. Around 40% of industrial machineries import is from China. And 30% of fertilizer import in Indonesia is also from China. This trend indicates China's growing importance in the three sectors, these are IT, manufacturing and agriculture, in Indonesia.

Beyond trade, Indonesia has been actively sought foreign direct investment (FDI) from China. In fact, under Jokowi administration, the Investment Coordinating Board (BKPM) has been tasked to promote investment from China, which has relatively lower realization

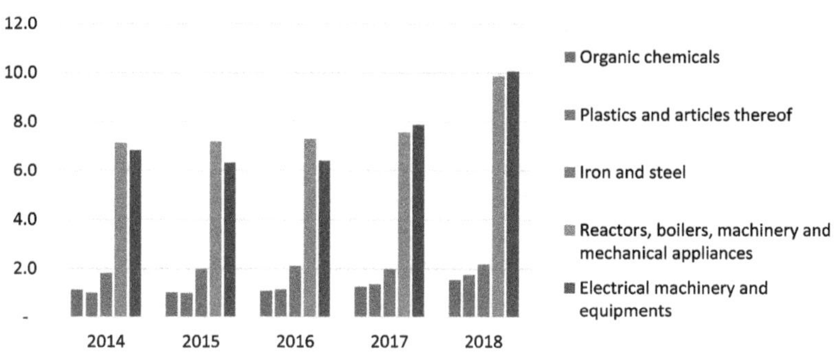

Source: BPS via CEIC.

Figure 5. Indonesia's Top Five Imports Categories from China, 2014–2018 ($ Billion)

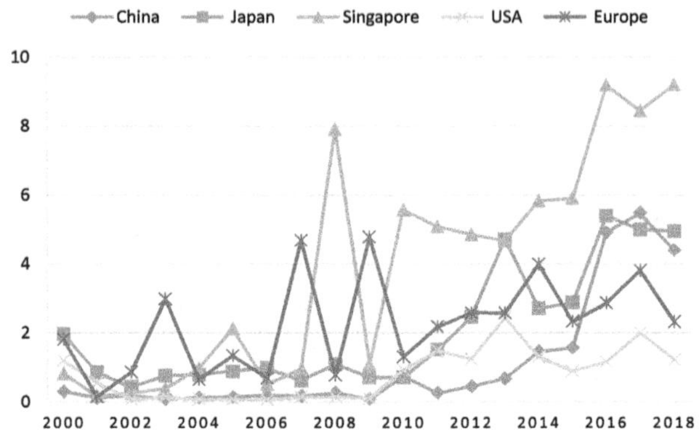

Note: BKPM via CEIC.
Source: BKPM via CEIC.

Figure 6. Realized FDI by Select Countries, 2000–2018 ($ Billion)

rate (percentage of realized investment from its commitment) when compared with that of Singaporean or Japanese FDI (BKPM, 2016a). As such, the BKPM has established a special desk dedicated to Chinese investors Investor Daily (2016).[4] This team provides consultation, facilitation and information service in Chinese language for investors from China. Moreover, BKPM has actively conducted investment promotions in China in partnership with China's banks and business association.[5]

The efforts have come to fruition, in which Chinese outward FDI to Indonesia has increased dramatically since 2016. China's ranking as a source of Indonesian inward FDI moved up from 10th in 2008 to 3rd in 2016 (BKPM, 2016b). Based on BKPM data, the realization of Chinese outward FDI has increased considerably from $0.6 billion in 2015 to $3.4 billion in 2017. However, due to widespread global economic uncertainties, China postponed some of its FDI commitments in Indonesia, as a consequence, the figure has dropped to $2.4 billion in 2018 (Figure 6).[6]

Generally, China's FDI realization in Indonesia remains below that of Singapore and Japan, two traditionally main FDI sources in the country. Figure 7 indicates that in 2018, China accounts for around 8% of total FDI realization in Indonesia. This is still quite low when compared with those of Singapore and Japan, which reached 31% and 17%, respectively (Figure 7). However, there are some anecdotal evidences that China's investment may also go through other entities such as Hong Kong or Singapore before flowing to Indonesia. This may underestimate the real value of their FDI in Indonesia.

What are factors attracting China's FDI into Indonesia? Based on some interviews with a number of Chinese companies' representatives in Indonesia, there are several factors

[4] Investor Daily (2016).
[5] Interview with BKPM's officers on October 26, 2017.
[6] https://finance.detik.com/berita-ekonomi-bisnis/d-4280400/realisasi-investasi-china-berkurang-drastis-hingga-33 (accessed on March 14, 2019).

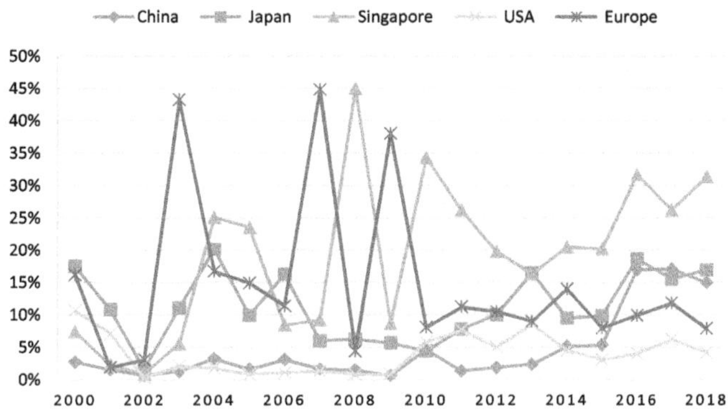

Note: FDI share is defined as total realized FDI value by specific country divided by total FDI that Indonesia received in that particular year.
Source: BKPM via CEIC.

Figure 7. FDI Share by Select Countries, 2000–2018 (Percentage Share to Total FDI)

affecting their decision to come to Indonesia.[7] The factors range from Indonesia's specific mineral and commodity resources needed by China to Indonesia's growing population of middle-class consumers. The former has attracted China's mining companies, such as Tsingshan Group and Delong Group. While the latter has attracted China's electronics companies, such as Xiaomi and Oppo; automotive companies, such as SAIC and Wuling and e-commerce companies, such as Alibaba, Tencent and JD.com.

These pull factors are reflected in the spatial distribution of Chinese FDI in Indonesia. As shown in Figure 8, Chinese companies have significant presence in resource-rich areas, in particular Sulawesi. Based on BKPM data, Sulawesi alone has received 43% of total China's investment in Indonesia. One of the biggest Chinese investments to date is located in Morowali, Central Sulawesi province. According to one estimate, Morowali has around 370 million tons of nickel deposits (Damuri *et al.*, 2018). The second biggest recipient of Chinese FDI is Java, the most populated island in Indonesia, home to around 60% of the country's population. While in Sulawesi, Chinese companies are seeking to explore mineral resources, in Java, they are seeking to explore Indonesia's growing middle class consumer.

Table 1 shows the distribution of China's FDI by sectors. It can be seen that in the last three years (2016–2018), there has been a significant increase in FDI realization, especially in metal and machinery industry. This investment trend is in line with Indonesia's policy to promote smelters development for processing mineral ores into higher value-added products (Negara and Suryadinata, 2018b).

[7] The interviews were conducted between 2017 and 2018 with companies involved in smelting, industrial park and electronics sectors.

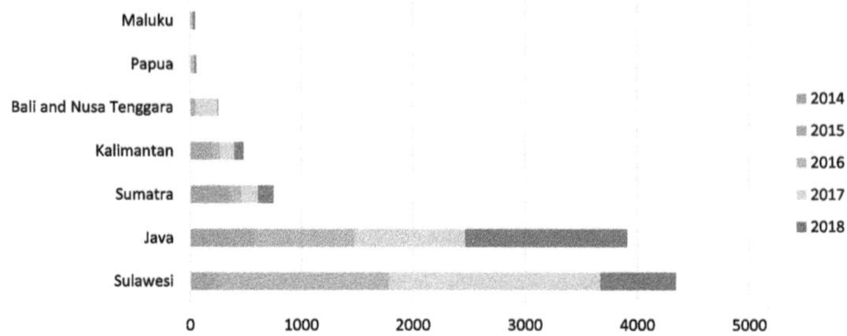

Source: BKPM.

Figure 8. China's Realized FDI by Locations (2014–2018) ($ Million)

Table 1. China's Realized FDI by Sectors (2014–2018) ($ Million)

	2014	2015	2016	2017	2018	Total (2014–2018)
Basic metal, metal goods, machinery and electronics	92.4	99.6	1,519.0	1,718.5	594.0	4,023.5
Electricity, gas and water	319.5	49.1	324.9	938.0	615.5	2,247.0
Transportation, warehouse and telecommunication	3.6	33.1	84.2	160.7	551.3	832.9
Housing, industrial estate and office	72.9	36.9	18.3	83.0	147.3	358.4
Trade and reparation	43.3	102.6	53.8	104.9	65.5	370.1
Chemical and pharmaceutical	8.9	4.1	175.9	90.1	47.2	326.2
Non-metal mineral	41.6	17.5	197.1	27.4	6.8	290.4
Food manufacturing	9.3	48.6	109.3	30.3	47.8	245.3
Food crops, plantation and livestock	2.0	139.8	8.3	30.8	73.0	253.9
Medical instruments and electrical equipment	6.8	20.3	24.5	51.2	107.2	210.0
Other sectors	199.8	76.7	149.9	126.3	120.9	673.6

Source: BKPM.

4. Connecting China's Projects with Indonesia's Industrial and Sub-national Development

The stylized facts above illustrate China's growing economic influence in Indonesia. The question is how will this bring benefits to Indonesia's development aspirations? Will China be able to offer benefits that other countries could not give? This section attempts to link some Chinese major projects with industrial and sub-national development in Indonesia.

As stated earlier, there is no official BRI project in Indonesia yet. If we look at the projects begun after Xi assumed the Chinese presidency, there is only one major project: the Jakarta–Bandung High Speed Rail project (HSR), the agreement for which was signed in October 2015. The project cost is estimated to reach around $6 billion and is financed by loans from China Development Bank, with 2.8% fixed interest. Arguably, this is the most important project in the context of China–Indonesia relations Salim and Negara (2016), which is likely to determine the future of BRI projects in Indonesia.

The Jakarta–Bandung HSR project was initially proposed by Japan during the SBY presidency (Negara and Suryadinata, 2018a; Yoshimatsu, 2018). It was believed Japan would win the project as it had the technology and had conducted various studies. However, when Jokowi became president, China was invited to join the competition. During the last stage of project bidding, Jokowi altered the conditions on capital and government guarantee and Japan was unable to fulfil these new requirements (Negara and Suryadinata, 2018a; Yoshimatsu, 2018). In contrast, China quickly accepted Jokowi's conditions and hence won the project.

This high-speed railway project shows an interesting new dynamic in a relatively new "high-tech" sector, in which China comes to challenge Japan's domination (Yoshimatsu, 2018). Despite China winning the project, the project construction has not been smooth-sailing. There were reports in foreign press that there were a lot of difficulties that the project contractor had to overcome with regard to land acquisition (Mcbeth, 2017). The implementation is more difficult than it was first thought. China may have missed an important aspect in their project calculation, in which the state could not freely acquire the people's land in Indonesia Tempo.co (2017b). This hurdle has delayed the completion of the project.

As of December 2018, the progress on the construction remained less than 5%, whereas land acquisition for the project had only reached 86%.[8] This means the completion deadline of the project would be delayed until 2021, two years later than the original deadline for the project's completion. However, the Chinese government appears to be optimistic. The *People's Daily* delegation visited Indonesia and filed a report on 15 January 2019 regarding the Jakarta–Bandung HSR. It is noted that this Jakarta–Bandung HSR is "an important landmark project." There were "breakthroughs in the 22 control points, and the project has entered a new phase of comprehensive implementation." The report mentioned that Tunnel No. 1 (which is the first tunnel from Jakarta, whose length was 1885 m) and the Walini Tunnel (which is about 40 min by car from Bandung, which is 600 m long) have achieved great progress (Figure 9). It also reported that the project benefited 2000 local employees and would create more additional jobs. It further reports that the Jakarta–Bandung HSR Construction Site School (Gongdi Xuexiao) was established and had trained 200 Indonesian workers and the target was to train 2000 workers Renmin Ribao (2019).[9]

[8] Tempo.co, "*Proyek Kereta Cepat Jakarta-Bandung Ditargetkan Rampung* 2021", 13 December 2018. https://bisnis.tempo.co/read/1154875/proyek-kereta-cepat-jakarta-bandung-ditargetkan-rampung-2021 (accessed on January 14, 2019).

[9] See "Wan Ya Gao Tie, Shuli shiwu hezuo xin biaogan" (Jakarta-Bandung HSR), to establish the new benchmark of pragmatic cooperation, *Renmin Ribao* (People's Daily), 15 January 2019. No information is available in the Indonesian newspapers on the details of the Jakarta–Bandung HSR project. It is also worth noting that the People's Daily report appeared to respond to criticism made in Indonesia about China's projects that primarily used mainland Chinese workers. Nevertheless, these have not really answered the questions as no percentage and number of Indonesian workers are available in Indonesian press that can be verified.

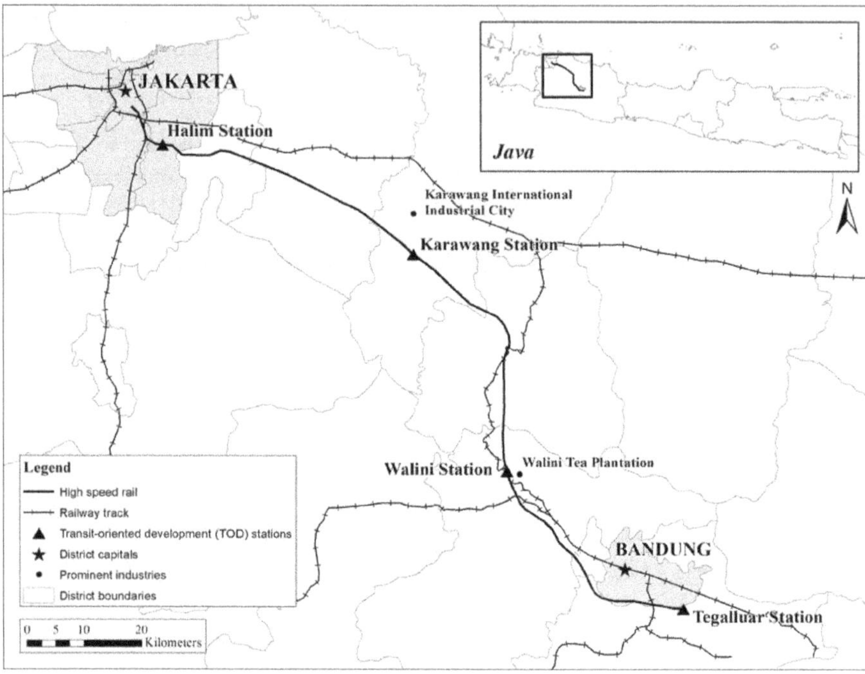

Source: Map provided by ISEAS-Yusof Ishak Institute @ (2019).

Figure 9. Jakarta–Bandung High-Speed Railway Project

Nevertheless, the report did not indicate how much of the project has been accomplished and when it would be completed.

Apart from the high-speed railway project, during the SBY presidency (Jokowi's predecessor), there were also a number of electricity generators projects built by Chinese contractors under the so-called Fast-Track Program (FTP), which aimed to accelerate the development of 10,000 MW of new power capacity. China constructed 90% of the total number of electricity projects under FTP-1. In total, there were 22 projects constructed by Chinese companies (Negara and Suryadinata, 2018b). All of these companies relied on financing from the China Export–Import Bank. It was reported that the Chinese built power plants were of mixed quality. Regardless of the mixed reporting, under Jokowi's administration, Indonesia's state-owned electricity company (PLN) still uses a great number of China's contractors in the 35,000 MW national electricity projects. This is because they are able to offer minimum bidding price.

Another major Chinese project that is worth further discussion is the development of Indonesia Morowali Industrial Park (IMIP) (Figure 10). In 2009, Shanghai Decent Group of China formed a JV with PT Sulawesi Mining Investment (SMI) of Indonesia in nickel ore mining and export. Since then, the JV has been developing ferronickel smelter in response to government's program to increase value added in minerals export. In 2014, Shanghai Decent Group and Bintangdelapan Group (owner of SMI) established an industrial park, called PT Indonesia Morowali Industrial Park (IMIP). Decent Group control 49.7% of the share of IMIP. In mid-2017, Tsingshan Group and Delong Group signed an MoU with IMIP to develop $980 million carbon-steel factory, with capacity of 3.5 million ton per year.

This private-sector-led project has been perceived by the Indonesian policymakers as an ideal model for BRI investment in Indonesia. The project is developed based on a business-to-business (B-to-B) scheme with least government involvement (financing). For Indonesia, this business model is more favorable since it will not burden the state budget. In addition, if completed the project is expected to create significant local jobs; promote exports and foster technology transfer to the local partners. Hence, if this really happens, the project can be considered as a win-win project. Nevertheless, it is difficult to assess real economic impact of the project as construction of the industrial park has not been completed and it will take more time to see the economic outputs stemming from the project.

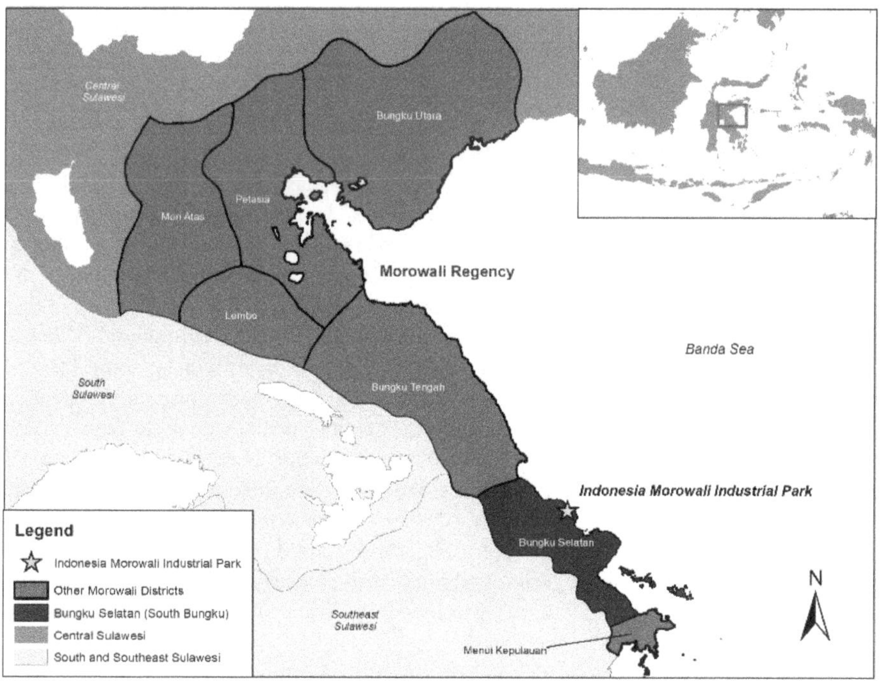

Source: Map provided by ISEAS-Yusof Ishak Institute @ (2019).

Figure 10. Morowali Industrial Park Project

All the above-mentioned major projects built by China might have different implications to industrial and sub-national development in Indonesia. In the case of high-speed railway project, it is designed to improve connectivity between two major cities, Jakarta and Bandung. The project is meant to anticipate growing traffic frequency driven by mega-urbanization in the two cities. It also links to future transit-oriented development (TOD) and services sector development. From the manufacturing sector aspect, the project might be linked with Indonesia's objective to develop its own railway industry by learning from imported Chinese technology. In the JV agreement, China has agreed to transfer the technology related to the development and management of high-speed railway technology.[10]

In the case of electricity project, most of the projects are under engineering, procurement and construction (EPC) contracts by Chinese contractors. The project aims to anticipate growing electricity demand needed by the industry. It was reported in local news that Chinese contractors dominated the 35,000 MW electricity project, while the Japanese were reluctant due to their disagreement with the bidding requirement.[11] Nevertheless, the low price might also relate to lower quality and overall higher life-cycle cost. In view of this, since China is not the only contractor involved in this sector, therefore it will be a good case study to assess the quality, life-cycle cost and technological aspects of Chinese built power plants vis-à-vis non-China's made power plants. This is beyond the scope of this paper.

And the last example, the development of industrial park is meant to promote sub-national development (especially outside Java) by focussing on the comparative advantage (including natural resources) in the related region. Compared with other investors, China has been more willing to invest in the outer islands, which has lower population density. By inviting China investment in the outer-island provinces, Indonesian government expects to promote a more balanced development in the country, i.e., creating the needed infrastructure, opening new jobs opportunity and boosting the local economy. This is one of the reasons why the Indonesian government has been inviting China's FDI, while other investors have shied away. The Indonesian government has been encouraging Chinese investors to form JV with local partners, in the hope that there will be some kind of technology transfer. While there is high expectation with regard to project benefits, however learning from past experience, Indonesia should perhaps be more realistic and may need to adapt its strategy going forward. An important issue is whether these JV projects allow Indonesian firms to assimilate and master the imported technologies to its specific needs. Past studies show that JVs do not guarantee transfer of innovative capabilities (Lall, 1998; Lindblad and Thee, 2002; Thee, 2005). Eventually, the successful development of local technological capabilities will determine whether the imported technologies can be successfully applied in Indonesia. This is a tricky exercise.

[10] https://properti.kompas.com/read/2016/05/17/150000621/KCIC.dan.CRIC.Siap.Alih.Teknologi.Kereta.Cepat (accessed on June 6, 2019).

[11] https://sains.kompas.com/read/2016/01/14/074400926/Proyek.Listrik.35.000.MW.Jepang.Ogah.Ikut.China.Mendominasi (accessed June 6, 2019).

A number of studies on international technology transfer in Indonesia's manufacturing sector show that foreign direct investment, technical licensing agreements, imports of capital goods and technical and marketing assistance from foreign buyers of manufactured exports have been the four important channels for international technology transfer in Indonesia (Lall, 1998; Thee, 2005). That said, many Indonesian companies have worked with foreign companies prior to Chinese companies, but the process of technology transfer has not been impressive so far (Lall, 1998; Thee, 2005). As a technology-importing country, Indonesia has been unsuccessful in maximizing the international transfer of the most relevant technologies on the best available terms (Thee, 2005, p. 217). As a result, most firms in Indonesia remain highly dependent on imports of "ready-made" technology. They have not been able to upgrade their capacity to absorb and improve upon complex imported technologies.

For some years, the government has been trying to encourage foreign companies to establish their R&D facilities in Indonesia. While effort to force Japanese companies to transfer their innovative capabilities to their local partner has failed, it seems unrealistic to expect Chinese enterprises to be different if the current bottlenecks are not addressed. A major factor which has often hampered transfer of technology through FDI and other channels has been the country's lack of absorptive capacity. This is because of acute shortage of adequately trained and skilled local workers able to fully comprehend and master the technologies transferred to them (Thee, 2005, p. 233). This shortage is by product of poor quality of education in Indonesia at all levels (Kurniawati *et al.*, 2018). For foreign companies to move their R&D facilities, they need a sufficiently large scale of market operations and a sufficient pool of highly qualified and experienced scientists and engineers who are in short supply in Indonesia. Therefore, local R&D in the foreign-controlled JV would remain highly dependent on the fully-fledged R&D department at the headquarters of the foreign principal (Lindblad and Thee, 2002, pp. 29–30).

Back to the case of the JV running a ferronickel smelter, Indonesia should be more realistic in terms of technology transfer and may need to adjust its strategy. To improve the process of international technology transfer, Indonesia should promote its ability to move from a passive dependence on technology transfer to a more active role in mastering and building upon imported technologies (Lall, 1998, p. 137). It needs to tackle significant obstacles for local companies to obtain new knowledge/technologies from foreign partners. Moreover, it might need to create the required ecosystem of innovation and offer certain incentive system for the foreign-controlled enterprises to transfer their innovative capabilities and for local enterprises to develop local technological capabilities. The questions will be what kind of incentives that will be powerful enough to make Chinese companies willing to transfer their technology. This can be part of the bargaining for future BRI projects. An important target would be to promote the development of capital goods sector, a crucial element of industrial deepening, which is relatively underdeveloped in Indonesia (Thee, 2005).

Finally, it is difficult to assess which business scheme can maximize the benefits of BRI. While the Indonesian government prefers "business-to-business" (B-to-B) model, however, not all BRI projects can apply similar scheme. B-to-B scheme works in the case of Morowali project since the area has large nickel deposits, which attract companies like Shanghai Decent Investment Group, Tsingshan Group, Delong Group and Bintangdelapan Groups to form a JV. The lucrative mining business also attracts other nickel-based companies to locate in the park. Certainly, not every BRI project possesses similar potential to attract investors. For instance, infrastructure projects in remote or sparsely populated areas will be difficult to find private investors to come. In this case, the role of public sector and state-owned enterprises might be critical. For sure, the benefits of BRI should be assessed beyond industrial development but also covering its impact on society and environment.

5. Criticisms and Other Issues

Beyond its growing investment, in recent years, Indonesia has also received more financing from China. This is amidst widespread concerns with regard to Chinese lending practices. Critics often allege that loans associated with China's BRI projects might put countries into a debt trap situation (Pavlićević and Kratz, 2017; Rimmer, 2018).[12] For Indonesia, the issue is not about debt trap but how the debt is used (for what purposes). According to Bank Indonesia data, China's loan to Indonesia is still relatively small compared with those from Singapore and Japan; however in terms of share, it has increased noticeably. In nominal term, the total loan from China has increased from $11.4 billion in 2008 to $194.7 billion in 2018. This has increased China's share from around 3% in 2008 to 9% of Indonesia's total outstanding external debt in 2018 (Figure 11). Importantly, Singapore's share remains high at around 16%, whereas Japan's share has plunged from 23% in 2008 to 8% in 2018. Of note, private sector loans collectively account for the lion's share (about 90%) of China's loans to Indonesia (Figure 12). This is in contrast to loans from Japan. The latter remains the key creditor for public sector in Indonesia. That said, over time, we see that the share of debt-financing from Japan that goes to private sector has been increasing. Unfortunately, we do not have information on where or to which sectors/ projects all these loans go.

In addition, critics of China's BRI assert that many projects related to BRI are dominated by Chinese contractors and hired Chinese workers with little spillover to the local community and host economies (He, 2019; Rimmer, 2018; Damuri *et al.*, 2018; Negara and Suryadinata, 2018b). For the case of Indonesia, we have seen an increase in the number of Chinese workers especially during the period of 2013–2018. The number of Chinese workers in Indonesia has doubled from 16,000 in 2011 to 32,000 by 2018 (Tempo.co (2017a)). Most of the Chinese workers are employed in Chinese-funded and operated projects. Based on an interview, Chinese contractors and Indonesian business counterpart perceive that using Chinese workers can speed up the project implementation

[12] Debt trap is a term used in international relations to describe a situation in which one creditor country intentionally extending excessive credit to another debtor country with the alleged intention of extracting economic or political concessions from the debtor country when it becomes unable to honor its debt obligations.

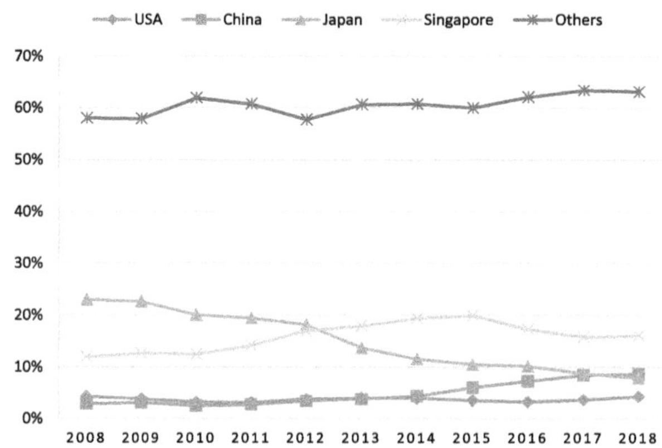

Notes: (1) Debt share is defined as total debt value from specific source divided by total external debt value that Indonesia recorded in that particular year. (2) China's figure is combined with Hong Kong.
Source: Ministry of Finance.

Figure 11. Debt Composition by Sources (Percentage Share of Total External Debt)

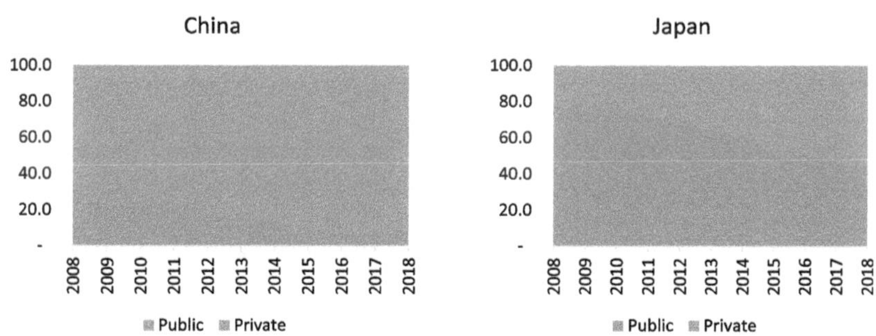

Note: Public sector debt includes offshore ownership of government bonds.
Source: Ministry of Finance.

Figure 12. Debt Composition by Public Versus Private Source, 2008–2018 (%)

since the local workers are less skillful/equipped to handle even the basic tasks, e.g., manual labor.[13] There has been a growing effort by some Chinese companies to train local workers, including by sending them to China for a few months training. However, this will take some time to have an impact on the quality of local workers.

Finally, Figure 13 shows that there has been a significant increase of Chinese visitors to Indonesia since 2005, which coincided with the former President Susilo Bambang

[13] Interview with owner of an industrial park in Galang Batang, Bintan, Riau Islands Province in February 2019. The industrial park is a JV between Chinese investor and local investor.

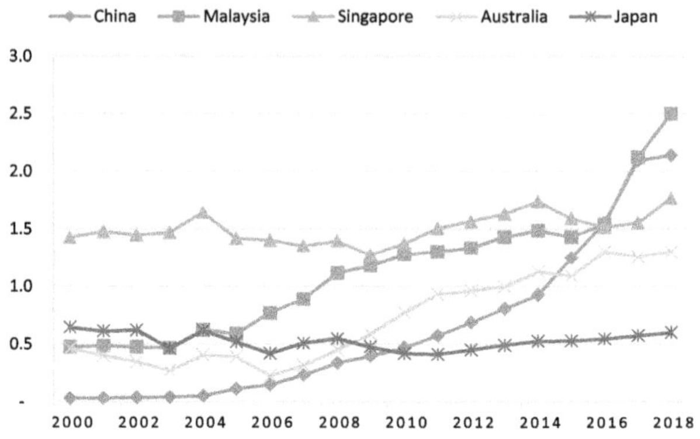

Source: Ministry of Tourism.

Figure 13. Number of Tourists by Country of Residence, 2000–2018 (Million)

Yudhoyono (SBY) period. In 2005, there were only around 100 thousand Chinese tourists visiting Indonesia. By 2018, the number of tourists from China has reached 2.14 million (Figure 11). Currently, China has been one of the largest sources of tourists for Indonesia, aside from Malaysia, Singapore and Australia. The rapid increase in Chinese visitors has contributed positively to the local economy and has been welcomed as such by the Indonesian government. Nevertheless, it is important to consider potential adverse effect from rapid tourism growth on the environment and community. These issues are often neglected if the central and local governments are only concern about the number of tourists and revenue from tourism.

In sum, to date, China is one of Indonesia's most important economic partners. It is Indonesia's largest trading partner, though the trade balance favors China. That said, trade with China is important to support Indonesia's industrialization in agricultural, manufacturing and IT sectors. In fact, most of the products being imported from China are intermediate inputs or necessary equipment for local industries. Moreover, China has quickly become one of the main investors in Indonesia after Singapore and Japan. It remains to be seen, however, whether Chinese FDI can surpass Japan and whether their FDI might become the catalyst for technology transfer and help boosting Indonesia's exports of higher value-added goods. On financing side, China is increasingly becoming a major source of funding for Indonesia's companies.

6. Conclusions

This paper attempts to apply the flying geese model in explaining potential benefits of China's BRI in Indonesia. The original flying geese model puts Japan at the central of Asian industrial development. As China has rapidly industrialized and become one of the leaders in the industrial and economic field, developing countries such as Indonesia come to rely more on China, especially in trade, technology, investment, financing and tourism. Despite its limitation, the flying geese framework is still useful to provide some insight into possible benefits that China's BRI could bring to the host economy.

As this paper argues, China has become one of the leading geese in Asia, thus it offers opportunities for other developing countries to follow its trajectory/path. In some specific sectors, China might have a competitive edge against Japan, South Korea and other developed economies, e.g., AI and 5G technology. In other aspects, it might also offer complementarities, e.g., infrastructure development. As such, developing countries like Indonesia are now facing more options in relation to their source of financing, technology and capital.

In view of broader Chinese investment (including BRI), it might be linked with Indonesia's ambition to build its industrial capacity and promote its sub-national development. The Indonesian government remains confident that China's BRI offers opportunities that other countries could not (or hesitate to) give. Under the Jokowi administration, Indonesia's response to BRI has been positive and is willing to invite BRI investment to promote industrialization and sub-national development. However, to make any concrete assessment of the benefits of BRI project is not possible, given there is no official completed BRI project yet in Indonesia. Therefore, at the moment, there are no sufficient empirical data to show benefits and costs of BRI in relation to either industrial or sub-national development in Indonesia. There are more anecdotal evidences than rigorous statistical data for assessing the impact.

While concrete assessment of the benefits of BRI project in Indonesia cannot be made, however, we argue that BRI might have initiated a new type of investment that might in turn change the industrial trends, structure and performance in the country. For instance, in recent years, there has been a new wave of Chinese investment in the manufacturing sector, including in electronics and mineral processing as well. If this change leads to improvement in products quality or value added, industrial upgrading, technological transfer and export boost, then one may argue that China's investment has brought promised benefits to Indonesia. In addition, China's BRI might also offer assistance to promote balanced development in the outer islands of the country. The latter have long suffered from poor infrastructure and low economic activities. This is why the Indonesian government has been trying to direct BRI investments outside Java.

While China is offering opportunity, eventually both country-specific and firm-specific variables are important in determining the impact of BRI on the host economy. For sure, there are many hindrances in tapping the benefits from BRI. The constraints include Indonesia's own weak business environment, infrastructure deficit and low human resource quality. Some of its industrial and trade policies are also not compatible with the foreign business interest. For instance, policies related to manpower (Manning and Roesad, 2007) and local content (Negara, 2017) are perceived less conducive to business. Without solving those bottlenecks, it is difficult to expect significant number of Chinese investors would be prepared to invest in the country.

Acknowledgments

The authors would like to thank two anonymous reviewers for their useful comments on our earlier draft. We thank Yudha Tri Utama, Taruna Ikhwanuddin (Indonesia Investment Coordinating Board or BKPM) and Yose Rizal Damuri (Center for Strategic International Studies or CSIS), Jakarta for their information on China's investment in Indonesia. We also would like to thank Benjamin Hu and Juen Tan for their assistance in producing maps in this paper. In this paper, all figures, unless otherwise noted, are given in United States dollars (USD).

References

Ahearne, AG, JG Fernald, P Loungani and JW Schindler (2006). Flying geese or sitting ducks: China's impact on the trading fortunes of other Asian economies. *Board of Governors of the Federal Reserve System International Finance Discussion Papers*. No. 887 (December).

Akamatsu, K (1962). A historical pattern of economic growth in developing countries. *The Developing Economies*, 1, 3–25.

Bernard, M and J Ravenhill (1995). Beyond product cycles and flying geese: Regionalization, hierarchy, and the industrialization of East Asia. *World Politics*, 47, 171–209.

BKPM (2016a). Siaran Press: Rencana Investasi PMA Tahun 2015 Terbesar dari Tiongkok, 4 January 2016 (accessed on January 14, 2019). Available at: http://www2.bkpm.go.id/images/uploads/file_siaran_pers/Siaran_Pers_BKPM_04012016_ Rencana_Investasi_PMA_Tahun_2015_Terbesar_dari_Tiongkok.pdf.

BKPM (2016b). Realisasi Penanaman Modal PMDN-PMA Triwulan I Tahun 2016, Press Release, 25 April 2016 (accessed on January 14, 2019). Available at: http://www5.bkpm.go.id/images/uploads/investasi_indonesia/file/PRESS_ RELEASE_REALISASI_INVESTASI_TW_I_2016_-_IND.pdf.

Chen, EKY and CH Kwan (1997). The emergence of subregional economic zones in Asia. In *Asia's Borderless Economy: The Emergence of Sub-regional Zones*, EKY Chen and CH Kwan (eds.), pp. 1–27. St Leonards, NSW: Allen and Unwin.

Damuri, YR, V Perkasa, R Atje and F Hirawan (2018). Perceptions and readiness of Indonesia towards the Belt and Road Initiative: Understanding local perspectives, capacity and governance, CSIS Report.

Edgington, DW and R Hayter (2000). Foreign direct investment and the flying geese model: Japanese electronics firms in Asia-Pacific. *Environment and Planning A*, 32, 281–304.

Hallgren, H and R Ghiasy (2017). Security and economy on the belt and road: Three country case studies. *SIPRI Insights on Peace and Security* No. 2017/4. December.

Hayter, R and DW Edgington (2004). Flying geese in Asia: The impacts of Japanese MNCs as a source of industrial learning. *Tijdschrift voor Economische en Sociale Geografie*, Royal Dutch Geographical Society KNAG, 95(1), 3–26.

Hatch, W and K Yamamura (1996). *Asia in Japan's Embrace: Building a Regional Production Alliance*, Cambridge University Press.

He, B (2019). The domestic politics of the Belt and Road Initiative and its implications. *Journal of Contemporary China*, 28(116), 180–195.

Investor Daily (2016). BKPM Siapkan Desk Khusus Tiongkok, 2 May 2016 (accessed on January 14, 2019). Available at: http://www5.bkpm.go.id/id/publikasi/detail/berita-investasi/bkpm-siapkan-desk-khusus-tiongkok.

Kurniawati, S, D Suryadarma, L Bima and A Yusrina (2018). Education in Indonesia: A white elephant? *Journal of Southeast Asian Economies*, 35(2), 185–199.

Lall, S (1998). Technology policies in Indonesia. In *Indonesia's Technological Challenge*, H Hill and Thee Kian Wie (eds.), pp. 136–168. Singapore: Institute of Southeast Asian Studies.

Lin, JY (2011). From flying geese to leading dragons: New opportunities and strategies for structural transformation in developing countries. WIDER Lecture, May 4, 2011 (accessed on January 14, 2019). Available at: http://siteresources.worldbank.org/INTMOZAMBIQUE/Resources/WIDER_Lecture-Justin_Lin-05-03-11.pdf.

Lindblad, JTh and KW Thee (2002). Indonesian economic development and Japanese technology. *ICSEAD Working Paper Series* 2002-09, Kitakyushu: International Centre for the Study of East Asian Development.

Liu, H and G Lim (2019). The political economy of a rising China in Southeast Asia: Malaysia's response to the Belt and Road Initiative. *Journal of Contemporary China*, 28(116), 216–231.

Manning, C and K Roesad (2007). The Manpower Law of 2003 and its implementing regulations: Genesis, key articles and potential impact. *Bulletin of Indonesian Economic Studies*, 43(1), 59–86.

Mcbeth, J (2017). Indonesia high-speed train, backed by China, comes untracked. *Asia Times*, 28 March 2017 (accessed on January 14, 2019). Available at: http://www.atimes.com/article/indonesia-high-speed-train-backed-china-comes-untracked/.

McKay, H and L Song (Eds.) (2012). *Rebalancing and Sustaining Growth in China*. ANU Press.

Nakagane, K (2013). China's economic development and Sino-Japanese economic relationships: Beyond the flying geese pattern theory. *Journal of Contemporary East Asia Studies*, 2(1), 29–54.

Negara, SD (2017). Assessing the impact of local content requirements on Indonesia's manufacturing. In *The Indonesian Economy: Trade and Industrial Policies*, L Yan-Ing, G Hanson and SM Indrawati (eds.). Routledge.

Negara, SD and L Suryadinata (2018a). Jakarta–Bandung High Speed Rail Project: Little Progress, Many Challenges. *ISEAS Perspective* No. 2.

Negara, SD and L Suryadinata (2018b). Indonesia and China's Belt and Road Initiatives: Perspectives, issues and prospects. *Trends in Southeast Asia Series*, No. 11/18.

Pavlićević, D and A Kratz (2017). Testing the China Threat paradigm: China's high-speed railway diplomacy in Southeast Asia. *The Pacific Review*, DOI: 10.1080/09512748.2017.1341427.

Qu, Y, F Cai and X Zhang (2012). Has the 'flying geese' phenomenon in industrial transformation occurred in China? In *Rebalancing and Sustaining Growth in China*, H McKay and L Song (eds.), pp. 93–110. ANU Press.

Renmin Ribao (2019). Wan Ya Gao Tie, Shuli shiwu hezuo xin biaogan (Jakarta-Bandung HSR, to establish the new benchmark of pragmatic cooperation), 15 January 2019.

Rimmer, PJ (2018). China's Belt and Road Initiative: Underlying economic and international relations dimensions. *Asian Pacific Economic Literature*, 32(2), 3–26.

Salim, W and SD Negara (2016). Why is the high-speed rail project so important to Indonesia. *ISEAS Perspective* No. 16.

Shen, S and W Chan (2018). A comparative study of the Belt and Road Initiative and the Marshall Plan. *Palgrave Communications*, 4(32) (accessed on March 3, 2019). Available at: https://www.nature.com/articles/s41599-018-0077-9.pdf.

Steven, R (1996). *Japan and the New World Order: Global Investments, Trade and Finance* (Basingstoke, Hants: Macmillan).

Suryadinata, L (2017a). *The Rise of China and the Chinese Overseas: A Study of Beijing Changing Policies in Southeast Asia and Beyond*. Singapore: ISEAS.

Suryadinata, L (2017b). Anti-China campaign in Jokowi's Indonesia, *Straits Times*, 10 January 2017 (accessed on January 14, 2019). Available at: http://www.straitstimes.com/opinion/anti-china-campaign-in-jokowis-indonesia.

Suryadinata, L and M Izzudin (2017). The Natunas: Territorial integrity in the forefront of Indonesia–China relations. *Trends in Southeast Asia*, No. 5, ISEAS Publishing.

Tan, KY (2007). China's 11th five-year plan: A critical perspective. In *China's Surging Economy: Adjusting for More Balanced Development*, J Wong and W Liu (eds.), pp. 55–132. World Scientific.

Tempo (2015a). Sayonara to the Shinkansen (English Edition), 18 October 2015.

Tempo (2015b). Selamat Datang Buruh Cina, 29 August 2015.

Tempo (2016). Akrobat Proyek Kereta Cepat, 14 February 2016.

Tempo.co (2017a). EKSKLUSIF 2, Hanif: Tenaga Kerja Asal Cina Itu Ada, tapi..., 2 January 2017 (accessed on January 14, 2019). Available at: https://nasional.tempo.co/read/831938/eksklusif-2-hanif-tenaga-kerja-asal-cina-itu-ada-tapi.

Tempo.co (2017b). Luhut Ungkap Kelemahan Cina dalam Proyek Kereta Cepat, 12 April 2017 (accessed on January 14, 2019). Available at: https://bisnis.tempo.co/read/news/2017/04/12/090865109/luhut-ungkap-kelemahan-cina-dalam-proyek-kereta-cepat.

Thee, KW (2005). The major channels of international technology transfer to Indonesia: An assessment. *Journal of the Asia Pacific Economy*, 10(2), 214–236.

Wong, J (2007). China's economic growth in East Asian Context. In *China's Surging Economy: Adjusting for More Balanced Development*, J Wong and W Liu (eds.), pp. 31–54. World Scientific.

Yamazawa, I (1990). *Economic Development and International Trade: The Japanese Model*, East-West Centre, Honolulu, HA.

Yoshimatsu, H (2018). New Dynamics in Sino-Japanese Rivalry: Sustaining infrastructure development in Asia. *Journal of Contemporary China*, 27(113), 719–734.

Chapter 15

CHINA'S BELT AND ROAD INITIATIVE: A VIEW FROM A MAHATHIRIST IMAGINARY*

BOO TEIK KHOO

The National Graduate Institute for Policy Studies
7-22-1 Roppongi, Minato-ku, Tokyo 106-8677, Japan
khoo-bt@grips.ac.jp

Published Online 8 August 2019

Malaysia's Mahathir Mohamad stands in a delicate position vis-à-vis China's Belt and Road Initiative (BRI). The BRI's Silk Road-like scenarios of transcontinental rail links to extend market-facilitated trade and investment have a place within a *'Mahathirist imaginary'* that opposes inequities in a western-ruled global order and sees hope for the 'rise of Asia'. In vision he shares the 'Chinese Dream' of resurrecting ancient land and maritime trade routes as an 'imperative of globalization' despite attempts by others to entangle the BRI in narratives of geopolitics long repugnant to his deep non-aligned convictions. His unprecedented resumption of premiership in May 2018 gave Mahathir a dream-like chance to engage with the BRI but he has been jolted by some Malaysian-China projects contracted in the name of the BRI by the Najib Razak-headed regime (2009–2018). Concerned that those projects could strain Malaysia's debt burden and undermine its sovereignty, Mahathir must balance his support for BRI with undoing some of its local manifestations without jeopardizing long-term Malaysia-China trade, investment and diplomatic relations.

Keywords: Mahathir Mohamad; Mahathirist imaginary; Malaysia; China; Belt and Road Initiative; Rise of Asia; East Coast Rail Link.

JEL Classification: F54

> We are living the logical conclusion of silk-road processes begun millennia ago. But the evocations of the silk road in music, travel, games, food, fashion, pharmaceuticals, and even politics speak to something else: nostalgia for a world connected but discrete, a world still capable of surprising us .... That silk road may be a fantasy but we still hope to travel it.
>
> James A Millward, *The Silk Road: A Very Short Introduction*, 2013: 121

> Q (BBC): But do you see them as bringing about a new form of colonialism with their One Belt, One Road infrastructure projects?
>
> A (Mahathir): No, no, no, not at all. One Belt, One Road is okay.
>
> *The Edge Financial Daily*, 3 October 2018

China's Belt and Road Initiative (BRI), like other economic and political developments with international ramifications — the 'East Asian miracle', the 'East Asian financial crisis', the 'global financial crisis', or the 'Arab Spring' — has spawned a 'cottage

*This article originally appeared in *The Singapore Economic Review*, **66**(1), pp. 293–312

industry, fuelling numerous events, dozens of studies, and hundreds of news articles and Op-Ed pieces' (Blanchard, 2018, 329). Many products of the industry offer assessments of security implications; others aim at popular edification (understood positively or negatively). On whether the BRI would benefit China and/or its partner states, for example, the literature ranges from detached analyses to partisan assessments, and from enthusiastic 'win-win' endorsements to dismissive 'zero-sum' judgments. Most readings of BRI are based on considerations of political economy and/or geopolitics, statist in their perspectives, and occupied with prognostications of a new Sino-centric world order that is shaped by the 'rise', the 'threat', the 'domination' or, come to that, the 'containment' of China.

This essay gives a novel reading of the BRI by viewing it from the imaginary of Prime Minister Dr Mahathir Mohamad of Malaysia. That might seem strange at first glance because Mahathir has not said much on the BRI. He had retired as prime minister in November 2003, a decade before China's President Xi Jinping announced the BRI in 2013. To the media Mahathir had mentioned that he had written Xi a letter of support for the BRI but the contents of the letter have not been made public. Mahathir was no doubt aware of the scenarios of global economic and strategic rivalry that surrounded the reception of the BRI. But he only faced the implementation of the BRI directly when he became Prime Minister again in May 2018.

'Viewing the BRI from Mahathir's imaginary', this essay suggests, can show an original non-Chinese perspective on related issues of development, regional cooperation, the global order, and so on, that Mahathir articulated as a national leader and a spokesperson of the 'Third World'. Precisely because Mahathir had borne 'maverick' criticisms of the global order, his views of the vision, possibilities, and even imperatives of the BRI might inform, complement or subvert well-rehearsed narratives of the BRI. For its purpose this essay has four parts. The first part reconstructs an ideological profile of Mahathir to show the complex imaginary that lies in his background, convictions, and experiences as a national leader and a spokesperson of the 'dispossessed states of the world'. The second part interprets the meanings and images that China held for Mahathir when Malaysia, Asia, and the world were or were not transformed in ways that were central to Mahathir's worldview and practical concerns. Third, the essay shows that the BRI's discursive reenactment of the Silk Road was not alien to Mahathir's view of world history and the requirements of transnational development. The essay concludes with Mahathir's paradoxical encounter with the BRI in reality after the country's 'regime change' on 9 May 2018.

1. Mahathirist Imaginary

Mahathir's imaginary may be flexibly demarcated by three things — generational, personal, and ideological — respectively, what he is, what he is not, and what he has. Being prime minister at the age of 93 now, Mahathir is the last politically active national leader to have emerged from Asia's, particularly Southeast Asia's, anti-colonial generation.[1] As he recalled

[1] I wish to thank Takashi Shiraishi for stressing the significance of this facet of Mahathir's life and career to me.

> I grew up in a world where so many of the young from Asia learned about liberty and freedom and democracy in the citadels of civilisation: in London and Paris and Amsterdam; only to return home to lands which remained subjugated and colonised. We heard about *liberté*. We heard about *égalité*. We heard about *fraternité*. But we knew mostly about colonial imperialism; authoritarian dictatorship and total subjugation (1999, 3 June).

'Therefore', Mahathir added, 'we yearned for freedom, for most of us were figuratively in chains' (1999, 3 June). But ideals for the one was illusions for the other. He once remarked of the Americans that, 'When they won the Pacific War and freed us from Japanese imperialism, I thought I would forever be pro-American' but he soon found that they were 'no longer the liberators [but had] become the dominators' (2001, 18 January). These formative experiences shaped his lifelong conviction that the good intentions of the West merely paved the roads to its domination of the 'Rest'.

The principal figures of the Asian anti-colonial generation had a range of ambitions and causes. Although the differences over those sometimes plunged them into internecine warfare during the Cold War period, they shared the traits of being nationalist, anti-colonialist, and developmentalist.[2] In sum they harbored deep aspirations of attaining a more egalitarian order, not necessarily within their own states but among the states of the world (Golub, 2016, 154). Mahathir is not an incidental remnant from that generation. He remains nationalist in his worldview, anti-imperialist in many disputes of world politics, and developmentalist in his vision of a global economic order. All that has caused him to be typed as being 'anti-West'. The appellation earned him the disdain of 'the West' — its politicians, media, intellectuals, and non-governmental organizations — but gained him the admiration of the 'non-West' — its anti-establishment elements, critical intelligentsia, and dissident populace. When the Bandung Conference was held in 1955, Malaya was two years away from gaining independence while Mahathir was a young politically conscious but unknown doctor. Yet he retained the spirit of 'Bandung' and the cause of 'non-alignment' throughout his political career. Hardly anyone still active among the leaders and proponents of the 'global South' can match his devotion to 'South-South' cooperation, for example, while in regional development he legitimately belongs with the political elites of an 'Asian resurgence' (Golub, 2016).

Mahathir's personality and temperament matched or served his convictions. He eschewed dogmatic rigidity in economics or politics (or religion, for that matter). He was not fixated on any trend of economic thought but eclectically drew his ideas of economic management from a variety of 'paradigms' — dependency, structuralism, developmental state, liberalization, and so on. In practice, he held to a 'disorder-treating' course which he credited to his doctor's training and experience. He so trusted to his ability to diagnose and treat the body politick that he rarely heeded 'dominant narratives' or orthodoxies that issued from states, markets, or institutions if he suspected their motives of being inimical to

[2] He was known to 'make a passionate plea for ...compassionate widespread developmentalism, for the development and prosperity of all the children of Adam — for not only the strong, the rich and the incredibly empowered ... but also for the disadvantaged, the poor and the miserably disenfranchised' (2001, 26 February).

the interests he had to safeguard. He identified with overlapping disadvantaged communities and refused to behave obsequiously on any stage towards economically developed and politically powerful states. He was pro-South but not hostile to the North as an export market or a source of foreign direct investment, transfer of technology, and learning. While he practiced state economic intervention, he neither suppressed the private sector nor rejected privatization. When he promoted his 'Malaysia Incorporated' and Privatization policies soon after he became prime minister in 1981 he was not, so to speak, far from empathizing with Deng Xiaoping's 'black or white cat' dictum.

What Mahathir is, and is not, form a piece with what he has in personal and discursive terms — a coherent reading of history, a 'periphery-derived' view of the world, and a recalcitrant sense of mission. His reading of history, centrally concerned with the rise and decline, and the advance or retrogress of states, regions, societies, and cultures, is extensive rather than startling (Khoo, 1995). It serves his didactic purpose of drawing 'lessons from history' in the spirit of Santayana's aphorism that, 'Those who cannot remember the past are doomed to repeat it.' He most keenly expresses this point at home when he laments that the Malays 'easily forget' the history of their subjection to colonial rule, and risk undoing their post-independent progress and reliving their domination by others. Abroad he taught that Southeast Asia, *his* region, had been 'a cockpit of big-power rivalries since the early days of colonialism' and suffered 'a psychological division of the region into pockets of varying political orientations from which we have never completely recovered' (1983, 8 March). That did not make Mahathir sanguine about the future of the developing world. Wherever he looked he saw inter-regional rivalry and inter-state inequalities, an unbridged divide between developing and developed nations, and the latter's self-serving manipulation of international trade and investment regimes. To that degree he views the world from its periphery. Most of the time he would be painfully conscious of how the 'global South' served as the plaything of the far richer and more powerful but 'insensitive' North. At one historic moment in the mid-1990s, though, when East Asia exhilarated in its 'economic miracle', he did not just defend but praised 'Asian values' as being superior to the 'universal vales' promoted by the West. It was, among others, his way of imagining Asia from its periphery (Khoo, 1999).

Mahathir has this saving grace: he does not succumb to passive anxiety but sets himself a mission to bestir disadvantaged states from angst towards cooperation in search of practical remedies for their conditions. Mahathir declared himself 'a great believer of cooperation for mutual benefit among all countries, especially among countries of the South, so many of which have for so long been deprived of any real benefits from their international economic and political relations' (1997, 3 November). In 1983 he advised leaders of non-aligned countries: 'If we are weak, let us unite ourselves into regional and international groups, aiding and trading with each other to the extent that we are capable. If we lack the skills, let us acquire them from whatever source available' (1983, 8 March). But he sounded a note of recalcitrance: 'it is better that we fall back on our own resources than to place our hopes on understanding and help from the unfeeling North' (1983, 8 March). Noting that Malaysia, though limited in capability, had ventured 'to the South Pacific, and to Africa, in order to seek meaningful South-South cooperation', he urged others towards the same goal so that 'we will not only survive' but 'will one day be free from the economic and technological oppression of an insensitive North' (1983, 8 March).

2. China in His Mind: Images and Realities

Mahathir took heart from the experience of nations, East Asian nations, which had delivered themselves from that condition of oppression. For him, recent world history suggested the parallel decline of the West and the rise of Asia. Barely a few months before the East Asian financial crisis of 1997, he predicted that, 'Short of a nuclear war ... there can be no stopping the emergence of East Asia as an economic powerhouse of the same stature as the European Union or NAFTA in the 21st Century' (1997, 27 March). In his view of the rise of Asia, two states, Japan and China, featured most prominently but in somewhat different ways given changes in Asia and the world as well as their impact on Malaysia.

Between the 1970s and the 1980s, Japan's economic ascendancy was iconic of what the World Bank later billed as the East Asian Miracle. Mahathir had a personal fascination with Japan's success which he translated into policy innovations. His 'Malaysia Incorporated' policy took Japan for Malaysia's model of late industrialization while his 'Look East' policy exhorted Malaysians to emulate the 'Japanese work ethic'. By the late 1980s, though, Japan's economy had suffered a 'high yen' condition, contrived by the G-7 via its 1985 Plaza Accord, and beginning economic stagnation. At home, Mahathir faced higher repayments of yen-denominated loans and a severe recession. Abroad, his hopes died of seeing Japan lead East Asian regionalism to counter the impending 'Fortress Europe' and North American Free Trade Agreement: Japan demurred while USA objected. Mahathir was led to lament at a conference in Osaka that, 'Japan understands Asia and East Asia better than the West, except when it chooses to listen to those people who do not understand Asians' (2001, 18 January). A decade later, Mahathir chided 'the Europeans on both sides of the Atlantic [who had] dominated the world for four centuries' for reacting to any vision of a 'strong cooperative Asia' by clinging to their 'outdated and silly' idea of 'domination and hegemony' and 'dictating the terms of trade, the systems of Government and the whole value system of the world' (1997, 27 March). He regretted that, 'The Asians, the only people capable of balancing European influence, are divided and unwilling to play a meaningful role in world affairs' (1997, 27 March).

By then the narrative of 'the rise of Asia' had melded with that of 'the rise of China', and an earlier 'fear of Asia' had mutated into a contemporary 'fear of China'. The China parts of these discursive changes imposed themselves on Mahathir's imaginary to novel outcomes.

Since the colonial era Southeast Asian states had apprehended China in multiple and often 'unstable' images, meanings and metaphors that partly reflected the former's own socioeconomic situation and security concerns. The social and political significance of this dimension to China-Southeast Asia ties has been variously explored for the Southeast Asian region, notably Indonesia (Liu, 2011) and Malaysia (Lee, 2015). In a way, Mahathir exemplifies this matter. In his life and career, he did not face a single, static China but a moving sequence of 'changing Chinas' as it were. For example, China in the guise of the massive influx of Chinese immigrants into colonial Malaya and their transformative impact on the domestic economy and politics, which were pressing matters for a 'native Malay' before Malaya's independence, shaped Mahathir's formative consciousness of world affairs (Khoo, 1995). Later, he strove to formulate a 'China policy' that befitted his aim of maintaining Malaysia as a non-aligned, pro-South, trade-dependent, export-oriented, and eastward-looking 'small neighbour' of China's.[3] By the time China had passed certain key economic moments, the Deng Xiaoping-initiated spurt, the 1997 East Asian financial crisis, and the 2007 global financial crisis, Mahathir had developed a nuanced assessment of China's position in the world and bearing on the fortunes of Malaysia and Southeast Asia. He had drawn inspiration from Japan in economic development before. Now he noted that China had become the model's model, showing 'every sign of becoming another Japan, only five times bigger' (2000, 28 October). It took nothing special for anyone to foresee that frenetic growth and transformation made China a powerful competitor to Southeast Asia in exports and the attraction of foreign direct investment. But it took Mahathir historical imagination and political equanimity to posit a definitive difference between the 'modernisation impetus of the Great Powers — Britain, Germany, France, the United States and Japan' (1985, 22 November) and that of China's. The former impetus came 'when most of Asia was weak and economically backward' and led the 'big-powers ... to seek hegemony over us' (1985, 22 November). China's modernization, undertaken while the smaller Asian countries were themselves industrializing, created 'a unique opportunity to establish a more just and equitable regional order and avoid many of the past mistakes of the former imperial powers' (1985, 22 November).

That was not an incidental comment from Mahathir. 'Due to sheer size alone, China must become a major economic power in the region' (1997, 27 March), he noted as he watched China emerge as an 'industrial giant' after being 'insular at first and refus[ing] to join in the Asian industrialisation programme' (2002, 7 March). That did not unsettle him. He coolly calculated that 'the combined size and wealth of the other North East Asian countries together with the South East Asian countries can easily balance that of China' (1997, 27 March). If so, if 'China will not be [economically] as big as the rest of East Asia' it was 'unnecessary', indeed 'counter-productive', Mahathir reasoned, for the 'rest of Asia' to adopt 'an antagonistic stance towards China' (1997, 27 March). 'We are being urged to fear [China as a major economic power],' he warned as he advocated a regionalist non-Sino-centric approach to the issue: 'cooperation between all the countries of East Asia including China, not in military or even economic terms, but in promoting justice and equitability worldwide, in arguing on behalf of weak nations, would create the kind of understanding which will diminish the possibility of conflicts and confrontations in East Asia' (1997, 27 March). Such regional cooperation 'by extension ... would contribute towards building a peaceful and more equitable world (1997, 27 March). During the 1990s, Mahathir was ambivalent towards predictions of 'the 21st Century becoming the Asian

[3] Mahathir's diplomacy in this area built on the breakthrough in China–Malaysia relations that was achieved, on the Malaysian side, by Prime Minister Abdul Razak whose government supported the 1971 vote of the United Nations General Assembly to transfer China's representation from Taiwan to the People's Republic of China (Santha, 2014).

Century', but if others chose to indulge in 'much talk' of the sort he was unperturbed in one sense: 'The Europeans were not going to have things their way much longer' (2000, 28 October).

The Mahathirist imaginary held scorn for the 'glorification of power politics' or the belief in the 'wonders of imperial dominance or "benign" hegemony' which for East Asia 'today and in the future ... will be clearly catastrophic' (2003, 4 August). He had his regionalist dream of an 'East Asian Community of Cooperative Peace and Prosperity' (2003, 4 August) but he was not naïve. The community had to have a critical role for China as it 'continues to be the powerhouse of regional and global growth' (2003, 4 August). Nor was he partisan. He considered it 'desirable' and 'inevitable' that the 'governmental leadership' of the community must 'come from various sources, on various issues, at various times' (2003, 4 August). But he gave an unambiguous answer to the question, 'Who should be the entrepreneurs, architects, engineers and builders of our East Asian community?' Having had his previous regionalist initiative frustrated by non-Asian Pacific nations, Mahathir bluntly insisted that not outsiders but 'we, the nations of East Asia' would build 'our community': 'We are not cows to be led by the nose. We are not children to be led by the hand.... We must act together and advance together' (2003, 4 August).

In his construction of East-West relations, he crucially absolved China of the sins committed by 'the Europeans on both sides of the Atlantic' at two historic moments. At the first moment, when the colonial powers subjugated weak states in Southeast Asia, China played no role in being an invader, conqueror or occupier. Although it 'had pretensions about being the ... the Middle Kingdom ... historically China had not colonized other countries' but European powers 'conquered and colonized Asian countries thousands of miles away from Europe' (2002, 21 May). Mahathir repeatedly recounted the fate of the Malay States which had experienced 'submission ... never more than' sending tributes 'of gold and silver flowers to the Emperor of China' (2002, 21 May) in several millennia's relations between them.[4] But within a much shorter duration of contact with the West the Malay States were seized and colonized by Portugal, the Netherlands and Britain in turn. Practically the entire Southeast Asia was annexed to the empires of the West. At the second historic moment, when the global market wrecked the financial systems of Asia's emerging economies in 1997, China had no hand in the currency speculation that lay at the heart of the crisis. China did not join the western chorus of *schadenfreude*, bashing Southeast Asian regimes over crony capitalism, non-transparent governance, and 'Asian values'. Nor did the Chinese join

> those who insisted to us over and over again that the road to our recovery and salvation lay simply in selling off the modest family valuables it has taken all our lives to earn; those who have insisted that we must sell, at 'fire sale prices', our homes, our factories, our banks, yes, most especially our banks (1999, 3 June).

[4] 'Yet as a tradition [the Chinese tributary system] stands in stark contrast to that of the West: to lend emphasis to this point, while the colonial system was for several centuries fundamental to Europe's relationship with the world, it was never part of the Chinese world order' (Jacques, 2012, 348).

Instead China displayed solidarity with the suffering nations by not devaluing the renminbi to protect its competitiveness. Although China's stance rendered its products less competitive than Southeast Asian products, affected its growth and raised its unemployment, 'China was steadfast in not making matters worse for Southeast Asia' (1999, 3 June). It was China's right to devalue its currency then, Mahathir stressed appreciatively, but that would have reduced the Southeast Asian economies' chances of exporting their way out of the crisis.[5]

It was sometimes and unflatteringly said that Mahathir defended China against western criticisms over its failings in democracy, civil liberties, and human rights. He did, without any apology to the detractors or obsequiousness before their target.[6] He also did from a perspective beyond polemics. So to speak, he swore by history where others affected to divine the future. He learnt from the past to spurn those whose records of villainy persisted to the present, exactly those who spread alarms of threats from others that lay in the future. How could Chinese leaders, possessed of a deep sense of history and memory of their 'century of melancholy', not see Mahathir as a kindred spirit when he was prime minister? Why should they not regard him as an old friend long after he was out of office?

3. Bonding along the Silk Road

The past offered other lessons. 'The fruits of our labour, our ingenuity and our resources must be exported if we ourselves are to be able to import the things we need or desire. This is a simple fact of the market place. It was true at the time of the great silk caravans and it is no less true today.' Xi Jinping could have spoken words to that effect when he enunciated a vision of the 'Silk Road Economic Belt' in Astana, Kazakhstan, in September 2013 (Xi, 2014, 247–249), or when he introduced the idea of a '21st Century Maritime Silk Road' in Jakarta, Indonesia, in October 2013 (Xi, 2014, 250–252). In fact, that passage, which contemplated a timeless and border-less nexus between an imperative (of trade), a facility (of the market place) and a mode (of connectivity), was part of a speech on 'the challenges and prospects of regional cooperation' that Mahathir delivered in Tsinghua University, Beijing, on 22 November 1985, nearly 28 years before Xi promulgated China's BRI.

The timing and broad context of Mahathir's address bear some reflection. When he spoke in Tsinghua University in 1985, he faced a difficult task in stimulating economic growth at home. Malaysia had a severe recession partly caused by a global slump in commodity prices, and a weak fiscal situation partly exacerbated by the post-Plaza Accord appreciation of the Japanese yen. Abroad, slow growth in the developed economies reduced their demand for Malaysia's exports, including manufactured goods, while rising protectionism obstructed trade expansion. In a rather gloomy environment, Mahathir

[5] In response to Japan's solidarity offered by the different route of direct financial assistance, Mahathir said, 'I would like to place on record my personal appreciation and the gratitude of the Malaysian people for the helping hand that Japan extended through the Miyazawa Plan and many other steps. Japan has not been a fine-weather friend. Japan has been an invaluable friend. Japan has been a friend in time of grievous need. Many of us will never forget this for as long as we live' (1999, 3 June).

[6] For instance, he dismissed as hypocrisy western calls for Hong Kong, which Britain ruled undemocratically for 150 years, to have democracy upon its return to China in 1997.

looked for antidotes to the vulnerability of his small, open, export-dependent economy. He made quite a few diplomatic overtures to broaden and deepen regional economic cooperation in East Asia but he and Malaysia were not sufficiently powerful to realize his initiatives in practice. In pursuit of other solutions, he called for closer South-South co-operation to strengthen and diversify trade and investment relationships even among far-flung non-traditional partners. But, arguably, they did not have much to share beyond economic distress and the weaknesses of uninfluential economies.

November 1985 marked four years and five months since Mahathir came to power, during which period he had instituted new policies of administrative reform and major projects of economic transformation. But it was only a year after he had launched a program of heavy industrialization. From his vantage point, Mahathir later said, only 'a few years' had passed since 'Deng Xiaoping dragged the country into the world of competitive trade … and China became an industrial giant' (2002, 7 March). In short, the development of Malaysia and China had each struck out on a late-industrializing, pro-growth and pro-market trajectory. Their immediate and latent complementarities began to overturn an older, post-1949 situation when Malaysia and China were not especially engrossed with each other's *economic* affairs beyond maintaining low-level trading relations.[7] Now, however, both sides had reason to foster closer and deeper trade and investment partnerships. A 'newly open' China could value Malaysia as a source of commodities and 'Overseas Chinese' investment. A 'newly industrialising' Malaysia had to evaluate China's potential as an export market and a rival for foreign direct investment.[8]

In thought and policy, Mahathir focused on global trade and market access, particularly their flaws and inequities. He blamed the rich yet protectionist North for its trade barriers, non-tariff barriers and 'pressures exerted in the name of human rights and the environment and through social clauses' (1996, 8 January) that harmed the interests of the global South. No one could bypass the global trading system but he was prepared to consider options for the South beyond being trapped in inequitable trading relations between unequal partners. For example, could the poor economies of the South weigh the feasibility of conducting 'counter-trade' among themselves? Come to it, he reasoned in his hard-headed manner, it would be better for cash-strapped economies to 'regress' to barter trade than to have no trade at all (Khoo, 1995). Even where there was trade or especially where there was substantial trade, could the partners not look to engage in direct trade? He held up Malaysia and China for his examples. They needed to aim for 'more balanced trade and greater direct trade' (1985, 20 November); they 'should not ignore the question of direct trade, the absence of which results in the under-utilisation of our ports and higher retail prices for Malaysian consumers' (1985, 22 November). 'Bearing in mind that Shanghai is also a great port,' Mahathir said at an official banquet, 'I see a lot of prospects for strengthening

[7] Mahathir expressed his hope that 'just as politics dominated the first decade of our relations, economics will come to dominate the next decade. This task is all the more important when one considers that trade barriers are going up in many parts of the world' (1985, 20 November).

[8] Seventeen years later Mahathir could summarize a record of much stronger economic ties (2002, 8 October).

shipping links between Shanghai and Malaysian ports which could contribute to the enhancement of direct trade ties between our two countries' (1985, 23 November).

From trade and markets, Mahathir moved logically to connectivity and infrastructure. He placed great hopes in infrastructure to extend communications and linkages. More than merely support trade, constructing infrastructure would spur development: 'Physical communication in terms of roads, railways, ports and airports never fails to stimulate the growth of a country' (2003, 5 June). If one truly wanted to help them, one should 'give a fishing rod to the poor countries by building for them the necessary infrastructures so they may export their products and import their needs at reasonable prices. Ports, airports, railways, roads, water supply and electricity, will do this' (2003, 3 June). It was a common enough idea that the 'mere construction of infrastructure can provide jobs and contracts for the locals' (2001, 27 February) and that the benefits accruing to them 'will be self-multiplying' (2003, 3 June). It was a more startling call from Mahathir to have infrastructure constructed by donor countries on a 'Build, Operate and Transfer' arrangement and handed over to recipient countries after a period (2003, 5 June). But he was virtually radical to suggest that, given the high cost of infrastructure, the inability of the poor to build it, and the inadequacy of foreign development aid for the purpose, 'It is time the world thinks of taxing the rich countries on a sliding scale in order to gather sufficient funds to finance the construction of infrastructure in the poor countries' (2001, 27 February). Did Mahathir expect his proposal to receive a hearing from the world's 'unfeeling' rich? He mused that 'the expenditure on infrastructure development from the tax on the rich will benefit the rich' because only they had the technology, machinery and expertise to carry out the construction and 'get back a good portion of the money they paid for the world infrastructure tax' (2001, 27 February). But his proposal, made at the Boao Forum in China in 2001, met 'deafening silence', leaving him indignant that, 'It is right to advocate the removal of borders so the wealth of a country can be exploited by the rich but to return some of that wealth to the exploited country meets with utter silence' (2003, 3 June).

In his restive search for ways to emerge from the impasse that confronted the South Mahathir's imaginary fastened on three fundamental factors, transnational trade, open markets, and enabling linkages. Perhaps then and surely wistfully at first, his sense of history drew him back to the Silk Road. That ancient transnational highway captured what he thought the world needed to prosper — a timeless and borderless nexus between the imperative of trade, the facility of a global market, and the connectivity of infrastructure. The BRI was still a long way off as concept or dream, let alone reality. But how could one evoke the historical Silk Road without conceding, correctly or otherwise, a privileged position along it for 'Cathay'?[9] Not coincidentally Mahathir's imaginary had begun to envision a place for China in the East Asian zone of rapid growth and, conversely, space for the smaller states of Southeast Asia in China's emergence as the economy that sustained the most rapid growth.

[9] 'The narrow conception of the silk road as an east-west route between China and Rome … obscures the fact that there was not one "road" but a skein of routes linking many entrepōts. Historians think of the silk road more as a network than as a linear route; to map it by simply drawing a couple of horizontal lines across the center of Eurasia and the Indian Ocean, as textbooks tend to do, gives a false impression' (Millward, 2013, 7).

Mahathir did not merely talk about building infrastructure in poorer countries that he could not help. In Malaysia, his first administration implemented several large-scale projects of new construction or facility upgrading, among the best known being the Penang Bridge, the North-South Highway, Tanjung Pelepas Port, and the Kuala Lumpur International Airport. From home, he looked across mainland Southeast Asia to China and proposed a railway link between the two. He suggested that the railway, 'the most important infrastructure for land-locked countries', would be cheaper to operate in Asia compared, say, to truck transport in Europe (2003, 5 June). Bearing 'our vision in Southeast Asia', he became one of the prime movers of an ASEAN scheme to 'send heavy goods by rail from Singapore to Europe via Kunming in China, Central Asia and on to the existing railway system which links it to Europe' (2003, 5 June).[10] Such a project might have been mulled but not carried out during the era of French Indochina and British Malaya (including Burma). Now Southeast Asia and China began to build a 6617-km Singapore-Kunming Rail Link. Mahathir accepted that the project would take much time to implement but he expected it to provide a faster alternative to sea transport. Not least he proudly considered it to be a project 'Asians can do'[11] since they had sufficient funds (2003, 5 June).

With railways, which Mahathir likened to 'the ships of the desert in these days of mass consumption', his imaginary knew few bounds. Beyond Southeast Asia and China:

> What Central Asia needs is a vast network of railways of super sizes and length. Two-mile long trains running on ultra-wide gauge tracks would reduce the cost of transporting raw materials and goods across the vast expanse of Central Asia. Just as tankers are built to transport ever increasing quantities of oil across vast oceans, there is no reason why the railways cannot be improved in the same way (2000, 28 October).

In the second decade of the 21st century, when '[t]rains half a mile long have started carrying millions of laptops, shoes, clothes and other non-perishable items in one direction and electronics, car parts and medical equipment in the other on a [China-Germany] journey that takes sixteen days — considerably faster than the sea route from China's Pacific ports' (Frankopan, 2015, 516), it does not seem fanciful that Mahathir had contemplated what Xi Jinping later announced — the revival of the Silk Road of antiquity. If 'asserting a common heritage of commercial and intellectual exchange' through 'old connections' was 'helpful for the future' (Frankopan, 2015, 516), it even seems natural for Mahathir to have written to Xi Jinping to support the BRI.

Only circumstantial evidence supports such speculation about an ideational link to the eventual '21st century Silk Road' in the Mahathirist imaginary. There was nothing much Mahathir could do beyond contemplation for almost 15 years after he retired in November

---

[10] China credited Mahathir as the originator of the 'Pan-Asia' (later called the SKRL) proposal: 'Sources from the Planning Department of [China's] Ministry of Railways said, the idea of the Pan-Asia railway was first put forward by Malaysian Prime Minister Mahathir at the fifth ASEAN summit meeting seven years ago [1995]' (*People's Daily online*, 2002). See Wu (2016) for an assessment of the SKRL project which was only later subsumed under the BRI.

[11] Maybe he was mocking the 'non-Asian' (French and British) failure to launch such a project in the early 20th century.

2003. When the BRI was announced, he no longer commanded the means to connect Malaysia to China and the rest of the world via the Silk Road. He could only gaze upon its progress if it was brought to life. But a twist of history brought him to face the BRI in reality.

4. 'New Malaysia' and the BRI: Undesired Entanglements

At Malaysia's 14th General Election (GE14), held on 9 May 2018, the opposition coalition, Pakatan Harapan (Harapan, or Pact of Hope), defeated the incumbent coalition, Barisan Nasional (BN, or National Front) and returned Mahathir, now 92 years and 10 months old, as the prime minister again![12] Whatever else arose with it, his resumption of national leadership landed him with unforeseen problems with 'BRI in Malaysia'.

The core problem lay in several large-scale projects contracted between the previous Najib Abdul Razak-headed regime and some Malaysian corporations, and state-owned or private corporations from China. The projects included the East Coast Rail Link (ECRL), two gas pipelines (one in Sabah and the other in northern Peninsular Malaysia), the Malaysia-China Kuantan Industrial Park (MCKIP), and the Forest City property development in Johor. Except for Forest City, these projects were promoted as components of Malaysia's link to the BRI. But they were controversial for their deployment of China-sourced finance, investment, management, and labor. Some observers regarded the projects as being detrimental in conception (to Malaysia), excessive in borrowings (from China), 'lopsided' in contractual terms (between contracting parties), opaque in execution (by the corporations), 'shady' in dealings (with outside interests), and so on. They issued warnings of mounting debt, financial infeasibility, economic dependence, compromised autonomy, and even loss of sovereignty (Ignatius, 2017a,b,c,d; Lim, 2018; Liew, 2018; Loh, 2018).

Circumstances forced Mahathir's hand over the BRI projects. It was *not* that the projects were 'not doable' and '[w]e may even require them,' he conceded, but 'at this moment we have no money, and we have a huge debt to repay' (Zurairi, 2018) because of the Najib regime's borrowings 'not only from China but also from other sources' (Jaipragas, 2018a). Rarely had Mahathir sounded more desperate over a problem than when he said that his government would abort or postpone the single most costly project, the ECRL,[13] or reduce its scale — '[a]nything that will [save] us from having to spend precious money' (Zurairi, 2018). He denounced Najib for entering into agreements 'very detrimental to our interests' (Jaipragas, 2018b). In exasperation he insisted that, 'It is not about the Chinese, it is about the [former] Malaysian government', and 'Malaysians playing around with money, not even doing proper feasibility studies and due diligence before going into business' (Jaipragas, 2018a). Even as he hoped for China's understanding, 'If we have to pay

[12] Mahathir was the de facto leader of Harapan's campaign although Dr Wan Azizah Wan Ismail was President of Parti Keadilan Rakyat (PKR, or People's Justice Party), the party in whose name all Harapan candidates contested GE14. Wan Azizah became Deputy Prime Minister.

[13] For critical pre-GE14 commentaries on the ECRL, see a researcher's view in Lim (2018) and a politician's in Liew (2018).

compensation, we have to pay. This is the stupidity of the negotiations before. We must find a way to exit these projects … this is our own people's stupidity' (Jaipragas, 2018b). Soon after GE14 Mahathir, some of his ministers, and his special adviser, Daim Zainuddin, met China's leaders, including Xi Jinping and Prime Minister Li Keqiang, in China and Kuala Lumpur. Official statements issued after the meetings reaffirmed the importance of China-Malaysia ties in trade, investment and regional security.[14] Mahathir was hopeful that China's leadership appreciated his need to review the feasibility of the BRI projects. At a press conference held on 22 January 2019, Daim said that the Malaysian government hoped that ongoing negotiations over ECRL would 'be finalized as soon as possible' (Boo, 2019).

In this unsettled situation, a lot of global media coverage fastened on the economic and geopolitical implications of Mahathir's comments and moves, for Malaysia, of course, but more widely for the countries drawn to the BRI. For example, Mahathir's harsh disapproval of the high costs and high debts of the ECRL was seen to belong with criticisms of the BRI's supposed 'cheque book diplomacy' that laid a 'debt trap' for recipient countries.[15] His allusions to 'lopsided contracts' and 'unequal treaties' were interpreted not merely as a reversal of Najib's 'tilt to China' but a growing resistance beyond Malaysia to China's domination of its BRI partners. Sometimes Mahathir, once the despised *bête noir* of the 'western media', was recast as an ideal elder statesman, because of his 'age and stature … to warn of a new colonialism' (*Asia Sentinel*, 2018) threatening Southeast Asia in particular.[16] It was wishful conjecture to link Mahathir's particularistic unhappiness over Malaysia's troubled projects to what China's detractors propagated as spreading global disaffection with virtually any aspect of the BRI.[17] He resisted attempts to portray him as being anti-BRI, let alone anti-China. When a BBC interviewer asked him if China was 'bringing about a new form of colonialism with their One Belt, One Road infrastructure projects', he firmly replied, 'No, no, no, not at all. One Belt, One Road is okay' (*The Edge Financial Daily*, 2018).[18]

[14] China's Foreign Minister Wang Yi said during his visit to Kuala Lumpur from 31 July to 1 August 2018 that his visit was to 'send a clear message to the international community that … Malaysia occupies an important place in our foreign relations — particularly among our neighbours' (Ho, 2018b).

[15] Wright and Hope (2019) is the latest news report of this kind. It claims to be based on 'the minutes of previously undisclosed meetings' that secretly arranged for China to rescue Najib from his 1MDB scandal with funds and influence in return for Malaysia's acceptance of the BRI projects. To date, Mahathir's government has disclaimed knowledge of the documents cited by Wright and Hope (Ho, 2019a). For a skeptical comment on the Wright and Hope story, see Bunn (2019). There had been earlier suspicion, not quite documented, that loans meant for the Sabah pipeline project had been misused to pay off 1MDB debts (*Malaysiakini*, 2018). For the ECRL, there were allegations that its RM55 billion cost had been inflated to divert a part of it to 'retire 1MDB debts' (Ho, 2018a).

[16] More nuanced assessments of Mahathir's approach to China over the BRI projects and, broadly, maritime disputes in the South China Sea are offered by Bowring (2018), Vatsayana (2018), Liew (2018) which introduced the idea of a 'Mahathir Doctrine', and Kuik and Liew (2018) which expanded on the idea of the 'doctrine'. As far back as 2002 Mahathir had advised Southeast Asians not to 'participate in trying to contain China' which would create 'an atmosphere of confrontation' and they would 'certainly stand to lose in the ensuing tension' (2002, 21 May).

[17] See Maru (2019) for a recent comment on how China's involvement in Africa has received favorable and not just unhappy responses from Africans. Brautigam (2009) offers a judiciously framed assessment of China's record of development aid in Africa, not least when to compared to the practices of western donors.

[18] Two months after Mahathir's visit to China, Minister of Economic Affairs Mohamed Azmin Ali maintained that Malaysia, 'a smallish economy … strategically located in the Asean region' would 'have much to gain from the Belt and Road Initiative' (Asila, 2018).

There was a diplomatic angle to Mahathir's reply. However, much this proud nationalist resented having to negotiate with China from a status he would consider degraded by Najib's BRI entanglements, he was too experienced to adopt any stance that might jeopardize a satisfactory renegotiation of the Malaysia-China projects.[19] Indeed, 'Mahathir has no intention of cutting ties with China ... and has continued to underscore the role of regional integration and cooperation in managing tensions in the South China Sea and mitigating the effects of the deepening rivalry between the United States and China' (Vatsayana, 2018). Nor would China's leaders sacrifice long-term China-Malaysia relations to limited short-term gains,[20] particularly if China's global popularity was indeed declining. Those relations had been assiduously cultivated by Mahathir for years before Najib was prime minister. With tact China's leaders could retain the 'new prime minister' as a 'trusted old friend',[21] where they have shrugged off the discredited Najib as a liability.

But Mahathir's reply bespeaks a deeper resonance that BRI has for him. He could not have predicted previously the concrete shapes that the BRI would take but he would not have found many of its dimensions alien or hostile. He had worked as part of ASEAN with China to launch the Singapore-Kunming Rail Link which was effectively a prototypical link in the vast BRI network. His expansive imaginary intuitively empathized with the historical immensity of the BRI, a 'biblical-size trade and infrastructure endeavour' (Holmes, 2018), inasmuch as 'The world will increasingly look to China in imagining the infrastructural future. Indeed, this can already be counted as part of China's emergent soft power, not only in the developing but the developed world' (Jacques, 2012, 612). Mahathir had long interpreted the world and sought to change it. He yearned to finish with the framework of globalization dictated by the West/North that discriminated against the South in economic development, international trade and investment, distribution of power, regional cooperation and inter-regional competition. Asia, he had counselled before, should not seek to 'manage the present concept of globalisation, to make it work, to benefit from it, but 'to influence the thinking on globalisation, to reshape it, to reduce the chances of it going awry and destroying economies and countries' (2002, 3 February). Some assailed China for lacking 'rules-based' transnational governance and bypassing international financial institutions in its lending to poor countries, for example. Would their argument find favor with Mahathir? He never forgot that when 'currency traders impoverished our countries merely by devaluing our currencies ... [t]he International institutions in which we had placed our trust claim[ed] that they [were] powerless to act against

[19] During his joint press conference with Li Keqiang after their meeting in Beijing, Mahathir might have made a *faux pas* by mentioning 'neo-colonialism' as a rejoinder to Li's call to maintain 'free trade'. When he was asked about this in a BBC interview, Mahathir explained that, 'I did not accuse the Chinese. I merely said that there are other forms of colonialism and one of them is neo colonialism, which was coined by President Sukarno. That's what I said. I didn't accuse the Chinese' (*The Edge Financial Daily*, 2018). The BBC interviewer, as did most other reporters, referred to 'a new form of colonialism', which has different connotations from Sukarno's 'neo-colonialism' to which Mahathir alluded.

[20] China is now Malaysia's largest trading partner. Between 2000 and 2017, Malaysia's trade with China rose from 3.5% of total trading volume to 16.4%. Over the same period, Malaysia's trade with USA fell from 18.7% to 8.7%, and Malaysia's trade with Japan declined from 16.7% to 7.9% (Zurairi, 2019). In the first nine months of 2018, the value of Chinese FDI entering Malaysia was US$3.77 billion, or 32% of total FDI received (Ho, 2019a).

[21] During his state visit to Malaysia in 2013, Xi Jinping paid an unofficial courtesy call on Mahathir.

these traders. The rules of trading [were] devised solely by the traders and … designed to benefit them' (1997, 3 November). Besides, he had made no secret of his contempt for the international financial and regulatory institutions:

> [The United Nations's] organs have been cut out, dissected and reshaped so they may perform the way the puppet masters want. The World Bank, the International Monetary Fund, the World Trade Organisation have now been turned into instruments of hegemony, to impoverish the poor, to enrich the rich. It is not surprising that today the disparities between rich and poor are far greater (2003, 25 September).[22]

The rich could well afford to talk of the 'debt trap' of the BRI. But would they show their money to the man with the quirky idea of instituting a tax on the rich countries precisely for the purpose of building infrastructure in poor countries?[23] And perhaps Mahathir had anticipated the warning of China's 'world domination' via the BRI long ago when he rejected 'Pax Nipponica, Pax Americana, [or] Pax Sinica' as being all 'neither desirable nor possible' (2003, 4 August).

Finally, the BRI holds some paradoxes for Mahathir insofar as his imaginary has had to contend with contemporary reality. Formerly, he facilitated the expansion of Malaysia-China trade and welcomed foreign direct investment from China. As prime minister again he was compelled to renegotiate, defer or cancel Najib's projects. Before GE14 Mahathir had attacked the MCKIP and Forest City projects in particular as threats to Malaysia's sovereignty.[24] After, he had to make sure that his 'China policy' would protect long-term China-Malaysia trade, investment and diplomatic relations. He used to dismiss alarmist warnings of a 'China threat' and advocated regional cooperation with a prominent role for China; now he had to consider the latter's strategic intents more guardedly. At heart, he probably shared the 'Chinese Dream' of re-resurrecting ancient land and maritime trade routes as an 'imperative of globalization' only to find the dream mired in the geopolitics repugnant to his deep non-aligned convictions.[25] He had warmed to Xi Jinping's vision only to be offended by Najib's rendition of it. Mahathir had visualized BRI's transcontinental connectivity in world historical grandeur but he saw it arrive in Malaysia corrupted

[22] See, for example, his call for 'a new globalisation that works less in the service of the very wealthy and much harder in the service of the very poor … to ensure that development is brought to the very centre of the global agenda as our principal objective' (2001, 26 February).

[23] Once he quoted Bill Clinton thus: 'If the wealthiest countries ended our agricultural subsidies, leveling the playing field for the world's farmers, that alone could increase the income of developing countries by $20 billion a year.' Then Mahathir asked, 'So why not do it? Why not remove the subsidies? Why not play fair? Why not level the playing field? Why not give the hundreds of millions of farmers in the developing world a better chance to put food in the mouths of their children and a few cents in their pocket?' (2001, 26 February).

[24] When he was warned that stopping the Forest City property development would undermine investors' confidence in his policy on foreign direct investment, Mahathir said: '… you see some people sell land, big pieces of land, to the Chinese where they are going to build a city which is very, very luxurious meant for their people to come and live there – 700,000 of them. That is not foreign direct investment. Foreign direct investment is about bringing money, bringing investment, setting up plants in Malaysia, employing Malaysians. That we accept' (*The Edge Financial Daily* 2018). Lim (2015) is a meticulous and fascinating study of the complex ways in which FDI from China has engaged with domestic capital. Moser (2017) views Forest City as a case of 'Chinese expansionism'.

[25] Xi Jinping's 'Chinese Dream' encompasses many other things, of course (Xi, 2014: 49–73).

and vulgarized. His unprecedented resumption of premiership gave him a dream-like chance to engage with the BRI but only to the extent of undoing its local manifestations. None of this meant that Mahathir's imaginary rejected a future Silk Road,[26] but only that neither Mahathir nor Malaysia could realize more than a small part of it.

5. Epilogue

The original pre-review version of this essay was submitted to the journal in early March 2019. This Epilogue merely provides an update on the ECRL project as a way to close the essay without bringing up fresh arguments.

On 3 July 2018, the Malaysian government suspended all work on the ECRL project. On 12 April 2019, after months of negotiations, led on Malaysia's side by Mahathir's special envoy, Daim Zainuddin, Malaysia and China announced the resumption of the project according to a re-negotiated agreement. The salient terms of the new agreement, which covered the engineering, procurement, construction, and commissioning aspects of the ECRL, were: a reduction of the project cost from the original sum of RM65.5 billion to RM44 billion, a reduction of the length of the entire link by 48 km (to 640 km), an increase in the participation rate of local contractors in civil works from 30% to 40%, and the establishment of a 50:50 joint-venture between China Communications Construction Company and Malaysia Rail Link to share operations upon completion of the project (Raganathini, 2019).

Mahathir noted that Malaysia chose to re-negotiate for a more favorable new contract instead of terminating the project and paying compensation of RM21.78 billion to CCCC. To Daim the new agreement ended the 'shady conception, lack of transparency, lack of integrity, hasty approval, its vague details, its hefty cost, the absence of accountability' (The Malaysian Insight, 2019) which Mahathir's government had opposed.

Media speculation and occasional official statements during the months of negotiations had probably prepared observers to expect a successful re-negotiation. In the event, not much surprise was evinced in the international media with contemporaneous coverage deciding that the new deal brought mutual benefit to China and Malaysia. On that score, perhaps the most important point was the ability of the two sides to salvage the project and thereby maintain good relations in many areas. When Mahathir attended the 2nd Belt Road Forum (BRF) held on 25–27 April in Beijing, he declared Malaysia's support for the BRI, reportedly noting that, 'The BRI is not a "domination plan" by China, one of the world's superpowers, to gain control of participating countries' (Ho, 2019b). Mahathir's view can be more fully reviewed when additional information and discussion of other responses to the BRF become available later. Here, it suffices to say, apropos of our theme, that re-solving Mahathir's inherited entanglement with China has left intact the conception of BRI in the Mahathirist imaginary.

[26] Mahathir is reported to have accepted Xi's invitation to attend the next 'Belt and Road Initiative Summit' in Beijing in April 2019 (Ho, 2019a).

Acknowledgments

I wish to thank Liu Hong, Guanie Lim and Tan Khong Yam for inviting me join the project that produced this Special Issue. I would also like to thank Ho Wah Foon, Lee Kam Hing, and Trin Aiyara for making some resources available to me. Funding support from the Japanese Government's Grant-in-Aid for Scientific Research Grant No. 17H02230 is gratefully acknowledged.

References

Entries for non-western names are cited and arranged alphabetically according to surnames or first names, without the use of commas, except where the first name is an honorific or where the name follows western convention in the original source.

I. Speeches by Mahathir Mohamad (cited by date, chronologically listed; sourced from Prime Minister's Office, Malaysia, Speech Collection Archives of Chief Executives, and Current Speeches

(1983, 8 March). Speech at the 7th Conference of Heads of State/Government of Non-Aligned Countries, New Delhi, Available at http://www.pmo.gov.my/ucapan/?m=p&p=mahathir&id=29 (accessed on 8 October 2018).

(1985, 20 November) Speech at The Welcoming Banquet Hosted by H.E. Zhao Ziyang, Premier of the State Council of The People, Beijing, Available at http://www.pmo.gov.my/ucapan/?m=p&p=mahathir&id=1635 (accessed on 8 October 2018).

(1985, 22 November). Regional Co-Operation: Challenges and Prospects, Tsinghua University, Beijing, http://www.pmo.gov.my/ucapan/?m=p&p=mahathir&id=846 (accessed on 8 October 2018).

(1985, 23 November) Speech at a Banquet in Shanghai, Shanghai, Available at http://www.pmo.gov.my/ucapan/?m=p&p=mahathir&id=5 (accessed on 8 October 2018).

(1996, 8 January) The Second Pacific Dialogue, Kuala Lumpur, Available at http://www.pmo.gov.my/ucapan/?m=p&p=mahathir&id=1573 (accessed on 3 October 2018).

(1997, 27 March). The Future of Asia and the Role of Japan: Challenges of the 21st Century to Youth, Waseda University, Tokyo, Available at http://www.pmo.gov.my/ucapan/?m=p&p=mahathir&id=1138 (accessed on 2 October 2018).

(1997, 3 November). The Opening of the 7th Summit Level Meeting of the Group of 15, Sg Besi, Selangor, Available at http://www.pmo.gov.my/ucapan/?m=p&p=mahathir&id=1499 (accessed on 2 October 2018).

(1999, 3 June). 5th Nikkei Conference, Tokyo, Available at http://www.pmo.gov.my/ucapan/?m=p&p=mahathir&id=977 (accessed on 29 September 2018).

(2000, 28 October). Agenda for a New Asia, The Asia Society Gala Forum, Hong Kong, Available at http://www.pmo.gov.my/ucapan/?m=p&p=mahathir&id=1018 (accessed on 29 September 2018).

(2001, 18 January) Conference Organised by *The Mainichi Shimbun*, Osaka, Available at http://www.pmo.gov.my/ucapan/?m=p&p=mahathir&id=1057 (accessed on 27 September 2018).

(2001, 26 February). A New Globalisation in a New World Order, Kuala Lumpur, Available at http://www.pmo.gov.my/ucapan/?m=p&p=mahathir&id=16 (accessed on 28 September 2018).

(2001, 27 February). Speech at the Official Launching of the Boao Forum for Asia, Boao, Hainan Province, Available at http://www.pmo.gov.my/ucapan/?m=p&p=mahathir&id=1397 (accessed on 28 September 2018).

(2002, 3 February). Globalisation: Challenges and Impact on Asia, New York, Available at http://www.pmo.gov.my/ucapan/?m=p&p=mahathir&id=135 (accessed on 29 September 2018).

(2002, 7 March). Future of Asia in the 21st Century: Redefining an East Asia Economic Grouping, Speech at the Asia Economic Summit, Kuala Lumpur, Available at http://www.pmo.gov.my/ucapan/?m=p&p=mahathir&id=25 (accessed on 26 September 2018).

(2002, 21 May). China — A Challenge or an Opportunity for Asean?, 8th Nikkei Conference on The Future of Asia, Tokyo, Available at http://www.pmo.gov.my/ucapan/?m=p&p=mahathir&id=989 (accessed on 26 September 2018).

(2002, 8 October). Speech at the 'Malaysia-China Economic Conference – Challenges, Impact and Prospects, Available at http://www.pmo.gov.my/ucapan/?m=p&p=mahathir&id=1654 (accessed on 27 September 2018).

(2003, 3 June). The Asian Dimension under the New World Order – Evolving Paradigms in Asia and Japan', 15th Anniversary Symposium of The Institute for International Policy Studies (IIPS), Tokyo, Available at http://www.pmo.gov.my/ucapan/?m=p&p=mahathir&id=939 (accessed on 26 September 2018).

(2003, 5 June). Genesis of a New Asia Order, 9th Nikkei Conference on The Future of Asia, Tokyo, Available at http://www.pmo.gov.my/ucapan/?m=p&p=mahathir&id=994 (accessed on 26 September 2018).

(2003, 25 September). Speech at the UN General Assembly, New York, Available at http://www.pmo.gov.my/ucapan/?m=p&p=mahathir&id=1632 (accessed on 26 September 2018).

II. Other publications

Asia Sentinel, 2018. Mahathir Shuts Down China, 22 August, Available at https://www.asiasentinel.com/politics/mahathir-mohamad-shuts-down-china (accessed on 23 October 2018).

Jalil, A (2018). Malaysia welcomes FDI, including China, says Azmin, The Malaysian Insight, 30 October, https://www.themalaysianinsight.com/s/107681 (accessed on 12 January 2019).

Blanchard, J-MF (2018). China's Maritime Silk Road Initiative (MSRI) and Southeast Asia: A Chinese "pond" not "lake" in the works. *Journal of Contemporary China*, 27(111), 329–343.

Boo, S-L (2019). ECRL still on table, says Daim who zips lips on Jho Low as "bargaining chip. *Malay Mail*, 22 January, Available at https://www.malaymail.com/news/malaysia/2019/01/22/ecrl-still-on-table-says-daim-who-zips-lips-on-jho-low-as-bargaining-chip/1715190 (accessed on 22 January 2019).

Bowring, P (2018). Commentary: Caution rising in China beneath the Belt and Road Initiative's shiny façade. *Channel NewsAsia*, 27 September 2018, https://www.channelnewsasia.com/news/commentary/cracks-beneath-the-shiny-facade-of-the-belt-and-road-initiative-10701696 (accessed on 23 October 2018).

Brautigam, D (2009). *The Dragon's Gift: The Real Story of China in Africa*. Oxford: Oxford University Press.

Bunn, N (2019). More clarity still needed. *The Star online*, January 13, Available at https://www.thestar.com.my/opinion/columnists/behind-the-headlines/2019/01/13/more-clarity-still-needed-nothing-should-be-assumed-too-easily-about-even-an-established-scandal-lik/ (accessed on 21 January 2019).

Frankopan, P (2015). *The Silk Roads: A New History of the World*. London and New York: Bloomsbury Paperbacks.

Golub, P (2016). *East Asia's Resurgence*. Cambridge, UK: Polity Press.

Ho, WF (2018a). Dr M jolts China's Belt-Road plan. *The Star Online*, 3 June, Available at https://www.thestar.com.my/news/nation/2018/06/03/dr-m-jolts-chinas-beltroad-plan-there-are-mixed-reactions-from-chinese-investors-after-malaysias-dec/ (accessed on 6 September 2018).

Ho, WF (2018b). A fruitful Beijing visit awaits Dr M. *The Star Online*, 3 August, Available at https://www.thestar.com.my/news/nation/2018/08/03/a-fruitful-beijing-visit-awaits-dr-m-there-is-a-lot-of-economic-interdependence-between-malaysia-and/ (accessed on 6 September 2018).

Ho, WF (2019a). Icy Malaysia-China relations set to thaw. *The Star Online*, 20 January, Available at https://www.thestar.com.my/news/nation/2019/01/20/icy-malaysiachina-relations-set-to-thaw-the-worst-of-malaysiachina-ties-may-be-over-with-talk-that-d/ (accessed on 21 January 2019).

Ho, WF (2019b). Malaysia set to see new wave of China FDI. *The Star Online*, 5 May, Available at https://www.thestar.com.my/news/nation/2019/05/05/malaysia-set-to-see-new-wave-of-china-fdi/ (accessed on 6 May 2019).

Holmes, F (2018). China's Belt And Road Initiative opens up unprecedented opportunities. *Forbes*, September 4, Available at https://www.forbes.com/sites/greatspeculations/2018/09/04/chinas-belt-and-road-initiative-opens-up-unprecedented-opportunities/#27826ed93e9a (accessed on 5 September 2018).

Kuik, C-C and CT Liew (2018). What Malaysia's "Mahathir Doctrine" means for China-US Rivalry. *SCMP*, 20 August, Available at https://www.scmp.com/week-asia/geopolitics/article/2160552/what-malaysias-mahathir-doctrine-means-china-us-rivalry (accessed on 3 September 2018).

Ignatius, D (2017a). New Silk Road: Pathway to prosperity or subjugation. *Malaysiakini*, 29 May, Available at https://www.malaysiakini.com/news/383905 (accessed on 14 November 2018).

Ignatius, D (2017b). New Silk Road: Is there a China plan for M'sia. *Malaysiakini*, 30 May, Available at https://www.malaysiakini.com/news/383919 (accessed on 14 November 2018).

Ignatius, D (2017c). New Silk Road: Demons within, dragons without. *Malaysiakini*, 31 May, Available at https://www.malaysiakini.com/news/384039 (accessed on 14 November 2018).

Ignatius, D (2017d). New Silk Road: Dancing with dragons. *Malaysiakini*, 5 June, Available at https://www.malaysiakini.com/news/384547 (accessed on 14 November 2018).

Jacques, M (2012). *When China Rules the World: The End of the Western World and the Birth of a New Global Order*. New York: Penguin.

Jaipragas, B (2018a). "It is not about the Chinese": Malaysia's Mahathir blames previous government for debt to Beijing and project woes. *South China Morning Post*, 19 August, Available at https://www.scmp.com/news/china/article/2160390/it-not-about-chinese-malaysias-mahathir-blames-previous-government-debt (accessed on 3 September 2018).

Jaipragas, B (2018b). Chinese "projects will not go on": Mahathir blasts Najib's "stupidity". *South China Morning Post*, 21 August, Available at https://www.scmp.com/news/china/diplomacy-defence/article/2160627/chinese-projects-will-not-go-mahathir-blasts-najibs (accessed on 3 September 2018).

Khoo, BT (1995). *Paradoxes of Mahathirism: An Intellectual Biography of Mahathir Mohamad*. Kuala Lumpur: Oxford University Press.

Khoo, BT (1999). The value(s) of a miracle: Malaysian and Singaporean Elite constructions of Asia. *Asian Studies Review*, 23, 181–192.

Lee, KH (2015). Images and the shaping of Malaysia's China Policy: 1957–1974. *International Journal of China Studies*, 6(2), 107–127.

Lim, G (2015). China's investments in Malaysia: Choosing the "Right" Partners. *International Journal of China Studies*, 6(1), 1–30.

Lim, G (2018). Resolving the Malacca dilemma: Malaysia's role in the Belt and Road Initiative. In *Securing the Belt and Road Initiative: Risk Assessment, Private Security and Special Insurances Along the New Wave of Chinese Outbound Investments*, AArduino and XGong (eds.), pp. 81–99. Basingstoke, UK: Palgrave Macmillan.

Liew, CT (2018). The Mahathir Doctrine and Malaysia-China Relations. *Liew Chin Tong*, 13 July, Available At https://www.liewchintong.com/2018/07/13/the-mahathir-doctrine-and-malaysia-china-relations/ (accessed on 29 October 2018).

Liu, H (2011). *China and the Shaping of Indonesia, 1949–1965*, Kyoto: Kyoto University Press.

Loh, F (2018). BRI and increased Chinese investments in Malaysia. In *Regime Change in MALAYSIA: GE14 and the end of UMNO-BN's 60-year Rule*, F Loh and A Netto (eds.), pp. 36–50. Petaling Jaya: SIRD.

Malaysiakini (2018). China company paid 1MDB RM2.7 billion for nothing in return. 30 July, Available at https://www.malaysiakini.com/news/436538 (accessed on 11 August 2018).

Maru, MT (2019). Why Africa loves China. *Al-Jazeera*, 6 January, Available at https://www.aljazeera.com/indepth/opinion/africa-loves-china-190103121552367.html (accessed on 8 January 2019).

Millward, JA (2013). *The Silk Road: A Very Short Introduction*. New York: Oxford University Press.

Moser, S (2017). Forest city, Malaysia, and Chinese expansionism. *Urban Geography*, 39(6), 935–943.

People's Daily online (2002). Asian Countries to Build Railway Linking China and Singapore. July 2, http://en.people.cn/200207/02/print20020702_98967.html (accessed on 16 November 2018).

Raganathini, V (2019). China firm to refund part of RM3.1 billion advance for ECRL, says PM. *The Malaysian Insight*, 15 April, Available at https://www.themalaysianinsight.com/s/147952 (accessed on 16 May 2019).

Santha, O (2014). A solemn declaration at a solemn time. *The Star online*, 26 May, Available at https://www.thestar.com.my/news/nation/2014/05/26/a-solemn-declaration-at-a-solemn-time/ (accessed on 5 January 2019).

The Edge Financial Daily (2018). Dr M: I didn't accuse the Chinese. 3 October, Available at https://www.theedgemarkets.com/article/dr-m-i-didnt-accuse-chinese (accessed on 4 October 2018).

The Malaysian Insight (2019). Daim says Najib ignored advice on ECRL. 21 April, Available at https://www.themalaysianinsight.com/s/149351 (accessed on 22 April 2019).

Wright, T and B Hope (2019). WSJ Investigation: China offered to bail out troubled Malaysian fund in return for deals. *Wall Street Journal*, 7 January, Available at https://www.wsj.com/articles/how-china-flexes-its-political-muscle-to-expand-power-overseas-11546890449?emailToken=9778a7fa1be650a3e7c1a702967c211coS3tcnrl/2O41KoqMp/kvau9aRapFfqOaY2TGhV4fQDRo0WifPv1RryYxdS+6jLfnRHEJDcy+75eU0BbTmvuJYwWLfZSULXVv7IPZOPUTinT3fjaqmghTw4XMW/sEeV9&reflink=article_whatsapp_share (accessed on 8 January 2019).

Vatsayana, M (2018). Back in Power, Malaysia's Prime Minister moves away from China. *Strafor*, 24 August, Available at https://worldview.stratfor.com/article/back-power-malaysias-prime-minister-moves-away-china (accessed on 25 September 2018).

Wu, SS (2016). Singapore-Kunming Rail Link: A "Belt and Road" case study. *The Diplomat*, June 17, Available at https://thediplomat.com/2016/06/singapore-kunming-rail-link-a-belt-and-road-case-study/ (accessed on 16 November 2018).

Xi, Jinping (2014). *The Governance of China*. Beijing: Foreign Languages Press.

Zurairi, AR (2018). Continue ECRL? We would if we could, says Dr M. *Malay Mail*, 13 November, Available at https://www.malaymail.com/s/1693030/continue-ecrl-we-would-if-we-could-says-dr-m (accessed on 14 November 2018).

Zurairi, AR (2019). Miti: Despite trade war, China to continue being Malaysia's top investor. *Malay Mail*, 22 January, Available at https://www.malaymail.com/news/malaysia/2019/01/22/miti-despite-trade-war-china-to-continue-being-malaysias-top-investor/1715142 (220119).

Lightning Source UK Ltd.
Milton Keynes UK
UKHW022146020921
389932UK00002B/153